"No other gu
a pleasure to

". . . Excellently organized for the casual traveler who is looking for a mix of recreation and cultural insight."
Washington Post

★★★★★ (5-star rating) "Crisply written and remarkably personable. Cleverly organized so you can pluck out the minutest fact in a moment. Satisfyingly thorough."
Réalités

"The information they offer is up-to-date, crisply presented but far from exhaustive, the judgments knowledgeable but not opinionated." *New York Times*

"The individual volumes are compact, the prose succinct, and the coverage up-to-date and knowledgeable . . . The format is portable and the index admirably detailed."
John Barkham Syndicate

". . . An abundance of excellent directions, diversions, and facts, including perspectives and getting-ready-to-go advice — succinct, detailed, and well organized in an easy-to-follow style." *Los Angeles Times*

"They contain an amount of information that is truly staggering, besides being surprisingly current."
Detroit News

"These guides address themselves to the needs of the modern traveler demanding precise, qualitative information . . . Upbeat, slick, and well put together."
Dallas Morning News

". . . Attractive to look at, refreshingly easy to read, and generously packed with information." *Miami Herald*

"These guides are as good as any published, and much better than most." *Louisville* (Kentucky) *Times*

Stephen Birnbaum Travel Guides

Acapulco
Bahamas, Turks & Caicos
Barcelona
Bermuda
Boston
Canada
Cancun, Cozumel, and Isla Mujeres
Caribbean
Chicago
Disneyland
Eastern Europe
Europe
Europe for Business Travelers
Florence
France
Great Britain
Hawaii
Honolulu
Ireland
Italy
Ixtapa & Zihuatanejo
Las Vegas
London
Los Angeles
Mexico
Miami & Ft. Lauderdale
Montreal & Quebec City
New Orleans
New York
Paris
Portugal
Puerto Vallarta
Rome
San Francisco
South America
Spain
Toronto
United States
USA for Business Travelers
Vancouver
Venice
Walt Disney World
Washington, DC
Western Europe

CONTRIBUTING EDITORS

David Baird, F. Lisa Beebe, Frederick H. Brengelman, Kevin Causey, Peter Collis, Thomas Fitzmaurice de la Cal, Martha de la Cal, Piers A. C. Gallie, Dwight V. Gast, Judith Glynn, Michael Hudec, Arline Inge, Donald A. Jeffrey, Jill Jolliffe, Robert Latona, Suzanne Lavenas, Charles Leocha, Jan S. McGirk, Jeanne Muchnick, Joan Kane Nichols, Clare Pedrick, Allan Seiden, Richard Slovak, Tracy Smith, Melinda Tang, David Wickers, Mark Williams, Peter Wise, Maria Emília Zino

MAPS B. Andrew Mudryk

SYMBOLS Gloria McKeown

A Stephen Birnbaum Travel Guide

Birnbaum's PORTUGAL 1993

Alexandra Mayes Birnbaum
EDITOR

Lois Spritzer
EXECUTIVE EDITOR

Laura L. Brengelman
Managing Editor

Mary Callahan
Jill Kadetsky
Susan McClung
Beth Schlau
Dana Margaret Schwartz
Associate Editors

Gene Gold
Assistant Editor

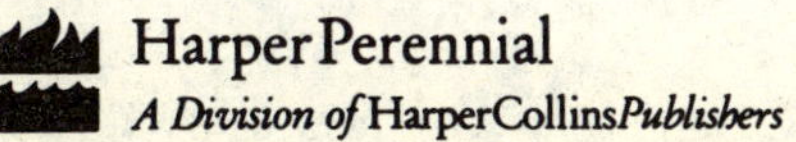

To Stephen, who merely made all this possible.

FIRST EDITION

ISSN 0749-2561 (Stephen Birnbaum Travel Guides)
ISSN 1055-5668 (Portugal)
ISBN 0-06-278051-4 (pbk.)

92 93 94 95 96 CC/WP 10 9 8 7 6 5 4 3 2 1

Contents

GETTING READY TO GO

All the practical travel data you need to plan your vacation down to the final detail.

When and How to Go

Preparing

On the Road

Sources and Resources

PERSPECTIVES

A cultural and historical survey of Portugal's past and present, its people, politics, and heritage.

THE CITIES

Thorough, qualitative guides to each of the 5 cities most often visited by vacationers and businesspeople. Each section, a comprehensive report of the city's most appealing attractions and amenities, is designed to be used on the spot. Directions and recommendations are immediately accessible because each guide is presented in a consistent form.

DIVERSIONS

A selective guide to 20 active and cerebral vacations, including the places to pursue them where your quality of experience is likely to be highest.

For the Experience

For the Body

For the Mind

DIRECTIONS

The most spectacular routes and roads; most arresting natural wonders; and most magnificent castles, manor houses, and gardens — all organized into 8 specific driving tours.

A Word from the Editor

My first memory of Portugal is wrapped up in a whirl of shirtwaist dresses, hula hoops, getting the braces off my teeth, and preparing to celebrate my sixteenth birthday. I was on my first Grand Tour of the Continent, complete with parents and older sister. My father asked me where I would like to spend this momentous moment of my life, and although I later confessed to my husband Steve Birnbaum that I had heard of Lisbon and possibly vaguely remembered some geography text relating to the Iberian Pensinsula, that was the full extent of my expertise on things Portuguese. Yet for reasons unknown, I replied firmly, "Portugal." That long-ago granted birthday wish turned out to stand me in splendid stead.

Above all, I (and later on Steve) developed a fondness for Portugal that neither of us ever lost, and I must say that I waited with some extra eagerness to finally focus on a guide to Portugal — Spain's understated and underrated Iberian neighbor.

In Portugal, a traveler first discovers, above all, that he or she is not visiting a suburb of Spain. Language, food, history, and music are all dramatically Portuguese, and despite its modest size, Portugal offers travelers tastes of its remarkable heritage that are both pungent and wonderfully pleasurable. Steve and I tried to make some sense of the often awkward relationship between these two often misunderstood nations that somehow emerged from a singular, separate square of European real estate.

Once again, the opportunity to present a single corner of the European continent in great detail has been a large part of the pleasure of preparing this guide. It gives us the opportunity to deal with Portuguese destinations in the sort of detail that they truly deserve, and to provide a modern traveler with the perspectives and insights that are required to do more than just superficially see one of Europe's most intriguing countries.

Such thorough treatment only mirrors an increasingly pervasive trend among travelers — the frequent return to treasured foreign travel spots. Once upon a time, even the most dedicated travelers would visit distant parts of the world no more than once in a lifetime — usually as part of that fabled Grand Tour (remember my introduction to Portugal). But greater numbers of would-be sojourners are now availing themselves of the opportunity to visit favored parts of the world over and over again.

So where once it was routine to say you'd "seen" a particular country after a very superficial, once-over-lightly encounter, the more perceptive travelers of today recognize that it's entirely possible to have only skimmed the surface of a specific destination even after having visited that place more than a dozen times. Similarly, repeated visits to a single site permit true exploration of special interests, whether they be sporting, artistic, or intellectual in nature.

For those of us who spent several years working out the special system under which we present information in this series, the luxury of being able to devote nearly as much space as we'd like to just a single country is as close to paradise for guide writers and editors as any of us expects to come. But clearly this is not the first guide to the pleasures of Portugal — guides of one sort or another have existed for centuries, so a traveler might logically ask why a new one is suddenly necessary.

Our answer is that the nature of travel to Portugal — and even of the travelers who now routinely make the trip — has changed dramatically. For the past 2,000 years or so, travel to and through Portugal was an extremely elaborate undertaking, one that required extensive advance planning. Even as recently as the 1950s, a person who had actually been to Lisbon or the Algarve could dine out on his or her experiences for years, since such adventures were quite extraordinary and usually the province of the privileged alone.

With the advent of jet air travel in the late 1950s, however, and of increased-capacity, wide-body aircraft during the late 1960s, travel to and around this once distant land became extremely common. In fact, in more than 2 decades of nearly unending inflation, airfares may be the only commodity in the world that has actually gone down in price.

Attitudes, as well as costs, also have changed significantly in the last couple of decades. Beginning with the so-called flower children of the 1960s, international travel lost much of its aura of mystery. Whereas their parents might have been happy with just a superficial sampling of Estoril or the Minho, these young people simply picked up and settled in various parts of Europe for an indefinite stay. While living as inexpensively as possible, they adapted to the local lifestyle, and generally immersed themselves in things European.

Thus began an explosion of travel to and through both Spain and Portugal. and over the years, the development of inexpensive charter flights and packages fueled the new American interest in and appetite for more extensive exploration.

Now, in the 1990s, those same flower children who were in the forefront of the modern travel revolution have undeniably aged. While it may be impolite to point out that many are probably well into their untrustworthy 30s and (often) 40s, their original zeal for travel remains undiminished. For them it's hardly news that the way to get from Lisbon to the Azores is to head 900 miles west in the Atlantic, and then watch for the outline of what some think is the lost continent of Atlantis. Such experienced and knowledgeable travelers know precisely where they want to go, and are more often searching for ideas and insights to expand their already sophisticated travel consciousness.

Obviously, any new guidebook to Portugal must keep pace with and answer the real needs of today's travelers. That's why we've tried to create a guide that's specifically organized, written, and edited for the more demanding modern traveler, one for whom qualitative information is infinitely more desirable than mere quantities of unappraised data. We think that this book, along with all the other guides in our series, represents a new generation of travel guides — one that is especially responsive to modern needs and interests.

For years, dating back as far as Herr Baedeker, travel guides have tended to be encyclopedic, seemingly much more concerned with demonstrating expertise in geography and history than with a real analysis of the sorts of things that actually concern a typical tourist. But today, when it is hardly necessary to tell a traveler where the Algarve is (in many cases, the traveler has been to a given Portuguese destination nearly as often as the guidebook editors), it becomes the responsibility of those editors to provide new perspectives and to suggest new directions in order to make the guide genuinely valuable.

That's exactly what we've tried to do in this series. I think you'll notice a different, more contemporary tone to the text, as well as an organization and focus that are distinctive and more functional. And even a random reading of what follows will demonstrate a substantial departure from the standard guidebook orientation, for we've not only attempted to provide information of a more compelling sort, but we also have tried to present the data in a format that makes it particularly accessible.

Needless to say, it's difficult to decide just what to include in a guidebook of this size — and what to omit. Early on, we realized that giving up the encyclopedic approach precluded our listing every single route and restaurant, a realization that helped define our overall editorial focus. Similarly, when we discussed the possibility of presenting certain information in other than strict geographic order, we found that the new format enabled us to arrange data in a way that we feel best answers the questions travelers typically ask.

Large numbers of specific questions have provided the real editorial skeleton for this book. The volume of mail we regularly receive emphasizes that modern travelers want very precise information, so we've tried to organize our material in the most responsive way possible. Readers who want to know the most evocative sights around Lisbon or the best places to dine in Porto will have no trouble extracting that data from this guide.

Travel guides are, understandably, reflections of personal taste, and putting one's name on a title page obviously puts one's preferences on the line. But I think I ought to amplify just what "personal" means. Like Steve, I don't believe in the sort of personal guidebook that's a palpable misrepresentation on its face. It is, for example, hardly possible for any single travel writer to visit thousands of restaurants (and nearly as many hotels) in any given year and provide accurate appraisals of each. And even if it were physically possible for one human being to survive such an itinerary, it would of necessity have to be done at a dead sprint, and the perceptions derived therefrom would probably be less valid than those of any other intelligent individual visiting the same establishments. It is, therefore, impossible (especially in a large, annually revised and updated guidebook *series* such as we offer) to have only one person provide all the data on the entire world.

I also happen to think that such individual orientation is of substantially less value to readers. Visiting a single hotel for just one night or eating one hasty meal in a random restaurant hardly equips anyone to provide appraisals that are of more than passing interest. No amount of doggedly alliterative or oppressively onomatopoeic text can camouflage a technique that is essentially specious. We have, therefore, chosen what I like to describe as the "thee and me" approach to restaurant and hotel evaluation and, to a somewhat more limited degree, to the sites and sights we have included in the other sections of our text. What this really reflects is a personal sampling tempered by intelligent counsel from informed local sources, and these additional friends-of-the-editor are almost always residents of the city and/or area about which they are consulted.

Despite the presence of several editors, writers, researchers, and local contributors, very precise editing and tailoring keep our text fiercely subjective. So what follows is the gospel according to Birnbaum, and it represents as much of our own taste and instincts as we can manage. It is probable, therefore, that if you like your cities stylish and prefer hotels with personality to high-rise anonymities, we're likely to have a long and meaningful relationship. Readers with dissimilar tastes may be less enraptured.

I also should point out something about the person to whom this guidebook is directed. Above all, he or she is a "visitor." This means that such elements as restaurants have been specifically picked to provide the visitor with a representative, enlightening, stimulating, and above all pleasant experience. Since so many extraneous considerations can affect the reception and service accorded a regular restaurant patron, our choices can in no way be construed as an exhaustive guide to resident dining. We think we've listed all the best places, in various price ranges, but they were chosen with a visitor's enjoyment in mind.

Other evidence of how we've tried to tailor our text to reflect modern travel habits is most apparent in the section we call DIVERSIONS. Where once it was common for travelers to spend a foreign visit in a determinedly passive state, the emphasis is far more active today. So we've organized every activity we could reasonably evaluate and arranged the material in a way that is especially accessible to activists of either athletic or cerebral bent. It is no longer necessary, therefore, to wade through a pound or two of superfluous prose just to find the very best shop or the most picturesque *pousada* within a reasonable distance of your destination.

If there is a single thing that best characterizes the revolution in and evolution of current holiday habits, it is that most travelers now consider travel a right rather than a privilege. No longer is a family trip to the far corners of the world necessarily a once-in-a-lifetime thing; nor is the idea of visiting exotic, faraway places in the least worrisome. Travel today translates as the enthusiastic desire to sample all of the world's opportunities, to find that elusive quality of experience that is not only enriching but comfortable. For that reason, we've tried to make what follows not only helpful and enlightening, but the sort of welcome companion of which every traveler dreams.

Finally, I should point out that every good travel guide is a living enterprise; that is, no part of this text is carved in stone. In our annual revisions, we refine, expand, and further hone all our material to serve your travel needs better. To this end, no contribution is of greater value to us than your personal reaction to what we have written, as well as information reflecting your own experiences while using the book. We earnestly and enthusiastically solicit your comments about this guide *and* your opinions and perceptions about places you have recently visited. In this way, we will be able to provide the most current information — including the actual experiences of recent travelers — and to make those experiences more readily available to others. Please write to us at 10 E. 53rd St., New York, NY 10022.

We sincerely hope to hear from you.

ALEXANDRA MAYES BIRNBAUM

How to Use This Guide

A great deal of care has gone into the special organization of this guidebook, and we believe it represents a real breakthrough in the presentation of travel material. Our aim is to create a new, more modern generation of travel books, and to make this guide the most useful and practical travel tool available today.

Our text is divided into five basic sections in order to present information in the best way on every possible aspect of a vacation to Portugal. This organization itself should alert you to the vast and varied opportunities available, as well as indicate all the specific data necessary to plan a successful visit. You won't find much of the conventional "swaying palms and shimmering sands" text here; we've chosen instead to deliver more useful and practical information. Prospective Portuguese itineraries tend to speak for themselves, and with so many diverse travel opportunities, we feel our main job is to highlight what's where and to provide the basic information — how, when, where, how much, and what's best — to assist you in making the most intelligent choices possible.

Here is a brief summary of the five sections of this book, and what you can expect to find in each. We believe that you will find both your travel planning and en route enjoyment enhanced by having this book at your side.

GETTING READY TO GO

This mini-encyclopedia of practical travel facts is a sort of know-it-all companion with all the precise information necessary to create a successful trip to and through Portugal. There are entries on more than 2 dozen separate topics, including how to get where you're going, what preparations to make before leaving, how to deal with possible emergencies while traveling, what to expect in the different parts of the country, what your trip is likely to cost, and how to avoid prospective problems. The individual entries are specific, realistic, and, where appropriate, cost-oriented.

We expect you to use this section most in the course of planning your trip, for its ideas and suggestions are intended to simplify this often confusing period. Entries are intentionally concise, in an effort to get to the meat of the matter with the least extraneous prose. These entries are augmented by extensive lists of specific sources from which to obtain even more specialized data, plus some suggestions for obtaining travel information on your own.

PERSPECTIVES

Any visit to an unfamiliar destination is enhanced and enriched by an understanding of the cultural and historical heritage of that area. We have, therefore, provided just such an introduction to Portugal, its history, people and politics, architecture, literature, traditional music, and food and drink.

THE CITIES

Individual reports on the five Portuguese cities most visited by travelers and businesspeople have been created with the assistance of researchers, contributors, professional journalists, and experts who live in the cities. Although useful at the planning stage, THE CITIES is really designed to be taken along and used on the spot. Each report offers a short-stay guide to its city, including an essay introducing the city as a historic entity and as a place to visit. *At-a-Glance* material is actually a site-by-site survey of the most important, interesting, and sometimes most eclectic sights to see and things to do. *Sources and Resources* is a concise listing of pertinent tourism information meant to answer myriad potentially pressing questions as they arise — from simple things such as the address of the local tourism office, how to get around, which sightseeing tours to take, and when special events and holidays occur to something more difficult like where to find the best nightspot, where to hail a taxi, which are the shops that have the finest merchandise and/or the most irresistible bargains, and where the best golf, tennis, fishing, and swimming, as well as the best museums and theaters, are to be found. *Best in Town* lists our collection of cost-and-quality choices of the best places to eat and sleep on a variety of budgets.

DIVERSIONS

This section is designed to help travelers find the best places in which to engage in a wide range of physical and cerebral activities, without having to wade through endless pages of unrelated text. This very selective guide lists the broadest possible range of activities, including all the best places to pursue them.

We start with a list of special places to stay and eat, and move to activities that require some perspiration — sports preferences and other rigorous pursuits — and go on to report on a number of more spiritual vacation opportunities. In every case, our suggestion of a particular location — and often our recommendation of a specific resort or hotel — is intended to guide you to that special place where the quality of experience is likely to be highest. Whether you opt for shopping or swimming, attending theater festivals or country fairs, the most stylish hotels or most esoteric museums, or tours of spectacular resorts, each category is the equivalent of a comprehensive checklist of the absolute best in Portugal.

DIRECTIONS

Here are eight itineraries that range all across Portugal, along the most beautiful routes and roads, past the most spectacular natural wonders, through the most historic cities and countrysides and the most idyllic islands. DIRECTIONS is the only section of this book that is organized geographically, and its itineraries cover the touring highlights of Portugal in short, independent journeys of 3 to 5 days' duration. Itineraries can be "connected" for longer sojourns or used individually for short, intensive explorations.

Each entry includes a guide to sightseeing highlights; a cost-and-quality guide to accommodations and food along the road (small inns, *pousadas,* castle hotels, country hotels); and hints and suggestions for activities.

Although each of the book's sections has a distinct format and a special function, they have all been designed to be used together to provide a complete inventory of travel information. To use this book to full advantage, take a few minutes to read the table of contents and random entries in each section to get a firsthand feel for how it all fits together.

Pick and choose needed information. Assume, for example, that you always have wanted to take that typically Portuguese vacation, a walking tour through rural Portugal — but you never really knew how to organize it or where to go. Start by reading the informative section on camping and hiking in GETTING READY TO GO, as well as the chapters on planning a trip, accommodations, and climate and clothes. But where to go and what to see? Turn next to DIRECTIONS. Routes and desirable detours are all clearly set forth. Your trip will likely begin or end in Lisbon, and for a complete rundown on this remarkable city, you should read the Lisbon chapter of THE CITIES. Finally, turn to DIVERSIONS to peruse the chapters on sports, hotels, antiques, and other activities in which you are especially interested, to make sure you don't miss anything along your chosen route.

In other words, the sections of this book are building blocks designed to help you put together the best possible trip. Use them selectively as a tool, a source of ideas, a reference work for accurate facts, and a guidebook to the best buys, the most exciting sights, the most pleasant accommodations, the tastiest food — *the best travel experience* that you can possibly have.

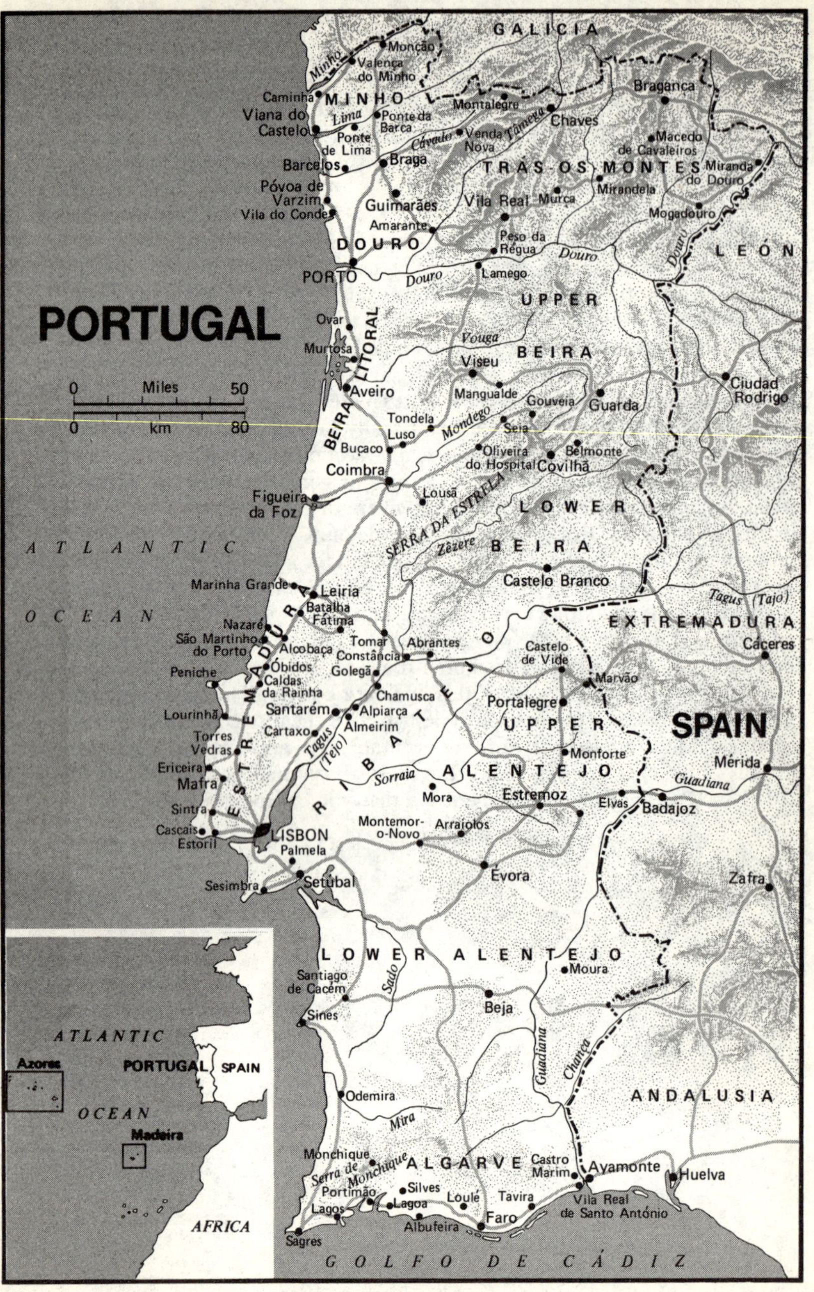
PORTUGAL
0 Miles 50
0 km 80
ATLANTIC OCEAN
GALICIA
MINHO
TRAS-OS-MONTES
DOURO
UPPER BEIRA
BEIRA LITORAL
LOWER BEIRA
ESTREMADURA
RIBATEJO
UPPER ALENTEJO
LOWER ALENTEJO
ALGARVE
LEÓN
EXTREMADURA
SPAIN
ANDALUSIA
GOLFO DE CÁDIZ
Monção
Valença do Minho
Caminha
Viana do Castelo
Ponte de Lima
Ponte da Barca
Montalegre
Chaves
Bragança
Macedo de Cavaleiros
Miranda do Douro
Mirandela
Mogadouro
Venda Nova
Barcelos
Braga
Póvoa de Varzim
Vila do Conde
Guimarães
Vila Real
Murça
Amarante
Peso da Régua
Lamego
PORTO
Ovar
Murtosa
Aveiro
Viseu
Mangualde
Gouveia
Guarda
Ciudad Rodrigo
Tondela
Luso
Buçaco
Seia
Oliveira do Hospital
Belmonte
Covilhã
Coimbra
Figueira da Foz
Lousã
SERRA DA ESTRELA
Castelo Branco
Marinha Grande
Leiria
Batalha
Fátima
Nazaré
São Martinho do Porto
Alcobaça
Tomar
Abrantes
Constância
Óbidos
Golegã
Peniche
Caldas da Rainha
Chamusca
Santarém
Alpiarça
Almeirim
Cartaxo
Lourinhã
Torres Vedras
Ericeira
Mafra
Sintra
Cascais
Estoril
LISBON
Palmela
Sesimbra
Setúbal
Castelo de Vide
Marvão
Portalegre
Cáceres
Monforte
Mérida
Mora
Estremoz
Elvas
Badajoz
Montemor-o-Novo
Arraiolos
Évora
Zafra
Moura
Santiago de Cacém
Sines
Beja
Odemira
Monchique
Serra de Monchique
Castro Marim
Ayamonte
Huelva
Portimão
Silves
Lagos
Lagoa
Loulé
Tavira
Vila Real de Santo António
Faro
Albufeira
Sagres
Minho
Lima
Cávado
Tâmega
Douro
Vouga
Mondego
Zêzere
Tagus (Tejo)
Sorraia
Guadiana
Sado
Mira
Chança
ATLANTIC
OCEAN
Azores
PORTUGAL
SPAIN
Madeira
AFRICA

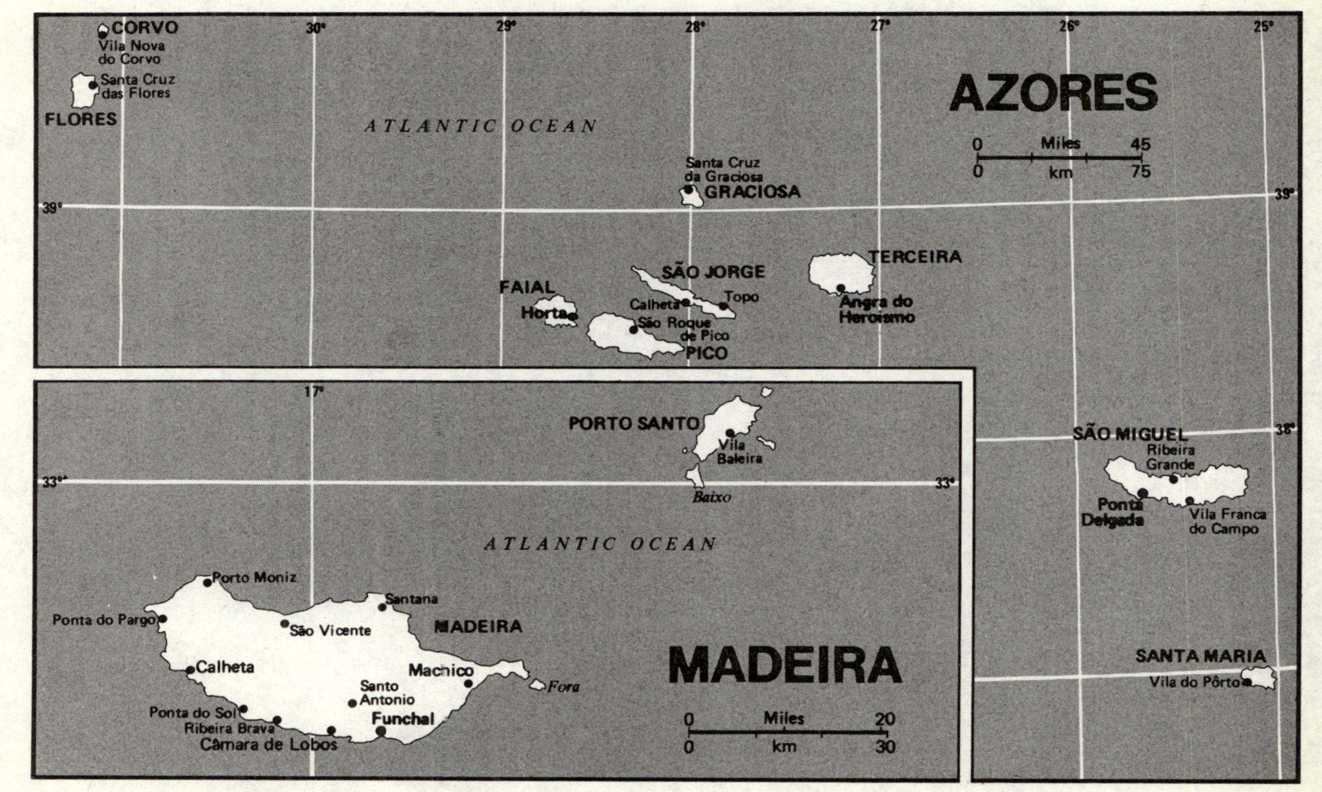
AZORES
0 Miles 45
0 km 75
ATLANTIC OCEAN
CORVO
Vila Nova do Corvo
Santa Cruz das Flores
FLORES
Santa Cruz da Graciosa
GRACIOSA
SÃO JORGE
Calheta
Topo
TERCEIRA
Angra do Heroismo
FAIAL
Horta
São Roque de Pico
PICO
SÃO MIGUEL
Ribeira Grande
Ponta Delgada
Vila Franca do Campo
SANTA MARIA
Vila do Pôrto
30°
29°
28°
27°
26°
25°
39°
38°
MADEIRA
0 Miles 20
0 km 30
ATLANTIC OCEAN
PORTO SANTO
Vila Baleira
Baixo
Porto Moniz
Ponta do Pargo
São Vicente
Santana
MADEIRA
Calheta
Machico
Santo Antonio
Funchal
Fora
Ponta do Sol
Ribeira Brava
Câmara de Lobos
17°
33°

GETTING READY TO GO

When and How to Go

What's Where

Portugal spans the west coast of what is most often referred to as the Iberian Peninsula — a rectangle jutting out from the southwest corner of Europe — which it shares with Spain. Its eastern boundaries with this larger nation are marked less by rivers and mountains than by lack of people: For much of its length, the Spanish-Portuguese border is a wasteland. Portugal always has turned its back on its big brother, facing not toward Spain but west, toward the Atlantic. Including the islands of the Azores and Madeira to the west, the country covers a total of 35,553 square miles and has a population of about 10.3 million.

Portugal, to most people, means either Lisbon — the sophisticated capital, rich in monuments, museums, and churches — or the Algarve — the famed vacation area, with its congenial mixture of sea, beaches, luxurious hotels, and varied cuisine. However, beyond Lisbon's city limits and away from the southern shore lies a country of ancient towns, walled villages, and captivating scenery. Portugal's landscape encompasses a wide variety of contrasts — the lush green valley of the Minho River, the rugged mountains of the Trás-os-Montes region, the steep, hilly vineyards of the Alto Douro, and the Beiras' flat coast. In the south, the pale gold wheat fields and olive and cork groves of the Alentejo give way to the cosmopolitan resorts of the Algarve, where beaches and imposing cliffs are washed by the warm waves of the Gulf Stream.

Portugal's Atlantic seaboard runs from the mouth of the Minho to the mouth of the Guadiana. The destiny of Portugal — its history, economy, and climate — has been formed by the sea. Most people live along the coasts, and its greatest cities — Lisbon and Porto, both excellent ports — are located there. Two-thirds of the coast — from the north to just below Lisbon — is low and sandy. In the south, especially in the Algarve, there are sea marshes and sand banks, estuaries, beaches, and coves. Much of Portugal is mild and moist, but the agricultural benefits of climate are mainly offset by poor soil.

Much of northern Portugal is mountainous. The Minho, on the northwest, is, along with the area to the south around Porto, the original nucleus of the country, a land of rolling hills and soft, misty countryside. Trás-os-Montes, "behind the mountains," in the northeast, is isolated and sparsely settled. A little farther south, the Douro River slices through steep slopes whose neatly terraced vineyards produce port wine. The Beiras region is the heart of the country. Here the distinction between coast and interior is not so sharp. The area encompasses high pastures, charming forests and valleys, lagoons and beaches. High above the pretty valley of the Mondego River is the city of Coimbra, the seat of a famous university and the center of intellectual life.

The Tagus River bisects the country, dividing north from south. Its broad valley contains both small holdings and large estates, irrigated fields, extensive pastures, and half-wild herds of cattle. The Tagus, which begins in Spain, ends at last in an inland sea on the Atlantic coast. This is the site of Lisbon and its suburbs. The Alentejo, in southern Portugal, is a large area but sparsely settled, even on the coast. Inland is mainly flat, dry heath with a few oak groves, no shade, little water, and intense summer heat. A low range of mountains divides it from the southern coastal area, the Algarve. Here grow almonds, figs, oranges, olives, wheat, vegetables, and flowers. Fisheries dot the coast. The Algarve's eastern side is temperate and lush, but its western coast is less sheltered from Atlantic storms. The wind continuously sweeps across Cape St. Vincent, the southwesternmost point on the Iberian Peninsula, close to where Prince Henry the Navigator watched his ships set off to circle the globe.

Portugal contains a number of architectural highlights: in the north, the extravagant mountaintop castle built by Fernando II between 1846 and 1850 in Sintra; the imposing marble monastery in Mafra, built in 1717 for King João V; the walled towns of Obidos; and the ruins of Conimbriga, the most important Roman settlement on the Iberian Peninsula. Tomar, in central Portugal, offers the magnificent Convento de Cristo, a fortified castle and convent, and blends styles of architecture from the 12th through the 17th century. Other notable sites include Marvão, a medieval village; Elvas, where a 15th-century aqueduct still carries water to the town; Estremoz, whose artisans are famous for their pottery figurines of people and animals; and Evora, with its 2nd-century Roman temple.

AZORES AND MADEIRA: Two archipelagoes lie off the coast of Portugal, both consisting of the tips of volcanoes. Madeira lies some 560 miles southwest of Lisbon. Its main island, also called Madeira, has produced the eponymous wine for almost 400 years. With its semi-tropical climate, abundance of flowers, and beautiful scenery, the island easily earns its nickname, "Enchanted Island." Funchal, its main city, is a lively resort town. Farther out in the Atlantic are the Azores, according to legend the mountaintops of the lost colony of Atlantis. Warm and wet, with luxuriant vegetation, black beaches, and mountains shrouded in mist, these islands, well off the beaten track, warrant a visit by the more adventurous traveler.

When to Go

There really isn't a "best" time to visit Portugal. For North Americans, as well as Europeans, the period from mid-May to mid-September has long been — and remains — the peak travel period, traditionally the most popular vacation time.

It is important to emphasize that Portugal is hardly a single-season destination; more and more travelers who have a choice are enjoying the substantial advantages of off-season travel. Though lesser tourist attractions may close during the off-season — roughly November to *Easter* — the major ones remain open and tend to be less crowded, as are some cities and other parts of the country. During the off-season, people relax and Portuguese life proceeds at a more leisurely pace. What's more, travel generally is less expensive.

For some, the most convincing argument in favor of off-season travel is the economic one. Getting there and staying there is more affordable during less popular travel periods, as airfares, hotel rooms, and car rental rates go down and less expensive package tours become available; the independent traveler can go farther on less, too. Europe is not like the Caribbean, however, where high and low seasons are precisely defined and rates drop automatically on a particular date, but many Portuguese hotels do reduce rates during the off-season. Although smaller establishments in some areas may close during the off-season in response to reduced demand, there still are plenty of alternatives, and in cities, cut-rate "mini-break" packages — for stays of more than 1 night, especially over a weekend (when business travelers traditionally go home) — are more common.

A definite bonus to visiting during the off-season is that even the most basic services are performed more efficiently. In theory, off-season service is identical to that offered during high season, but the fact is that the absence of demanding crowds inevitably begets much more thoughtful and personal attention. The very same staff that barely can manage to get fresh towels onto the racks during the height of summer at coastal resort areas has the time to chat pleasantly in the spring or fall. And it is not only hotel service that benefits from the absence of the high-season mobs.

There also are some notable exceptions to this rule. For example, in April, *Holy Week* — especially in Braga — is not exactly a time when hoteliers need to drum up business. Even in off-season, high-season rates may prevail because of an important local event. Particularly in the larger cities, special events and major trade shows or conferences held at the time of your visit are sure to affect the availability not only of discounts, but even of a place to stay. And traveling in the dead of winter is not for everyone. While most of Portugal does not suffer freezing temperatures, the rain, fog, and cold gray skies in some regions are not always conducive to relaxed sightseeing.

It also should be noted that the months immediately before and after the peak summer months — what the travel industry refers to as shoulder seasons — often are sought out because they offer fair weather and somewhat smaller crowds. But be aware that very near high-season prices can prevail, notably in certain popular resort areas such as the Algarve.

In short, like many other popular places, Portugal's vacation appeal has become multi-seasonal. But the noted exceptions notwithstanding, most travel destinations are decidedly less trafficked and less expensive during the winter.

CLIMATE: The basic distinction in climate in Portugal is the amount of rainfall, which varies among the northern, central, and southern regions. Precipitation is not uncommon in any region, and the Portuguese climate tends to be damp and relatively temperate, due to the winds that blow off the Atlantic. To the east, however, it becomes drier, with almost no rain in summer. Frosts are uncommon in Portugal and snow rarely falls.

Those planning on traveling during the high season should note that Portugal's Algarve can be extremely hot throughout the summer. If sightseeing is a priority, the months of May, June, and September may offer more comfortable weather. In the coastal regions, mild weather is not uncommon during February and November.

The following chart lists average low and high temperatures in major Portuguese cities at different times of the year to help in planning. *(Please note that although temperatures usually are recorded on the Celsius scale in Portugal, for purposes of clarity we use the more familiar Fahrenheit scale throughout this guide.)*

AVERAGE TEMPERATURES (in °F)

	January	*April*	*July*	*October*
Coimbra	41–57	48–70	59–84	54–73
Evora	43–54	50–66	61–88	56–72
Faro	43–61	52–66	64–81	59–73
Lisbon	46–57	54–68	63–81	57–72
Madeira Island	57–64	59–68	64–75	64–75
Porto	41–55	48–64	59–77	52–70
Santarém	41–58	49–69	61–87	54–75

Travelers can get current readings and extended forecasts through the *Weather Channel Connection,* the worldwide weather report center of the *Weather Channel,* a cable television station. By dialing 900-WEATHER and punching in the first four letters of the city (or island), an up-to-date recording will provide such information as current temperature, barometric pressure, relative humidity, and wind speed, as well as a general 2-day forecast for over 225 international destinations. For instance, to hear the weather report for Lisbon, punch in LISB. (To find out which cities or locations in a given country are covered, enter the first four letters of the *country* name.) Callers also can access information on the weather patterns for any time of the year in the area requested, as well as international travel information such as entry requirements, US State Department travel advisories, tipping, and voltage requirements. Portuguese destinations included in this service are Lisbon and Porto. This 24-hour service can be accessed from any touch-tone phone in the US, and costs 95¢ per minute. The charge will show up on your phone bill. For additional information, contact the *Weather Channel Connection,* 2600 Cumberland Pkwy., Atlanta, GA 30339 (phone: 404-434-6800).

SPECIAL EVENTS: Travelers may want to schedule a trip to Portugal to coincide with some special event. For a music lover, a concert in a great cathedral or in a splendid natural setting may be an especially thrilling experience, and much more memorable than seeing the same place on an ordinary sightseeing itinerary. A folklore or harvest festival can bring nearly forgotten traditions alive or underscore their continuing significance in modern life.

Portugal has literally hundreds of fiestas or festivals each year, particularly from *Easter* through October. City and town squares are festooned with brightly colored arches and lanterns, houses are adorned with flags, and people of all ages dress in folk costumes handed down for generations to take part in parades, folk dances, singing, and fantastic fireworks displays. No one is a stranger and everyone is drawn into the merriment.

The events that follow are the major ones, listed according to the months in which they usually occur. Where possible, we have indicated the exact dates for the festivities this year. However, for those events for which specific dates were not yet available as we went to press, and to guard against inevitable scheduling changes, it is best to check with the Portuguese National Tourist Office for the exact dates of anything that may be of interest and for current schedules of festivals, fairs, and other events. Also keep in mind that some events, particularly festivals, may vary by a few days to several weeks from town to town and region to region; again, it's best to check with the tourist authorities for the most up-to-date information (see *Tourist Information Offices,* in this section, for addresses).

February

Carnaval: Pre-*Lenten* festivities celebrated throughout Portugal. Typically held for 4 days, ending at midnight on *Shrove Tuesday.* February 21–24, this year.

April

Holy Week A week of religious observances, processions, and pageantry throughout the country, especially in Braga. (For additional information about events in Braga during this period, see the individual city chapter in THE CITIES.)

Festa da Flor (Flower Festival): This annual festival at the end of April celebrates Madeira's botanic abundance with flower-decked floats and a parade of over 2,000 children carrying blossoms pieced together as a floral Wall of Hope. The festivities have a heavy folk flavor, with plenty of Madeiran music, singing, and dancing. April 25. Funchal, Madeira.

May

Festival of the Crosses: Celebrates the Miracle of the Crosses in early May, attracting thousands of visitors who take part in Minho folk dancing, a pottery fair, fun fair, eating, drinking, and fireworks. May 1–3. Barcelos.

Festival of the Roses: A splendid display of roses on parade and one of Portugal's most popular folkloric celebrations. May 8–9. Vila Franca do Lima.

Fátima Pilgrimage: Thousands of pilgrims from all parts of the world converge on Fátima to honor the appearance of Our Lady of Fátima in 1917. Religious ceremonies, processions, and masses are held on May 12–13 (and again on October 12–13). Fátima.

June

Grand International Fair of Santarém: Beginning the first Friday in June, 10 days of horsemanship and bullfighting heroics, handicraft and livestock exhibitions, folk dancing, singing, and fireworks. June 5–13. Santarém.

Festa de São Antônio: Celebration honoring the birthday of St. Anthony, the patron saint of young lovers. Lisbon's Old Quarter comes alive on the eve: Dances are held in streets festooned with colored lanterns, and throughout the night gallons of good, rough wine are drunk to wash down mountains of sardines roasted on open barbecues. The saint is a powerful matchmaker, so this is the night when the city's young girls hope to meet their future husbands. June 12–13. Lisbon.

Festas de São João: A Christian holiday with roots in pagan rites celebrating the summer solstice. Parties go on until all hours of the night, the *vinho verde* flows freely, and the aroma of festive food, including roast goat, invades the popular neighborhoods. Festivities include parades, fireworks, folk music, medieval dancing, and ancient customs, such as passing around leeks and throwing scented herbs and thistles into large bonfires to make divinations. June 23–24. Braga and Porto.

Festival de São Pedro: Nationwide celebrations honoring St. Peter, the patron saint of fishermen, includes a blessing of the ships; a display of regional products, handicrafts, and the famous *queijadas de Sintra,* delicious sweet cheese tarts, in Sintra and Lisbon; solemn processions and "Sword Dancing" in Ribeira Brava (Madeira); running of the bulls through the streets of Montijo, outside Lisbon; and *Cavalhadas de São Pedro* — a parade of masked riders, dating from the 15th century — through the streets of Ribeira Grande (São Miguel, Azores). June 28–29.

July

Festival of the Colete Encarnado: Open-air festivities the first week in July, featuring the parade of the *campinos* (Portuguese cowboys), running of the bulls, bullfights, fireworks, and folkloric exhibitions. July 2–4. Vila Franca de Xira.

August

Festas Gualteriãnas: A huge folk fair featuring regional foods and wines, religious parades, music, and costumed singers and dancers satirizing the Middle Ages. August 6–9. Guimarães.

Festas de Nossa Senhora da Agonia (Festival of Our Lady of Suffering): In mid-August, 3 days of colorful festivities attract pilgrims from the most varied parts of the country to take part in the grand procession. Other activities include fairs, music, dancing, and fireworks. August 20–22. Viano do Castel.

Festa de São Bartolomeu: This festival, held on the third Sunday in August, has evolved into a *cortejo de papel,* or "paper parade," in which people dress in paper costumes to satirize public personages and politicians. They follow a float carrying Neptune and Sirens to the beach, where they battle "pirates" from the sea; the battle ends with all the participants and some of the onlookers rushing into the water for a holy bath, a practice no doubt related to the old superstition that a dip in the sea can cast out the devil. Porto.

September

Festival of Our Lady of Boa Viagem (Good Voyage): Street fairs, amusements, running of the bulls, and other festivities. September 10–16. Moita.

Feiras Novas (New Fairs): This popular celebration, dating from the 12th century, now includes a procession to Our Lady of Sorrows. September 18–20. Ponte de Lima.

October

Fátima Pilgrimage: Pilgrimages (also held earlier, in May) to honor the appearance of Our Lady of Fátima in 1917. Religious ceremonies, processions, and masses on October 12 and 13. Fátima.

November

Feira Nacional do Cavalo (Feira de São Martinho): One of Europe's largest horse fairs, featuring daring exhibitions by Portuguese cowboys, parades, and various equestrian events, fireworks, and folk dancing. The horse show coincides with the *Feast of St. Martin,* which includes eating roasted chestnuts and drinking local wine. November 6–14. Golegã.

December

Festa do São Silvestre: Wild *New Year's Eve* celebration featuring singing, dancing, and a harborfront fireworks display. Funchal, Madeira.

Traveling by Plane

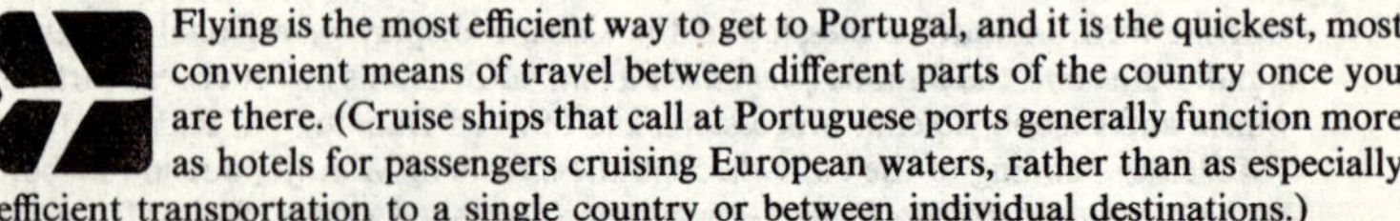

Flying is the most efficient way to get to Portugal, and it is the quickest, most convenient means of travel between different parts of the country once you are there. (Cruise ships that call at Portuguese ports generally function more as hotels for passengers cruising European waters, rather than as especially efficient transportation to a single country or between individual destinations.)

The air space between North America and Europe is the most heavily trafficked in the world. It is served by dozens of airlines, almost all of which sell seats at a variety of prices, under a vast spectrum of requirements and restrictions. Since you probably will spend more for your airfare than for any other single item in your travel budget, try to take advantage of the lowest fares offered by either scheduled airlines or charter companies. You should know what kinds of flights are available, the rules under which air travel operates, and all the special package options.

SCHEDULED AIRLINES: *TAP Air,* the Portuguese national airline, operates four nonstop flights a week from New York to Lisbon; *Delta* offers three; and *TWA* provides daily service on this route. *TAP* also flies nonstop from Newark to Lisbon four times a week, and nonstop from Boston once a week. Two weekly flights out of Boston travel to Lisbon via the Azores, with one stop on São Miguel, the other on Terceira.

In addition, *British Airways* offers connecting flights from its 17 US gateways through London's Heathrow and Gatwick airports to Faro and Lisbon. *Air France* also offers connections through Paris, from Boston, Chicago, Houston, Los Angeles, Miami, New York, and Washington, DC, to Lisbon and Porto, among other Portuguese cities. *KLM* offers connecting flights from Atlanta, Baltimore, Chicago, Detroit, Houston, Los Angeles, Minneapolis, New York, and Orlando, via Amsterdam to Lisbon and Porto. *Sabena* flies from Boston, Chicago, and New York, with connections made in Brussels for flights to Lisbon and Porto.

Gateways – At present, nonstop flights to Portugal leave from Boston, New York, and Newark. Additional connecting flights depart from some of the above cities and a few others as well. Nonstop or direct, nearly all of these flights land at major Portuguese destinations.

Tickets – When traveling on one of the many regularly scheduled flights, a full-fare ticket provides maximum travel flexibility (although at considerable expense) because there are no advance booking requirements. A prospective passenger can buy a ticket for a flight right up to the minute of takeoff — if a seat is available. If your ticket is for a round trip, you can make the return reservation whenever you wish — months before you leave, or the day before you return. Assuming the foreign immigration requirements are met, you can stay at your destination for as long as you like. (Tickets generally are good for a year and can be renewed if not used.) You also can cancel your flight at any time without penalty. However, while it is true that this category of ticket can be purchased at the last minute, it is advisable to reserve well in advance during popular vacation periods and around holiday times.

Fares – Airfares continue to change so rapidly that even the experts find it difficult to keep up with them. This ever-changing situation is due to a number of factors, including airline deregulation, volatile labor relations, increasing fuel costs, and vastly increased competition. Note that, at press time, the recent restructuring of air fares by a number of major US carriers applied only to domestic flights and some flights to Canada, the Caribbean, and Mexico. These changes had *not* been adopted on transatlantic and other international routes by either US or foreign carriers.

Perhaps the most common misconception about fares on scheduled airlines is that the cost of the ticket determines how much service will be provided on the flight. This is true only to a certain extent. A far more realistic rule of thumb is that the less you pay for your ticket, the more restrictions and qualifications are likely to come into play before you board the plane (as well as after you get off). These qualifying aspects relate to the months (and the days of the week) during which you must travel, how far in advance you must purchase your ticket, the minimum and maximum amount of time you may or must remain away, your willingness to decide on a return date at the time of booking — and your ability to stick to that decision. It is not uncommon for passengers sitting side by side on the same wide-body jet to have paid fares varying by hundreds of dollars, and all too often the traveler paying more would have been equally willing (and able) to accept the terms of the far less expensive ticket.

In general, the great variety of fares between the US and Portugal can be reduced to four basic categories, including first class, coach (also called economy or tourist class), and excursion or discount fares. A fourth category, called business class, has been added by many airlines in recent years. In addition, Advance Purchase Excursion (APEX) fares offer savings under certain conditions.

In a class by itself is the *Concorde,* the supersonic jet developed jointly by France and Great Britain, which cruises at speeds of 1,350 miles an hour (twice the speed of sound) and makes transatlantic crossings in half the time (3¾ hours from New York to Paris) of conventional, subsonic jets. *Air France* offers *Concorde* service from New York to Paris; *British Airways* flies from New York and Washington, DC, to London. Service is "single" class (with champagne and caviar all the way), and the fare is expensive, about 20% more than a first class ticket on a subsonic aircraft. Some discounts have been offered, but time is the real gift of the *Concorde.* For travelers to Portuguese destinations, this "gift" may be more or less valuable as compared to a direct flight when taking connections from London or Paris into account.

A **first class** ticket is your admission to the special section of the aircraft, with larger seats, more legroom, sleeperette seating on some wide-body aircraft, better (or at least more elaborately served) food, free drinks and headsets for movies and music channels, and above all, personal attention. First class fares are about twice those of full-fare economy, although both first class passengers and those paying full economy fares are entitled to reserve seats and are sold tickets on an open reservation system. An additional advantage of a first class ticket is that if you're planning to visit several cities within Portugal or elsewhere in Europe, you may include any number of stops en route to or from your most distant destination, provided that certain set, but generous, restrictions regarding maximum mileage limits and flight routes are respected.

Not too long ago, there were only two classes of air travel, first class and all the rest, usually called economy or tourist. Then **business class** came into being — one of the most successful recent airline innovations. At first, business class passengers were merely curtained off from the other economy passengers. Now a separate cabin or cabins — usually toward the front of the plane — is the norm. While standards of comfort and service are not as high as in first class, they represent a considerable improvement over conditions in the rear of the plane, with roomier seats, more leg and shoulder space between passengers, and fewer seats abreast. Free liquor and headsets, a choice of meal entrées, and a separate counter for speedier check-in are other inducements. As in first class, a business class passenger may travel on any scheduled flight he or she wishes, may buy a one-way or round-trip ticket, and have the ticket remain valid for a year. There are no minimum or maximum stay requirements, no advance booking requirements, and no cancellation penalties, and the fare allows the same free stopover privileges as first class. Airlines often have their own names for their business class service — such as Navigator Class on *TAP Air,* Medallion Class on *Delta,* and Ambassador Class on *TWA.*

The terms of the **coach** or **economy** fare may vary slightly from airline to airline, and in fact from time to time airlines may be selling more than one type of economy fare. Coach or economy passengers sit more snugly, as many as 10 in a single row on a wide-body jet, behind the first class and business class sections. Normally, alcoholic drinks are not free, nor are the headsets (except on *British Airways,* which does offer these free on its transatlantic flights). If there are two economy fares on the books, one (often called "regular economy") still may include a number of free stopovers. The other, less expensive fare (often called "special economy") may limit stopovers to one or two, with a charge (typically $25) for each one. Like first class passengers, however, passengers paying the full coach fare are subject to none of the restrictions that usually are attached to less expensive excursion and discount fares. There are no advance booking requirements, no minimum stay requirements, and no cancellation penalties. Tickets are sold on an open reservation system: They can be bought for a flight right up to the minute of takeoff (if seats are available), and if the ticket is round trip, the return reservation can be made anytime you wish. Both first class and coach tickets generally are good for a year, after which they can be renewed if not used, and if you ultimately decide not to fly at all, your money will be refunded. The cost of economy and business class tickets does not vary much in the course of the year between the US and Portugal, though on some transatlantic routes they vary from a basic (low-season) price in effect most of the year to a peak (high-season) price during the summer.

Excursion and other **discount** fares are the airlines' equivalent of a special sale and usually apply to round-trip bookings only. These fares generally differ according to the season and the number of travel days permitted. They are only a bit less flexible than full-fare economy tickets, and are, therefore, often useful for both business and holiday travelers. Most round-trip excursion tickets include strict minimum and maximum stay requirements, and reservations can be changed only within the specified time limits. So don't count on extending a ticket beyond the prescribed time of return or staying less time than required. Different airlines may have different regulations concerning the number of stopovers permitted, and sometimes excursion fares are less expensive during midweek. The availability of these reduced-rate seats is most limited at busy times such as holidays. Discount or excursion fare ticket holders sit with the coach passengers, and, for all intents and purposes, are indistinguishable from them. They receive all the same basic services, even though they may have paid anywhere between 30% and 55%

less for the trip. Obviously, it's wise to make plans early enough to qualify for this less expensive transportation if possible.

These discount or excursion fares may masquerade under a variety of names, they may vary from city to city (from the East Coast to the West Coast, especially), but they invariably have strings attached. A common requirement is that the ticket be purchased a certain number of days — usually between 7 and 21 days — in advance of departure, though it may be booked weeks or months in advance (it has to be "ticketed," or paid for, shortly after booking, however). The return reservation usually has to be made at the time of the original ticketing and often cannot be changed later than a certain number of days (again, usually 7 to 21 days) before the return flight. If events force a passenger to change the return reservation after the date allowed, the difference between the round-trip excursion rate and the round-trip coach rate probably will have to be paid, though most airlines allow passengers to use their discounted fares by standing by for an empty seat, even if they don't otherwise have standby fares. Another common condition is a minimum and maximum stay requirement; for example, 1 to 6 days or 6 to 14 days (but including at least a Saturday night). Last, cancellation penalties of up to 50% of the full price of the ticket have been assessed — if a refund is offered at all — so careful planning is imperative. Check the specific penalty in effect when you purchase your discount/excursion ticket.

Of even greater risk — and bearing the lowest price of all the current discount fares — is the ticket where no change at all in departure and/or return flights is permitted, and where the ticket price is totally nonrefundable. If you do buy a nonrefundable ticket, you should be aware of a policy followed by many airlines that may make it easier to change your plans if necessary. For a fee — set by each airline and payable at the airport when checking in — you *may* be able to change the time or date of a return flight on a nonrefundable ticket. However, if the nonrefundable ticket price for the replacement flight is higher than that of the original (as often is the case when trading in a weekday for a weekend flight), you will have to pay the difference. Any such change must be made a certain number of days in advance — in some cases as little as 2 days — of either the original or the replacement flight, whichever is earlier; restrictions are set by the individual carrier. (Travelers holding a nonrefundable or other restricted ticket who must change their plans due to a family emergency should know that some carriers may make special allowances in such situations; for further information, see *Staying Healthy,* in this section.)

In the past, some excursion fares offered for travel to Portugal came unencumbered by advance booking requirements and cancellation penalties, permitted one stopover (though not a free one) in each direction, and had "open jaws," meaning that you could fly to one city and depart from another, arranging and paying for your own transportation between the two. Although, for the most part, such excursion fares are no longer offered on flights between the US and the majority of European destinations, they still exist on flights between the US and Portugal, where they cost about a third less than economy — during the off-season. High-season prices may be less attractive. The ticket currently is good for a minimum of 7 days and a maximum of 1 year abroad.

There also is a newer, often less expensive type of excursion fare, the **APEX**, or **Advanced Purchase Excursion**, fare. (On European routes, this type of fare also may be called a "Eurosaver" fare.) As with traditional excursion fares, passengers paying an APEX fare sit with and receive the same basic services as any other coach or economy passengers, even though they may have paid up to 50% less for their seats. In return, they are subject to certain restrictions. In the case of flights to Portugal, the ticket usually is good for a minimum of 7 days abroad and a maximum, currently, of 3 months (depending on the airline and the destination); and as its name implies, it must be "ticketed," or paid for in its entirety, a certain period of time before departure — usually 21 days, although in the case of Portugal it may be as little as 14 days.

The drawback to an APEX fare is that it penalizes travelers who change their minds — and travel plans. The return reservation must be made at the time of the original ticketing, and if for some reason you change your schedule while abroad, you will have to pay a penalty of $100 or 10% of the ticket value, whichever is greater, as long as you travel within the validity period of your ticket. But if you change your return to a date less than the minimum stay or more than the maximum stay, the difference between the round-trip APEX fare and the full round-trip coach rate will have to be paid. There also is a penalty of anywhere from $50 to $125 or more for canceling or changing a reservation *before* travel begins — check the specific penalty in effect when you purchase your ticket. No stopovers are allowed on an APEX ticket, but it is possible to create an open-jaw effect by buying an APEX on a split ticket basis; for example, flying to Lisbon and returning from Ponta Delgada, on the island of São Miguel in the Azores. The total price would be half the price of an APEX to Lisbon plus half the price of an APEX to Ponta Delgada. APEX tickets to Portugal are sold at basic and peak rates (peak season is around May through September) and may include surcharges for weekend flights.

There also is a Winter or Super APEX fare, which may go under different names for different carriers. Similar to the regular APEX fare, it costs slightly less but is more restrictive. Depending on the airline and destination, it usually is available only for off-peak winter travel and is limited to a stay of between 7 and 21 days. Advance purchase still is required (currently 30 days prior to travel), and ticketing must be completed within 48 hours of reservation. The fare is nonrefundable except in cases of hospitalization or death.

Note that *TAP Air* does not offer Super APEX fares, as such, on its transatlantic flights. Instead it markets competitive fares — "specials" — on an irregular basis, depending on what discounts other airlines that serve the same route are offering. These "specials" have many of the same restrictions as the Super APEX fares offered by other carriers. *TAP Air* also offers a PEX fare, which unlike their APEX fares, is offered on flights within Portugal and to cities in other European countries.

Another type of fare that sometimes is available is the **youth fare.** At present, most airlines flying to Portugal are using a form of APEX fare as a youth fare for those through age 24. The maximum stay is extended to a year, and the return booking must be left open. Seats usually can be reserved no more than 3 days before departure, and tickets must be purchased when the reservation is made. The return is booked from Portugal in the same manner, no more than 3 days before flight time. On most airlines (including *TAP Air*), there is no cancellation penalty, but the fare is subject to availability, so it may be difficult to book a return during peak travel periods, and as with the regular APEX fare, it may not even be available for travel to or from Portugal during high season and may be offered only on selected routes. For instance, *TAP Air* stresses that this fare is offered on a space-available basis.

Standby fares, at one time the rock-bottom price at which a traveler could fly to Europe, have become elusive. At the time of this writing, most major scheduled airlines did not regularly offer standby fares on direct flights to Portugal. Because airline fares and their conditions constantly change, however, bargain hunters should not hesitate to ask if such a fare exists at the time they plan to travel. Travelers to Portugal also should inquire about the possibility of connecting flights through other European countries that may be offered on a standby basis.

While the definition of standby varies somewhat from airline to airline, it generally means that you make yourself available to buy a ticket for a flight (usually no sooner than the day of departure), then literally stand by on the chance that a seat will be empty. Once aboard, however, a standby passenger has the same meal service and frills (or lack of them) enjoyed by others in the economy class compartment.

Something else to check is the possibility of qualifying for a **GIT** (Group Inclusive

Travel) fare, which requires that a specific dollar amount of ground arrangements be purchased, in advance, along with the ticket. The requirements vary as to the number of travel days and stopovers permitted, and the minimum number of passengers required for a group. The actual fares also vary, but the cost will be spelled out in brochures distributed by the tour operators handling the ground arrangements. In the past, GIT fares were among the least expensive available from the established carriers, but the prevalence of discount fares has caused group fares to all but disappear from some air routes. Travelers reading brochures on group package tours to Portugal will find that, in almost all cases, the applicable airfare given as a sample (to be added to the price of the land package to obtain the total tour price) is an APEX fare, the same discount fare available to the independent traveler.

The major airlines serving Portugal from the US also may offer individual excursion fare rates similar to GIT fares, which are sold in conjunction with ground accommodation packages. Previously called ITX, and sometimes referred to as individual tour-basing fares, these fares generally are offered as part of "air/hotel/car/transfer packages," and can reduce the cost of an economy fare by more than a third. The packages are booked for a specific amount of time, with return dates specified; rescheduling and cancellation restrictions and penalties vary from carrier to carrier. At the time of this writing, these fares were offered to popular destinations throughout Portugal by *TAP Air* and *TWA*. Although their offering did not represent substantial savings over standard economy fares, it is worth checking at the time you plan to travel. (For further information on package options, see *Package Tours,* in this section.)

Travelers looking for the least expensive possible airfares should, finally, scan the pages of their hometown newspapers (especially the Sunday travel section) for announcements of special promotional fares. Most airlines offer their most attractive special fares to encourage travel during slow seasons, and to inaugurate and publicize new routes. Even if none of these factors applies, prospective passengers can be fairly sure that the number of discount seats per flight at the lowest price is strictly limited, or that the fare offering includes a set expiration date — which means it's absolutely necessary to move fast to enjoy the lowest possible price.

Among other special airline promotional deals for which you should be on the lookout are discount or upgrade coupons sometimes offered by the major carriers and found in mail-order merchandise catalogues. For instance, airlines sometimes issue coupons that typically cost around $25 each and are good for a percentage discount or an upgrade on an international airline ticket — including flights to Portugal. The only requirement beyond the fee generally is that a coupon purchaser must buy at least one item from the catalogue. There usually are some minimum airfare restrictions before the coupon is redeemable, but in general these are worthwhile offers. Restrictions often include certain blackout days (when the coupon cannot be used at all), usually imposed during peak travel periods. These coupons are particularly valuable to business travelers who tend to buy full-fare tickets, and while the coupons are issued in the buyer's name, they can be used by others who are traveling on the same itinerary.

It's always wise to ask about discount or promotional fares and about any conditions that might restrict booking, payment, cancellation, and changes in plans. Check the prices from neighboring cities. A special rate may be offered in a nearby city but not in yours, and it may be enough of a bargain to warrant your leaving from that city. Ask if there is a difference in price for midweek versus weekend travel, or if there is a further discount for traveling early in the morning or late at night. Also be sure to investigate package deals, which are offered by virtually every airline. These may include a car rental, accommodations, and dining and/or sightseeing features, in addition to the basic airfare, and the combined cost of packaged elements usually is considerably less than the cost of the exact same elements when purchased separately.

If in the course of your research you come across a deal that seems too good to be true, keep in mind that logic may not be a component of deeply discounted airfares — there's not always any sane relationship between miles to be flown and the price to get there. More often than not, the level of competition on a given route dictates the degree of discount, and don't be dissuaded from accepting an offer that sounds irresistible just because it also sounds illogical. Better to buy that inexpensive fare while it's being offered and worry about the sense — or absence thereof — while you're flying to your desired destination.

When you're satisfied that you've found the lowest possible price for which you can conveniently qualify (you may have to call the airline more than once, because different airline reservations clerks have been known to quote different prices), make your booking. Then, to protect yourself against fare increases, purchase and pay for your ticket as soon as possible after you've received a confirmed reservation. Airlines generally will honor their tickets, even if the operative price at the time of your flight is higher than the price you paid; if fares go up between the time you *reserve* a flight and the time you *pay* for it, you likely will be out of luck. Finally, with excursion or discount fares, it is important to remember that when a reservations clerk says that you must purchase a ticket by a specific date, this is an absolute deadline. Miss it and the airline may automatically cancel your reservation without telling you.

■ **Note:** Another wrinkle in the airfare scene is that if the fares go *down* after you purchase your ticket, you *may* be entitled to a refund of the difference. However, this is only possible in certain situations — availability and advance purchase restrictions pertaining to the lower rate are set by the airline. If you suspect that you may be able to qualify for such a refund, check with your travel agent or the airline.

Frequent Flyers – Among the leading carriers serving Portugal, *TAP Air, British Airways, Delta,* and *TWA* offer a bonus system to frequent travelers. After the first 10,000 miles, for example, a passenger might be eligible for a first class seat for the coach fare; after another 10,000 miles, he or she might receive a discount on his or her next ticket purchase. The value of the bonuses continues to increase as more miles are logged. If you are signed up for such a program with a US carrier and fly to Europe on *British Airways* or another European airline, in some cases the miles flown may be applied towards your collective bonus mileage account with the US carrier.

Bonus miles also may be earned by patronizing affiliated car rental companies or hotel chains, or by using one of the credit cards that now offers this reward. In deciding whether to accept such a credit card from one of the issuing organizations that tempt you with frequent flyer mileage bonuses on a specific airline, first determine whether the interest rate charged on the unpaid balance is the same as (or less than) possible alternate credit cards, and whether the annual "membership" fee also is equal or lower. If these charges are slightly higher than those of competing cards, weigh the difference against the potential value in airfare savings. Also ask about any bonus miles awarded just for signing up — 1,000 is common, 5,000 generally the maximum.

For the most up-to-date information on frequent flyer bonus options, you may want to send for the monthly newsletter *Frequent.* Issued by Frequent Publications, it provides current information about frequent flyer plans in general, as well as specific data about promotions, awards, and combination deals to help you keep track of the profusion — and confusion — of current and upcoming availabilities. For a year's subscription, send $33 to Frequent Publications, 4715-C Town Center Dr., Colorado Springs, CO 80916 (phone: 800-333-5937).

There also is a monthly magazine called *Frequent Flyer,* but unlike the newsletter mentioned above, its focus is primarily on newsy articles of interest to business travelers and other frequent flyers. Published by Official Airline Guides (PO Box 58543, Boulder, CO 80322-8543; phone: 800-323-3537), *Frequent Flyer* is available for $24 for a 1-year subscription.

Low-Fare Airlines – Increasingly, the stimulus for special fares is the appearance of airlines associated with bargain rates. On these airlines, all seats on any given flight generally sell for the same price, which is somewhat below the lowest discount fare offered by the larger, more established airlines. It is important to note that tickets offered by the smaller airlines specializing in low-cost travel frequently are not subject to the same restrictions as the lowest-priced ticket offered by the more established carriers. They may not require advance purchase or minimum and maximum stays, may involve no cancellation penalties, and may be available one way or round trip. A disadvantage to some low-fare airlines, however, is that when something goes wrong, such as delayed baggage or a flight cancellation due to equipment breakdown, their smaller fleets and fewer flights mean that passengers may have to wait longer for a solution than they would on one of the equipment-rich major carriers.

One airline offering a consistently low fare to Europe is *Virgin Atlantic Airways* (phone: 800-862-8621 or 212-242-1330), which flies from Boston, Los Angeles, Miami, Newark, and New York to London's Gatwick and Heathrow airports. The airline sells tickets in several categories, including business or "Upper Class," economy, APEX, and nonrefundable variations on standby. Fares from New York to London include Late Saver fares — which must be booked or purchased no more than 20 days prior to travel — and Late Late Saver fares — which must be booked or bought no more than 3 days prior to travel. Travelers to Portugal will have to take a short second flight from London to Portugal, but still may save money. To determine the potential savings, add the cost of the transatlantic fare and the cost of connecting flights to come up with the total ticket price. Remember, too, that since Portugal is such a popular holiday destination with the British, ultra-low-priced package programs are frequently available from British-based tour operators and bucket shops.

In a class by itself is *Icelandair,* a scheduled airline long known as a good source of low-cost flights to Europe. *Icelandair* flies from Baltimore/Washington, DC, New York, and Orlando to Copenhagen (Denmark), Glasgow and London (Great Britain), Gothenburg and Stockholm (Sweden), Helsinki (Finland), Luxembourg (in the country of the same name), Oslo (Norway), Paris (France), and Reykjavik (Iceland). In addition, the airline increases the options for its passengers by offering "thru-fares" on connecting flights to other European cities. (The price of the intra-European flights — aboard Luxembourg's *Luxair* — is included in the price *Icelandair* quotes for the transatlantic portion of the travel to these additional destinations.)

Icelandair sells tickets in a variety of categories, from unrestricted economy fares to a sort of standby "3-days-before" fare (which functions just like the youth fares described above but has no age requirement). Travelers should be aware, however, that all *Icelandair* flights stop in Reykjavik for 45 minutes — a minor delay for most, but one that further prolongs the trip for passengers who will wait again to board connecting flights to their ultimate destination in Portugal. (At the time of this writing, *Icelandair* did not offer connecting flights to Portugal; however, connecting flight options are available through other carriers.) It may be a better choice for travelers intending to visit other destinations on the Continent when taking both this delay and the cost of connections into account. For reservations and tickets, contact a travel agent or *Icelandair* (phone: 800-223-5500 or 212-967-8888).

Intra-European Fares – The cost of the round trip across the Atlantic is not the only expense to be considered. Flights between European cities can be quite expensive. Note that discounts have recently been introduced on routes between some European cities.

Recent Common Market moves toward airline deregulation are expected to lead gradually to a greater variety of budget fares. In the meantime, however, the high cost of fares between most European cities can be avoided by careful use of stopover rights on the higher-priced transatlantic tickets — first class, business class, and full-fare economy. If your ticket doesn't allow stopovers, ask about APEX and other excursion fares. If you are able to comply with applicable restrictions and can use them, you may save as much as 35% to 50% off full-fare economy. Note that these fares, which once could be bought only after arrival in Europe, are now sold in the US and can be bought before departure.

It is not easy to inform yourself about stopover possibilities by talking to most airline reservations clerks. More than likely, an inquiry concerning any projected trip will prompt the reply that a particular route is nonstop aboard the carrier in question, thereby precluding stopovers completely, or that the carrier does not fly to all the places you want to visit. It may take additional inquiries, perhaps with the aid of a travel agent, to determine the full range of options regarding stopover privileges.

Travelers might be able to squeeze in visits to Amsterdam, Dublin, London, or Paris on a first class ticket to Lisbon, for instance; and Lisbon might only be the first of many free European stopovers possible on a one-way or round-trip ticket to a city in Eastern Europe or points beyond. The airline that flies you on the first leg of your trip across the Atlantic issues the ticket, though you may have to use several different airlines in order to complete your journey. There is no time limit on the validity of a first class ticket, so there's no rush.

TAP Air offers PEX fares for travel within Portugal, as well as thru-fares between Portuguese and other European destinations. These fares can be purchased either before you leave the US or once in Europe, and there are no advance purchase restrictions (tickets can be purchased up to the time of the flight). These fares are available only on certain flights and have varying minimum and maximum stay requirements (most require that you stay over a Saturday).

Taxes and Other Fees – Travelers who have shopped for the best possible flight at the lowest possible price should be warned that a number of extras will be added to that price and collected by the airline or travel agent who issues the ticket. In addition to the $6 International Air Transportation Tax — a departure tax paid by all passengers flying from the US to a foreign destination — there is a $10 US Federal Inspection Fee levied on all air and cruise passengers who arrive in the US from outside North America (those arriving from Canada, Mexico, the Caribbean, and US territories are exempt). Usually included in the price of a round-trip or incoming ticket, it combines a $5 customs inspection fee and a $5 immigration inspection fee, both instituted in 1986 to finance additional inspectors and reduce delays at gateways.

Still another fee is charged by some airlines to cover more stringent security procedures, prompted by recent terrorist incidents. The 10% Federal US Transportation Tax applies to travel within the US or US territories. It does not apply to passengers flying between US cities or territories en route to a foreign destination, unless the trip includes a stopover of more than 12 hours at a US point. Someone flying from Los Angeles to New York and stopping in New York for more than 12 hours before boarding a flight to Portugal, for instance, would pay the 10% tax on the domestic portion of the trip. Note that these taxes *usually* (but not always) are included in advertised fares and in the prices quoted by airline reservations clerks.

Reservations – For those who don't have the time or patience to investigate personally all possible air departures and connections for a proposed trip, a travel agent can be of inestimable help. A good agent should have all the information on which flights go where and when, and which categories of tickets are available on each. Most have computerized reservation links with the major carriers, so that a seat can be reserved and confirmed in minutes. An increasing number of agents also possess fare-comparison computer programs, so they often are very reliable sources of detailed competitive price data. (For more information, see *How to Use a Travel Agent,* in this section.)

When making plane reservations through a travel agent, ask the agent to give the airline your home phone number, as well as your daytime business phone number. All too often the agent uses the agency number as the official contact for changes in flight plans. Especially during the winter, weather conditions hundreds or even thousands of miles away can wreak havoc with flight schedules. Aircraft are constantly in use, and a plane delayed in the Orient or on the West Coast can miss its scheduled flight from the East Coast the next morning. The airlines are fairly reliable about getting this sort of information to passengers if they can reach them; diligence does little good at 10 PM if the airline has only the agency's or an office number.

Reconfirmation is strongly recommended for all international flights (though it is not usually required on US domestic flights) and in the case of flights to Portugal, it is essential to confirm your round-trip reservations — especially the return leg — as well as any point-to-point flights within Europe. Some (though increasingly fewer) reservations to and from international destinations are automatically canceled after a required reconfirmation period (typically 72 hours) has passed — even if you have a confirmed, fully paid ticket in hand. It always is wise to call ahead to make sure that the airline did not slip up in entering your original reservation, or in registering any changes you may have made since, and that it has your seat reservation and/or special meal request in the computer. If you look at the printed information on your ticket, you'll see the airline's reconfirmation policy stated explicitly. Don't be lulled into a false sense of security by the "OK" on your ticket next to the number and time of the flight. This only means that a reservation has been entered; a reconfirmation still may be necessary. If in doubt — call.

If you plan not to take a flight on which you hold a confirmed reservation, by all means inform the airline. Because the problem of "no-shows" is a constant expense for airlines, they are allowed to overbook flights, a practice that often contributes to the threat of denied boarding for a certain number of passengers (see "Getting Bumped," below).

Seating – For most types of tickets, airline seats usually are assigned on a first-come, first-served basis at check-in, although some airlines make it possible to reserve a seat at the time of ticket purchase. Always check in early for your flight, even with advance seat assignments. A good rule of thumb for international flights is to arrive at the airport *at least* 2 hours before the scheduled departure to give yourself plenty of time in case there are long lines.

Most airlines furnish seating charts, which make choosing a seat much easier, but there are a few basics to consider. You must decide whether you prefer a window, aisle, or middle seat. On flights where smoking is permitted, you also should indicate if you prefer the smoking or nonsmoking section.

The amount of legroom provided (as well as chest room, especially when the seat in front of you is in a reclining position) is determined by something called "pitch," a measure of the distance between the back of the seat in front of you and the front of the back of your seat. The amount of pitch is a matter of airline policy, not the type of plane you fly. First class and business class seats have the greatest pitch, a fact that figures prominently in airline advertising. In economy class or coach, the standard pitch ranges from 33 to as little as 31 inches — downright cramped.

The number of seats abreast, another factor determining comfort, depends on a combination of airline policy and airplane dimensions. First class and business class have the fewest seats per row. Economy generally has 9 seats per row on a DC-10 or an L-1011, making either one slightly more comfortable than a 747, on which there normally are 10 seats per row. Charter flights on DC-10s and L-1011s, however, often have 10 seats per row and can be noticeably more cramped than 747 charters, on which the seating normally remains at 10 per row.

Airline representatives claim that most aircraft are more stable toward the front and midsection, while seats farthest from the engines are quietest. Passengers who have long legs and are traveling on a wide-body aircraft might request a seat directly behind a door or emergency exit, since these seats often have greater than average pitch, or a seat in the first row of a given section, which offers extra legroom — although these seats are increasingly being reserved for passengers who are willing (and able) to perform certain tasks in the event of emergency evacuation. It often is impossible, however, to see the movie from these seats, which are directly behind the plane's exits. Be aware that the first row of the economy section (called a "bulkhead" seat) on a conventional aircraft (not a widebody) does *not* offer extra legroom, since the fixed partition will not permit passengers to slide their feet under it, and that watching a movie from this first-row seat can be difficult and uncomfortable. These bulkhead seats do, however, provide ample room to use a bassinet or safety seat and often are reserved for families traveling with children.

A window seat protects you from aisle traffic and clumsy serving carts and also provides a view, while an aisle seat enables you to get up and stretch your legs without disturbing your fellow travelers. Middle seats are the least desirable, and seats in the last row are the worst of all, since they seldom recline fully. If you wish to avoid children on your flight or if you find that you are sitting in an especially noisy section, you usually are free to move to any unoccupied seat — if there is one.

If you are overweight, you may face the prospect of a long flight with special trepidation. Center seats in the alignments of wide-body 747s, L-1011s, and DC-10s are about 1½ inches wider than those on either side, so larger travelers tend to be more comfortable there.

Despite all these rules of thumb, finding out which specific rows are near emergency exits or at the front of a wide-body cabin can be difficult because seating arrangements on two otherwise identical planes vary from airline to airline. There is, however, a quarterly publication called the *Airline Seating Guide* that publishes seating charts for most major US airlines and many foreign carriers as well. Your travel agent should have a copy, or you can buy the US edition for $39.95 per year and the international edition for $44.95. Order from Carlson Publishing Co., Box 888, Los Alamitos, CA 90720 (phone: 800-728-4877 or 310-493-4877).

Simply reserving an airline seat in advance, however, actually may guarantee very little. Most airlines require that passengers arrive at the departure gate at least 45 minutes (sometimes more) ahead of time to hold a seat reservation. *TAP Air,* for example, may cancel seat assignments and may not honor reservations of passengers who have not checked in 45 minutes before the scheduled departure time, and they *ask* travelers to check in 2 hours before all international flights. It pays to read the fine print on the back of your ticket carefully and plan ahead.

A far better strategy is to visit an airline ticket office (or one of a select group of travel agents) to secure an actual boarding pass for your specific flight. Once this has been issued, airline computers show you as checked in, and you effectively own the seat you have selected (although some carriers may not honor boarding passes of passengers arriving at the gate less than 10 minutes before departure). This also is good — but not foolproof — insurance against getting bumped from an overbooked flight and is, therefore, an especially valuable tactic at peak travel times.

Smoking – One decision regarding choosing a seat has been taken out of the hands of many travelers who smoke. Effective February 25, 1990, the US government imposed a ban that prohibits smoking on all flights scheduled for 6 hours or less within the US and its territories. The new regulation applies to both domestic and international carriers serving these routes.

In the case of flights to Portugal, these rules do not apply to nonstop flights from the US to Europe, or those with a *continuous* flight time of over 6 hours between stops in the US or its territories. Smoking is not permitted on segments of international flights where the time between US landings is under 6 hours — for instance, flights that include a stopover (even with no change of plane), or connecting flights. To further complicate the situation, several individual carriers are banning smoking altogether on certain routes, although as we went to press these bans had not yet extended to carriers flying between the US and Portugal — for instance, *TAP Air* allows smoking on all transatlantic flights. Smoking *has* been banned on domestic flights within Portugal, however.

On those flights that do permit smoking, the US Department of Transportation has determined that nonsmoking sections must be enlarged to accommodate all passengers who wish to sit in one. The airline does not, however, have to shift seating to accommodate nonsmokers who arrive late for a flight or travelers flying standby, and in general not all airlines can guarantee a seat in the nonsmoking section on international flights. Cigar and pipe smoking are prohibited on all flights, even in the smoking sections.

For a wallet-size guide, which notes in detail the rights of nonsmokers according to these regulations, send a self-addressed, stamped envelope to *ASH (Action on Smoking and Health),* Airline Card, 2013 H St. NW, Washington, DC 20006 (phone: 202-659-4310).

Meals – If you have specific dietary requirements, be sure to let the airline know well before departure time. The available meals include vegetarian, seafood, kosher, Muslim, Hindu, high-protein, low-calorie, low-cholesterol, low-fat, low-sodium, diabetic, bland, and children's menus (not all of these may be available on every carrier). There is no extra charge for this option. It usually is necessary to request special meals when you make your reservations — check-in time is too late. It's also wise to reconfirm that your request for a special meal has made its way into the airline's computer — the time to do this is 24 hours before departure. (Note that special meals generally are not available on intra-European flights on small local carriers. If this poses a problem, try to eat before you board, or bring a snack with you.)

Baggage – Travelers from the US face two different kinds of rules. When you fly on a US airline or on a major international carrier, US baggage regulations will be in effect. Though airline baggage allowances vary slightly, in general, all passengers are allowed to carry on board, without charge, one piece of luggage that will fit easily under a seat of the plane or in an overhead bin and whose combined dimensions (length, width, and depth) do not exceed 45 inches. A reasonable amount of reading material, camera equipment, and a handbag also are allowed. In addition, all passengers are allowed to check two bags in the cargo hold: one usually not to exceed 62 inches when length, width, and depth are combined, the other not to exceed 55 inches in combined dimensions. Generally no single bag may weigh more than 70 pounds. The weight restriction, however, may vary on transatlantic flights of other European airlines, ranging from as much as 88 pounds permitted for first class passengers to as little as 50 pounds for economy class — so check with the specific carrier in advance.

On many intra-European flights, including domestic service in Portugal, baggage allowances may be subject to the old weight determination, under which each economy or discount passenger is allowed only a total of 44 to 50 pounds of luggage without additional charge. First class or business passengers are allowed a total of 66 to 88 pounds. (If you are flying from the US to Europe and connecting to a domestic flight, you generally will be allowed the same amount of baggage as on the transatlantic flight. If you break your trip and then take a domestic flight, the local carrier's weight restrictions apply.)

Charges for additional, oversize, or overweight bags usually are made at a flat rate; the actual dollar amount varies from carrier to carrier. If you plan to travel with any special equipment or sporting gear, be sure to check with the airline beforehand. Most have specific procedures for handling such baggage, and you may have to pay for transport regardless of how much other baggage you have checked. Golf clubs may be checked through as luggage (most airlines are accustomed to handling them), but tennis rackets should be carried onto the plane. Some airlines require that bicycles be partially dismantled and packaged (see *Camping and Caravanning, Hiking and Biking,* in this section).

Airline policies regarding baggage allowances for children vary and usually are based on the percentage of full adult fare paid. Although on many US carriers children who are ticket holders are entitled to the same baggage allowance as a full-fare passenger, some carriers allow only one bag per child, which sometimes must be smaller than an adult's bag (around 39 to 45 inches in combined dimensions). Often there is no luggage allowance for a child traveling on an adult's lap or in a bassinet. Particularly for international carriers, it's always wise to check ahead. (For more information, see *Hints for Traveling with Children,* in this section.)

To reduce the chances of your luggage going astray, remove all airline tags from previous trips, and label each bag inside and out — with your business address rather than your home address on the outside, to prevent thieves from knowing whose house might be unguarded. Lock everything and double-check the tag that the airline attaches to make sure that it is correctly coded for your destination: LIS for Portela Airport in Lisbon, for instance.

If your bags are not in the baggage claim area after your flight, or if they're damaged, report the problem to airline personnel immediately. Keep in mind that policies regarding the specific time limit within which you have to make your claim vary from carrier to carrier. Fill out a report form on your lost or damaged luggage and keep a copy of it and your original baggage claim check. If you must surrender the check to claim a damaged bag, get a receipt for it to prove that you did, indeed, check your baggage on the flight. If luggage is missing, be sure to give the airline your destination and/or a telephone number where you can be reached. Also, take the name and number of the person in charge of recovering lost luggage.

Most airlines have emergency funds for passengers stranded away from home without their luggage, but if it turns out that your bags are truly lost and not simply delayed, do not then and there sign any paper indicating you'll accept an offered settlement. Since the airline is responsible for the value of your bags within certain statutory limits ($1,250 per passenger for lost baggage on a US domestic flight; $9.07 per pound or $20 per kilo for checked baggage, and up to $400 per passenger for unchecked baggage, on an international flight), you should take some time to assess the extent of your loss (see *Insurance,* in this section). It's a good idea to keep records indicating the value of the contents of your luggage. A wise alternative is to take a Polaroid picture of the most valuable of your packed items just after putting them in your suitcase.

Considering the increased incidence of damage to baggage, it's now more than ever a good idea to keep the sales slips that confirm how much you paid for your bags. These are invaluable in establishing the value of damaged luggage and eliminate any arguments. A better way to protect your precious gear from the luggage-eating conveyers is to try to carry it on board wherever possible.

Be aware that airport security increasingly is an issue all over Europe, and the Portuguese take it very seriously. Heavily armed police patrol the airports, and unattended luggage of any description may be confiscated and quickly destroyed. Passengers checking in at European airports may undergo at least two separate inspections of their tickets, passports, and luggage by courteous, but serious, airline personnel — who ask passengers if their baggage has been out of their possession between packing and the airport or if they have been given gifts or other items to transport — before checked items are accepted.

Airline Clubs – Some US and foreign carriers have clubs for travelers who pay for membership. These clubs are not solely for first class passengers, although a first class ticket *may* entitle a passenger to lounge privileges. Membership entitles the traveler to use of the private lounges at airports along their route, to refreshments served in these lounges, and to check-cashing privileges at most of their counters. Extras include special telephone numbers for individual reservations, embossed luggage tags, and a membership card for identification. Airlines serving Portugal that offer membership in such clubs include the following:

Delta: The *Crown Club.* Single yearly membership $150; spouse an additional $50 per year; 3-year and lifetime memberships also available.

TWA: The *Ambassador Club.* Single yearly membership $150 for the first year (spouse an additional $25); $125 yearly per couple thereafter; lifetime memberships also available.

Note that such companies do not have club facilities in all airports. Other airlines also offer a variety of special services in many airports.

Getting Bumped – A special air travel problem is the possibility that an airline will accept more reservations (and sell more tickets) than there are seats on a given flight. This is entirely legal and is done to make up for "no-shows," passengers who don't show up for a flight for which they have made reservations and bought tickets. If the airline has oversold the flight and everyone does show up, there simply aren't enough seats. When this happens, the airline is subject to stringent rules designed to protect travelers.

In such cases, the airline first seeks ticket holders willing to give up their seats voluntarily in return for a negotiable sum of money or some other inducement, such as an offer of upgraded seating on the next flight or a voucher for a free trip at some other time. If there are not enough volunteers, the airline may bump passengers against their wishes.

Anyone inconvenienced in this way, however, is entitled to an explanation of the criteria used to determine who does and does not get on the flight, as well as compensation if the resulting delay exceeds certain limits. If the airline can put the bumped passengers on an alternate flight that is *scheduled to arrive* at their original destination within 1 hour of their originally scheduled arrival time, no compensation is owed. If the delay is more than 1 hour but less than 2 hours on a domestic US flight, they must be paid denied-boarding compensation equivalent to the one-way fare to their destination (but not more than $200). If the delay is more than 2 hours beyond the original arrival time on a domestic flight or more than 4 hours on an international flight, the compensation must be doubled (not more than $400). The airline also may offer bumped travelers a voucher for a free flight instead of the denied-boarding compensation. The passenger may be given the choice of either the money or the voucher, the dollar value of which may be no less than the monetary compensation to which the passenger would be entitled. The voucher is not a substitute for the bumped passenger's original ticket; the airline continues to honor that as well.

Keep in mind that the above regulations and policies are only for flights leaving the US, and do *not* apply to charters or to inbound flights originating abroad, even on US carriers. Airlines carrying passengers between foreign destinations are free to determine what compensation they will pay to passengers who are bumped because of overbooking. They generally spell out their policies on airline tickets. Some foreign airline policies are similar to the US policy; however, don't assume all carriers will be as generous.

To protect yourself as best you can against getting bumped, arrive at the airport early, allowing plenty of time to check in and get to the gate. If the flight is oversold, ask immediately for the written statement explaining the airline's policy on denied-boarding compensation and its boarding priorities. If the airline refuses to give you this information, or if you feel it has not handled the situation properly, file a complaint with both the airline and the appropriate government agency (see "Consumer Protection," below).

Delays and Cancellations – The above compensation rules also do not apply if the flight is canceled or delayed, or if a smaller aircraft is substituted due to mechanical problems. Each airline has its own policy for assisting passengers whose flights are delayed or canceled or who must wait for another flight because their original one was overbooked. Most airline personnel will make new travel arrangements if necessary. If the delay is longer than 4 hours, the airline may pay for a phone call or telegram, a meal, and, in some cases, a hotel room and transportation to it.

■ **Caution:** If you are bumped or miss a flight, be sure to ask the airline to notify other airlines on which you have reservations or connecting flights. When your name is taken off the passenger list of your initial flight, the computer usually cancels all of your reservations automatically, unless *you* take steps to preserve them.

CHARTER FLIGHTS: By booking a block of seats on a specially arranged flight, charter operators offer travelers air transportation for a substantial reduction over the full coach or economy fare. These operators may offer air-only charters (selling transportation alone) or charter packages (the flight plus a combination of land arrangements such as accommodations, meals, tours, or car rentals). Charters are especially attractive to people living in smaller cities or out-of-the-way places, because they frequently leave from nearby airports, saving travelers the inconvenience and expense of getting to a major gateway.

From the consumer's standpoint, charters differ from scheduled airlines in two main respects: You generally need to book and pay in advance, and you can't change the itinerary or the departure and return dates once you've booked the flight. In practice, however, these restrictions don't always apply. Today, although most charter flights still require advance reservations, some permit last-minute bookings (when there are unsold seats available), and some even offer seats on a standby basis.

Though charters almost always are round-trip, and it is unlikely that you would be sold a one-way seat on a round-trip flight, on rare occasions one-way tickets on charters are offered. Although it may be possible to book a one-way charter in the US, giving you more flexibility in scheduling your return, note that US regulations pertaining to charters may be more permissive than the charter laws of other countries. For example, if you want to book a one-way foreign charter back to the US, you may find advance booking rules in force.

Some things to keep in mind about the charter game:

1. It cannot be repeated often enough that if you are forced to cancel your trip, you can lose much (and possibly all) of your money unless you have cancellation insurance, which is a *must* (see *Insurance,* in this section). Frequently, if the cancellation occurs far enough in advance (often 6 weeks or more), you may forfeit only a $25 or $50 penalty. If you cancel only 2 or 3 weeks before the flight, there may be no refund at all unless you or the operator can provide a substitute passenger.
2. Charter flights may be canceled by the operator up to 10 days before departure for any reason, usually underbooking. Your money is returned in this event, but there may be too little time for you to make new arrangements.
3. Most charters have little of the flexibility of regularly scheduled flights regarding refunds and the changing of flight dates; if you book a return flight, you must be on it or lose your money.
4. Charter operators are permitted to assess a surcharge, if fuel or other costs warrant it, of up to 10% of the airfare up to 10 days before departure.
5. Because of the economics of charter flights, your plane almost always will be full, so you will be crowded, though not necessarily uncomfortable. (There is, however, a new movement among charter airlines to provide flight accommodations that are more comfort-oriented, so this situation may change in the near future.)

To avoid problems, *always* choose charter flights with care. When you consider a charter, ask your travel agent who runs it and carefully check the company. The Better Business Bureau in the company's home city can report on how many complaints, if any, have been lodged against it in the past. Protect yourself with trip cancellation and interruption insurance, which can help safeguard your investment if you, or a traveling companion, are unable to make the trip and must cancel too late to receive a full refund from the company providing your travel services. (This is advisable whether you're buying a charter flight alone or a tour package for which the airfare is provided by charter or scheduled flight.)

Bookings – If you do fly on a charter, read the contract's fine print carefully and pay particular attention to the following:

Instructions concerning the payment of the deposit and its balance and to whom the check is to be made payable. Ordinarily, checks are made out to an escrow account, which means the charter company can't spend your money until your flight has safely returned. This provides some protection for you. To ensure the safe handling of your money, make out your check to the escrow account, the number of which must appear by law on the brochure, though all too often it is on the back in fine print. Write the details of the charter, including the destination and dates, on the face of the check; on the back, print "For Deposit Only." Your travel agent may prefer that you make out your check to the agency, saying that it will then pay the tour operator the fee minus commission. It is perfectly legal to write the check as we suggest, however, and if your agent objects too vociferously (he or she should trust the tour operator to send the proper commission), consider taking your business elsewhere. If you don't make your check out to the escrow account, you lose the protection of that escrow should the trip be canceled. Furthermore, recent bankruptcies in the travel industry have served to point out that even the protection of escrow may not be enough to safeguard a traveler's investment. More and more, insurance is becoming a necessity. The charter company should be bonded (usually by an insurance company), and if you want to file a claim against it, the claim should be sent to the bonding agent. The contract will set a time limit within which a claim must be filed.

Specific stipulations and penalties for cancellations. Most charters allow you to cancel up to 45 days in advance without major penalty, but some cancellation dates are 50 to 60 days before departure.

Stipulations regarding cancellation and major changes made by the charterer. US rules say that charter flights may not be canceled within 10 days of departure except when circumstances — such as natural disasters or political upheavals — make it impossible to fly. Charterers may make "major changes," however, such as in the date or place of departure or return, but you are entitled to cancel and receive a full refund if you don't wish to accept these changes. A price increase of more than 10% at any time up to 10 days before departure is considered a major change; no price increase at all is allowed during the 10 days immediately before departure.

At the time of this writing, the following two companies regularly offered charter flights to Portugal:

Relvas Tours (188 Pequonnock St., Bridgeport, CT 06604; phone: 800-243-3500 or 203-333-3322).

Suntrips (2350 Paragon Dr., San Jose, CA 95131; phone: 800-SUNTRIPS in California; 408-432-0700 elsewhere in the US).

For the full range of possibilities at the time you plan to travel, you may want to subscribe to the travel newsletter *Jax Fax,* which regularly features a list of charter companies and packagers offering seats on charter flights and may be a source for other charter flights to Portugal. For a year's subscription send a check or money order for $12 to *Jax Fax* (397 Post Rd., Darien, CT 06820; phone: 203-655-8746).

DISCOUNTS ON SCHEDULED FLIGHTS: Promotional fares often are called discount fares because they cost less than what used to be the standard airline fare — full-fare economy. Nevertheless, they cost the traveler the same whether they are bought through a travel agent or directly from the airline. Tickets that cost less if bought from some outlet other than the airline do exist, however. While it is likely that the vast majority of travelers flying to Portugal in the near future will be doing so on a promotional fare or charter rather than on a "discount" air ticket of this sort, it still is a good idea for cost-conscious consumers to be aware of the latest developments in the budget airfare scene. Note that the following discussion makes clear-cut distinctions among the types of discounts available based on how they reach the consumer; in actual practice, the distinctions are not nearly so precise.

Courier Travel – There was a time when traveling as a courier was a sort of underground way to save money and visit otherwise unaffordable destinations, but more and more, this once exotic idea of traveling as a courier is becoming a very "establishment" exercise. Being a courier means no more than accompanying freight of one sort or another, and typically that freight replaces what otherwise would be the traveler's checked baggage. Be prepared, therefore, to carry all your own personal travel gear in a carry-on bag. In addition, the so-called courier usually pays only a portion of the total airfare — the freight company pays the remainder — and the courier also may be assessed a small registration fee. Note that many courier flights can be booked in advance (sometimes as much as 3 months) and that flights often are round trip.

There are dozens of courier companies operating actively around the globe, and several publications provide information on courier opportunities:

A Simple Guide to Courier Travel, by Jesse L. Riddle, is a particularly good reference guide to courier travel. Published by the Carriage Group (PO Box 2394, Lake Oswego, OR 97035; phone: 800-222-3599), it's available for $15.95, including postage and handling.

Travel Secrets (PO Box 2325, New York, NY 10108; phone: 212-245-8703). Provides information useful to those considering traveling as a courier and often lists specific US and Canadian courier companies. Monthly; a year's subscription costs $33.

Travel Unlimited (PO Box 1058, Allston, MA 02134-1058; no phone). Lists courier companies and agents worldwide. Monthly; for a year's subscription send $25.

World Courier News (PO Box 77471, San Francisco, CA 94107; no phone). Provides information on courier opportunities, as well as useful tips. Each issue highlights a different destination. Monthly; for a year's subscription send $20.

Although, at press time, no companies were arranging courier flights to Portugal, those that regularly send couriers to Europe include *Discount Travel International* (152 W. 72nd Street, Suite 223, New York, NY 10023; phone: 212-362-3636) and *Courier Travel Service* (530 Central Ave., Cedarhurst, NY 11516; phone: 800-922-2FLY or 516-374-2299). Check with them when planning your trip to find out if current offerings include flights to Portugal. You also may want to consider contacting *Excaliber International Courier Inc.,* as this company often sends couriers to London (where you can catch a connecting flight to Portugal). For information, contact *Excaliber*'s representative, *Way to Go Travel* (6679 Sunset Blvd., Hollywood, CA 90028; phone: 213-466-1126). In addition, *Now Voyager* (74 Varick St., Suite 307, New York, NY 10013; phone: 212-431-1616) is a referral agency that matches up would-be couriers with courier companies.

Net Fare Sources – The newest notion for reducing the costs of travel services comes from travel agents who offer individual travelers "net" fares. Defined simply, a net fare is the bare minimum amount at which an airline or tour operator will carry a prospective traveler. It doesn't include the amount that normally would be paid to the travel agent as a commission. Traditionally, such commissions amount to about

10% on domestic fares and from 10% to 20% on international fares — not counting significant additions to these commission levels that are paid retroactively when agents sell more than a specific volume of tickets or trips for a single supplier. At press time, at least one travel agency in the US was offering travelers the opportunity to purchase tickets and/or tours for a net price. Instead of earning its income from individual commissions, this agency assesses a fixed fee that may or may not provide a bargain for travelers; it requires a little arithmetic to determine whether to use the services of a net travel agent or those of one who accepts conventional commissions. One of the potential drawbacks of buying from agencies selling travel services at net fares is that some airlines refuse to do business with them, thus possibly limiting your flight options.

Travel Avenue is a fee-based agency that rebates its ordinary agency commission to the customer. For domestic flights, they will find the lowest retail fare, then rebate 7% to 10% (depending on the airline selected) of that price minus a $10 ticket-writing charge. The rebate percentage for international flights varies from 5% to 16% (again depending on the airline), and the ticket-writing fee is $25. The ticket-writing charge is imposed per ticket; if the ticket includes more than eight separate flights, an additional $10 or $25 fee is charged. Customers using free flight coupons pay the ticket-writing charge, plus an additional $5 coupon-processing fee.

Travel Avenue will rebate its commissions on all tickets, including heavily discounted fares and senior citizen passes. Available 7 days a week, reservations should be made far enough in advance to allow the tickets to be sent by first class mail, since extra charges accrue for special handling. It's possible to economize further by making your own airline reservation, then asking *Travel Avenue* only to write/issue your ticket. For travelers outside the Chicago area, business may be transacted by phone and purchases charged to a credit card. For information, contact *Travel Avenue* at 641 W. Lake St., Suite 201, Chicago, IL 60606-1012 (phone: 312-876-1116 in Illinois; 800-333-3335 elsewhere in the US).

Consolidators and Bucket Shops – Other vendors of travel services can afford to sell tickets to their customers at an even greater discount because the airline has sold the tickets to them at a substantial discount (usually accomplished by sharply increasing commissions to that vendor), a practice in which many airlines indulge, albeit discreetly, preferring that the general public not know they are undercutting their own "list" prices. Airlines anticipating a slow period on a particular route sometimes sell off a certain portion of their capacity at a very great discount to a wholesaler, or consolidator. The wholesaler sometimes is a charter operator who resells the seats to the public as though they were charter seats, which is why prospective travelers perusing the brochures of charter operators with large programs frequently see a number of flights designated as "scheduled service." As often as not, however, the consolidator, in turn, sells the seats to a travel agency specializing in discounting. Airlines also can sell seats directly to such an agency, which thus acts as its own consolidator. The airline offers the seats either at a net wholesale price, but without the volume-purchase requirement that would be difficult for a modest retail travel agency to fulfill, or at the standard price, but with a commission override large enough (as high as 50%) to allow both a profit and a price reduction to the public.

Travel agencies specializing in discounting sometimes are called "bucket shops," a term once fraught with connotations of unreliability in this country. But in today's highly competitive travel marketplace, more and more conventional travel agencies are selling consolidator-supplied tickets, and the old bucket shops' image is becoming respectable. Agencies that specialize in discounted tickets exist in most large cities, and usually can be found by studying the smaller ads in the travel sections of Sunday newspapers.

Before buying a discounted ticket, whether from a bucket shop or a conventional, full-service travel agency, keep the following considerations in mind: To be in a position to judge how much you'll be saving, first find out the "list" prices of tickets to your destination. Then do some comparison shopping among agencies. Also bear in mind that a ticket that may not differ much in price from one available directly from the airline may, however, allow the circumvention of such things as the advance-purchase requirement. If your plans are less than final, be sure to find out about any other restrictions, such as penalties for canceling a flight or changing a reservation. Most discount tickets are non-endorsable, meaning that they can be used only on the airline that issued them, and they usually are marked "nonrefundable" to prevent their being cashed in for a list price refund.

A great many bucket shops are small businesses operating on a thin margin, so it's a good idea to check the local Better Business Bureau for any complaints registered against the one with which you're dealing — before parting with any money. If you still do not feel reassured, consider buying discounted tickets only through a conventional travel agency, which can be expected to have found its own reliable source of consolidator tickets — some of the largest consolidators, in fact, sell only to travel agencies.

A few bucket shops require payment in cash or by certified check or money order, but if credit cards are accepted, use that option. Note, however, if buying from a charter operator selling both scheduled and charter flights, that the scheduled seats are not protected by the regulations — including the use of escrow accounts — governing the charter seats. Well-established charter operators, nevertheless, may extend the same protections to their scheduled flights, and when this is the case, consumers should be sure that the payment option selected directs their money into the escrow account.

Among the numerous consolidators offering discount fares to Portugal (among other European destinations) are the following:

Bargain Air (655 Deep Valley Dr., Suite 355, Rolling Hills, CA 90274; phone: 800-347-2345 or 213-377-2919).

Council Charter (205 E. 42nd St., New York, NY 10017; phone: 800-800-8222 or 212-661-0311).

Maharaja Travel/Consumer Wholesale Travel (34 W. 33rd St., Suite 1014, New York, NY 10001; phone: 212-213-2020 in New York State; 800-223-6862 elsewhere in the US).

TFI Tours International (34 W. 32nd St., 12th Floor, New York, NY 10001; phone: 212-736-1140 in New York State; 800-825-3834 elsewhere in the US).

Travac Tours and Charters (989 Sixth Ave., New York, NY 10018; phone: 212-563-3303).

25 West Tours (2490 Coral Way, Miami, FL 33145; phone: 800-225-2582 or 305-856-0810).

Unitravel (1177 N. Warson Rd., St. Louis, MO 63132; phone: 314-569-0900 in Missouri; 800-325-2222 elsewhere in the US).

■ **Note:** Although rebating and discounting are becoming increasingly common, there is some legal ambiguity concerning them. Strictly speaking, it is legal to discount domestic tickets, but not international tickets. On the other hand, the law that prohibits discounting, the Federal Aviation Act of 1958, is consistently ignored these days, in part because consumers benefit from the practice and in part because many illegal arrangements are indistinguishable from legal ones. Since the line separating the two is so fine that even the authorities can't always tell the difference, it is unlikely that most consumers would be able to do so, and in fact it is not illegal to *buy* a discounted ticket. If the issue of legality bothers you, ask the agency whether any ticket you're about to buy would be permissible under the above-mentioned act.

OTHER DISCOUNT TRAVEL SOURCES: An excellent source of information on economical travel opportunities is the *Consumer Reports Travel Letter,* published monthly by Consumers Union. It keeps abreast of the scene on a wide variety of fronts, including package tours, rental cars, insurance, and more, but it is especially helpful for its comprehensive coverage of airfares, offering guidance on all the options from scheduled flights on major or low-fare airlines to charters and discount sources. For a year's subscription, send $37 ($57 for 2 years) to *Consumer Reports Travel Letter* (PO Box 53629, Boulder, CO 80322-3629; phone: 800-234-1970). For information on other travel newsletters, see *Books, Newspapers, Magazines, and Newsletters,* in this section.

Last-Minute Travel Clubs – Still another way to take advantage of bargain airfares is open to those who have a flexible schedule. A number of organizations, usually set up as last-minute travel clubs and functioning on a membership basis, routinely keep in touch with travel suppliers to help them dispose of unsold inventory at discounts of between 15% and 60%. A great deal of the inventory consists of complete package tours and cruises, but some clubs offer air-only charter seats and, occasionally, seats on scheduled flights.

Members pay an annual fee and receive a toll-free hotline telephone number to call for information on imminent trips. In some cases, they also receive periodic mailings with information on bargain travel opportunities for which there is more advance notice. Despite the suggestive names of the clubs providing these services, last-minute travel does not necessarily mean that you cannot make plans until literally the last minute. Trips can be announced as little as a few days or as much as 2 months before departure, but the average is from 1 to 4 weeks' notice.

Among the organizations regularly offering such discounted travel opportunities to Portugal are the following:

Discount Travel International (Ives Building, 114 Forrest Ave., Suite 205, Narberth, PA 19072; phone: 800-334-9294 or 215-668-7184). Annual fee: $45 per household.

Encore/Short Notice (4501 Forbes Blvd., Lanham, MD 20706; phone: 301-459-8020; 800-638-0930 for customer service). Annual fee: $36 per family for their Short Notice program only; $48 per family to join the Encore program, which provides additional travel services.

Last Minute Travel (1249 Boylston St., Boston MA 02215; phone: 800-LAST-MIN or 617-267-9800). No fee.

Moment's Notice (425 Madison Ave., New York, NY 10017; phone: 212-486-0500). Annual fee: $45 per family.

Spur-of-the-Moment Tours and Cruises (10780 Jefferson Blvd., Culver City, CA 90230; phone: 310-839-2418 in Southern California; 800-343-1991 elsewhere in the US). No fee.

Traveler's Advantage (3033 S. Parker Rd., Suite 1000, Aurora, CO 80014; phone: 800-548-1116). Annual fee: $49 per family.

Vacations to Go (2411 Fountain View, Suite 201, Houston, TX 77057; phone: 800-338-4962). Annual fee: $19.95 per family.

Worldwide Discount Travel Club (1674 Meridian Ave., Miami Beach, FL 33139; phone: 305-534-2082). Annual fee: $40 per person; $50 per family.

■ **Note:** For additional information on last-minute travel discounts, a new "900" number telephone service called *Last Minute Travel Connection* (phone: 900-446-8292) provides recorded advertisements (including contact information) for discount offerings on airfares, package tours, cruises, and other travel opportunities. Since companies update their advertisements as often as every hour, listings are current. This 24-hour service is available to callers using touch-tone phones; the cost is $1 per minute (the charge will show up on your phone bill). For more information, contact *La Onda, Ltd.,* 601 Skokie Blvd., Suite 224, Northbrook, IL 60062 (phone: 708-498-9216).

Generic Air Travel – Organizations that apply the same flexible-schedule idea to air travel only and arrange for flights at literally the last minute also exist. The service they provide sometimes is known as "generic" air travel, and it operates somewhat like an ordinary airline standby service except that the organizations running it do not guarantee flights to a specific destination, but only to a general region, and offer seats on not one but several scheduled and charter airlines.

One pioneer of generic flights is *Airhitch* (2790 Broadway, Suite 100, New York, NY 10025; phone: 212-864-2000), which arranges flights to Portugal from various US gateways. Prospective travelers stipulate a range of at least five consecutive departure dates and their desired destination, along with alternate choices, and pay the fare in advance. They are then sent a voucher good for travel *on a space-available basis* on flights to their destination *region* (i.e., not necessarily the specific destination requested) during this time period. The week before this range of departure dates begins, travelers must contact *Airhitch* for specific information about flights that will probably be available and instructions on how to proceed for check-in. (Return flights are arranged in the same manner as the outbound flights — a specified period of travel is decided upon, and a few days before this date range begins, prospective passengers contact *Airhitch* for details about flights that may be available.) If the client does not accept any of the suggested flights or cancels his or her travel plans after selecting a flight, the amount paid can be applied toward a future fare or the flight arrangements can be transferred to another individual (although, in both cases, an additional fee may be charged). No refunds are offered unless the prospective passenger does not ultimately get on any flight in the specified date range; in such a case, the full fare is refunded. (Note that *Airhitch*'s slightly more expensive "Target" program, which provides confirmed reservations on specific dates to specific destinations, offers passengers greater — but not guaranteed — certainty regarding flight arrangements.)

Bartered Travel Sources – Suppose a hotel buys advertising space in a newspaper. As payment, the hotel gives the publishing company the use of a number of hotel rooms in lieu of cash. This is barter, a common means of exchange among hotels, airlines, car rental companies, cruise lines, tour operators, restaurants, and other travel service companies. When a bartering company finds itself with empty airline seats (or excess hotel rooms, or cruise ship cabin space, and so on) and offers them to the public, considerable savings can be enjoyed.

Bartered travel clubs often offer discounts of up to 50% to members who pay an annual fee (approximately $50 at press time) which entitles them to select from the flights, cruises, hotel rooms, or other travel services that the club obtained by barter. Members usually present a voucher, club credit card, or scrip (a dollar-denomination voucher negotiable only for the bartered product) to the hotel, which in turn subtracts the dollar amount from the bartering company's account.

Selling bartered travel is a perfectly legitimate means of retailing. One advantage to club members is that they don't have to wait until the last minute to obtain flight or room reservations.

Among the companies specializing in bartered travel, several that frequently offer members travel services to and in Portugal include the following:

Travel Guild (18210 Redmond Way, Redmond, WA 98052; phone: 206-861-1900). Annual fee: $48 per family.

Travel World Leisure Club (225 W. 34th St., Suite 2203, New York, NY 10122; phone: 800-444-TWLC or 212-239-4855). Annual fee: $50 per family.

Another company, *IGT (In Good Taste) Services* (1111 Lincoln Rd., 4th Floor, Miami Beach, FL 33139; phone: 800-444-8872 or 305-534-7900) offers discounts on a variety of travel services and occasionally sells bartered travel arrangements as well. At press time, however, they were not offering bartered travel or other discounts to Portugal — call when planning your trip. Their annual membership fee is $48 per family.

CONSUMER PROTECTION: Consumers who feel that they have not been dealt with fairly by an airline should make their complaints known. Begin with the customer service representative at the airport where the problem occurs. If he or she cannot resolve your complaint to your satisfaction, write to the airline's consumer office. In a businesslike, typed letter, explain what reservations you held, what happened, the names of the employees involved, and what you expect the airline to do to remedy the situation. Send copies (never the originals) of the tickets, receipts, and other documents that back your claims. Ideally, all correspondence should be sent via certified mail, return receipt requested. This provides proof that your complaint was received.

Passengers with consumer complaints — lost baggage, compensation for getting bumped, violations of smoking and nonsmoking rules, deceptive practices by an airline, charter regulations — who are not satisfied with the airline's response should contact the US Department of Transportation (DOT), Consumer Affairs Division (400 Seventh St. SW, Room 10405, Washington, DC 20590; phone: 202-366-2220). DOT personnel stress, however, that consumers initially should direct their complaints to the airline that provoked them.

Travelers with an unresolved complaint involving a foreign carrier also can contact the US Department of Transportation. DOT personnel will do what they can to help resolve all such complaints, although their influence may be limited.

Although Portugal does not have a specific government bureau that deals with airline complaints, consumers with complaints against a Portuguese airline or other travel-related service company can write to the tourist authority in the area of Portugal where the problem occurred (see *Sources and Resources,* in this section, for addresses). Outline the specifics in as much detail as possible (preferably in Portuguese, but they generally will respond — in English — to a letter sent to them in English). They will try to resolve the complaint or, if it is out of their jurisdiction, will refer the matter to the proper authorities, and will notify you in writing of the result of their inquiries and/or any action taken.

Remember, too, that the federal Fair Credit Billing Act permits purchasers to refuse to pay for credit card charges for services which have not been delivered, so the onus of dealing with the receiver for a bankrupt airline falls on the credit card company. Do not rely on another airline to honor the ticket you're holding, since the days when virtually all major carriers subscribed to a default protection program that bound them to do so are long gone. Some airlines may voluntarily step forward to accommodate the stranded passengers of a fellow carrier, but this now is an entirely altruistic act.

The deregulation of US airlines has meant that the traveler must find out for himself or herself what he or she is entitled to receive. The US Department of Transportation's informative consumer booklet *Fly Rights* is a good place to start. To receive a copy, send $1 to the Superintendent of Documents (US Government Printing Office, Washington, DC 20402-9325; phone: 202-783-3238). Specify its stock number, 050-000-00513-5, and allow 3 to 4 weeks for delivery.

■ **Note:** Those who tend to experience discomfort due to the change in air pressure while flying may be interested in the free pamphlet *Ears, Altitude and Airplane Travel;* for a copy send a self-addressed, stamped, business-size envelope to the *American Academy of Otolaryngology* (One Prince St., Alexandria, VA 22314; phone: 703-836-4444). And for when you land, *Overcoming Jet Lag* offers some helpful tips on minimizing post-flight stress; it is available from Berkeley Publishing Group (PO Box 506, Mail Order Dept., East Rutherford, NJ 07073; phone: 800-631-8571) for $6.95, plus shipping and handling.

Traveling by Ship

There was a time when traveling by ship was extraordinarily expensive, time-consuming, utterly elegant, and was utilized almost exclusively for getting from one point to another. Alas, the days when steamships reigned as the primary means of transatlantic transportation are gone, days when European countries — and the US — had fleets of passenger liners that offered week-plus trips across the North Atlantic. Only one ship (*Cunard*'s *Queen Elizabeth 2*) continues to offer this kind of service between the US and Europe with any degree of regularity; others make "positioning" cruises a few times a year at most. At the same time, the possibility of booking passage to Europe on a cargo ship is becoming less practical. Fewer and fewer travelers, therefore, first set foot on Portuguese soil with sea legs developed during an ocean voyage.

Although fewer travelers to Europe are choosing sea travel as the means of transport to a specific destination, more and more people are cruising *around* Europe. No longer primarily pure transportation, cruising currently is riding a wave of popularity as a leisure activity in its own right, and the host of new ships (and dozens of rebuilt old ones) testifies dramatically to the attraction of vacationing on the high seas. And due to the growing popularity of travel along coastal and inland waterways, more and more travelers — particularly repeat travelers — are climbing aboard some kind of water-borne conveyance once they've arrived in Europe, and seeing Portugal while cruising around the Mediterranean or taking a ferry to one of the Portuguese islands.

Many modern-day cruise ships seem much more like motels-at-sea than the classic liners of a couple of generations ago, but they are consistently comfortable and passengers often are pampered. Cruise prices can be quite reasonable, and since the single cruise price covers all the major items in a typical vacation — transportation, accommodations, all meals, entertainment, and a full range of social activities, sports, and recreation — a traveler need not fear any unexpected assaults on the family travel budget.

When selecting a cruise, your basic criteria should be where you want to go, the time you have available, how much you want to spend, and the kind of environment that best suits your style and taste (in which case price is an important determinant). Rely on the suggestions of a travel agent — preferably one specializing in cruises (see "A final note on picking a cruise," below) — but be honest with the agent (and with yourself) in describing the type of atmosphere you're seeking. Ask for suggestions from friends who have been on cruises; if you trust their judgment, they should be able to suggest a ship on which you'll feel comfortable.

There are a number of moments in the cruise-planning process when discounts are available from the major cruise lines, so it may be possible to enjoy some diminution of the list price almost anytime you book passage on a cruise ship. For those willing to commit early — say 4 to 6 months before sailing — most of the major cruise lines routinely offer a 10% reduction off posted prices, in addition to the widest selection of cabins. For those who decide to sail rather late in the game — say, 4 to 6 weeks before departure — savings often are even greater — an average of 20% — as steamship lines try to fill up their ships. The only negative aspect is that the choice of cabins tends to be limited, although it is possible that a fare upgrade will be offered to make this limited selection more palatable. In addition, there's the option of buying from a discount travel club or a travel agency that specializes in last-minute bargains; these discounters and other discount travel sources are discussed at the end of *Traveling by Plane,* above.

Most of the time, the inclusion of air transportation in the cruise package costs significantly less than if you were to buy the cruise separately and arrange your own air transportation to the port. If you do decide on one of these economical air/sea packages, be forewarned that it is not unusual for the pre-arranged flight arrangements to be less than convenient. The problems often arrive with the receipt of your cruise ticket, which also includes the airline ticket for the flight to get you to and from the ship dock. This is normally the first time you see the flights on which you have been booked and can appraise the convenience of the departure and arrival times. The cruise ship lines generally are not very forthcoming about altering flight schedules, and your own travel agent also may have difficulty in rearranging flight times or carriers. That means that the only remaining alternative is to ask the line to forget about making your flight arrangements and to pay for them separately by yourself. This may be more costly, but it's more likely to give you an arrival and departure schedule that will best conform to the sailing and docking times of the ship on which you will be cruising.

Cruise lines promote sailings to and around Europe as "get away from it all" vacations. But prospective cruise ship passengers will find that the variety of cruises is tremendous, and the quality, while generally high, varies depending on shipboard services, the tone of shipboard life, the cost of the cruise, and operative itineraries. Although there are less expensive ways to see Europe, the romance and enjoyment of a sea voyage remain irresistible for many, so a few points should be considered by such sojourners before they sign on for a seagoing vacation (after all, it's hard to get off in mid-ocean). Herewith, a rundown on what to expect from a cruise, a few suggestions on what to look for and arrange when purchasing passage on one, and some representative sailings to and around Portugal.

CABINS: The most important factor in determining the price of a cruise is the cabin. Cabin prices are set according to size and location. The size can vary considerably on older ships, less so on newer or more recently modernized ones, and may be entirely uniform on the very newest vessels.

Shipboard accommodations utilize the same pricing pattern as hotels. Suites, which consist of a sitting room–bedroom combination and occasionally a small private deck that could be compared to a patio, cost the most. Prices for other cabins (interchangeably called staterooms) usually are more expensive on the upper passenger decks, less expensive on lower decks; if a cabin has a bathtub instead of a shower, the price probably will be higher. The outside cabins with portholes cost more than inside cabins without views and generally are preferred — although many experienced cruise passengers eschew the more expensive accommodations for they know they will spend very few waking hours in their cabins. As in all forms of travel, accommodations are more expensive for single travelers. If you are traveling on your own but want to share a double cabin to reduce the cost, some ship lines will attempt to find someone of the same sex willing to share quarters (also see *Hints for Single Travelers,* in this section).

FACILITIES AND ACTIVITIES: You may not use your cabin very much — organized shipboard activities are geared to keep you busy. A standard schedule might consist of swimming, sunbathing, and numerous other outdoor recreations. Evenings are devoted to leisurely dining, lounge shows or movies, bingo and other organized games, gambling, dancing, and a midnight buffet. Your cruise fare normally includes all of these activities — except the cost of drinks.

Most cruise ships have at least one major social lounge, a main dining room, several bars, an entertainment room that may double as a discotheque for late dancing, an exercise room, indoor games facilities, at least one pool, and shopping facilities, which can range from a single boutique to an arcade. Still others have gambling casinos and/or slot machines, card rooms, libraries, children's recreation centers, indoor pools (as well as one or more on open decks), separate movie theaters, and private meeting rooms. Open deck space should be ample, because this is where most passengers spend their days at sea.

Usually there is a social director and staff to organize and coordinate activities. Evening entertainment is provided by professionals. Movies are mostly first-run and drinks are moderate in price (or should be) because a ship is exempt from local taxes when at sea.

■ **Note:** To be prepared for possible illnesses at sea, travelers should get a prescription from their doctor for medicine to counteract motion sickness. All ships with more than 12 passengers have a doctor on board, plus facilities for handling sickness or medical emergencies.

Shore Excursions – These side trips almost always are optional and available at extra cost. Before you leave, do a little basic research about the Portuguese ports you'll be visiting and decide what sights will interest you. If several of the most compelling of these are some distance from the pier where your ship docks, the chances are that paying for a shore excursion will be worth the money.

Shore excursions usually can be booked through your travel agent at the same time you make your cruise booking, but this is worthwhile only if you can get complete details on the nature of each excursion being offered. If you can't get these details, better opt to purchase your shore arrangements after you're on board. Your enthusiasm for an excursion may be higher once you are on board because you will have met other passengers with whom to share the excitement of "shore leave." And depending on your time in port, you may decide to eschew the guided tour and venture out on your own.

Meals – All meals on board almost always are included in the basic price of a cruise, and the food generally is abundant and quite palatable. Evening meals are taken in the main dining room, where tables are assigned according to the passengers' preferences. Tables usually accommodate from 2 to 10; specify your preference when you book your cruise. If there are two sittings, you also can specify which one you want at the time you book or, at the latest, when you first board the ship. Later sittings usually are more leisurely. Breakfast frequently is available in your cabin, as well as in the main dining room. For lunch, many passengers prefer the buffet offered on deck, usually at or near the pool, but again, the main dining room is available.

DRESS: Most people pack too much for a cruise on the assumption that their daily attire should be chic and every night is a big event. Comfort is a more realistic criterion. Daytime wear on most ships is decidedly casual. Evening wear for most cruises is dressy-casual. Formal attire probably is not necessary for 1-week cruises, optional for longer ones. (For information on choosing and packing a basic wardrobe, see *How to Pack,* in this section.)

TIPS: Tips are a strictly personal expense, and you *are* expected to tip — in particular, your cabin and dining room stewards. The general rule of thumb (or palm) is to expect to pay from 10% to 20% of your total cruise budget for gratuities — the actual amount within this range is based on the length of the cruise and the extent of personalized services provided. Allow $2 to $5 a day for each cabin and dining room steward (more if you wish) and additional sums for very good service. (*Note:* Tips should be paid by and for each individual in a cabin, whether there are one, two, or more.) Others who may merit tips are the deck steward who sets up your chair at the pool or elsewhere, the wine steward in the dining room, porters who handle your luggage (tip them individually at the time they assist you), and any others who provide personal service. On some ships you can charge your bar tab to your cabin; throw in the tip when you pay it at the end of the cruise. Smart travelers tip twice during the trip: about midway through the cruise and at the end; even wiser travelers tip a bit at the start of the trip to ensure better service throughout.

Although some cruise lines do have a no-tipping policy and you are not penalized by the crew for not tipping, naturally, you aren't penalized for tipping, either. If you can restrain yourself, it is better not to tip on those few ships that discourage it. However, never make the mistake of not tipping on the majority of ships, where it is a common, expected practice. (For further information on calculating gratuities, see *Tipping,* in this section.)

SHIP SANITATION: The US Public Health Service (PHS) currently inspects all passenger vessels calling at US ports, so very precise information is available on which ships meet its requirements and which do not. The further requirement that ships immediately report any illness that occurs on board adds to the available data.

The problem for a prospective cruise passenger is to determine whether the ship on which he or she plans to sail has met the official sanitary standard. US regulations require the PHS to publish actual grades for the ships inspected (rather than the old pass or fail designation), so it's now easy to determine any cruise ship's status. Nearly 4,000 travel agents, public health organizations, and doctors receive a copy of each monthly ship sanitation summary, but be aware that not all travel agents fully understand what this ship inspection program is all about. The best advice is to deal with a travel agent who specializes in cruise bookings, for he or she is most likely to have the latest information on the sanitary conditions of all cruise ships (see "A final note on picking a cruise," below). To receive a copy of the most recent summary or a particular inspection report, write to Chief, Vessel Sanitation Program, Center for Environmental Health and Injury Control (1015 N. America Way, Room 107, Miami, FL 33132; phone: 305-536-4307). Note that the center requests that all inquiries be made in writing.

TRANSATLANTIC CROSSINGS: There are a number of cruise lines that sail between the US and Europe. Some include Portuguese ports as part of their European itineraries, while on others passengers may disembark at other ports on the Continent and sail, fly, or drive to Portugal.

For seagoing enthusiasts, *Cunard*'s *Queen Elizabeth 2* is one of the largest and most comfortable vessels afloat and each year the *QE2* schedules approximately a dozen round-trip transatlantic crossings between April and, usually, December. The ship normally sets its course from New York to Southampton, England (a 5-day trip), and then sails directly back to the US, although on a few of the crossings it proceeds from Southampton to Cherbourg, France, or to other European ports before turning back across the Atlantic. (Similarly, on some crossings, the ship calls at various East Coast US ports in addition to New York, thus giving passengers a choice of where to embark or disembark.)

If Portuguese ports are not included in the applicable itinerary, travelers can take an intra-European flight from Southampton or Cherbourg to Portugal, and then take a transatlantic flight home. For those sailing to Europe on the *QE2* and flying home, another option for travel to Portugal is based on the validity period of the return ticket. Following the transatlantic crossing, passengers have a specified time — up to 35 days for first class passengers and 15 days for the less expensive fares — during which they can take a trip to Portugal via a separate round-trip ticket on *British Airways* from London to Faro or Lisbon. The intra-European round-trip fare is subject to the availability of discounts, and the traveler must return to London in time to leave for home within the 15 or 35 days specified. The transatlantic flight included in these packages no longer must arrive at one of the 17 US gateways served by *British Airways; Cunard* now allows passengers to transfer free to connecting flights to another 60 gateways served by other carriers. Those who want to splurge can apply the air allowance included in such air/sea packages toward a ticket aboard *British Airways*' supersonic *Concorde,* although the difference between the basic allowance and the *Concorde* fare is substantial. The only maximum-stay restriction for passengers who upgrade to a return flight on the *Concorde* is that they must return on or before the end of the calendar year of their sailing. For further information on current air/sea offerings, check with your travel agent, call *British Airways* (phone: 800-AIRWAYS), or contact *Cunard* (555 Fifth Ave., New York, NY 10017; phone: 800-5-CUNARD or 800-221-4770).

Positioning Cruises – Another interesting possibility for those who have the time is what the industry calls a positioning cruise. This is the sailing of a US- or Caribbean-based vessel from its winter berth to the city in Europe from which it will be offering summer cruise programs. Eastbound positioning cruises take place in the spring; westbound cruises return in the fall. Since ships do not make the return trip until they need to position themselves for the next cruise season, most lines offering positioning cruises have some air/sea arrangement that allows passengers to fly home economically — though the cruises themselves are not an inexpensive way to travel.

Typically, the ships set sail from Florida or from San Juan, Puerto Rico, and cross the Atlantic to any one of a number of European ports where the trip may be broken — including Portuguese ports — before proceeding to cruise European waters (for example, the Mediterranean, the Baltic Sea, the Black Sea, the Norwegian fjords). Passengers can elect to stay aboard for the basic transatlantic segment alone or for both the crossing and the subsequent European cruise. Ports of call on such crossings and subsequent itineraries may vary substantially from year to year. For the most current information on operative itineraries, ask your travel agent or contact the cruise line directly.

Among the lines that offer positioning cruises to Portugal are the following:

Crystal Cruises (2121 Ave. of the Stars, Los Angeles, CA 90067; phone 800-446-6645). The *Crystal Harmony* makes an 11-day cruise in April from San Juan (Puerto Rico) to Lisbon that stops at Madeira.

Cunard (555 Fifth Ave., New York, NY 10017; phone: 800-5-CUNARD or 800-221-4770). The *Vistafjord* makes a 15-day westbound transatlantic sailing in November from Naples (Italy) to Ft. Lauderdale (Florida) that calls at Lisbon.

Ocean Cruise Lines (1510 SE 17th St., Ft. Lauderdale, FL 33316; phone: 800-556-8850). Offers a 15-day positioning cruise aboard the *Ocean Princess* from San Juan (Puerto Rico) to Nice (France) in April that stops at Madeira and Lisbon.

Paquet French Cruises (1510 SE 17th St., Ft. Lauderdale, FL 33316; phone: 800-556-8850). In early May, the *Mermoz* makes a 14-day transatlantic crossing from Guadeloupe to Le Havre (the port for Paris) that calls at Lisbon.

Princess Cruises (10100 Santa Monica Blvd., Los Angeles, CA 90067; phone: 800-421-0522). The *Star Princess* visits Madeira during its late fall westbound positioning cruise from Barcelona (Spain) to San Juan (Puerto Rico).

Royal Cruise Line (One Maritime Plaza, Suite 1400, San Francisco, CA 94111; phone: 800-227-5628 or 415-956-7200). The *Royal Odyssey* makes a 12-day transatlantic positioning cruise in February from Barbados to Málaga (Spain) — travelers to Portugal can disembark at Lisbon. The *Crown Odyssey* also stops at Lisbon on a 21-day sailing from San Juan (Puerto Rico) to Venice (Italy) in April, and at Madeira on a 21-day westbound cruise between Piraeus (Greece) and San Juan in November.

Royal Viking Line (95 Merrick, Coral Gables, FL 33134; phone: 800-422-8000). The *Royal Viking Sun* sails westward on a 10-day cruise from Lisbon to Ft. Lauderdale in October. Optional add-ons include air transportation from the US and a 2-night package in Lisbon before the cruise begins.

Seabourn Cruise Line (55 Francisco Street, Suite 710, San Francisco, CA 94133; phone: 800-351-9595). Offers a 12-day transatlantic positioning cruise aboard the *Seabourn Pride* in early May from Ft. Lauderdale to Bordeaux (France) that calls at Ponta Delgada, in the Azores.

Sun Line (1 Rockefeller Plaza, Suite 315, New York, NY 10020; phone: 800-468-

6400 or 212-397-6400). Departing in April, the *Stella Solaris* makes a 23-day positioning cruise between Galveston (Texas) and Piraeus (Greece) that includes Lisbon among its ports of call.

Windstar Cruises (300 Elliott Ave. West, Seattle, WA 98119; phone: 206-281-3535). The *Wind Spirit* calls at Lisbon and Madeira during a 22-day positioning cruise in April from St. Thomas to Civitavecchia (the port for Rome). In addition, travelers can book the 11-day Madeira–Rome segment of this cruise separately. The *Wind Star* also stops at Lisbon and Madeira during an October sailing from Monte Carlo (Monaco) to Barbados.

INTRA-EUROPEAN CRUISES: The Atlantic Ocean southwest of the Iberian Peninsula, where it laps Portugal's Madeira Islands, is a popular and picturesque cruising ground, attracting a wide range of pleasure-seeking cruise traffic. Thus, it's not difficult to find a cruise ship calling at Lisbon or some other Portuguese port. Less easy to find is a cruise devoting its time exclusively to Portuguese territory. Many Mediterranean cruises actually may begin in a Portuguese port, such as Lisbon, but end elsewhere — Genoa or Venice or even farther afield. (The reverse itinerary also is common.)

Classical Cruises (132 E. 70th St., New York, NY 10021; phone: 800-252-7745 or 212-794-3200 throughout the US; 800-252-7746 in Canada). This educational cruise specialist offers sailings aboard small ships — each accommodates 80 passengers. Cruises include lectures by guest speakers on the culture and history of the areas visited. Among its offerings is an 11-day Islands of the Western Mediterranean sailing between Lisbon and Venice aboard the *Illiria,* as well as several 16-day Mediterranean cruises aboard the *Aurora I* that either begin or end in Lisbon.

Costa Cruises (80 SW 8th St., Miami, FL 33130-7325; phone: 800-462-6782). The *Costa Classica*'s 29-day, late summer round-trip cruise from Genoa (Italy) to St. Petersburg (Russia) includes a stop at Lisbon. Several other cruises also include Portuguese ports of call, such as the *Eugenio Costa*'s 10-day and 11-day round-trip sailings from Genoa1

Crystal Cruises (2121 Ave. of the Stars, Los Angeles, CA 90067; phone 800-446-6645). The *Crystal Harmony* sails from Lisbon to Tilbury (England) on a 13-day cruise in May. It also stops at Lisbon during a 13-day Tilbury–Rome sailing in August.

Cunard (555 Fifth Ave., New York, NY 10017; phone: 800-221-4770). The *Vistafjord* stops at Lisbon during an 8-day cruise between Barcelona (Spain) and Hamburg (Germany) in June, and calls at Lisbon and Madeira on a 9-day Hamburg–Barcelona sailing in September.

Ocean Cruise Lines (1510 SE 17th St., Ft. Lauderdale, FL 33316; phone: 800-556-8850). The *Ocean Princess* makes an 11-day cruise from Nice to Paris in May that includes stops at Lisbon and Porto. Another 11-day sailing (in September) from London to Nice docks overnight in Lisbon en route.

P&O Cruises (c/o *Express Travel Services,* Empire State Building, Suite 7718, 350 Fifth Ave., New York, NY 10118; phone: 800-223-5799 or 212-629-3630). Offers several cruises that include Portugal in their itineraries, such as a 12-day Islands in the Sun cruise aboard the *Canberra* that stops in Lisbon and Madeira, and an Indian Summer trip aboard the *Sea Princess* that stops in those same ports.

Princess Cruises (10100 Santa Monica Blvd., Los Angeles, CA 90067; phone: 800-421-0522). The *Royal Princess* makes two 12-day cruises between Barcelona and London in the late spring that also stop in Lisbon. The *Star Princess* calls at Lisbon during its 14-day London–Piraeus sailing later in the summer.

Royal Cruise Line (One Maritime Plaza, Suite 1400, San Francisco, CA 94111; phone: 800-227-5628 or 415-956-7200). A number of 12- to 13-day cruises aboard the *Royal Odyssey* and the *Crown Odyssey* in the fall either begin or end in Lisbon. On three of these cruises, the *Royal Odyssey* also stops at Madeira. In addition, the *Crown Odyssey* makes a 13-day trip between Tilbury (England) and Venice (Italy) in October that calls at Lisbon and Porto.

Royal Viking Line (95 Merrick, Coral Gables, FL 33134; phone: 800-422-8000). The *Royal Viking Sun* makes two 12-day sailings in the spring — from Lisbon to Copenhagen (Denmark) and from Tilbury (England) to Barcelona (Spain), with a stop at Lisbon — and in the fall, it sails from Civitavecchia (Italy) back to Lisbon. The *Royal Viking Queen* stops at Lisbon on a 13-day sailing from London to Monte Carlo in August; optional add-ons include round-trip transportation from the US and 2-night packages at some of its ports of call, including Lisbon.

SeaQuest Cruises (600 Corporate Dr., Suite 410, Ft. Lauderdale, FL 33334; phone: 800-223-5688 or 305-772-7552). This adventure cruising specialist offers a 13-day sailing aboard the *Caledonian Star* between Dover (England) and Barcelona (Spain) that also stops at Lisbon and Porto.

Swan Hellenic Cruises (c/o *Esplanade Tours*, 581 Boylston St., Boston, MA 02116; phone: 800-426-5492 or 617-266-7465). The *Orpheus* sails on a number of 13- to 15-day cruises that call at Lisbon, as well as other ports in Europe and North Africa.

FREIGHTERS: An alternative to conventional cruise ships is travel by freighter. These are cargo ships that also take a limited number of passengers (usually about 12) in reasonably comfortable accommodations. The idea of traveling by freighter has long appealed to romantic souls, but there are a number of drawbacks to consider before casting off. Once upon a time, a major advantage of freighter travel was its low cost, but this is no longer the case. Though freighters usually are less expensive than cruise ships, the difference is not as great as it once was. Accommodations and recreational facilities vary, but freighters were not designed to amuse passengers, so it is important to appreciate the idea of freighter travel itself. Schedules are erratic, and travelers must fit their timetable to that of the ship. Passengers have found themselves waiting as long as a month for a promised sailing, and because freighters follow their cargo commitments, it is possible that a scheduled port could be omitted at the last minute or a new one added.

Anyone contemplating taking a freighter from a US port across the Atlantic to Portugal should be aware that at press time, no freighter line made regular stops at Portuguese ports. Nevertheless, it pays to check at the time you plan to travel. The following specialists deal only (or largely) in freighter travel and may be able to provide information on current freighter passage to Portugal. They provide information, schedules, and, when you're ready to sail, booking services.

Freighter World Cruises, Inc. (180 S. Lake Ave., Suite 335, Pasadena, CA 91101; phone: 818-449-3106). A freighter travel agency that acts as general agent for several freighter lines. Publishes the twice-monthly *Freighter Space Advisory*, listing space available on sailings worldwide. A subscription costs $27 a year, $25 of which can be credited toward the cost of a cruise.

Pearl's Travel Tips (9903 Oaks La., Seminole, FL 34642; phone: 813-393-2919). Run by Ilse Hoffman, who finds sailings for her customers and sends them off with all kinds of valuable information and advice.

TravLtips Cruise and Freighter Travel Association (PO Box 218, Flushing, NY 11358; phone: 800-872-8584 or 718-939-2400 throughout the US; 800-548-7823 from Canada). A freighter travel agency and club ($15 per year or $25 for 2 years) whose members receive the bimonthly *TravLtips* magazine of cruise and freighter travel.

Those interested in freighter travel also may want to subscribe to *Freighter Travel News,* a publication of the *Freighter Travel Club of America.* A year's subscription to this monthly newsletter costs $18. To subscribe, write to the club at 3524 Harts Lake Rd., Roy, WA 98580.

Another monthly newsletter that may be of interest to those planning to cruise Portuguese waters is *Ocean and Cruise News,* which offers comprehensive coverage of the latest on the cruise ship scene. A year's subscription costs $24. Contact *Ocean and Cruise News,* PO Box 92, Stamford, CT 06904 (phone: 203-329-2787).

■ **A final note on picking a cruise:** A "cruise-only" travel agency can best help you choose a cruise ship and itinerary. Cruise-only agents are best equipped to tell you about a particular ship's "personality," the kind of person with whom you'll likely be traveling on a particular ship, what dress is appropriate (it varies from ship to ship), and much more. Travel agencies that specialize in booking cruises usually are members of the *National Association of Cruise Only Agencies (NACOA).* For a listing of the agencies in your area (requests are limited to three states), send a self-addressed, stamped envelope to *NACOA,* PO Box 7209, Freeport, NY 11520, or call 516-378-8006.

Traveling by Train

Perhaps the most economical, and often the most satisfying, way to see a lot of a foreign country in a relatively short time is by rail. It certainly is the quickest way to travel between two cities up to 300 miles apart (beyond that, a flight normally would be quicker, even counting the time it takes to get to and from the airport). But time isn't always the only consideration. Traveling by train is a way to keep moving and to keep seeing at the same time. The fares usually are reasonable, and with the special discounts available to visitors, it can be an almost irresistible bargain. You only need to get to a station on time; after that, put your watch in your pocket and relax. You may not get to your destination exactly at the appointed hour, but you'll have a marvelous time looking out the window and enjoying the ride.

TRAINS AND ROUTES: While North Americans have been raised to depend on their cars, Europeans have long been able to rely on public transportation. As in other countries on the Continent, Portugal has a relatively extensive railway system. Portuguese trains operate within Portugal and cross the border into Spain.

Portuguese National Railways, or *CP (Companhia dos Caminhos de Ferro Portuguêses),* operates trains connecting most of the main cities and towns in the country. It operates 2,500 miles of track, 700 stations, and has express trains that can travel at speeds up to 90 miles per hour.

Towns across Portugal are served by "regular" express and local trains. The best trains are the *Rapidos.* These are comparable to the Europe-wide *Inter-City (IC)* trains; they provide a high standard of service and offer a full range of facilities including lounges, restaurant cars, bars, diaper-changing facilities, and so on. Both first and second class service usually are available and supplements usually must be paid to ride most of these trains, while reservations are obligatory only on those crossing the border. More common are the *Inter-Regional (IR)* trains, which offer only basic amenities (a few offer snacks and drinks) and make numerous local stops.

Lisbon has four train stations. Santa Apolónia, the main station, is the departure point for trains bound north and northeast and for international trains making connections into Spain (and onward into France). Terreiro do Paço station actually is the landing stage for ferries crossing the Tagus River to Barreiro, as well as the terminus for trains serving the Algarve and other points south and southeast. Electric commuter trains for Estoril-Cascais and for Sintra leave from Cais do Sodré and Rossio stations respectively; other trains traveling up the western coast of Portugal to Figueira da Foz and Coimbra also leave from Rossio.

Porto, the second-largest city in Portugal, has two main stations: São Bento, in the center of town, and Campanhã. Six express trains connecting Lisbon and Porto operate daily. One train, making only one stop, arrives at its destination in just 3 hours. Others make several stops and take 1 to 2 hours longer. Schedules are available at the train stations or through the Portuguese National Tourist Office. As in the US, tickets are bought at train stations throughout Portugal.

The track used in Portugal is broad gauge, not the narrow gauge used elsewhere in Europe (due to British influence and construction in the early days). Visitors to Portugal who plan on extending their trip by rail through Spain and into France (or elsewhere on the Continent) generally must change to another train when crossing the border into France. The only exception would be if traveling aboard one of the specially equipped (and increasingly common) *Talgos* trains, which can adjust their wheel base automatically to the standard narrow gauge and, therefore, may operate beyond the border into France.

Portugal also is part of the Eurorail System, and daily service from London via Paris goes to Portugal. Passengers headed for Lisbon must change trains at Irún/Hendaye, in Spain, and those going to Porto must change a second time at Pampilhosa. The trip from London to Paris takes 7 hours; Paris to Lisbon takes 25 hours; and Paris to Porto, an hour less. The trip from Paris to Porto is second class only, although sleepers and a mini-bar are available. The "Sud Express" between Paris and Lisbon has both first and second class carriages and dining and sleeping services in both classes.

ACCOMMODATIONS, FARES, AND SERVICES: Fares on European trains are based on the quality of accommodations the passenger enjoys. You pay on the basis of traveling first class or second class, and some trains, such as the *Rapidos,* require a supplement. Traditionally, seating is arranged in compartments, with three or four passengers on one side facing a like number on the other side, but increasingly, in the newer cars, compartments have been replaced by a central-aisle design.

Tickets, schedules, and departure information are available at train stations throughout Portugal. Domestic and international tickets usually are sold separately.

In order to save time, you may want to buy your rail tickets before leaving the US from travel agents or *Rail Europe* (226-230 Westchester Ave., White Plains, NY 10604; phone: 914-682-5172 in Connecticut, New Jersey, and New York State; 800-345-1990 elsewhere in the US), which is the North American representative of the *Portuguese National Railways. Rail Europe* can make reservations for train trips of at least 3 hours' duration, as well as overnight excursions; bookings require a minimum of 7 days for confirmation. Tickets, schedules, and departure information also are available at train stations throughout Portugal.

Most of the international ticket and reservations systems are computerized and efficient. Fares vary from route to route, but short hauls always are more expensive per mile than longer runs. There is a $3 fee for European reservations made in the US (plus a $5 telex fee). Normally, reservations can be made up to 2 months prior to the travel date, and when making a reservation, you can ask for a window seat, as well as for a smoking or nonsmoking section. Reservations reduce flexibility, but they are advisable during the summer on popular routes. They also are advisable at any time of the year if it is imperative that you be on a particular train.

Portuguese trains, like others in Europe, carry two basic kinds of sleeping quarters: "couchettes," the coach seats of a compartment converted to sleeping berths, and "wagon-lits," or sleepers, individual single or double bedrooms that compare favorably with the slumber coaches on transcontinental American trains. First class couchettes (not available on every train) have four berths per compartment; second class couchettes have six. The berth is narrow, with a pillow, blanket, and sheet provided. Couchettes are a relatively inexpensive way to get a night's rest aboard a train. However, they provide privacy only for those traveling with a family or other group that can use the whole compartment; individual travelers are mixed with passengers of either sex.

Couchettes cost a standard charge (around $20 per person if bought in the US) added to the basic first or second class fare. A private or semiprivate wagon-lit or sleeper is more expensive (anywhere from $30 and up, depending on your destination).

The wide range of dining facilities runs the gamut from prix fixe menus served in dining cars or at your seat to self-service cafeteria-style cars and mobile vendors dispensing snacks, sandwiches, and beverages. In-seat and dining car lunch and dinner reservations either are made in advance or after boarding by visiting the dining car or through the train steward. If you're sure you will want to eat en route, it's a good idea to inquire beforehand exactly what meal service is offered on the train you'll be taking and whether advance dining reservations are required.

A standardized pictorial code has been designed to indicate the various amenities offered at many train stations. These may include showers, as well as restaurants, post and telegraph offices, exchange bureaus, and diaper changing facilities. In those cities that have two or more stations (see above), make sure you know the name of the station for your train.

Baggage often can be checked through to your destination or can be checked overnight at most stations. Some stations also provide 24-hour luggage lockers where you can temporarily free yourself of surplus bags, but these are becoming less common throughout Europe, as lockers are being eliminated due to bomb threats. It always is a good idea to travel as light as possible: Porters are in short supply at most stations, and self-service carts frequently are scarce as well.

Those planning driving routes should be aware that all European railways have some form of auto ferry. In Portugal, it is called *Auto-Expreso.* This service is offered aboard *Rapido* lines running between Lisbon and Porto, Regua, Castelo Branco, Guarda, and Paris. During the summer, car-carrying service is available to the Algarve as well. *Note:* The *Auto-Expreso* can be booked only in Europe, and it is quite popular with Europeans, especially during the peak summer months. Your best bet is to make reservations as soon as you get to Europe, the earlier the better.

PASSES: Rail passes are offered by most European railroad companies. They allow unlimited train travel within a set time period, frequently include connecting service via other forms of transportation, and can save the traveler a considerable amount of money, as well as time. Previously, the only requirement was validation of the pass by an information clerk on the day of your first trip, but this is no longer the case. Your pass now can be validated *before* you travel, so there is no need to stand in line — and lines can be very long during peak travel periods — to buy individual tickets for subsequent trips. Designed primarily for foreign visitors, these passes must be bought in the US (or some other foreign location) prior to arrival in Europe. Although these passes can be among the best bargains around, be sure to look into the comparable cost of individual train tickets which — depending on the number of days you plan to travel — may work out to be less expensive.

The Eurailpass, the first and best-known of all rail passes, is valid for travel through Portugal and 16 other countries — Austria, Belgium, Denmark, Finland, France, Germany, Greece, Holland, Hungary, Ireland, Italy, Luxembourg, Norway, Spain, Sweden, and Switzerland. It entitles holders to 15 or 21 days or 1, 2, or 3 months of unlimited first class travel, plus many extras, including some ferry crossings (within and between countries in the Eurail network), river trips, lake steamers, and transportation by bus and private railroads, as well as scheduled *Europabus* services, and airport and city center rail connections. Since the Eurailpass is a first class pass, Eurail travelers can ride just about any European train they wish, including special express trains, without paying additional supplements. The only extras are the nominal reservation fee, meals, and sleeper and couchette costs.

A Eurailpass for children under 12 is half the adult price (children under 4 travel free) but includes the same features. The Eurail Youthpass, for travelers under 26 years of age, is slightly different, in that it is valid for travel in second class only.

The Eurail Saverpass resembles the basic Eurailpass, except that it provides 15 days of unlimited first class travel for three people traveling together during peak season; two people traveling together qualify if travel takes place entirely between October 1 and March 31. The Saverpass provides savings of approximately $100 per ticket as compared to the price of a 15-day Eurailpass.

Another option is the Eurail Flexipass, which can be used for first class travel on any 5 days within a 15-day period, 9 days within a 21-day period, or 14 days within a 30-day period. All of these passes must be bought before you go, either from travel agents or from *Rail Europe* (address above). A *Eurail Aid* office in Europe will replace lost passes when proper documentation is provided; a reissuance fee is charged. (A list of *Eurail Aid* offices throughout Europe is provided when you buy a Eurailpass; you also can ask at any *Portuguese National Railways* office for the nearest location.)

The Portuguese Flexipass is good for a total of 4 days of first class rail travel over a 15-day period or 7 days over a 30-day period. The Portuguese Rail 'n Drive with *Avis* combines 3 days of car travel with 3 days of rail travel in one month, with an option to add 5 more days of rail service and/or car rental days. Included is unlimited mileage and local taxes, as well as one-way drop-off privileges in Portugal for no extra charge. Reservations must be made in the US at least 7 days in advance by calling *Avis* at 800-331-1084.

- **Eurailpass Insurance:** When buying a Eurailpass, you may want to consider Pass Replacement Insurance, recently introduced by *Rail Europe* and *Travel Assistance International.* In the event of loss or theft of your Eurailpass en route, you will be reimbursed for the cost of purchasing a replacement pass valid for the remaining days of travel. The fee for this insurance policy is 3% of the price of the original Eurailpass. Note that the cost of the EurailDrive program and other special services are *not* covered. For further information, contact *Rail Europe* (address above) or *Travel Assistance International* (1133 15th St. NW, Suite 400, Washington, DC 20005; phone: 202-331-1609 in Washington, DC; 800-821-2828 elsewhere in the US).

The Eurailpass is a bargain for those who are combining a visit to Portugal with sightseeing elsewhere on the Continent. But for those traveling strictly within Portugal, a pass that allows unlimited travel for defined periods of time over this country's national transportation network is more economical.

Rail passes in Portugal include Tourist Tickets, which allow unlimited travel in any class and are good for 7, 14, and 21 days. There also is a Family Ticket, which can be purchased for a minimum of three family members traveling a minimum of 150 kilometers (93 miles). One family member pays full fare (according to the type of train and the class) while other family members age 12 or older pay half fare, and children from 4 to 11 pay one-quarter fare. Children under 4 ride free in Portugal. To obtain the pass, you must provide passports and documentation indicating that the travelers sharing the pass are related.

FURTHER INFORMATION: Particularly if Portugal is only a part of a more extensive trip through Europe or even farther afield, you may want to consult additional sources before finalizing plans. Both the *Eurail Traveler's Guide* (which contains a railroad map) and the *Eurail Timetable* are free from Eurailpass (Box 10383, Stamford, CT 06904-2383), as well as from the Eurail Distribution Centre (PO Box 4000, Station A, Mississauga, Ontario L5A 9Z9, Canada). The *Eurail Guide,* by Kathryn Turpin and Marvin Saltzman, is available in most travel bookstores; it also can be ordered from Eurail Guide Annuals (27540 Pacific Coast Hwy., Malibu, CA 90265: phone; 213-457-7286) for $13.95, plus shipping and handling. *Europe by Eurail,* by George Wright Ferguson, is available from Globe Pequot Press (PO Box Q, Chester, CT 06412; phone: 203-526-9571) for $14.95, plus shipping and handling. The latter two guides discuss train travel in general, contain information on Portugal and the other countries included in the Eurail network (the Saltzman book also discusses Eastern Europe and the rest of the world), and suggest numerous sightseeing excursions by rail from various base cities.

You also may want to buy the *Thomas Cook European Timetable,* a weighty and detailed compendium of European international and national rail services which constitutes the most revered and accurate railway reference in existence. The *Timetable* comes out monthly, but because most European countries — including Portugal — switch to summer schedules at the end of May (and back to winter schedules at the end of September), the June edition offers the first complete summer schedule (and October the first complete winter schedule). The February through May editions, however, contain increasingly more definitive supplements on upcoming summer schedules that can be used to plan a trip. The *Thomas Cook European Timetable* is available in some travel bookstores or can be ordered from the *Forsyth Travel Library* (PO Box 2975, Shawnee Mission, KS 66201-1375; phone: 800-367-7984 or 913-384-0496) for $23.95, plus shipping and handling; credit card orders by phone also are accepted.

Rail Europe is the North American representative of the *Portuguese National Railways,* or *CP (Companhia dos Caminhos de Ferro Portugueses).* Note that all inquiries and reservations are handled directly through their main office in the US (226-230 Westchester Ave., White Plains, NY 10604; phone: 914-682-5172 in Connecticut, New Jersey, and New York State; 800-345-1990 elsewhere in the US). *Rail Europe*'s regional offices now perform administrative functions only and no longer supply information or make reservations.

Once you have arrived in Portugal, rail information is available from the main office of *Portuguese National Railways* (Direção Commercial de Passageiros, Informação Publico, 66 Av. da Republica 3°, Lisbon 1000), as well as from offices at the Santa Apolónia (phone: 1-87-6025) and Rossio (phone: 1-346-5022) train stations, both in Lisbon. Additional branch offices are located at train stations throughout the country.

Finally, although any travel agent can assist you in making arrangements to tour Portugal by rail, you may want to consult a train travel specialist, such as *Accent on Travel,* 1030 Curtis St., Suite 201, Menlo Park, CA 94025 (phone: 800-347-0645 or 415-326-7330).

Traveling by Bus

Going from place to place by bus may not be the fastest way to get from here to there, but that (and, in some cases, a little less comfort) is the primary drawback to bus travel. A persuasive argument in its favor is its cost: Short of walking, it is the least expensive way to cover a long distance and at the same time enjoy the scenic view.

Buses also reach outposts remote from railroad tracks, for those so inclined. While train service in Portugal is more limited than it is in some other European countries, a map of the bus routes is not much different from a road map: If the way is paved, it's likely that a bus — some bus — is assigned to travel it. The network of express buses — those traveling long distances with few stops en route — is only slightly less extensive. Therefore, Portugal is particularly well suited to bus travel.

In Portugal, the buses are run by numerous small regional lines, all of which come under the auspices of *Rodoviaria Nacional, EP* (*RN;* 18 Av. Casal Ribeiro, Lisbon 1000; phone: 1-545439). This company can offer information on service to most cities and towns throughout the country and bus stations are located just about everywhere. The main bus terminal in Lisbon is at 18-B Av. Casal Ribeiro, Lisbon (phone: 1-545439). Schedule and fare information can be obtained at the terminal, through the Portuguese National Tourist Office in the US or Portugal, or through travel agents.

BOOKING: Reservations are not usually necessary on most local bus routes, which run on established and published schedules. As many rural lines are very crowded (since buses usually are the main form of transport for local residents), you may want to inquire about the possibility of making a reservation in order to ensure a seat. Tickets usually are bought on the bus and are valid for only that day and that ride. For long journeys, however, travelers must purchase tickets at the bus station before they leave. When you buy your ticket, ask about any discounts available.

SERVICES: Buses are not equipped for food service, but on long trips, as in the US, they do make meal and rest stops. If you plan to spend some time traveling around Portugal by bus, it's not a bad idea to bring some food aboard, although you're probably better off waiting until you reach a stop in a town or city where you can eat more comfortably at a restaurant. Toilet facilities are likely to be provided only on the newer buses on long-distance trips, and air conditioning is the exception rather than the rule — particularly on rural routes. If taking a motorcoach *tour,* however, you can expect special amenities such as air conditioning, toilets, upholstered and adjustable seats, and reading lamps.

FOR COMFORTABLE TRAVEL: Dress casually in loose-fitting clothes. Be sure you have a sweater or jacket (even in the summer) and, for when you disembark, a raincoat or umbrella is a must, particularly during the winter (December through March). Passengers are allowed to listen to radios or cassette players, but must use earphones. Choose a seat in the front near the driver for the best view or in the middle between the front and rear wheels for the smoothest ride.

BUS TOURS: Many American tour operators offer motorcoach tours, however, one company, *Rodoviaria Nacional, EP* (*RN Tours;* 38 Av. Fontes Pereira de Melo, Lisbon 1000; phone: 1-352-8683), which is the Portuguese affiliate of *Gray Line,* specializes in bus tours of Portugal. Among the itineraries offered are several tours in the vicinity of Porto, as well as Lisbon and surrounding areas. For further information on all-inclusive motorcoach tours offered by US tour operators, see *Package Tours,* in this section.

Traveling by Car

Driving certainly is the most flexible way to explore out-of-the-way regions of Portugal. The privacy, comfort, and convenience of touring by car can't be matched by any other form of transport. Trains often whiz much too fast past too many enticing landscapes, tunnel through or pass between hills and mountains rather than climb up and around them for a better view, frequently deposit passengers in an unappealing part of town, and skirt some areas of the country altogether. Buses have a greater range, but they still don't permit many spur-of-the-moment stops and starts. In a car you go where you want when you want, and can stop along the way as often as you like for a meal, a photograph, or a particularly appealing view.

Portugal is ideally suited for driving tours. Distances between major cities usually are reasonable, and the historical and cultural density is such that the flexibility of a car can be used to maximum advantage. A traveler can cover large amounts of territory, visit major cities and sites, or motor from one small village to another while exploring the countryside. (See DIRECTIONS for our choices of the most interesting routes.)

Travelers who wish to cover Portugal from end to end can count on a good system of highways to help them make time. Those who wish to explore only one region will find that the secondary and even lesser roads are well surfaced and generally in good condition, although farther off the beaten track, this may not always be the case. Either way, there is plenty of satisfying scenery en route.

But driving isn't an inexpensive way to travel. Gas prices are far higher in Europe than in North America, and car rentals seldom are available at bargain rates. Keep in mind, however, that driving becomes more economical with more passengers. Because the price of getting wheels abroad will be more than an incidental expense, it is important to investigate every alternative before making a final choice. Many travelers find this expense amply justified when considering that rather than just the means to an end, a well-planned driving route also can be an important part of the adventure.

Before setting out, make certain that everything you need is in order. If possible, discuss your intended trip with someone who already has driven the route to find out about road conditions and available services. If you can't speak to someone personally, try to read about others' experiences. Automobile clubs (see below) and the Portuguese National Tourist Office in the US can be a good source of driving information, although when requesting brochures and maps, be sure to specify the areas you are planning to visit. (Also see "Roads and Maps," below.)

DRIVING: A valid driver's license from his or her own state of residence enables a US citizen to drive in Portugal. Although not required, an International Driving Permit (IDP), which is a translation of the US license in 9 languages, is strongly recommended — particularly if you are considering driving across the border into Spain or other European countries.

You can obtain your IDP before you leave from most branches of the *American Automobile Association (AAA).* Applicants must be at least 18 years old, and the application must be accompanied by two passport-size photos (some *AAA* branches have a photo machine available), a valid US driver's license, and a fee of $10. The IDP is good for 1 year and must be accompanied by your US license to be valid.

Proof of liability insurance also is required and is a standard part of any car rental contract. (To be sure of having the appropriate coverage, let the rental staff know in advance about the national borders you plan to cross.) If buying a car and using it abroad, the driver must carry an International Insurance Certificate, known as a Green Card (called a *Cartão Verde* in Portugal). Your insurance agent or carrier at home can arrange for a special policy to cover you in Europe, and automatically will issue your Green Card.

Contrary to first impressions, Portuguese drivers tend to be skillful and disciplined. Also contrary to first impressions, rules of the road do exist. Driving in Portugal is on the right side of the road, as in most of Europe. Passing is on the left; the left turn signal must be flashing throughout the entire process and the right indicator must be used when pulling back to the right; it's also a common practice to flash your headlights to signal the driver in front what you're doing. On mountain roads, get used to flashing your headlights at night and beeping your horn when rounding blind curves during the day; traffic going up usually has priority over traffic coming down, though signposts may indicate who has the right of way and at what times. In most larger cities, honking is forbidden (except to avoid accidents); flash your headlights instead. Also, don't be intimidated by tailgaters — everyone does it.

According to law, those coming from the right at intersections have the right of way, as in the US, and pedestrians, provided they are in marked crosswalks, have priority over all vehicles. Unfortunately, however, this is not always the case. Exceptions are priority roads, marked by a sign with a yellow diamond on it; these have the right of way until the diamond reappears with a black bar and the right of way reverts to those coming from the right. In many areas, though, signposting is meager, and traffic at intersections converges from all directions, resulting in a proceed-at-your-own-risk flow.

Pictorial direction signs, generally found on the newer roads in Portugal, are standardized under the International Roadsign System, and their meanings are indicated by their shapes: Triangular signs indicate danger; circular signs give instructions; and rectangular signs are informative. Driving in European cities can be a tricky proposition, since many of them do not have street signs at convenient corners, but instead identify their byways with plaques attached to the walls of corner buildings. These often are difficult to spot until you've passed them, and since most streets don't run parallel to one another, taking the next turn can lead you astray. Fortunately, most European cities and towns post numerous signs pointing the way to the center of the city, and plotting a course to your destination from there may be far easier. In Portugal, look for the signs that read CENTRO. Also note that highway signs showing the distance from point to point are in kilometers rather than miles (1 mile equals approximately 1.6 kilometers; 1 kilometer equals .62 mile). And speed limits are in kilometers per hour, so think twice before hitting the gas when you see a speed limit of 100. That means 62 miles per hour.

In Portuguese cities and towns, the speed limit usually is 60 kph (37 mph). On main roads outside Portuguese towns, speed limits usually are 90 kph (56 mph) for cars or 70 kph (44 mph) for cars towing trailers. The minimum on highways is 50 kph (31 mph), the maximum, 120 kph (75 mph).

Keep in mind, when touring along Portugal's scenic roadways, that it is all too easy to inch up over the speed limit. And use alcohol sparingly prior to getting behind the wheel. Portugal has specific laws pertaining to drinking and driving and, as in other European countries, the Portuguese authorities are most zealous in prosecuting those who commit infractions under the influence. Police also have the power to levy on-the-spot fines for other violations such as speeding, failure to stop at a red light, and failure to wear seat belts (required by law for front-seat passengers).

■ **Note:** Pay particular attention to parking signs in large cities throughout Europe, especially those indicating "control zones," where an unattended parked car presents a serious security risk. If you park in a restricted zone, unlike in the US (where you chance only a ticket or being towed), you may return to find that the trunk and doors have been blown off by overly cautious security forces. (More likely, however, you'll return to find one of the car's wheels "clamped," a procedure that renders your car inoperable and involves a tedious — and costly — process to get it freed).

Roads and Maps – Western Europe's network of highways is as well maintained as any in North America, with a system comparable to the American highway system: expressways, first class roads, and well-surfaced secondary roads. Three decades ago, a pan-European commission established standards for international European routes, called E roads. Most European maps note E route numbers together with national route numbers. Single-country maps generally use only a national number.

Portugal maintains its own highway system, and continues to invest in road improvements, such as widening and repaving main thoroughfares. Coastal roads tend to be foggy in the morning, and in the north of Portugal traffic can be very heavy. Traffic in the north has been eased somewhat since last year, however, with the completion of the extended autostrada (main highway) linking Lisbon and Porto; and the recently built road between Lisbon and the Algarve should make traveling south faster and easier. However, pay special attention on newly surfaced roads throughout Portugal: there is a tendency to forget to install signals or to paint dividing lines.

Except for stretches of free autoroutes in the vicinity of cities, most of the autoroutes (designated by A on pan-European maps) are toll roads, and they are fairly expensive. They save time, gas, and wear and tear on the car, but they are obviously not the roads to take if you want to browse and linger along the way. The other main roads (designated by N) and the secondary, or regional (designated by D), are free, well maintained, and much more picturesque, while minor roads have their own charm.

Traffic congestion is at its worst on main roads, particularly those radiating from major cities. Look for signs pointing out detours or alternative routes to popular holiday destinations. Service stations, information points, and tourist offices often distribute free maps of the alternate routes, which may be the long way around but probably will get you to your destination faster in the end.

Be aware that in recent years, numerous changes have been taking place in the numbering of European roads. Many N roads have become D roads, some merely changing their prefix from N to D, some changing numbers as well. Another recent development is a new Europe-wide road numbering system. The European designations, prefaced by an E, appear together with the individual country's road numbers; so, for example, autoroute A1 in Portugal also could be called E5, but another country's A1 would have a different E number. Both designations appear on Michelin's newest maps, but expect discrepancies between the old and new numbers to appear on maps and in guidebooks and brochures for some time to come.

All Michelin publications — the red and green guides, as well as road maps (by far the best for visitors touring) — are available in bookstores and map shops throughout the US and all over Europe, and also can be ordered from Michelin Guides and Maps (PO Box 3305, Spartanburg, SC 29304-3305; phone: 803-599-0850 in South Carolina; 800-423-0485 elsewhere in the US). A new edition of each map appears every year; if you're not buying directly from the publisher, make sure that the edition you buy is no more than 2 years old by opening one fold and checking the publication date, given just under the black circle with the map number. A particularly good map of Portugal is Michelin's *No. 990,* which is on a scale of 1:1,000,000 (1 cm equals 10 km). It outlines scenic routes in green, and highlights national parks and interesting sights

Freytag & Berndt's excellent series of 28 road maps ($8.95 to $9.95 each) covers most major destinations throughout Europe, including the Iberian Peninsula. As the publisher is Austrian, this series is best ordered from the US distributor, *Map Link* (25 E. Mason St., Suite 201, Santa Barbara, CA 93101; phone: 805-965-4402), which also is a good source of just about any other kind of map of just about anywhere in the world. You may want to order their comprehensive guide to maps worldwide, *The World Map Directory* ($29.95). If they don't have the map you want in stock, they will do their best to get it for you. Their selection of Portuguese maps includes several country maps and a wide range of city and topographical maps. The *Freytag* maps and those of other publishers also may be available from some of the travel sources listed in *Books, Magazines, Newspapers, and Newsletters,* in this section.

Road maps also are sold at gas stations throughout Europe. Stateside, some free maps can be obtained from the national tourist offices. The Portuguese National Tourist Office has a free map of Portugal that, in addition to all road information, identifies gas stations that sell unleaded gas. *Avis,* the car rental company (see below), offers "Personally Yours," a travel packet complete with maps and information on places to see and things to do while driving through Portugal.

The *American Automobile Association (AAA)* also provides a number of useful reference sources, including an overall Europe planning map, several regional maps of

Portugal, the 600-page *Travel Guide to Europe* (the price varies from branch to branch), and the 64-page *Motoring in Europe* ($7.25). These are available through local *AAA* offices (see below — note that the price and availability of these publications, both for members and non-members, vary from branch to branch). Another invaluable guide, *Euroad: The Complete Guide to Motoring in Europe,* is available for $8.95, including postage and handling, from *VLE Limited,* PO Box 444, Tenafly, NJ 07024 (phone: 201-585-5080).

Automobile Clubs and Breakdowns – Most European automobile clubs offer emergency assistance to any breakdown victim, whether a club member or not; however, only members of these clubs or affiliated clubs may have access to certain information services and receive discounted or free towing and repair services.

Members of the *American Automobile Association (AAA)* often are automatically entitled to a number of services from foreign clubs. With over 31 million members in chapters throughout the US and Canada, the *AAA* is the largest automobile club in North America. *AAA* affiliates throughout the US provide a variety of travel services to members, including a travel agency, trip planning, fee-free traveler's checks, and *sometimes,* reimbursement for foreign roadside assistance (if no reciprocal service agreement exists between the foreign automobile club and the *AAA*). They will help plan an itinerary, send a map with clear routing directions, and even make hotel reservations. These services apply to travel in both the US and Europe. Although *AAA* members receive maps and brochures for no charge or at a discount, non-members also can order from an extensive selection of highway and topographical maps at most *AAA* branches. You can join the *AAA* through local chapters (listed in the telephone book under *AAA*) or contact the national office at 1000 AAA Dr., Heathrow, FL 32746-5063 (phone: 407-444-8544).

Through its association with the *Alliance Internationale de Tourisme* (*AIT;* International Touring Organization) in France, the *AAA* is affiliated with automobile clubs throughout Europe. Based on reciprocal agreements, club members may be provided with services such as free or low-cost travel information and road maps, towing, and limited emergency road service. Note that the *AAA* is not directly affiliated with Portuguese automobile clubs, such as the *Automóvel Club de Portugal* (24 Rua Rosa Araújo, Lisbon 1200; phone: 1-563931). If you call on this or another Portuguese automobile club for roadside assistance, it is likely that you will have to pay for any services provided. The *AAA* may or may not agree to reimburse you for these charges on your return from Portugal — such requests for reimbursement are handled on a case-by-case basis.

If you break down on the road, immediate emergency procedure is to get the car off the road. If the road has a narrow shoulder, try to get all the way off, even if you have to hang off the shoulder a bit. Better yet, try to make it to an area where the shoulder is wider — if you are crawling along well below the speed limit, use your emergency flashers to warn other drivers. Once you've pulled off the road, raise the hood as a signal that help is needed, and tie a white handkerchief or rag to the door handle or radio antenna. Don't leave the car unattended, and don't try any major repairs on the road. Note that motor patrols in Portugal usually drive small cars painted white with blue trim, and emergency call boxes are located on many major routes.

Aside from these options, a driver in distress will have to contact the nearest service center by pay phone. And, although English is spoken in most of the major tourist areas in Portugal, if language is a barrier in explaining your dilemma, your best bet may be to reach an English-speaking international operator who can stay on the line and act as interpreter. (For further information on calling for help, see *Mail, Telephone, and Electricity, Staying Healthy,* and *Legal Aid and Consular Services,* all in this section.) Car rental companies also make provisions for breakdowns, emergency service, and assistance; ask for a number to call when you pick up the vehicle.

Gasoline – In Portugal, gasoline is sold by the liter, which is slightly more than 1 quart; approximately 3.8 liters equal 1 US gallon. Regular or leaded gas generally is sold in two grades — called *gasolina normal* or *gasolina super.* Diesel (called diesel) also is widely available, but unleaded fuel (*gasolina sem chumbo*) has only recently been introduced in Portugal and may be difficult (or even impossible) to find. At least until all Portuguese gas stations sell unleaded, your safest bet is to rent a car that takes leaded gasoline.

Gas prices everywhere rise and fall depending on the world supply of oil, and an American traveling overseas is further affected by the prevailing rate of exchange, so it is difficult to say exactly how much fuel will cost when you travel. It is not difficult to predict, however, that gas prices will be substantially higher in Portugal than you are accustomed to paying in the US.

Particularly when traveling in rural areas, fill up whenever you come to a gas station. It may be a long way to the next open station. (Even in more populated areas, it may be difficult to find an open station on Sundays or holidays.) You don't want to get stranded on an isolated stretch — so it is a good idea to bring along an extra few gallons in a steel container. (Plastic containers tend to break when a car is bouncing over rocky roads. This, in turn, creates the danger of fire should the gasoline ignite from a static electricity spark. Plastic containers also may burst at high altitudes.)

Considering the cost of gas in Portugal relative to US prices, gas economy is of particular concern. The prudent traveler should plan an itinerary and make as many reservations as possible in advance in order not to waste gas figuring out where to go, stay, or eat. Drive early in the day, when there is less traffic. Then leave your car at the hotel and use local transportation whenever possible after you arrive at your destination.

Although it may be as dangerous to drive at a speed much below the posted limit as it is to drive above it — particularly on major highways, where the speed limit is 120 kph (75 mph) — at 88 kph (55 mph) a car gets 25% better mileage than at 112 kph (70 mph). The number of miles per liter or gallon also is increased by driving smoothly.

RENTING A CAR: Although there are other options, such as leasing or outright purchase, most travelers who want to drive in Europe simply rent a car. Travelers to Portugal can rent a car through a travel agent or international rental firm before leaving home, or from a local company once they are in Europe. Another possibility, also arranged before departure, is to rent the car as part of a larger travel package (see "Fly/Drive Packages," below, as well as *Package Tours,* in this section).

Renting a car in Portugal is not inexpensive, but it is possible to economize by determining your own needs and then shopping around among the car rental companies until you find the best deal. As you comparison shop, keep in mind that rates vary considerably, not only from city to city, but also from location to location within the same city. For instance, it might be less expensive to rent a car in the center of a city rather than at the airport. Ask about special rates or promotional deals, such as weekend or weekly rates, bonus coupons for airline tickets, or 24-hour rates that include gas and unlimited mileage.

Rental car companies operating in Europe can be divided into three basic categories: large international companies; national or regional companies; and smaller local companies. Because of aggressive local competition, the cost of renting a car can be less expensive once a traveler arrives in Portugal, compared to the prices quoted in advance in the US. Local companies usually are less expensive than the international giants.

Given this situation, it's tempting to wait until arriving to scout out the lowest-priced rental from the company located the farthest from the airport high-rent district and offering no pick-up services. But if your arrival coincides with a holiday or a peak travel period, you may be disappointed to find that even the most expensive car in town was spoken for months ago. Whenever possible, it is best to reserve in advance, anywhere from a few days in slack periods to a month or more during the busier seasons.

Renting from the US – Travel agents can arrange foreign rentals for clients, but it is just as easy to call and rent a car yourself. Listed below are some of the major international rental companies represented in Portugal that have information and reservations numbers that can be dialed toll-free from the US:

Avis (phone: 800-331-1084). Has 24 locations in Portugal.

Budget (phone: 800-527-0700). Has 15 locations in Portugal.

Dollar Rent A Car (known throughout most of Europe as *Eurodollar Rent A Car;* phone: 800-800-6000). Has 6 locations in Portugal, 2 each in Faro, Lisbon, and Porto.

Hertz (phone: 800-654-3001). Has 21 locations in Portugal.

National (known in Europe as *Europcar;* phone: 800-CAR-EUROPE). Has 24 locations in Portugal.

Thrifty Rent-A-Car (phone: 800-367-2277). Has 1 location in Lisbon and 2 in the Algarve (in Altura and Tavira).

Note that *Avis* also offers two helpful free services for customers traveling in Portugal, as well as in numerous other European countries: the "Know Before You Go" US hotline (phone: 914-355-AVIS); and an "On Call Service" for customers calling once in Europe. Both provide travelers with tourist information on Portugal. Topics may range from questions about driving (distances, gasoline prices, and license requirements) to queries about currency, customs, tipping, and weather. (Callers to the US number receive a personal letter confirming the information discussed.) For the European service, there is a different toll-free number in each country; the numbers are given to you when you rent from *Avis* (personnel at these numbers speak English).

Another special service is *Avis*'s Europe Message Center, which operates like any answering service in that it will take phone messages 24 hours a day for *Avis* customers. *Avis* renters are given a telephone number in Europe that they can leave with anyone who wants to contact them while they are touring; if your rental car comes with a car phone, *Avis* will give this number to callers (with your permission). The tourers themselves can call a toll-free number to pick up messages or leave word for family, friends, or business colleagues. To utilize the service, a renter picks up his or her car at an *Avis* outlet in Europe, and then simply calls the Message Center and registers with the rental agreement number. It's even possible to leave an itinerary — which can be altered later if necessary — making messages easy to leave and/or pick up.

It also is possible to rent a car before you go by contacting any of a number of smaller or less well known US companies that do not operate worldwide. These organizations specialize in European auto travel, including leasing and car purchase in addition to car rental, or actually are tour operators with well-established European car rental programs. These firms, whose names and addresses are listed below, act as agents for a variety of European suppliers, offer unlimited mileage almost exclusively, and frequently manage to undersell their larger competitors by a significant margin.

There are legitimate bargains in car rentals provided you shop for them. Call all the familiar car rental names whose toll-free numbers are given above (don't forget to ask about their special discount plans), and then call the smaller companies listed below. In the recent past, the latter have tended to offer significantly lower rates, but it always pays to compare. Begin your comparison shopping early, because the best deals may be booked to capacity quickly and may require payment 14 to 21 days or more before picking up the car.

Auto Europe (PO Box 1097, Sharps Wharf, Camden, ME 04843; phone: 207-236-8235; 800-223-5555 throughout the US and Canada). Offers rentals in Albufeira, Cascais, Faro, Lisbon, and Porto.

Europe by Car (One Rockefeller Plaza, New York, NY 10020; phone: 212-581-3040 in New York State; 800-223-1516 elsewhere in the US; and 9000 Sunset Blvd., Los Angeles, CA 90069; phone: 800-252-9401 in California; 213-272-0424 elsewhere in the US). Offers rentals in Faro, Lisbon, and Porto.

European Car Reservations (349 W. Commercial St., Suite 2950, East Rochester, NY 14445; phone: 800-535-3303). Offers rentals in Albufeira, Estoril, Faro, Lisbon, Porto, and Praia de Rocha.

Foremost Euro-Car (5430 Van Nuys Blvd., Suite 306, Van Nuys, CA 91401; phone: 818-786-1960 or 800-272-3299). Offers rentals in Carvoeiro, Estoril, Faro, Lagos, Lisbon, Portimão, Porto, and Quarteira.

Kemwel Group Inc. (106 Calvert St., Harrison, NY 10528; phone: 800-678-0678 or 914-835-5555). Offers rentals in Estoril, Faro, Lisbon, and Porto.

Meier's World Travel, Inc. (6033 W. Century Blvd., Suite 1080, Los Angeles, CA 90045; phone: 800-937-0700). In conjunction with major car rental companies arranges economical rentals throughout Portugal.

One of the ways to keep the cost of car rentals down is to deal with a car rental consolidator, such as *Connex International* (23 N. Division St., Peekskill, NY 10566; phone: 800-333-3949 or 914-739-0066). *Connex*'s main business is negotiating with virtually all of the major car rental agencies for the lowest possible prices for its customers. This company arranges rentals throughout Europe, including 20 cities and towns in Portugal.

Local Rentals – It long has been common wisdom that the least expensive way to rent a car is to make arrangements in Europe. This is less true today than it used to be. Many medium to large European car rental companies have become the overseas suppliers of stateside companies such as those mentioned previously, and often the stateside agency, by dint of sheer volume, has been able to negotiate more favorable rates for its US customers than the European firm offers its own. Still lower rates may be found by searching out small, strictly local rental companies overseas, whether at less than prime addresses in major cities or in more remote areas. But to find them you must be willing to invest a sufficient amount of vacation time comparing prices on the scene. You also must be prepared to return the car to the location that rented it; drop-off possibilities are likely to be limited.

Once overseas, local branches of the Portuguese National Tourist Office may be able to supply the names of Portuguese car rental companies. The local yellow pages is another good place to begin. (For further information on local rental companies, see the individual reports in THE CITIES.).

In Portugal, major national car rental companies include *Olivauto* (21 Av. João XXI 12D, Lisbon; phone: 1-893588) and *Viata Rent A Car* (26A Rua Filipe da Mata, Lisbon; phone: 1-293-3148).

Also bear in mind that *Hertz* offers a rail-and-drive pass, called EurailDrive Pass, which is valid throughout all the countries that are included in the Eurail network, including Portugal. (For further information on rail-and-drive packages, see *Traveling by Train,* above.)

Requirements – Whether you decide to rent a car in advance from a large international rental company with European branches or wait to rent from a local company, you should know that renting a car is rarely as simple as signing on the dotted line and roaring off into the night. If you are renting for personal use, you must have a valid driver's license and will have to convince the renting agency that (1) you are personally creditworthy, and (2) you will bring the car back at the stated time. This will be easy if you have a major credit card; most rental companies accept credit cards in lieu of a cash deposit, as well as for payment of your final bill. If you prefer to pay in cash, leave your credit card imprint as a "deposit," then pay your bill in cash when you return the car.

If you are planning to rent a car once in Portugal, *Avis, Budget, Hertz,* and other US rental companies usually *will* rent to travelers paying in cash and leaving either a credit card imprint or a substantial amount of cash as a deposit. This is not necessarily standard policy, however, as some of the other international chains, and a number of local and regional European companies will *not* rent to an individual who doesn't have a valid credit card. In this case, you may have to call around to find a company that accepts cash.

Also keep in mind that although the minimum age to drive a car in Portugal is 18 years, the minimum age to rent a car is set by the rental company. (Restrictions vary from company to company, as well as at different locations.) Many firms have a minimum age requirement of 21 years, some raise that to between 23 and 25 years, and for some models of cars it rises to 30 years. The upper age limit at many companies is between 69 and 75; others have no upper limit or may make drivers above a certain age subject to special conditions.

Costs – Finding the most economical car rental will require some telephone shopping on your part. As a *general* rule, expect to hear lower prices quoted by the smaller, strictly local companies than by the well-known international names, with those of the national Portuguese companies falling somewhere between the two.

Comparison shopping always is advisable, however, because the company that has the least expensive rentals in one country or city may not have the least expensive cars in another, and even the international giants offer discount plans whose conditions are easy for most travelers to fulfill. For instance, *Budget* and *National* offer discounts of anywhere from 10% to 30% off their usual rates (according to the size of the car and the duration of the rental), provided that the car is reserved a certain number of days before departure (usually 7 to 14 days, but it can be less), is rented for a minimum period (5 days or, more often, a week), is paid for at the time of booking, and, in most cases, is returned to the same location that supplied it or to another in the same country. Similar discount plans include *Hertz*'s Affordable Europe and *Avis*'s Supervalue Rates Europe.

If driving short distances for only a day or two, the best deal may be a per-day, per-mile (or per-kilometer) rate: You pay a flat fee for each day you keep the car, plus a per-mile (or per-kilometer) charge. An increasingly common alternative is to be granted a certain number of free miles or kilometers each day and then be charged on a per-mile or per-kilometer basis over that number.

A better alternative for touring the countryside may be a flat per-day rate with unlimited free mileage; this certainly is the most economical rate if you plan to drive over 100 miles (160 km). Make sure that the low, flat daily rate that catches your eye, however, is indeed a per-day rate: Often the lowest price advertised by a company turns out to be available only with a minimum 3-day rental — fine if you want the car that long, but not the bargain it appears if you really intend to use it no more than 24 hours for in-city driving. Flat weekly rates also are available, as are some flat monthly rates that represent a further saving over the daily rate. (*Note:* When renting a car in Portugal, the term "mileage" may refer either to miles or kilometers.)

Another factor influencing cost is the type of car you rent. Rentals generally are based on a tiered price system, with different sizes of cars — variations of budget, economy, regular, and luxury — often listed as A (the smallest and least expensive) through F, G, or H, and sometimes even higher. Charges may increase by only a few dollars a day through several categories of subcompact and compact cars — where most of the competition is — then increase by great leaps through the remaining classes of full-size and luxury cars and passenger vans. The larger the car, the more it costs to rent and the more gas it consumes, but for some people the greater comfort and extra luggage space of a larger car (in which bags and sporting gear can be safely locked out of sight) may make it worth the additional expense. Be warned, too, that relatively few European cars have automatic transmissions, and those that do are more likely to be in the F than the A group. Similarly, cars with air conditioning are likely to be found in the more expensive categories only. Most expensive are sleek sports cars, but, again, for some people the thrill of driving such a car — for a week or a day — may be worth it.

Electing to pay for collision damage waiver (CDW) protection will add considerably to the cost of renting a car. You may be responsible for the *full value* of the vehicle being rented, but you can dispense with the possible obligation by buying the offered waiver at a cost of about $10 to $13 a day. Before making any decisions about optional collision damage waivers, check with your own insurance agent and determine whether your personal automobile insurance policy covers rented vehicles; if it does, you probably won't need to pay for the waiver. Be aware, too, that increasing numbers of credit cards automatically provide CDW coverage if the car rental is charged to the appropriate credit card. However, the specific terms of such coverage differ sharply among individual credit card companies, so check with the credit card company for information on the nature and amount of coverage provided. Business travelers also should be aware that, at the time of this writing, *American Express* had withdrawn its automatic CDW coverage from some corporate *Green* card accounts — watch for similar cutbacks by other credit card companies.

Overseas, the amount renters may be liable for should damage occur has not risen to the heights it has in the US. In addition, some European car rental agreements include collision damage waiver coverage. In this case, the CDW supplement frees the renter from liability for the *deductible* amount — as opposed to the standard CDW coverage, described above, which releases the driver from liability for the full value of the car. In Portugal, this deductible typically ranges from $1,500 to $2,500 at present, but can be higher for some luxury car groups. As with the full collision damage waiver, the cost of waiving this liability — which can be as high as $25 a day — is far from negligible, however. Drivers who rent cars in the US often are able to decline the CDW because many personal automobile insurance policies (subject to their own deductibles) extend to rental cars; unfortunately, such coverage usually does not extend to cars rented for use outside the US and Canada. Similarly, CDW coverage provided by some credit cards if the rental is charged to the card may be limited to cars rented in the US or Canada.

When inquiring about CDW coverage and costs, you should be aware that a number of the major international car rental companies now are automatically including the cost of this waiver in their quoted prices. This does not mean that they are absorbing this cost and you are receiving free coverage — total rental prices have increased to include the former CDW charge. The disadvantage of this inclusion is that you probably will not have the option to refuse this coverage, and will end up paying the added charge — even if you already are adequately covered by your own insurance policy or through a credit card company.

Additional costs to be added to the price tag include drop-off charges or one-way service fees. The lowest price quoted by any given company may apply only to a car that is returned to the same location from which it was rented. A slightly higher rate may be charged if the car is to be returned to a different location (even within the same city), and a considerably higher rate may prevail if the rental begins in one country and ends in another.

A further consideration: Don't forget that all car rentals are subject to Value Added Tax (VAT — known in Portugal as IVA). This tax rarely is included in the rental price that's advertised or quoted, but it always must be paid — whether you pay in advance in the US or pay it when you drop off the car. In Portugal, the VAT rate on car rentals is 17%.

There is a wide variation in this tax from country to country. One-way rentals bridging two countries used to be exempt from tax, but this is no longer the case. In general, the tax on one-way rentals is determined by the country in which the car has been rented, so if your tour plans include several countries, you should examine your options regarding the pick-up and drop-off points. Even if you intend to visit only one country in Europe, you still might consider a nearby country as a pick-up point if it will provide substantial savings. For instance, for a tourer planning to explore Portugal, there's a financial incentive (particularly for long-term rentals) to pick up his or her rental car in Spain, and then drive across the border (at a 4% cost saving).

Some rental agencies that do not maintain their own fleets use a contractor, whose country of registration determines the rate of taxation. An example is *Kemwel Group,* whose one-way inter-country rentals are taxed at the Danish rate of 25%. Round-trip rentals, where the car is picked up and returned in the same country, are taxed at that country's national rate — in the case of Portugal, 17%. *Kemwel*'s special programs offer savings to the client planning to tour Europe (particularly through countries where the tax rate is higher). Their UltraSaver and UltraSaver Plus tariffs offer inclusive rentals in some 45 cities across Europe, including Lisbon. The UltraSaver Plus program includes full insurance coverage and all European VATs. Weekly rentals, including unlimited mileage, are available. If part of a fly/drive package (see below) booked through *Kemwel,* rates may be even lower. Although reservations should be made earlier, bookings must be paid for at least 7 days before delivery of the car, and the vehicle must be returned to the *Kemwel* garage from which it was originally rented. For further information, contact *Kemwel Group,* 106 Calvert St., Harrison, NY 10528 (phone: 800-678-0678 or 914-835-5555).

Also, don't forget to factor in the price of gas. Rental cars usually are delivered with a full tank of gas. (This is not always the case, however, so check the gas gauge when picking up the car, and have the amount of gas noted on your rental agreement if the tank is not full.) Remember to fill the tank before you return the car or you will have to pay to refill it, and gasoline at the car rental company's pump always is much more expensive than at a service station. This policy may vary for smaller local and regional companies; ask when picking up the vehicle. Before leaving the lot, also check that the rental car has a spare tire and jack in the trunk.

Finally, currency fluctuation is another factor to consider. Most brochures quote rental prices in US dollars, but these dollar amounts frequently are only guides; that is, they represent the prevailing rate of exchange at the time the brochure was printed. The rate may be very different when you call to make a reservation, and different again when the time comes to pay the bill (when the amount owed may be paid in cash in foreign currency or as a charge to a credit card, which is recalculated at a still later date's rate of exchange). Some companies guarantee rates in dollars (often for a slight surcharge), but this is an advantage only when the value of the dollar is steadily declining overseas. If the dollar is growing stronger overseas, you may be better off with rates guaranteed in Portuguese escudos.

Fly/Drive Packages – Airlines, charter companies, car rental companies, and tour operators have been offering fly/drive packages for years, and even though the basic components of the package have changed somewhat — return airfare, a car waiting at the airport, and perhaps a night's lodging all for one inclusive price used to be the rule — the idea remains the same. You rent a car *here* for use *there* by booking it along with other arrangements for the trip. These days, the very minimum arrangement possible is the result of a tie-in between a car rental company and an airline, which entitles customers to a rental car for less than the company's usual rates, provided they show proof of having booked a flight on that airline. For information on these packages, check with the airline or your travel agent.

Slightly more elaborate fly/drive packages are listed under various names (go-as-you-please, self-drive, or, simply, car tours) in the independent vacations sections of tour catalogues. Their most common ingredients are the rental car plus some sort of hotel voucher plan, with the applicable airfare listed separately. You set off on your trip with a block of prepaid accommodations vouchers, a list of hotels that accept them (usually members of a hotel chain or association), and a reservation for the first night's stay, after which the staff of each hotel books the next one for you or you make your own reservations. Naturally, the greater the number of establishments participating in the scheme, the more freedom you have to range at will during the day's driving and still be near a place to stay for the night. Less flexible car tours provide a rental car, a hotel plan, and a set itinerary that permits no deviation because the hotels all are reserved in advance.

The cost of these combination packages generally varies according to the size of the car and the quality of the hotels; there usually is an additional drop-off charge if the car is picked up in one city and returned in another. Most packages are offered at several different price levels, ranging from a standard plan covering stays in hotels to a budget plan using accommodations such as small inns or farmhouses. Airlines also have special rental car rates available when you book their flights, often with a flexible hotel voucher program. For additional information, see *Package Tours,* in this section.

LEASING: Anyone planning to be in Europe for 3 weeks or more should compare the cost of renting a car with that of leasing one for the same period. While the money saved by leasing — rather than renting for a 23-day (the minimum) or 30-day period — may not be great, what is saved over the course of a long-term lease — 45, 60, 90 days, or more — amounts to hundreds, even thousands, of dollars. Part of the saving is due to the fact that leased cars are exempt from the stiff taxes applicable to rented cars. In addition, leasing plans provide for collision insurance with no deductible amount, so there is no need to add the daily cost of the collision damage waiver protection (an option offered by rental car companies — see above). A further advantage of a car lease — actually, a financed purchase/repurchase plan — is that you reserve your car by specific make and model rather than by group only, and it is delivered to you fresh from the factory.

Unfortunately, leasing as described above is offered only in Belgium and France, and the savings it permits can be realized to the fullest only if the cars are picked up and returned in these countries. While leased cars can be delivered to other countries there is a charge for this service, to which must be added an identical return charge. If you don't intend to keep the car very long, the two charges could nullify the amount saved by leasing rather than renting, so you will have to do some arithmetic.

It is possible to lease a car in countries other than Belgium and France, but most of the plans offered are best described as long-term rentals at preferential rates. They differ from true leasing in that you will pay tax and collision damage waiver protection (though it may be included in the quoted price), and the cars usually are late-model used cars rather than brand new.

One of the major car leasing companies is *Renault,* offering leases of new cars for 23 days to 6 months. The cars are exempt from tax, all insurance is included, and there is no mileage charge. *Renault* offers free pick-up/drop-off at *Renault* branch offices in most major French cities; substantial pick-up/drop-off charges apply to selected cities elsewhere in Europe. Although *Renault* does not offer the service in Portugal, cars can be picked up in Spain (in Barcelona, Madrid, Seville, or Vigo for a charge, at press time, of about $150), driven into Portugal, and returned in Spain. For further information and reservations, ask your travel agent or contact *Renault USA,* 650 First Ave., New York, NY 10016 (phone: 212-532-1221 in New York State; 800-221-1052 elsewhere in the US).

Peugeot also offers a similar arrangement, called the "Peugeot Vacation Plan." In accordance with the standard type of financed purchase/repurchase plan, travelers pick up the car in France, paying at the time of pick-up to use the car for a specified period of time (anywhere between 23 and 180 days), and at the end of this pre-arranged period return it to *Peugeot.* The tax-free temporary "purchase" includes unlimited mileage, factory warranty, full collision damage waiver coverage (no deductible), and 24-hour towing and roadside assistance. Pick-up and drop-off locations and charges are similar to *Renault*'s. *Peugeot*'s "European Delivery" program is a full-purchase program, including shipment of the car to the US, as discussed below. For further information, contact *Peugeot Motors of America* (1 Peugeot Plaza, PO Box 607, Lyndhurst, NJ 07071; phone: 201-935-8400). Some of the car rental firms listed above — *Auto Europe, Europe by Car, Foremost Euro-Car,* and *Kemwel Group* — also arrange European car leases.

BUYING A CAR: If your plans include both buying a new car of European make and a driving tour of Europe, it's possible to combine the two ventures and save some money on each. By buying the car abroad and using it during your vacation, you pay quite a bit less for it than the US dealer would charge and at the same time avoid the expense of renting a car during your holiday. There are two basic ways to achieve this desired end, but one, factory delivery, is far simpler than the other, direct import.

Factory delivery means that you place an order for a car in the US, then pick it up in Europe, often literally at the factory gate. It also means that your new car is built to American specifications, complying with all US emission and safety standards. Because of this, only cars made by manufacturers who have established a formal program for such sales to American customers may be bought at the factory. At present, the list includes Audi, BMW, Jaguar, Mercedes-Benz, Peugeot, Porsche, Saab, Volkswagen, and Volvo, among others (whose manufacturers generally restrict their offerings to those models they ordinarily export to the US). The factory delivery price, in US dollars, usually runs about 5% to 15% below the sticker price of the same model at a US dealership and sometimes (depending on the manufacturer) includes the cost of shipping the car home. All contracts include US customs duty, but the cost of the incidentals and the insurance necessary for driving the car around Europe are extra, except in BMW's plan.

One of the few disadvantages of factory delivery is that car manufacturers make only a limited number of models available each year, and for certain popular models you may have to get in line early in the season. Another is that you must take your trip when the car is ready, not when you are, although you usually will have 8 to 10 weeks' notice. The actual place of delivery can vary; it is more economical to pick up the car at the factory, but arrangements sometimes — but not always — can be made to have it delivered elsewhere for an extra charge. For example, cars made by Jaguar (now owned by Ford) must be ordered through a US dealer and picked up at the factory in Coventry, England, although they also can be dropped off for shipment home in any number of European cities. For information, write to *Jaguar Cars,* 555 MacArthur Blvd., Mahwah, NJ 07430 (phone: 201-818-8500).

Cars for factory delivery usually can be ordered either through one of the manufacturer's authorized dealers in the US or through companies — among them *Europe by Car, Foremost Euro-Car,* and *Kemwel Group* (see above for contact information) — that specialize in such transactions. (Note that *Foremost Euro-Car* serves all of the US for rentals and leasing, but they arrange *sales* only for California residents.) Another company arranging car sales abroad is *Ship Side Tax Free World on Wheels BV,* 600B Lake St., Suite A, Ramsey, NJ 07446 (phone: 201-818-0400).

Occasionally an auto manufacturer offers free or discounted airfare in connection with a European delivery program. This year, Mercedes-Benz has a program including discounted round-trip airfare ($500 for two economy fare seats or one business class seat) from any US gateway served by *Delta, KLM,* or *Lufthansa* to Stuttgart (where the buyer picks up the car), plus a 2-night stay at the local *Hilton* or *Ramada* hotel, and 15 days' comprehensive road insurance. For details, contact *Mercedes-Benz of North America,* 7700 Wisconsin Ave., Suite 1100, Bethesda, MD 20814 (phone: 800-458-8202).

The other way to buy a car abroad, **direct import**, sometimes is referred to as "gray market" buying. It is perfectly legal, but not totally hassle-free. Direct import means that you buy abroad a car that was meant for use abroad, not one built according to

US specifications. It can be new or used, and may even include — if made for use in Ireland or Great Britain — a steering wheel on the right side. The main drawback to direct import is that the process of modification to bring the car into compliance with US standards is expensive and time-consuming: it typically costs from $5,000 to $7,000 in parts and labor and takes from 2 to 6 months. In addition, the same shipping, insurance, and miscellaneous expenses (another $2,000 to $5,000, according to estimates) that would be included in the factory delivery price must be added to the purchase price of the car, and the considerable burden of shepherding it on its journey from showroom to home garage usually is borne by the purchaser. Direct import dealers do exist (they are not the same as your local, factory-authorized foreign car dealer, with whom you are now in competition), but even if you use one, you still need to do a great deal of paperwork yourself.

Once upon a time, the main advantage of the direct import method — besides the fact that it can be used for makes and models not available in factory delivery programs — was that much more money could be saved importing an expensive car. Given today's exchange rates, however, the method's potential greater gain is harder to realize and must be weighed against its greater difficulties. Still, if direct importing interests you, you can obtain a list of those makes and models approved for conversion in this country, and of the converters licensed to bring them up to US specifications, by contacting the Environmental Protection Agency, Manufacturers' Operations Division, EN-340-F, Investigations/Imports Section, 401 M St. SW, Washington, DC 20460 (phone: 202-260-2479).

If you have special problems getting your car into the US, you might consider contacting a specialist in vehicle importation, such as Daniel Kokal, an independent regulatory consultant. His address is 15014 Kamputa Dr., Centerville, VA 22020 (phone: 703-818-9009).

Package Tours

If the mere thought of buying a package for travel to and through Portugal conjures up visions of a race through ten cities in as many days in lockstep with a horde of frazzled fellow travelers, remember that packages have come a long way. For one thing, not all packages necessarily are escorted tours, and the one you buy does not have to include any organized touring at all — nor will it necessarily include traveling companions. If it does, however, you'll find that people of all sorts — many just like yourself — are taking advantage of packages today because they are economical and convenient, save you an immense amount of planning time, and exist in such variety that it's virtually impossible not to find one that suits at least the majority of your travel preferences. Given the high cost of travel these days, packages have emerged as a particularly wise buy.

In essence, a package is just an amalgam of travel services that can be purchased in a single transaction. A package (tour or otherwise) to and through Portugal may include any or all of the following: round-trip transatlantic transportation, local transportation (and/or car rentals), accommodations, some or all meals, sightseeing, entertainment, transfers to and from the hotel at each destination, taxes, tips, escort service, and a variety of incidental features that might be offered as options at additional cost. In other words, a package can be any combination of travel elements, from a fully escorted tour offered at an all-inclusive price to a simple fly/drive booking allowing you to move about totally on your own. Its principal advantage is that it saves money: The cost of the combined arrangements invariably is well below the price of all of the same elements if bought separately, and particularly if transportation is provided by charter or discount flight, the whole package could cost less than just a round-trip economy airline ticket on a regularly scheduled flight. A package provides more than economy and convenience: It releases the traveler from having to make individual arrangements for each separate element of a trip.

Tour programs generally can be divided into two categories — "escorted" (or locally hosted) and "independent." An escorted tour means that a guide will accompany the group from the beginning of the tour through to the return flight; a locally hosted tour means that the group will be met upon arrival at each location by a different local host. On independent tours, there generally is a choice of hotels, meal plans, and sightseeing trips in each city, as well as a variety of special excursions. The independent plan is for travelers who do not want a totally set itinerary, but who do prefer confirmed hotel reservations. Whether choosing an escorted or independent tour, always bring along complete contact information for your tour operator in case a problem arises, although US tour operators often have European affiliates who can give additional assistance or make other arrangements on the spot.

To determine whether a package — or, more specifically, *which* package — fits your travel plans, start by evaluating your interests and needs, deciding how much and what you want to spend, see, and do. Gather whatever package tour information is available for your schedule. Be sure that you take the time to read the brochure *carefully* to determine precisely what is included. Keep in mind that travel brochures are written to entice you into signing up for a package tour. Often the language is deceptive and devious. For example, a brochure may quote the lowest prices for a package tour based on facilities that are unavailable during the off-season, undesirable at any season, or just plain nonexistent. Information such as "breakfast included" (as it often is in packages to Portugal) or "plus tax" (which can add up) should be taken into account. Note, too, that the prices quoted in brochures almost always are based on double occupancy: The rate listed is for each of two people sharing a double room, and if you travel alone, the supplement for single accommodations can raise the price considerably (see *Hints for Single Travelers,* in this section).

In this age of erratic airfares, the brochure most often will *not* include the price of an airline ticket in the price of the package, though sample fares from various gateway cities usually will be listed separately, as extras to be added to the price of the ground arrangements. Before figuring your actual cost, check the latest fares with the airlines, because the samples invariably are out of date by the time you read them. If the brochure gives more than one category of sample fares per gateway city — such as an individual tour-basing fare, a group fare, an excursion, APEX, or other discount ticket — your travel agent or airline tour desk will be able to tell you which one applies to the package you choose, depending on when you travel, how far in advance you book, and other factors. (An individual tour-basing fare is a fare computed as part of a package that includes land arrangements, thereby entitling a carrier to reduce the air portion almost to the absolute minimum. Though it always represents a saving over full-fare coach or economy, lately the individual tour-basing fare has not been as inexpensive as the excursion and other discount fares that also are available to individuals. The group fare usually is the least expensive fare, and it is the tour operator, not you, who makes up the group.) When the brochure does include round-trip transportation in the package price, don't forget to add the cost of round-trip transportation from your home to the departure city to come up with the total cost of the package.

Finally, read the general information regarding terms and conditions and the responsibility clause (usually in fine print at the end of the descriptive literature) to determine the precise elements for which the tour operator is — and is not — liable. Here the tour operator frequently expresses the right to change services or schedules as long as equivalent arrangements are offered. This clause also absolves the operator of responsibility for circumstances beyond human control, such as floods, or injury to you or your property. While reading, ask the following questions:

1. Does the tour include airfare or other transportation, sightseeing, meals, transfers, taxes, baggage handling, tips, or any other services? Do you want all these services?
2. If the brochure indicates that "some meals" are included, does this mean a welcoming and farewell dinner, two breakfasts, or every evening meal?
3. What classes of hotels are offered? If you will be traveling alone, what is the single supplement?
4. Does the tour itinerary or price vary according to the season?
5. Are the prices guaranteed; that is, if costs increase between the time you book and the time you depart, can surcharges unilaterally be added?
6. Do you get a full refund if you cancel? If not, be sure to obtain cancellation insurance.
7. Can the operator cancel if too few people join? At what point?

One of the consumer's biggest problems is finding enough information to judge the reliability of a tour packager, since individual travelers seldom have direct contact with the firm putting the package together. Usually, a retail travel agent is interposed between customer and tour operator, and much depends on his or her candor and cooperation. So ask a number of questions about the tour you are considering. For example:

- Has the travel agent ever used a package provided by this tour operator?
- How long has the tour operator been in business? Check the Better Business Bureau in the area where the tour operator is based to see if any complaints have been filed against it.
- Is the tour operator a member of the *United States Tour Operators Association* (*USTOA;* 211 E. 51st St., Suite 12B, New York, NY 10022; phone: 212-944-5727)? The *USTOA* will provide a list of its members on request; it also offers a useful brochure, *How to Select a Package Tour.*
- How many and which companies are involved in the package?
- If air travel is by charter flight, is there an escrow account in which deposits will be held; if so, what is the name of the bank?

This last question is very important. US law requires that tour operators place every charter passenger's deposit and subsequent payment in a proper escrow account. Money paid into such an account cannot legally be used except to pay for the costs of a particular package or as a refund if the trip is canceled. To ensure the safe handling of your money, make your check payable to the escrow account — by law, the name of the depository bank must appear in the operator-participant contract, and usually is found in that mass of minuscule type on the back of the brochure. Write the details of the charter, including the destination and dates, on the face of the check; on the back, print "For Deposit Only." Your travel agent may prefer that you make your check out to the agency, saying that it will then pay the tour operator the fee minus commission. But it is perfectly legal to write your check as we suggest, and if your agent objects too strongly (the agent should have sufficient faith in the tour operator to trust him or her to send the proper commission), consider taking your business elsewhere. If you don't make your check out to the escrow account, you lose the protection of that escrow should the trip be canceled or the tour operator or travel agent fail. Furthermore, recent bankruptcies in the travel industry have served to point out that even the protection of escrow may not be enough to safeguard your investment. Increasingly, insurance is becoming a necessity (see *Insurance,* in this section), and payment by credit card has become popular since it offers some additional safeguards if the tour operator defaults.

■ **A word of advice:** Purchasers of vacation packages who feel they're not getting their money's worth are more likely to get a refund if they complain in writing to the operator — and bail out of the whole package immediately. Alert the tour operator or resort manager to the fact that you are dissatisfied, that you will be leaving for home as soon as transportation can be arranged, and that you expect a refund. They may have forms to fill out detailing your complaint; otherwise, state your case in a letter. Even if difficulty in arranging immediate transportation home detains you, your dated, written complaint should help in procuring a refund from the operator.

SAMPLE PACKAGES TO PORTUGAL: There are so many packages available to Portugal today that it's probably safe to say that just about any arrangement anyone might want is available for as long as it is wanted. The keynote is flexibility. Some packages tour the country, while others explore only a selected region or visit only major cities.

Packages to Portugal do tend to break down into two regions, north and south, with tours of either beginning in Lisbon. Combined Spain-Portugal trips also are common, frequently beginning in Lisbon, cutting across the Alentejo Plains and the Spanish border to Seville, and ending in Madrid. The same itinerary in reverse — Madrid to Lisbon — also is common, as is a full circle, Lisbon to Lisbon or Madrid to Madrid. In this case, the northern link generally is via the Portuguese city of Coimbra, the Beira Mountains, and the Spanish cities of Salamanca and Avila.

Escorted Tours – Those seeking the maximum in structure will find that the classic sightseeing tour by motorcoach, fully escorted and all-inclusive (or nearly), has withstood the test of time and still is well represented among the programs of major tour operators. Typically, these tours begin in a major city and last from 1 to 2 weeks. A good many tour operators offer such tours of Portugal in combination with Spain and/or other European destinations.

Hotel accommodations in these packages usually are characterized as first class or better, with private baths or showers accompanying all rooms, although more than a few tour packagers offer less expensive alternatives by providing more modest lodgings. These packages tend to be all-inclusive, although the number of included meals may vary considerably. Among such packages are the following:

Abreu Tours (317 E. 34th St., New York, NY 10016; phone: 800-223-1580 or 212-661-0555). Offers a 7- or 11-day Northern Portugal escorted motorcoach tour. Other packages combine tours to Portugal and Spain.

American Express Travel Related Services (offices throughout the US; phone: 800-241-1700 for information and local branch offices). On their motorcoach tours of Europe, travelers can choose from a number of different itineraries, such as a 14-day, 7-city Iberian Sun Seeker package, which includes visits to Faro and Lisbon; a 17-day, 11-city Moroccan Fiesta tour which visits Faro, Funchal, and Lisbon; and a 14-day, 9-city Andalusian tour which takes in the Algarve, Coimbra, Fátima, and Guarda, among other cities.

Globus-Gateway **and** *Cosmos* (95-25 Queens Blvd., Rego Park, NY 11374; phone: 800-221-0090; or 150 S. Los Robles Ave., Pasadena, CA 91101; phone: 800-556-5454 or 818-449-2019). These affiliated agencies offer numerous tours of Europe, including a 12-day Best of Spain and Portugal package; a 14-day Spain-Portugal-Tangier itinerary; a 15-day Spain-Portugal-Morocco tour; a 23-day Treasures of France, Spain, and Portugal tour; and a 15-day Portugal In Depth package. (Bookings for these agencies must be made through travel agents; however, both can be contacted for information.)

Maupintour (PO Box 807, Lawrence, KS 66044; phone: 800-255-4266). Offers several round-trip tours from Lisbon that tour the countryside (some also visiting Spanish destinations). Their Pousadas and Paradores tour deviates from the norm by scheduling the majority of overnights in these government-run establishments. Other packages include a 14-day Iberian Highlights tour and a 21-day Mallorca, Spain, and Portugal trip.

Melia International (450 Seventh Ave., Suite 1805, New York, NY 10103; phone: 212-967-6565 in New York State; 800-848-2314 elsewhere in the US). Offers 7- and 14-day tours of the Iberian Peninsula that include a visit to Lisbon.

Mill-Run Tours (20 E. 49th St., New York, NY 10017; phone: 212-486-9840 in New York State, 800-MILL-RUN elsewhere). Offers a number of tours throughout Portugal, including the Azores and Madeira.

Olson Travelworld (1334 Parkview Ave., Suite 210, Manhattan Beach, CA 90266; phone: 213-546-8400 in California or abroad; 800-421-5785 in California; 800-421-2255 elsewhere in the US). Offers escorted, highly structured packages to Portugal, including a 22-day Casbah and Castinets tour that takes in Cascais, Fátima, and Lisbon, and a 17-day deluxe Connoisseur's Iberia tour of Portugal, Spain, and Gibraltar.

Skyline Travel Club (376 New York Ave., Huntington, NY 11743; phone: 516-222-9090 in New York State; 800-645-6198 elsewhere in the US). Offers a 13-day Portuguese Sun Seeker motorcoach tour (with stays in *pousadas*) that explores southern Portugal, including the Algarve, and an 11- or 15-day Best of Portugal trip that covers the rest of the country, including the Azores and Madeira.

TAP Air Portugal Discovery Vacations (399 Market St., Newark, NJ 07105; phone: 800-247-8686). Offers a wide variety of escorted tours throughout Portugal, Spain, Morocco, and other destinations in Africa and Europe. The 11-day Toast to Portugal trip begins and ends in Lisbon, and visits Fátima, Minho, Porto, and several other Portuguese cities.

Thomas Cook (Headquarters: 45 Berkeley St., Piccadilly, London W1A 1EB; phone: 44-71-499-4000). The best known of all British tour operators, its name is practically synonymous with the Grand Tour of Europe, but *Cook*'s wide range of itineraries spans the world. Among the packages to Portugal are a 17-day Treasures of Spain, Portugal, and Morocco trip that travels to Batalha, Fátima, and Lisbon, and a 15-day Best of Spain and Portugal tour that visits many of the same sites. Other escorted and stay-put packages also are offered. (Note that although this company is a wholesaler, you can book a tour directly through any of its offices in major cities in North America or through travel agents.)

Trafalgar Tours (21 E. 26th St., New York, NY 10010; phone: 212-689-8977 in New York City; 800-854-0103 elsewhere in the US). Offers numerous first class (as well as some budget) motorcoach itineraries of the Continent. Among the regular itineraries are a 14-day, 8-city, Highlights of Spain and Portugal motorcoach tour, and a 17-day trip that offers the same itinerary plus a short additional trip to Morocco. (As this operator is a wholesaler, bookings must be made through a travel agent.)

Travcoa (PO Box 2630, Newport Beach, CA 92658; phone: 714-476-2800; 800-992-2004 in California; 800-992-2003 elsewhere in the US). Offers a lineup of escorted motorcoach tours, including 18-, 26-, or 29-day packages in Portugal that include all meals.

TWA Getaway Tours (phone: 800-GETAWAY). Offers a wide variety of escorted motorcoach tours throughout Europe, including a 14-day Flamenco package that visits Coimbra, Fátima, Lisbon, and several other Portuguese cities, as well as destinations in Spain.

Independent Tours – Less restrictive arrangements for travelers who prefer more independence than that found on escorted tours are listed in the semi-escorted and hosted sections of tour catalogues. These may combine some aspects of an escorted tour, such as moving from place to place by motorcoach, with longer stays in one spot, where participants are at liberty but a host or hostess — that is, a representative of the tour company — is available at a local office or even in the hotel to answer questions and assist in arranging activities and optional excursions.

Another equally common type of package to Portugal is the car tour or fly/drive arrangement, often described in brochures as a self-drive or go-as-you-please tour. These are independent vacations, geared to travelers who want to cover as much ground as they might on an escorted group sightseeing tour but who prefer to do it on their own. The most flexible plans include no more than a map, a rental car, and a block of as many prepaid hotel vouchers as are needed for the length of the stay (the packages typically are 4 or 7 days long, extendable by individual extra days or additional package segments), along with a list of participating hotels at which the vouchers are accepted. In most cases, only the first night's accommodation is reserved; from then on, travelers book their rooms one stop ahead as they drive from place to place, creating their own itinerary as they go. When the hotels are members of a chain or association — which they usually are — the staff of the last hotel will reserve the next one for you. In other cases, there may be a choice of reserving all accommodations before departure — usually for a fee. Operators offering these packages usually sell vouchers in more than one price category; travelers may have the option of upgrading accommodations by paying a supplement directly to more expensive establishments or can economize by choosing to stay in a modest inn or guesthouse. Another type of fly/drive arrangement is slightly more restrictive in that the tour packager supplies an itinerary that must be followed day by day, with a specific hotel to be reached each night. Often these plans are more deluxe as well.

Fly/drive packages to and around Portugal include the following:

AutoVenture (425 Pike St., Suite 502, Seattle, WA 98101; phone: 206-624-6033 in Washington State; 800-426-7502 elsewhere in the US). Their deluxe car tours feature overnight stays in hotels that are elegant converted castles or manor houses or old and distinctive country inns. Some itineraries, which range from 6 to 14 days in length, cover Portugal and can be bought in either a self-drive or chauffeured version.

Cavalcade Tours (2200 Fletcher Ave., Ft. Lee, NJ 07024; phone: 800-356-2405 or 201-346-9061). In conjunction with international car rental companies, offers a variety of European fly/drive programs, including Portugal. (As this tour operator is a wholesaler, bookings must be made through a travel agent.)

Extra Value Travel (683 S. Collier Blvd., Marco Island, FL 33937; phone: 800-255-2847). In conjunction with international car rental companies, offers week-long fly/drive bookings throughout Portugal.

Ibero Travel (109-21 72nd Rd., Forest Hills, New York, NY 11375; phone: 800-654-2376 in New York State; 800-882-6678 elsewhere in the US). Offers packages featuring accommodations in *pousadas,* primarily in metropolitan locations.

Marsans International Travel (90 W. 34th St., Suite 302, New York, NY 10001; phone: 212-239-3880 in New York State; 800-777-9110 elsewhere in the US). Offers 3- to 7-day car rental packages that can be booked along with airfare and accommodations for a custom fly/drive vacation.

Plus Ultra Tours (174 7th Ave., New York, NY 10011; phone: 800-242-0394 or 212-242-0393). Offers economical 9- to 14-day fly/drive packages to Portugal.

Stay-Put City and Resort Packages – A further possibility for independent travelers is a "stay-put" package, such as the popular Portugal city packages. These appeal to travelers who want to be on their own and remain in one place for the duration of their vacation, although it is not unusual for travelers to buy more than one package at a time. Basically, a city package — no matter what the city — includes round-trip transfers between airport and hotel, a choice of hotel accommodations (usually including breakfast) in several price ranges, plus any of a number of other features you may not need or want but would lose valuable time arranging if you did. Common package features are 1 or 2 half-day guided tours of the city; a boat cruise; passes for unlimited local travel by bus or train; discount cards for shops, museums, and restaurants; temporary membership in and admission to clubs, discotheques, or other nightspots; and car rental for some or all of your stay. Other features may include anything from a souvenir travel bag to a tasting of local wines, or dinner and a show.

These packages usually are a week long — although 4-day and 14-day packages also are available, and most packages can be extended by extra days — and often are hosted; that is, a representative of the tour company may be available at a local office or even in the hotel to answer questions, handle problems, and assist in arranging activities and optional excursions. A similar stay-put resort package generally omits the sightseeing tour and may offer some sort of daily meal plan if accommodations are in hotels; accommodations in apartment hotels with kitchenettes are another common alternative.

Among the stay-put packages offered in Portugal are the following:

Abreu Tours (317 E. 34th St., New York, NY 10016; phone: 212-661-0555 in New York State; 800-223-1580 elsewhere in the US). Offers 3- to 6-night packages in Lisbon and Porto.

American Express Travel Related Services (offices throughout the US; phone: 800-241-1700 for information and local branch offices). Offers 3- to 6-night city packages in Lisbon.

Marsans International (19 W. 34th St., Suite 302, New York, NY 10001; phone: 212-239-3880 in New York State; 800-223-6114 elsewhere in the US). Offers 3- to 6-night packages in Estoril and Lisbon.

Mill-Run Tours (20 E. 49th St., New York, NY 10017; phone: 212-486-9840 in New York State, 800-MILL-RUN elsewhere). Offers 3-night packages in Lisbon and Porto.

Spanish Heritage Tours (116-47 Queens Blvd., Forest Hills, NY 11375; phone: 718-520-1300 or 800-221-2580). Offers two 6-night packages, one in Estoril, the other in Lisbon.

TWA Getaway Tours (phone: 800-GETAWAY). Offers numerous city packages throughout Europe, including Lisbon

The Algarve, Portugal's southern coast, is the most common destination for resort packages in Portugal; the islands of the Azores and Madeira also are offered by many tour packagers. Besides the tour operators mentioned above, so many others offer packages to one or more of these resorts (often in combination with cities or other resorts) that it's best to consult a travel agent. *TAP Air* collaborates with *Abreu Tours* (317 E. 34th St., New York, NY 10016; phone 800-223-1580 or 212-661-0555), *Cavalcade Tours* (2200 Fletcher Ave., Ft. Lee, NJ 07024; phone: 800-356-2405 or 201-346-9061), and several other tour packagers to offer a large selection of combined air/land packages. (They don't publish a tour catalogue, however.) For information, contact *Abreu Tours, Cavalcade Tours,* or your travel agent.

Another good example of a stay-put vacation is the resort package offered by *Club Med* (40 W. 57th St., New York, NY 10019; phone: 800-CLUB-MED), which operates its own resort villages around the world and has one resort in Portugal, in Da Balaia near Albufeira in the Algarve.

Special-Interest Packages – Special-interest tours are a growing sector of the travel industry. Programs focusing on food and wine are prominent among the packages of this sort. Note, though, that they tend to be quite structured arrangements rather than independent ones, and they rarely are created with the budget traveler in mind. Also note that inclusive as they may be, few food and wine tours include *all* meals in the package price. This is not necessarily a cost-cutting technique on the part of the packager; rather, because of the lavishness of some of the meals, others may be left to the discretion of the participants, not only to allow time for leisure, but also to allow for differing rates of metabolism. Similarly, even on wine tours that spend entire days in practically full-time tasting, unlimited table wine at meals may not always be included in the package price. The brochures usually are clear about what comes with the package and when.

Among the various food and wine tours are *Bacchants' Pilgrimages*' tours of vineyards and wine cellars. Included are winery-hosted luncheons, picnics, dinners in three-star restaurants, and other luncheons and dinners in restaurants of lesser renown. This year's itineraries will include a tour to Portugal, in combination with Spain. Bookings are through travel agents or *Bacchants' Pilgrimages* (475 Sansome St., Suite 840, San Francisco, CA 94111; phone: 415-981-8518). For groups of ten or more travelers, *Travel Concepts* (62 Commonwealth Ave., Suite 3, Boston, MA 02116; phone: 617-266-8450) offers a variety of custom-designed food and wine tours throughout Europe. Although there is no pre-planned itinerary in Portugal, they can design one for individuals or groups. And finally, *X.O. Travel Consultants* (38 W. 32nd St., Suite 1009, New York, NY 10001; phone: 800-262-9682 or 212-947-5530) offers a Ports and Sherries of Iberia tour, as well as other customized tours focusing on Portugal's food, wine, and gardens.

There also are special-interest packages catering to travelers particularly interested in the arts and/or cultural studies. Among these are the packages for music and opera lovers offered by *Dailey-Thorp* (330 W. 58th St., New York, NY 10019; phone: 212-307-1555), which focus on European musical events and sometimes visit Portuguese cities such as Lisbon. *Prospect Art Tours* (454-458 Chiswick High Rd., London W45TT; phone: 44-81-995-2151 or 44-81-995-2163) offers 5- to 15-day packages visiting key museums, private galleries, and art collections throughout Europe, including Portugal.

Golf courses in many European countries are a fairly new addition; however, the courses in Portugal have been around for quite some time. Among the companies offering golf tours to Portugal are the following:

Adventure Golf Holiday (815 North Rd., Westfield, MA 01085; phone: 800-628-9655 or 413-568-2855). Offers packages to Portugal's Algarve.

Adventures in Golf (29 Valencia Dr., Nashua, NH 03062; phone: 603-882-8367). Offers a 14-day combined Spain and Portugal tour that includes a rental car. The company also can custom-design golf holidays for individuals and groups.

Golf Intercontinental/Marsans (19 W. 34 St., New York, NY 10001; phone: 212-239-3880 in New York State; 800-223-6114 elsewhere in the US). Offers customized self-drive tours through Portugal — for serious golfers only.

Golfing Holidays (231 E. Millbrae Ave., Millbrae, CA 94030; phone: 415-697-0230). Arranges customized golf tours to the Algarve and the vicinity of Lisbon.

InterGolf (745 Atlantic Ave., Suite 730, Boston, MA 02111; phone: 617-426-6383). Offers self-drive golf tours throughout Portugal.

ITC Golf Tours (4134 Atlantic Ave., Suite 205, Long Beach, CA 90807; phone: 800-257-4981 or 310-595-6905). Arranges custom golf packages anywhere and any way you want it — including in Portugal.

Perry Golf (8302 Dunwoody Pl., Suite 305, Atlanta, GA 30350; phone: 800-344-5257 or 404-641-9696). Has fly/drive golf packages to Portugal's Algarve, as well as a 12-day package visiting greens in both Spain and Portugal.

Value Holidays (10224 N. Port Washington Rd., Mequon, WI 53092; phone: 800-558-6850). Offers golf packages to Portugal's Algarve.

Wide World of Golf (PO Box 5217, Lincoln St. at Fifth St., Carmel, CA 93921; phone: 408-624-6667). Offers a 10-day golf package to Portugal, including courses in the vicinity of Lisbon and the Algarve, as well as a 2-week combined Spain and Portugal golf tour. Also arranges customized packages.

Horseback riding holidays are the province of *FITS Equestrian* (2011 Alamo Pintado Rd., Solvang, CA 93463; phone: 800-666-FITS or 805-688-9494), which offers two 8-day riding packages departing from Lisbon: The Silver Coast Ride follows the coastline north of Lisbon and the Lusitano Ride heads inland. *Equitour* (PO Box 807, Dubois, WY 82513; phone: 307-455-3363 in Wyoming; 800-545-0019 elsewhere in the US) also offers packages — not for beginners — that include 8 days discovering Portugal on the back of the country's Lusitano breed. On both company's tours, accommodations may be in small hotels or inns, or on ranches.

Fisherfolk might enjoy the opportunity to fish for tuna in the Portuguese Azores that's offered by *Fishing International* (Hilltop Estate, 4010 Montecito Ave., Santa Rosa, CA 95404; phone: 800-950-4242 or 707-542-4242). These week-long packages include accommodations in a small country inn and breakfast daily, and the opportunity to exchange fish stories about the one that got away. This company also designs custom fishing packages.

Special-interest tours for practitioners and spectators of other sports include many hiking and biking tours of varying levels of difficulty. For the names and addresses of their organizers, see *Camping and Caravanning, Hiking and Biking,* below.

Camping and Caravanning, Hiking and Biking

CAMPING AND CARAVANNING: Portugal welcomes campers, whether they come alone or with a group, with tents or in recreational vehicles — generally known in Europe as "caravans" (a term that technically refers to towable campers as opposed to fully motorized vehicles, known as "minibuses" or "minivans"). Camping probably is the best way to enjoy the Portuguese countryside. And, fortunately, campgrounds in Portugal are plentiful.

Where to Camp – Caravanning is extremely popular with European vacationers, and many parks cater more to the caravanner than to the tent dweller. Some campgrounds have minimal facilities, and others are quite elaborate, with a variety of amenities on the premises. Most sites are open from about *Easter* through October.

Although there may be an occasional language barrier, directors of campgrounds often have a great deal of information about their region, and some even will arrange local tours or recommend sports facilities or attractions in the immediate area. Campgrounds also provide the atmosphere and opportunity to meet other travelers and exchange useful information. Too much so, sometimes — the popularity of European campgrounds causes them to be quite crowded during the summer, and campsites can be so close together that any attempt at privacy or getting away from it all is sabotaged. As campgrounds fill quickly throughout the season, and the more isolated sites always go first, it's a good idea to arrive early in the day and reserve your chosen spot — which leaves you free to explore the area for the rest of the day. (Whenever possible, try to call ahead and arrange a "pitch" in advance. At the height of the season, if you do not have advance reservations, you may be lucky to get even a less desirable site.)

In some communities, it is possible to camp free on public grounds. Ask the local police or local tourism information office about regulations. To camp on private property you first must obtain the permission of the landowner or tenant — and assume the responsibility of leaving the land exactly as you found it in return for the hospitality.

Portuguese campgrounds generally are well marked. Still, it's best to have a map or check the information available in one of the numerous comprehensive guides to sites across the Continent. It may not be easy to find camping facilities open before June or after September, so a guide that gives this information comes in particularly handy off-season. When in difficulty, remember that tourist offices throughout Portugal can direct visitors to sites in the areas they serve.

In the US, maps, brochures, and other information for campers are distributed by the Portuguese National Tourist Office, including a useful brochure called *Roteiro Campisto* (which is available in English). A variety of useful publications also are available from American and European automobile clubs and other associations.

The *American Automobile Association (AAA)* offers a number of useful resources, including its 600-page *Travel Guide to Europe* and the 64-page *Motoring Europe,* as well as a variety of useful maps; contact the nearest branch of *AAA* or the national office (see *Traveling by Car,* in this section). In addition, the *Automobile Association of Great Britain (AA)* publishes a comprehensive guide, *Camping and Caravanning in Europe* ($14.95), which lists about 4,000 sites throughout Europe, inspected and rated by the *AA,* and provides other information of interest to campers. It is available from AA Publishing (Farnum House, Basingstoke, Hampshire RG21 2EA, England; phone: 44-256-20123). Another useful guide, *The Camper's Companion to Southern Europe,* also includes camping information about Portugal; unfortunately, it's recently gone out of print, so check your local library.

The French international camping organization *Fédération Internationale de Camping et Caravaning* issues a pass, called a *carnet,* that entitles the bearer to a modest discount on camping fees at many campgrounds throughout Europe, including Portugal. It is available in the US from the *National Campers and Hikers Association* (4804 Transit Rd., Bldg. 2, Depew, NY 14043; phone: 716-668-6242) for a fee of $30, which includes membership in the organization as well as camping information.

Most experienced campers prefer to bring their own tried and true equipment, but camping equipment is available for sale or rent in Portugal — particularly in metropolitan areas such as Lisbon. For information on outfitters, consult the above-mentioned guides to camping and caravanning or contact the national tourist offices in the US which may be able to refer you to reliable Portuguese dealers.

Keep in mind that accessible food will lure scavenging wildlife, which may invade tents and vehicles. Also, even if you are assured that the campground where you are staying provides potable water, it is safer to use bottled, purified, or boiled water for drinking. To purify tap water, either use a water purification kit (available at most camping supply stores) or bring the water to a full, *rolling,* boil over a campstove. It also is generally inadvisable to use water from streams, rivers, or lakes — even purified.

Organized Camping Trips – A packaged camping tour abroad is a good way to have your cake and eat it, too. The problems of advance planning and day-to-day organizing are left to someone else, yet you still reap the benefits that shoestring travel affords and can enjoy the insights of experienced guides and the company of other campers. Be aware, however, that these packages usually are geared to the young, with ages 18 to 35 as common limits. Transfer from place to place is by bus or van (as on other sightseeing tours), overnights are in tents or shelters, and meal arrangements vary. Often there is a kitty that covers meals in restaurants or in the camps; sometimes there is a chef, and sometimes the cooking is done by the participants themselves. When considering a packaged camping tour, be sure to find out if equipment is included and what individual participants are required to bring.

Recreational Vehicles – Known in Europe as caravans (or minibuses or minivans), recreational vehicles (RVs) will appeal most to the kind of person who prefers the flexibility of accommodations — there are countless campgrounds throughout Portugal and a number of them provide RV hookups — and enjoys camping with a little extra comfort.

An RV undoubtably saves a traveler a great deal of money on accommodations; in-camp cooking saves money on food as well. However, it is important to remember that renting an RV is a major expense; also, any kind of RV increases gas consumption considerably.

Although the term "recreational vehicle" is applied to all manner of camping vehicles, whether towed or self-propelled, generally the models available for rent in Portugal and nearby countries are either towable campers (caravans) or motorized RVs. The motorized models usually are minivans or minibuses — vans customized in various ways for camping, often including elevated roofs — or larger, coach-type, fully equipped homes on wheels, requiring electrical hookups at night to run the TV set, air conditioning, and kitchen appliances. Although most models are equipped with standard shift, occasionally automatic shift vehicles may be available for an additional charge.

Towed vehicles can be hired overseas, but usually are not offered by US companies. At present, however, the only type of motorized caravan rented in Portugal is a van or minibus with an elevated roof. These are available from international and regional car rental companies in the major cities (see *Traveling by Car,* earlier in this section), although you probably will have to do some calling around to find one. You can rent other types of RVs in other European countries and drive them across the border through Spain and into Portugal (see list below). In this event, inform the rental company of your plans.

If you are planning to caravan all over Europe, make sure that whatever vehicle you choose is equipped to deal with the electrical and gas standards of all the countries on your itinerary. There are differences, for instance, among the kinds of bottled stove gas supplied in various countries. You should have either a sufficient supply of the type the camper requires or equipment that can use more than one type. When towing a camper, note that nothing towed is automatically covered by the liability insurance of the primary vehicle, so the driver's Green Card must carry a specific endorsement that covers the towed vehicle. (For further information, see *Traveling by Car,* above.)

Whether driving a camper or towing, it is essential to have some idea of the terrain you'll be encountering en route. In some regions of Portugal, where the terrain can be quite steep, only experienced drivers should drive large campers. In fact, grades sometimes can be too steep for certain vehicles to negotiate, and some roads are off limits to towed caravans. Car tunnels, or "piggyback" services on trains, usually bypass those summits too difficult to climb, but they also impose dimension limitations and often charge high fees. The *AAA* guides noted above provide detailed information on the principal European passes and tunnels, as do tourist offices.

As mentioned above, only customized vans (minibuses or minivans) are available in Portugal; however, rentals of RVs in neighboring France (or other nearby countries for those planning to do more extensive touring in addition to visiting Portugal) are available. Among companies offering minivan and/or RV rentals for Portuguese camping are the following:

Auto Europe (PO Box 1907, Camden, ME 04843; phone: 207-236-8235 in Maine; 800-223-5555 elsewhere in the US). Offers minibus rentals in Coimbra, Faro, Lisbon, and Porto.

Avis Rent-A-Car (4500 S. 129 East Ave., Suite 100, Tulsa, OK 74134; phone: 800-331-1084). Offers minibus rentals at most of its locations in Portugal; larger

RVs can be rented at locations in France, the Netherlands, and Switzerland and driven through Spain and into Portugal. Arrangements must be made through the US office.

Connex International (23 N. Division St., Peekskill, NY 10566; phone: 800-333-3949 or 914-739-0066). Rents minibuses in Portugal and motorized RVs in Germany, Great Britain, and the Netherlands.

Europe by Car (One Rockefeller Plaza, New York, NY 10020; phone: 212-581-3040 in New York State; or 9000 Sunset Blvd., Los Angeles, CA 90069; phone: 800-252-9401 or 213-272-0424 in California; elsewhere in the US, call 800-223-1516). Rents minibuses in Portugal, as well as Austria, Belgium, Denmark, France, Germany, Greece, Hungary, Ireland, Italy, Luxembourg, and Switzerland, and RVs in Germany.

The general policy with the above agencies is to make reservations far enough in advance to receive a voucher required to pick up the vehicle at the designated location in Europe. (Early reservations also are advisable as the supply of RVs is limited and the demand great.)

Among the French companies offering RV rentals in France — which by special arrangement may be driven over the border through Spain and into Portugal (but usually must be returned in France) — are the following:

FCI Location (Zone Industrielle de St-Brendan, Quentin 22800, France; phone: 33-96-74-08-36). Rents motorized RVs in France.

Trois Soleils (Maison Trois Soleils, 2 Rte. de Paris, Ittenheim 67117, France; phone: 33-88-69-17-17). Rents motorized RVs, as well as some basic campers throughout France; a number of pick-up and drop-off locations are offered.

As in the US, numerous smaller, local companies that rent both motorized and towable campers are to be found throughout Europe. For minivan and minibus rentals in Portugal, ask at local car rental companies and tourism offices.

Useful information on RVs is available from the following sources:

Living on Wheels, by Richard A. Wolters. Provides useful information on how to choose and operate a recreational vehicle. As it's currently out of print, check your library.

Recreational Vehicle Industry Association (*RVIA;* PO Box 2999, Reston, VA 22090-0999). Issues a useful complimentary package of information on RVs, as well as a 24-page magazine-size guide, *Set Free in an RV* ($3), and a free catalogue of RV sources and consumer information. Write to the association for these and other publications.

Recreational Vehicle Rental Association (*RVRA;* 3251 Old Lee Hwy., Suite 500, Fairfax, VA 22030; phone: 800-336-0355 or 703-591-7130). This RV dealers' group publishes an annual rental directory, *Who's Who in RV Rentals* ($7.50).

TL Enterprises (29901 Agoura Rd., Agoura, CA 91301; phone: 818-991-4980) publishes two monthly magazines for RV enthusiasts: *Motorhome* ($17.98 for a year's subscription) and *Trailer Life* ($14.98 for a year's subscription). Members of the *TL Enterprises' Good Sam Club* can subscribe to these magazines at discounted rates ($12 and $11, respectively), and also receive discounts on a variety of RV services. Membership costs $19 per year.

Trailblazer (1000 124th Ave. NE, Bellevue, WA 98005; phone: 206-455-8585). A recreational-vehicle and motorhome magazine. A year's subscription costs $24.

Although most RV travelers head off independently, traveling in a "caravan" where several RVs travel together offers the best of both worlds for an RV trip: Since caravan members are provided with detailed itineraries and directions, they can, if they wish, travel independently — or with one or two other RVs — to and from pre-arranged destinations, yet when the full caravan convenes, they can enjoy the fellowship of the group and participate in planned activities. Caravans usually include from 20 to 40 vehicles, which are lead by a "wagonmaster," who functions as tour escort, keeping things running smoothly and on schedule. His assistant, the "tailgunner," brings up the rear and handles any mechanical problems. The caravan tour operator takes care of trip planning and routing, insurance, campground reservations and fees, and so forth. Besides the planned sightseeing, social activities can include group dinners, shows and other entertainment, cookouts at campsites, and more, but again, caravan members always have the option of spending as much time by themselves as they wish. One operator of such RV caravan trips is *Creative World Rallies and Caravans* (606 N. Carrollton Ave., New Orleans, LA 70119; phone: 800-732-8337 or 504-486-7259), which arranges trips throughout Europe. At press time, the company had no current offerings to Portugal; however, future trips were under consideration, so call when planning your visit.

HIKING: If you would rather eliminate all the gear and planning and take to the outdoors unencumbered, park the car and go for a day's hike. By all means, cover as much area as you can by foot; you'll see everything in far more detail than you would from the window of any conveyance. For information on suggested hikes throughout Portugal, see *Great Walks and Mountain Rambles* in DIVERSIONS.

Trails abound in Portugal. Preliminary information on where to hike is available from the Portuguese tourist office in the US, and local tourist authorities often distribute information sheets on popular trails in their respective regions upon request. (Even those tourist offices that do not have literature on hand — or have little in English — may be able to direct you to associations in their areas that supply maps, guides, and further information.) There are other sources for those intent on getting about on their own steam; however, as material on hiking in these countries may be difficult to find in the US, you may want to contact international hiking organizations for information. One useful walking guide for those exploring Portugal afoot is *Landscapes of Madeira* (Hunter; $9.95) by John and Pat Underwood; it's recently gone out of print, however, so check your local library.

For those who are hiking on their own, without benefit of a guide or group, a map of the trail is a must. Particularly helpful for those heading out afoot are the Topographical Series maps, which, for Portugal, are on a detailed scale of 1:200,000. There are 174 of these maps and they are available for $10 each, plus postage and handling, from *Map Link* (25 E. Mason St., Santa Barbara, CA 93101; phone: 805-965-4402).

BIKING: For young and/or fit travelers, the bicycle offers a marvelous tool for exploring Portugal. Throughout the country there is an abundance of secondary roads that thread through picturesque stretches of countryside. Biking does have its drawbacks: Little baggage can be carried, travel is slow, and cyclists are exposed to the elements. However, should a cyclist need rest or refuge from the weather, there always is a welcoming tavern or comfortable inn around the next bend.

Besides being a viable way to tour Portugal — and to burn calories to make room for larger portions of regional food — biking is a great way to meet people. Remember, however, that although many residents of Portugal do speak some English, this is less likely to be true in rural areas, so pack a good copy of a Portuguese-English phrase book if your command of Portuguese is not up to par. (For a list of helpful terms and basic expressions, see *Useful Words and Phrases,* in this section.)

A good book to help you plan a trip is *Bicycle Touring in Europe,* by Karen and Gary Hawkins (Random House; $11.95); it offers information on buying and equipping a touring bike, useful clothing and supplies, and helpful techniques for the long-distance biker. Another good general book is *Europe by Bike,* by Karen and Terry Whitehall (Mountaineers Books; $10.95). The *International Youth Hostel Handbook, Volume One: Europe and the Mediterranean* ($10.95) is a guide to all the hostels of Europe to which *AYH* members have access; a map of their locations is included. (For information on joining *American Youth Hostels,* see *Hints for Single Travelers,* in this section.)

Detailed maps will infinitely improve a biking tour and are available from a number of sources. Comprehensive Michelin maps covering Portugal (on a scale of 1:200,000), as well as much of the rest of Europe, are available from Michelin Guides and Maps, PO Box 3305, Spartanburg, SC 29304-3305 (phone: 803-599-0850 in South Carolina; 800-423-0485 elsewhere in the US).

One of the best sources for detailed topographical maps and just about any other type of map (of just about anywhere in the world) is *Map Link* (25 E. Mason St., Santa Barbara, CA 93101; phone: 805-965-4402). Their comprehensive guide *The World Map Directory* ($29.95) includes a wealth of sources for travelers afoot, and if they don't stock a map of the area in which you are interested (or the type of map best suited to your outdoor exploration), they will order it for you. But it is likely that they'll have something to suit your needs — they stock numerous maps of Portugal.

An additional source of maps and other information useful to cyclists are the local tourist authorities (see *Tourist Information Offices,* in this section, for addresses), which can often offer recommendations on popular scenic and historical routes.

Choosing, Renting, and Buying a Bike – Although many bicycling enthusiasts choose to take along their own bikes, bicycles can be rented throughout Europe. Long and short rentals are available; however, in Portugal, particularly in rural areas, it is recommended that you check ahead. Almost all European trains have facilities for bike transport at nominal fees.

As an alternative to renting, you might consider buying a bicycle in Europe. Bicycle shops that rent bikes often also sell them and buying a used bike might be even less expensive than a long-term rental. If you do buy a bike and plan on taking it home, remember that it will be subject to an import duty by US Customs if its price (or the total of all purchases made abroad) exceeds $400. (A European bicycle purchased in the US should have proof-of-purchase papers to avoid potential customs problems.) Bicycle shops exist in most metropolitan areas, so you should be able to replace or add to gear; however, because tires and tubes are sized to metric dimensions in Portugal, when riding your own bike, bring extras from home.

Airlines going from the US (or elsewhere) to Europe generally allow bicycles to be checked as baggage; they require that the pedals be removed, handlebars be turned sideways, and the bike be in a shipping carton (which some airlines provide, subject to availability — call ahead to make sure). If buying a shipping carton from a bicycle shop, check the airline's specifications and also ask about storing the carton at the destination airport so that you can use it again for the return flight. Although some airlines charge only a nominal fee, if the traveler already has checked two pieces of baggage, there may be an excess baggage charge of $40 to $80 for the bicycle. As regulations vary from carrier to carrier, be sure to call well before departure to find out your airline's specific regulations. As with other baggage, make sure that the bike is thoroughly labeled with your name, a business address and phone number, and the correct airport destination code.

Biking Tours – A number of organizations offer bike tours in Portugal. Linking up with a bike tour is more expensive than traveling alone, but with experienced leaders, an organized tour often becomes an educational, as well as a very social, experience.

One of the attractions of a bike tour is that shipment of equipment — the bike — is handled by the organizers, and the shipping fee is included in the total tour package. Travelers simply deliver the bike to the airport, already disassembled and boxed; shipping cartons can be obtained from most bicycle shops with little difficulty. Bicyclists not with a tour must make their own arrangements with the airline, and there are no standard procedures for this (see above). Although some tour organizers will rent bikes, most prefer that participants bring a bike with which they are already familiar. Another attraction of *some* tours is the existence of a "sag wagon" to carry extra luggage, fatigued cyclists, and their bikes, too, when pedaling another mile is impossible.

Most bike tours are scheduled from May to October, last 1 or 2 weeks, are limited to 20 or 25 people, and provide lodging in inns or hotels, though some use hostels or even tents. Tours vary considerably in style and ambience, so request brochures from several operators in order to make the best decision. When contacting groups, be sure to ask about the maximum number of people on the trip, the maximum number of miles to be traveled each day, and the degree of difficulty of the biking; these details should determine which tour you join and can greatly affect your enjoyment of the experience. Planning ahead is essential because trips often fill up 6 months or more in advance.

SAMPLE PACKAGE TOURS: A number of companies offer tours that feature camping, hiking, and biking, as well as other outdoor activities. While many of them specialize in outdoor adventure packages, others include these activities as part of broader tour programs. Among such companies are the following:

Alternative Travel Groups ((69-71 Banbury Rd., Oxford OX2 6PE, England; phone: 800-527-5997). The motto of this company is "The best way to see a country is on foot." Among their numerous itineraries worldwide are walking tours in Portugal.

Blue Marble Travel (c/o *Odyssey Adventures,* 89 Auburn St., Suite 1199, Portland, ME 04103; phone: 800-544-3216 or 207-878-8650). This company, specializing in trips for those between the ages of 20 and 45, offers a 30-day Trans-Iberian Biking tour that departs from Biarritz in France and travels through northern Portugal along the Minho River, and to Coimbra and Porto, as well as to several cities in Spain.

Cycle Through the Centuries (PO Box 877, San Antonio, FL 33576; phone: 800-245-4226 or 904-588-4132). Most of this company's itineraries focus on Spain and Portugal. Among its offerings are 8- to 10-day biking trips along the coast from Lisbon to Faro (in the Algarve), and in the vineyards of the Minho wine country, as well as a 15-day trip from Porto to Madrid.

Easy Rider Tours (PO Box 1384, E. Arlington, MA 02174; phone: 800-488-8332 or 617-643-8332). Offers a 1-week tour on São Miguel Island in the Azores and 1 to 2-week bicycling programs in the Alentejo and Minho regions.

Eurobike (PO Box 40, DeKalb, IL 60115; phone: 815-758 8851). Offers a 14-day, hotel-to-hotel biking tour departing from Porto.

An alternative to dealing directly with the above companies is to contact *All Adventure Travel,* a specialist in hiking and biking trips worldwide. This company, which acts as a representative for numerous special tour packagers offering such outdoor adventures, can provide a wealth of detailed information about each packager and programs offered. They also will help you design and arrange all aspects of a personalized itinerary. This company operates much like a travel agency, collecting commissions from the packagers. Therefore, there is no additional charge for these services. For information, contact *All Adventure Travel,* PO Box 4307, Boulder, CO 80306 (phone: 800-537-4025 or 303-939-8885).

■ **Note:** The *Specialty Travel Index* (305 San Anselmo Ave., Suite 313, San Anselmo, CA 94960; phone: 415-459-4900 in California; 800-442-4922 elsewhere in the US) is a directory of special-interest travel and an invaluable resource. Listings include tour operators specializing in camping, as well as myriad other interests that combine nicely with a camping trip, such as biking, motorcycling, horseback riding, ballooning, and boating. It costs $6 per copy, $10 for a year's subscription of two issues.

ADDITIONAL RESOURCES: Other useful sources of information on camping, hiking, and biking in Portugal include the following organizations, most of which also sponsor tours of their own:

American Youth Hostels (PO Box 37613, Washington, DC 20013-7613; phone: 202-783-6161). This nonprofit organization and its local chapters regularly sponsor a number of foreign hiking and biking tours. Membership is open to all ages, but departures are geared to various age groups and levels of skill; tours frequently feature accommodations in hostels — along with hotels for adults and campgrounds for younger participants. Although, at press time, no trips to Portugal were being offered, call when planning your trip for current information.

Cyclists' Touring Club (*CTC;* Cotterell House, 69 Meadrow, Godalming, Surrey GU7 3HS, England; phone: 44-0483-41-7217). Britain's largest cycling association, this group organizes tours of numerous countries, including Portugal. *CTC* has a number of planned routes available in pamphlet form for bikers on their own and helps members plan their own tours. The club also publishes a yearly handbook, as well as magazines.

International Bicycle Touring Society (*IBTS;* PO Box 6979, San Diego, CA 92106-0979; phone: 619-226-TOUR). Regularly sponsors low-cost bicycle tours led by member volunteers. Participants must be over 21. For information, send $2 plus a self-addressed, stamped envelope.

League of American Wheelmen (190 W. Ostend St., Suite 1208, Baltimore, MD 21230; phone: 301-539-3399 or 301-944-3399). This organization publishes *Tourfinder,* a list of groups that sponsor bicycle tours worldwide. The list is free with membership ($25 individual, $30 family) and can be obtained by nonmembers for $5. The *League* also can put you in touch with biking groups in your area.

Sierra Club (Outing Dept., 730 Polk St., San Francisco, CA 94109; phone: 415-776-2211). Dedicated to preserving and protecting the natural environment, this nonprofit organization also offers numerous trips each year, including both walking tours and trips that combine hiking and biking. Some are backpacking trips, moving to a new camp each day; others make day hikes from a base camp. This year, a 2-week walking and sightseeing tour of Portugal, including Evora and Porto, is being offered.

Preparing

Calculating Costs

A realistic appraisal of travel expenses is the most crucial bit of planning you will undertake before any trip. It also is, unfortunately, one for which it is most difficult to give precise, practical advice.

After several years of living relatively high on the hog, travel from North America to Europe dropped off precipitously in 1987, in response, among other considerations, to the relative weakness of the US dollar on the Continent. Many Americans, who had enjoyed bargain prices while touring through Europe only a couple of years before, found that disadvantageous exchange rates really put a crimp in their travel planning. But even though the halcyon days of dollar domination seem over for the present, discount fares and the availability of charter flights can greatly reduce the cost of a European vacation. Package tours can even further reduce costs, as European providers of travel services try to win back their American clients in the 1990s.

Although most travelers have to plan carefully before they go and manage their travel funds prudently, in general, a holiday in Portugal still is a good value. Even though the major cities — like our own — suffer from a relatively high cost of living, travel in the countryside still can be very reasonable (and sometimes even inexpensive) as compared to other destinations in Europe. Portugal always has been popular with both the first-time and the seasoned traveler, and the competition for American visitors often works to inspire surprisingly affordable travel opportunities.

In Portugal, estimating travel expenses depends on the mode of transportation you choose, the part or parts of the country you plan to visit, how long you will stay, and in some cases, what time of year you plan to travel. In addition to the basics of transportation, hotels, meals, and sightseeing, you have to take into account seasonal price changes that apply on certain air routings and at popular vacation destinations, as well as the vagaries of currency exchange.

In general, it's usually also a good idea to organize your trip so that you pay for as much of it as you can in Portugal, using escudos purchased from Portuguese banks (which, barring interim variations, generally offer a more advantageous rate of exchange than US sources). That means minimizing the amount of advance deposits paid in US greenbacks and deferring as many bills as possible until you arrive in Europe, although the economies possible through prepaid package tours and other special deals may offset the savings in currency exchange. (For further information on managing money abroad, see *Credit and Currency,* in this section.)

DETERMINING A BUDGET: When calculating costs, start with the basics, the major expenses being transportation, accommodations, and food. However, don't forget such extras as local transportation, shopping, and such miscellaneous items as laundry and tips. The reasonable cost of these items usually is a positive surprise to your budget. Ask about special discount passes that provide unlimited travel by the day or the week on regular city transportation. Entries in the individual city reports in THE CITIES give helpful information on local transportation options.

Other expenses, such as the cost of local sightseeing tours and excursions, will vary from city to city. Tourist information offices are plentiful throughout Portugal, and most of the better hotels will have someone at the front desk to provide a rundown on the costs of local tours and full-day excursions in and out of the city. Travel agents or railway booking offices (see *Traveling by Train,* in this section) can provide information on rail tours.

Budget-minded families can take advantage of some of the more economical accommodations options to be found in Portugal (see our discussion of accommodations in *On the Road,* in this section). Campgrounds are particularly inexpensive and they are located throughout the country (see *Camping and Caravanning, Hiking and Biking*). Picnicking is another excellent way to cut costs, and Portugal abounds with well-groomed parks and idyllic pastoral settings, particularly along the coast. A stop at a local market can provide a feast of regional specialties at a surprisingly economical price compared to the cost of a restaurant lunch. (Do, however, read our warnings about seafood in *Staying Healthy,* in this section.)

In planning any travel budget, it also is wise to allow a realistic amount for both entertainment and recreation. Are you planning to spend time sightseeing and visiting local museums? Do you intend to spend your days sailing or horseback riding? Is daily golf or tennis a part of your plan? Will your children be disappointed if they don't take a guided tour of Roman ruins? Finally, don't forget that if haunting clubs, discotheques, or other nightspots is an essential part of your vacation, or you feel that one performance at the *Teatro Nacional de São Carlos* in Lisbon may not be enough, allow for the extra cost of nightlife.

If at any point in the planning process it appears impossible to estimate expenses, consider this suggestion: The easiest way to put a ceiling on the price of all these elements is to buy a package tour. A totally planned and escorted one, with almost all transportation, rooms, meals, sightseeing, local travel, tips, and a dinner show or two included and prepaid, provides a pretty exact total of what the trip will cost beforehand, and the only surprise will be the one you spring on yourself by succumbing to some irresistible, expensive souvenir. And keep in mind, particularly when calculating the major expenses, that costs vary according to fluctuations in the exchange rate — that is, how much of a given foreign currency a dollar will buy.

Also note that a sales tax or VAT (value added tax, known as IVA in Portugal) is added to both goods and services in many European countries. In Portugal, the rate ranges from a low of 17% on food to a high of 30% for luxury items. The VAT is buried in the prices of hotel rooms and restaurant meals, so you won't even notice it. It also is included in the amount shown on the price tag of retail goods. There is no escaping the tax on services, but for foreigners the tax on purchases frequently can be reimbursed. Another alternative is to have the goods sent directly to your home address — if the store is willing to do so. For a full discussion of VAT refunds, see *Duty-Free Shopping and Value Added Tax,* in this section.

■ **Note:** The volatility of exchange rates means that between the time you originally make your hotel reservations and the day you arrive, the price in US dollars may vary substantially from the price originally quoted. To avoid paying more than you expected, it's wise to confirm rates by writing directly to hotels or by calling their representatives in the US.

Planning a Trip

123 Travelers fall into two categories: those who make lists and those who do not. Some people prefer to plot the course of their trip to the finest detail, with contingency plans and alternatives at the ready. For others, the joy of a voyage is its spontaneity; exhaustive planning only lessens the thrill of anticipation and the sense of freedom.

For most travelers, however, any week-plus trip to Portugal can be too expensive for an "I'll take my chances" type of attitude. Even perennial gypsies and anarchistic wanderers have to take into account the time-consuming logistics of getting around, and even with minimal baggage, they need to think about packing. Hence, at least some planning is crucial.

This is not to suggest that you work out your itinerary in minute detail before you go; but it's still wise to decide certain basics at the very start: where to go, what to do, and how much to spend. These decisions require a certain amount of consideration. So before rigorously planning specific details, you might want to establish your general travel objectives:

1. How much time will you have for the entire trip, and how much of it are you willing to spend getting where you're going?
2. What interests and/or activities do you want to pursue while on vacation? Do you want to visit one, a few, or several different places?
3. At what time of year do you want to go?
4. What kind of topography or climate would you prefer?
5. Do you want peace and privacy or lots of activity and company?
6. How much money can you afford to spend for the entire vacation?

You now can make almost all of your own travel arrangements if you have time to follow through with hotels, airlines, tour operators, and so on. But you'll probably save considerable time and energy if you have a travel agent make arrangements for you. The agent also should be able to advise you of alternate arrangements of which you may not be aware. Only rarely will a travel agent's services cost a traveler any money, and they may even save you some (see *How to Use a Travel Agent,* below).

If it applies to your schedule and destination, pay particular attention to the dates when off-season rates go into effect. In major tourism areas, accommodations may cost less during the off-season (and the weather often is perfectly acceptable at this time). Off-season rates frequently are lower for car rentals and other facilities, too. In general, it is a good idea to be aware of holiday weeks, as rates at hotels generally are higher during these periods and rooms normally are heavily booked.

Make plans early. During the summer season and other holiday periods, make hotel reservations at least a month in advance in all major cities. If you are flying at peak times and want to benefit from savings of discount fares or charter programs, purchase tickets as far ahead as possible. (Charter flights to Lisbon and other popular destinations may be completely sold out months in advance.) The less flexible your schedule requirements, the earlier you should book. Many Portuguese hotels require deposits before they will guarantee reservations, and this most often is the case during peak travel periods. (Be sure you have a receipt for any deposit or use a credit card.) Religious and national holidays also are times requiring reservations well in advance in Portugal.

Before your departure, find out what the weather is likely to be at your destination. Consult *When to Go,* in this section, for information on climatic variations and a chart of average temperatures. See *How to Pack,* also in this section, for some suggestions on how to decide what clothes to take. Also see *When to Go,* as well as the individual city reports in THE CITIES for information on special events that may occur during your stay. The city chapters also provide essential information on local transportation and other services and resources.

Make a list of any valuable items you are carrying with you, including credit card numbers and the serial numbers of your traveler's checks. Put copies in your purse or pocket and leave other copies at home. Put a label with your name and home address on the inside of your luggage for identification in case of loss. Put your name and business address — *never your home address* — on a label on the outside of your luggage. (Those who run businesses from home should use the office address of a friend or relative.)

Review your travel documents. If you are traveling by air, check that your ticket has been filled in correctly. The left side of the ticket should have a list of each stop you will make (even if you are only stopping to change planes), beginning with your departure point. Be sure that the list is correct, and count the number of copies to see that you have one for each plane you will take. If you have confirmed reservations, be sure that the column marked "status" says "OK" beside each flight. Have in hand vouchers or proof of payment for any reservation for which you've paid in advance; this includes hotels, transfers to and from the airport, sightseeing tours, car rentals, and tickets to special events.

Although policies vary from carrier to carrier, it's still smart to reconfirm your flight 48 to 72 hours before departure, both going and returning; reconfirmation is particularly recommended for point-to-point flights within Europe. If you will be driving while in Portugal, bring your driver's license, International Driver's Permit (which is recommended), and any other necessary documentation — such as proof of insurance.

Before traveling to Portugal, you should consider learning some basic Portuguese. Although you can get by in Portugal without speaking Portuguese — particularly if you stick to the major resort areas and other popular tourist destinations — your trip will be much more rewarding and enjoyable (and, in some instances, safer) if you can communicate with the people who live in the areas you will be visiting. (Even a rudimentary knowledge of Spanish may be of some use.) The Portuguese will not make you feel silly or stupid if you don't pronounce words properly — in fact they will openly appreciate your efforts if you do try to converse.

Some adult education programs and community colleges offer courses in Portuguese. *Living Language,* among others, has a series of teach-yourself language courses on audiocassette tapes with accompanying books, which are available for $20 (plus postage and handling) from Random House (400 Hahn Rd., Westminster, MD 21157; phone: 800-726-0600). For information on pronunciation and a list of common travel terms, see *Useful Words and Phrases,* in this section; an introduction to a number of native drinks and dishes that you may encounter can be found in *Food and Drink,* in PERSPECTIVES.

Finally, you always should bear in mind that despite the most careful plans, things do not always occur on schedule. If you maintain a flexible attitude and try to accept minor disruptions as less than cataclysmic, you will enjoy yourself a lot more.

How to Use a Travel Agent

A reliable travel agent remains the best source of service and information for planning a trip abroad, whether you have a specific itinerary and require an agent only to make reservations or you need extensive help in sorting through the maze of airfares, tour offerings, hotel packages, and the scores of other arrangements that may be involved in a trip to Portugal.

Know what you want from a travel agent so that you can evaluate what you are getting. It is perfectly reasonable to expect your agent to be a thoroughly knowledgeable travel specialist, with information about your destination and, even more crucial, a command of current airfares, ground arrangements, and other wrinkles in the travel scene.

Most travel agents work through computer reservations systems (CRS). These are used to assess the availability and cost of flights, hotels, and car rentals, and through them they can book reservations. Despite reports of "computer bias," in which a computer may favor one airline over another, the CRS should provide agents with the entire spectrum of flights available to a given destination, as well as the complete range of fares, in considerably less time than it takes to telephone the airlines individually — and at no extra charge to the client.

Make the most intelligent use of a travel agent's time and expertise; understand the economics of the industry. As a client, traditionally you pay nothing for the agent's services; with few exceptions, it's all free, from hotel bookings to advice on package tours. Any money the travel agent makes on the time spent arranging your itinerary — booking hotels or flights, or suggesting activities — comes from commissions paid by the suppliers of these services — the airlines, hotels, and so on. These commissions generally run from 10% to 15% of the total cost of the service, although suppliers often reward agencies that sell their services in volume with an increased commission, called an override. In most instances, you'll find that travel agents make their time and experience available to you at no cost, and you do not pay more for an airline ticket, package tour, or other product bought from a travel agent than you would for the same product bought directly from the supplier.

Exceptions to the general rule of free service by a travel agent are the agencies beginning to practice net pricing. In essence, such agencies return their commissions and overrides to their customers and make their income by charging a flat fee per transaction instead (thus adding a charge after a reduction for the commissions has been made). Net fares and fees are a growing practice, though hardly widespread.

Even a conventional travel agent sometimes may charge a fee for special services. These chargeable items may include long-distance telephone or cable costs incurred in making a booking, for reserving a room in a place that does not pay a commission (such as a small, out-of-the-way hotel), or for special attention such as planning a highly personalized itinerary. A fee also may be assessed in instances of deeply discounted airfares.

Choose a travel agent with the same care with which you would choose a doctor or lawyer. You will be spending a good deal of money on the basis of the agent's judgment, so you have a right to expect that judgment to be mature, informed, and interested. At the moment, unfortunately, there aren't many standards within the travel agent industry to help you gauge competence, and the quality of individual agents varies enormously.

At present, only nine states have registration, licensing, or other forms of travel agent–related legislation on their books. Rhode Island licenses travel agents; Florida, Hawaii, Iowa, and Ohio register them; and California, Illinois, Oregon, and Washington have laws governing the sale of transportation or related services. While state licensing of agents cannot absolutely guarantee competence, it can at least ensure that an agent has met some minimum requirements.

Perhaps the best-prepared agents are those who have completed the CTC Travel Management program offered by the *Institute of Certified Travel Agents* and carry the initials CTC (Certified Travel Counselor) after their names. This indicates a relatively high level of expertise. For a free list of CTCs in your area, send a self-addressed, stamped, #10 envelope to *ICTA,* 148 Linden St., Box 82-56, Wellesley, MA 02181 (phone: 617-237-0280 in Massachusetts; 800-542-4282 elsewhere in the US).

An agent's membership in the *American Society of Travel Agents (ASTA)* can be a useful guideline in making a selection. But keep in mind that *ASTA* is an industry organization, requiring only that its members be licensed in those states where required; be accredited to represent the suppliers whose products they sell, including airline and cruise tickets; and adhere to its Principles of Professional Conduct and Ethics code. *ASTA* does not guarantee the competence, ethics, or financial soundness of its members, but it does offer some recourse if you feel you have been dealt with unfairly. Complaints may be registered with *ASTA* (Consumer Affairs Dept., 1101 King St.,

Alexandria, VA 22314; phone: 703-739-2782). First try to resolve the complaint directly with the supplier. For a list of *ASTA* members in your area, send a self-addressed, stamped, #10 envelope to *ASTA,* Public Relations Dept., at the address above.

There also is the *Association of Retail Travel Agents (ARTA),* a smaller but highly respected trade organization similar to *ASTA.* Its member agencies and agents similarly agree to abide by a code of ethics, and complaints about a member can be made to *ARTA*'s Grievance Committee, 1745 Jeff Davis Hwy., Arlington, VA 22202-3402 (phone: 800-969-6069 or 703-553-7777).

Perhaps the best way to find a travel agent is by word of mouth. If the agent (or agency) has done a good job for your friends over a period of time, it probably indicates a certain level of commitment and competence. Always ask not only for the name of the company, but for the name of the specific agent with whom your friends dealt, for it is that individual who will serve you, and quality can vary widely within a single agency. There are some superb travel agents in the business, and they can facilitate vacation or business arrangements.

Entry Requirements and Documents

A valid US passport is the only document a US citizen needs to enter Portugal, and that same passport also is needed to reenter the US. As a general rule, a US passport entitles the bearer to remain in Portugal for up to 60 days as a tourist. Resident aliens of the US should inquire at the nearest Portuguese consulate (see *Tourist Information Offices,* in this section, for addresses) to find out what documents they need to enter Portugal; similarly, US citizens intending to work, study, or reside in Portugal should address themselves to the consulate.

Vaccination certificates are required only if the traveler is entering from an area of contagion as defined by the World Health Organization, and as the US is considered an area "free from contagion," an international vaccination certificate no longer is required for entering Portugal for a short period of time. Because smallpox is considered eradicated from the world, only a few countries continue to require visitors to have a smallpox vaccination certificate. You certainly will not need one to travel to Portugal or return to the US.

VISAS: Visas are required, however, for study, residency, or work, and US citizens should address themselves to the the Portuguese embassy or consulate, well in advance of a proposed trip. Visas of this type are available for stays in Portugal of up to 1 year. Note that although visas for study often are issued, it is much more difficult to get a visa permitting you to work in the country. The ready processing of a visa application also may be based on the duration of the visa you are requesting — visas for studying in Portugal for several months are likely to be processed more quickly than residency visas good for 1 year or longer. Proof of substantial means of independent financial support during the stay also is pertinent to the acceptance of any long-term–stay application.

At least two items are necessary to apply for a visa: a valid passport and a completed visa form. (These forms may be obtained by sending a self-addressed, stamped envelope to any Portuguese consulate with a written request.) Depending on the type of visa you are requesting, additional documentation may be required. There is no charge for the issuance of visas. Application can be made through the mail or in person at the Portuguese embassy or a consulate (see *Tourist Information Offices,* in this section, for addresses). If applying in person, it is a good idea to call ahead to check during what hours and days visa requests are accepted.

PASSPORTS: While traveling in Portugal, carry your passport with you at all times (for an exception to this rule, see our note "When Checking In," below). If you lose your passport while abroad, immediately report the loss to the nearest US consulate or embassy (see *Legal Aid and Consular Services,* in this section, for locations in Portugal). You can get a 3-month temporary passport directly from the consulate, but you must fill out a "loss of passport" form and follow the same application procedure — and pay the same fees — as you did for the original (see below). It's likely to speed things up if you have a record of your passport number and the place and date of its issue (a photocopy of the first page of your passport is perfect). Keep this information separate from your passport — you might want to give it to a traveling companion to hold or put it in the bottom of your suitcase.

US passports now are valid for 10 years from the date of issue (5 years for those under age 18). The expired passport itself is not renewable, but must be turned in along with your application for a new and valid one (you will get it back, voided, when you receive the new one). Normal passports contain 24 pages, but frequent travelers can request a 48-page passport at no extra cost. Every individual, regardless of age, must have his or her own passport. Family passports no longer are issued.

Passports can be renewed by mail with forms obtained at designated locations only if the expired passport was issued no more than 12 years before the date of application for renewal and if it was not issued before the applicant's 16th birthday. The rules for renewal regarding teens under 16 and younger applicants vary depending on age and when their previous passport was issued. Those who are eligible to apply by mail must send the completed form with the expired passport, two photos (see description below), and $40 (which includes a $10 execution fee) to the nearest passport agency office. Delivery can take as little as 2 weeks or as long as 6 weeks during the busiest season — from approximately mid-March to mid-September.

Adults applying for the first time and younger applicants who must apply for a passport in person (as well as those who cannot wait for mail application turnaround) can do so at one of the following places:

1. The State Department has passport agencies in Boston, Chicago, Honolulu, Houston, Long Beach (California), Miami, New Orleans, New York City, Philadelphia, San Francisco, Seattle, Stamford, CT, and Washington, DC.
2. A federal or state courthouse.
3. Any of the 1,000 post offices across the country with designated acceptance facilities.

Application blanks are available at all these offices and must be presented with the following:

1. Proof of US citizenship. This can be a previous passport or one in which you were included. If you are applying for your first passport and were born in the United States, an original or certified birth certificate is the required proof. If you were born abroad, a Certificate of Naturalization, a Certificate of Citizenship, a Report of Birth Abroad of a Citizen of the United States, or a Certification of Birth is necessary.
2. Two 2-by-2-inch, front-view photographs in color or black and white, with a light, plain background, taken within the previous 6 months. These must be taken by a photographer rather than a machine.
3. A $65 passport fee ($40 for travelers under 16), which includes a $10 execution fee. *Note:* Your best bet is to bring the exact amount in cash (no change is given), or a separate check or money order for each passport (although a family can combine several passport fees on one check or money order).
4. Proof of identity. Again, this can be a previous passport, a Certificate of Naturalization or of Citizenship, a driver's license, or a government ID card with a physical

description or a photograph. Failing any of these, you should be accompanied by a blood relative or a friend of at least 5 years' standing who will testify to your identity. Credit cards or social security cards do not suffice as proof of identity — but note that since 1988, US citizens *must* supply their social security numbers.

As getting a passport — or international visa — through the mail can mean waiting as much as 6 weeks or more, a new mini-industry has cropped up in those cities where there is a US passport office. The yellow pages currently list quite a few organizations willing to wait on line to expedite obtaining a visa or passport renewal; there's even one alternative for those who live nowhere near the cities mentioned above. In the nation's capital there's an organization called the *Washington Passport and Visa Service.* It may be the answer for folks in need of special rapid action, since this organization can get a passport application or renewal turned around in a single day. What's more, their proximity to an embassy or consulate of every foreign country represented in the US helps to speed the processing of visa applications as well. The fee for a 5- to 7-day turnaround is $30; for next-day service the charge is $50; for same-day service they charge $90. For information, application forms, and other prices, contact *Washington Passport and Visa Service,* 2318 18th St. NW, Washington, DC 20009 (phone: 800-272-7776). Another company in Washington providing a similar service is *Travisa* (2122 P St. NW, Washington, DC 20037; phone: 800-222-2589). They charge $30 for an 8- to 10-day turnaround on passport applications.

If you need an emergency passport, it also is possible to be issued a passport in a matter of hours by going directly to your nearest passport office (there is no way, however, to avoid waiting in line). Explain the nature of the emergency, usually as serious as a death in the family; a ticket in hand for a flight the following day also will suffice. Should the emergency occur outside of business hours, all is not lost. There's a 24-hour telephone number in Washington, DC (phone: 202-647-4000), that can put you in touch with a State Department duty officer who may be able to expedite your application. Note that if a passport is obtained after regular business hours, a nominal charge will be added to the standard passport fee.

- **When Checking In:** It is not at all unusual for a Portuguese hotel to ask you to surrender your passport for 24 hours. While we all get a little nervous when we're parted from our passports, the US State Department's passport division advises that it's a perfectly acceptable procedure. The purpose usually is to check the validity of the passport and ascertain whether the passport holder is a fugitive or has a police record. Many hotels merely will ask that you enter your passport number on your registration card. If a hotel does take your passport, make sure it's returned to you the next day.

DUTY AND CUSTOMS: As a general rule, the requirements for bringing the majority of items into Portugal is that they must be in quantities small enough not to imply commercial import.

Among the items that may be taken into Portugal duty-free are 200 cigarettes or 250 grams of tobacco, 2 bottles of wine, and 1 bottle of liquor. Personal effects and sports equipment appropriate for a pleasure trip also are allowed.

If you are bringing along a computer, camera, or other electronic equipment for your own use that you will be taking back to the US, you should register the item with the US Customs Service in order to avoid paying duty both entering and returning from Portugal. (Also see *Customs and Returning to the US,* in this section.) For information on this procedure, as well as for a variety of informative pamphlets on US customs regulations, contact the local office of the US Customs Service or the central office, PO Box 7474, Washington, DC 20044 (phone: 202-566-8195).

Additional information regarding customs regulations is available from the Portuguese National Tourist Office. See *Tourist Information Offices,* in this section, for addresses of offices in the US.

■ **One rule to follow:** When passing through customs, it is illegal not to declare dutiable items; penalties range from stiff fines and seizure of the goods to prison terms. So don't try to sneak anything through — it just isn't worth it.

Insurance

It is unfortunate that most decisions to buy travel insurance are impulsive and usually are made without any real consideration of the traveler's existing policies. Therefore, the first person with whom you should discuss travel insurance is your own insurance broker, not a travel agent or the clerk behind the airport insurance counter. You may discover that the insurance you already carry — homeowner's policies and/or accident, health, and life insurance — protects you adequately while you travel and that your real needs are in the more mundane areas of excess value insurance for baggage or trip cancellation insurance.

TYPES OF INSURANCE: To make insurance decisions intelligently, however, you first should understand the basic categories of travel insurance and what they cover. Then you can decide what you should have in the broader context of your personal insurance needs, and you can choose the most economical way of getting the desired protection: through riders on existing policies; with onetime short-term policies; through a special program put together for the frequent traveler; through coverage that's part of a travel club's benefits; or with a combination policy sold by insurance companies through brokers, automobile clubs, tour operators, and travel agents.

There are seven basic categories of travel insurance:

1. Baggage and personal effects insurance
2. Personal accident and sickness insurance
3. Trip cancellation and interruption insurance
4. Default and/or bankruptcy insurance
5. Flight insurance (to cover injury or death)
6. Automobile insurance (for driving your own or a rented car)
7. Combination policies

Baggage and Personal Effects Insurance – Ask your insurance agent if baggage and personal effects are included in your current homeowner's policy, or if you will need a special floater to cover you for the duration of a trip. The object is to protect your bags and their contents in case of damage or theft anytime during your travels, not just while you're in flight and covered by the airline's policy. Furthermore, only limited protection is provided by the airline. Baggage liability varies from carrier to carrier, but generally speaking, on domestic flights, luggage usually is insured to $1,250 — that's per passenger, not per bag. For most international flights, including domestic portions of international flights, the airline's liability limit is approximately $9.07 per pound or $20 per kilo (which comes to about $360 per 40-pound suitcase) for checked baggage and up to $400 per passenger for unchecked baggage. These limits should be specified on your airline ticket, but to be awarded any amount, you'll have to provide an itemized list of lost property, and if you're including new and/or expensive items, be prepared for a request that you back up your claim with sales receipts or other proof of purchase.

If you are carrying goods worth more than the maximum protection offered by the airline, bus, or train company, consider excess value insurance. Additional coverage is available from airlines at an average, currently, of $1 to $2 per $100 worth of coverage, up to a maximum of $5,000. This insurance can be purchased at the airline counter when you check in, though you should arrive early enough to fill out the necessary forms and to avoid holding up other passengers.

Major credit card companies also provide coverage for lost or delayed baggage — and this coverage often also is over and above what the airline will pay. The basic coverage usually is automatic for all cardholders who use the credit card to purchase tickets, but to qualify for additional coverage, cardholders generally must enroll.

American Express: Provides $500 coverage for checked baggage; $1,250 for carry-on baggage; and $250 for valuables, such as cameras and jewelry.

Carte Blanche and Diners Club: Provide $1,250 free insurance for checked or carry-on baggage that's lost or damaged.

Discover Card: Offers $500 insurance for checked baggage and $1,250 for carry-on baggage — but to qualify for this coverage cardholders first must purchase additional flight insurance (see "Flight Insurance," below).

MasterCard and Visa: Baggage insurance coverage set by the issuing institution.

Additional baggage and personal effects insurance also is included in certain of the combination travel insurance policies discussed below.

■ **A note of warning:** Be sure to read the fine print of any excess value insurance policy; there often are specific exclusions, such as cash, tickets, furs, gold and silver objects, art, and antiques. And remember that insurance companies ordinarily will pay only the depreciated value of the goods rather than their replacement value. The best way to protect the items you're carrying in your luggage is to take photos of your valuables and keep a record of the serial numbers of such items as cameras, typewriters, laptop computers, radios, and so on. This will establish that you do, indeed, own the objects. If your luggage disappears en route or is damaged, deal with the situation immediately. If an airline loses your luggage, you will be asked to fill out a Property Irregularity Report before you leave the airport. If your property disappears at other transportation centers, tell the local company, but also report it to the police (since the insurance company will check with the police when processing the claim). When traveling by train, if you are sending excess luggage as registered baggage, remember that some trains may not have provisions for extra cargo; if your baggage does not arrive when you do, it may not be lost, just on the next train!

Personal Accident and Sickness Insurance – This covers you in case of illness during your trip or death in an accident. Most policies insure you for hospital and doctor's expenses, lost income, and so on. In most cases, it is a standard part of existing health insurance policies, though you should check with your broker to be sure that your policy will pay for any medical expenses incurred abroad. If not, take out a separate vacation accident policy or an entire vacation insurance policy that includes health and life coverage.

Two examples of such comprehensive health and life insurance coverage are the travel insurance packages offered by *Wallach & Co:*

HealthCare Global: This insurance package, which can be purchased for periods of 10 to 180 days, is offered for two age groups: Men and women up to age 75 receive $25,000 medical insurance and a $50,000 death benefit; those from age 76 to 84 are eligible for $12,500 medical insurance and a $25,000 death benefit. For either policy, the cost for a 10-day period is $25, with decreasing rates up to 75 days, after which the rate is $1.50 a day.

HealthCare Abroad: This program is available to individuals up to age 75. For $3 per day (minimum 10 days, maximum 90 days), policy holders receive $100,000 medical insurance and $25,000 death benefit.

Both of these basic programs also may be bought in combination with trip cancellation and baggage insurance at extra cost. For further information, write to *Wallach & Co.,* 107 W. Federal St., Box 480, Middleburg, VA 22117-0480 (phone: 703-687-3166 in Virginia; 800-237-6615 elsewhere in the US).

Trip Cancellation and Interruption Insurance – Most charter and package tour passengers pay for their travel well before departure. The disappointment of having to miss a vacation because of illness or any other reason pales before the awful prospect that not all (and sometimes none) of the money paid in advance might be returned. So cancellation insurance for any package tour is a must.

Although cancellation penalties vary (they are listed in the fine print of every tour brochure, and before you purchase a package tour you should know exactly what they are), rarely will a passenger get more than 50% of this money back if forced to cancel within a few weeks of scheduled departure. Therefore, if you book a package tour or charter flight, you should have trip cancellation insurance to guarantee full reimbursement or refund should you, a traveling companion, or a member of your immediate family get sick, forcing you to cancel your trip or *return home early.*

The key here is *not* to buy just enough insurance to guarantee full reimbursement for the cost of the package or charter in case of cancellation. The proper amount of coverage should be sufficient to reimburse you for the cost of having to catch up with a tour after its departure or having to travel home at the full economy airfare if you have to forgo the return flight of your charter. There usually is quite a discrepancy between a charter fare and the amount charged to travel the same distance on a regularly scheduled flight at full economy fare.

Trip cancellation insurance is available from travel agents and tour operators in two forms: as part of a short-term, all-purpose travel insurance package (sold by the travel agent); or as specific cancellation insurance designed by the tour operator for a specific charter tour. Generally, tour operators' policies are less expensive, but also less inclusive. Cancellation insurance also is available directly from insurance companies or their agents as part of a short-term, all-inclusive travel insurance policy.

Before you decide on a policy, read each one carefully. (Either type can be purchased from a travel agent when you book the charter or package tour.) Be certain that your policy includes enough coverage to pay your fare from the farthest destination on your itinerary should you have to miss the charter flight. Also, be sure to check the fine print for stipulations concerning "family members" and "pre-existing medical conditions," as well as allowances for living expenses if you must delay your return due to bodily injury or illness.

Default and/or Bankruptcy Insurance – Although trip cancellation insurance usually protects you if *you* are unable to complete — or begin — your trip, a fairly recent innovation is coverage in the event of default and/or bankruptcy on the part of the tour operator, airline, or other travel supplier. In some travel insurance packages, this contingency is included in the trip cancellation portion of the coverage; in others, it is a separate feature. Either way, it is becoming increasingly important. Whereas sophisticated travelers long have known to beware of the possibility of default or bankruptcy when buying a charter flight or tour package, in recent years more than a few respected airlines unexpectedly have revealed their shaky financial condition, sometimes leaving hordes of stranded ticket holders in their wake. Moreover, the value of escrow protection of a charter passenger's funds lately has been unreliable. While default/bankruptcy insurance will not ordinarily result in reimbursement in time to pay for new arrangements, it can ensure that you will get your money back, and even independent travelers buying no more than an airplane ticket may want to consider it.

Flight Insurance – Airlines have carefully established limits of liability for injury to or the death of passengers on international flights. For all international flights to, from, or with a stopover in the US, all carriers are liable for up to $75,000 per passenger.

For all other international flights, the liability is based on where you purchase the ticket: If booked in advance in the US, the maximum liability is $75,000; if arrangements are made abroad, the liability is $10,000. But remember, these liabilities are not the same thing as insurance policies; every penny that an airline eventually pays in the case of injury or death may be subject to a legal battle.

But before you buy last-minute flight insurance from an airport vending machine, consider the purchase in light of your total existing insurance coverage. A careful review of your current policies may reveal that you already are amply covered for accidental death, sometimes up to three times the amount provided for by the flight insurance you're buying at the airport.

Be aware that airport insurance, the kind typically bought at a counter or from a vending machine, is among the most expensive forms of life insurance coverage, and that even within a single airport, rates for approximately the same coverage vary widely. Often policies sold in vending machines are more expensive than those sold over the counter, even when they are with the same national company.

If you buy your plane ticket with a major credit card, you generally receive automatic insurance coverage at no extra cost. Additional coverage usually can be obtained at extremely reasonable prices, but a cardholder must sign up for it in advance. (Note that rates vary slightly for residents of some states.) As we went to press, the travel accident and life insurance policies of the major credit cards were as follows:

American Express: Automatically provides $100,000 in insurance to its *Green, Gold,* and *Optima* cardholders, and $500,000 to *Platinum* cardholders. With *American Express,* $4.50 per ticket buys an additional $250,000 worth of flight insurance; $7.50 buys $500,000 worth; and $14 provides an added $1 million worth of coverage.

Carte Blanche: Automatically provides $150,000 flight insurance.

Diners Club: Provides $350,000 free flight insurance. An additional $250,000 worth of insurance is available for $4; $500,000 costs $6.50.

Discover Card: Provides $500,000 free flight insurance. An additional $250,000 worth of insurance is available for $4.50; $500,000 costs $6.50.

MasterCard and Visa: Insurance coverage set by the issuing institution.

Automobile Insurance – Public liability and property damage (third-party) insurance is compulsory in Europe, and whether you drive your own or a rental car you must carry insurance. Car rentals in Portugal usually include public liability, property damage, fire, and theft coverage and, sometimes (depending on the car rental company), collision damage coverage with a deductible.

In your car rental contract, you'll see that for about $9 to $15 a day, you may buy optional collision damage waiver (CDW) protection. (If partial coverage with a deductible is included in the rental contract, the CDW will cover the deductible in the event of an accident, and can cost as much as $25 per day.)

If you do not accept the CDW coverage, you may be liable for as much as the full retail value of the rental car, and by paying for the CDW you are relieved of all responsibility for any damage to the car. Before agreeing to this coverage, however, check with your own broker about your existing personal automobile insurance policy. It very well may cover your entire liability exposure without any additional cost, or you automatically may be covered by the credit card company to which you are charging the cost of your rental. To find out the amount of rental car insurance provided by major credit cards, contact the issuing institutions.

You also should know that an increasing number of the major international car rental companies automatically are including the cost of the CDW in their basic rates. Car rental prices have increased to include this coverage, although rental company ad campaigns may promote this as a new, improved rental package "benefit." The disadvantage of this inclusion is that you may not have the option to turn down the CDW — even if you already are adequately covered by your own insurance policy or through a credit card company.

Your rental contract (with the appropriate insurance box checked off), as well as proof of your personal insurance policy, if applicable, are required as proof of insurance. If you will be driving your own car in Portugal, you must carry an International Insurance Certificate (called a Green Card — *Cartão Verde* in Portugal), available through insurance brokers in the US.

Combination Policies – Short-term insurance policies, which may include a combination of any or all of the types of insurance discussed above, are available through retail insurance agencies, automobile clubs, and many travel agents. These combination policies are designed to cover you for the duration of a single trip.

Policies of this type include the following:

Access America International: A subsidiary of the Blue Cross/Blue Shield plans of New York and Washington, DC, now available nationwide. Contact *Access America,* PO Box 90310, Richmond, VA 23230 (phone: 800-424-3391 or 804-285-3300).

Carefree: Underwritten by The Hartford. Contact *Carefree Travel Insurance,* Arm Coverage, PO Box 310, Mineola, NY 11501 (phone: 800-645-2424 or 516-294-0220).

NEAR Services: In addition to a full range of travel services, this organization offers a comprehensive travel insurance package. An added feature is coverage for lost or stolen airline tickets. Contact *NEAR Services,* 450 Prairie Ave., Suite 101, Calumet City, IL 60409 (phone: 708-868-6700 in the Chicago area; 800-654-6700 elsewhere in the US and Canada).

Tele-Trip: Underwritten by the Mutual of Omaha Companies. Contact *Tele-Trip Co.,* 3201 Farnam St., Omaha, NE 68131 (phone: 402-345-2400 in Nebraska; 800-228-9792 elsewhere in the US).

Travel Assistance International: Provided by Europ Assistance Worldwide Services, and underwritten by Transamerica Occidental Life Insurance. Contact *Travel Assistance International,* 1133 15th St. NW, Suite 400, Washington, DC 20005 (phone: 202-331-1609 in Washington, DC; 800-821-2828 elsewhere in the US).

Travel Guard International: Underwritten by the Insurance Company of North America, it is available through authorized travel agents, or contact *Travel Guard International,* 1145 Clark St., Stevens Point, WI 54481 (phone: 715-345-0505 in Wisconsin; 800-826-1300 elsewhere in the US).

Travel Insurance PAK: Underwritten by The Travelers. Contact *The Travelers Companies,* Ticket and Travel Plans, One Tower Sq., Hartford, CT 06183-5040 (phone: 203-277-2319 in Connecticut; 800-243-3174 elsewhere in the US).

How to Pack

No one can provide a completely foolproof list of precisely what to pack, so it's best to let common sense, space, and comfort guide you. Keep one maxim in mind: Less is more. You simply won't need as much clothing as you think, and you are far more likely to need a forgotten accessory — or a needle and thread or scissors — than a particular piece of clothing.

As with almost anything relating to travel, a little planning can go a long way.

1. Where are you going — city, country, or both?
2. How many total days will you be gone?
3. What's the average temperature likely to be during your stay?

The goal is to remain perfectly comfortable, neat, clean, and fashionable, but to pack as little as possible. Learn to travel light by following two firm packing principles:

1. Organize your travel wardrobe around a single color — blue or brown, for example — that allows you to mix, match, and layer clothes. Holding firm to one color scheme will make it easy to eliminate items of clothing that don't harmonize.
2. Never overpack to ensure a supply of fresh clothing — shirts, blouses, underwear — for each day of a long trip. Use hotel laundries to wash and dry-clean clothes. There are self-service laundries (called *lavandarias*) in most towns of any size.

CLIMATE AND CLOTHES: Exactly what you pack for your trip will be a function of where you are going and when and the kinds of things you intend to do. A few degrees can make all the difference between being comfortably attired and very real suffering, so your initial step should be to find out what the general weather conditions are likely to be in the areas you will visit.

Portugal is roughly parallel with the US; Lisbon (at 39°) is about even with Washington, DC. The climate throughout Portugal ranges from moderate to hot during the summer and mild in spring and fall, though it can be damp and chilly in the winter months. Residents of the US will find that the same wardrobe they would wear in the southern United States will, with a few adjustments, also be appropriate for most parts of Portugal in the same season.

Anyone going to Portugal from the late fall through the early spring, however, should take into account that while central heating is prevalent, interiors usually are not heated to the same degree they would be in the US. Thus, although there is no need to prepare for sub-zero winters, most people probably will feel more comfortable wearing heavier clothing indoors than they might at home — for instance, sweaters rather than lightweight shirts and blouses.

Particularly during the winter months, rain gear also is advisable. A raincoat with a zip-out lining — and a hood or rain hat — is a versatile choice. If you do decide to take an umbrella, a compact telescoping model is best.

More information about the climate in Portugal, along with a chart of average low and high temperatures for different cities, is given in *When to Go,* in this section; other sources of information are airlines and travel agents.

Keeping temperature and climate in mind, consider the problem of luggage. Plan on one suitcase per person (and in a pinch, remember it's always easier to carry two small suitcases than to schlepp one that is roughly the size of downtown Detroit). Standard 26- to 28-inch suitcases can be made to work for 1 week or 1 month, and unless you are going for no more than a weekend, never cram wardrobes for two people into one suitcase. Hanging bags are best for dresses, suits, and jackets.

Before packing, lay out every piece of clothing you think you might want to take. Select clothing on the basis of what can serve several functions (wherever possible, clothes should be chosen that can be used for both daytime and evening wear). Pack clothes that have a lot of pockets for traveler's checks, documents, and tickets. Eliminate items that don't mix, match, or coordinate with your color scheme. If you can't wear it in at least two distinct incarnations, leave it at home. Accessorize everything beforehand so you know exactly what you will be wearing with what.

Layering is the key to comfort — particularly when touring in parts of the countryside where mornings and evenings can be chilly even when the days are mild. No matter where you are traveling in Portugal, however, layering is a good way to prepare for atypical temperatures or changes in the weather and even in a heat wave, an extra layer will be welcome for exploring cathedrals and wine cellars. Recommended basics are T-shirts and lightweight cotton shirts or sweaters, which can be worn under another shirt and perhaps a third layer, such as a pullover sweater, jacket, or windbreaker. In cooler weather, substitute a lightweight wool or heavier cotton turtleneck for the lighter layers. As the weather changes, you can add or remove clothes as required.

And finally — since the best touring of Portuguese monuments, churches, and countryside is done on foot — it is essential to bring comfortable shoes (often this means an old pair, already broken in). Sneakers or other rubber-soled shoes are good for walking up and down stairs, up and down hills, and to distant archaeological sites and back. And even in the evening, when walking no farther than to the nearest restaurant, women should avoid spike heels. Cobblestones are ubiquitous, and chunkier heels have a better chance of not getting caught — and ruined.

Your carry-on luggage should contain a survival kit with the basic things you will need in case your luggage gets lost or stolen: a toothbrush, toothpaste, all medications, a sweater, nightclothes, and a change of underwear. With these essential items at hand, you will be prepared for any sudden, unexpected occurrence that separates you from your suitcase. If you have many 1- or 2-night stops scheduled, you can live out of your survival case without having to unpack completely at each hotel.

Sundries – If you are traveling in the heat of summer and will be spending a lot of time outdoors, be sure to take along a sun hat (to protect hair as well as skin) and sunscreen.

Other items you might consider packing are a a pocket-size flashlight with extra batteries, a small sewing kit, a first-aid kit (see *Staying Healthy,* in this section, for recommended components), binoculars, and a camera or camcorder (see *Cameras and Equipment,* also in this section).

■ **Note:** For those on the go, *Travel Mini Pack* offers numerous products — from toilet articles to wrinkle remover spray — in handy travel sizes, as well as travel accessories such as money pouches, foreign currency calculators, and even a combination hair dryer/iron. For a catalog, contact *Travel Mini Pack* (PO Box 571, Stony Point, NY 10980; phone: 914-429-8281). *Pacific Traveler's Supply* (529 State St., Santa Barbara, CA 93101; phone: 805-963-4438) also carries a variety of similar items, as well as an extensive collection of travel guides and maps.

PACKING: The basic idea of packing is to get everything into the suitcase and out again with as few wrinkles as possible. Simple, casual clothes — shirts, jeans and slacks, permanent press skirts — can be rolled into neat, tight sausages that keep other packed items in place and leave the clothes themselves amazingly unwrinkled. However, for items that are too bulky or delicate for even careful rolling, a suitcase can be packed with the heaviest items on the bottom, toward the hinges, so that they will not wrinkle more perishable clothes. Candidates for the bottom layer include shoes (stuff them with small items to save space), a toilet kit, handbags (stuff them to help keep their shape), and an alarm clock. Fill out this layer with things that will not wrinkle or will not matter if they do, such as sweaters, socks, a bathing suit, gloves, and underwear.

If you get this first, heavy layer as smooth as possible with the fill-ins, you will have a shelf for the next layer — the most easily wrinkled items, like slacks, jackets, shirts, dresses, and skirts. These should be buttoned and zipped and laid along the whole length of the suitcase with as little folding as possible. When you do need to make a fold, do it on a crease (as with pants), along a seam in the fabric, or where it will not show (such as shirttails). Alternate each piece of clothing, using one side of the suitcase, then the other, to make the layers as flat as possible. Make the layers even and the total contents of your bag as full and firm as possible to keep things from shifting around during transit. On the top layer put the things you will want at once: nightclothes, a bathing suit, an umbrella or raincoat, a sweater.

With men's two-suiter suitcases, follow the same procedure. Then place jackets on hangers, straighten them out, and leave them unbuttoned. If they are too wide for the suitcase, fold them lengthwise down the middle, straighten the shoulders, and fold the sleeves in along the seam.

While packing, it is a good idea to separate each layer of clothes with plastic cleaning bags, which will help preserve pressed clothes while they are in the suitcase. Unpack your bags as soon as you get to your hotel. Nothing so thoroughly destroys freshly cleaned and pressed clothes as sitting for days in a suitcase. Finally, if something is badly wrinkled and can't be professionally pressed before you must wear it, hang it for several hours in a bathroom where the bathtub has been filled with very hot water; keep the bathroom door closed so the room becomes something of a steamroom. It really works miracles.

SOME FINAL PACKING HINTS: Apart from the items you pack as carry-on luggage (see above), always keep all necessary medicines, valuable jewelry, and travel or business documents in your purse, briefcase, or carry-on bag — *not in the luggage you will check.* Tuck a bathing suit into your handbag or briefcase, too; in the event of lost baggage, it's frustrating to be without one. And whether in your overnight bag or checked luggage, cosmetics and any liquids should be packed in plastic bottles or at least wrapped in plastic bags and tied.

Golf clubs may be checked through as luggage (most airlines are accustomed to handling them), but tennis rackets should be carried onto the plane. Some airlines require that bicycles be partially dismantled and packaged (see *Camping and Caravanning, Hiking and Biking,* in this section). Check with the airline before departure to see if there is a specific regulation concerning any special equipment or sporting gear you plan to take.

Hints for Handicapped Travelers

From 40 to 50 million people in the US alone have some sort of disability, and over half this number are physically handicapped. Like everyone else today, they — and the uncounted disabled millions around the world — are on the move. More than ever before, they are demanding facilities they can use comfortably, and they are being heard.

Portugal, a country of many hills and steps, has been comparatively slow in developing access for the handicapped. Generally, only the best or newest hotels and restaurants are easily accessible to a person in a wheelchair, and unless you are on a special tour for the handicapped, you will need to rely mostly on taxis for transportation. Nevertheless, with ingenuity and the help of an able-bodied traveling companion, you can get around Portugal well enough to thoroughly enjoy its varied delights. What the Portuguese lack in facilities for the handicapped they more than make up for in willingness to help.

PLANNING: Collect as much information as you can about your specific disability and facilities for the disabled in Portugal. Make your travel arrangements well in advance and specify to all services involved the exact nature of your condition or restricted mobility, as your trip will be much more comfortable if you know that there are accommodations and facilities to suit your needs. The best way to find out if your intended destination can accommodate a handicapped traveler is to write or call the local tourist authority or hotel and ask specific questions. If you require a corridor of a certain width to maneuver a wheelchair or if you need handles on the bathroom walls for support, ask the hotel manager. A travel agent or the local chapter or national office of the organization that deals with your particular disability — for example, the *American Foundation for the Blind* or the *American Heart Association* — will supply the most up-to-date information on the subject. The following organizations offer general information on access:

ACCENT on Living (PO Box 700, Bloomington, IL 61702; phone: 309-378-2961). This information service for persons with disabilities provides a free list of travel agencies specializing in arranging trips for the disabled; for a copy send a self-addressed, stamped envelope. Also offers a wide range of publications, including a quarterly magazine ($10 per year; $17.50 for 2 years) for persons with disabilities.

Information Center for Individuals with Disabilities (Fort Point Pl., 1st Floor, 27-43 Wormwood St., Boston, MA 02210; phone: 800-462-5015 in Massachusetts; 617-727-5540/1 elsewhere in the US; both numbers provide voice and TDD — telecommunications device for the deaf). The center offers information and referral services on disability-related issues, publishes fact sheets on travel agents, tour operators, and other travel resources, and can help you research your trip.

Mobility International USA (*MIUSA;* PO Box 3551, Eugene, OR 97403; phone: 503-343-1284; both voice and TDD). This US branch of *Mobility International* (the main office is at 228 Borough High St., London SE1 1JX, England; phone: 44-71-403-5688), a nonprofit British organization with affiliates worldwide, offers members advice and assistance — including information on accommodations and other travel services, and publications applicable to the traveler's disability. *Mobility International* also offers a quarterly newsletter and a comprehensive sourcebook, *A World of Options for the 90s: A Guide to International Education Exchange, Community Service and Travel for Persons with Disabilities* ($14 for members; $16 for non-members). Membership includes the newsletter and is $20 a year; subscription to the newsletter alone is $10 annually.

National Rehabilitation Information Center (8455 Colesville Rd., Suite 935, Silver Spring, MD 20910; phone: 301-588-9284). A general information, resource, research, and referral service.

Paralyzed Veterans of America (*PVA;* PVA/ATTS Program, 801 18th St. NW, Washington, DC 20006; phone: 202-416-7708 in Washington, DC; 800 424 8200 elsewhere in the US). The members of this national service organization all are veterans who have suffered spinal cord injuries, but it offers advocacy services and information to all persons with a disability. *PVA* also sponsors *Access to the Skies (ATTS),* a program that coordinates the efforts of the national and international air travel industry in providing airport and airplane access for the disabled. Members receive several helpful publications, as well as regular notification of conferences on subjects of interest to the disabled traveler.

Royal Association for Disability and Rehabilitation (*RADAR;* 25 Mortimer St., London W1N 8AB, England; phone: 44-71-637-5400). Offers a number of publications for the handicapped, including *Holidays and Travel Abroad 1993/94 — A Guide for Disabled People,* a comprehensive guidebook focusing on international travel. This publication can be ordered by sending payment in British pounds to *RADAR.* As we went to press, it cost just over £3; call for current pricing before ordering.

Society for the Advancement of Travel for the Handicapped (*SATH;* 347 Fifth Ave., Suite 610, New York, NY 10016; phone: 212-447-7284). To keep abreast of developments in travel for the handicapped as they occur, you may want to join *SATH,* a nonprofit organization whose members include consumers, as well as travel service professionals who have experience (or an interest) in travel for the handicapped. For an annual fee of $45 ($25 for students and travelers who are 65 and older) members receive a quarterly newsletter and have access to extensive information and referral services. *SATH* also offers two useful publications: *Travel Tips for the Handicapped* (a series of informative fact sheets) and *The United States Welcomes Handicapped Visitors* (a 48-page guide covering domestic transportation and accommodations that includes useful hints for travelers with disabilities abroad); to order, send a self-addressed, #10 envelope and $1 per title for postage.

Travel Information Service (Moss Rehabilitation Hospital, 1200 W. Tabor Rd., Philadelphia, PA 19141-3099; phone: 215-456-9600 for voice; 215-456-9602 for TDD). This service assists physically handicapped people in planning trips and supplies detailed information on accessibility for a nominal fee.

Blind travelers should contact the *American Foundation for the Blind* (15 W. 16th St., New York, NY 10011; phone: 800-829-0500 or 212-620-2147) and *The Seeing Eye* (Box 375, Morristown, NJ 07963-0375; phone: 201-539-4425); both provide useful information on resources for the visually impaired. *Note:* In Portugal, Seeing Eye dogs must be accompanied by a certificate of inoculation against rabies, issued within the previous year and certified by the attending veterinarian. These certificates must be authorized by a Portuguese consul (for a fee of about $7 at press time), and the certificate should include the type, prescription number, and manufacturer of the vaccine. *The American Society for the Prevention of Cruelty to Animals* (*ASPCA,* Education Dept., 441 E. 92 St., New York, NY 10128; phone: 212-876-7700) offers a useful booklet, *Traveling With Your Pet,* which lists inoculation and other requirements by country. It is available for $5 (including postage and handling).

In addition, there are a number of publications — from travel guides to magazines — of interest to handicapped travelers. Among these are the following:

Access to the World, by Louise Weiss, offers sound tips for the disabled traveler. Published by Facts on File (460 Park Ave. S., New York, NY 10016; phone: 212-683-2244 in New York State; 800-322-8755 elsewhere in the US; 800-443-8323 in Canada), it costs $16.95. Check with your local bookstore; it also can be ordered by phone with a credit card.

The Diabetic Traveler (PO Box 8223 RW, Stamford, CT 06905; phone: 203-327-5832) is a useful quarterly newsletter. Each issue highlights a single destination or type of travel and includes information on general resources and hints for diabetics. A 1-year subscription costs $15. When subscribing, ask for the free fact sheet including an index of special articles; back issues are available for $4 each.

Guide to Traveling with Arthritis, a free brochure available by writing to the Upjohn Company (PO Box 307-B, Coventry, CT 06238), provides lots of good, commonsense tips on planning your trip and how to be as comfortable as possible when traveling by car, bus, train, cruise ship, or plane.

Handicapped Travel Newsletter is regarded as one of the best sources of information for the disabled traveler. It is edited by wheelchair-bound Vietnam veteran Michael Quigley, who has traveled to 93 countries around the world. Issued every 2 months (plus special issues), a subscription is $10 per year. Write to *Handicapped Travel Newsletter,* PO Box 269, Athens, TX 75751 (phone: 903-677-1260).

Handi-Travel: A Resource Book for Disabled and Elderly Travellers, by Cinnie Noble, is a comprehensive travel guide full of practical tips for those with disabilities affecting mobility, hearing, or sight. To order this book, send $12.95, plus shipping and handling, to the *Canadian Rehabilitation Council for the*

Disabled, 45 Sheppard Ave. E., Suite 801, Toronto, Ontario M2N 5W9, Canada (phone: 416-250-7490; both voice and TDD).

The Itinerary (PO Box 2012, Bayonne, NJ 07002-2012; phone: 201-858-3400). This quarterly travel magazine for people with disabilities includes information on accessibility, listings of tours, news of adaptive devices, travel aids, and special services, as well as numerous general travel hints. A subscription costs $10 a year.

The Physically Disabled Traveler's Guide, by Rod W. Durgin and Norene Lindsay, rates accessibility of a number of travel services and includes a list of organizations specializing in travel for the disabled. It is available for $9.95, plus shipping and handling, from Resource Directories, 3361 Executive Pkwy., Suite 302, Toledo, OH 43606 (phone: 419-536-5353 in the Toledo area; 800-274-8515 elsewhere in the US).

Ticket to Safe Travel offers useful information for travelers with diabetes. A reprint of this article is available free from local chapters of the *American Diabetes Association.* For the nearest branch, contact the central office at 505 Eighth Ave., 21st Floor, New York, NY 10018 (phone: 212-947-9707 in New York State; 800-232-3472 elsewhere in the US).

Travel for the Patient with Chronic Obstructive Pulmonary Disease, a publication of the George Washington University Medical Center, provides some sound practical suggestions for those with emphysema, chronic bronchitis, asthma, or other lung ailments. To order, send $2 to Dr. Harold Silver, 1601 18th St. NW, Washington, DC 20009 (phone: 202-667-0134).

Traveling Like Everybody Else: A Practical Guide for Disabled Travelers, by Jacqueline Freedman and Susan Gersten, offers the disabled tips on traveling by car, cruise ship, and plane, as well as lists of accessible accommodations, tour operators specializing in tours for disabled travelers, and other resources. It is available for $11.95, plus postage and handling, from Modan Publishing, PO Box 1202, Bellmore, NY 11710 (phone: 516-679-1380).

Travel Tips for Hearing-Impaired People, a free pamphlet for deaf and hearing-impaired travelers, is available from the *American Academy of Otolaryngology* (One Prince St., Alexandria, VA 22314; phone: 703-836-4444). For a copy, send a self-addressed, stamped, business-size envelope to the academy.

Travel Tips for People with Arthritis, a 31-page booklet published by the *Arthritis Foundation,* provides helpful information regarding travel by car, bus, train, cruise ship, or plane, planning your trip, medical considerations, and ways to conserve your energy while traveling. It also includes listings of helpful resources, such as associations and travel agencies that operate tours for disabled travelers. For a copy, contact your local *Arthritis Foundation* chapter, or send $1 to the national office, PO Box 19000, Atlanta, GA 30326 (phone: 404-872-7100).

A few more basic resources to look for are *Travel for the Disabled,* by Helen Hecker ($19.95), and by the same author, *Directory of Travel Agencies for the Disabled* ($19.95). *Wheelchair Vagabond,* by John G. Nelson, is another useful guide for travelers confined to a wheelchair (hardcover, $14.95; paperback, $9.95). All three titles are published by Twin Peaks Press, PO Box 129, Vancouver, WA 98666 (phone: 800-637-CALM or 206-694-2462). The publisher offers a catalogue (the cost is $2) of 26 other books on travel for the disabled.

Other good sources of information are the branches of the Portuguese National Tourist Office, although brochures specifically for the handicapped may not be in English. (For the US addresses of these government tourist authorities, see *Tourist Information Offices,* in this section.)

Two organizations based in Great Britain offer information for handicapped persons traveling throughout Europe, including Portugal. *Tripscope* (63 Esmond Rd., London W4 1JE, UK; phone: 44-81-994-9294) is a telephone-based information and referral service (not a booking agent) that can help with transportation options for journeys throughout Europe. It may, for instance, be able to recommend outlets leasing small family vehicles adapted to accommodate wheelchairs. *Tripscope* can put such information on cassette for blind or visually-impaired travelers, and accepts written requests for information from those with speech impediments. And for general information, there's *Holiday Care Service* (2 Old Bank Chambers, Station Rd., Horley, Surrey RH6 9HW, UK; phone: 44-293-774535), a first-rate, free advisory service on accommodations, transportation, and holiday packages throughout Europe for disabled visitors.

Regularly revised hotel and restaurant guides use the symbol of access (person in a wheelchair; see the symbol at the beginning of this section) to point out accommodations suitable for wheelchair-bound guests. The red *Michelin Guide to Spain and Portugal,* found in general and travel bookstores, is one such publication. It can be ordered for $19.95 from Michelin Guides and Maps, PO Box 3305, Spartanburg, SC 29304-3305 (phone: 803-599-0850 in South Carolina; 800-423-0485 elsewhere in the US).

PLANE: The US Department of Transportation (DOT) has ruled that US airlines must accept all passengers with disabilities. As a matter of course, US airlines were pretty good about accommodating handicapped passengers even before the ruling, although each airline has somewhat different procedures. Foreign airlines also generally are good about accommodating the disabled traveler, but again, policies vary from carrier to carrier. Most carriers can accommodate passengers in wheelchairs, although advance notice usually is required. Ask for specifics when you book your flight.

Disabled passengers always should make reservations well in advance, and should provide the airline with all relevant details of their condition. These details include information on mobility and equipment that you will need the airline to supply — such as a wheelchair for boarding or portable oxygen for in-flight use. Be sure that the person to whom you speak fully understands the degree of your disability — the more details provided, the more effective help the airline can give you.

On the day before the flight, call back to make sure that all arrangements have been prepared, and arrive early on the day of the flight so that you can board before the rest of the passengers. It's a good idea to bring a medical certificate with you, stating your specific disability or the need to carry particular medicine.

Because most airports have jetways (corridors connecting the terminal with the door of the plane), a disabled passenger usually can be taken as far as the plane, and sometimes right onto it, in a wheelchair. If not, a narrow boarding chair may be used to take you to your seat. Your own wheelchair, which will be folded and put in the baggage compartment, should be tagged as escort luggage to assure that it's available at planeside upon landing rather than in the baggage claim area. Travel is not quite as simple if your wheelchair is battery-operated: Unless it has non-spillable batteries, it might not be accepted on board, and you will have to check with the airline ahead of time to find out how the batteries and the chair should be packaged for the flight. Usually people in wheelchairs are asked to wait until other passengers have disembarked. If you are making a tight connection, be sure to tell the attendant.

Passengers who use oxygen may not use their personal supply in the cabin, though it may be carried on the plane as cargo (the tank must be emptied) when properly packed and labeled. If you will need oxygen during the flight, the airline will supply it to you (there is a charge) provided you have given advance notice — 24 hours to a few days, depending on the carrier.

Useful information on every stage of air travel, from planning to arrival, is provided in the booklet *Incapacitated Passengers Air Travel Guide.* To receive a free copy, write to the *International Air Transport Association* (Publications Sales Department, 2000

Peel St., Montreal, Quebec H3A 2R4, Canada; phone: 514-844-6311). Another helpful publication is *Air Transportation of Handicapped Persons,* which explains the general guidelines that govern air carrier policies. For a copy of this free booklet, write to the US Department of Transportation (Distribution Unit, Publications Section, M-443-2, Washington, DC 20590) and ask for "Free Advisory Circular #AC-120-32." *Access Travel: A Guide to the Accessibility of Airport Terminals,* a free publication of the *Airport Operators Council International,* provides information on more than 500 airports worldwide — including major airports throughout Europe — and offers ratings of 70 features, such as wheelchair-accessible bathrooms, corridor width, and parking spaces. For a copy contact Consumer Information Center (Pueblo, CO 81009; phone: 719-948-3334).

Note: At the time of this writing, the only carriers serving Portugal that provide TDD toll-free lines in the US for the hearing-impaired were *TWA* (phone: 800-252-0622 in California; 800-421-8480 elsewhere in the US) and *Delta* (phone: 800-831-4488).

SHIP: Among the ships calling at Portuguese ports, *Cunard*'s *Queen Elizabeth 2, Crystal Cruises' Crystal Harmony,* and *Royal Cruise Line*'s *Crown Odyssey* are considered the best-equipped vessels for the handicapped. Handicapped travelers are advised to book reservations at least 90 days in advance to reserve specialized cabins.

For those in wheelchairs or with limited mobility, one of the best sources for evaluating a ship's accessibility is the free chart issued by the *Cruise Lines International Association* (500 Fifth Ave., Suite 1407, New York, NY 10110; phone: 212-921-0066). The chart lists accessible ships and indicates whether they accommodate standard-size or only narrow wheelchairs, have ramps, wide doors, low or no doorsills, handrails in the rooms, and so on. (For information on ships cruising around Portugal, see *Traveling by Ship,* in this section.)

GROUND TRANSPORTATION: Perhaps the simplest solution to getting around is to travel with an able-bodied companion who can drive. Another alternative in Portugal is to hire a driver/translator with a car — be sure to get a recommendation from a reputable source. The organizations listed above may be able to help you make arrangements — another source is your hotel concierge.

If you are accustomed to driving your own hand-controlled car and are determined to rent one, you may have to do some extensive research, as in Portugal it is difficult to find rental cars fitted with hand controls. If agencies do provide hand-controlled cars, they are apt to be offered only on a limited basis in major metropolitan areas and usually are in high demand. For instance, although *Budget* rents hand-controlled cars throughout Portugal, you must call ahead and make arrangements at least 30 days in advance, and the selection of vehicles is very limited. The best course is to contact the major car rental agencies listed in *Traveling by Car,* in this section, well before your departure, but be forewarned, you still may be out of luck. Other sources for information on vehicles adapted for the handicapped are the organizations discussed above.

The *American Automobile Association (AAA)* publishes a useful book, *The Handicapped Driver's Mobility Guide.* Contact the central office of your local *AAA* club for availability and pricing, which may vary at different branch offices.

Although taxis and public transportation are available in Portugal, accessibility for the disabled varies and may be limited in rural areas, as well as in some cities. Check with a travel agent or the Portuguese tourist authorities for information.

TRAIN: Train travel in Portugal is not well adapted to wheelchairs, although timetables may specify which, if any, departures are accessible. For information on accessible trains and timetables, contact *Rail Europe,* the Portuguese rail service representative in the US (226-230 Westchester Ave., White Plains, NY 10604; phone: 914-682-5172 in Connecticut, New Jersey, and New York State; 800-345-1990 elsewhere in the US), or ask for information at regional rail offices abroad.

BUS: In general, bus travel is not recommended for travelers who are totally wheelchair-bound, unless they have someone along who can lift them on and off or they are members of a group tour designed for the handicapped and are using a specially outfitted bus. If you have some mobility, however, you'll find local personnel usually quite happy to help you board and exit.

TOURS: Programs designed for the physically impaired are run by specialists who have researched hotels, restaurants, and sites to be sure they present no insurmountable obstacles. The following travel agencies and tour operators specialize in making group and individual arrangements for travelers with physical or other disabilities.

Access: The Foundation for Accessibility by the Disabled (PO Box 356, Malverne, NY 11565; phone: 516-887-5798). A travelers' referral service that acts as an intermediary with tour operators and agents worldwide, and provides information on accessibility at various locations.

Accessible Journeys (412 S. 45th St., Philadelphia, PA 19104; phone: 215-747-0171). Arranges for traveling companions who are medical professionals — registered or licensed practical nurses, therapists, or doctors (all are experienced travelers). Several prospective companions' profiles and photos are sent to the client for perusal and if one is acceptable, the "match" is made. The client usually pays all travel expenses for the companion, plus a set fee to compensate for wages the companion would be making at his or her usual job. This company also offers tours and cruises for people with special needs, although you don't have to take one of their tours to hire a companion through them.

Accessible Tours/Directions Unlimited (720 N. Bedford Rd., Bedford Hills, NY 10507; phone: 914-241-1700 in New York State; 800-533-5343 elsewhere in the continental US). Arranges group or individual tours for disabled persons traveling in the company of able-bodied friends or family members. Accepts the unaccompanied traveler if completely self-sufficient.

Dialysis at Sea Cruises (611 Barry Place, Indian Rocks Beach, FL 34635; phone: 800-544-7604 or 813-596-7604). Offers cruises that include the medical services of a nephrologist (a specialist in kidney disease) and a staff of dialysis nurses. Family, friends, and companions are welcome to travel on these cruises, but the number of dialysis patients usually is limited to roughly ten travelers per trip.

Evergreen Travel Service (4114 198th St. SW, Suite 13, Lynnwood, WA 98036-6742; phone: 800-435-2288 or 206-776-1184). Offers worldwide tours and cruises for the disabled (Wings on Wheels Tours), sight-impaired/blind (White Cane Tours), and hearing-impaired/deaf (Flying Fingers Tours). Most programs are first class or deluxe, and include a trained escort.

Flying Wheels Travel (143 W. Bridge St., Box 382, Owatonna, MN 55060; phone: 800-535-6790 or 507-451-5005). Handles both tours and individual arrangements.

The Guided Tour (613 W. Cheltenham Ave., Suite 200, Melrose Park, PA 19126; phone: 215-782-1370). Arranges tours for people with developmental and learning disabilities and sponsors separate tours for members of the same population who also are physically disabled or who simply need a slower pace.

Sprout (893 Amsterdam Ave., New York, NY 10025; phone: 212-222-9575). Arranges travel programs for mildly and moderately disabled teens and adults.

USTS Travel Horizons (11 E. 44th St., New York, NY 10017; phone: 800-487-8787 or 212-687-5121). Travel agent and registered nurse Mary Ann Hamm designs trips for individual travelers requiring all types of kidney dialysis and handles arrangements for the dialysis.

Whole Person Tours (PO Box 1084, Bayonne, NJ 07002-1084; phone: 201-858-3400). Owner Bob Zywicki travels the world with his wheelchair and offers a lineup of escorted tours (many conducted by him) for the disabled. *Whole*

Person Tours also publishes *The Itinerary,* a quarterly newsletter for disabled travelers (see the publication source list above).

Travelers who would benefit from being accompanied by a nurse or physical therapist also can hire a companion through *Traveling Nurses' Network,* a service provided by Twin Peaks Press (PO Box 129, Vancouver, WA 98666; phone: 800-637-CALM or 206-694-2462). For a $10 fee, clients receive the names of three nurses, whom they can then contact directly; for a $125 fee, the agency will make all the hiring arrangements for the client. Travel arrangements also may be made in some cases — the fee for this further service is determined on an individual basis.

A similar service is offered by *MedEscort International* (ABE International Airport, PO Box 8766, Allentown, PA 18105; phone: 800-255-7182 in the continental US; elsewhere, call 215-791-3111). Clients can arrange to be accompanied by a nurse, paramedic, respiratory therapist, or physician through *MedEscort.* The fees are based on the disabled traveler's needs. This service also can assist in making travel arrangements.

Hints for Single Travelers

Just about the last trip in human history on which the participants were neatly paired was the voyage of Noah's Ark. Ever since, passenger lists and tour groups have reflected the same kind of asymmetry that occurs in real life, as countless individuals set forth to see the world unaccompanied (or unencumbered, depending on your outlook) by spouse, lover, friend, or relative. Unfortunately, traveling alone can turn a traveler into a second class citizen.

The truth is that the travel industry is not very fair to people who vacation by themselves. People traveling alone almost invariably end up paying more than individuals traveling in pairs. Most travel bargains, including package tours, accommodations, resort packages, and cruises, are based on *double-occupancy* rates. This means that the per-person price is offered on the basis of two people traveling together and sharing a double room (which means they each will spend a good deal more on meals and extras). The single traveler will have to pay a surcharge, called a single supplement, for exactly the same package. In extreme cases, this can add as much as 35% and sometimes more — to the basic per-person rate.

Don't despair, however. Throughout Portugal, there are scores of smaller hotels and other hostelries where, in addition to a cozier atmosphere, prices still are quite reasonable for the single traveler. Some ship lines have begun to offer special cruises for singles, and some resorts cater to the single traveler.

The obvious, most effective alternative is to find a traveling companion. Even special "singles' tours" that promise no supplements usually are based on people sharing double rooms. Perhaps the most recent innovation along these lines is the creation of organizations that "introduce" the single traveler to other single travelers, somewhat like a dating service. Some charge fees, others are free, but the basic service offered is the same: to match an unattached person with a compatible travel mate, often as part of the company's own package tours. Among such organizations are the following:

Odyssey Network (118 Cedar St., Wellesley, MA 02181; phone: 617-237-2400). Originally founded to match single women travelers, this company now includes men in its enrollment. *Odyssey* offers a quarterly newsletter for members who are seeking a travel companion, and occasionally organizes small group tours. A newsletter subscription is $50.

Partners-in-Travel (PO Box 491145, Los Angeles, CA 90049; phone: 213-476-

4869). Members receive a list of singles seeking traveling companions; prospective companions make contact through the agency. The membership fee is $40 per year and includes a chatty newsletter (6 issues per year).

Singleworld (401 Theodore Fremd Ave., Rye, NY 10580; phone: 800-223-6490 or 914-967-3334). For a yearly fee of $25, this club books members on tours and cruises and arranges shared accommodations, allowing individual travelers to avoid the single supplement charge; members also receive a quarterly newsletter. *Singleworld* also offers its own package tours for singles in two categories: for those 35 or younger or for all ages.

Travel Companion Exchange (PO Box 833, Amityville, NY 11701; phone: 516-454-0880). This group publishes a newsletter for singles and a directory of individuals looking for travel companions. On joining, members fill out a lengthy questionnaire and write a small listing (much like an ad in a personal column). Based on these listings, members can request copies of profiles and contact prospective traveling companions. It is wise to join well in advance of your planned vacation so that there's enough time to determine compatibility and plan a joint trip. Membership fees, including the newsletter, are $36 for 6 months or $60 a year for a single-sex listing; $66 and $120, respectively, for a complete listing.

Also note that certain cruise lines offer guaranteed share rates for single travelers, whereby cabin mates are selected on request. For instance, three cruise lines that provide guaranteed share rates are *Cunard* (phone: 800-221-4770), *Princess Cruises* (phone: 800-421-0522), and *Royal Cruise Line* (phone: 415-956-7200 or 800-622-0538 in California; 800-227-4534 elsewhere in the US).

In addition, a number of tour packagers cater to single travelers. These companies offer packages designed for individuals interested in vacationing with a group of single travelers or in being matched with a traveling companion. Among the better established of these agencies are the following:

Club Europa/VET (802 W. Oregon St., Urbana, IL 61801; phone: 800-331-1882 or 217-344-5863). Specializes in travel for 18- to 30-year-olds. Offers multi-country escorted tours ranging from 2 weeks to 2 months, including itineraries in Portugal.

Contiki Holidays (1432 E. Katella Ave., Anaheim, CA 92805; phone: 800-466-0610 or 714-937-0611). Specializes in vacations for 18- to 35-year-olds. As this packager is a wholesaler, reservations must be booked through a travel agent.

Cosmos: This tour operator offers budget motorcoach tours of Europe — including Portugal — with a guaranteed-share plan whereby singles who wish to share rooms (and avoid paying the single supplement) are matched by the tour escort with individuals of the same sex and charged the basic double-occupancy tour price. Contact the firm at one of its three North American branches: 95-25 Queens Blvd., Rego Park, NY 11374 (phone: 800-221-0090 from the eastern US); 150 S. Los Robles Ave., Pasadena, CA 91101 (phone 818-449-0919 or 800-556-5454 from the western US); 1801 Eglinton Ave. W., Suite 104, Toronto, Ontario M6E 2H8, Canada (phone: 416-787-1281).

Gallivanting (515 E. 79th St., Suite 20F, New York, NY 10021; phone 800-933-9699 or 212-988-0617). Offers 1- to 2-week tours for singles ages 25 through 55, including cruises and outdoor activities such as hiking, rafting, hot-air ballooning, snorkeling, and sailing. *Gallivanting* also matches singles of the same sex willing to share accommodations in order to avoid paying single supplement charges, and the agency guarantees this arrangement if bookings are paid for at least 75 days in advance.

Grand Circle Travel (347 Congress St., Boston, MA 02210; phone: 617-350-7500 or 800-221-2610). Arranges extended vacations, escorted tours and cruises for the over-50 traveler, including singles. Membership, which is automatic when you book a trip through *Grand Circle,* includes travel discounts and other extras, such as a Pen Pals service for singles seeking traveling companions.

Insight International Tours (745 Atlantic Ave., Boston MA 02111; phone: 800-582-8380 or 617-482-2000). Offers a matching service for single travelers. Several tours are geared for travelers in the 18 to 35 age group.

Marion Smith Singles (611 Prescott Pl., North Woodmere, NY 11581; phone: 516-791-4652, 516-791-4865, or 212-944-2112). Specializes in tours for singles ages 20 to 50, who can choose to share accommodations to avoid single supplement charges.

Saga International Holidays (222 Berkeley St., Boston MA 02116; phone: 800-343-0273 or 617-451-6808). A subsidiary of a British company specializing in older travelers, many of them single, *Saga* offers a broad selection of packages for people age 60 and over or those 50 to 59 traveling with someone 60 or older. Anyone can book a *Saga* trip, but a club membership (no fee) includes a subscription to their newsletter, as well as other publications and travel services — such as a matching service for single travelers.

Singles in Motion (545 W. 236th St., Suite 1D, Riverdale, NY 10463; phone: 718-884-4464). Offers a number of packages for single travelers, including tours, cruises, and excursions focusing on outdoor activities such as hiking and biking.

Solo Flights (63 High Noon Rd., Weston, CT 06883; phone: 203-226-9993). Represents a number of packagers and cruise lines and books singles on individual and group tours.

Suddenly Single Tours (161 Dreiser Loop, Bronx, NY 10475; phone: 718-379-8800). Specializes in group tours for singles; many participants are over 40.

Travel in Two's (239 N. Broadway, Suite 3, N. Tarrytown, NY 10591; phone: 914-631-8409). This company books solo travelers on packages offered by a number of companies (at no extra cost to clients), offers its own tours, and matches singles with traveling companions. Many offerings are listed in their quarterly *Singles Vacation Newsletter,* which costs $7.50 per issue or $20 per year.

A good book for single travelers is *Traveling On Your Own* by Eleanor Berman, which offers tips on traveling solo and includes information on trips for singles, ranging from outdoor adventures to educational programs. Available in bookstores, it also can be ordered by sending $12.95, plus postage and handling, to Random House, Order Dept., 400 Hahn Rd., Westminster, MD 21157 (phone: 800-733-3000).

Single travelers also may want to subscribe to *Going Solo,* a newsletter that offers helpful information on going on your own. Issued eight times a year, a subscription costs $36. Contact Doerfer Communications, PO Box 1035, Cambridge, MA 02238 (phone: 617-876-2764).

An attractive alternative for the single traveler is *Club Med,* which operates scores of resorts in more than 37 countries worldwide and caters to the single traveler, as well as couples and families. Though the clientele often is under 30, there is a considerable age mix: the average age is 37. *Club Med* has one resort in Albufeira, Portugal and most of the guests at its resort are European. *Club Med* offers single travelers package-rate vacations including airfare, food, wine, lodging, entertainment, and athletic facilities. The atmosphere is relaxed, the dress informal, and the price reasonable. For information, contact *Club Med,* 3 E. 54th St., New York, NY 10022 (phone: 800-CLUB-MED). For further information on *Club Med* and other alternatives suitable for singles, see our discussions of accommodations in *On the Road,* in this section.

Not all single travelers are looking for a swinging scene. Some take vacations to rest and relax, and they prefer being by themselves. Generally, people who want this quieter mode of travel have to accept that their accommodations will cost more than if they were part of a couple.

Other possibilities that include an opportunity to visit with the Portuguese are *pensões,* which often are family-run, and home stays. See our discussion of accommodations in *On the Road,* in this section, for information on these and other accommodations alternatives suitable for single travelers. And there's always camping. Many areas along the coast, as well as some sites around the countryside, have a place to pitch a tent and enjoy the scenery. (For more information, see *Camping and Caravanning, Hiking and Biking,* in this section.)

WOMEN AND STUDENTS: Two specific groups of single travelers deserve special mention: women and students. Countless women travel by themselves in Portugal, and such an adventure need not be feared. Recommended is Linda White's *The Independent Woman's Guide to Europe* (Fulcrum Books; $13.95), which discusses subjects from tipping to transportation, as well as coping with illness, accidents, and crime.

One lingering inhibition many female travelers still harbor is that of eating alone in public places. The trick here is to relax and enjoy your meal and surroundings; while you may run across the occasional unenlightened waiter, a woman dining solo is no longer uncommon.

Studying Abroad – A large number of single travelers are students. Travel *is* education. Travel broadens a person's knowledge and deepens his or her perception of the world in a way no media or "armchair" experience ever could. In addition, to study a country's language, art, culture, or history in one of its own schools is to enjoy the most productive method of learning.

By "student" we do not necessarily mean a person who wishes to matriculate at a foreign university to earn a degree. Nor do we necessarily mean a younger person. A student is anyone who wishes to include some sort of educational program in a trip to Portugal.

There are many benefits for students abroad, and the way to begin to discover them is to consult the *Council on International Educational Exchange (CIEE).* This organization, which runs a variety of well-known work, study, and travel programs for students, is the US sponsor of the International Student Identity Card (ISIC). Reductions on airfare, other transportation, and entry fees to most museums and other exhibitions are only some of the advantages of the card. To apply for it, write to *CIEE* at one of the following addresses: 205 E. 42nd St., New York, NY 10017 (phone: 212-661-1414); 312 Sutter St., Suite 407, San Francisco, CA 94108 (phone: 415-421-3473); and 919 Irving St., Suite 102, San Francisco, CA 94122 (phone: 415-566-6222). Mark the letter "Attn. Student ID." Application requires a $14 fee, a passport-size photograph, and proof that you are a matriculating student (this means either a transcript or a letter or bill from your school registrar with the school's official seal; high school and junior high school students can use their report cards). There is no maximum age limit, but participants must be at least 12 years old. The *International Student Travel Guide,* which gives details of the discounts country by country, is free with membership. Another free publication of *CIEE* is the informative, annual, 72-page *Student Travel Catalog,* which covers all aspects of youth-travel abroad for vacation trips, jobs, or study programs, and also includes a list of other helpful publications. You can order the catalogue from the Information and Student Services Department at the New York address given above.

Another card of value in Europe, and also available through *CIEE,* is the Federation of International Youth Travel Organizations (FIYTO) card, which provides many of the benefits of the ISIC card. In this case, cardholders need not be students, merely under age 26. To apply, send $14 with a passport-size photo and proof of birth date to *CIEE* at one of the addresses above.

CIEE also sponsors charter flights to Europe that are open to students and non-students of any age. Although, unfortunately, Lisbon is no longer among the destinations served, flights are offered between New York and Madrid (with budget-priced add-ons available from Chicago, Cleveland, Miami, Minneapolis, Phoenix, Portland, Salt Lake City, San Diego, Seattle, and Spokane), where travelers can catch a connecting flight to Lisbon or continue their journey by land. These flights arrive and depart at least three times a week from Kennedy (JFK) Airport during the high season. Youth fares also may be offered by some scheduled airlines offering transatlantic service to Portugal. To find out about current discounts and restrictions, contact the individual carriers. (Also see *Traveling by Plane,* in this section.)

For extensive travel throughout Europe, there is a version of the Eurailpass restricted to travelers (including non-students) under 26 years of age. The Eurail Youthpass entitles the bearer to either 1 or 2 months of unlimited second class rail travel in 17 countries, including Portugal. In addition, it is honored on many European steamers and ferries and on railroad connections between the airport and the center of town in various cities. The pass also entitles the bearer to reduced rates on some bus lines in several countries. The Eurail Youthpass can be purchased only by those living outside Europe or North Africa, and it must be purchased before departure. Eurailpasses can be bought from a US travel agent or from the national railway offices of the countries in the Eurail network (for further information and addresses, see *Traveling by Train,* in this section).

Students and singles in general should keep in mind that youth hostels exist in many cities throughout Portugal. They always are inexpensive, generally clean and well situated, and they are a sure place to meet other people traveling alone. Hostels are run by the hosteling associations of 68 countries that make up the *International Youth Hostel Federation (IYHF);* membership in one of the national associations affords access to the hostels of the rest. To join the American affiliate, *American Youth Hostels (AYH),* contact the national office (PO Box 37613, Washington, DC 20013-7613; phone: 202-783-6161), or the local *AYH* council nearest you. As we went to press, the following membership rates were in effect: $25 for adults (between 18 and 54), $10 for youths (17 and under), $15 for seniors (55 and up), and $35 for family membership. *Hosteling North America,* which lists hostels in the US and Canada, comes with your *AYH* card (non-members can purchase this book for $5, plus postage and handling); the *Guide to Budge Accommodations,* Volume 1, covers hostels in Europe (Volume 2 covers North and South America, as well as Africa, Asia, and Australia) and must be purchased ($10.95, plus postage and handling, for each volume).

Those who go abroad without an *AYH* card may purchase youth hostel International Guest Cards (for the equivalent of about $18), and obtain information on local youth hostels by contacting *Associação Portuguesa de Pousadas de Juventude* (46 Rua Andrade de Corvo, Lisbon 1000, Portugal; phone: 1-539725). This association also provides information on hostels throughout Portugal. Another source of information is the tourist boards, which may provide information sheets on hostels in their areas (see the individual city reports in THE CITIES for locations).

Opportunities for study range from summer or academic-year courses in the language and civilization of Portugal designed specifically for foreigners (including those whose school days are well behind them) to long-term university attendance by those intending to take a degree.

Complete details on more than 3,000 available courses abroad (including at Portuguese universities) and suggestions on how to apply are contained in two books published by the *Institute of International Education* (IIE Books, Publications Office, 809 UN Plaza, New York, NY 10017; phone 212-984-5412): *Vacation Study Abroad* ($31.95, plus shipping and handling) and *Academic Year Abroad* ($39.95, plus shipping and handling). A third book, *Teaching Abroad,* is out of print; check your local library. IIE Books also offers a free pamphlet called *Basic Facts on Study Abroad.*

The *National Registration Center for Study Abroad* (*NRCSA,* PO Box 1393, Milwaukee, WI 53201; phone: 414-278-0631) also offers a publication called the *Worldwide Classroom: Study Abroad and Learning Vacations in 40 Countries: 1993-1994,* available for $8.50, plus shipping and handling, which includes information on over 160 schools and cultural centers that offer courses for Americans, with the primary focus on foreign language and culture.

Those who are interested in a "learning vacation" abroad also may be interested in *Travel and Learn* by Evelyn Kaye. This guide to educational travel discusses a wide range of opportunities — everything from archaeology to whale watching — and provides information on organizations that offer programs in these areas of interest. The book is available in bookstores for $23.95; or you can send $26 (which includes shipping charges) to Blue Penguin Publications (147 Sylvan Ave., Leonia, NJ 07605; phone: 800-800-8147 or 201-461-6918). *Learning Vacations* by Gerson G. Eisenberg also provides extensive information on seminars, workshops, courses, and so on — in a wide variety of subjects. Available in bookstores, it also can be ordered from Peterson's Guides (PO Box 2123, Princeton, NJ 08543-2123; phone: 800-338-3282 or 609-243-9111) for $11.95, plus shipping and handling.

Work, Study, Travel Abroad: The Whole World Handbook, issued by the *Council on International Educational Exchange (CIEE),* is an informative, chatty guide on study programs, work opportunities, and travel hints, and includes information on Portugal. It is available for $10.95, plus shipping and handling, from *CIEE* (address above).

AFS Intercultural Programs (313 E. 43rd St., New York, NY 10017; phone 800-AFS-INFO or 212-949-4242) sets up exchanges between US and foreign high school students on an individual basis for a semester or whole academic year.

National Association of Secondary School Principals (*NASSP,* 1904 Association Dr., Reston, VA 22091; phone: 703-860-0200), an association of administrators, teachers, and state education officials, sponsors *School Partnership International,* a program in which secondary schools in the US are linked with partner schools abroad for an annual short-term exchange of students and faculty.

WORKING ABROAD: Jobs for foreigners in Portugal are not easy to come by and in general do not pay well enough to cover all the expenses of a trip. They do provide an invaluable learning experience, however, while helping to make a trip more affordable.

For individuals age 18 (or 16 in Germany) and up who are interested in working abroad as volunteers, the *CIEE* also publishes a helpful book, *Volunteer!,* which includes volunteer programs with nonprofit organizations worldwide, many of which are located in Portugal. It is available for $8.95, plus shipping and handling, from the *CIEE* at one of the addresses given above. *CIEE* also may be able to provide other information or assistance to those interested in working in Portugal.

For a complete list of programs administered by Portuguese institutions, contact the Portuguese National Tourist Office in North America (see *Tourist Information Offices,* in this section, for addresses).

Hints for Older Travelers

Special discounts and more free time are just two factors that have given Americans over age 65 a chance to see the world at affordable prices. Senior citizens make up an ever-growing segment of the travel population, and the trend among them is to travel more frequently and for longer periods of time.

PLANNING: When planning a vacation, prepare your itinerary with one eye on your own physical condition and the other on a topographical map. Keep in mind variations in climate, terrain, and altitudes, which may pose some danger for anyone with heart or breathing problems.

Older travelers may find the following publications of interest:

The Discount Guide for Travelers Over 55, by Caroline and Walter Weintz, is an excellent book for budget-conscious older travelers. Published by Penguin USA, it is currently out of print; check your local library.

Going Abroad: 101 Tips for the Mature Traveler offers tips on preparing for your trip, commonsense precautions en route, and some basic travel terminology. This concise, free booklet is available from *Grand Circle Travel,* 347 Congress St., Boston, MA 02210 (phone: 800-221-2610 or 617-350-7500).

The International Health Guide for Senior Citizen Travelers, by Dr. W. Robert Lange, covers such topics as trip preparations, food and water precautions, adjusting to weather and climate conditions, finding a doctor, motion sickness, jet lag, and so on. Also includes a list of resource organizations that provide medical assistance for travelers. It is available for $4.95 postpaid from Pilot Books, 103 Cooper St., Babylon, NY 11702 (phone: 516-422-2225).

The Mature Traveler is a monthly newsletter that provides information on travel discounts, places of interest, useful tips, and other topics of interest for travelers 49 and up. To subscribe, send $24.95 to GEM Publishing Group, PO Box 50820, Reno, NV 89513 (phone: 702-786-7419).

Take a Camel to Lunch and Other Adventures for Mature Travelers, by Nancy O'Connell, offers offbeat and unusual adventures for travelers over 50. Available at bookstores or directly from Bristol Publishing Enterprises, PO Box 1737, San Leandro, CA 94577 (phone: 800-346-4889 or 510-895-4461) for $8.95 (plus shipping and handling).

Travel Tips for Older Americans is a useful booklet that provides good, basic advice. This US State Department publication (stock number: 044-000-02270-2) can be ordered by sending a check or money order for $1 to the Superintendent of Documents (US Government Printing Office, Washington, DC 20402) or by calling 202-783-3238 and charging the order to a credit card.

Unbelievably Good Deals & Great Adventures That You Absolutely Can't Get Unless You're Over 50, by Joan Rattner Heilman, offers travel tips for older travelers, including discounts on accommodations and transportation, as well as a list of organizations for seniors. It is available for $7.95 (plus shipping and handling) from Contemporary Books, 180 N. Michigan Ave., Chicago, IL 60601 (phone: 312-782-9181).

HEALTH: Health facilities in Portugal generally are excellent; however, an inability to speak the language can pose a serious problem, not in receiving treatment at large hospitals, where many doctors and other staff members will speak English, but in getting help elsewhere or in getting to the place where help is available. A number of organizations help travelers avoid or deal with a medical emergency overseas. For information on these services, see *Staying Healthy,* in this section.

Pre-trip medical and dental checkups are strongly recommended. In addition, be sure to take along any prescription medication you need, enough to last *without a new prescription* for the duration of your trip; pack all medications with a note from your doctor for the benefit of airport authorities. If you have specific medical problems, bring prescriptions and a "medical file" composed of the following:

1. A summary of your medical history and current diagnosis.
2. A list of drugs to which you are allergic.
3. Your most recent electrocardiogram, if you have heart problems.
4. Your doctor's name, address, and telephone number.

DISCOUNTS AND PACKAGES: Since guidelines change from place to place, it is a good idea to inquire in advance about discounts for accommodations, transportation, tickets to theater performances, concerts, and movies, entrance fees to museums, national monuments, and other attractions.

Many hotel chains, airlines, cruise lines, bus companies, car rental companies, and other travel suppliers offer discounts to older travelers. For instance, *TAP Air* offers those age 60 and over (and one traveling companion per qualifying senior citizen) discounts on flights from Boston, Los Angeles, and New York to Portugal. *Delta* and *TWA* airlines also offer discounts for passengers age 60 (or 62) and over, which also may apply to one traveling companion per senior. For information on current prices and applicable restrictions, contact the individual carriers.

Some discounts, however, are extended only to bona fide members of certain senior citizens organizations. For instance, *Sheraton* offers a 25% discount to any senior citizen and participating *Holiday Inns* offer 10% discounts for *AARP* members — in both cases, these discounts may not apply during certain "blackout" periods. (See listings below for more information on *AARP* benefits.) Because the same organizations frequently offer package tours to both domestic and international destinations, the benefits of membership are twofold: Those who join can take advantage of discounts as individual travelers and also reap the savings that group travel affords. In addition, because the age requirements for some of these organizations are quite low (or nonexistent), the benefits can begin to accrue early.

In order to take advantage of these discounts, you should carry proof of your age (or eligibility). A driver's license, membership card in a recognized senior citizens organization, or a Medicare card should be adequate. Among the organizations dedicated to helping older travelers see the world are the following:

American Association of Retired Persons (*AARP;* 601 E St. NW, Washington, DC 20049; phone: 202-434-2277). The largest and best-known of these organizations. Membership is open to anyone 50 or over, whether retired or not; dues are $8 a year, $20 for 3 years, or $45 for 10 years, and include spouse. The *AARP* Travel Experience Worldwide program, available through *American Express Travel Related Services* offers members tours, cruises, and other travel programs worldwide designed exclusively for older travelers. Members can book these services by calling *American Express* at 800-927-0111 for land and air travel, or 800-745-4567 for cruises.

Golden Companions (PO Box 754, Pullman, WA 99163-0754; phone: 509-334-9351). This club assists members in finding suitable traveling companions. Its Travel Companion Network includes a mail exchange service and bimonthly newsletter for those age 45 and over. Other services include vacation home exchanges, discounts on hotels and package tours, and group trips and cruises, some of which are sponsored by the club.

Mature Outlook (Customer Service Center, 6001 N. Clark St., Chicago, IL 60660; phone: 800-336-6330). Through its *Travel Alert,* tours, cruises, and other vacation packages are available to members at special savings. Hotel and car rental discounts and travel accident insurance also are available. Membership is open to anyone 50 years of age or older, costs $9.95 a year, and includes a bimonthly newsletter and magazine, as well as information on package tours.

National Council of Senior Citizens (1331 F St. NW, Washington, DC 20004; phone: 202-347-8800). Here, too, the emphasis is on keeping costs low. This nonprofit organization offers members a different roster of package tours each year, as well as individual arrangements through its affiliated travel agency *(Vantage Travel Service).* Although most members are over 50, membership is open to anyone (regardless of age) for an annual fee of $12 per person or couple. Lifetime membership costs $150.

Certain travel agencies and tour operators offer special trips geared to older travelers. Among them are the following:

Evergreen Travel Service (4114 198th St. SW, Suite 13, Lynnwood, WA 98036-6742; phone: 800-435-2288 or 206-776-1184). This specialist in trips for persons with disabilities recently introduced Lazybones Tours, a program offering leisurely tours for older travelers. Most programs are first class or deluxe, and include an escort.

Gadabout Tours (700 E. Tahquitz Canyon Way, Palm Springs, CA 92262; phone: 619-325-5556 or 800-521-7309 in California; 800-952-5068 elsewhere in the US). Offers escorted tours and cruises to a number of destinations, including Portugal.

Grand Circle Travel (347 Congress St., Boston, MA 02210; phone: 800-221-2610 or 617-350-7500). Caters exclusively to the over-50 traveler and packages a large variety of escorted tours, cruises, and extended vacations. Membership, which is automatic when you book a trip through *Grand Circle,* includes discount certificates on future trips and other travel services, such as a matching service for single travelers and a helpful free booklet, *Going Abroad: 101 Tips for Mature Travelers* (see the source list above).

Insight International Tours (745 Atlantic Ave., Boston, MA 02111; phone: 800-582-8380 or 617-482-2000). Offers a matching service for single travelers. Several tours are geared for mature travelers.

OmniTours (104 Wilmot Rd., Deerfield, IL 60015; phone: 800-962-0060 or 708-374-0088). Offers combination air and rail group tours designed for travelers 50 years and older.

Saga International Holidays (222 Berkeley St., Boston MA 02116; phone: 800-343-0273 or 617-451-6808). A subsidiary of a British company catering to older travelers, *Saga* offers a broad selection of packages for people age 60 and over or those younger traveling with someone in this age bracket. Although anyone can book a *Saga* trip, club membership includes a subscription to their newsletter, as well as other publications and travel services. You need only call to join; there is no membership fee.

Sun Holidays (26 Sixth St., Suite 603, Stamford, CT 06905; phone: 203-323-1166 in Connecticut; 800-243-2057 elsewhere in the US). This company specializes in extended-stay packages for senior citizens, including stays in Portugal's Algarve.

Many travel agencies, particularly the larger ones, are delighted to make presentations to help a group of senior citizens select destinations. A local chamber of commerce should be able to provide the names of such agencies. Once a time and place are determined, an organization member or travel agent can obtain group quotations for transportation, accommodations, meal plans, and sightseeing. Larger groups usually get the best breaks.

Another choice open to older travelers is a trip that includes an educational element. *Elderhostel,* a nonprofit organization, offers programs at educational institutions worldwide, including Braga, Evora, and Sintra, in Portugal. The foreign programs generally last about 3 weeks, and include double-occupancy accommodations in hotels or student residence halls and all meals. Travel to the programs usually is by designated scheduled flights, and participants can arrange to extend their stay at the end of the program. Elderhostelers must be at least 60 years old (younger if a spouse or companion qualifies), in good health, and not in need of special diets. For a free catalogue describing the program and current offerings, write to *Elderhostel* (75 Federal St., Boston, MA 02110; phone: 617-426-7788). Those interested in the program also can purchase an informational videotape for $5.

Interhostel, a program sponsored by the Division of Continuing Education of the

University of New Hampshire, sends travelers back to school at cooperating institutions in 25 countries on 4 continents. Participants attend lectures on the history, economy, politics, and cultural life of the country they are visiting, go on field trips to pertinent points of interest, and take part in activities meant to introduce them to their foreign contemporaries. In Portugal, participants study in both Lisbon and Porto. Trips are for 2 weeks; accommodations are on campus in university residence halls or off campus in modest hotels (double occupancy). Groups are limited to 35 to 40 participants who are at least 50 years old (or at least 40 if a participating spouse is at least 50), physically active, and not in need of special diets. For further information or to receive the three free seasonal catalogues, contact *Interhostel,* UNH Division of Continuing Education, 6 Garrison Ave., Durham, NH 03824 (phone: 800-733-9753 or 603-862-1147).

Hints for Traveling with Children

What better way to encounter the world's variety than in the company of the young, wide-eyed members of your family? Their presence does not have to be a burden or excessive expense. The current generation of discounts for children and family package deals can make a trip together quite reasonable.

A family trip will be an investment in your children's future, making geography and history come alive to them, and leaving a sure memory that will be among the fondest you will share with them someday. Their insights will be refreshing to you; their impulses may take you to unexpected places with unexpected dividends.

PLANNING: Here are several hints for making a trip with children easy and fun.

1. Children, like everyone else, will derive more pleasure from a trip if they know something about their destination before they arrive. Begin their education about a month before you leave. Using maps, travel magazines, and books, give children a clear idea of where you are going and how far away it is.
2. Children should help to plan the itinerary, and where you go and what you do should reflect some of their ideas. If they already know something about the sites they'll visit, they will have the excitement of recognition when they arrive.
3. Children also will enjoy learning some Portuguese phrases — a few basics like *ola* (hello), *adeus* (good-bye), and *obrigado/obrigada* (thanks).
4. Familiarize your children with escudos. Give them an allowance for the trip, and be sure they understand just how far it will or won't go.
5. Give children specific responsibilities: The job of carrying their own flight bags and looking after their personal things, along with some other light chores, will give them a stake in the journey.
6. Give each child a diary or scrapbook to take along.

Children's books about Portugal provide an excellent introduction to to the country and its culture. Sources of children's books include libraries, general bookstores, and the following stores specializing in children's books:

Books of Wonder (132 7th Ave., New York, NY 10011; phone: 212-989-3270; or 464 Hudson St., New York, NY 10014; phone: 212-645-8006). Carries both new and used books for children.

Cheshire Cat (5512 Connecticut Ave. NW, Washington, DC 20015; phone: 202-244-3956). Specializes in books for children of all ages.

Eeyore's Books for Children (2212 Broadway, New York, NY 10024; phone:

212-362-0634; or 25 E. 83rd St., New York, NY 10028; phone: 212-988-3404). Carries an extensive selection of children's books; features a special travel section.

Reading Reptile, Books and Toys for Young Mammals (4120 Pennsylvania St., Kansas City, MO 64111; phone: 816-753-0441). Carries books for children and teens to age 15.

Red Balloon (891 Grand Ave., St. Paul, MN 55105; phone: 612-224-8320). Carries both new and used books for children.

White Rabbit Children's Books (7755 Girard Ave., La Jolla, CA 92037; phone: 619-454-3518). Carries books and music for children (and parents).

Another source of children's books perfect to take on the road is *The Family Travel Guides Catalogue.* This detailed booklet contains informative and amusing titles focusing on numerous countries, including Portugal. For instance, the *Travel Papers,* a series of short articles full of useful facts for families, covers Portugal. The *Travel Papers* and the catalogue are available from Carousel Press (PO Box 6061, Albany, CA 94706; phone: 415-527-5849), which also is the mail-order supplier of all titles.

For older children and parents alike, *Castle* (Houghton Mifflin; $14.95 hardcover; $7.95 paperback), by David Macaulay, uses text and drawings to show how castles were built in the 13th century, and is particularly suited to helping children learn about the castles they may see in Portugal. *Cathedral: The Story of Its Construction* (Houghton Mifflin; $15.95 hardcover; $7.95 paperback), by the same author, also is interesting and informative.

And just for parents, *Travel With Your Children* (*TWYCH;* 80 Eighth Ave., New York, NY 10011; phone: 212-206-0688) publishes a newsletter, *Family Travel Times,* that focuses on families with young travelers and offers helpful hints. An annual subscription (10 issues) is $35 and includes a copy of the "Airline Guide" issue (updated every other year), which focuses on the subject of flying with children. This special issue is available separately for $10.

Another newsletter devoted to family travel is *Getaways.* This quarterly publication provides reviews of family-oriented literature, activities, and useful travel tips. To subscribe, send $25 to *Getaways,* Att. Ms. Brooke Kane, PO Box 8282, McLean, VA 22107 (phone: 703-534-8747).

Also of interest to parents traveling with their children is *How to Take Great Trips With Your Kids,* by psychologist Sanford Portnoy and his wife, Joan Flynn Portnoy. The book includes helpful tips from fellow family travelers, tips on economical accommodations and touring by car, recreational vehicle, and train, as well as over 50 games to play with your children en route. It is available for $8.95, plus shipping and handling, from Harvard Common Press, 535 Albany St., Boston, MA 02118 (phone: 617-423-5803). Another title worth seeking is *Great Vacations with Your Kids,* by Dorothy Jordan (Dutton; $12.95)

Another book on family travel, *Travel with Children* by Maureen Wheeler, offers a wide range of practical tips on traveling with children, and includes accounts of the author's family travel experiences. It is available for $10.95, plus shipping and handling, from Lonely Planet Publications, Embarcadero West, 112 Linden St., Oakland, CA 94607 (phone: 510-893-8555).

Finally, parents arranging a trip with their children may want to contact *Let's Take the Kids* (1268 Devon Ave., Los Angeles, CA 90024; phone: 800-726-4349 or 213-274-7088), an information service specializing in family travel. Although they do not arrange or book trips, this organization provides parents with information and advice on questions they may have about accommodations, itineraries, transportation, and other aspects of a planned vacation. They also offer a parent travel network, whereby parents who have been to a particular destination can evaluate it for others.

GETTING THERE AND GETTING AROUND: Begin early to investigate all available discounts and charter flights, as well as any package deals and special rates offered by the major airlines. Booking is sometimes required up to 2 months in advance. You may well find that charter companies offer no reductions for children, or not enough to offset the risk of last-minute delays or other inconveniences to which charters are subject. The major scheduled airlines, on the other hand, almost invariably provide hefty discounts for children on flights to and from Europe. If traveling by ship, note that children under 12 usually travel at considerably reduced fares on cruise lines. When using local transportation such as a bus or train, ask about lower fares for children or family rates.

Plane – When you make your reservations, tell the airline that you are traveling with a child. Children ages 2 through 12 generally travel at about a half to two-thirds of the regular full-fare adult ticket price on most international flights. This regular children's fare, however, usually is much higher than the excursion fare (which also may be even further reduced for children). On many international flights, children under 2 travel at about 10% of the adult fare if they sit on an adult's lap. A second infant without a second adult would pay the fare applicable to children ages 2 through 11.

Although some airlines will, on request, supply bassinets for infants, most carriers encourage parents to bring their own safety seat on board, which then is strapped into the airline seat with a regular seat belt. This is much safer — and certainly more comfortable — than holding the child in your lap. If you do not purchase a seat for your baby, you have the option of bringing the infant restraint along on the off chance that there might be an empty seat next to yours — in which case some airlines will let you use that seat at no charge for your baby and infant seat. However, if there is no empty seat available, the infant seat no doubt will have to be checked as baggage (and you may have to pay an additional charge), since it generally does not fit under airplane seats or in the overhead racks. The safest bet is to pay for a seat.

Be forewarned: Some safety seats designed primarily for use in cars do not fit into plane seats properly. Although nearly all seats manufactured since 1985 carry labels indicating whether they meet federal standards for use aboard planes, actual seat sizes may vary from carrier to carrier. At the time of this writing, the FAA was in the process of reviewing and revising the federal regulations regarding infant travel and safety devices — it was still to be determined if children should be *required* to sit in safety seats and whether the airlines will have to provide them.

If using one of these infant restraints, you should try to get bulkhead seats, which will provide extra room to care for your child during the flight. You also should request a bulkhead seat when using a bassinet — again, this is not as safe as strapping the child in. On some planes bassinets hook into a bulkhead wall; on others they are placed on the floor in front of you. (Note that bulkhead seats often are reserved for families traveling with children.) As a general rule, babies should be held during takeoff and landing.

Request seats on the aisle if you have a toddler or if you think you will need to use the bathroom frequently. Carry onto the plane all you will need to care for and occupy your children during the flight — formula, diapers, a sweater, books, favorite stuffed animals, and so on. Dress your baby simply, with a minimum of buttons and snaps, because the only place you may have to change a diaper is at your seat or in a small lavatory. The flight attendant can warm a bottle for you.

On US carriers, you also can ask for a hot dog, hamburger, or even a fruit plate, instead of the airline's regular lunch or dinner if you give at least 24 hours' notice. Some, but not all, airlines have baby food aboard. While you should bring along toys from home, also ask about children's diversions. Some carriers have terrific free packages of games, coloring books, and puzzles.

When the plane takes off and lands, make sure your baby is nursing or has a bottle, pacifier, or thumb in its mouth. This sucking will make the child swallow and help to clear stopped ears. A piece of hard candy will do the same thing for an older child.

Parents traveling by plane with toddlers, children, or young teenagers may want to consult *When Kids Fly,* a free booklet published by *Massport* (Public Affairs Department, 10 Park Plaza, Boston, MA 02116-3971; phone: 617-973-5600), which includes helpful information on airfares for children, infant seats, what to do in the event of overbooked or cancelled flights, and so on.

■ **Note:** Newborn babies, whose lungs may not be able to adjust to the altitude, should not be taken aboard an airplane. And some airlines may refuse to allow a pregnant woman in her 8th or 9th month to fly. Check with the airline ahead of time, and carry a letter from your doctor stating that you are fit to travel — and indicating the estimated date of birth.

Ship, Train, and Bus – Some shipping lines offer cruises that feature special activities for children, particularly during periods that coincide with major school holidays like *Christmas, Easter,* and the summer months. On such cruises, children may be charged special cut-rate fares, and there are youth counselors to organize activities. Occasionally, a shipping line even offers free passage during the summer months for children under age 16 occupying a stateroom with two (full-fare) adult passengers. Your travel agent should know which cruise lines offer such programs.

If you plan to travel by train when abroad, note that on some Portuguese railways children under 4 (accompanied by an adult) travel free, provided they do not occupy a seat; children under 4 occupying a seat and from ages 4 through 11 also often travel at a lower fare. The Eurailpass, which is good for unlimited train travel throughout Europe, including Portugal, is half price for children ages 4 through 12. It must be bought before leaving the US, so plan ahead. Some regional bus lines also may have lower fares for children or family rates. For more information, see *Traveling by Ship, Traveling by Train,* and *Traveling by Bus,* all in this section.

Car – Touring by car allows the greatest flexibility for traveling and packing. Games and simple toys, such as magnetic checkerboards or drawing pencils and pads, also provide a welcome diversion. And frequent stops so that children can run around make car travel much easier.

ACCOMMODATIONS AND MEALS: Often a cot for a child will be placed in a hotel room at little or no extra charge. If you wish to sleep in separate rooms, special rates sometimes are available for families; some places do not charge for children under a certain age. In many of the larger chain hotels, the staffs are more used to children. These hotels also are likely to have swimming pools or gamerooms — both popular with most youngsters. Many large resorts also have recreation centers for children. Cabins, bungalows, condominiums, and other rental options offer families privacy, flexibility, some kitchen facilities, and often lower costs.

You might want to look into accommodations along the way that will add to the color of your trip. For instance, the many *pousadas* and *pensões* in Portugal provide a delightful experience for the whole family and permit a view of Portuguese life different from that gained by staying in a conventional hotel. Children will love them.

Among the least expensive options is a camping facility; many are situated in beautiful, out-of-the-way spots, and generally are good and well equipped, and less expensive than any hotel. For further information on accommodations options for the whole family, see our discussions in *On the Road,* and for information on camping facilities, see *Camping and Caravanning, Hiking and Biking,* in this section.

Although it is difficult to find adequate baby-sitting services in most Portuguese cities, most better hotels will try to arrange for a sitter for the times you will want to be without the children — for an evening's entertainment or a particularly rigorous stint of sightseeing. Whether the sitter is hired directly or through an agency, ask for and check references and keep in mind that the candidates may not speak much, if any, English.

At mealtime, don't deny yourself or your children the delights of a new style of cooking. Encourage them to try new foods. Children like to know what kind of food to expect, so it will be interesting to look up Portuguese dishes before leaving. In metropolitan and resort areas, you may be able to find American-style food, but you probably will have to settle for local fare everywhere else. And don't forget about picnics. Note that although milk is pasteurized and water is potable in Portugal, it's wise to stick to bottled water for small children and for those with sensitive stomachs.

Things to Remember

1. If you are spending your vacation touring many places, pace the days with children in mind. Break the trip into half-day segments, with running around or "doing" time built in. Keep travel time on the road to a maximum of 4 to 5 hours a day.
2. Don't forget that a child's attention span is far shorter than an adult's. Children don't have to see every sight or all of any sight to learn something from their trip; watching, playing with, and talking to other children can be equally enlightening.
3. Let your children lead the way sometimes; their perspective is different from yours, and they may lead you to things you would never have noticed on your own.
4. Remember the places that children love to visit: aquariums, zoos, amusement parks, beaches, nature trails, and so on. Among the activities that may pique their interest are bicycling, snorkeling, boat trips, horseback riding, visiting children's museums, and viewing natural habitat exhibits.

On the Road

Credit and Currency

It may seem hard to believe, but one of the greatest (and least understood) costs of travel is money itself. If that sounds simplistic, consider the fact that you can lose as much as 30% of your dollar's value simply by changing money at the wrong place or in the wrong form. Your one single objective in relation to the care and retention of your travel funds is to make them stretch as far as possible. When you do spend money, it should be on things that expand and enhance your travel experience, with no buying power lost due to carelessness or lack of knowledge. This requires more than merely ferreting out the best airfare or the most charming budget hotel. It means being canny about the management of money itself. Herewith, a primer on making money go as far as possible overseas.

CURRENCY: The basic unit of Portuguese currency is the *escudo.* This is divided into 100 *centavos.* The escudo is abbreviated with a dollar sign, which takes the place of the decimal point in US currency. Coins are issued for 2$50, 5, 10, 20, 50, and 100 escudos. Bank notes are in denominations of 100, 500, 1,000, 5,000, and 10,000 escudos. The value of Portuguese currency in relation to the US dollar fluctuates daily, affected by a wide variety of phenomena.

Although US dollars may be accepted in Portugal (particularly at points of entry), you certainly will lose a percentage of your dollar's buying power if you do not take the time to convert it into escudos. By paying for goods and services in the local currency, you save money by not negotiating invariably unfavorable exchange rates for every small purchase, and avoid difficulty where US currency is not readily — or happily — accepted. *Throughout this book, unless specifically stated otherwise, prices are given in US dollars.*

There is no limit to the amount of US currency that can be brought into Portugal. To avoid problems anywhere along the line, it's advisable to fill out any customs forms provided when leaving the US on which you can declare all money you are taking with you — cash, traveler's checks, and so on. US law requires that anyone taking more than $10,000 into or out of the US must report this fact on customs form No. 4790, which is available at all international airports or from any office of US Customs. If taking over $10,000 out of the US, you must report this *before* leaving the US; if returning with such an amount, you must include this information on your customs declaration. Although travelers usually are not questioned by customs officials about currency when entering or leaving, the sensible course is to observe all regulations just to be on the safe side.

FOREIGN EXCHANGE: Because of the volatility of exchange rates, be sure to check the current value of the Portuguese escudo before finalizing any travel budget. And before you actually depart on your trip, be aware of the most advantageous exchange rates offered by various financial institutions — US banks, currency exchange firms (at home or abroad), or Portuguese banks.

For the best sense of current trends, follow the rates posted in the financial section of your local newspaper or in such international newspapers as the *International Herald Tribune.* You also can check with your own bank or with *Thomas Cook Foreign Exchange* (for the nearest location, call 800-972-2192 in Illinois; 800-621-0666 elsewhere in the US). *Harold Reuter and Company,* a currency exchange service in New York City (200 Park Ave., Suite 332 E., New York, NY 10166; phone: 212-661-0826), is particularly helpful in determining current trends in exchange rates. *Ruesch International* offers up-to-date foreign currency information and currency-related services (such as converting foreign currency VAT refund checks into US dollars; see *Duty-Free Shopping and Value Added Tax,* in this section). *Ruesch* also offers a pocket-size *Foreign Currency Guide* (good for estimating equivalents while planning) and a helpful brochure, *6 Foreign Exchange Tips for the Traveler.* Contact *Ruesch International* at one of the following addresses: 3 First National Plaza, Suite 2020, Chicago, IL 60602 (phone: 312-332-5900); 1925 Century Park E., Suite 240, Los Angeles, CA 90067 (phone: 213-277-7800); 608 Fifth Ave., "Swiss Center," New York, NY 10020 (phone: 212-977-2700); or 1350 Eye St. NW, 10th Floor and street level, Washington, DC 20005 (phone: 800-424-2923 or 202-408-1200).

In Portugal, you will find the official rate of exchange posted in banks, airports, money exchange houses, hotels, and some shops. As a general rule, expect to get more local currency for your US dollar at banks than at any other commercial establishment. Exchange rates do change from day to day, and most banks offer the same (or very similar) exchange rates. (In a pinch, the convenience of exchanging money in your hotel — sometimes on a 24-hour basis — *may* make up for the difference in the exchange rate.) Don't try to bargain in banks or hotels — no one will alter the rates for you.

Money exchange houses *(cambios)* are financial institutions that charge a fee for the service of exchanging dollars for local currency. When considering alternatives, be aware that although the rate varies among these establishments, the rates of exchange offered are bound to be slightly less favorable than the terms offered at nearby banks — again, don't be surprised if you get fewer escudos for your dollar than the rate published in the papers.

That said, however, the following rules of thumb are worth remembering:

Rule number one: Never (repeat: *never*) exchange more than $10 dollars for foreign currency at hotels, restaurants, or retail shops. If you do, you are sure to lose a significant amount of your US dollar's buying power. If you do come across a storefront exchange counter offering what appears to be an incredible bargain, there's too much counterfeit specie in circulation to take the chance. (See Rule number three, below.)

Rule number two: Estimate your needs carefully; if you overbuy, you lose twice — buying and selling back. Every time you exchange money, someone is making a profit, and rest assured it isn't you. Use up foreign notes before leaving, saving just enough for last-minute incidentals and tips.

Rule number three: Don't buy money on the black market. The exchange rate may be better, but it is a common practice to pass off counterfeit bills to unsuspecting foreigners who aren't familiar with the local currency. It's usually a sucker's game, and you almost always are the sucker; it also can land you in jail.

Rule number four: Learn the local currency quickly and keep abreast of daily fluctuations in the exchange rate. These are listed in the English-language *International Herald Tribune* daily for the preceding day, as well as in every major newspaper in Europe. Rates change to some degree every day. For rough calculations, it is quick and safe to use round figures, but for purchases and actual currency exchanges, carry a small pocket calculator to help you compute the exact rate. Inexpensive calculators specifically designed to convert currency amounts for travelers are widely available.

When changing money, don't be afraid to ask how much commission you're being charged, and the exact amount of the prevailing exchange rate. In fact, in any exchange of money for goods or services, you should work out the rate before making any payment.

TIP PACKS: It's not a bad idea to buy a *small* amount of Portuguese coins and banknotes before your departure. But note the emphasis on "small," because, for the most part, you are better off carrying the bulk of your travel funds to Portugal in US dollar traveler's checks (see below). Still, the advantages of tip packs are threefold:

1. You become familiar with the currency (really the only way to guard against making mistakes or being cheated during your first few hours in a new country).
2. You are guaranteed some money should you arrive when a bank or exchange counter isn't open or available.
3. You don't have to depend on hotel desks, porters, or taxi drivers to change your money.

A "tip pack" is the only foreign currency you should buy before you leave. If you do run short upon arrival, US dollars often are accepted at points of entry. In other areas, they either *may* be accepted, or someone may accommodate you by changing a small amount — though invariably at a less than advantageous rate.

TRAVELER'S CHECKS: It's wise to carry traveler's checks while on the road instead of (or in addition to) cash, since it's possible to replace them if they are stolen or lost; you usually can receive partial or full replacement funds the same day if you have your purchase receipt and proper identification. Issued in various denominations and available in both US dollars and Portuguese escudos, with adequate proof of identification (credit cards, driver's license, passport), traveler's checks are as good as cash in most hotels, restaurants, stores, and banks.

You will be able to cash traveler's checks fairly easily throughout Portugal, but don't expect to meander into a small village and be able to get instant cash. Also, even in metropolitan areas, don't assume that restaurants, small shops, and other establishments are going to be able to change checks of large denominations. Worldwide, more and more establishments are beginning to restrict the amount of traveler's checks they will accept or cash, so it is wise to purchase at least some of your checks in small denominations — say, $10 and $20. Also, don't expect to change them into US dollars except at banks and international airports.

Although traveler's checks are available in some foreign currencies, such as Portuguese escudos — at press time, only from *Thomas Cook* — the exchange rates offered by the issuing companies in the US generally are far less favorable than those available from banks both in the US and abroad. Therefore, it usually is better to carry the bulk of your travel funds abroad in US dollar–denomination traveler's checks.

Every type of traveler's check is legal tender in banks around the world, and each company guarantees full replacement if checks are lost or stolen. After that the similarity ends. Some charge a fee for purchase, others are free; you can buy traveler's checks at almost any bank, and some are available by mail. Most important, each traveler's check issuer differs slightly in its refund policy — the amount refunded immediately, the accessibility of refund locations, the availability of a 24-hour refund service, and the time it will take for you to receive replacement checks. For instance, *American Express* guarantees replacement of lost or stolen traveler's checks in under 3 hours at any *American Express* office — other companies may not be as prompt. (Note that *American Express*'s 3-hour policy is based on a traveler's being able to provide the serial numbers of the lost checks. Without these numbers, refunds can take much longer.)

We cannot overemphasize the importance of knowing how to replace lost or stolen checks. All of the traveler's check companies have agents around the world, both in their own name and at associated agencies (usually, but not necessarily, banks), where refunds can be obtained during business hours. Most of them also have 24-hour toll-free telephone lines and some will provide emergency funds to tide you over on a Sunday.

Be sure to make a photocopy of the refund instructions that will be given to you by the issuing institution at the time of purchase. To avoid complications should you need to redeem lost checks (and to speed up the replacement process), keep the purchase receipt and an accurate list, by serial number, of the checks that have been spent or cashed. You may want to incorporate this information in an "emergency packet," also including your passport number and date of issue, the numbers of the credit cards you are carrying, and any other bits of information you shouldn't be without. Always keep these records separate from the checks and the original records themselves (you may want to give them to a traveling companion to hold).

Although most people understand the desirability of carrying funds in the form of traveler's checks as protection against loss or theft, an equally good reason is that US dollar traveler's checks invariably get a better rate of exchange than cash does — usually by at least 1% (although the discrepancy has been known to be substantially higher). The reasons for this are technical, but potential savings exist and it is a fact of travel life that should not be ignored.

That 1% won't do you much good, however, if you already have spent it *buying* your traveler's checks. Several of the major traveler's check companies charge 1% for the acquisition of their checks. To receive fee-free traveler's checks you may have to meet certain qualifications — for instance, *Thomas Cook*'s checks issued in US currency are free if you make your travel arrangements through its travel agency. *American Express* traveler's checks are available without charge to members of the *American Automobile Association.* Holders of some credit cards (such as the *American Express Platinum* card) also may be entitled to free traveler's checks. The issuing institution (e.g., the particular bank at which you purchase them) may itself charge a fee. If you purchase traveler's checks at a bank in which you or your company maintains significant accounts (especially commercial accounts of some size), the bank may absorb the 1% fee as a courtesy.

■ **Note:** *American Express* cardholders now can order traveler's checks by phone through a new service called *Cheques On Call.* By dialing 800-55-FOR-TC, *Green* cardholders can order up to $1,000, *Gold* cardholders, $2,500, and *Platinum* cardholders, $10,000 of *American Express* traveler's checks during any 7-day period. In addition, the usual 1% acquisition fee is waived for *Gold* and *Platinum* cardholders. There is no postage charge if the checks are sent by first class mail; *Federal Express* delivery is available for a fee.

American Express, Bank of America, Citicorp, Thomas Cook, MasterCard, and *Visa* all offer traveler's checks. Here is a list of the major companies issuing traveler's checks and the numbers to call in the event that loss or theft makes replacement necessary:

American Express: To report lost or stolen checks in the US, call 800-221-7282. In Europe, *American Express* advises travelers to call 44-273-571600 (in Brighton, England), collect. Another (slower) option is to call 801-964-6665 (in the US), collect; or contact the nearest *American Express* office.

Bank of America: To report lost or stolen checks in the US, call 800-227-3460. In Portugal and elsewhere worldwide, call 415-624-5400 or 415-622-3800, collect.

Citicorp: To report lost or stolen checks in the US, call 800-645-6556 or 800-541-8882. In Portugal and elsewhere worldwide, call 813-623-1709 or 813-626-4444, collect. Customers also can contact *Citicorp*'s office in England, by calling 44-81-318-8950 or 44-71-982-4044, collect.

MasterCard: Note that *Thomas Cook MasterCard* (below) is now handling all *MasterCard* traveler's check inquiries and refunds.

Thomas Cook MasterCard: To report lost or stolen checks in the US, call 800-223-7373. In Portugal, call 609-987-7300 (in the US) or 44-733-502995 (in England), collect, and they will direct you to the nearest branch of *Thomas Cook.*

Visa: To report lost or stolen checks in the continental US, call 800-227-6811. In Portugal, call 415-574-7111, collect. In Europe, you also can call this London number collect: 44-71-937-8091.

CREDIT CARDS: Some establishments you might encounter during the course of your travels may not honor any credit cards and some may not honor all cards, so there is a practical reason to carry more than one. Most US credit cards, including the principal bank cards, are honored in Portugal; however, keep in mind that some cards may be issued under different names in Europe. For example, *MasterCard* may go under the name *Access* or *Eurocard,* and *Visa* often is called *Carte Bleue* — wherever these equivalents are accepted, *MasterCard* and *Visa* may be used. The following is a list of credit cards that enjoy wide domestic and international acceptance:

American Express: Cardholders can cash personal checks for traveler's checks and cash at *American Express* or its representatives' offices in the US up to the following limits (within any 21-day period): $1,000 for *Green* and *Optima* cardholders; $5,000 for *Gold* cardholders; and $10,000 for *Platinum* cardholders. Check cashing also is available to cardholders who are guests at participating hotels (up to $250), and for holders of airline tickets, at participating airlines (up to $50). Free travel accident, baggage, and car rental insurance if ticket or rental is charged to card; additional insurance also is available for additional cost. For further information or to report a lost or stolen *American Express* card, call 800-528-4800 throughout the continental US; in Portugal, contact a local *American Express* office or call 212-477-5700, collect.

Carte Blanche: Free travel accident, baggage, and car rental insurance if ticket or rental is charged to card; additional insurance also is available at additional cost. For medical, legal, and travel assistance worldwide, call 800-356-3448 throughout the US; in Portugal, call 214-680-6480, collect. For further information or to report a lost or stolen *Carte Blanche* card, call 800-525-9135 throughout the US; in Portugal, call 303-790-2433, collect.

Diners Club: Emergency personal check cashing for cardholders staying at participating hotels and motels (up to $250 per stay). Free travel accident, baggage, and car rental insurance if ticket or rental is charged to card; additional insurance also is available for an additional fee. For medical, legal, and travel assistance worldwide, call 800-356-3448 throughout the US; in Portugal, call 214-680-6480, collect. For further information or to report a lost or stolen *Diners Club* card, call 800-525-9135 throughout the US; in Portugal, call 303-790-2433, collect.

Discover Card: Offered by a subsidiary of Sears, Roebuck & Co., it provides cardholders with cash advances at numerous automatic teller machines and *Sears* stores throughout the US. For further information and to report a lost or stolen *Discover* card, call 800-DISCOVER throughout the US; elsewhere worldwide, call 302-323-7652, collect. Note that, at press time, the *Discover* card was not yet accepted in Portugal; call for current information when planning your trip.

MasterCard: Cash advances are available at participating banks worldwide. Check with your issuing bank for information. *MasterCard* also offers a 24-hour emergency lost card service; call 800-826-2181 throughout the US; in Portugal and elsewhere worldwide, call 314-275-6690, collect.

Visa: Cash advances are available at participating banks worldwide. Check with your issuing bank for information. *Visa* also offers a 24-hour emergency lost card service; call 800-336-8472 throughout the US. In Portugal, call 415-574-7700, collect.

One of the thorniest problems relating to the use of credit cards abroad concerns the rate of exchange at which a purchase is charged. Be aware that the exchange rate in effect on the date that you make a foreign purchase or pay for a foreign service has nothing at all to do with the rate of exchange at which your purchase is billed to you when you get the invoice (sometimes months later) in the US. The amount that the credit card company charges is either a function of the exchange rate at which the establishment's bank processed it or the rate in effect on the day your charge is received at the credit card center. (There is a 1-year limit on the time a hotel or other business can take to forward its charge slips.)

The principle at work in this credit card–exchange rate roulette is simple, but very hard to predict. You make a purchase at a particular dollar versus local currency exchange rate. If the dollar gets stronger in the time between purchase and billing, your purchase actually costs you less than you anticipated. If the dollar drops in value during the interim, you pay more than you thought you would. There isn't much you can do about these vagaries except to follow one very broad, very clumsy rule of thumb: If the dollar is doing well at the time of purchase, its value increasing against the local currency, use your credit card on the assumption that it still will be doing well when billing takes place. If the dollar is doing badly, assume it will continue to do badly and pay with traveler's checks or cash. If you get too badly stuck, the best recourse is to complain, loudly. Be aware, too, that most credit card companies charge an unannounced, un-itemized 1% fee for converting foreign currency charges to US dollars.

SENDING MONEY ABROAD: If you have used up your traveler's checks, cashed as many emergency personal checks as your credit card allows, drawn on your cash advance line to the fullest extent, and still need money, it is possible to have it sent to you via the *Western Union Telegraph Company* (phone: 800-325-4176 throughout the US). A friend or relative can go, cash in hand, to any *Western Union* office in the US, where, for a *minimum* charge of $13 (it rises with the amount of the transaction), plus a $25 surcharge, the funds will be transferred to a participating *Banco Espirito Santo, Western Union*'s correspondent bank in Portugal. (The Portuguese cities to which money can be wired via *Western Union* are Coimbra, Faro, Lisbon, and Porto.) When the money arrives, you will not be notified — you must go to the bank to inquire. Transfers generally take anywhere from 2 to 5 business days, although the wait may be much longer, particularly in remote areas. The funds will be turned over in local currency, based on the rate of exchange in effect on the day of receipt. For a higher fee, the US party to this transaction may call *Western Union* with a *MasterCard* or *Visa* number to send up to $2,000, although larger transfers will be sent to a predesignated location.

If you are literally down to your last centavo, and you have no other way to obtain cash, the nearest US consulate (see *Legal Aid and Consular Services,* in this section) will let you call home to set these matters in motion.

CASH MACHINES: Automatic teller machines (ATMs) are increasingly common worldwide. Some financial institutions offer exclusive automatic teller machines for their own customers only at bank branches. If your bank participates in one of the international ATM networks (most do), the bank will issue you a "cash card" along with a personal identification code or number (also called a PIC or PIN). You can use this card at any ATM in the same electronic network to check your account balances, transfer monies between checking and savings accounts, and — most important for a traveler — withdraw cash instantly. Network ATMs generally are located in banks, commercial and transportation centers, and near major tourist attractions. The cash or credit cards accepted by a given machine usually are clearly indicated.

At the time of this writing, the ATMs which *are* connected generally belong to one of two international networks, *CIRRUS* (phone: 800-4-CIRRUS), which is owned by *MasterCard*, or *PLUS* (phone: 800-THE-PLUS), which is owned by *Visa*.

As we went to press, *CIRRUS/MasterCard* was expanding its operations into Portugal, with more than 1,200 locations scheduled to be opened this year. Although *PLUS/Visa* had no immediate plans to add Portuguese ATM locations, travelers can use their *Visa* cards at more than 1,300 ATMs in Portugal to withdraw cash against their credit lines.

Information about the *CIRRUS* and *PLUS* systems also is available at member bank branches, where you can obtain free booklets listing the locations of machines worldwide. Note that a recent change in banking regulations permits financial institutions *in the US* to subscribe to *both* the *CIRRUS* and *PLUS* systems, allowing users of either network to withdraw funds from ATMs at participating banks. This change does not, however, apply to banks in Portugal (and in Europe in general), and remember, regulations there may vary.

Accommodations

From elegant, centuries-old castle resorts to modern, functional high-rises and modest, inexpensive inns, it's still possible to be comfortable and well cared for on almost any budget in Portugal. Admittedly, prices for hotel accommodations in the major cities, such as Lisbon, have risen somewhat in recent years, and the Algarve is full of deluxe establishments providing expensive services to people with money to burn, but more affordable alternatives always have been available, particularly in the countryside.

In fact, generally speaking, those watching their wallets will be pleased to find as broad a selection of accommodations in their price range as at home, with probably more inexpensive to moderately priced establishments than in many other countries in Europe. Portugal has long been one of the European destinations where the cost of living is lowest, and it still is relatively affordable, despite inflation and the recent decline in the strength of the US dollar. At the lower end of the price scale, you will not necessarily have to forgo charm. While a fair number of inexpensive establishments are simply no-frills, "generic" places to spend the night, even the sparest room may have the cachet of once having been the nightly retreat of a monk or nun. And some of the most delightful places to stay in Portugal are the smaller, less expensive, often family-run small inns, and *pensões*.

Once upon a time, such things as the superiority of New World plumbing made many of the numerous, less expensive accommodations alternatives unacceptable for North Americans. Today, the gap has closed considerably, and in Portugal the majority of hostelries catering to the tourist trade are likely to be at least adequate in their basic facilities.

HOTELS, INNS, AND GUESTHOUSES: Information on accommodations is available from the Portuguese National Tourist Office in the US. In addition to a broad range of individual brochures focusing on particular types of accommodation and regions of Portugal, they offer a large, comprehensive guide to accommodations throughout the country called *Portugal Hotel Guide*. Each listing in this publication includes detailed information on and standardized ratings of the type and quality of facilities.

Portuguese hotels are classified from 5 stars (the highest rating) through 1 star (the lowest). Other rated accommodations include *estalagens* (*estalagem* in the singular), which are 5-star and 4-star inns, and *albergarias*, also inns, but all 4 stars (historically, these were less sophisticated hostelries than *estalagens*, although there is little difference between the two today). Generally more modest are *pensões* (*pensão* in the singular), 4-star through 1-star boardinghouses that often occupy only part of a building otherwise devoted to apartments or offices. Some *pensões* require guests to take one or more meals besides breakfast, while others may not serve any other meals than breakfast. In Portugal, any hotel, inn, or pension that calls itself a *residência* (an R follows its name in publications of the tourist office) serves breakfast but no other meals.

The Portuguese National Tourist Office also provides information on Portugal's *pousadas* (see below), its few motels, and a variety of apartment hotels and other furnished apartments suitable for vacationers (see "Rental Options," below). Their various publications include the star category of each establishment, its address and phone number, and the number of rooms with and without private baths. Prices are not given, although the tourist office also distributes information sheets showing average room rates in high season and low season for each category of accommodation, apartments excepted. Generally, high season runs from April through October everywhere in Portugal but Madeira, where winter is the busy season accompanied by the highest prices.

Establishments in Portugal have signs outside showing the category to which they belong and their star ratings. Room prices, which include a 10% to 15% service charge and 17% Value Added Tax (IVA), are posted in individual bedrooms, along with the prices of meals if they are offered. Note that the price of the room always includes a continental breakfast. A single room is a *quarto individual,* a double room a *quarto duplo,* or, more specifically, a *quarto com duas camas* (with twin beds) or a *quarto de casal* (with a double bed). Rooms with private baths are *com banho;* those without are *sem banho.* In most establishments, however, rooms that have no private bathroom do have a sink with hot and cold running water. When one person occupies a double room, the price of one breakfast is deducted from the room rate. When an extra bed is added to a room, the price increases by 30% in most accommodations, by 25% in apartment hotels and motels. Should there be any complaints, hotels in Portugal often have an official complaints book — *livro de reclamações* — in which guests may register serious dissatisfaction.

For those who prefer to reserve in advance, a number of well-known hotel chains or associations have properties in Portugal, particularly in major cities. Among these are the following (with toll-free reservations numbers to call in the US):

Best Western (phone: 800-528-1234). Has over 25 properties in Portugal.

Forte Hotels International (formerly *Trusthouse Forte;* phone: 800-225-5843). Has 2 properties in the Algarve — in Pinina and in Vala de Lobo.

Hilton International (phone: 800-445-8667). Owned by the Ladbroke's gambling group of Great Britain, there is no proprietary connection with the US *Hilton* chain. Has 1 hotel in Lisbon.

Holiday Inn (phone: 800-465-4329). Has 2 properties in Lisbon.

Inter-Continental (phone: 800-327-0200). Has 1 property in Lisbon.

Meridien (phone: 800-543-4300). Has 1 hotel in Lisbon and 1 in Porto.

Minotels Europe (phone: 800-336-4668). Has 6 properties in Portugal; one each in Albufeira, Cascais, Faro, and Leiria, and 2 in Lisbon.

Sheraton (phone: 800-325-3535). Has 3 properties, one each in Albufeira, Lisbon, and Porto.

Among other large European chains which have a US office that will provide information and take reservations is *Pullman Sofitel.* This group, comprising the recently merged *Pullman* and *Sofitel* chains, has 1 property in Portugal. *Novotel,* under the same ownership, has approximately 250 3-star hotels throughout Europe, 3 of them in Portugal. *Pullman Sofitel* and *Novotels* are represented by *Resinter Reservations* (2 Overhill Rd., Scarsdale, NY 10583; phone: 800-221-4542). Reservations for all *Pull-*

man Sofitel properties also can be made through *Utell International* (810 N. 96th St., Omaha, NE 68114; phone: 800-44-UTELL), which represents over 2,000 properties throughout Europe, including over 50 in Portugal. Note, finally, that *Marketing Ahead* (433 Fifth Ave., New York, NY 10016; phone: 212-686-9213) represents numerous independent hotels in Portugal, and also makes reservations for Portugal's *pousadas* (see below). There are several other stateside reservations services for individual Portuguese hotels. The Portuguese tourist offices should be able to tell you who in the US represents a particular property.

Pousadas – Portugal boasts a network of state-owned inns — *pousadas* — that are among the most interesting hostelries in Europe. In 1940, Portugal took its cue from Spain's system of *paradores* and began this network of *pousadas,* which now is 32 inns strong. The program sponsors the reclaiming of abandoned historic or architecturally notable structures where private investment lags. Although only some *pousadas* are in historic buildings — such as those in the castles of Obidos, Palmela, and Estremoz or in the Lóios Monastery of Evora — all are in scenic areas and in regional styles of architecture that complement their surroundings. *Pousadas* tend to be small, ranging from 6 rooms to a maximum of 55 in the largest (*Pousada de Santa Marinha da Costa,* near Guimarães). All have modern conveniences and restaurants. *Pousadas* are not given a star rating along with the rest of Portugal's hotels; instead, they are divided into three categories (B, C, and CH, corresponding to inexpensive, moderate, and deluxe historic building).

The Portuguese tourist authority distributes an illustrated booklet — *Pousadas de Portugal* — that provides a somewhat better view of the background and attractions of the individual inns and details of the facilities at each. Prices are omitted, however, so ask for a rate sheet giving the average prices for inns in each category. Since *pousadas* are very popular, reservations are strongly recommended, particularly during the high season. In the US, they can be made through travel agents or *Marketing Ahead* (433 Fifth Ave., New York, NY 10016; phone: 212-686-9213). Note that some travel agents will make reservations only for stays of 3 or more nights per establishment; for shorter stays you may want to contact the *pousada* directly. In addition, several tour operators offer fly/drive packages featuring accommodations in *pousadas* (see *Package Tours,* in this section).

Manor Houses and Farmhouses – Travelers who prefer to stay in establishments that are less commercial than hotels, inns, or even *pousadas,* and who like to leave the beaten track and meet people as much as possible should investigate Portugal's *Turismo no Espaço Rural* (Tourism in the Country) program. This is a network of privately owned properties, from aristocratic 16th- and 17th-century manor houses to rustic farmhouses, that accommodate paying guests.

The program — which is like the *pousada* program in its origin as an attempt to preserve the country's heritage through tourism — began in the early 1980s, when the owners of many of Portugal's finest old estates received low-interest government loans to restore their homes and open them to overnight visitors. Initially, the program was known as *Turismo de Habitação* (Tourism in Private Houses), and its properties, largely concentrated in northern Portugal, were the country manors of some of the nation's oldest families. Indeed, a number of the properties were (and are) not merely *solares* and *quintas* — manor houses and country mansions — but *paços,* a word indicating that, at some time in the past, a king slept on the premises. Given the success of the program, it rapidly spread to the rest of Portugal and grew to include other types of country properties. Thus, *Turismo de Habitação (TH)* was joined by *Turismo Rural (TR),* which includes homes that are more modest than the manor houses but still characteristically regional in their architecture (they can be in the countryside or in villages), and by *Agroturismo (AG),* which includes rustic farmhouses. The new name, *Turismo no Espaço Rural (TER),* came into being to cover them all.

Whatever its classification, a house can offer as few as 1 or 2 double or single rooms or as many as 10, usually with private baths; at some properties, entirely independent apartments are available. Amenities can include swimming pools, tennis courts, gardens to walk in, and horses to ride. Prices cover a full range (depending on the level of luxury) for two people per day, including breakfast; some of the houses also serve lunch and dinner, if requested — in which case guests may eat with other paying guests or even with the host family, since, in most cases, the owner continues to live on the property.

The Portuguese National Tourist Office provides a list of participating houses. Reservations are then made directly with the proprietors or through the central booking offices of three owners' associations in Portugal. One of them, the *Associação de Turismo de Habitação (Turihab;* Praça da República, Ponte de Lima 4990, Portugal; phone: 58-942729), handles houses in the northern Minho region only (where the network of houses is thickest, however). The two others, representing properties throughout the country, are the *Associação das Casas em Turismo (ACT;* Alto da Pampilheira, Torre D-2 8-A, Cascais 2750, Portugal), whose marketing arm, *PIT* (phone: 1-286-7958), books the properties, and the *Associação Portuguesa de Turismo de Habitação (Privetur;* 209 Rua Castilho, Lisbon 1000, Portugal), whose reservations are handled by a travel agent, *Feriasol, Viajens e Turismo* (phone: 1-286-8232). Note that some houses do not belong to any association and, therefore, have to be booked directly. Note, too, that a minimum stay, 3 nights in the case of *Turihab,* 2 or 3 nights elsewhere, usually is imposed. Information on the program also is available from the *Direção Geral de Turismo, Divisão de Turismo no Espaço Rural* (86 Av. António Augusto de Aguiar, Lisbon 1000, Portugal; phone: 1-575015).

Relais & Châteaux – Most members of this association are in France, but the group has grown to include dozens of establishments in many other countries. At the time of this writing, this association had one member property in Portugal — *La Réserve* in Faro.

Relais & Châteaux members are of particular interest to travelers who wish lodgings reflecting the ambience, style, and, frequently, the history of the places they are visiting. Some properties actually are ancient castles or palaces — dating back more than 1,000 years — which have been converted into hotels. Others — the *relais* — are old inns, manor houses, even converted mills, convents, and monasteries. A few well-known city and resort establishments are included, but most are in quiet country settings, and frequently are graced with parks, ponds, and flowering gardens.

Members of the *Relais & Châteaux* group often are expensive, though no more than you would pay for deluxe, authentically elegant accommodations and service anywhere in the world (and many are not all that costly). Accommodations and service from one *relais* or château to another can range from simple but comfortable to elegantly deluxe, but they all maintain very high standards in order to retain their memberships, as they are reviewed annually. Most also have good restaurants.

An illustrated catalogue of all the *Relais & Châteaux* properties is published annually and is available for $7 from *Relais & Châteaux* (2400 Lazy Hollow, Suite 152D, Houston, TX 77063; phone: 800-743-8033 or 713-783-8033). The association also can provide information on member properties. Reservations can be made directly with the establishments or through a travel agency.

RENTAL OPTIONS: An attractive alternative for the visitor content to stay in one spot for a week or more is to rent one of the numerous properties available throughout Portugal. These offer a wide range of luxury and convenience, depending on the price you want to pay. One of the advantages of staying in a house, apartment (usually called a "flat" overseas), or other rented vacation home is that you will feel much more like a visitor than a tourist.

Known to Europeans as a "holiday let" or a "self-catering holiday," a vacation in a furnished rental has both the advantages and disadvantages of living "at home" abroad. It can be less expensive than staying in a first class hotel, although very luxurious and expensive rentals are available, too. It has the comforts of home, including a kitchen, which can mean potential savings on food. Furthermore, it gives a sense of the country that a large hotel often cannot. On the other hand, a certain amount of housework is involved because if you don't eat out, you have to cook, and though some rentals (especially the luxury ones) include a cleaning person, most don't. (If the rental doesn't include daily cleaning, arrangements often can be made with a nearby service.)

For a family, two or more couples, or a group of friends, the per-person cost — even for a luxurious rental — can be quite reasonable. Weekly and monthly rates are available to reduce costs still more. But best of all is the amount of space that no conventional hotel room can equal. As with hotels, the rates for properties in some areas are seasonal, rising during the peak travel season, while for others they remain the same year-round. To have your pick of the properties available, you should begin to make arrangements for a rental at least 6 months in advance.

There are several ways of finding a suitable rental property. Some of the possibilities are listed in the accommodations guides published by the Portuguese tourist authority. The choices include a variety of apartment hotels (rated 4 through 2 stars) and tourist apartments (1st, 2nd, and 3rd categories, with the 1st category the highest), as well as tourist villages, or *aldeamentos turistícos* (deluxe, 1st, and 2nd categories), all particularly prevalent in the Algarve. The information distributed by the Portuguese National Tourist Office in the US lists all three types, but the manor house program discussed above should also be considered as a source of rentals, since a number of properties have made independent apartments out of servants' quarters, wine cellars, stables, and other buildings on their estates.

Many tour operators regularly include a few rental packages among their offerings; these generally are available through a travel agent. In addition, a number of companies specialize in rental vacations. Their plans typically include rental of the property (or several properties, but usually for a minimum stay per location), a rental car, and airfare.

The companies listed below rent a wide range of properties in Portugal. They handle the booking and confirmation paperwork and can be expected to provide more information about the properties than that which might ordinarily be gleaned from a short listing in an accommodations guide.

At Home Abroad (405 E. 56th St., Apt. 6H, New York, NY 10022; phone: 212-421-9165). Modest to luxurious houses (some with pools) and a few apartments in the Algarve. Photographs of properties and a newsletter are available for a $50 registration fee applicable to the rental.

Eastone Overseas Accommodations (79 Forest Circle, Cooper City, FL 33458; phone: 305-435-3800). Handles a few apartments, but mostly villas and houses in northern Portugal and along the Atlantic coast.

Europa-Let (PO Box 3537, 92 N. Main St., Ashland, OR 97520; phone: 800-462-4486 or 503-482-5806). Rentals range from modest apartments to luxurious villas in the Algarve, north of Lisbon, and the Porto area.

Hideaways International (15 Goldsmith St., PO Box 1270, Littleton, MA 01460; phone: 800-843-4433 or 508-486-8955). Rents apartments, private homes, and villas throughout Portugal.

International Lodging Corp. (300 1st Ave., Suite 7C, New York, NY 10009; phone: 212-228-5900). Flats, villas, and some country homes in the vicinity of the Algarve.

Rent a Home International (7200 34th Ave. NW, Seattle, WA 98117; phone: 800-488-RENT or 206-789-9377). Represents a wide variety of properties in the Algarve and in and around Lisbon, including luxury villas and apartments.

Rent a Vacation Everywhere (*RAVE;* 383 Park Ave., Rochester, NY 14607; phone: 716-256-0760). Moderate to luxurious villas in the Algarve.

VHR Worldwide (235 Kensington Ave., Norwood, NJ 07648; phone: 201-767-9393 in New Jersey; 800-NEED-A-VILLA elsewhere in the US). Rents villas in the Algarve and in Sintra.

Villas International (605 Market St., Suite 510, San Francisco, CA 94105; phone: 800-221-2260 or 415-281-0910). The choices range from simple to luxurious houses and apartments in the Algarve, in Lisbon and its environs, and along the coast up to Porto.

And for further information, including a general discussion of all forms of vacation rentals, evaluating costs, and information on rental opportunities in Portugal, see *A Traveler's Guide to Vacation Rentals in Europe,* by Michael and Laura Murphy (Penguin; $11.95).

In addition, a useful publication, the *Worldwide Home Rental Guide,* lists properties throughout Portugal, as well as the managing agencies. Issued twice annually, single copies may be available at newsstands for $10 an issue. For a year's subscription, send $18 to *Worldwide Home Rental Guide,* PO Box 2842, Santa Fe, NM 87504 (phone: 505-988-5188).

When considering a particular vacation rental property, look for answers to the following questions:

- How do you get from the airport to the property?
- If the property is on the shore, how far is the nearest beach? Is it sandy or rocky, and is it safe for swimming?
- What size and number of beds are provided?
- How far is the property from whatever else is important to you, such as a golf course or nightlife?
- If there is no grocery store on the premises (which may be comparatively expensive, anyway), how far is the nearest market?
- Are baby-sitters, cribs, bicycles, or anything else you may need for your children available?
- Is maid service provided daily?
- Are air conditioning and/or a phone provided?
- Is a car rental part of the package? Is a car necessary?

Before deciding which rental is for you, make sure you have satisfactory answers to all your questions. Ask your travel agent to find out or call the company involved directly.

HOME EXCHANGES: Still another alternative for travelers who are content to stay in one place during their vacation is a home exchange: The Smith family from St. Louis moves into the home of the Cardoso family in Evora, while the Cardosos enjoy a stay in the Smiths' home. The home exchange is an exceptionally inexpensive way to ensure comfortable, reasonable living quarters with amenities that no hotel could possibly offer; often the trade includes a car. Moreover, it allows you to live in a new community in a way that few tourists ever do: For a little while, at least, you will become something of a resident.

Several companies publish directories of individuals and families willing to trade homes with others for a specific period of time. In some cases, you must be willing to list your own home in the directory; in others, you can subscribe without appearing in it. Most listings are for straight exchanges only, but each directory also has a number of listings placed by people interested in either exchanging or renting (for instance, if they own a second home). Other arrangements include exchanges of hospitality while owners are in residence, or youth exchanges, where your teenager is received as a guest in return for your welcoming their teenager at a later date. A few house-sitting opportunities also are available. In most cases, arrangements for the actual exchange take place directly between you and the foreign host. There is no guarantee that you will find a listing in the area in which you are interested, but each of the organizations noted below includes Portuguese homes among its hundreds or even thousands of foreign listings.

Home Base Holidays (7 Park Ave., London N13 5PG England; phone: 44-81-886-8752). For $48 a year, subscribers receive four listings, with an option to list in all four.

Intervac US/International Home Exchange Service (PO Box 590504, San Francisco, CA 94159; phone: 800-756-HOME or 415-435-3497). For $45 (plus postage) subscribers receive copies of the three directories published yearly, and are entitled to list their home in one of them; a photograph may be included with the listing for an additional $11. A $5 discount is given to travelers over age 62.

Loan-A-Home (2 Park La., Apt. 6E, Mt. Vernon, NY 10552; phone: 914-664-7640). Specializes in long-term (4 months or more — excluding July and August) housing arrangements worldwide for students, professors, businesspeople, and retirees, although its two annual directories (with supplements) carry a small list of short-term rentals and/or exchanges. $35 for a copy of one directory and one supplement; $45 for two directories and two supplements.

Vacation Exchange Club (PO Box 820, Haleiwa, HI 96712; phone: 800-638-3841). Some 10,000 listings. For $50, the subscriber receives two directories — one in late winter, one in the spring — and is listed in one.

Worldwide Home Exchange Club (13 Knightsbridge Green, London SW1X 7QL, England; phone: 44-71-589-6055; or 806 Brantford Ave., Silver Spring, MD 20904; phone: 301-680-8950). Handles over 1,500 listings a year worldwide, including homes throughout Portugal. For $25 a year, you will receive two listings yearly, as well as supplements.

Better Homes and Travel (formerly *Home Exchange International*), with offices in New York and representatives in Los Angeles, London, Paris, and Milan, functions differently in that it publishes no directory and shepherds the exchange process most of the way. Interested parties supply the firm with photographs of themselves and their homes, information on the type of home they want and where, and a registration fee of $50. The company then works with its other offices to propose a few possibilities, and only when a match is made do the parties exchange names, addresses, and phone numbers. For this service, *Better Homes and Travel* charges a closing fee, which ranges from $150 to $500 for switches from 2 weeks to 3 months in duration, and from $300 to $600 for longer switches. Contact *Better Homes and Travel,* 33 E. 33rd St., New York, NY 10016 (phone: 212-689-6608).

HOME STAYS: Although travelers taking advantage of Portugal's Tourism in the Country program (see above) often come away feeling they've been one of the family, Portugal does not offer a formal "meet the Portuguese" program. If the idea of actually staying in a private home as the guest of a Portuguese family appeals to you, check with the *United States Servas Committee,* which maintains a list of hosts throughout the world (at present, there are 23 in Portugal) willing to throw open their doors to foreign visitors, entirely free of charge.

The aim of this nonprofit cultural program is to promote international understanding and peace, and every effort is made to discourage freeloaders. *Servas* will send you an application form and the name of the nearest of some 200 interviewers around the US for you to contact. After the interview, if you're approved, you'll receive documentation certifying you as a *Servas* traveler. There is a membership fee of $45 for an individual, and there also is a deposit of $15 to receive the host list, refunded on its return. The list gives the name, address, age, occupation, and other particulars of each host, including languages spoken. From then on, it is up to you to write to prospective hosts directly, and *Servas* makes no guarantee that you will be accommodated.

Servas stresses that you should choose only people you really want to meet, and that during your stay (which normally lasts between 2 nights and 2 weeks) you should be interested mainly in your hosts, not in sightseeing. It also suggests that one way to show your appreciation once you've returned home is to become a host yourself. The minimum age of a *Servas* traveler is 18 (however, children under 18 may accompany their parents), and though quite a few are young people who have just finished college, there are travelers (and hosts) in all age ranges and occupations. Contact *Servas* at 11 John St., Room 407, New York, NY 10038-4009 (phone: 212-267-0252).

You also might be interested in a publication called *International Meet-the-People Directory,* published by the *International Visitors Information Service.* It lists several agencies in a number of foreign countries (37 worldwide, 18 in Europe) that arrange home visits for Americans, either for dinner or overnight stays. To order a copy, send $5.95 to the *International Visitors Information Service* (1623 Belmont St. NW, Washington, DC 20009; phone: 202-939-5566). For other local organizations and services offering home exchanges, contact the local tourist authority.

Time Zones, Business Hours, and Public Holidays

TIME ZONES: The countries of Europe fall into three time zones. Greenwich Mean Time — the time in Greenwich, England, at longitude 0°0′ — is the base from which all other time zones are measured. Areas in zones west of Greenwich have earlier times and are called Greenwich Minus; those to the east have later times and are called Greenwich Plus. For example, New York City — which falls into the Greenwich Minus 5 time zone — is 5 hours earlier than Greenwich, England.

Portugal is in the Greenwich Mean Time zone — which means that the time in Portugal is the same as it is in Greenwich, England, and when it is noon in Lisbon, it is 7 AM in New York and Washington, DC. Madeira also is in the Greenwich Mean Time zone; however, the time in the Azores is 1 hour earlier than on mainland Portugal.

Like most Western European nations, Portugal moves its clocks ahead an hour in late spring and an hour back in the fall, although the date of the change tends to be about a week earlier (in spring) and a week later (in fall) than the dates we have adopted in the US. For about 2 weeks a year, then, the time difference between the US and Portugal is 1 hour more or less than usual.

Portuguese and other European timetables use a 24-hour clock to denote arrival and departure times, which means that hours are expressed sequentially from 1 AM. By this method, 9 AM is recorded as 0900, noon as 1200, 1 PM as 1300, 6 PM as 1800, midnight as 2400, and so on. For example, the departure of a train at 7 AM will be announced as "0700"; one leaving at 7 PM will be noted as "1900."

BUSINESS HOURS: Throughout Portugal, most businesses and shops are open Mondays through Fridays from 9 AM to 1 or 2 PM, and then from 3 or 4 PM until 7 or 8 PM. Many shops also are open on Saturdays from 9 AM to 1 PM. In small towns and villages, shops may close on one weekday at 1 PM; others may skip the early closing and simply not open on Mondays (or another day of the week). Larger stores in shopping centers generally stay open through midday and may close as late as 9 PM.

In Portugal, weekday banking hours are from 8:30 AM to 3 PM, usually without a break for lunch. Certain banks (particularly in Lisbon) may remain open until 1 PM on Saturdays, and also may have late hours from 6 to 11 PM on weekdays. Most banks are closed on Sundays and public holidays, although major airport banks may be open 7 days a week.

Restaurant hours are similar to those in the US. Most restaurants are open all week during the high season and close 1 day each week during the off-season — the day varies from restaurant to restaurant. Hours in general also tend to be a bit later in summer, and they vary from city to city; check local listings in THE CITIES and DIRECTIONS, as well as *Dining in Portugal,* in PERSPECTIVES.

PUBLIC HOLIDAYS: In Portugal, the public holidays are as follows:

New Year's Day (January 1)
Good Friday (April 9)
Liberty Day (April 25)
Labor Day or May Day (May 1)
Portugal's and Camões Day (June 10)
St. Anthony's Day (June 13)
Corpus Christi (June 20)
Assumption Day (August 15)
Republic Day (October 5)
All Saints' Day (November 1)
Restoration of Independence (December 1)
Immaculate Conception (December 8)
Christmas Day (December 25)

For further information on holidays celebrated throughout Portugal, see "Special Events" in this section, as well as in each of THE CITIES.

Mail, Telephone, and Electricity

MAIL: Most post offices in Portugal are open Mondays through Saturdays from 9 AM to 5:30 PM. Stamps *(selos)* can be bought at the post office and at authorized tobacconists *(tabacarias);* mail rates change frequently, following the upward trend of everything else. As in the US, letters can be mailed in letter boxes found on the street, but it is better to mail them (and certainly packages) directly from post offices. Portuguese mailboxes are red, with *correio* printed on them.

Mailing a letter or package, however, is not as straightforward as in the US. Post offices have different windows for each step in the procedure (one window to buy stamps, another to weigh a package, and so on), and standing in line for service may take a while. Be advised that delivery from Portugal can be slow (especially if you send something any distance by surface mail) and erratic (postcards often are given lowest priority, so don't use them for important messages). Send your correspondence via air mail if it's going any distance, and to ensure or further speed delivery of important letters, send them registered mail or express or special delivery.

If your correspondence is important, you may want to send it via one of the special courier services: *Federal Express, DHL,* and other international services are available in Portugal. The cost is considerably higher than sending something via the postal service — but the assurance of its timely arrival is worth it.

If you're mailing to an address within Portugal, another way to ensure or speed delivery is to use the postal code. And since small towns in Portugal may have similar names, the postal code always should be specified — delivery of a letter may depend on it. If you do not have the correct postal code, call the Portuguese National Tourist Office (see *Tourist Information Offices,* in this section, for telephone numbers) — they should be able to look it up for you. Alternatively, you could call the addressee directly — if you have the telephone number — and although this will be costly, it may be worth it to ensure delivery of your correspondence.

There are several places that will receive and hold mail for travelers in Portugal. Mail sent to you at a hotel and clearly marked "Guest Mail, Hold for Arrival" is one safe approach. Post offices also will extend this service to you if the mail is addressed to the Portuguese equivalent of US general delivery — called *Posta Restante.* This probably is the best way for travelers to have mail sent if they do not have a definite address. Have your correspondents print your last name in big block letters on the envelope (lest there be any doubt as to which is your last name), and as there often are several post office locations in major cities, it is important that the address and/or specific name of the office be indicated (not just the name of the city), in addition to the words *Posta Restante.* Be sure to call at the correct office when inquiring about mail. Also, don't forget to take your passport with you when you go to collect it. Most Portuguese post offices require formal identification before they will release anything; there also may be a small charge for picking up your mail.

If you are an *American Express* customer (a cardholder, a carrier of *American Express* traveler's checks, or traveling on an *American Express Travel Related Services* tour), you can have mail sent to most of its offices in cities along your route. Letters are held free of charge — registered mail and packages are not accepted. You must be able to show an *American Express* card, traveler's checks, or a voucher proving you are on one of the company's tours to qualify for mail privileges. Those who aren't clients cannot use the service. There also is a forwarding fee ($5 at press time). Mail should be addressed to you, care of *American Express,* and should be marked "Client Mail Service." Additional information on its mail service and the addresses of *American Express* offices in Portugal are listed in the pamphlet *American Express Travelers' Companion,* available from any US branch of *American Express.*

While US embassies and consulates abroad will not under ordinary circumstances accept mail for tourists, they *may* hold mail for US citizens in an emergency situation, or if the papers are particularly important. It is best to inform them either by separate letter or cable, or by phone (particularly if you are in the country already), that you will be using their address for this purpose.

TELEPHONE: The Portuguese telephone system is not too different from our own. It includes direct dialing, operator-assisted calls, collect calls, reduced rates for certain times of the day and days of the week, and so on. The number of digits does vary somewhat within the country, and to further confuse matters, an area code may be included in the digits quoted as the "local" number. If you dial a number directly and your call does not go through, either the circuits are busy or you may need to add or delete one or several digits. If you have tried several times and are sure that you have the correct number, have an international operator place the call — however, this will be more expensive than dialing directly. (To reach an international operator in the US, dial "0" for a local operator and ask him or her to connect you.)

The procedure for calling anywhere in Portugal from the US is as follows: dial 011 (the international access code) + 34 (the country code) + the area code (if you don't know this, ask the international operator) + the local number. For example, to place a call from anywhere in the US to Lisbon, dial 011 + 351 + 1 (the area code for Lisbon) + the local number.

The procedure for making a direct call from Portugal to the US (usually a more expensive proposition) is similar to the procedure described above: dial 097 (the international access code) + 1 (the US country code) + the US area code + the local number. For instance, to call a number in New York City from Portugal, dial 097 + 1 + 212 + the local number.

For calling from one Portuguese city to another, dial 0 + the area code + the local number; and for calls within the same area code coverage, simply dial the local number. Note that Portuguese telephone directories and other sources may include the preceding 0, which should be used only for dialing within the country; when dialing from the US, follow the procedure described above, *leaving off the 0.*

If you don't know the area code, check the front of a telephone book (if calling within Portugal) or ask an operator. To reach a local operator in Portugal, dial 16. To reach an international operator, dial 098 (you also can dial 16 for a local operator who can connect you). For information on what to do in the event of an emergency, see *Staying Healthy,* in this section.

Making connections in Europe sometimes can be hit or miss — all exchanges are not always in operation on the same day. If the number dialed does not go through, try later or the next day. So be warned: Those who have to make an important call — to make a hotel reservation in another city, for instance — should start to do so a few days ahead.

Public Telephones – Pay telephones in Portugal are located much as in the US — in restaurants, hotel lobbies, booths on the street, and at most tourist centers. A useful tip: Coins are fed into a slot at the top of the phone box and automatically drop down as the price of your call increases. It pays to use more coins than you think you may need to avoid being cut off during your conversation; when you are done with the call, the unused amount will be returned.

Although the majority of Portuguese pay phones still take coins, phones that take specially designated phone cards are increasingly common in Portugal. Instituted to cut down on vandalism, the phone cards free callers from the necessity of carrying around a pocketful of change, and are sold in various escudo or centavo denominations. The units per card, like message units in US phone parlance, are a combination of time and distance. To use the card, you insert it into a slot in the phone and dial the number you wish to reach. A display gradually will count down the value (in escudos) that remains on your card. When you run out of units on your card, you can insert another.

In Portugal, pay phones that take phone cards generally are found in metropolitan areas and in major tourism areas, particularly on the coast. Phone cards can be purchased at post offices or national phone company offices, as well as from some tobacconists.

Although you can use a telephone-company credit card number on any phone, pay phones that take major credit cards (*American Express, MasterCard, Visa,* and so on) are increasingly common worldwide, particularly in transportation and tourism centers. Also now available is the "affinity card," a combined telephone calling card/bank credit card that can be used for domestic and international calls. Cards of this type include the following:

AT&T/Universal (phone: 800-662-7759). Cardholders can charge calls to the US from overseas.

Executive Telecard International (phone: 800-950-3800). Cardholders can charge calls to the US from overseas, as well as between most European countries.

Sprint Visa (phone: 800-877-4646). Cardholders can charge calls to the US from overseas.

Similarly, *MCI VisaPhone* (phone: 800-866-0099) can add phone card privileges to the services available through your existing *Visa* card. This service allows you to use your *Visa* account number, plus an additional code, to charge calls on any touch-tone phone in the US and Europe.

Hotel Surcharges – A lot of digits may be involved once a caller starts dialing beyond national borders, but avoiding operator-assisted calls can cut costs considerably and bring rates into a somewhat more reasonable range — except for calls made through hotel switchboards. One of the most unpleasant surprises travelers encounter in many foreign countries is the amount they find tacked on to their hotel bill for telephone calls, because foreign hotels routinely add on astronomical surcharges. (It's not at all uncommon to find 300% or 400% added to the actual telephone charges.)

Until recently, the only recourse against this unconscionable overcharging was to call collect from abroad or to use a telephone credit card — available through a simple procedure from any local US phone company. (Note, however, that even if you use a telephone credit card, some hotels still may charge a fee for line usage). Now *American Telephone and Telegraph (AT&T)* offers *USA Direct,* through which users can dial an access number — 050-171288 in Portugal — that will connect them to an *AT&T* operator in the US, who can then put the call through at the standard international rate. One feature of this service is "Sequential Calling," which enables customers to place up to 10 consecutive calls without having to redial the access number. Travelers abroad also can reach US toll-free (800) numbers — provided the 800 numbers are supplied by *AT&T* — through this service. Charges for all calls made through *USA Direct* appear on the caller's regular US phone bill. (This service is now available from any touch-tone phone in Portugal; the special *USA Direct* telephones that used to be found at some airports, hotels, and phone centers are being phased out.) For a brochure and wallet card listing toll-free numbers by country, contact International Information Service, *AT&T Communications,* 635 Grand St., Pittsburgh, PA 15219 (phone: 800-874-4000).

It's wise to ask about surcharge rates *before* calling from a hotel. If the rate is high, it's best to use a telephone credit card, or the direct-dial service described above (where it is available); make a collect call; or place the call and ask the party to call right back. If none of these choices is possible, to avoid surcharges, make international calls from the local post office or special telephone center. Another way to keep down the cost of telephoning from Portugal is to leave a copy of your itinerary and telephone numbers with people in the US so that they can call you instead.

Other Resources – Travelers to Portugal who don't speak fluent Portuguese may be interested in *AT&T*'s Language Line Service. By calling 800-628-8486, you will be connected with an interpreter in any one of 143 languages and dialects (including Portuguese), who will provide on-line interpretive services for $3.50 a minute. From the US, this service is particularly useful for booking travel services in Europe where English is not spoken or not fluently spoken — such as Portugal. Once in Europe, this number can be reached by using the *USA Direct* toll-free (800) number connection feature described above — it will enable you to make arrangements at foreign establishments or to reach emergency or other vital services with which you would otherwise have trouble communicating due to the language barrier. For frequent business travelers, *AT&T* offers this service on a membership basis. For further information, contact *AT&T* at the address above, or call 800-752-6096.

Particularly useful for planning a trip is *AT&T*'s *Toll-Free 800 Directory,* which lists thousands of companies with 800 numbers, both alphabetically (white pages) and by category (yellow pages), including a wide range of travel services — from travel agents to transportation and accommodations. Issued in a consumer edition for $9.95 and a business edition for $14.95, both are available from *AT&T Phone Centers* or by calling 800-426-8686. Other useful directories for use before you leave and on the road include the *Toll-Free Travel & Vacation Information Directory* ($5.95 postpaid from Pilot Books, 103 Cooper St., Babylon, NY 11702; phone: 516-422-2225) and *The Phone Booklet,* which lists the nationwide, toll-free (800) numbers of travel information sources and suppliers — such as major airlines, hotel and motel chains, car rental companies, and tourist information offices (send $2 to *Scott American Corporation,* Box 88, W. Redding, CT 06896).

ELECTRICITY: The US runs on 110-volt, 60-cycle alternating current. Portugal runs on 220-volt, 50-cycle alternating current, as does much of the rest of Europe. Note that in some remote areas of Portugal 110-volt current still may be in use. (Some large tourist hotels *may* offer 110-volt current for your convenience — but don't count on it.) The difference between US and Portuguese voltage means that, without a converter, the motor of a US appliance used overseas at 220 or 240 volts — twice the voltage at which it was meant to be operated — would quickly burn out.

Travelers can solve the problem by buying a lightweight converter to transform foreign voltage into the US kind (there are several types of converters, depending on the wattage of the appliance) or by buying dual-voltage appliances, which convert from one to the other at the flick of a switch (hair dryers of this sort are common). The difference between the 50- and 60-cycle currents will cause no problem — the American appliance simply will run more slowly — but it still will be necessary to deal with differing socket configurations before plugging in. To be fully prepared, bring along an extension cord (in older or rural establishments the electrical outlet may be farther from the sink than the cord on your razor or hair dryer can reach), and a wall socket adapter with a full set of plugs to ensure that you'll be able to plug in anywhere.

One good source for sets of plugs and adapters for use worldwide is the *Franzus Company* (PO Box 142, Beacon Falls, CT 06403; phone: 203-723-6664). *Franzus* also publishes a useful brochure, *Foreign Electricity Is No Deep Dark Secret,* which provides information about converters and adapter plugs for electric appliances to be used abroad but manufactured for use in the US. To obtain a free copy, send a self-addressed, stamped envelope to *Franzus* at the above address; a catalogue of other travel accessories is available on request.

Staying Healthy

The surest way to return home in good health is to be prepared for medical problems that might occur on vacation. As is always the case with both diseases and accidents, prevention is the best cure. Below, we've outlined some things you need to think about before your trip.

BEFORE YOU GO: Older travelers or anyone suffering from a chronic medical condition, such as diabetes, high blood pressure, cardiopulmonary disease, asthma, or ear, eye, or sinus trouble, should consult a physician before leaving home. Those with conditions requiring special consideration when traveling should consider seeing, in addition to their regular physician, a specialist in travel medicine. For a referral in a particular community, contact the nearest medical school or ask a local doctor to recommend such a specialist. Dr. Leonard Marcus, a member of the *American Committee on Clinical Tropical Medicine and Travelers' Health,* provides a directory of more than 100 travel doctors across the country. For a copy, send a 9- by 12-inch, self-addressed, stamped envelope to Dr. Marcus at 148 Highland Ave., Newton, MA 02165 (phone: 617-527-4003).

Also be sure to check with your insurance company ahead of time about the applicability of your hospitalization and major medical policies away from home; many policies do not apply, and others are not accepted in Europe. Older travelers should know that Medicare does not make payments outside the US and its territories. If your medical policy does not protect you while you're traveling, there are comprehensive combination policies specifically designed to fill the gap. (For a discussion of medical insurance and a list of inclusive combination policies, see *Insurance,* in this section.)

First Aid – Put together a compact, personal medical kit including Band-Aids, first-aid cream, antiseptic, nose drops, insect repellent, aspirin (or non-aspirin tablets), an extra pair of prescription glasses or contact lenses (and a copy of your prescription for glasses or contact lenses), sunglasses, over-the-counter remedies for diarrhea, indigestion, and motion sickness, a thermometer, and a supply of those prescription medicines you take regularly.

In a corner of your kit, keep a list of all the drugs you have brought and their purpose, as well as duplicate copies of your doctor's prescriptions (or a note from your doctor). As brand names may vary in different countries, it's a good idea to ask your doctor for the generic name of any drugs you use so that you can ask for their equivalent should you need a refill. It also is a good idea to ask your doctor to prepare a medical identification card that includes such information as your blood type, your social security number, any allergies or chronic health problems you have, and your medical insurance information. Considering the essential contents of your kit, keep it with you, rather than in your checked luggage.

MINIMIZING THE RISKS: Travelers to Portugal — and to Western Europe in general — do not face the same health risks entailed in traveling to some other destinations (such as Mexico or South America). Although traveling always entails *some* risk of injury or illness, neither is inevitable and, with some basic precautions, your trip will proceed untroubled by ill health.

Sunburn – The burning power of the sun can quickly cause severe sunburn or sunstroke. To protect yourself against these ills, wear sunglasses, take along a broad-brimmed hat and cover-up, and, most important, use a sunscreen lotion.

Water Safety – Portugal is famous for its beaches, but it's important to remember that the sea can be treacherous. A few precautions are necessary. Beware of the undertow, that current of water running back down the beach after a wave has washed ashore; it can knock you off your feet and into the surf. Even more dangerous is the riptide, a strong current of water running against the tide, which can pull you out to sea. If you get caught offshore, don't panic or try to fight the current, because it will only exhaust you; instead, ride it out while waiting for it to subside, which usually happens not too far from shore, or try swimming away parallel to the beach.

Sharks are sometimes sighted, but they usually don't come in close to shore, and they are well fed on fish. Should you meet up with one, just swim away as quietly and smoothly as you can, without shouting or splashing. Although not aggressive, eels can be dangerous when threatened. If snorkeling or diving in coastal waters or freshwater lakes or streams, beware of crevices where these creatures may be lurking. The tentacled Portuguese man-of-war and other jellyfish also may drift in quiet salt waters for food and often wash up onto the beach; the long tentacles of these creatures sting whatever they touch — a paste made of household vinegar and unseasoned meat tenderizer is the recommended treatment.

Insects and Other Pests – Flies and mosquitoes can be troublesome, so it is a good idea to use some form of topical insect repellent — those containing DEET (N,N-diethyl-m-toluamide) are among the most common and effective. The US Environmental Protection Agency (EPA) stresses that you should not use any pesticide that has not been approved by the EPA (check the label) and that all such preparations should be used in moderation. (Use products containing no more than a 15% solution of DEET on children, for example, and apply only to clothing, not directly to the skin.) If picnicking or camping, burn mosquito coils or candles containing allethrin, pyrethrin, or citronella, or use a pyrethrum-containing flying-insect spray. For further information about active ingredients in repellents, call the *National Pesticide Telecommunications Network*'s 24-hour hotline number: 800-858-7378.

If you do get bitten — by mosquitoes, horse or black flies, or other bugs — the itching can be relieved with baking soda, topical first-aid cream, or antihistamine tablets. Should a bite become infected, treat it with a disinfectant or antibiotic cream.

Though rarer, bites from snakes, spiders, and — in southern Portugal — the occasional scorpion can be serious. If possible, always try to catch the villain for identification purposes. If bitten by these creatures or *any* wild animal, the best course of action may be to head directly to the nearest emergency ward or outpatient clinic of a hospital. Cockroaches, waterbugs, and termites thrive in warm climates, but pose no serious health threat.

If complications, allergic reactions (such as breathlessness, fever, or cramps), or signs of serious infection result from any of the above circumstances, *see a doctor.*

Food and Water – Tap water generally is clean and potable throughout most of Portugal. Ask if the water is meant for drinking, but if you're at all unsure, bottled water is readily available in stores. In general, it is a good idea to drink bottled water at least at the beginning of the trip. This is not because there is something wrong with the water as far as the residents are concerned, but microbes to which you have not become accustomed may cause mild stomach or intestinal upsets. Particularly in rural areas, the water supply may not be thoroughly purified, and local residents either have developed immunities to the natural bacteria or boil the water for drinking. You also should avoid swimming in or drinking water from freshwater streams, rivers, or pools, as they may be contaminated with leptospira, which causes a bacterial disease called leptospirosis (the symptoms resemble influenza). In campgrounds, water usually is indicated as drinkable or for washing only — again, if you're not sure, ask.

Milk is pasteurized throughout Portugal, and dairy products are safe to eat, as are fruit, vegetables, meat, poultry, and fish. Because of Mediterranean pollution, however, fish and shellfish should be eaten cooked, and make sure it is *fresh,* particularly in the heat of the summer, when inadequate refrigeration is an additional concern.

Following all these precautions will not guarantee an illness-free trip, but should minimize the risk. For more information regarding preventive health care for travelers, contact the *International Association for Medical Assistance to Travelers* (*IAMAT;* 417 Center St., Lewiston, NY 14092; phone: 716-754-4883). This organization also assists travelers in obtaining emergency medical assistance while abroad (see list of such organizations below).

MEDICAL ASSISTANCE IN PORTUGAL: Nothing ruins a vacation or business trip more effectively than sudden injury or illness. Fortunately, should you need medical attention, competent health professionals perfectly equipped to handle any medical problem can be found throughout the country. Most Portuguese towns and cities of any size have a public hospital, and even the tiniest of villages has a medical clinic or private physician nearby. All hospitals are prepared for emergency cases, and many hospitals also have walk-in clinics to serve people who do not really need emergency service, but who have no place to go for immediate medical attention. The level of medical care in Portugal, especially in the larger cities, generally is quite good, providing the same basic specialties and services that are available in the US.

Emergency Treatment – You will find, in the event of an emergency, that most tourist facilities — transportation companies, hotels, and resorts — are equipped to handle the situation quickly and efficiently. Outside such facilities, however, an inability to speak Portuguese can pose a serious problem, not in receiving treatment at a large teaching hospital, where many doctors and other staff members will speak English, but in getting help elsewhere or in getting to the place where help is available. If a bona fide emergency occurs, the fastest way to get attention may be to take a taxi to the emergency room of the nearest hospital. An alternative is to dial the free national "emergency" number used to summon the police, fire trucks, and ambulances — 115 in Portugal.

Most emergency services send out well-equipped and well-staffed ambulances, although ambulances in Portugal may not be equipped with the advanced EMS technology found in the US and may provide only basic medical attention and be used mainly for transportation. When calling for help, state immediately that you are a foreign tourist and then describe the nature of your problem and your location. Note that the ambulance dispatcher may not be bilingual, and unless you speak Portuguese, he or she will be unable to determine the nature of the emergency, what equipment will be needed, or even where to send the ambulance. Travelers with little or no Portuguese language ability should try to get someone else to make the call. If the situation is desperate, dial 098 or 099 (throughout Portugal) for an international operator who may be able to make the call to the local emergency service and stay on the line as interpreter.

Portugal has socialized medicine and there are two types of hospitals: public and private. Medical services at *policlinicas,* or clinics which are for less serious medical matters, are free (or relatively inexpensive) for Portuguese citizens, but foreign travelers will have to pay full fees for such service. There may not be an English-speaking health worker there, however, and, although they will not turn you away if there is an opening, you generally need to make an appointment, rather than simply walk in off the street. Although private local services are the preferred option, in an extreme medical emergency the US military hospital on the base in Lajes, Portugal, may treat travelers (of any nationality) who are seriously ill or injured until their conditions are stabilized — assuming that the US hospital has the facilities for the treatment required — and then transfer the patient to other hospitals.

Non-Emergency Care – If a doctor is needed for something less than an emergency, there are several ways to find one. If you are staying in a hotel or at a resort, ask for help in reaching a doctor or other emergency services, or for the house physician, who may visit you in your room or ask you to visit an office. Travelers staying at a hotel of any size probably will find that the doctor on call speaks at least a modicum of English — if not, request one who does. When you register at a hotel, it's not a bad idea to include your home address and telephone number; this will facilitate the process of notifying friends, relatives, or your own doctor in case of an emergency.

Dialing the nationwide emergency number (115) also may be of help in locating a physician in a non-emergency situation (again, if you can speak the language). If you require a specialist, call the appropriate department of a teaching hospital (if one exists nearby) or the nearest US consulate, or the Embassy (see *Legal Aid and Consular Services,* below), as these also maintain lists of English-speaking doctors and dentists. If you are already at the hospital, you can see the specialist there or make an appointment to be seen at his or her office.

Pharmacies and Prescription Drugs – Portuguese drug stores, *farmácias,* are identified by a red cross out front. There should be no problem finding a 24-hour drugstore in any major Portuguese city. Each pharmacy is part of a network within a given city, so that there always should be a drugstore somewhere that is open. In many areas, night duty rotates among pharmacies; closed pharmacies generally will have a sign in the window telling you the location of the pharmacy staying open for 24 hours on that day — the name and address follow the words *farmácia de serviço.* A call to the emergency room of the local hospital also may produce this information. In small towns, where none may be open after normal business hours, you may be able to have one open in an emergency situation — such as a diabetic needing insulin — although you may be charged a fee for this off-hour service.

Again, bring along a copy of any prescription you may have from your doctor in case you should need a refill. In the case of minor complaints, Portuguese pharmacists *may* agree to fill a foreign prescription; however, do not count on this. In most cases, you will need a local doctor to rewrite the prescription. Even in an emergency, a traveler will more than likely be given only enough of a drug to last until a local prescription can be obtained.

Travelers also will notice that some drugs sold only by prescription in the US are sold over the counter in Portugal (and vice versa). Although this can be very handy, be aware that common cold medicines and aspirin that contain codeine or other controlled substances will not be allowed back into the US.

ADDITIONAL RESOURCES: A wealth of additional information also is available from various organizations. Some also offer programs designed to assist travelers who have chronic ailments or whose illness requires them to return home. Among these are the following:

International Association of Medical Assistance to Travelers (*IAMAT;* 417 Center St., Lewiston, NY 14092; phone: 716-754-4883). Entitles members to the services of participating English-speaking doctors around the world, as well as clinics and hospitals in various locations. Participating physicians agree to adhere to a basic charge of around $50 to see a patient referred by *IAMAT.* To join, simply write to *IAMAT;* in about 3 weeks you will receive a membership card, a booklet of members, and an inoculation chart. A nonprofit organization, *IAMAT* appreciates donations; with a donation of $25 or more, you will receive a set of worldwide climate charts detailing weather and sanitary conditions. (Delivery can take up to 5 weeks, so plan ahead.)

International Health Care Service (New York Hospital–Cornell Medical Center, 525 E. 68th St., Box 210, New York, NY 10021; phone: 212-746-1601). This service provides a variety of travel-related health services, including a complete range of immunizations at moderate per-shot rates. A pre-travel counseling and immunization package costs $255 for the first family member and $195 for each additional member; a post-travel consultation is $175 to $275, plus lab work. Consultations are by appointment only, from 4 to 8 PM Mondays through Thursdays, although 24-hour coverage is available for urgent travel-related problems. In addition, sending $4.50 (with a self-addressed envelope) to the address above will procure the service's publication, *International Health Care Travelers Guide,* a compendium of facts and advice on health care and diseases around the world.

International SOS Assistance (PO Box 11568, Philadelphia, PA 19116; phone: 800-523-8930 or 215-244-1500). Subscribers are provided with telephone access — 24 hours a day, 365 days a year — to a worldwide, monitored, multilingual network of medical centers. A phone call brings assistance ranging from a telephone consultation to transportation home by ambulance or aircraft, or, in some cases, transportation of a family member to wherever you are hospitalized. Individual rates are $35 for 2 weeks of coverage ($3.50 for each additional day), $70 for 1 month, or $240 for 1 year; couple and family rates also are available.

Medic Alert Foundation (2323 N. Colorado, Turlock, CA 95380; phone: 800-ID-ALERT or 209-668-3333). If you have a health condition that may not be readily perceptible to the casual observer — one that might result in a tragic error in an emergency situation — this organization offers identification emblems specifying such conditions. The foundation also maintains a computerized central file from which your complete medical history is available 24 hours a day by phone (the telephone number is clearly inscribed on the emblem). The onetime membership fee (between $35 and $50) is based on the type of metal from which the emblem is made — the choices range from stainless steel to 10K gold-filled.

TravMed (PO Box 10623, Baltimore, MD 21204; phone: 800-732-5309 or 410-296-5225). For $3 per day, subscribers receive comprehensive medical assistance while abroad. Major medical expenses are covered up to $100,000, and special transportation home or of a family member to wherever you are hospitalized is provided at no additional cost.

Helpful Publications – Practically every phase of health care — before, during, and after a trip — is covered in *The New Traveler's Health Guide,* by Drs. Patrick J. Doyle and James E. Banta. It is available for $4.95, plus postage and handling, from Acropolis Books Ltd., 13950 Park Center Rd., Herndon, VA 22071 (phone: 800-451-7771 or 703-709-0006). In addition, *Travelers' Medical Resource: A Guide to Health and Safety Worldwide,* by Dr. William W. Forgey, is a compendium of medical advice, information, and resources. It is available directly from the publisher (ICS Books, One Tower Plaza, 107 E. 89th Ave., Merrillville, IN 46410; phone: 219-769-0585) for $19.95, plus shipping and handling, as well as from general bookstores.

The *Traveling Healthy Newsletter,* which is published six times a year, also is brimming with health-related travel tips. For a year's subscription, which costs $24 (sample issues are available for $4), contact Dr. Karl Neumann (108-48 70th Rd., Forest Hills, NY 11375; phone: 718-268-7290). Dr. Neumann also is the editor of the useful free booklet *Traveling Healthy,* which is available by contacting the *Travel Healthy Program,* Clark O'Neill, Inc., 1 Broad Ave., Fairview, NJ 07022 (phone: 201-945-3400).

The Centers for Disease Control publishes an interesting booklet, *Health Information for International Travel.* To order send a check or money order for $5 to the Superintendent of Documents (US Government Printing Office, Washington, DC 20402), or charge it to your credit card by calling 202-783-3238. For information on vaccination requirements, disease outbreaks, and other health information pertaining to traveling abroad, you also can call the Centers for Disease Control's 24-hour International Health Requirements and Recommendations Information Hotline: 404-332-4559.

■ **Note:** Those who are unable to take a reserved flight due to personal illness or who must fly home unexpectedly due to a family emergency should be aware that airlines may offer a discounted airfare (or arrange a partial refund) if the traveler can demonstrate that his or her situation is indeed a legitimate emergency. Your inability to fly or the illness or death of an immediate family member usually must be substantiated by a doctor's note or the name, relationship, and funeral home from which the deceased will be buried. In such cases, airlines often will waive certain advance purchase restrictions or you may receive a refund check or voucher for future travel at a later date. Be aware, however, that this bereavement fare may not necessarily be the least expensive fare available and, if possible, it is best to have a travel agent check all possible flights through a computer reservations system (CRS).

Legal Aid and Consular Services

There is one crucial place to keep in mind when outside the US, namely, the American Services section of the US Consulate. If you are injured or become seriously ill, the consulate will direct you to medical assistance and notify your relatives. If, while abroad, you become involved in a dispute that could lead to legal action, the consulate, once again, is the place to turn.

It usually is far more alarming to be arrested abroad than at home. Not only are you alone among strangers, but the punishment can be worse. Granted, the US Consulate can advise you of your rights and provide a list of English-speaking lawyers, but it cannot interfere with the local legal process. Except for minor infractions of the local traffic code, there is no reason for any law-abiding traveler to run afoul of immigration, customs, or any other law enforcement authority.

The best advice is to be honest and law-abiding. If you get a traffic ticket, pay it. If you are approached by drug hawkers, ignore them. The penalties for possession of marijuana, cocaine, and other narcotics are even more severe abroad than in the US. (If you are picked up for any drug-related offense, do not expect US foreign service officials to be sympathetic. Chances are, they will notify a lawyer and your family and that's about all. See "Drugs," below.)

In the case of minor traffic accidents (such as a fender bender), it often is most expedient to settle the matter before the police get involved. If, however, you are involved in a serious accident, where an injury or fatality results, the first step is to contact the nearest US consulate (for addresses, see below) and ask the consul to locate an attorney to assist you. If you have a traveling companion, ask him or her to call the consulate (unless either of you has a local contact who can help you quickly). Competent English-speaking lawyers practice throughout Europe, and it is possible to obtain good legal counsel on short notice.

The US Department of State in Washington, DC, insists that any US citizen who is arrested abroad has the right to contact the US embassy or consulate "immediately," but it may be a while before you are given permission to use a phone. Do not labor under the illusion, however, that in a scrape with foreign officialdom the consulate can act as an arbitrator or ombudsman on a US citizen's behalf. Nothing could be farther from the truth. Consuls have no power, authorized or otherwise, to subvert, alter, or contravene the legal processes, however unfair, of the foreign country in which they serve. Nor can a consul oil the machinery of a foreign bureaucracy or provide legal advice. The consul's responsibilities do encompass "welfare duties," including providing a list of lawyers and information on local sources of legal aid, informing relatives in the US, and organizing and administrating any defense monies sent from home. If a case is tried unfairly or the punishment seems unusually severe, the consul can make a formal complaint to the authorities. For questions about US citizens arrested abroad, how to get money to them, and other useful information, call the *Citizens' Emergency Center* of the Office of Special Consular Services in Washington, DC, at 202-647-5225. (For further information about this invaluable hotline, see below.)

Other welfare duties, not involving legal hassles, cover cases of both illness and destitution. If you should get sick, the US consul can provide names of English-speaking doctors and dentists, as well as the names of all local hospitals and clinics; the consul also will contact family members in the US and help arrange special ambulance service for a flight home. In a situation involving "legitimate and proven poverty" of an US citizen stranded abroad without funds, the consul will contact sources of money (such as family or friends in the US), apply for aid to agencies in foreign countries, and in a last resort — which is *rarely* — arrange for repatriation at government expense, although this is a loan that must be repaid. And in case of natural disasters or civil unrest, consulates around the world handle the evacuation of US citizens if it becomes necessary.

The consulate is not occupied solely with emergencies and is certainly not there to aid in trivial situations, such as canceled reservations or lost baggage, no matter how important these matters may seem to the victimized tourist. The main duties of any consulate are administrating statutory services, such as the issuance of passports and visas; providing notarial services; distributing VA, social security, and civil service benefits to US citizens; taking depositions; handling extradition cases; and reporting to Washington, DC, the births, deaths, and marriages of US citizens living within the consulate's domain.

We hope that none of the information in this section will be necessary during your stay in Portugal. If you can avoid legal hassles altogether, you will have a much more pleasant trip. If you become involved in an imbroglio, the local authorities may spare you legal complications if you make clear your tourist status. And if you run into a confrontation that might lead to legal complications developing with a Portuguese citizen or with local authorities, the best tactic is to apologize and try to leave as gracefully as possible. Do not get into fights with residents, no matter how belligerent or provocative they are in a given situation.

Following are the US embassies and consulates in Portugal. If you are not in any of the cities mentioned when a problem arises, contact the nearest office. If you are not a US citizen, contact the consulate of your own nation. Note that mailing addresses may be different — so call before sending anything to these offices. We have included the phone number prefix (0) as you are most likely to dial these numbers once in Portugal; if calling from the US, leave off the 0.

Lisbon: US Embassy (Av. das Forças Armadas, Lisbon 1600; phone: 01-726-6600).

Ponta Delgada: US Consulate (Av. D. Henrique, Ponta Delgada 09406; phone: 09-622216).

Porto: US Consulate (65 Praça Conde de Samadaes, Porto 4000; phone: 02-606-3094).

You can obtain a booklet with addresses of most US embassies and consulates around the world by writing to the Superintendent of Documents (US Government Printing Office, Washington, DC 20402; phone: 202-783-3238) and asking for publication #744-006-0000-7, *Key Offices of Foreign Service Posts.*

As mentioned above, the US State Department operates a *Citizens' Emergency Center,* which offers a number of services to US citizens traveling abroad and their families at home. In addition to giving callers up-to-date information on trouble spots, the center will contact authorities abroad in an attempt to locate a traveler or deliver an urgent message. In case of illness, death, arrest, destitution, or repatriation of a US citizen on foreign soil, it will relay information to relatives at home if the consulate is unable to do so. Travel advisory information is available 24 hours a day to people with touch-tone phones (phone: 202-647-5225). Callers with rotary phones can get information at this number from 8:15 AM to 10 PM (eastern standard time) on weekdays; 9 AM to 3 PM on Saturdays. In the event of an emergency, this number also may be called during these hours. For emergency calls only, at all other times, call 202-634-3600 and ask for the Duty Officer.

Drinking and Drugs

DRINKING: It is more than likely that some of the warmest memories of a trip to Portugal will be moments of conviviality shared over a drink in a neighborhood bar or sunlit café. Visitors will find that liquor, wine, and brandies in Portugal are distilled to the same proof and often are the same labels as those found at home. However, Portuguese beer tends to be about 5% higher in alcoholic content than beer brewed in the US.

You'll want to try the country's specialties. Beer and wine are favorites in bars and cafés. Portuguese beer *(cerveja)* is served cold in a *cervejaria,* or tavern. Sagres is a popular national brand, available in regular, light *(leve),* and dark *(preta).* Draft beer is called *cerveja fino.* Portuguese wines are as world-renowned as they are varied, with each region boasting its own specialty. *Vinho verde,* or green wine, is a clear and refreshing, light, young "white" wine (8% to 14% alcohol). *Colares* is available either as a full, smooth red, or a sweet, full-bodied white, while *bucelas* is a drier, fresh white. *Rosé,* a national favorite, is a heavier, fruity, and fragrant red wine. (For a more thorough discussion of Portuguese beverages, see *Dining in Portugal,* PERSPECTIVES, and *Visitable Vineyards,* DIVERSIONS.)

Portuguese bars and cafés open at 8:30 AM or earlier to serve coffee and breakfast, although alcohol generally is not served until at least 10 AM. Most remain open until midnight, but others may stay open until as late as 4 AM. The legal age for drinking in Portugal is 18, though it is not strictly enforced.

As in the US, national taxes on alcohol affect the prices of liquor in Portugal, and, as a general rule, mixed drinks — especially imported liquors such as whiskey and gin — are more expensive than at home. If you like a drop before dinner, a good way to save money is to buy a bottle of your favorite brand at the airport before leaving the US and enjoy it in your hotel before setting forth.

Visitors to Portugal may bring in 2 liters of wine and 1 liter of liquor per person duty-free. If you are buying any quantity of alcohol (such as a case of wine) in Portugal and traveling through other European countries on your route back to the US, you will have to pass through customs and pay duty at each border crossing, so you might want to arrange to have it shipped home. Whether bringing it with you or shipping, you will have to pay US import duties on any quantity over the allowed 1 liter (see *Customs and Returning to the US,* in this section).

DRUGS: Illegal narcotics are as prevalent in Portugal as in the US, but the moderate legal penalties and vague social acceptance that marijuana has gained in the US have no equivalents in Portugal. Due to the international war on drugs, enforcement of drug laws is becoming increasingly strict throughout the world. Local European narcotics officers and customs officials are renowned for their absence of understanding and lack of a sense of humor — especially where foreigners are involved.

Opiates and barbiturates, and other increasingly popular drugs — "white powder" substances like heroin, cocaine, and "crack" (the cocaine derivative) — continue to be of major concern to narcotics officials. Most European countries — including Portugal — have toughened laws regarding illegal drugs and narcotics, and it is important to bear in mind that the type or quantity of drugs involved is of minor importance. Particularly for foreigners, the maximum penalties may be imposed for possessing even *traces* of illegal drugs. There is a high conviction rate in these cases, and bail for foreigners is rare. Persons arrested are subject to the laws of the country they are visiting, and there isn't much that the US consulate can do for drug offenders beyond providing a list of lawyers. The best advice we can offer is this: Don't carry, use, buy, or sell illegal drugs.

Those who carry medicines that contain a controlled drug should be sure to have a current doctor's prescription with them. Ironically, travelers can get into almost as much trouble coming through US customs with over-the-counter drugs picked up abroad that contain substances that are controlled in the US. Cold medicines, pain relievers, and the like often have codeine or codeine derivatives that are illegal, except by prescription, in the US. Throw them out before leaving for home.

- **Be forewarned:** US narcotics agents warn travelers of the increasingly common ploy of drug dealers asking travelers to transport a "gift" or other package back to the US. Don't be fooled into thinking that the protection of US law applies abroad — accused of illegal drug trafficking, you will be considered guilty until you prove your innocence. In other words, do not, under any circumstances, agree to take anything across the border for a stranger.

Tipping

Throughout Portugal (and in most of the rest of Europe), you will find the custom of including some kind of service charge in a bill for a meal or accommodations more common than in the US. This can confuse Americans not familiar with the custom. On the one hand, many a traveler, unaware of this policy, has left many a superfluous tip. On the other hand, travelers aware of this policy may make the mistake of assuming that it takes care of everything. It doesn't.

While "service included" in theory eliminates any question about how much and whom to tip, in practice there still are occasions when on-the-spot tips are appropriate. Among these are tips to show appreciation for special services, as well as tips meant to say "thank you" for services rendered. So keep a pocketful of 100 escudo bills and 50 escudo coins ready, and hand these out like dollar bills.

In Portuguese restaurants, the service charge (called *serviço incluido*) may appear in one of two ways: It either already is calculated in the prices listed or will be added to the final bill. For the most part, if you see a notation at the bottom of the menu without a percentage figure, the charge should be included in the prices; if a percentage figure is indicated, the service charge has not yet been added. To further confuse the issue, not every restaurant notes if its policy is to include service and at what point the charge is added. If you are at all unsure, you should feel no embarrassment about asking a waiter.

This service charge generally ranges from 10% to 15%. In the rare instance where it isn't added, a 15% tip to the waiter — just as in the US — usually is a safe figure, although one should never hesitate to penalize poor service or reward excellent and efficient attention by leaving less or more. If the tip has been added, no further gratuity is expected — though it's a common practice in Europe to leave a few extra coins on the table. The emphasis is on *few,* and the current equivalent of $1 usually is quite adequate.

Although it's not necessary to tip the maître d' of most restaurants — unless he has been especially helpful in arranging a special party or providing a table (slipping him something in a crowded restaurant *may* get you seated sooner or procure a preferred table) — when tipping is desirable or appropriate, the least amount should be the current equivalent of $5. In the finest restaurants, where a multiplicity of servers are present, plan to tip 5% to the captain. The sommelier (wine waiter) is entitled to a gratuity of approximately 10% of the price of the bottle. Tipping in bars and cafés is similar to tipping in restaurants: Service may be included, but you still may wish to leave a few extra coins on the table.

In allocating gratuities at a restaurant, pay particular attention to what has become the standard credit card charge form, which now includes separate places for gratuities for waiters and/or captains. If these separate boxes are not on the charge slip, simply ask the waiter or captain how these separate tips should be indicated. Be aware, too, of the increasingly common — and devious — practice of placing the amount of an entire restaurant bill (in which service already has been included) in the top box of a charge slip, leaving the "tip" and "total" boxes ominously empty. Don't be intimidated: Leave the "tip" box blank and just repeat the total amount next to "total" before signing. In some establishments, tips indicated on credit card receipts may not be given to the help, so you may want to leave tips in cash.

As in restaurants, visitors often — though not always — will find a service charge of 10% to 15% included in their final bill at Portuguese hotels. No additional gratuities are required — or expected — beyond this billed service charge. It is unlikely, however, that a service charge will be added to bills in small family-run guesthouses or other modest establishments. In these cases, guests should let their instincts be their guide; no tipping is expected by members of the family who own the establishment, but it is a nice gesture to leave something for others — such as a dining room waiter or a maid — who may have been helpful. The equivalent of around $1 per night is adequate in most cases.

If a hotel does not automatically add a service charge, it is perfectly proper for guests to ask to have an extra 10% to 15% added to their bill, to be distributed among those who served them. This may be an especially convenient solution in a large hotel, where it's difficult to determine just who out of a horde of attendants actually performed particular services.

For those who prefer to distribute tips themselves, a chambermaid generally is tipped at the rate of $1 per day. Tip the concierge or hall porter for specific services only, with the amount of such gratuities dependent on the level of service provided. (Remember, if he has obtained theater or concert tickets for you, he most likely has included a service charge in the price — if in doubt, ask. You still may want to tip in advance to encourage him to use his influence in obtaining hard-to-get tickets.) For any special service you receive in a hotel, a tip is expected — the current equivalent of $1 being the minimum for a small service.

Bellhops, doormen, and porters at hotels and transportation centers generally are tipped at the rate of $1 per piece of luggage, along with a small additional amount if a doorman helps with a cab or car. Once upon a time, taxi drivers in Europe would give you a rather odd look if presented with a tip for a fare, but times have changed, and 10% to 15% of the amount on the meter is now a standard gratuity.

Miscellaneous tips: Tipping ushers in a movie house, theater, or concert hall used to be the rule, but is becoming less common — the best policy is to check what other patrons are doing and follow suit. Most of the time, the program is not free, and in lieu of a tip it is common practice to purchase a program from the person who seats you. Sightseeing tour guides also should be tipped. If you are traveling in a group, decide together what you want to give the guide and present it from the group at the end of the tour ($1 per person is a reasonable tip). If you have been individually escorted, the amount paid should depend on the degree of your satisfaction, but it should not be less than 10% of the total tour price. Museum and monument guides also are usually tipped, and it is a nice touch to tip a caretaker who unlocks a small church or turns on the lights in a chapel for you in some out-of-the-way town.

In barbershops and beauty salons, tip as you would at home, keeping in mind that the percentages vary according to the type of establishment — 10% in the most expensive salons; 15% to 20% in less expensive establishments. (As a general rule, the person who washes your hair should get a small additional tip.) Washroom attendants should get a small tip — they usually set out a little plate with a coin already on it indicating the suggested denomination. Coat checks are worth about 50¢ to $1 a coat. And don't forget service station attendants, for whom a tip of around 50¢ for cleaning the windshield or other attention is not unusual.

Tipping always is a matter of personal preference. In the situations covered above, as well as in any others that arise where you feel a tip is expected or due, feel free to express your pleasure or displeasure. Again, never hesitate to reward excellent and efficient attention and to penalize poor service. Give an extra gratuity and a word of thanks when someone has gone out of his or her way for you. Either way, the more personal the act of tipping, the more appropriate it seems. And if you didn't like the service — or the attitude — don't tip.

Duty-Free Shopping and Value Added Tax

DUTY-FREE SHOPS: Note that at the time of this writing, because of the newly integrated European economy, there were some questions as to the fate and number of duty-free shops that would be maintained at international airports in European Economic Community (EEC) member countries. It appears, however, that those traveling between EEC countries and any country *not* a member of the Common Market will still be entitled to buy duty-free items. Since the United States is not a Common Market member, duty-free purchases by US travelers will, presumably, remain as is for the forseeable future.

If common sense says that it always is less expensive to buy goods in an airport duty-free shop than to buy them at home or in the streets of a foreign city, travelers should be aware of some basic facts. Duty-free, first of all, does not mean that the goods travelers buy will be free of duty when they return to the US. Rather, it means that the shop has paid no import tax acquiring goods of foreign make because the goods are not to be used in the country where the shop is located. This is why duty-free goods are available only in the restricted, passengers-only area of international airports or are delivered to departing passengers on the plane. In a duty-free store, travelers save money only on goods of foreign make because they are the only items on which an import tax would be charged in any other store. There usually is no saving on locally made items, but in countries such as Portugal that impose Value Added Taxes (see below) that are refundable to foreigners, the prices in airport duty-free shops also are minus this tax, sparing travelers the often cumbersome procedures they otherwise have to follow to obtain a VAT refund.

Beyond this, there is little reason to delay buying locally made merchandise and/or souvenirs until reaching the airport (for information on local specialties, see the individual city chapters in THE CITIES, and *Shopping Spree,* in DIVERSIONS). In fact, because airport duty-free shops usually pay high rents, the locally made goods sold in them may well be more expensive than they would be in downtown stores. The real bargains are foreign goods, but — let the buyer beware — not all foreign goods are automatically less expensive in an airport duty-free shop. You can get a good deal on even small amounts of perfume, costing less than the usually required minimum purchase, tax-free. Other fairly standard bargains include spirits, smoking materials, cameras, clothing, watches, chocolates, and other food and luxury items — but first be sure to know what these items cost elsewhere. Terrific savings do exist (they are the reason for such shops, after all), but so do overpriced items that an unwary shopper might find equally tempting. In addition, if you wait to do your shopping at airport duty-free shops, you will be taking the chance that the desired item is out of stock or unavailable.

Duty-free shops are located in most major international airports throughout Europe. In Portugal, they are located at the Lisbon and Porto airports.

VALUE ADDED TAX: Commonly abbreviated as VAT, this is a tax levied by various European countries, including Portugal, and added to the purchase price of most goods and services. The standard VAT (known as IVA in Portugal) is 17% (slightly higher in the Azores and Madeira) on most purchases, with a higher rate of 30% applying to luxury goods such as watches, jewelry, furs, glass, and cameras (food and transportation are exempt).

The tax is intended for residents (and already is included in the price tag), but visitors are required to pay it, too, unless they have purchases shipped directly to an address abroad by the store. If visitors pay the tax and take purchases with them, however, they generally are entitled to a refund under a retail export scheme that has been in operation for several years. In the past, returning travelers have complained of delays in receiving the refunds and of difficulties in converting checks written in foreign currency into dollars, but a service called *IVA Refund* has recently been introduced that greatly streamlines the procedure.

In order to qualify for a refund, a minimum purchase is required. For items taxable at the 17% VAT rate, purchases must total at least 11,700 escudos (about $83 US at press time); for items taxable at the 30% rate, the minimum purchase is 13,000 escudos (about $90 US at press time). In both cases, these minimum amounts apply to purchases at a single store — purchases from several stores cannot be combined. In most cases, stores will provide the appropriate refund forms on request. If the store does not have this form, it can be obtained at the refund office at the airport, which also can provide information on the procedure for submitting the paperwork to obtain the refund. Visitors leaving Portugal must have all of their receipts for purchases and refund vouchers stamped by customs; as customs officials may well ask to see the merchandise, it's a good idea not to pack it in the bottom of your suitcase. Refund checks (in escudos) are sent out within 6 to 8 weeks of receipt of the vouchers; refunds by credit card also are possible — if the shopkeeper agrees to this arrangement.

A VAT refund by dollar check or by credit to a credit card account is relatively hassle-free. If it arrives in the form of a foreign currency check and if the refund is less than a significant amount, charges imposed by US banks for converting foreign currency refund checks — which can run as high as $15 or more — could make the whole exercise hardly worth your while.

Far less costly is sending the foreign currency check (after endorsing it) to *Ruesch International,* which will covert it to a check in US dollars for a $2 fee (deducted from the dollar check). Other services include commission-free traveler's checks and foreign currency which can be ordered by mail. Contact *Ruesch International* at one of the following addresses: 191 Peachtree St., Atlanta, GA 30303 (phone: 404-222-9300); 3 First National Plaza, Suite 2020, Chicago, IL 60602 (phone: 312-332-5900); 1925 Century Park E., Suite 240, Los Angeles, CA 90067 (phone: 213-277-7800); 608 Fifth Ave., "Swiss Center," New York, NY 10020 (phone: 212-977-2700); and 1350 Eye St. NW, 10th Floor and street level, Washington, DC 20005 (phone: 800-424-2923 or 202-408-1200).

- **Buyer Beware:** You may come across shops *not* at airports that call themselves duty-free shops. These require shoppers to show a foreign passport but are subject to the same rules as other stores, including paying import duty on foreign items. What "tax-free" means in the case of these establishments is something of an advertising strategy: They are announcing loud and clear that they do, indeed, offer the VAT refund service — sometimes on the spot (minus a fee for higher overhead). Prices may be no better at these stores and could be even higher due to the addition of this service.

Religion on the Road

Portugal is predominantly Catholic, and every town, right down to the most isolated village, has its own church. In larger, more heavily populated areas, some amount of religious variety is reflected in the churches of other denominations, synagogues, and the occasional mosque or temple.

The surest source of information on English-language religious services in an unfamiliar country is the desk clerk of the hotel or guesthouse in which you are staying; the local tourist information office, a US consul, or a church of another religious affiliation also may be able to provide this information. If you aren't in an area with services held in your own denomination, you might find it interesting to attend the service of another religion. You also might enjoy attending a service in Portuguese — even if you don't understand all the words. There are many beautiful churches throughout Portugal, and whether in a stately cathedral or a small village chapel, visitors are welcome.

Customs and Returning to the US

Whether you return to the United States by air or sea, you must declare to the US Customs official at the point of entry everything you have bought or acquired while in Europe. The customs check can go smoothly, lasting only a few minutes, or can take hours, depending on the officer's instinct. To speed up the process, keep all your receipts handy and try to pack your purchases together in an accessible part of your suitcase. It might save you from unpacking all your belongings.

DUTY-FREE ARTICLES: In general, the duty-free allowance for US citizens returning from abroad is $400. This duty-free limit is based on the provision that your purchases accompany you and are for personal use. This limit includes items used or worn while abroad, souvenirs for friends, and gifts received during the trip. A flat 10% duty based on the "fair retail value in country of acquisition" is assessed on the next $1,000 worth of merchandise brought in for personal use or gifts. Amounts over the basic allotment and the 10% dutiable amount are dutiable at a variety of rates. The average rate for typical tourist purchases is about 12%, but you can find out rates on specific items by consulting *Tariff Schedules of the United States* in a library or at any US Customs Service office.

Families traveling together may make a joint declaration to customs, which permits one member to exceed his or her duty-free exemption to the extent that another falls short. Families also may pool purchases dutiable under the flat rate. A family of three, for example, would be eligible for up to a total of $3,000 at the 10% flat duty rate (after each member had used up his or her $400 duty-free exemption) rather than three separate $1,000 allowances. This grouping of purchases is extremely useful when considering the duty on a high-tariff item, such as jewelry or a fur coat.

Personal exemptions can be used once every 30 days; in order to be eligible, an individual must have been out of the country for more than 48 continuous hours. If any portion of the exemption has been used once within any 30-day period or if your trip is less than 48 hours long, the duty-free allowance is cut to $25.

There are certain articles, however, that are duty-free only up to certain limits. The $25 allowance includes the following: 10 cigars (not Cuban), 50 cigarettes, and 4 ounces of perfume. Individuals eligible for the full $400 duty-free limit are allowed 1 carton of cigarettes (200), 100 cigars, and 1 liter of liquor or wine if the traveler is over 21. Under federal law, alcohol above this allowance is liable for both duty and an Internal Revenue tax. Note, however, that states are allowed to impose additional restrictions and penalties of their own, including (in Arizona and Utah, for example) confiscation of any quantities of liquor over the statutory limit. Antiques, if they are 100 or more years old and you have proof from the seller of that fact, are duty-free, as are paintings and drawings if done entirely by hand.

To avoid paying duty twice, register the serial numbers of computers, watches, and electronic equipment with the nearest US Customs bureau before departure; receipts of insurance policies also should be carried for other foreign-made items. (Also see the note at the end of *Entry Requirements and Documents,* in this section.)

Gold, gold medals, bullion, and up to $10,000 in currency or negotiable instruments may be brought into the US without being declared. Sums over $10,000 must be declared in writing.

The allotment for individual "unsolicited" gifts mailed from abroad (no more than one per day per recipient) is $50 retail value per gift. These gifts do not have to be declared and are not included in your duty-free exemption (see below). Although you should include a receipt for purchases with each package, the examiner is empowered to impose a duty based on his or her assessment of the value of the goods. The duty owed is collected by the US Postal Service when the package is delivered (also see below). More information on mailing packages home from abroad is contained in the US Customs Service pamphlet *Buyer Beware, International Mail Imports* (see below for where to write for this and other useful brochures).

CLEARING CUSTOMS: This is a simple procedure. Forms are distributed by airline or ship personnel before arrival. (Note that a $5-per-person service charge — called a user fee — is collected by airlines and cruise lines to help cover the cost of customs' checks, but this is included in the ticket price.) If your purchases total no more than the $400 duty-free limit, you need only fill out the identification part of the form and make an oral declaration to the customs inspector. If entering with more than $400 worth of goods, you must submit a written declaration.

Customs agents are businesslike, efficient, and not unkind. During the peak season, clearance can take time, but this generally is because of the strain imposed by a number of jumbo jets simultaneously discharging their passengers, not because of unwarranted zealousness on the part of the customs people.

Efforts to streamline procedures used to include the so-called Citizens' Bypass Program, which allowed US citizens whose purchases were within their duty-free allowance to go to the "green line," where they simply showed their passports to the customs inspector. Although at the time of this writing this procedure still is being followed at some international airports in the US, most airports have returned to an earlier system. US citizens arriving from abroad now have to go through a passport check by the Immigration & Naturalization Service (INS) prior to recovering their baggage and proceeding to customs. (US citizens will not be on the same line as foreign visitors, but this additional wait does delay clearance on re-entry into the US.) Although all passengers have to go through this obligatory passport inspection, those entering with purchases within the duty-free limit may be spared a thorough customs inspection; however, inspectors still retain the right to search any luggage they choose — so don't do anything foolish.

It is illegal not to declare dutiable items; not to do so, in fact, constitutes smuggling, and the penalty can be anything from stiff fines and seizure of the goods to prison sentences. It simply isn't worth doing. Nor should you go along with the suggestions of foreign merchants who offer to help you secure a bargain by deceiving customs officials in any way. Such transactions frequently are a setup, using the foreign merchant as an agent of US Customs. Another agent of US Customs is TECS, the Treasury Enforcement Communications System, a computer that stores all kinds of pertinent information on returning citizens. There is a basic rule to buying goods abroad, and it should never be broken: *If you can't afford the duty on something, don't buy it.* Your list or verbal declaration should include all items purchased abroad, as well as gifts received abroad, purchases made at the behest of others, the value of repairs, and anything brought in for resale in the US.

Do not include in the list items that do not accompany you, i.e., purchases that you have mailed or had shipped home. As mentioned above, these are dutiable in any case, even if for your own use and even if the items that accompany your return from the same trip do not exhaust your duty-free exemption. It is a good idea, if you have accumulated too much while abroad, to mail home any personal effects (made and bought in the US) that you no longer need rather than your foreign purchases. These personal effects pass through US Customs as "American goods returned" and are not subject to duty.

If you cannot avoid shipping home your foreign purchases, however, the US Customs Service suggests that the package be clearly marked "Not for Sale," and that a copy of the bill of sale be included. The US Customs examiner usually will accept this as indicative of the article's fair retail value, but if he or she believes it to be falsified or feels the goods have been seriously undervalued, a higher retail value may be assigned.

FORBIDDEN IMPORTS: Narcotics, plants (unless specifically exempt and free of soil), and many types of food are not allowed into the US. Drugs are totally illegal, with the exception of medication prescribed by a physician. It's a good idea not to travel with too large a quantity of any given prescription drug (however, in the event that a pharmacy is not open when you need it, bring along several extra doses) and to have the prescription on hand in case any question arises either abroad or when reentering the US.

Any sculpture that is part of an architectural structure, any authentic archaeological find, or other artifacts may not be exported from Portugal without the permission of the *Instituto Português do Patrimônio Cultural,* Palácio Nacional da Ajuda, Lisbon 1400; phone: 1-363-1677). If you do not obtain prior permission of the proper regulatory agencies, such items will be confiscated at the border, and you will run the risk of being fined or imprisoned.

Tourists have long been forbidden to bring into the US foreign-made US trademarked articles purchased abroad (if the trademark is recorded with US Customs) without written permission. It's now permissible to enter with one such item in your possession as long as it's for personal use.

The US Customs Service implements the rigorous Department of Agriculture regulations concerning the importation of vegetable matter, seeds, bulbs, and the like. Living vegetable matter may not be imported without a permit, and everything must be inspected, permit or not. Approved items (which do not require a permit) include dried bamboo and woven items made of straw; beads made of most seeds (but not jequirity beans — the poisonous scarlet and black seed of the rosary pea) and some viable seeds; cones of pine and other trees; roasted coffee beans; most flower bulbs; flowers (without roots); dried or canned fruits, jellies, or jams; polished rice, dried beans and teas; herb plants (not witchweed); nuts (but not acorns, chestnuts, or any nuts with outer husks); dried lichens, mushrooms, truffles, shamrocks, and seaweed; and most dried spices.

Other processed foods and baked goods usually are okay. Regulations on meat products generally depend on the country of origin and manner of processing. As a rule, commercially canned meat, hermetically sealed and cooked in the can so that it can be stored without refrigeration, is permitted, but not all canned meat fulfills this requirement. Be careful when buying European-made pâté, for instance. Goose liver pâté in itself is acceptable, but the pork fat that often is part of it, either as an ingredient or a rind, may not be. Even canned pâtés may not be admitted for this reason. (The imported ones you see in US stores have been prepared and packaged according to US regulations.) So before stocking up on a newfound favorite, it pays to check in advance — otherwise you might have to leave it behind.

The US Customs Service also enforces federal laws that prohibit the entry of articles made from the furs or hides of animals on the endangered species list. Beware of shoes, bags, and belts made of crocodile and certain kinds of lizard, and anything made of tortoiseshell; this also applies to preserved crocodiles, lizards, and turtles sometimes sold in gift shops. And if you're shopping for big-ticket items, beware of fur coats made from the skins of spotted cats. They are sold in Europe, but they will be confiscated upon your return to the US, and there will be no refund. For information about other animals on the endangered species list, contact the Department of the Interior, US Fish and Wildlife Service (Publications Unit, 4401 N. Fairfax Dr., Room 130, Arlington, VA 22203; phone: 703-358-1711), and ask for the free publication *Facts About Federal Wildlife Laws.*

Also note that some foreign governments prohibit the export of items made from certain species of wildlife, and the US honors any such restrictions. Before you go shopping in any foreign country, check with the US Department of Agriculture (G110 Federal Bldg., Hyattsville, MD 20782; phone: 301-436-8413) and find out what items from the country you will be visiting are prohibited.

The US Customs Service publishes a series of free pamphlets with customs information. It includes *Know Before You Go,* a basic discussion of customs requirements pertaining to all travelers; *Buyer Beware, International Mail Imports; Travelers' Tips on Bringing Food, Plant, and Animal Products into the United States; Importing a Car; GSP and the Traveler; Pocket Hints; Currency Reporting; Pets, Wildlife, US Customs; Customs Hints for Visitors (Nonresidents);* and *Trademark Information for Travelers.* For the entire series or individual pamphlets, write to the US Customs Service (PO Box

7474, Washington, DC 20044) or contact any of the seven regional offices — in Boston, Chicago, Houston, Long Beach (California), Miami, New Orleans, and New York.

Note that the US Customs Service has a tape-recorded message whereby callers using touch-tone phones can obtain free pamphlets on various travel-related topics; the number is 202-566-8195. These pamphlets provide great briefing material, but if you still have questions when you're in Europe, contact the nearest US consulate or the US Embassy.

Sources and Resources

Tourist Information Offices

North American branches of the Portuguese National Tourist Office generally are the best sources of travel information, and most of their many, varied publications are free for the asking. For the best results, request general information on specific provinces or cities, as well as publications relating to your particular areas of interest: accommodations, restaurants, special events, sports, guided tours, and facilities for specific sports. There is no need to send a self-addressed, stamped envelope with your request, unless specified.

The best places for tourist information in Portuguese cities are listed in the individual reports in THE CITIES. The following North American tourist information offices are best equipped to handle written or telephone inquiries from potential visitors on this side of the Atlantic.

New York: 590 Fifth Ave., Fourth Floor, New York, NY 10036-4704 (phone: 212-354-4403).

Canada: 60 Bloom St. W., Suite 1005, Toronto, Ontario M4W 3B8 (phone: 416-921-7376).

The Portuguese Embassy and Consulates in the US

The Portuguese government maintains an embassy and a number of consulates in the US. One of their primary functions is to provide visas for certain resident aliens (depending on their country of origin) and for Americans planning to visit for longer than 60 days, or to study, reside, or work in Portugal. Consulates also are empowered to sign official documents and to notarize copies or translations of US documents, which may be necessary for those papers to be considered legal abroad.

Listed below are the Portuguese embassy and consulates in the US.

Embassy: 2125 Kalorama Rd. NW, Washington, DC 20008 (phone: 202-328-8610).

Consulates:

- 899 Boylston St., Second Floor, Boston, MA 02115 (phone: 617-536-8740).
- 1180 Raymond Blvd., Suite 222, Newark, NJ 07102 (phone: 201-622-7300).
- 628 Pleasant St., Suite 204, New Bedford, MA 02740 (phone: 508-997-6151).
- 630 Fifth Ave., Suite 655, New York, NY 10111 (phone: 212-246-4580).
- 56 Pine St., Sixth Floor, Providence, RI 02903 (phone: 401-272-2003).
- 3298 Washington St., San Francisco, CA 94115 (phone: 415-346-3400).

Theater and Special Event Tickets

In more than one section of this book you will read about events that spark your interest — everything from music festivals and special theater seasons to sporting championships — along with telephone numbers and addresses to which to write for descriptive brochures, reservations, or tickets. The Portuguese National Tourist Office can supply information on these and other special events and festivals that take place in Portugal, though they cannot in all cases provide the actual program or detailed information on ticket prices.

Since many of these occasions often are fully booked well in advance, think about having your reservation in hand before you go. In some cases, tickets may be reserved over the phone and charged to a credit card, or you can send an international money order or foreign draft. If you do write, remember that any request from the US should be accompanied by an International Reply Coupon to ensure a response (send two of them for an airmail response). These international coupons, money orders, and drafts are available at US post offices.

For further information, write for the *European Travel Commission*'s extensive list of events scheduled for the entire year for its 24 member countries (including Portugal). For a free copy, send a self-addressed, stamped, business-size (4 x 9½) envelope, to "European Events," *European Travel Commission* (PO Box 1754, New York, NY 10185). They also publish a free brochure called *Planning Your Trip to Europe.* To order a copy, send a self-addressed, stamped (postage is 52¢) envelope to the *European Travel Commission* at a different ordering address: PO Box 9012, East Setauket, NY 11723.

Books, Magazines, Newspapers, and Newsletters

BOOKS: Throughout GETTING READY TO GO, numerous books and brochures have been recommended as good sources of further information on a variety of topics.

Suggested Reading – The list below comprises books we have seen and think worthwhile; it is by no means complete — but meant merely to start you on your way. Unless indicated, all the books listed here are in print, but you also may want to do some additional research at your local library. These titles include some informative guides to special interests, solid fiction and poetry, and books that call your attention to things you might not notice otherwise.

Food & Wine

Around Mama's Kitchen: Authentic Portuguese Recipes by Gussie De Faria (Woods Hole Press; $6.95).

The Food of Portugal by Jean Anderson (Morrow; $24.95).

Food of Spain and Portugal: The Complete Iberian Cuisine by Elizabeth Ortiz (Macmillan; $22.50).

Wines of Portugal by Jan Reed (Faber & Faber; $11.95).

Art and Architecture

Country Manors of Portugal by Marcus Binney (Scala Books; $55).

Gardens of Portugal by Patrick Bowe (Rizzoli International Publications; $50).

Lives of the Artists by Giorgio Vasari (Penguin Classics; volume I $6.95, volume II $5.95).

The Story of Art by E. H. Gombrich (Prentice Hall; $43).

Culture

Long Stays in Portugal by Roger W. Hicks and Francis Schultz (Hippocrene Books; $19.95).

Living in Portugal: A Complete Guide by Susan Thackery (Trans-Atlantic Publications; $33.50).

Roads to Today's Portugal by Nelson Vieria (Gava-Brown; $8).

Women of the Praia: Work and Lives in a Portuguese Coastal Community by Sally Cooper Cole (Princeton University Press; $39.50).

History

The English in Portugal by Fernão Lopes (Aris & Phillips; $25).

The European Discovery of America by Samuel Eliot Morison (Oxford University Press; published in two volumes, $39.95 each)

Explorer World Atlas: Commemorating the Age of Discovery by Rand McNally Staff (Rand McNally; $29.95).

Inquisition by Edward Peters (University of California Press; $12.95).

Ocean Traders: From the Portuguese Discoveries to the Present Day by Michael Marshall (Facts on File; $24.95).

Portugal: Ancient Country, Young Democracy edited by Kenneth Maxwell and Michael H. Haltzel (Wilson Center Press; $22.75).

Portugal: From Monarchy to Pluralist Democracy by Walter C. Opello, Jr. (Westview; part of the Nations of Contemporary Western Europe Series; $34.95).

Portugal of Salazar by Michael Derrick (Ayer Company Publishers; $12.50).

Literature

Always Astonished: Selected Prose by Fernando Pessoa (City Lights; $8.95).

Book of Disquiet by Fernando Pessoa (Serpents Tail; $15.99).

By the Rivers of Babylon by Jorge de Sena (Rutgers University Press; $10.95).

The Cold Stove League by Thomas Boyle (Academy Chicago Publishers; $5.95).

The Inhabited Heart: The Selected Poems of Eugenio de Andrade (Perivale; $7.95).

The Lusiads by Luis de Camões (Penguin; $8.95).

Marine Rose by Sophia de Mello Breyner (Black Swan; $20).

The Muse Reborn: The Poetry of Antonio Ferreira edited by T. F. Earle (Oxford University Press; $55).

Salazar Blinks by David R. Slavitt (Collier Books; $8.95).

Travels in My Homeland by Viscount Almeida Garrett (Dufour; $22.50).

General Travel

The Mandarins by Simone de Beauvoir (W. W. Norton; $12.95).

Portugal in Pictures Visual Geography Series (Lerner Publications; $12.95).

The Portugal Traveler: Great Sights and Hidden Treasures by Barbara Radcliffe Rogers and Stillman Rogers (Mills & Sanderson; $9.95).

They Went to Portugal by Rose Macaulay (G. Cape, London; $36.95)

Portuguese Language Phrasebooks and Dictionaries

Common Usage Dictionary: Portuguese-English/English-Portuguese by Oscar Fernandez (Crown Publishing; $4).

Living Portuguese: The Complete Living Language Course (Crown Publishing; includes two 60-minute cassettes and manual; $20).

Portuguese-English/English-Portuguese Dictionary (Hippocrene Books; $11.95).

Portuguese Phrase Book (Berlitz Publishing Co.; $5.95).

In addition, *Culturgrams* is a handy series of pamphlets that provides a good sampling of information on the people, cultures, sights, and bargains to be found in over 90 countries around the world. Each four-page, newsletter-size leaflet covers one country, and Portugal is included in the series. The topics included range from customs and courtesies to lifestyles and demographics. These fact-filled pamphlets are published by the David M. Kennedy Center for International Studies at Brigham Young University; for an order form contact the group c/o Publication Services (280 HRCB, Provo, UT 84602; phone: 801-378-6528). When ordering from 1 to 5 *Culturgrams,* the price is $1 each; 6 to 49 pamphlets cost 50¢ each; and for larger quantities, the price per copy goes down proportionately.

Another source of cultural information, is *Do's and Taboos Around the World,* compiled by the Parker Pen Company and edited by Roger E. Axtell. It focuses on protocol, customs, etiquette, hand gestures and body language, gift giving, the dangers of using US jargon, and so on, and can be fun to read even if you're not going anyplace. It's available for $10.95 in bookstores or through John Wiley & Sons, 1 Wiley Dr., Somerset, NJ 08875 (phone: 212-850-6418).

Sources – The books listed above may be ordered directly from the publishers or found in the travel section of any good general bookstore or any sizeable public library. If you still can't find something, the following stores and/or mail-order houses also specialize in travel literature. They offer books on the US along with guides to the rest of the world, and in some cases, even an old Baedeker or two.

Book Passage (51 Tamal Vista Blvd., Corte Madera, CA 94925; phone: 415-927-0960 in California; 800-321-9785 elsewhere in the US). Travel guides and maps to all areas of the world. A free catalogue is available.

The Complete Traveller (199 Madison Ave., New York, NY 10016; phone: 212-685-9007). Travel guides and maps. A catalogue is available for $2.

Forsyth Travel Library (PO Box 2975, Shawnee Mission, KS 66201-1375; phone: 800-367-7984 or 913-384-3440). Travel guides and maps, old and new, to all parts of the world, including Portugal. Ask for the "Worldwide Travel Books and Maps" catalogue.

Phileas Fogg's Books and Maps (87 *Stanford Shopping Center,* Palo Alto, CA 94304; phone: 800 533-FOGG or 415-327-1754). Travel guides, maps, and language aids.

Powell's Travel Store (Pioneer Courthouse Sq., 701 SW 6th Ave., Portland, OR 97204; phone: 503-228-1108). A panoply of travel-related books and materials (over 15,000 titles, as well as globes, maps, language aids, and videos), supplies and accessories (luggage, travel irons, electrical converters, and so on), and service (there is even a travel agency on the premises) — essentially "one-stop shopping" for the traveler.

The Reader's Catalog (250 W. 57th St., Suite 1330, New York, NY 10107; phone: 800-733-BOOK or 212-262-7198). This general mail-order catalogue business will make recommendations on travel — and other — books, and ship them anywhere in the world.

Tattered Cover (2955 E. First Ave., Denver, CO 80206; phone: 800-833-9327 or 303-322-7727). The travel department alone of this enormous bookstore carries over 7,000 books, as well as maps and atlases. No catalogue is offered (the list is too extensive), but a newsletter, issued three times a year, is available on request.

Thomas Brothers Maps & Travel Books (603 W. Seventh St., Los Angeles, CA 90017; phone: 213-627-4018). Maps (including road atlases, street guides, and wall maps), guidebooks, and travel accessories.

Traveller's Bookstore (22 W. 52nd St., New York, NY 10019; phone: 212-664-

0995). Travel guides, maps, literature, and accessories. A catalogue is available for $2.

In addition, *Luso Brazilian* specializes in Portuguese and Brazilian books, some in English translation. The store has a mail-order facility and can be reached at PO Box 170286, Brooklyn, NY 11217 (phone: 718-624-4000).

NEWSPAPERS AND MAGAZINES: A subscription to the *International Herald Tribune* is a good idea for dedicated travelers. This English-language newspaper is written and edited mostly in Paris and is *the* newspaper read most regularly and avidly by Americans abroad to keep up with world news, US news, sports, the stock market (US and foreign), fluctuations in the exchange rate, and an assortment of help-wanted ads, real estate listings, and personals, global in scope. Published 6 days a week (no Sunday paper), it is available at newsstands throughout the US and in cities worldwide. Although you may have some difficulty finding it on newsstands in Portugal, larger hotels may have copies in the lobby for guests — if you don't see a copy, ask the hotel concierge if it is available. A 1-year's subscription in the US costs $369 (believe it or not, it's $20 less in New York City: $349). To subscribe, write or call the Subscription Manager, *International Herald Tribune,* 850 Third Ave., 10th Floor, New York, NY 10022 (phone: 800-882-2884 or 212-752-3890).

Among the major US publications that can be bought (generally a day or two after distribution in the US) in some of the larger cities and resort areas, at hotels, airports, and newsstands, are *The New York Times, USA Today,* and the *Wall Street Journal.* As with other imports, expect these and other US publications to cost considerably more in Portugal than in the US.

As sampling the regional fare is likely to be one of the highlights of any visit, you will find reading about local edibles worthwhile before you go or after you return. *Gourmet,* a magazine specializing in food, now and then features articles on Portuguese cooking and touring, although its scope is much broader. It is available at newsstands throughout the US for $2.50 an issue or for $18 a year from *Gourmet* (PO Box 53780, Boulder, CO 80322-2886; phone: 800-365-2454). There are numerous additional magazines for every special interest available; check at your library information desk for a directory of such publications, or look over the selection offered by a well-stocked newsstand.

NEWSLETTERS: Throughout GETTING READY TO GO we have mentioned specific newsletters which our readers may be interested in consulting for further information. One of the very best sources of detailed travel information is *Consumer Reports Travel Letter.* Published monthly by Consumers Union (PO Box 53629, Boulder, CO 80322-3629; phone: 800-999-7959), it offers comprehensive coverage of the travel scene on a wide variety of fronts. A year's subscription costs $37; 2 years, $57.

In addition, the following travel newsletters provide useful up-to-date information on travel services and bargains:

Entree (PO Box 5148, Santa Barbara, CA 93150; phone: 805-969-5848). This newsletter caters to a sophisticated, discriminating traveler with the means to explore the places mentioned. Subscribers have access to a 24-hour hotline providing information on restaurants and accommodations around the world. Monthly; a year's subscription costs $59.

The Hideaway Report (Harper Associates, Subscription Office, PO Box 300, Whitefish, MO 59937; phone: 406-862-3480). This monthly source highlights retreats — including Portuguese idylls — for sophisticated travelers. A year's subscription costs $90.

Romantic Hideaways (217 E. 86th St., Suite 258, New York, NY 10028; phone: 212-969-8682). This monthly newsletter leans toward those special places made for those traveling in twos. A year's subscription costs $65.

Travel Smart (Communications House, 40 Beechdale Rd., Dobbs Ferry, NY 10522; phone: 914-693-8300 in New York; 800-327-3633 elsewhere in the US). This monthly covers a wide variety of trips and travel discounts. A year's subscription costs $44.

■ **Computer Services:** Anyone who owns a personal computer and a modem can subscribe to a database service providing everything from airline schedules and fares to restaurant listings. Two such services of particular use to travelers are *CompuServe* (5000 Arlington Center Blvd., Columbus, OH 43220; phone: 800-848-8199 or 614-457-8600; $39.95 to join, plus usage fees of $6 to $12.50 per hour) and *Prodigy Services* (445 Hamilton Ave., White Plains, NY 10601; phone: 800-822-6922 or 914-993-8000; $12.95 per month's subscription, plus variable usage fees).

Before using any computer bulletin-board services, be sure to take precautions to prevent downloading of a computer "virus." First install one of the programs designed to screen out such nuisances.

Genealogy Hunts

Some of the most extensive pedigrees in the world are to be found in Portugal, where bloodlines date back to Roman times. The country's isolation on the Iberian Peninsula between Spain and the sea has produced a unique race: proud, brave, and independent, with a distinctive history. Facing outward toward the waters of the Atlantic, the Portuguese people developed with a passion for maritime exploration of lands beyond the horizon.

Few immigrants have settled in Portugal, but many have emigrated since the 1500s — for Portugal was a major world power at this time — and settled in Portuguese colonies in South America (Brazil), Africa (Angola, Mozambique, Guinea, St. Thomas), India, and Asia (Macao). Of these, only Macao remains under Portuguese administration today. The Atlantic islands of Madeira and the Azores always have been considered an integral part of Portugal. During the 19th century, a great many Portuguese from these islands came to North America, settling chiefly in California, Hawaii, Massachusetts, and Rhode Island.

Happily for contemporary ancestor-worshipers, the Portuguese have kept pretty good records, beginning as far back as the 14th century in some cases, and legitimate evidence of Iberian forebears — no matter how humble their origins — usually is yours for the searching. With a little digging around, you'll probably at least be able to visit the church where your great-uncle Julio married your great-aunt Celina before leaving for America, or the port where your grandfather waved good-bye to the Old Country, or the cemetery where your mother's family has been resting quietly for centuries.

While there is not much written on how to conduct research in Portugal, if dig you must, try to do as much preliminary research as possible before your trip. One of the challenges of this sort of project is the need for creativity, since most people don't have convenient pedigree charts they can consult. Family Bibles are a good source, as are old letters, documents, photographs, or heirlooms, even anecdotes from the oldest members of your family (that's how Alex Haley began when he traced his own *Roots*). What follows is, hopefully, a helpful primer on how to tackle what may at first appear to be a daunting project.

To begin with, check your library and state offices for local published records, regional archives, and local history. The *US Library of Congress* (Local History and Genealogy Reading Room, Jefferson Building, Washington, DC 20540; phone: 202-707-5537) and the *New York Public Library* (Division of US History, Local History and Genealogy, Room 315N, 42nd St. & Fifth Ave., New York, NY 10018; phone: 212-930-0828) both have extensive facilities for personal research; however, you may want to call ahead to find out if they have material relevant to your particular search.

Those wishing to trace their Portuguese ancestry may wish to join the *American-Portuguese Genealogical Society.* For information, contact Cecilia Rose (PO Box 644, Taunton, MA 02780; phone: 508-823-3330). This society has amassed a large number (65,000) of ancestral records — primarily on individuals who lived before the turn of the century — which are housed in the nearby Taunton Public Library (12 Pleasant St., Taunton, MA 02780; phone: 508-821-1411). Both are a good source of information on researching your Portuguese ancestry.

Another source of Portuguese information is the *Genealogical Society of the Church of Jesus Christ of Latter-Day Saints,* which has thousands of reels of genealogical records on microfilm, available for consultation in person at its headquarters, the Family History Library (35 NW Temple St., Salt Lake City, UT 84150; phone: 801-240-2331; open Mondays through Saturdays), or through any of its branch libraries. Ruth Gomez de Scheirmacher (phone: 801-240-2881) will guide anyone who asks through the first steps to be taken in a search. Using the Mormons' index reels, you can, for a small fee, order from Salt Lake City the microfilm records of most Portuguese towns. The film should arrive at the branch library in about 6 to 8 weeks, and loans are renewable for 2-week periods up to 6 months. There is no charge for reviewing a film at the headquarters in Salt Lake City.

An indispensable resource found in most libaries is the scholarly reference guide, *The World of Learning* (Europa Publications), which lists libraries and archives throughout Portugal. Also look in your library for T. Beard's and D. Demong's comprehensive *How to Find Your Family Roots* (McGraw-Hill, 1977), which contains an excellent list of available genealogical resources. *In Search of Your European Roots* by Angus Baxter (Genealogical Publishing Co., 1985) has chapters on Portugal, as does Noel Currer-Briggs's *Worldwide Family History* (Routledge & Kegan Paul, 1982). For general information, take a look at Jeane Eddy Westin's *Finding Your Roots* (J. P. Tarcher, distributed by St. Martin's Press). Another book of particular relevance to genealogical studies in Portugal is *Silva Descendents* (out of print, but found in some libraries).

You also may want to subscribe to the excellent *Ancestry Newsletter,* edited by Robb Barr and published bimonthly by Ancestry Incorporated (PO Box 476, Salt Lake City, UT 84110; phone: 800-531-1790); a yearly subscription costs $12.

Constructing a family tree is a backward process: You need to start with your parents' dates and places of birth, their parents' dates and places, and so on, as far back as you can. It should be a considerable stretch since it's quite possible to trace back several hundred years. To obtain the relevant documents, make sure you have the exact names of each ancestor (remember, many immigrants' surnames were irrevocably, if unwittingly, changed through clerical misspellings at Ellis Island and other ports of entry), as well as the names of any family members closely related to the ancestor you are researching. You can request many different types of documents that contain information about a previous generation: for example, birth and death certificates, marriage licenses, emigration and immigration records, and baptism and christening records.

In Portugal, unless your ancestors were members of the aristocracy, parish records weren't kept consistently until about the early 16th century, though again, it may be possible to go back as far as 1390, when the writing of parish records first was promulgated by King Afonso IV. The Council of Trent (1545–63) was convened in northern Italy to reestablish discipline in the Catholic church, and one of the ways it did this was by insisting that parish priests all over the world keep a register of church events. In Portugal, there was an almost 100% compliance with this edict. Although the registers are a little unorthodox, they almost certainly will have the personal observations of the local priest and details of baptisms and burials. Something to bear in mind in the case of Portugal, however, are three events that caused great destruction of records: the 1755 earthquake in Lisbon; the French invasions that devastated the provinces of Beira, Baixa, and Ribatejo; and the invasion of Alentejo by the Spanish.

REQUESTING RECORDS: Before about 1870, personal records — baptism, confirmation, marriage, and death — were kept, for the most part, only by parish churches. Thus, to obtain information on your family before 1865, you should begin by writing either to the parish priest or to the bishop holding territorial jurisdiction. Since about 1865, birth, marriage, death, and citizenship records have been kept by municipalities, so, after discovering where your ancestors came from, you must write to the local authorities. There are important archives in all the major centers, as well as in smaller towns and villages. Again, on the local level you will find civil registration *(registo civil)* as well as church registers *(registos paroquiais).*

It's worth noting that because of the close ties between Great Britain and Portugal and the number of British businessmen living in the country, there were Church of England (Anglican) churches in Lisbon and Madeira. Registers for the period from 1721 to 1890 are in the custody of the Bishop of London in England. Bear in mind also that in Portugal, records of the notorious Catholic Inquisition trials held in Lisbon, Coimbra, and Evora in particular (roughly from the 15th to the 18th century) often include very detailed personal biographies of the accused people. They all can be found in the Portuguese National Archives in Lisbon.

DIGGING DEEPER: Once you've done your basic research, you might want to turn to some older records or even use them as duplicates to verify information you've already accumulated. The following are some of the most readily available records by mail or in person.

Certificates of Family Genealogy – Write to the archives office in the town where your family member lived to obtain a certificate of your family genealogy, giving names, relationships, birth dates, and birthplaces of all living family members at the time of recording.

Emigration Records – Passenger lists *(listas de passageiros),* passports *(passaportes),* and other emigration records also can be helpful. Again, try the local archives of the province of the emigrant's birthplace or port of departure to obtain documentation of emigration. In Portugal, passports were first issued in 1757. The records are in the District Archives and list name, date, place of birth, date of the voyage, and destination.

Clerical Surveys and Civil Records – To obtain Catholic parish records in Portugal, write to the particular church or, if it is no longer in existence, the District Archives or the National Archives. The oldest parish register in existence is that of Nabainhos, near Gouveia, which began with a baptism in 1529. Other early ones include Cheleiros and Santiago. If you are writing to the parish priest, ask if he has a list of the names appearing on the tombstones *(pedras tumulares).*

The Portuguese national archives *(Arquivo Nacional da Torre do Tombo)* are in a central office at Alameda da Universidade, Lisbon 1600; Civil Registration Archives *(Conservatórias do Registo Civil)* are kept in Lisbon, as are the Property Registration Archives *(Conservatórias do Registo Predial)* and the National Identification Archives *(Conservatórias de Identificação Civil e Criminal).*

With the above information and a little patience, you should have a firm grasp for a lengthy climb up your family tree.

Weights and Measures

When traveling in Portugal, you'll find that just about every quantity, whether it is length, weight, or capacity, will be expressed in unfamiliar terms. In fact, this is true for travel almost everywhere in the world, since the US is one of the last countries to make its way to the metric system. Your trip to Portugal may serve to familiarize you with what one day may be the weights and measures at your grocery store.

There are some specific things to keep in mind during your trip. Fruits and vegetables at a market generally are recorded in kilos (kilograms), as are your luggage at the airport and your body weight. (This latter is particularly pleasing to people of significant size, who, instead of weighing 220 pounds, hit the scales at a mere 100 kilos.) A kilo equals 2.2 pounds and 1 pound is .45 kilo. Body temperature usually is measured in degrees centigrade or Celsius rather than on the Fahrenheit scale, so that a normal body temperature is 37C, not 98.6F, and freezing is 0 degrees C rather than 32F.

Gasoline is sold by the liter (approximately 3.8 liters to 1 gallon). Tire pressure gauges and other equipment measure in kilograms per square centimeter rather than pounds per square inch. Highway signs are written in kilometers rather than miles (1 mile equals 1.6 km; 1 km equals .62 mile). And speed limits are in kilometers per hour, so think twice before hitting the gas when you see a speed limit of 100. That means 62 miles per hour.

The tables and conversion factors listed below should give you all the information you will need to understand any transaction, road sign, or map you encounter during your travels.

CONVERSION TABLES
METRIC TO US MEASUREMENTS

Multiply:	by:	to convert to:
LENGTH		
millimeters	.04	inches
meters	3.3	feet
meters	1.1	yards
kilometers	.6	miles
CAPACITY		
liters	2.11	pints (liquid)
liters	1.06	quarts (liquid)
liters	.26	gallons (liquid)
WEIGHT		
grams	.04	ounces (avoir.)
kilograms	2.2	pounds (avoir.)

US TO METRIC MEASUREMENTS

LENGTH		
inches	25.	millimeters
feet	.3	meters
yards	.9	meters
miles	1.6	kilometers
CAPACITY		
pints	.47	liters
quarts	.95	liters
gallons	3.8	liters
WEIGHT		
ounces	28.	grams
pounds	.45	kilograms

TEMPERATURE

°F = (°C × 9/5) + 32 °C = (°F − 32) × 5/9

APPROXIMATE EQUIVALENTS

Metric Unit	Abbreviation	US Equivalent
LENGTH		
meter	m	39.37 inches
kilometer	km	.62 mile
millimeter	mm	.04 inch
CAPACITY		
liter	l	1.057 quarts
WEIGHT		
gram	g	.035 ounce
kilogram	kg	2.2 pounds
metric ton	MT	1.1 ton
ENERGY		
kilowatt	kw	1.34 horsepower

Cameras and Equipment

Vacations are everybody's favorite time for taking pictures and home movies. After all, most of us want to remember the places we visit — and show them off to others. Here are a few suggestions to help you get the best results from your travel photography or videography.

BEFORE THE TRIP

If you're taking your camera or camcorder out after a long period in mothballs, or have just bought a new one, check it thoroughly before you leave to prevent unexpected breakdowns or disappointing pictures.

1. Still cameras should be cleaned carefully and thoroughly, inside and out. If using a camcorder, run a head cleaner through it. You also may want to have your camcorder professionally serviced (opening the casing yourself will violate the manufacturer's warranty). Always use filters to protect your lens while traveling.
2. Check the batteries for your camera's light meter and flash, and take along extras just in case yours wear out during the trip. For camcorders, bring along extra Nickel-Cadmium (Ni-Cad) batteries; if you use rechargeable batteries, a recharger will cut down on the extras.
3. Using all the settings and features, shoot at least one test roll of film or one videocassette, using the type you plan to take along with you.

EQUIPMENT TO TAKE ALONG

Keep your gear light and compact. Items that are too heavy or bulky to be carried comfortably on a full-day excursion will likely remain in your hotel room.

1. Invest in a broad camera or camcorder strap if you now have a thin one. It will make carrying the camera much more comfortable.
2. A sturdy canvas, vinyl, or leather camera or camcorder bag, preferably with padded pockets (not an airline bag), will keep your equipment organized and easy to find. If you will be doing much shooting around the water, a waterproof case is best.
3. For cleaning, bring along a camel's hair brush that retracts into a rubber squeeze bulb. Also take plenty of lens tissue, soft cloths, and plastic bags to protect equipment from dust and moisture.

■ **Note:** If you are planning on using your camcorder in Europe, note that most European countries (including Portugal) operate on a different electrical current than the US, so you should make sure that the battery charger that comes with your camcorder is compatible with the current in the countries you're visiting. You'll also need a plug adapter kit to cope with the variations in plug configurations found in Europe. And don't expect to be able to play back your tape through a European TV set or VCR. The US and Canada use a different television standard than most European countries; these systems are incompatible with each other and multiple-standard TV sets are rare.

FILM AND TAPES: If you are concerned about airport security X-rays damaging undeveloped film (X-rays do not affect processed film) or tapes, store them in one of the lead-lined bags sold in camera shops. This possibility is not as much of a threat as it used to be, however. In the US and Canada, incidents of X-ray damage to unprocessed film (exposed or unexposed) are few because low-dosage X-ray equipment is used virtually everywhere. However, when crossing international borders, travelers should know that foreign X-ray equipment used for carry-on baggage may deliver higher levels of radiation and that even more powerful X-ray equipment may be used for checked luggage, so it's best to carry your film on board.

If you're traveling without a protective bag, you may want to ask to have your photo equipment inspected by hand. In the US, Federal Aviation Administration regulations require that if you request a hand inspection, you get it, but overseas the response may depend on the humor of the inspector. One type of film that should never be subjected to X-rays is the very high speed ASA 1000; there are lead-lined bags made especially for it — and, in the event that you are refused a hand inspection, this is the only way to save your film. The walk-through metal detector devices at airports do not affect film, though the film cartridges may set them off. Because cassettes have been favorite carriers for terrorist explosives over the years, airport officials probably will insist that you put these through the X-ray machine as well. If you don't have a choice, put them through and hope for the best.

You should have no problem finding film or tapes throughout Europe. When buying film, tapes, or photo accessories the best rule of thumb is to stick to name brands with which you are familiar. Different countries have their own ways of labeling camcorder tapes, and although the variations in recording and playback standards won't affect your ability to use the tape, they will affect how quickly you record and how much time you actually have to record on the tape. The availability of film processing labs and equipment repair shops will vary from area to area.

- **A note about courtesy and caution:** When photographing individuals in Portugal (and anywhere else in the world), ask first. It's common courtesy. Furthermore, some governments have security regulations regarding the use of cameras and will not permit the photographing of certain subjects, such as particular government and military installations. When in doubt, ask.

Useful Words and Phrases

Unlike the French, who tend to be a bit brusque if you don't speak their language perfectly, the Portuguese do not expect you to speak their native tongue — but are very flattered when you try. In many circumstances, you won't have to, because the staffs at most hotels, as well as at a fair number of restaurants, speak serviceable English, or at least a modicum of it, which they usually are eager to try — and that means practicing with you. If you find yourself in a situation where your limited Portuguese turns out to be the only means of communication, take the plunge. Don't be afraid of misplaced accents or misconjugated verbs — in most cases you will be understood.

The list that follows is a selection of commonly used words and phrases to speed you on your way. Note that in Portuguese, nouns either are masculine or feminine, as well as singular or plural, and that the adjectives that modify them must agree in both gender and quantity. Most nouns ending in *o* in the singular are masculine; the *o* becomes *os* in the plural. Most nouns ending in *a* in the singular are feminine; the *a* becomes *as* in the plural. Nouns may have other endings.

In Portuguese, the letter *a* is pronounced as in *watch.* The *e* in stressed syllables sounds like *eh,* as in English *pear* or *era.* Unstressed final *e* is pronounced like the *i* in *pin.* The *i* in Portuguese is a simple vowel similar to the *i* in *pique.* Initial *i* before a vowel is pronounced like English *y* in *yet.* Stressed *o* also is a simple vowel pronounced as in *orb;* when written *ô* it is pronounced like the *o* in *mote.* Unstressed final *o* is pronounced like the *u* in *put.* The stressed *u* is pronounced as in *toot.* When vowels either bear a tilde (˜) or are followed by *m, n,* or *nh,* the pronunciation is nasal; that is, some air is emitted through the nose while the vowel is being pronounced. The French pronunciations of *dance* and *cent* illustrate this sound. The *ei* is "long a," *ai* stands for "long i," *ou* stands for "long o," and *au* has the vowel sound of *how.* Portuguese words are generally stressed on the vowel preceding the last consonant. A nasalized vowel preceding a final vowel will be stressed.

Portuguese consonants are pronounced much like English with these exceptions: In Portuguese as in English, *c* always is hard before *a, o, u,* or a consonant, as in *car, core,* and *climb;* however *ch* has a soft sound like *sh* in *show.* (The letter *x* is also pronounced like *sh.*) *C* is soft when it falls before *e* or *i* or is marked with a cedilla (ç), as in *century.* The *s* following a stressed vowel is pronounced with a *z* sound, as in *rose.* The letter *i* is pronounced like *si* in *vision.* The letter *t* before a final unstressed *e* is pronounced like English *ch; d* in the same position is pronounced like English *i.*

These are only the most basic rules, and even they may seem daunting at first, but they shouldn't remain so for long. Nevertheless, if you can't get your mouth to speak Portuguese, try your hands at it: With a little observation, you'll pick it up quickly and be surprised at how often your message will get across.

Greetings and Everyday Expressions

Good morning! (also, Good day)	*Bom dia!*
Good afternoon/evening!	*Boa tarde/noite!*
Hello!	*Ola!*
How are you?	*Como esta?*
Pleased to meet you. (How do you do?)	*Muito prazer em conhecê-lo (-la).*
Good-bye!	*Adeus!*
So long!	*Até logo!*
Goodnight! (when leaving)	*Boa noite!*
Yes	*Sim*
No	*Não*
Please	*Se faz favor/Por favor*
Thank you	*Obrigado(a)*
You're welcome	*De nada*
I beg your pardon (Excuse me)	*Perdão*
I don't speak Portuguese.	*Não falo português.*
Do you speak English?	*Fala inglês?*
I don't understand.	*Não compreêndo.*
Do you understand?	*Compreênde?/Entende?*
My name is . . .	*Chamo-me . . .*
What is your name?	*Como se chama?*
miss	*menina*
madame	*senhora*
mister	*senhor*
open	*aberto/a*
closed	*encerrado(a)/fechado(a)*
entrance	*entrada*
exit	*saída*
push	*empurre*
pull	*puxe*
today	*hoje*
tomorrow	*amanhã*
yesterday	*ontem*

Checking In

I would like . . .	*Queria/Costaria . . .*
I have a reservation	*Mandei reservar*
a single room	*um quarto individual*
a double room	*um quarto duplo*
a quiet room	*um quarto tranquilo*

with bath	*com banho*
with shower	*com chuveiro*
with a sea view	*com vista para o mar*
with air conditioning	*com ar condicionado*
with balcony	*com varanda*
overnight only	*só uma noite*
a few days	*alguns dias*
a week (at least)	*uma semana (pelo menos)*
with full board	*com pensão completa*
with half board	*com meia-pensão*
Does that price include	*O preço está incluido*
breakfast	*cafe da manhâ*
taxes	*os impostos*
VAT (Value Added Tax)	*IVA*
It doesn't work.	*Não funciona*
Do you accept traveler's checks?	*Aceitam cheques de viagem?*
Do you accept credit cards?	*Posso pagar com cartão de crédito?*

Eating Out

ashtray	*um cinzeiro*
bottle	*uma garrafa*
(extra) chair	*uma cadeira (mais)*
cup	*uma chávena*
fork	*um garfo*
knife	*uma faca*
napkin	*um guardanapo*
plate	*um prato*
spoon	*uma colher*
table	*uma mesa*
beer	*uma cerveja*
hot cocoa	*um cacau*
black coffee	*um café*
coffee with milk	*café com leite*
cream	*creme*
milk	*leite*
tea	*um chá*
fruit juice	*um sumo de fruta*
lemonade	*um gasosa*
water	*água*
mineral water	*água mineral*
(carbonated)	*(com gás)*
(not carbonated)	*(sem gas)*
orangeade	*uma laranjada*
port	*vinho do Porto*
sherry	*vinho de Xerez*
red wine	*vinho tinto*
white wine	*vinho branco*
cold	*frio/a*
hot	*quente*

sweet	*doce*
(very) dry	*(extra) seco/a*
bacon	*bacon/toucinho Americano*
bread	*pão*
butter	*manteiga*
eggs	*ovos*
hard-boiled	*ovo cozido*
fried	*ovos estrelados*
omelette	*omeleta*
soft-boiled	*ovo(s) quente(s)*
scrambled	*ovos mexidos*
honey	*mel*
jam/marmalade	*doce de fruta/marmelada*
orange juice	*sumo de laranja*
pepper	*pimenta*
salt	*sal*
sugar	*açúcar*
Waiter	*Criado*
I would like	*Queria*
a glass of	*um copo de*
a bottle of	*uma garrafa de*
a half bottle of	*uma meia-garrafa de*
a carafe of	*um jarro de*
a liter of	*um litro de*
The check, please.	*A conta, por favor.*
Is a service charge included?	*E serviço incluido?*
I think you made a mistake in this bill.	*Creio que se enganou na conta.*

Shopping

bakery	*a padaria*
bookstore	*a livraria*
butcher shop	*o talho*
camera shop	*a loja de artigos fotográficos*
cosmetics store	*perfumaria*
delicatessen	*charcuteria*
department store	*o grande armazém*
grocery	*mercearia*
jewelry store	*a ourivesaria*
newsstand	*o quiosque a banca de jornais*
pastry shop	*a pastelaria*
pharmacy/drugstore	*a farmácia*
shoestore	*a sapataria*
supermarket	*o supermercado*
tobacconist	*a tabacaria*
inexpensive	*barato/a*
expensive	*caro/a*
large	*grande*
larger	*maior*

too large	*muito grande*
small	*pequeno/a*
smaller	*mais pequeno/a*
too small	*muito pequeno/a*
long	*comprido/a*
short	*curto/a*
old	*velho/a*
new	*novo/a*
used	*usado/a*
handmade	*feito/a à mão*
Is it machine washable?	*Pode lavar-sè à máquina?*
How much does it cost?	*Quanto custa isto?*
What is it made of?	*De que é feito?*
camel's hair	*pêlo de camelo*
cotton	*algodão*
corduroy	*bombazina*
filigree	*filigrana*
lace	*renda*
leather	*couro/pele*
linen	*linho*
silk	*seda*
suede	*camurça*
synthetic	*sintético/a*
tiles	*os azulejos*
wool	*lã*
brass	*latão*
copper	*cobre*
gold	*ouro*
gold plate	*banho de ouro*
silver	*prata*
silver plate	*banho de prata*
stainless steel	*aço inoxidável*
wood	*madeira*

Colors

beige	*bege*
black	*prêto/a*
blue	*azul*
brown	*castanho/a*
green	*verde*
gray	*cinzento/a*
orange	*laranja*
pink	*cor de rosa*
purple	*roxo/a*
red	*vermelho/a*
white	*branco/a*
yellow	*amarelo/a*
dark	*escuro/a*
light	*claro/a*

Getting Around

north	*norte*
south	*sul*
east	*este*

west	*oeste*
right	*direita*
left	*esquerda*
Go straight ahead	*Vá sempre em frente*
far	*longe*
near	*perto*
gas station	*estação de serviço*
train station	*a estação de comboios*
bus stop	*a paragem do autocarro*
subway station	*estação de metrô*
airport	*aeroporto*
tourist information	*informações de turismo*
map	*mapa*
one-way ticket	*um bilhete ida*
round-trip ticket	*um bilhete ida e volta*
track/platform	*o cais/a plataforma*
first class	*primeira classe*
second class	*segunda classe*
no smoking	*não fumadores*
gasoline	*gasolina*
normal leaded	*gasolina normal*
super leaded	*gasolina super*
unleaded	*gasolina sem chumbo*
diesel	*diesel*
tires	*pneus*
oil	*o óleo*
Fill it up, please.	*Encha o depósito, por favor.*
Where is . . . ?	*Onde fica . . . ?*
Where are . . . ?	*Onde ficam . . . ?*
How far is it to . . . from here?	*A que distância estamos de . . . ?*
Does this bus go to . . . ?	*Este autocarro pára em . . . ?*
What time does it leave?	*A que horas parte?*
Danger	*Perigo*
Caution	*Cuidado*
Detour	*Desvio*
Do Not Enter	*Entrada Proibida*
No Parking	*Estacionamento Proibido*
No Passing	*Proibido Ultrapassar*
One Way	*Sentido Unico*
Pay Toll	*Pedagio*
Pedestrian Zone	*Pedestres*
Reduce Speed	*Afrouxe/Devagar*
Steep Incline	*Descida Perigosa*
Stop	*Alto*
Use Headlights	*Acender as Luzes*
Yield	*Dê Passagem*

Personal Items and Services

barbershop	*o barbeiro*
beauty shop	*o instituto de beleza*

dry cleaner	*o lavandaria a seco*
hairdresser (salon)	*o cabeleireiro*
launderette	*a lavandaria automática*
laundry	*a lavandaria*
post office	*correio*
aspirins	*aspirinas*
Band-Aids	*pensos rápidos*
condoms	*preservativos*
sanitary napkins	*pensos higiênicos*
shampoo	*um shampoo*
shaving cream	*um creme de barba*
soap	*um sabonete*
stamps	*selos*
tampons	*tampões*
tissues	*lenços de papel*
toilet paper	*papel higiênico*
toothbrush	*uma escova de dentes*
toothpaste	*pasta de dentes*
Where is the bathroom?	*Onde fica a casa de banho?*
The bathroom door will say:	
for the men's room	*Cavalheiros/Homens*
for the women's room	*Senhoras*

Days of the Week

Monday	*Segunda-feira*
Tuesday	*Terça-feira*
Wednesday	*Quarta-feira*
Thursday	*Quinta-feira*
Friday	*Sexta-feira*
Saturday	*Sábado*
Sunday	*Domingo*

Months

January	*Janeiro*
February	*Fevereiro*
March	*Março*
April	*Abril*
May	*Maio*
June	*Junho*
July	*Julho*
August	*Agosto*
September	*Setembro*
October	*Outubro*
November	*Novembro*
December	*Dezembro*

Numbers

zero	*zero*
one	*um/uma*
two	*dois/duas*
three	*três*
four	*quatro*
five	*cinco*

six	*seis*
seven	*sete*
eight	*oito*
nine	*nove*
ten	*dez*
eleven	*onze*
twelve	*doze*
thirteen	*treze*
fourteen	*catorze*
fifteen	*quinze*
sixteen	*dezesseis*
seventeen	*dezessete*
eighteen	*dezoito*
nineteen	*dezenove*
twenty	*vinte*
thirty	*trinta*
forty	*quarenta*
fifty	*cinquenta*
sixty	*sessenta*
seventy	*setenta*
eighty	*oitenta*
ninety	*noventa*
one hundred	*cem*
one thousand	*mil*
1993	*mil novecentos e noventa e três*

PERSPECTIVES

History

For a country that prides itself on its *brandos costumes* (mild manners), Portugal has had a dramatic history. Though a minimum of bloodshed accompanied its 1974 coup (red carnations rather than bullets sprouted from soldiers' rifles), the factions that followed the "Carnation Revolution," the rulers who preceded it, and the clashes of the original prehistoric tribes all belie any idea of excessive mildness in the Portuguese character.

For several millennia, Portugal and Spain, which share the Iberian Peninsula, also shared a common history. The southern end of the peninsula was inhabited in Paleolithic times — no doubt by the same emigrants from Africa who settled elsewhere in southern Europe. By 3000 BC, Mesolithic peoples had settled in the north.

Recorded history, however, begins with three waves of invaders: the Iberians, who came from the eastern Mediterranean or northern Africa in the 3rd millennium BC and spread across the peninsula to which they gave their name; the Celts (the same people who inhabited Ireland, Scotland, and Wales), whose matriarchal, pastoral societies trudged south across the Pyrenees around 900 BC to settle north of the Douro River; and the Lusitanians, a patriarchal, warring society, who occupied the lands between the Tagus and the Minho rivers. Mythically, these Lusitanians, who were known to the Roman writers Polybius and Strabo, are considered the true ancestors of the Portuguese.

Around 1200 BC, more civilized visitors — the Phoenicians — explored the area on Iberia's western coast that would become Portugal's eventual homeland; Phoenician colonists from Carthage soon followed and, about 400 years later, so did the Greeks. During the 3rd century BC, the future country of Portugal shared the fate of most of western Europe: conquest by Rome. Hannibal, the Carthaginian general, had hired Lusitanian mercenaries to fight the Romans. To stop them, the Romans invaded Iberia in 212 BC. Hampered by fierce Lusitanian heroes like Viriatus, still revered in Portuguese (and Spanish) folklore, it took the Romans almost 200 years to conquer the peninsula, which they renamed Hispania; its southernmost portion — part of present-day Portugal — they named Lusitania.

The Romans founded several towns in Lusitania, including Bracara Augusta (Braga), Pax Julia (Beja), and Olisipo (Lisbon). This last, according to legend, was originally founded by Ulysses. Another town, Portus Cale — which became first Portucale and eventually the city of Porto (meaning port) — gave the country of Portugal its name.

As elsewhere in Europe, northern barbarians invaded as Rome grew weak. In AD 409, Suevians swept down from the Pyrenees and established a government seat at Braga. These were rather non-barbaric barbarians. In no time they converted to Christianity, which had arrived on the peninsula from Roman North Africa some 200 years earlier. Nor did they find it troublesome to live at peace with the Visigoths who ruled Hispania under Roman auspices.

The Moors — arguably the most civilized invaders of all — came to Spain in 711 to battle King Rodrigo and his Visigoths, decided to stay, and by the end of the decade had conquered most of the peninsula. In the western part of the peninsula, they did not adapt well to the climate — either political or meteorological — north of the Douro River, where resistance by the Visigothic chieftain Pelayo began almost immediately, and so they settled down instead in the Algarve (from the Arabic *Al-Gharb,* "the west"), south of the Tagus River. There they reigned peacefully over Jews and Christians alike. Though the tolerant Moors allowed both to continue to practice their own religions, Christians in the south — like those in Spain — became so imbued with Islamic culture that they were known as Mozarabs.

But not all Christians. The reconquest of the peninsula, begun in the north by Pelayo early in the 8th century, continued — on and off — for 5 centuries in Portugal, and even longer in Spain. The Christian kings of northern Asturias-León quickly retook Braga, Porto, Viseu, and Guimarães, cities that lay between the Douro and Minho rivers — an area that a 9th-century document calls for the first time *Provincia Portucalense,* Province of Portugal. For the next 200 years, this northern section of present-day Portugal acted as a buffer zone for the Christians struggling to regain the peninsula. By the late 11th century, Christian-held territory extended as far south as Coimbra.

Portugal's independence from Spain began in 1096, when Alfonso VI, King of Castile and León, awarded the northern county of Portucale — an area extending roughly from the Minho River down to the Mondego at Coimbra — to his son-in-law, Henry of Burgundy, the French nobleman and crusader, for helping to fight the Moors at Toledo. Henry died in 1112, leaving his wife, Teresa, regent for their young son, Afonso Henriques.

Some 16 years later, at the urging of the Portuguese, Afonso Henriques assumed his father's role of vassal to Castile and León. Not for long, however. After defeating the armies of his overlord, he triumphed over the Moors at a famous battle in Ourique. Then he supposedly saw a vision of the Cross in the heavens, and taking this as a sign, he proclaimed himself King of Portugal.

King Afonso Henriques and his Burgundian heirs continued the Reconquest southward, taking Lisbon in 1147, the Alentejo in 1225, and finally, the Algarve, Portugal's southernmost edge, in 1249. The nation's boundaries were now defined. King Afonso III transferred the court from Coimbra to Lisbon in about 1260, and his son, King Dinis (who ruled from 1279 to 1325), made Portuguese the country's official language and, in 1290, established its first university (in Lisbon, but later moved to Coimbra). In 1297, the Treaty of Alcañices fixed the border with Spain.

When Ferdinand, the last king of the House of Burgundy, died in 1383, he left no legitimate male heir — only a daughter, Beatrice, and an illegitimate brother, João. Beatrice had married the King of Castile, who, as her consort, would also become King of Portugal. The Cortes (Parliament) would not submit to Spanish rule, however, so they elected the brother, João of Avis, to the throne instead.

The new king reinforced his position by defeating the Spaniards at Aljubarrota in 1385. Aiding him was a contingent of English mercenaries. As a result, England and Portugal signed the Treaty of Windsor in 1386, which decreed perpetual friendship between the two countries; to this day, it remains the longest unbroken alliance in the history of the west. To seal it, King João married Philippa of Lancaster, daughter of John of Gaunt, granddaughter of Edward III, and sister of Henry IV.

The marriage of João and Philippa heralded the beginning of Portugal's greatest age and produced four remarkable sons — Duarte, Pedro, Fernando, and Dom Henrique. One became king, one regent, one a crusader, and the fourth, Prince Henry the Navigator. The great Portuguese writer Luís de Camões called them the "wonderful generation."

In 1415 João I, three of his sons, and a fleet of over 200 ships seized the Moroccan town of Ceuta, a center of the spice trade. Inspired by this victory, Prince Henry founded a school of navigation in Sagres, at Portugal's southwesternmost point, 3 years later. Here on this windswept coast, the scientific-minded prince and his assistants collected information from returning sailors, charted the seas, drew maps, invented nautical instruments, and encouraged exploration.

And so the Age of Discovery began — an era that would turn a small, rather insignificant country into the ruler of one of the world's great empires. No wonder the Portuguese look back to this time with the longing and nostalgia they call *saudade.* Those intrepid explorers who set out from Portugal's Atlantic coast in quest of a route to India discovered Madeira in 1419 and the Azores in 1427 (some say in 1431), and rounded Cape Bojador, on the coast of northwestern Africa, in 1434. Their travels led them to the farthest reaches known to Europe. Henry died in 1460, but Portuguese exploration continued: In 1482, Diogo Cão reached the mouth of the Congo River. In 1488, when Bartholomeu Dias rounded the Tempest Cape on Africa's southern tip, King João II quickly renamed it the Cape of Good Hope.

Four years later, Christopher Columbus discovered the New World; Spain had joined Portugal in the race for empire. To prevent future conflicts between the two nations, Pope Alexander VI drew a vertical line just west of the Cape Verde Islands, dividing the world between them. In 1493, the Treaty of Tordesillas moved the line some 1,000 miles to the west — thus incorporating into Portuguese territory the eastern part of Brazil — leading historians to believe that the Portuguese may already have known of Brazil's existence. Officially, Pedro Alvares de Cabral discovered Brazil in 1500, having been blown off course while following Vasco da Gama's route to India. Da Gama himself, probably Portugal's greatest explorer, reached Mozambique and then India in 1488.

Though Gaspar Corte Real discovered westward-lying Newfoundland in 1501, the then king, Manuel, encouraged eastward voyages. In 1510, Afonso de Albuquerque established a fort at Goa; by 1515, the Portuguese commanded the Indian Ocean from that spot. Meanwhile, Portuguese navigators continued to discover the rest of the world. Under Spanish auspices, the Portuguese Fernão de Magalhães (Ferdinand Magellan) set sail in 1519, landed in India 2 years later, and continued on to the Philippines. Although he was killed there, one of his ships completed the journey, becoming the first ever to circumnavigate the globe.

Under King Manuel, Portugal experienced its golden age. The empire garnered enormous wealth, most of it from the East Indies spice trade. The prosperous trade in gold, ivory, and slaves poured even more riches into the country. The arts flourished, and people lived well.

But it was not to last: The empire, Portugal's greatest strength, was also its weakness. The Casa da India, the holding company largely owned and financed by the Portuguese crown, controlled a trade monopoly on spice and pepper, which were brought to Lisbon for re-export to the rest of Europe. By the beginning of the 16th century, profits had peaked; as imports increased, however, the value of individual goods decreased. Gold from Guinea, which was the medium of exchange, was also decreasing. By 1560, Portuguese resources had become taxed to such an extent that the Casa da India had to solicit foreign investors just to stay in business.

To add to Portugal's troubles, King Sebastian and many of the nation's nobles died in 1578 in a battle against the Moors at Alcázarquivir in Morocco, leaving the king's uncle, the aged Cardinal Henrique, to assume the throne. Two years later, the Hapsburg Philip II of Spain moved against the weakened empire; once again the Spanish were in control.

Portugal, however, enjoyed an autonomous existence under the Hapsburgs, who also controlled similarly independent kingdoms in Spain, Italy, and the Netherlands. But now that Portugal belonged to Spain, its colonies became prey to Spain's enemies. The Dutch attacked and acquired Portuguese colonies in Ceylon, Malacca, the East Indies, Africa, and parts of Brazil (only Brazil would eventually revert back to Portugal). Another drawback of belonging to Spain was the heavy taxes Spanish wars extracted from Portuguese coffers.

In 1640, the Portuguese rose up against the Spanish and regained their complete independence. At the urging of Portuguese nobles, the Duke of Bragança (from an illegitimate line descended from the House of Avis) assumed the throne as King João IV of Portugal. The new ruler renewed the alliance with England, and enhanced the credibility of the Bragança line by marrying his daughter Catherine to Charles II of England. In 1703, Portugal signed the Methuen Treaty with its old ally, agreeing to import British textiles in exchange for exporting Portuguese wine, chiefly port. (This after-dinner wine, which English gentlemen traditionally sipped at the table when the ladies retired to the drawing room, was no doubt one compelling reason for the durability of the Anglo-Portuguese alliance.) Shortly afterward, in 1706, João V, known as the Magnificent, came to the throne. The splendor of his reign, which lasted until 1750, was due to the steady trickle of Brazilian gold, discovered at the end of the 17th century, into Portuguese coffers, and the lavish application of gilt to the nation's churches. The sudden wealth also freed the monarchy from dependence on the Cortes and set it on an absolutist course.

In the world of late-18th-century Portuguese politics, one figure stands out — Sebastião José de Carvalho e Melo, Marquês de Pombal. Pombal, who held various ministerial posts under King José, eventually became the power behind the throne. His regime was notorious for anti-clericalism and the cruel treatment of its opponents. His leadership abilities, however, were more than welcome on November 1, 1775, the date of the catastrophic Lisbon earthquake. Combined with the fire and tidal wave that followed, the earthquake destroyed the city and killed 40,000 people. Pombal gained international fame with his directive to "bury the dead and relieve the living." Upon the death of King José in 1777, Pombal's dictatorship came to an end.

The early 19th century brought Napoleon's troops to Portugal in 1807, and the royal family escaped to Brazil to rule in exile. The French were defeated in 1810 at Buçaco by Portuguese and British troops under the command of Sir Arthur Wellesley, later the Duke of Wellington, but the royal family remained in Brazil as their country became a virtual British protectorate.

When João VI returned to Lisbon to rule, it was within the restrictions of the 1822 Constitution, which established a constitutional government with a limited monarchy. King João had left his son Dom Pedro in charge in Rio de Janeiro; Pedro promptly declared Brazil independent and himself emperor. When his father died, Pedro returned to Portugal — at British insistence — to urge a restructuring of the government that would give the sovereign more power. Having accomplished this (in the liberal Charter of 1826), Pedro returned to Brazil, leaving behind his young daughter Maria as queen under the regency of her uncle Miguel.

But Miguel was not to be trusted. His seizure of power and abolition of the charter prompted Pedro to return to Portugal again, and in 1832 he led an expeditionary force to Porto. After a civil war in which liberals and conservatives battled for power, Pedro, with the help of the British, regained control in 1834. The middle class ruled as a liberal oligarchy for the rest of the century.

The 20th century began in turmoil: King Carlos was assassinated in Lisbon in 1908. Coups and counter-coups followed. In 1910, King Manuel II abdicated and fled to England. The liberals declared a republic and, in 1911, adopted a new constitution that established a parliamentary government, with Afonso Costa becoming prime minister. Further struggles ensued as Portugal entered World War I on the side of the Allies, primarily to protect its African colonies.

This unpopular move resulted in Sidónio Pais taking over the government, provoking further turmoil until 1919, when elections restored an orderly Democratic party majority. More and more, though, prime ministers came from the military; anti-clericalism was on the rise; and finances were a shambles. Finally, in 1926, the right-wing military seized power. General António Oscar de Fragoso Carmona, who took control under a dictatorship, would remain president until 1951.

In 1928, Dr. António de Oliveira Salazar, an economics professor from the University of Coimbra, became Minister of Finance. He managed to pull the country out of its financial straits and assumed the post of prime minister in 1932. In 1933, a new constitution established Portugal's Estado Novo, or New State, and gave Salazar dictatorial powers. The New State, a repressive regime, suppressed individual rights, muffled the press, and outlawed political parties.

It's not surprising, therefore, that Portugal favored Franco during the Spanish Civil War; afterwards, Portugal and Spain formally cemented an alliance by signing the Iberian Pact. During World War II, Portugal remained neutral, though it did allow the Allies to maintain bases in the Azores. More trouble followed the war, as the government became increasingly repressive, introducing censorship and encouraging the growth of a secret police force — the Polícia Internacional e de Defesa do Estado, or PIDE.

During the 1960s, the last shreds of empire crumbled. India seized Portugal's holdings there, and independence movements erupted in Angola and Mozambique. The young Portuguese sent to crush these insurrections sympathized with them instead. The fighting drained the economy and put great stress on the military.

Then, in 1968, after a blood clot formed in his brain, Salazar slipped into an irreversible coma. He was succeeded by Marcello Caetano, who more or less followed Salazar's policies. And so dissatisfaction continued to grow until, on April 25, 1974, the so-called Young Captains staged a coup with flowers in their rifles — the *Day of the Red Carnations* — to oust Caetano and restore democratic principles to Portugal.

The changing winds of liberalism sweeping across the country transcended Portugal's borders, reaching the farthest limits of the empire. By the end of 1975, Portugal's African possessions had gained their independence. Foreign Minister Mário Soares traveled to Africa with the intention of organizing free elections; instead, Cuban-inspired Marxist-Leninists took over the governments, provoking a massive emigration of some 750,000 *retornados* (refugees) from the colonies to Portugal, equivalent to about 10% of its population. Finally, after 2 years of jockeying for power between right and left, a new Portuguese constitution and elections ushered in a more moderate government (about 35% Socialist). Socialist leader Soares became prime minister in 1976.

In 1987, under Prime Minister Anibal Cavaco Silva, the moderate Social Democrat party won a parliamentary majority in a republican government presided over by Socialist President Mário Soares. Having joined the Common Market in 1986, Portugal is already benefiting from the newly integrated European economy. Last year its monetary unit, the escudo, was linked to other currencies in the European Monetary System; today, Portugal leads all Western industrial nations in attracting foreign capital (on a per capita basis). Portugal's economic recovery has even been proposed as a model for many economically devastated Eastern European countries to follow.

Literature

Saudade, a powerful sense of yearning and nostalgia, has long permeated Portuguese literature, as it does the Portuguese character. Because this literature is so rich in lyrical poetry and not often translated into English, a knowledge of Portuguese is useful for reading and appreciating it. Its greatest works, however, especially those of Luís de Camões, are available in English. Happily transcending the limitations of translation, these magnificent poems and stories spring to life in English as easily as in their native tongue. Newer works also have become more available recently, as the success of Brazilian writers writing in Portuguese — among them Joaquim Maria Machado de Assis and Jorge Amado — has led to translations of the works of contemporary writers from Portugal as well.

From the very beginning, the great glory of Portuguese literature has been its lyric poetry. This literary tradition began shortly after the creation of the country at the end of the 11th century, when Henry of Burgundy brought French scholars with him to his court in the county of Portucale, the court into which Afonso Henriques, Portugal's first king, was born. Afonso's son, Sancho I (1154–1211), along with King Alfonso X of Castile and León (ca. 1226–84) and King Dinis I (1261–1325) of Portugal, created a body of Provençal-style poems written in Galician, the language of northwestern Iberia that foreshadowed both modern Spanish and modern Portuguese. Although the tradition began during the 12th century, only a few works survive from before 1200, one of them a brief verse said to be the work of Sancho I. About 2,000 of these songs — *cantigas de amor* (love songs), *cantigas de amigo* (songs of friendship), and *cantigas de maldizer* (satirical songs) — survive from the 12th and 13th centuries, however. Many of them were written by Dinis himself, the same king who founded the University of Coimbra during his reign and made the dialect of northern Portugal the official language of the entire kingdom.

During the 14th century, Portuguese literary efforts turned away from poetry and toward such prose works as detailed *livros de linhagem* (genealogical registers) and *cronicas* (chronicles). Of greater interest as documentation than as literature, they remained the dominant literary form until the Galician troubador Macias o Enamorado (Macias the Enamored) briefly revived the tradition of Provençal poetry.

King Duarte (Edward) I (1391–1438) and his brother Dom Pedro (1392–1449) were the great patrons of prose writing during the 15th century, using the essay form to write treatises on philosophy. They also created the position of royal chronicler. Among these chroniclers, Fernão Lopes (1380–1460) was one of the best. He compiled a factual, well-documented history of the Kings of Portugal, distinguished by its vivid style.

The great voyages of discovery in the 16th century led to scholarly and personal accounts of the Portuguese conquests. Fernão Lopes de Castanheda (1500–1559) and João de Barros (1496–1570) both published monumental histories of Portuguese expansion; Gaspar Correia (1495–1565) and Diego do Couto (1543–1616) wrote unofficial accounts of those years. Their histories — full of reported abuses of authority and generally unflattering accounts of Portuguese behavior in the colonies — were suppressed for centuries. Another personal account of years spent in the Orient, the widely read *Peregrinação* (Pilgrimage) of Fernão Mendes Pinto (1510–83), earned its author, noted for his colorful exaggerations, the epithet "the father of all lies."

Earlier in the century, Gil Vicente (1470–ca. 1536), one of Portuguese literature's greatest figures and often considered Portugal's Shakespeare and the father of the modern play, had introduced drama to the court. His popular farces and religious dramas (*autos*), though still medieval in their stereotypical characters, were full of ribald wit.

Portugal's first Renaissance poet, Francisco de Sá de Miranda (1481–1558), wrote comedies and sonnets, in which he displayed his mastery of the Petrarchan sonnet form. At around the same time, the concept of *saudade* entered the literature — in the form of bucolic poems, a pastoral novel entitled *Livro das Saudades* (Book of Yearnings), and other works by Bernardim Ribeiro (1482–1552), as well as in the lyric poetry of António Ferreira (1528–69) and Diogo Bernardes (1530–1600).

Until this time, the literature of Portugal largely had been a reflection of other cultures. But with the appearance of Luís de Camões (1524–80), Portuguese literature came into its own. Camões, who is to Portugal what Dante is to Italy, lived a life full of suitably romantic incidents. After studying at the University of Coimbra, he fell out of favor with the king and was banished from court. Embarking on a military career, he lost an eye in a Moroccan campaign, then moved on to India and Macao, where he was dismissed from an official post. During his return to Portugal, he was shipwrecked.

Having regained favor with the court under the patronage of King Sebastian, Camões published a work in 1572 named after Lusus, legendary ancestor of the Portuguese people — *Os Lusíadas* (The Lusiads). In chronicling the voyage of Vasco da Gama and retracing Portugal's history, he created the country's great national epic. Along with his *Ten Songs* and *Sonnets, The Lusiads* ranks Camões among the most important figures of world literature.

Foreign influence returned to Portuguese literature with the Spanish domination of 1580 to 1640. During this period, Francisco Manuel de Melo (1611–66) wrote his histories, poems, and letters primarily in Castilian, but Portuguese was preserved in the letters of António de Vieira (1608–97), a Jesuit missionary in Brazil. The most popular "Portuguese" work of the century, however, was *Lettres portugaises* (1669), a collection of letters in French reputedly written by a nun from Beja, Sister Marianna Alcoforado, and sent to her lover, the French Comte de Chamilly.

Despite their popularity, the authenticity of the *Portuguese Letters* was always doubtful, and in 1926 it was proved that their true author was Gabriel de Lavergne. Nevertheless, the letters, and the tale they tell of a passionate love affair, strongly influenced the epistolary novel, and provided the English

Victorian poet Elizabeth Barrett Browning with the inspiration for her famous love poems *Sonnets from the Portuguese.*

In spite of the Enlightenment, the 18th century was a largely uneventful period for Portuguese literature. While poet Pedro António Correa Garção (1724–72) was making a determined effort to eradicate the Spanish influence from Portuguese literature, Filinto Elísio (pseudonym of Padre Francisco Manoel do Nascimento, 1734–1819) was being influenced by nearby France to take an interest in neo-classical poetry and radical politics. Manuel Maria Barbosa du Bocage (1765–1805), of French descent, moved toward Romanticism with the Nova Arcadia group of poets' revolutionary and antireligious writing.

It was João Baptista da Silva Leitão de Almeida Garrett (1799–1854) who firmly implanted Romanticism in Portugal. A participant in the liberal revolution of 1820, he was forced into exile in Great Britain and France during the reaction to it. But on his return to Portugal, he entered politics, founded a national theater, and produced a prolific amount of verse, epic poetry, and drama that influenced a generation of writers. Alexandre Herculano de Carvalho e Araújo (1810–77), the other principal Romantic writer, was a historian and historical novelist. The Portuguese novel per se began with *Amor de perdição* (Love of Perdition) by Camillo Castello-Branco (1826–90) and was further developed by Júlio Dinis (pseudonym of Joaquim Guilherme Gomes Coelho, 1839–71), who moved the form away from Romanticism toward realism.

Another prime mover was Antero Tarquinio de Quental (1842–91), an Azorean aristocrat and intellectual known especially for his darkly pessimistic sonnets. He became a Socialist, helped found the Portuguese branch of the International, and was the major inspiration for the so-called Generation of 1870, which included such writers as José Duarte Ramalho Ortigão (1836–1915) and José Maria de Eça de Queirós (1843–1900) and the poet Abílio Manuel Guerra Junqueiro (1850–1923). Ortigão and Eça de Queirós founded a satirical review, *As Farpas,* and Ortigão went on to write travel books, among them *John Bull* and *A Holanda.* Eça de Queirós's novels, all translated into English, had a tremendous impact in their day. His early works, *O crime do Padre Amaro* (The Sin of Father Amaro) and *O primo Basílio* (Cousin Basilio), are social commentaries on the clergy and the middle class.

In the spirit of *saudade,* many of the Generation of 1870 became disillusioned in later years (Quental committed suicide and Ortigão became *vencido da vida* — "vanquished by life" — another recurrent phenomenon among Portuguese writers), even as nostalgic poetry and historical fiction underwent a revival during the 1890s. Teixeira de Pascoais (1877–1952) developed the spirit of *saudade* into a literary theory he called *saudosismo,* a belief that Portugal's magnificent past would forever hold back its present and future.

Fernando António Nogueira Pessoa (1888–1935), on the other hand, had great faith in Portugal's progress, and with José Regio (the pseudonym of José Maria dos Reis Pereira, 1901–69) introduced Modernism to Portuguese literature. Pessoa, who grew up in South Africa and occasionally wrote poetry in English, also wrote under a variety of pseudonyms, each with its own distinctive stylistic personality. Though he only published one volume of poetry,

Mensagem (Message), his work influenced Portuguese poets well into the 1940s and 1950s. Regio, also a playwright, was concerned with religious themes.

This century also saw the beginnings of regional writing, best exemplified by the works of Aquilino Ribeiro (1885–1963) about the Beiras, Miguel Torga (the pseudonym of Adolfo Correia da Rocha, b. 1907) about Trás-os-Montes, and Fernando Namora (b. 1919) about the Alentejo. The Portuguese presence in Brazil was explored by Ferreira de Castro (1893–1974), who based his social novels *Emigrantes* (Emigrants) and *A Selva* (The Jungle) on experiences in Brazil.

Among contemporary writers are Maria Teresa Horta, Maria Isabel Berreno, and Maria Fátima Velho da Costa. Known collectively as the "three Marias," they published *Novas cartas portugueses* (New Portuguese Letters) in 1972. With Sister Marianna Alcoforado's (1640–1723) 17th-century letters as its inspiration, the work is a compilation of letters, stories, and poetry about the repression of women in a male-dominated society. More recently, Maria Fátima Velho da Costa published the autobiographical *Missa in Albis.* Contemporary Portuguese writers who have been translated into English include António Lobo Antunes, whose *Os cus de Judas* was published as *South of Nowhere,* and the rising literary star José Saramago, whose historical novel *Balthazar and Blimunda* was published in the US in 1987. His latest work, translated into English as *The Year of the Death of Ricardo Reis,* is a historical tour de force whose eponymous character — in reality one of the great Pessoa's *noms de plume* — is brought to life as a melancholy poet.

Painting and Sculpture

Portugal has been so affected by certain national experiences, including foreign interventions, that it never established a great school of national art. While few, if any, Portuguese artists' names are recognized beyond the country's borders, Portuguese painting and sculpture are nevertheless rich in personality, combining the best techniques of Flemish, Italian, French, and Spanish art as a point of departure for its own. Compared with Spanish art — which overshadows it and with which it is too often confused — it is gentle and bright, a reflection of the warm spirit of the Portuguese people.

THE BRONZE AGE TO THE ROMANESQUE

Although no cave paintings such as the remarkable ones at Altamira in Spain have been found in Portugal, archaeologists have unearthed Bronze Age rock engravings, tools, ornaments, sculptures, and stunning examples of the goldsmith's art. Pottery and metal relics left by the successive waves of Portugal's invaders — Celts, Phoenicians, and Greeks — also remain, as do the more valuable artistic objects formed by the Iberians, such as statues, pottery, works of bronze, and some fine jewelry. Of all the works of art dating from before the Middle Ages, Roman remains are the most extensive. Scattered about Portugal are rather crude mural paintings, along with multicolored and black-and-white mosaics, but sculptures are the most prevalent. Statues and reliefs of gods and goddesses, portraits of Roman emperors, and sarcophagi abound.

The battles of the Reconquest and the ravages of the Moors destroyed most works of art fashioned during the earliest period of the Middle Ages, and a mere handful of funerary plaques, sarcophagi, and fragments of ornamental reliefs attest to the artistry of the Visigoths. Nor do many paintings other than a few shabby church frescoes remain from the Romanesque period, which succeeded the Middle Ages. Because the Koran forbade representation of the human form and since the Moors were not expelled from all of Portugal until the 13th century, it was not until the age of Romanesque art that Portuguese sculpture began to develop in earnest. As the reconquest spread southward, the Italian-inspired style spread with it.

THE FOURTEENTH CENTURY

Romanesque art maintained its sway longer in Portugal than in the rest of Europe, and the new Gothic style did not really begin to manifest itself until the 1300s. Little now remains of 14th-century painting. Among the few frescoes still extant are some attributed to Gonçalo Anes of Lisbon in the

Cathedral of Braga. Romanesque sculpture, however, is profusely represented, especially in architectural ornaments. Byzantine-style capitals carved with stylized animals, birds, and people are noteworthy examples and are located mostly in northern Portugal, the first part of the kingdom to be reconquered from the Moors.

Because of the availability of the easily worked local Ança stone, Coimbra became Portugal's sculpture center. Almost exclusively religious in theme, sculpture sprouted and flourished in the form of Gothic funerary pieces and religious icons. The creativity and nobility of the Coimbra school are apparent in such exemplary tombs of the period as the Gonçalo Pereira tomb by Master Pero of Coimbra and Telo Garcia of Lisbon in the Cathedral of Braga, and the sepulcher with the recumbent Christ in the *Museum of Machado de Castro* in Coimbra. The very finest monuments of Portuguese Gothic sculpture, however, are the tombs of Dom Pedro I (1320–1367) and the beautiful Spanish noblewoman Inês de Castro in the monastery church at Alcobaça. Intricate carvings of religious scenes decorate the sides of these magnificent tombs. Appreciation is enhanced by knowledge of their inhabitants' tragic story: Inês was the beloved of Dom Pedro, heir to the Portuguese throne. They loved each other for 10 years, until she was murdered by King Afonso IV. Dom Pedro then openly rebelled against his father and upon ascending the throne in 1357 had Inês — after death — honored as his queen.

THE FIFTEENTH CENTURY

The years from 1450 on were fertile ones for Portuguese painting and sculpture. As the first great sea power in Renaissance Europe, Portugal could afford to commission the best foreign artists and send its own budding painters abroad. Jan van Eyck's arrival in Lisbon in 1428 signaled the beginning of a Flemish domination that would last well into the 16th century. A royal marriage that linked Portugal and the Netherlands — including what is present-day Belgium — allowed Portuguese artists to train at Antwerp, while Flemish painters worked in Portugal or sent their works to Lisbon. The Age of Discovery also acquainted Portugal with the art of Africa, India, and the Orient, implanting influences that would last for hundreds of years.

The great painter Nuno Gonçalves appeared on the scene around 1450 with a Flemish style learned, presumably, from van Eyck. His most famous work and the treasure of Lisbon's *National Museum of Ancient Art,* the six-panel polyptych known as the *St. Vincent Panels,* attracted attention because of its twist on its Flemish roots. Gonçalves used yellow in places normally reserved for gold and accentuated the personalities of his subjects, rather than the precise indoor or outdoor setting, as was common in Flemish art. This attention to detail in his human subjects — the deep-set oval eyes, long nose, full lips, and slightly protruding jaw of the main figures — also can be found in many sculptures of this era. Today, the panels attract attention not only for their artistic merit, but also as a document of Portuguese society of the time. Among the crowd paying homage to the saint — a gathering of 60 or so, including many who have been identified — are Portuguese from all walks of life, from the king to fishermen, monks from Alcobaça, the Archbishop of

Lisbon, a rabbi, Prince Henry the Navigator, and, possibly, Gonçalves himself.

Outside of Gonçalves's work, little of interest remains. Alvaro Pires of Evora and Luís de Portugal, among the first Portuguese painters whose works can be identified, worked for a time in Italy and display Tuscan and Florentine influences in their painting. Also, a few frescoes still can be found, such as the one in the Abbey of Florença, attributable to João Gonçalves. A typical painting of the century is the *Ecce Homo* by an unknown artist in the *National Museum of Ancient Art* in Lisbon. By the end of the century, multi-panel retables, or altarpieces, similar to Gonçalves's religious homage to St. Vincent, became the backbone of Portuguese art.

The work of the traditional school of sculptors at Coimbra continued into the 15th century. Its great leaders created such fine works as Master Pero's *Virgins of the Annunciation,* a wooden Christ in the Monastery of Almoster, and the *Corpus de Deus* retable in the *Museum of Machado de Castro.* The Coimbra school was joined by two others: one at Santarém, where the funerary sculpture adheres to the traditions of the Coimbra masters, and one at Batalha — under the direction of Huguet, a northern master — where the sculpture deviates from the Coimbra school. Examples of the work created by the Batalha school are the tombs created for João I and Philippa of Lancaster and for King Duarte and Queen Leonor, now in the Monastery at Batalha.

THE SIXTEENTH CENTURY

Due to Portugal's epic expansion overseas, the 16th century was a golden era. The air crackled with the excitement of the discoveries of da Gama, Cabral, and Magellan, an excitement that found expression in artistic vitality and vigor. The reigning king at the beginning of the century, Manuel I, was a lavish spender, commissioning the best foreign artists available — one reason for the eclecticism of Portuguese art. By the time of his accession to the throne in 1495, Flemish painters and sculptors, attracted by visions of wealth, were swarming into Portugal. Under the reign of Dom Manuel's successor, João III, Italian artists introduced the style of the Renaissance, which eventually merged with the highly ornamental Manueline style. Despite the large number of foreign artists, the mood of the country was nationalistic, and the art it produced — retaining as it did Moorish elements — was distinctly Portuguese.

In Portugal, as elsewhere in Europe at this time, painters worked in groups, or studios. Each master artist had assistants who helped complete a work; masters also sometimes worked together to fulfill a commission. These master painters clustered in three major centers: Lisbon, Evora, and Viseu. Jorge Afonso, court painter to Manuel and João, headed the Lisbon school, where he taught and worked with many of the important painters of his time. His paintings display both a penchant for order and a fascination with the human anatomy. The panels at the Convento de Cristo in Tomar, the Igreja de Madre de Deus in Lisbon, and the Jesus Church at Setúbal are his greatest works and significantly influenced subsequent Portuguese painters. Another member of the Lisbon school, Afonso's brother-in-law Francisco Henriques, who died in the plague of 1518, is most famous for his work on the altars in the Church of São Francisco at Evora. These paintings, such as the *Pentecost* and the *Presentation in the Temple,* give an overall impression of calm while simultaneously foreshadowing the excitement of the mannerist style.

In southern Portugal lived Frei Carlos, a Flemish painter and monk at the Espinheiro monastery in Evora, for which he painted a series of panels in the Flemish style. His work is remarkable for the mysticism of its figures and its general mood of sweetness and strength. Also painting for the Espinheiro monastery was a painter known only as the Master of Lourinhã, noted for the harmony, delicacy, and rich colors of his work. In Viseu, a third school centered around Vasco Fernandes (1475–1541) — better known as "Grão," or "Great" Vasco — who was one of Portugal's most famous painters and also a friend of Afonso. Vasco painted panels for the high altar of Lamego Cathedral, now in the *Lamego Museum.* Typical of his style are the 16 panels he executed for the high altar in Freixo-de-Espada-a-Cinta. The powerful, vigorous *Saint Peter* that he painted for the Cathedral of Viseu (now housed in the *Grão Vasco Museum*) is considered one of his greatest works.

Gregório Lopes (1490–1550), Cristóvão de Figueiredo, and Garcia Fernandez — three of Afonso's pupils, sometimes called the Masters of Ferreirim — introduced mannerism to Portugal. Related by bonds of friendship and marriage, the three often worked together on the same projects. Among their fine individual works are Figueiredo's *Entombment of Christ,* Fernandez's *Christ Appearing to the Virgin,* and Lopes's *Mass of St. Gregory,* the latter a panel from the altarpiece of the Church of São João Baptista at Tomar, in which Lopes emphasized the dramatic emotions of his subjects — a group of chanting monks.

During the second half of the 16th century, many of Portugal's best painters — in particular the gifted Vasco Perieira — worked at the Spanish court in Madrid. Those that remained in Portugal — including Gaspar Dias, Francisco Venegas, Diogo Teixeira, and Simão Rodrigues — were strongly influenced by Italian art. One genre that developed during this period was the art of portraiture, as evidenced by the remarkable *Portrait of a Lady with a Rosary* by an unknown painter, now hanging in the *National Museum of Ancient Art* in Lisbon. Painting also flourished in the form of illustrations of charts and atlases — a natural outcome of the intensive study of navigation launched by Prince Henry the Navigator and his brothers.

Sculpture made its way from a medieval technique to a kind of architectural decoration. Olivier de Gand, a Fleming, carved the last Gothic masterpiece in Portugal — the main altar of Coimbra's Old Cathedral. Also working in Coimbra, which remained a major center for sculptors, were the leading exponents of the Manueline style, a style that embraced crocodiles, exotic plants, ropes, sea shells, and other motifs drawn from Portugal's heroic enterprise in navigation and discovery. Diogo Pires the Younger, the greatest of the Manueline sculptors, sculpted tombs in Leça do Bailio, at Montemor-o-Velho, and in the Monastery of São Marcos, near Tentúgal.

Along with traditional sculptors like de Gand and Pires, four French sculptors — Filipe Udarte (Hodart), Nicolas Chanterène, Jacques Loguin, and João de Ruão (Jean de Rouen) — worked at Coimbra, where they introduced the Renaissance style. Udarte modeled a bigger-than-life *Last Supper* in terra cotta for Coimbra's Santa Cruz Church; Chanterène created strong, lifelike tomb effigies of the first two Kings of Portugal; Loguin created the pulpit at Santa Cruz, very different from the similarly shaped Manueline pulpit at Belém; and the less talented de Ruão, primarily an architectural contractor, also did work for the Church of Santa Cruz. De Ruão's more talented associate, Tomé Velho, created works such as his masterpiece *St. Elizabeth* that were more Portuguese in character than de Ruão's. During the last quarter of the 16th century, stone sculpture declined in importance and the majority of retables were made of gilt and polychromed (decorated in several colors) wood.

THE SEVENTEENTH CENTURY

By 1580, Portugal's reign as a supreme power had come to an end. Philip II of Spain seized control, and the royal court, which moved to Madrid, no longer was able to patronize or send promising young painters to study in other countries. Not surprisingly, Portugal's creative juices dried up, and its art world began a long period of decline. Even after the 1640 Restoration, both court and country were too poor to support art for another half a century. In both painting and sculpture, mannerism ended and Portugal entered its baroque phase (1590–1710). Baroque is a grander, more melodramatic and expansive version of Renaissance classicism; colors are strong and definite, parts are subordinate to the whole, and light fuses all into one. The portraits of Domingo Vieira (1627–1652) exemplify the baroque style and show the Spanish influence — his technique seems indebted to Velázquez — yet in their modest dignity and warm humanity manage to express some of the best traits of the Portuguese character.

Despite its artistic atrophy and general impoverishment in the 17th century, Portugal did experience one area of growth: The great expansion of monastic churches that occurred between 1580 and 1640 brought a demand for retables and images that continued for several generations. Pious scenes encircled by flower garlands adorned walls, ceilings, and altars. The leading practitioner of this devout and ingenious genre was Josefa d'Ayala (ca. 1830–1884), known as Josefa d'Obidos. Born in Spain to a Spanish mother and a Portuguese father (the painter Baltasar Gomes Figueira), she was soon brought to Portugal to live. Beginning as an etcher and a painter of small scenes on copper, she progressed to still lifes and religious scenes on canvas, such as the exciting late-baroque painting *The Mystic Marriage of St. Catherine* on the main altar in the Capuchins church in Cádiz, Spain. Brightly colored, exquisitely detailed, and expertly designed, her work — especially in scenes of the Holy Family — manages to combine the festive with the devout.

Most 17th-century sculpture consists of portraits and carvings of retables, usually influenced by Spanish and Italian art. More typically Portuguese is the high altar and Chapel of St. Bernardo in the monastery at Alcobaça, which combines terra cotta and wood. A group like the *Death of St. Bernard,* though badly mutilated, represents the epitome of Portuguese high baroque.

The only notable native sculptor of the period, Manuel Pereira (1588–1683), spent most of his time in Madrid, where he could command better commissions. He is the leading representative of Portuguese classicism.

THE EIGHTEENTH CENTURY

Like the 16th century — and for much the same reason — the 18th century was a golden era for Portuguese art. The discovery of gold in Brazil in the late 17th century brought wealth to the royal court, enabling art to flourish once again. João V (1706–50) called foreign artists to Portugal and sent promising young Portuguese to Rome. Not surprisingly, for most of the century, Portuguese painting was strongly influenced by Italian styles. The predominant painter in the first half of the century was Francisco Vieira do Matos Lusitano, called Vieira Lusitano (1699–1783), who became the court painter in 1733, succeeding the Frenchman Pierre-Antoine Quillard. Vieira, who had studied in Rome, was a brilliant designer, engraver, and painter, known primarily for his altarpieces. His is an intellectual art full of symbolism and allegory. Other artists of the time, like their Italian mentors, produced a wealth of ceiling paintings.

Unfortunately, the Lisbon earthquake of 1755 destroyed much of the best Portuguese art. Undaunted, the Portuguese began reconstruction under the Marquês de Pombal, who, like his forefathers, provided many commissions in sculpture and painting. Under Maria I (1734–1816), the statesman Pina Manique founded a Royal Academy of Design and sustained the Portuguese Academy in Rome, founded in 1791. A second Francisco Vieira, known as Vieira Portuense (1765–1805), studied at the Portuguese Academy, traveled in Europe, and worked in London for 2 years. His eclectic style can be seen in his *Jupiter and Leda* and *Pieta,* both at the *National Museum of Ancient Art* in Lisbon. Vieira's delicate, gently harmonious paintings show him to be a forerunner of early 19th-century Romanticism. A far greater artist — and future Romantic — was Domingos António de Sequeira (1768–1837), who studied first in Pina Manique's Royal Academy of Design and later in Rome. His 18th-century canvasses, such as *Gentleman,* now in the *National Museum of Ancient Art,* are still neo-classical in style. His major works, however, were created in the 19th century.

Among the foreign sculptors attracted to Portugal by its new-found Brazilian wealth was the Frenchman Claude de Laprade, active in Portugal from 1699 to 1730, whose best work is the monument to Bishop Moura at Vista Alegre near Aveiro. The Italian Alessandro Giusti (1715–1799), the most famous sculptor of the period, settled in 1753 in Mafra, where he founded Portugal's first school of sculpture, which produced a number of highly skilled artists. Despite the multitude of foreign artists in Portugal during the 18th century, native sculpture flourished. Working with Giusti in Mafra, for example, was Joaquim Machado de Castro, Portugal's leading native sculptor. The equestrian statue of King José I in the Praça do Comércio in Lisbon is his masterpiece. Other noteworthy sculptors of the time include José de Almeida (1700–1769), the leading exponent of high rococo, and João José de Aguiar (1769–1841), the leader in the neo-classical style.

THE NINETEENTH AND TWENTIETH CENTURIES

Though Portuguese art flourished in the 18th century, no single cohesive style had emerged — until the arrival of Domingos António de Sequeira, who studied first in Lisbon and later in Rome. Sequeira was a portraitist who used light to express the dramatic. Possessing a strong sense of faith in life that is typically Portuguese, Sequeira brought to the art world a hopeful optimism, using brighter colors, lighter shadows, realistic overtones — in sum, a pre-Impressionistic style. His first works were mainly symbolic, such as the huge *Allegory of the Casa Pia,* which he painted in Rome in 1792 in honor of the intendant Pina Manique, the founder of his art school. But perhaps his most famous work is his portrait of the *Viscount of Santarém and His Family* (1805–10), which has often been compared to Goya's *Charles IV of Spain.* There is no evidence, however, that Sequeira ever visited Spain or saw Goya's work.

Sequeira was Portugal's last great heroic artist. A staunch liberal, he painted scenes that expressed his contempt for contemporary politics, especially the French invasion of Portugal in 1807. His allegory of *Lisbon Sheltered by Junot* cost him 9 months in prison (1808–9). Eventually, like Goya, he sought voluntary exile. His last works, the *Ascension* and *Last Judgment of 1832,* were painted in Rome and tell of his obsession with religious themes. Most of his works are in the *National Museum of Ancient Art* in Lisbon.

The painters who followed Sequeira were attracted to the new European movement of romanticism and later to the naturalism that rose in reaction to it. Impressionism, too, had its Portuguese adherents, among them José Vital Branco Malôa (1855–1933), noted for his treatment of light, and Columbano Bordalo Pinheiro (1857–1934), a major portrait painter. Another Pinheiro, Rafael Bordalo (1847–1905), one of the two leading sculptors of the 19th century, was known for his clay caricature figures. The outstanding Portuguese sculptor of that century, however, was António Soares dos Reis (1847–1889). A master of sensitive character delineation, he demonstrated the power of his technique in statues such as the *Exile* and numerous portrait busts, including the *Count of Ferreira* — both in the *National Museum of Soares dos Reis* in Porto.

Today, a new revolution seems to be gaining speed in Portugal. Long inhibited by the rule of the Salazar government, which considered modern art subversive, Portuguese art once again is struggling to come into its own. Recent styles such as Impressionism, cubism, Expressionism, and futurism have all had their Portuguese adherents; still, there is no common ground that ties Portugal's art together, nor one great Portuguese master. Art is as eclectic as ever.

Several Portuguese painters have achieved international standing, although none have the world class status of many contemporary Spanish artists. Amadeu de Sousa Cardoso (1887–1918) began the modern movement in Portuguese painting. A cubist, he was influenced by Robert Delaunay, but later developed a more personal style of his own. Another cubist and one of the more prominent figures in modern Portuguese art, Eduardo Viana was influenced by Cézanne and also by Delaunay, with whom he worked closely in northern Portugal during World War I. Viana's brilliant color relationships and geometric configurations reveal Delaunay's imprint.

Probably the greatest modern Portuguese painter is Maria Helena Vieira da Silva. Her vibrant abstractions, which look like golden towers, are noted for the richness of their texture. Other Portuguese painters of the present century include José de Almada Negreiros (1893–1970), who painted murals and frescoes; two adherents of the poetic style of surrealism, António Pedro and António Dacosta; Fernado Lanhas, noted for his images, which are simple and vivid, yet rigid and hard-edged; and Paulo-Guilherme, whose linear patterns constitute a sensitive and very personal style.

Francisco Franco (1885–1955) led the reaction against the weak, decadent sculpture of the late 19th century. Leopoldo de Almeida, a member of Franco's generation, created the sculptures for the Monument of the Discoveries (1940) on the Tajo River — designed by José Angelo Cottinelli Telmo (1897–1948) — which may well be the outstanding examples of 20th-century Portuguese sculpture. After World War II, an abstract school of sculpture sprang up among artists who had studied at fine arts schools in Porto and Lisbon. Among this generation is the very gifted Jorge Vieira, who attracted some notice internationally. His is a bare, simplified style with bronze figures reminiscent of insect skeletons cast in a rigid yet flowing design.

Architecture

Along with influences from the outside world, a plethora of indigenous and invading cultures has contributed to the richness of Portuguese architecture. It reached its creative peak during the Manueline period, a time that, not surprisingly, coincided with the increased confidence (and coffers) of the Age of Discovery. Today, due to extensive remodeling over the years, most buildings exhibit a mélange of historic styles. Still, certain characteristics have remained constant for almost 3 millennia: the use of a wide variety of local stone, uncomplicated ground plans, and simple architectural orders.

Not surprisingly in a practical country filled with granite and limestone, Portuguese architecture is founded on stone. Its earliest remains, dating from the 8th century BC, are the stone walls that surround the fortified hill towns of the northern *casteja* civilization. When excavated, many of these *castros* and *citanias,* like Briteiros and Sabroso, reveal both round and rectangular granite houses.

Much remains of the Roman presence — well-engineered roads, the bridges at Chaves and Ponte de Lima, aqueducts, and the still unexplained pink granite tower outside Belmonte. Left behind from Lisbon's Roman incarnation as Olisipo are numerous baths and ruins, including — beneath today's Baixa section — a theater built when Nero was Emperor of Rome. The ruins at Conímbriga, a Celtic city inhabited and fortified by the Romans, date from the 2nd century BC, and are among the most extensive on the Iberian Peninsula. The peninsula's best single Roman site, however, is the temple at Evora, built during the 2nd or 3rd century.

But the people who inhabited the peninsula during the next few centuries left little architectural evidence of their presence in the area that is Portugal today. The Visigoths built the Church of São Pedro de Balsemão near Lamego in the 7th century; Christians, under Moorish domination, built São Pedro de Lourosa near Oliveira do Hospital in the 10th century and rebuilt the Visigoths' São Frutuoso, near Braga, in the 11th century.

Present-day Portugal began to take shape late in the 11th century under the Burgundian dynasty. Alfonso VI of León and Castile had granted the county of Portucale to Henry of Burgundy, whose son, Afonso I, became Portugal's first king. This led, throughout northern Portugal, to an impressive number of churches built in the Romanesque style on the model of the Burgundian monastery at Cluny. Braga, Porto, Lisbon, Evora, and Coimbra all boast cathedrals from this period, though only the last two have remained relatively unaltered. Among smaller Romanesque churches, São Martinho de Cedofeita in Porto and São Salvador de Bravães on the Lima River are the best examples. Other outstanding Romanesque buildings include the *domus municipalis* in Bragança and the polygonal church — the Charola — built by the Knights Templar order in Tomar, and later surrounded by the convent-castle of the Knights of Christ.

The transition from Romanesque to Gothic began in the late 12th century, when Cistercian monks summoned from France by Afonso I built a monastery at Alcobaça. The rigidly simple architecture they used provides Europe's best example of the Cistercian style. During the next century, when the monks built the Cloister of Santa Maria de Celas in Coimbra, they used a much freer hand in the decoration of its capitals.

The Gothic style dominated Portuguese architecture until the 16th century, its austere local variation quite suited to the castles built during this increasingly militant time. Almourol, Guimarães, Leiria, Lisbon, Monsaraz, and Obidos provide examples. The fortress at Vila Viçosa was the first of many that also were built during this period.

In sacred architecture, the outstanding example of the Gothic style is the monastery Church of Santa Maria da Vitória in Batalha. This church marks a turning point, a moment when local architects used the international influences they had absorbed to develop a highly original national style. Begun during the late 14th century by Afonso Domingues, a Portuguese architect, its construction was taken over at the turn of the century by an architect named Huguet (or Ougete), who may have come from Ireland or France and introduced English and French influences to the design. Martin Vasques and Fernão d'Evora continued the work, and, with a flourish, the Spanish architect João de Castilho completed it. The use of golden limestone throughout the church gives an overall unity to the work of these numerous hands.

Castilho, Diogo Biotac, and the brothers Diogo and Francisco de Arruda were the principal architects of the Manueline style, a late Gothic phenomenon peculiar to Portugal. Though named for King Manuel I (who reigned from 1495 to 1521), the period actually extends from about 1490 to 1550. Highly decorative, exuberant, and characterized by the free use of nautical motifs, the Manueline style celebrates the Portuguese Age of Discovery. Waves, shells, ropes, and anchors cavort with such symbols as Prince Henry the Navigator's Order of the Garter and the King's Cross of Christ. Outstanding examples, in addition to the church in Batalha, include the Mosteiro dos Jerónimos (Hieronymite Monastery) in Belém, the Igreja Matriz do São João Baptista in Vila do Conde, the Igreja de Jesus in Setúbal, and the convent-castle of the Knights of Christ at Tomar.

The best examples of secular Manueline style are the wings that were added to Sintra's Palácio Real during Manuel's reign. The palace interior contains lavish examples of another characteristic of Portuguese architecture, hand-painted ornamental tiles called *azulejos.* Those at Sintra were imported from Spain — where Moorish craftsmen made them — in the 16th century. Portugal began producing its own *azulejos,* based on Italian and then Flemish tiles, at about the same time.

Another peculiarly Portuguese phenomenon that flourished during the Manueline era are *pelhourinhos* (pillories). Introduced by the Romans, these were columns used for publicly displaying caged or chained criminals. Eventually, they became symbols of municipal authority, which burgeoned under King Manuel, and as a result, the Manueline versions are particularly numerous and elaborate.

Because Portugal remained in the grip of the Manueline style until well into the 16th century, the Renaissance architecture prevalent elsewhere in Europe arrived relatively late. Not until 1541, with the publication of Diego de Sagredo's textbook *Medidas del Romano,* was Renaissance neo-classicism formally introduced to Portugal. Its center was the university town of Coimbra, where the north portal of the Sé Velha (Old Cathedral) and its São Pedro chapel are among the best examples of Renaissance architecture in the country. Most Renaissance-style churches, however, including Coimbra's Sé Nova (New Cathedral) and the cathedrals at Leiria, Portalegre, and Miranda do Douro, were built later, when the neo-classical style had evolved into Mannerism.

Spanish Hapsburg rule in Portugal between 1580 and 1640 coincided with the construction of numerous religious buildings throughout the country. These combined Spanish monumentality with a neo-classicism that came from an interest in Palladian architecture. Filippo Terzi, an Italian architect who worked for the Hapsburgs, was responsible for the churches of São Roque and São Vicente de Fora in Lisbon, which were built at this time.

Baroque architecture, though it took its name from the Portuguese word for a misshapen pearl, *barroco,* originated in Italy during the 17th century. At the time, Portuguese wealth was being used to fight against Spain. The discovery of gold in the Portuguese colony of Brazil at the end of the century, however, resulted in money and materials for such projects as the palace designed by the German architect Johann Friedrich Ludwig for João V at Mafra, and the numerous churches decorated in gilded wood called *talha dourada.* Manor houses and country estates (called *solares* and *quintas* in Portuguese), which had long been a tradition in Portugal, also took a sumptuous turn. The royal palace at Queluz, with its formal gardens and lavish *azulejos,* is the most accessible.

Like the ill wind that blows somebody good, the devastating earthquake of 1755 gave Lisbon's city planners a clean slate. Under the Marquês de Pombal, José I's dictatorial chief minister, Eugénio dos Santos laid out the new Lisbon in a grid plan. The first buildings were in a rococo style that came to be known as Pombaline. The city's Praça do Comércio is the best example. When Pombal was dismissed upon José's death in 1777, rebuilding continued in a more neo-classical vein. Neo-classicism also extended to the north. It can be seen in the Cadeia da Relação (Law Courts) building and the Carrancas Palace in Porto, and in the Church of Bom Jesus do Monte near Braga, built atop a baroque staircase.

As elsewhere in Europe during the 19th century, architects in Portugal were seized with a passion for reviving historical styles. Given the diverse styles of Portugal's history, however, they produced forms seen nowhere else. The *Palace* hotel in Buçaco, for example, is neo-Manueline, and the *Campo Pequeno* bullfighting arena in Lisbon is neo-Moorish. Alexandre-Gustave Eiffel, the engineer responsible for the Paris tower that bears his name, designed the Dona Maria Pia railroad bridge in Porto, while his disciples were responsible for other engineering feats in Portugal — the Ponte de Dom Luís in Porto and the Elevador de Santa Justa in Lisbon.

During the 20th century, Portuguese architecture has continued to reflect European trends. Art Nouveau, in vogue at the beginning of the century, left its mark in Lisbon, Leiria, and Coimbra. The functional architecture that sprang up next is most pleasantly exemplified by the modern *Calouste Gulbenkian Museum,* designed by Alberto Pessoa, Pedro Cid, and Ruy Anthoguia, and begun in Lisbon in 1966. That year also saw the building of the Ponte 25 de Abril suspension bridge — the longest in Europe — connecting Lisbon to southern Portugal. After the 1974 revolution, the so-called *style méditerranéen* (Mediterranean style), ubiquitous in southern European resort communities, erupted all over the Algarve, site of an outbreak of intense tourism development. Even more recently, post-modernism arrived in the person of Tomás Taveira, who designed the colorful and controversial Amoreiras residential and industrial complex in western Lisbon.

Traditional Music

Just as the Portuguese are, generally speaking, less flamboyant than their Spanish neighbors, their signature musical tradition, the *fado* (from the Latin word meaning "fate"), is more subdued than the bold flamenco, and no dance is involved. While drawing upon the same wellspring of raw emotion, the tragic despair of flamenco becomes in *fado* an abiding melancholy. Though flamenco and *fado* seem to have much in common superficially — the coarse quality of the voice, the vocal glissandos and trills, the note of anguish — allegations of a common Moorish foundation are belied by the Algarve, the southernmost province of Portugal, where the Moorish presence was most prolonged but where there is no trace of a *fado* tradition.

First referred to formally in 1833, *fado* has been assigned various theoretical lineages. Most plausible among them deems it a blend of the African dance called the *lundum,* brought to Brazil by slaves and to Portugal by 18th-century sailors, and the more sophisticated *modinhas,* adaptations of the sentimental Italian operatic airs that were popular in Lisbon at about the same time. Originally a song form of sailors, it premiered in the dock areas of Lisbon and spread quickly through the city's Alfama, Mouraria, and Bairro Alto districts. Full of the loneliness and nostalgia of life at sea, the early *fados* were taught by sailors to their long-suffering wives, their prostitutes, their local vendors, and their neighbors. Until the 1830s, *fado* was strictly a working class diversion that chronicled the daily life of the Lisbon citizenry, commenting not only on love affairs but also on the popular figures of the day, political events, and, of course, scandals.

Ironically, it was a scandal that eventually made the art form upwardly mobile. During the first half of the 19th century, Maria Severa, an attractive, temperamental young prostitute whose mother was a Gypsy, had become Lisbon's most popular *fadista.* Succumbing to her numerous charms, the Count of Vimioso fell in love with her, despite the profound discrepancy in their social standings. His persistent attentions to Maria and her art finally made *fado* respectable among the nobility. But Maria died young — at the age of 26 — prompting all *fado* singers of the time to don black to mourn her premature passing. Whether out of a lingering sentiment or its eminent suitability for the *fado* mood, the black costume remains to this day the traditional garb of the *fadista.*

The traditional themes of the *fado* continue to focus on *saudade,* a poignant yearning for the impossible that is akin to the Spanish *soledad.* Note the following *fado* verse:

I look at the earth and at the sky
And everything reminds me of you.

When I lost your love
I lost every reason for living.
There is only one truth
Remaining in our love:
It is the image of "saudade,"
Beautiful but covered with sadness.
"Saudade" go away
Depart from my tired heart
Take it to a distant land
This fado of mine.
Written on the wind:
At night my brother is the wind
Trying to forget the storm
As I long to forget
This "saudade."
But alas, I cannot.
Come back, my love to me.
The pain goes and gaiety returns;
Love dies and friendship remains;
Only this profound "saudade"
Will not from my heart depart.
Please come back, my love.
Let me hold you in my arms.
Why do you keep me distant,
Knowing that I long to be near you?

Lisbon *fados* are the saddest of them all, bemoaning the sorrow and strife of life and love. When the lights dim in the capital's *fado* cafés, the time for the song has arrived. Typically, two guitars — one 12-stringed Portuguese and one 6-stringed Spanish — begin to play. The *fadista* (male or female) emerges from the shadows. If the singer is a woman, she will wear a black woolen shawl. True to tradition, she will clasp her hands in front of her, lean her head back, and close her eyes, retreating to the inner recesses of passion. If she is good, she will draw the audience in with her. Her throaty voice, singing in syncopated (2/4) time, matches the sad texture of the lyrics.

Unfortunately, *fado* has suffered much the same fate as flamenco. Those today who sing for love of art or from the agony of their souls are rare. Most often visitors will find those who sing for a salary, the emotional edge of their tired songs dulled by nightly repetition.

Unlike contemporary flamenco, *fado* is strictly a song form. Like flamenco, it also has its lighter side. The *fado corrido* from the Ribatejo, the bull-raising area along the Tagus River, is faster and more spirited than its Lisbon counterpart. And the more polished and lyrical *fado de Coimbra,* from the north's famed university town, is actually a romantic serenade that has little in common with its melancholy cousin from Lisbon.

Traditionally, many *fado* songs have taken their lyrics from Portuguese poets, although new lyrics are often written expressly for individual *fadistas.* Though *fado* is more melodic than flamenco, many visitors consider its earthy vocals and exotic halftones an acquired taste. Many of Lisbon's *fado* houses are full-fledged restaurants that offer folk dancing and popular songs. "Before midnight," says a native *fado* connoisseur, "the *fado* they sing is fit only for tourists. After midnight, only for Portuguese." As Amália Rodrigues, the most famous *fadista* of all time, once sang so eloquently, "All this exists, all this is sad, all this is *fado.*"

Fado is not all there is to folk art in Portugal. Perhaps best-known of all the Portuguese folk dances is the *vira,* a product of the northern Minho region. Though widely heard throughout the area extending from Porto to the country's northern border and running 30 miles inland from the coast, its two main focal points are Vila do Conde and Vila Nova de Famalição. Traditionally, the *vira* is a round dance for four couples, but any number may participate. Similar to waltz rhythm, the *vira*'s 6/8 time is frequently accentuated by the Minhotan women's wooden clogs.

A variation occurs in the fishing villages of Estremadura and, most notably, in Nazaré. Though the tempo here is also waltz-like, it's quicker and livelier. Another difference between the two versions of *vira* lies in the instruments played. The north favors the ukelele and fife; the south, the accordion. Both use the *bombo* (an earthenware pot) for percussion. A further difference lies in the chorus. Curiously, the Minhotan *vira* uses castanets, a custom not normally found in Portuguese folk music.

Bullfighting

Bullfighting, or *tourada,* has taken place since the 17th century in Portugal. Today it is second only to soccer as the nation's spectacle of choice, although its use of sharp darts that penetrate the bull's hide, not to mention the risk taken by the bullfighter and the horse upon which he conducts his end of the fight, are not to everyone's taste.

Nevertheless, bloodshed is kept to a minimum. Unlike his Spanish counterpart, the Portuguese bullfighter does not kill the beast. A gory incident in which the Count of Arcos was mauled by a bull in the 18th century prompted the Marquês de Pombal, King José I's chief minister, to prohibit the practice. That act reflects the Portuguese attitude toward the bullfight as an elegant, dignified pastime. In fact, on the occasions when the bullfight is preceded by a *corrida de gala à antiga portuguesa* — a gala fight in the old Portuguese style — the ring assumes the pageantry of a fairy tale. Costumed and mounted musicians, footmen bearing the coats of arms of the noble old bullfighting families, brightly bedecked mules carrying baskets of darts to stick the bull, and white horses drawing coaches that carry the *cavaleiros* (horsemen) who will later engage the bulls on horseback, all parade around the ring.

A Portuguese bullfight, while it doesn't always include the *corrida de gala,* is customarily fought in 17th-century costume and divided into distinct segments. Like Spain's, it begins with a parade (*cortesia*): Horseback riders ceremoniously drive the bulls through the streets to the ring, where, to a trumpet fanfare, the cast of players enters the arena. First come the *campinos,* countrified bull handlers; next, the six *peões de brega* (capemen), wearing their glittering suits of lights, and the *forcados* — youths who will tackle the bull in the second half of the *tourada* — dressed in short jackets, breeches, white stockings, and green-and-red-tasseled stocking caps; and finally the mounted *cavaleiros,* the real stars of the spectacle. Dressed in plumed, tricornered hats, lace jabots, brilliantly decorated three-quarter-length coats, white breeches, and black boots, the *cavaleiros* bow gracefully to the *intelligente* (director of the bullfight) before circling the ring. Their high-spirited and skillful horses have plaited tails and manes. The high-backed saddles are heavily studded and decorated. At the sound of the bugle, all participants leave the arena and the segment ends.

Another bugle call sounds to signal the second segment. A lone *cavaleiro* returns. His horse stops short to gaze across the ring at a closed gate. It opens and the bull charges into the arena, its horns covered with leather sheaths called *embolados.* As the *peões de brega* toy with the bull, the *cavaleiro* sizes up his adversary. Then his task begins.

In a series of *sortes,* or strikes, he must plunge into the bull's neck muscle several darts — usually six, three long and three short — which release small flags upon impact. At the discretion of the *intelligente,* the rider can throw a seventh and shorter stick, but to do so he practically has to fall out of the saddle.

The *sortes* take different forms. The *sorte de gaiola* is a surprise strike: The bull charges directly from the gate past the gatemen to the *cavaleiro* — without benefit of a warm-up period — to receive its first dart, or *farpa.* The dart's length, about a yard, allows the *cavaleiro* to keep a certain distance as he swoops down on the bull. The usual encounter, however, after bull and *cavaleiro* have had time to assess each other during the cape play, is *poder-a-poder,* a frontal charge that ends with the placement of the *farpa.*

The shorter darts are called *bandarilhas,* and after the last one — just a few inches long — has been inserted, the *cavaleiro* rides victoriously around the ring to a cheering crowd — or a booing mob if he has not lived up to expectations. The *cavaleiro*'s circular saunter ends the segment.

Next, the eight-man team of *forcados* jumps over a barrier into the ring. Their role — as well as their costume — is based on the one played by servants of the original bullfighting nobility, who often turned the bull over to attendants before killing it. (*Forcados* are amateurs — unlike *cavaleiros,* who enjoy professional status.) Their leader taunts the bull, calling it names until it charges, at which time he lunges forward between the bull's horns and holds on tight, a maneuver called *pega de cara.* His mates then surround the bull, grab its tail, and dig in their heels until they bring it to a halt.

After the *forcados* jump back over the barriers, the bull is escorted out of the ring by a herd of bullocks gaily decorated with bells and bits of colorful material. Badly injured bulls are slaughtered; others are returned to pasture for breeding.

Variations liven up the customary *tourada.* The *cavaleiro* may perform tricks, or *adornos,* such as riding the bull's horns while carrying a dart in either hand, or breaking a dart to decrease the distance between rider and bull. Sometimes the *cavaleiro* will alternate with a *toureiro,* who enters the ring on foot, teases the bull with a cape, and pretends to kill it with a sword. (Actual slaughter of the bull can result in a heavy fine.) In some villages, such as in the Azores, the entire town participates in the bullfight; a roped bull is given the freedom of the streets, and local youths display their prowess in subduing it.

There are about 40 bullrings in Portugal, most in the center of the country. Bullfighting, however, is most popular in the Alentejo and Ribatejo regions of southern Portugal, where fighting bulls and the specially trained horses used in the fights are bred. The best-known bullfighters appear at town festivals — in Santarém in June and Vila Franca de Xira in July — though the most famous arena is the *Praça de Touros do Campo Pequeno* in Lisbon, which seats 8,000 spectators. The season runs from *Easter* to October. *Touradas* take place on Sundays and occasionally Thursdays. During the month of June, when Lisbon honors Saint Anthony, its patron saint, there are bullfights at the *Campo Pequeno* every Thursday night from 10 o'clock on.

Dining in Portugal

When Vasco da Gama rounded the Cape of Good Hope late in the 15th century, he made world history — and forever altered the course of Portuguese cooking. He and his seafaring countrymen introduced pepper, cloves, curry, nutmeg, cinnamon, rice, tea, coffee, hot and sweet peppers, and a host of other savory foods to Portuguese larders. Portuguese cooks, in turn, added and blended these exotic ingredients into their fish and meat dishes, their soups, and their desserts. The result is a tasty, wholesome, and sometimes surprising cuisine that makes dining in Portugal both a pleasant experience and an adventure.

The foundation of Portuguese cooking consists of olive oil, garlic, onions, salt, and pepper. Potatoes, tomatoes, peppers, beans, and rice are its basic ingredients; coriander, cumin, and paprika its most popular spices. Parsley both flavors and decorates. It's a balanced cuisine: spicy, but not overtly spiked; savory, but not too seasoned; smooth, but not bland. And it's bold — the Portuguese, after all, have the audacity to combine potatoes and rice in the same dish and get away with it. Credit goes to the Moors for introducing honey, almonds, and eggs into the country's dessert diet.

The Portuguese love affair with the sea and its bounty is intense. Wherever people go along the coast, the aroma of sardines — cooking in earthenware charcoal grills outside corner *tascas* (taverns) — greets them, as does the sight of mounds of *mariscos* (seafood) in the window displays of *marisquerias* (fish restaurants). Of all fish, *bacalhau* (codfish) is dearest to the Portuguese palate. Portuguese fishermen have been catching it off Newfoundland banks for over 500 years, and Portuguese cooks are reputed to have invented over 365 ways to prepare it. Codfish is so highly prized that it makes up the main course at *Christmas* dinner. Governments have been known to falter when cod is in short supply.

Caldeirada (fish stew), Portugal's bouillabaisse, is the second national seafood dish. Although its content varies from region to region and with the day's catch, a good *caldeirada* should include about nine varieties of fish and shellfish, including clams, mussels, squid, and octopus. Carnivores need not despair. Portugal's third national dish, *cozido à portuguesa* (Portuguese boiled dinner), is a stew made up of a hearty selection of meats, sausages, and vegetables.

Portuguese dining hours are more in tune with those of northern Europe than with the late schedules kept by neighboring Spain. Breakfast, *pequeno almoço,* is light, usually *chá* (tea) or *café* (coffee) *com leite* (with milk) or *sem leite* (without milk). Coffee shops serve a strong, flavorful *bica* (demitasse) and a creamy, machine-steamed *galão* (coffee and milk in a glass). Accompaniments can include *torradas* (toast) or *bolos* (sweet cakes) and cinnamon-covered *pastéis de nata* (egg and custard pastries). Lunch (*almoço*) is served between 1 and 3 PM. For travelers on the move, quick meals are available at *cervejarias* (beer halls), which specialize in *petiscos* (tidbits, or snacks, the equivalent of Spanish *tapas),* sandwiches, and simple meat and fish platters.

For *lanches* or *merendas* (afternoon snacks), artists head for the *café* (coffee shop), society women to the *salão de chá* (tea salon), and the general public to the *pastelaria* (pastry shop). This last offers a large choice — everything from sweet *pastéis* (pastries) to *croquetes* filled with cod, shrimp, chicken, and meat. By late afternoon, the *tascas* and *cervejarias* begin to fill up with the after-work crowd tossing down *imperiais* (glasses of draft lager), *cerveja preta* (dark beer), and *copos de vinho* (glasses of wine), both *tinto* (red) and *branco* (white), while munching on *caracois* (snails), *gambas* (prawns), *codornizes* (stewed quails), *polvo* (octopus), *bifanas* (miniature paprika-laced pork steaks), and *pregos* (steak sandwiches).

Restaurants serve dinner (*jantar*) between 7 and 10 PM, or even later in some cosmopolitan restaurants and modern shopping malls. Menus are à la carte, although many places carry a fixed-price, three-course *menu do dia* (daily menu) at reasonable rates.

A typical dinner starts with a selection of appetizers (*aperitivos*) such as *queijinhos* (fresh sheep or goat cheeses), a mild pâté, and *azeitonas* (olives), along with mouth-watering bread: the rich *pão de milho* (maize bread), the wholesome, dark *pão de centeio* (barley bread), and the lusty, golden *broa* (yeast-based corn bread). Specialties may include *presunto* (smoked ham) from Chaves, Lamego, and Monchique; a plate of *amêijoas* (clams) in white wine, garlic, and parsley sauce; or *gambas na prancha* (grilled prawns).

The Portuguese excel at *sopa* (soup). The light *canja de galinha* (chicken and rice), the creamy *sopa de marisco* (shellfish), the nutritious *sopa de verdura* (vegetable), the heavy *sopa de grão* (chickpea), and the wholesome *sopa de feijão* (bean) are among the more common. Regional soups include the northern *caldo verde* (cabbage soup), the thick, breaded *açordas* from the Alentejo and Estremadura, and the cold, vinegary *gaspacho* soup of the Algarve.

A soup from Ribatejo called *sopa de pedra* (rock soup) contains beans, vegetables, and a stone. According to the story, whenever a certain roaming mendicant priest was refused a meal, he would simply light a fire, then fill a pot with water, put a stone in it, and set it to boil. As curious villagers approached, he slowly coaxed them into adding the ingredients necessary to make a real soup.

There's plenty of fish (*peixe*) on the menu, including boiled or batter-fried *pescada* (hake), grilled *linguado* (sole), and *salmão* (salmon), Tagus River *sável* (shad), *tamboril* (monkfish), ham-stuffed river *truta* (trout), *robalo* (sea bass), wine- or blood-stewed *lampreia* (eel) from the Minho and Tomar rivers, smoked *espadarte* (swordfish), *cherne* (stone bass), Algarve *carapau* (mackerel), and the ubiquitous sardine. Stewed, grilled, and stuffed *lulas* (squid), along with *santola no carro* (cold crab salad in a shell), are coveted seafood dishes, though *lagosta* (lobster) from Peniche is a luxury item for Portuguese and visitors alike.

Carne (meat) and *ave* (poultry) can be *assada* (baked), *grelhada* (grilled), *frita* (fried), *cozida* or *estufada* (stewed), and *recheada* (stuffed). In Portugal, where farmers feed their pigs chestnuts and acorns, *porco* (pork) is the most abundant and tasty meat. Each region has its pork dish: stewed in a copper pot with white wine, clams, and sausages in the Algarve; stewed in red wine in the Minho; and *leitão assado* (roast suckling pig) in the Coimbra region. But the most interesting — and sublime — pork dish in Portugal is probably *carne de porco à alentejana* (pork and clams Alentejo-style), which means seasoned in a savory sauce of paprika, white wine, *pimentão* (sweet red peppers), garlic, oil, bay leaves, onions, and tomato paste.

Cordeiro (lamb) and *cabrito* (kid) dishes are best in the northern and central mountain regions. Steaks, not Portugal's forte, are still worth sampling when accompanied by the mushroom, cream, and mustard sauces used in the best restaurants. Especially good, however, are *bitoques,* thin beefsteaks cooked in butter and served with egg and French fries in hot earthenware dishes. Grilled *frango* (chicken) is becoming more and more popular, particularly in coastal areas, where chickens compete with sardines for space on outdoor grills. The waiter may ask if you want yours with *piri-piri* sauce. Be warned — *piri-piri,* made by mixing Angolan red peppers with oil and vinegar, may be the most tongue-searing sauce in the cooking almanac. Use it sparingly.

In Portugal, sausages are a staple — as appetizers, in stews and soup, and grilled. They come in several shapes, tastes, and sizes. The dry and garlicky *chouriço* is especially popular, and so is *linguiça,* its thinner cousin, sometimes cooked in alcohol to be eaten with bread in *fado* music houses. Smoked *paio* (pork sausage) is popular in the Alentejo, while *morcelas* (blood sausages) come mainly from the north. During the 15th century, at the time of the Inquisition, Jews, under duress and masquerading as Christians, invented *alheiras,* mixed-meat sausages disguised to resemble pork.

Sobremesa (dessert) is an ode to the Portuguese sweet tooth and the bane of cholesterol watchers. Some egg-based desserts such as *toucinho do céu* (bacon of the sky) require as many as 12 egg yolks, and the already rich flans (custard puddings) are thickened with eggs and caramelized. There are also sweets with amusing names such as *barrigas de freira* (nuns' tummies). These stem, apparently, from the 19th century, when the religious orders were banned and, in order to earn a living, nuns became cooks.

Other seductive desserts include *pudim Molotov,* a poached meringue with caramel or peach topping; golden *sonhos* (dreams), deep-fried batter puffs sprinkled with sugar and cinnamon; *arroz doce* (rice pudding); *doce de chila* (caramelized chila gourd); and *torta de amêndoa* (almond tart). For weight watchers, *fruta fresca* (fresh fruit), or *melão* (melon) or *ananás* (pineapple) with razor-thin strips of *presunto,* are lighter alternatives. *Queijo* (cheese) is another dessert option; the ones made from sheep's milk are the most coveted. The queen of Portugal's cheese is *serra,* a brie-like cheese from the central Serra da Estrela range. Following closely on its heels are the smooth *castelo branco* cheeses, the Alentejo's salty beja, and the semi-sharp and buttery *serpa,* brushed with paprika and oil.

Along with their love of a *boa mesa* (well-laid out table), the Portuguese love their wine. With its endless number of producers and labels, the country is like one huge wine cellar, and a tour of Portugal, where wine changes from valley to valley and from town to town, is a wine lover's dream. The traveler can discover young local wines and visit the shrine of the venerated port wine in the Douro Valley. This area is also the home of the superb Barca Velha reds and Monopólio whites and Portugal's best *vinhos espumantes* (sparkling wines): Lamego's Raposeira *brutos* (dry) and *semi-secos* (medium dry) bubblies.

The young, crisp *vinhos verdes* (green wines) from the Minho region, which are drunk chilled, go well with fish and shellfish. These wines have a lower alcohol content but higher acidity than more mature wines, however, so it's wise to resist the temptation to drink too much of them before going to bed. Other important demarcated-zone wines are the tart, white *bucelas,* grown on the sandy banks of the Tagus River east of Lisbon, the robust red *dão* wines from the upper Beira region, the fruity *bairrada* reds from the coastal areas near Coimbra, the chilled *colares* reds and whites from the salty cliffs near Sintra west of Lisbon, the full-bodied and sweet muscatel from Setúbal south of Lisbon, and the light Algarve reds and whites. And then there are the fruity rosés — such as the Mateus rosé from Trás-os-Montes — so popular with tourists.

Portugal's after-dinner drinks are also unique. Liqueurs range from *medronho,* made from the smooth nectar of the arbutus berry, to the bitter almond *amêndoa amarga* from the Algarve. The sweet cherry *ginginha* brandy from Alcobaça, west of Lisbon, is popular, as is the rougher *bagaço,* a clear brandy-like liquor distilled from grape leaves and drunk chilled. Aged *aguardente velha* is a more refined, cognac-flavored spirit favored by connoisseurs and the well-to-do.

Part of the charm of dining in Portugal can be the history lesson consumed along with the meal. Consider, for example, *tripas à moda do Porto* (tripe, Porto-style). Back in the 15th century, Prince Henry the Navigator, in order to provision an armada, commandeered almost all the meat in the city of Porto, leaving its citizens nothing but tripe. However, they immediately fashioned this into a delicious and spicy dish of tripe and beans. Today, culinary ingenuity and resourcefulness, together with the Portuguese flair for blending, still delight those fortunate enough to dine in Portugal.

THE CITIES

BRAGA

Porto earns, Lisbon spends, Coimbra studies, and Braga prays. So goes the popular Portuguese saying, and the description fits Braga to a tee. With a reputed 300 churches and only 140,000 inhabitants, the city can boast one of the highest church-to-resident ratios in all Christendom. The capital of the northern Minho province, Braga has been Portugal's religious center and the home of its archbishops since the birth of the nation in the 12th century. At the height of the Church's power, not even the nobility was allowed to own land inside the city walls, and all industries centered around the Church's needs.

Today, the medieval walls have come down, the city's economic base has been diversified, and a sprawling, ugly metropolis is springing up around the old center. Yet despite these changes, the Old Quarter of Braga, with its ornate Renaissance and Manueline palaces, baroque churches, and narrow medieval streets, still charms the visitor and attests to the city's former glory.

The strategic location of Braga, in a fertile valley at the foot of three mountain ranges, always has made it ripe for occupation and development. The Goidelic Celts, also known as the Bracari, are believed to have founded the city and given it a name several thousand years ago. The Romans occupied it in 250 BC and made it the hub of five major roads, all leading to Rome. Through them Christianity and the first Bishops of Braga eventually came. The Suevians overran the city in AD 409, but were replaced in 485 by Visigoth invaders, who, in turn, were vanquished in 711 by a Moorish army. For more than 3 centuries, the Christians and the Moors jousted over Braga, until the Muslims were finally expelled at the end of the 11th century.

It was a Spanish king, Alfonso (VI of León and I of Castile), who, with the help of French Crusaders, succeeded in wresting this part of northern Iberia from the Moors. Thus, the bishops barely had returned to Braga when, in 1095, the king rewarded a French nobleman, Henry of Burgundy, with the hand of his daughter Teresa in marriage. The county of "Portucale" — not yet the kingdom, but a smaller entity to which Braga belonged — came as part of her dowry, and Henry became Count of Portucale. The new masters of Braga arrived with its first archbishop, a French prelate eventually canonized as St. Gerald, and work began on the cathedral. Later, in 1112, Henry granted a city charter to another archbishop, Dom Maurício Bourdin, making him Lord of Braga, a title the archbishops continued to hold until the late 18th century.

In the mid-12th century, when the Count of Portucale, Henry's son Dom Afonso Henriques, broke away from León and Castile and established the kingdom of Portugal, Braga's archbishops were his allies. They became the spiritual heads of the new nation and waged their own war against their Spanish arch-rivals in Santiago de Compostela and Toledo. But their energies ultimately were diverted southward to the business of driving out the Moors and, later, to evangelizing the new continents discovered by the Portuguese mariners of the late 15th century.

During the 16th century, a dynamic archbishop named Dom Diogo de Sousa used money from Portugal's new spice trade with India to embellish the city. Sousa imported artists from neighboring Spain, built a Renaissance palace, and commissioned the construction of new churches. The building boom came to an end soon after his death, however, as the same discoveries that had brought the country prosperity also drained it of manpower and cash. To make matters worse, the Portuguese king and a large part of the nobility perished in a disastrous campaign against Morocco in 1578, prompting Philip II of Spain to seize the opportunity to invade his neighbor and put an end to Portugal's golden age.

Independence returned to the nation in the 17th century, and the euphoria of that event, heightened by the religious zeal of the Counter-Reformation and by the flow of gold from Brazil, breathed new life into 18th-century Braga. Two prelates, Dom Rodrigo de Moura Teles — a midget of a man who made up in energy what he lacked in size — and Dom Gaspar de Bragança (son of King João V), used the newfound wealth to fund large construction projects. They turned Braga into the center of baroque art in Portugal (it was from the Portuguese word *barroco,* meaning "rough pearl," that the style got its name). The Raio Palace and elegant Town Hall were built during this prolific period, as was the impressive staircase leading to the Bom Jesus Church. Braga artists also popularized the use of *talha dourada,* heavily gilded, carved wood, in church interiors. The archbishops were at the zenith of their power. They patronized the arts, dressed in satin and jewels, and even had their own private orchestra.

The social upheavals and revolutions that swept through Europe during the late 18th century, however, eventually reached Braga and eroded the power of the Church. In 1792, the archbishops were forced to give up their feudal title as Lords of Braga and to hand over control of the city administration to a growing bourgeoisie. In 1808, Napoleon's forces overran the city and sacked the churches. Finally, in 1910, church properties were confiscated by the first Portuguese Republic. Although some of these were later restored, the Church in Braga never regained administrative control of the city.

Today, Braga is enduring the growing pains of modernity, with all its motorized traffic and noxious fumes. Instead of cathedrals and chapels, industrial parks and shopping malls are going up. New industries, such as graphic design and the manufacture of auto accessories, are functioning alongside traditional crafts such as candlemaking and the fashioning of religious artifacts and vestments. Chic cafés are popping up next to dowager coffeehouses. Church institutions such as the Catholic University are being forced to compete with modern counterparts. And for the first time since the Inquisition, Roman Catholicism is being challenged by new religious sects such as the Mormons and Jehovah's Witnesses.

Yet despite the changes, Braga remains Portugal's Eternal City. Its numerous street altars and chapels are constantly lit with votive candles, and dozens of shops sell a vast assortment of religious artifacts to a constant influx of pilgrims from all over the world. *Holy Week* in Braga, a time of sumptuous processions and colorful religious pageantry, remains the most important event of the year, the most spectacular festival of its kind in Portugal. And the people of Braga — serious, hardworking, and contemplative — are considered the most religious in the country, so religious that it is said no citizen of Braga makes a major decision without lighting a candle and praying to any one of hundreds of saints, many of whom, incidentally, come from Braga.

BRAGA AT-A-GLANCE

SEEING THE CITY: For a spectacular view of Braga and its surroundings, leave town by Avenida João XXI and drive east 5½ miles (9 km) on N103-3 via Bom Jesus to the Monte Sameiro sanctuary and park. The reward for a climb up 265 steps to the lantern tower in the cupola of the Sanctuary to the Virgin at the park's summit is a breathtaking panorama of the Minho region. On a clear day, the Atlantic coastline can be sighted 20 miles to the west, and the Serra do Gerês and Serra do Marão peaks are visible to the northeast and southeast; closer are Braga itself to the west and the prehistoric city of Briteiros to the east. Feast on the marvelous view, then settle down to a meal on the ground at the *Sameiro* restaurant (see *Eating Out*), one of the area's best eating establishments. The sanctuary is open daily, from 8 AM to 8 PM; there is an admission charge for the tower.

The Torre de Menagem, in Braga on Largo de São Francisco, across from the tourist office, is also open to visitors. The crenelated tower, an 18th-century addition to the city's medieval fortifications and the only part of them to survive urban expansion, provides a nice view of the Old Town. It is open daily from 10 AM to noon and from 2 to 6 PM. Admission charge.

SPECIAL PLACES: Although Braga is a sprawling metropolis, the city center, which includes the historic section, is concentrated enough to explore on foot. Leave your car at the municipal parking lot on Praça Conde de Agrolongo, walk past the Torre de Menagem, and turn into Rua do Souto, a pedestrian walkway that is the site of the city's most elegant shops and picturesque outdoor cafés and which, together with Rua Dom Diogo de Sousa, cuts through the Old Town and religious heart of the city. Before this east-west parallel ends its trajectory at the Porta Nova arch, it passes several of the city's major landmarks: the Largo do Paço fountain and square and the former Archbishops' Palace to the north, and the Misericórdia Church and the cathedral to the south. Nearby, to the northwest, are the *Biscainhos Palace,* now a museum, and Braga's baroque Town Hall, on the Praça do Município, while to the southeast are two notable houses, the Casa dos Coimbras and the Casa dos Crivos, both on São João de Souto Square, and the São Marcos Hospital, in the adjoining square, Largo Carlos Amarante. A 5-minute walk southeast from the hospital leads to the striking Raio Palace and, next door, the pre-Roman Fountain of the Idol; its cool and relaxing setting makes it an ideal place to unwind after a day's walking tour.

THE SÉ (CATHEDRAL) COMPLEX

Sé (Cathedral) – When the Portuguese want to point out the antiquity of something, they say it's "as old as the cathedral of Braga." Work on the Sé was begun in the 12th century by Henry of Burgundy and his wife, Teresa, at a site previously occupied by a 6th-century church destroyed by the Moors and, before that, by a Roman temple built in AD 43. The present building has undergone changes and additions over the centuries; the charming south door and the arching over the west (main) door are two of the most notable remnants of its early, Romanesque period. During the 16th century, the Gothic portico was added to the west door by Biscayan artists imported from Spain by Archbishop Dom Diogo de Sousa, who also rebuilt the apse in a Flamboyant ogival style. Archbishop Dom Rodrigo de Moura Teles was responsible for the 18th-century bell towers and the building's baroque façade. Several chapels line the cloister and courtyard of the cathedral. The plan was to incorporate the area where the courtyard stands as part of a five-nave structure so the Sé could compete with the cathedral in Santiago de Compostela, Spain. But financial restraints forced the archbishops to pare down their ambitions.

On the cathedral grounds are several statues of Nossa Senhora do Leite (Our Lady of Milk, or the Madonna Suckling the Holy Child); some of them are surrounded by wax and plastic votive offerings in the shape of breasts. These are left by pregnant women imploring the Virgin to provide them with ample milk to nurse their babies, a practice that is possibly a holdover from Roman days, since the Roman temple originally on this spot was dedicated to Isis, the goddess of fertility and motherhood.

Upon entering the cross-shaped cathedral, a visitor sees a baptismal font carved in the ornate 16th-century Manueline style immediately to the left, and a chapel with the bronze tomb of the Infante Dom Afonso (a brother of Henry the Navigator), the work of 16th-century Flemish artisans, to the right. Still at the cathedral's west end, the *coro baixo* (lower choir) is flanked by two magnificent 18th-century organs, richly decorated in brass, marble, and gilded wood, while the *coro alto* (raised choir), the gallery above it, contains 18th-century stalls in black wood that can be seen during the Treasury visit (see below). Look across the nave to the east end of the cathedral and the rib-vaulted chancel, its high altar carved in stone; above the altar is a statue of St. Mary of Braga, the patron saint of the city. To the right of the chancel is the Chapel of the Holy Sacrament, with a 17th-century polychrome wood altar representing the Triumph of the Church; to the left is the Chapel of São Pedro de Rates, the first Bishop of Braga, with 18th-century *azulejos,* glazed and painted tiles, depicting his life.

Tesouro (Treasury) – The cathedral's treasury — otherwise known as Braga's *Museum of Sacred Art* — contains religious objects dating as far back as the 10th century and is well worth a visit. There are rooms filled with gold and silver embroidered vestments and chalices from the 15th and 16th centuries, including a silver monstrance (a vessel used during mass) encrusted with 450 precious stones that belonged to Dom Gaspar de Bragança. Other treasures include a 10th-century Hispano-Arab (Mozarabic) ivory casket, a 17th-century silver reliquary cross, an iron cross said to have been used in the first mass celebrated in Brazil, a working 17th-century traveling organ, a 17th-century saddle embroidered in gold and silver used in Corpus Christi processions, and huge 17th- and 18th-century liturgical books. Most amusing are the giant platform shoes used by the diminutive archbishop Dom Rodrigo de Moura Teles, who was only 3'11" tall and needed the enormous heels to reach the altar. The treasury is open daily from 8:30 AM to 6 PM in summer (8:30 AM to 12:30 PM and 1:30 to 5:30 PM in winter) and can be seen by guided tours only. Both the tour (conducted in Portuguese) and the admission charge cover a visit to the cathedral's *coro alto* (for a close view of the organ cases and the choir stalls) and to the three chapels listed below.

Capela dos Reis (Chapel of Kings) – This Gothic-style structure off the cathedral's cloister contains the tombs of the founders, Dom Henrique (Henry of Burgundy) and Dona Teresa. Teresa is buried beside her husband, although she took up with a Galician count after his death; in the early 16th century, Dom Diogo de Sousa had her placed in the same tomb as her husband, but a later archbishop had it opened and the bones separated into adjoining tombs. The chapel also contains the embalmed remains of a 14th-century warrior archbishop, Dom Lourenço Vicente, who distinguished himself in the famous battle of Aljubarrota, where a small Portuguese force and British archers defeated a much larger Spanish army. For opening hours and admission information, see the Tesouro above.

Capela de São Geraldo (St. Gerald's Chapel) – The walls of this handsome Gothic chapel, located across the courtyard from the Chapel of Kings, are covered with *azulejos* depicting the life of St. Gerald, the first Archbishop of Braga. On December 5, the public brings baskets of fruit to the chapel as an offering to the saint. The tradition is said to derive from St. Gerald's first miracle — saving the life of a sick child by conjuring up fresh fruit in the middle of winter. For opening hours and admission information, see the Tesouro above.

Capela da Glória (Chapel of Glory) – Next to St. Gerald's Chapel is a third elegant Gothic chapel, this one built by Archbishop Gonçalo Pereira as his burial chamber. Vestiges of Renaissance frescoes and Mudéjar paintings can be traced on one of the walls. The archbishop's finely sculptured tomb is set on six sleeping lions, its sides bearing reliefs of the Crucifixion, the Apostles, the Virgin and Child, and a "theory of deacons" chanting the Litany of the Dead. The reclining statue of Dom Gonçalo looks up at an 18th-century ceiling of painted wood. For opening hours and admission information, see the Tesouro above.

ELSEWHERE

Igreja da Misericórdia (Misericórdia Church) – The Renaissance church next to the cathedral doesn't catch the eye, but its dazzling altarpiece does. The baroque wooden altar, intricately carved and gilded by Marcelino de Araújo, is considered one of the best — and certainly one of the most sumptuous — examples of *talha dourada* in Portugal. The two figures at the top, practically lost in this sea of swirls and lines, are Mary and her sister Elizabeth. Rua Dom Diogo de Sousa.

Antigo Paço Episcopal (Former Archbishops' Palace) – The former residence of the Archbishops of Braga is made up of wings from the 14th, 17th, and 18th centuries — although the latter burned at the end of the last century and was remodeled in the 1930s. The palace now serves as the city library and headquarters of the University of the Minho. Part of the 14th-century wing is used for university seminars and can be visited, as can the library reading room in the 18th-century wing, notable for its carved wood ceiling. The library houses over 300,000 volumes and is considered the second most important source of civil documents in Portugal, after Lisbon's Torre do Tombo. Its priceless parchments, some stored in wooden drawers inlaid with ivory in the Sala do Arcaz, date back as far as the 9th century and include detailed family genealogies, compiled during the Inquisition, of those persons who applied to enter church service. (Special permission is required to visit the rooms with these collections.) The lobby of the university rectory has a small but fine display of 17th- and 18th-century Portuguese tiles taken from various churches and homes in the region. The library is open Mondays through Fridays from 9 AM to noon and from 2 to 8 PM. No admission charge. Praça do Município (phone: 612234).

Chafariz do Largo do Paço (Largo do Paço Fountain) – In the picturesque square between the Archbishops' Palace and the cathedral stands a fountain built in 1723 by Archbishop Dom Rodrigo de Moura Teles to glorify his family. The fountain's basin is supported by angels and encircled by the city's six towers; a seventh tower, prominently displaying the Moura Teles family coat of arms, serves as a base for the Madonna, or St. Mary of Braga, the city's patron saint. Largo do Paço.

Arco da Porta Nova (Arch of the New Door) – The story behind this arch typifies the struggle between the church and the nobility for control of the city. In 1512, Archbishop Dom Diogo de Sousa had a door constructed to serve as the main gate to the city. In 1778, it was torn down and replaced by a wider structure on which, to the displeasure of the reigning archbishop, King José I placed his coat of arms. The situation was later resolved by the municipality, which simply added an episcopal hat on top of the royal coat of arms and encircled it with ecclesiastical tassels. Rua Dom Diogo de Sousa.

Palácio dos Biscainhos (Biscainhos Palace) – This nobleman's palace was built during the 17th century, but has undergone several alterations since then. It now serves as a museum, focusing on the lifestyle of the Portuguese nobility between the late 17th and the 19th centuries. Granite figures of pages welcome visitors to a spacious atrium leading to terraced gardens with interesting *casas de fresco,* or cool houses — large umbrella-shaped trees with square openings cut into them, which the nobility used to escape the hot sun. The Salão Nobre (Grand Salon) is lined with early-18th-century *azulejos* depicting the life of the leisure class (not always a life of ease, as can be seen in the painting on the ceiling portraying a missionary member of the household being burned at the stake in Japan in 1624). Several large rooms with ornate stucco ceilings contain elaborate Indo-Portuguese furniture, inlaid with ivory; handsome Portuguese, Chinese, and Dutch (Delft) pottery; glassware; silverware; and 18th- and 19th-century objets d'art. The salon of the Romantic period, with its rich reds and flamboyant furniture, is in sharp contrast to the more austere elegance of the neo-classical dining room, while the 18th-century bedroom is decorated in the Queen Dona Maria style, a period characterized by its emphasis on religious decoration. Open for guided tours (in Portuguese only) from 10 AM to 12:15 PM and from 1:30 to 5:15 PM; closed Mondays. Admission charge (no charge on Sunday mornings). Rua dos Biscainhos (phone: 27645).

Câmara Municipal (Town Hall) – The façade on this 18th-century building, attributed to the architect André Soares, is considered one of the best examples of baroque architecture in Portugal. Although its grand stairway is lined with tiles depicting the arrival in Braga of a new archbishop, Dom José de Bragança (the bastard brother of King João V), the building was constructed specifically as a Town Hall, demonstrating that secular power was already beginning to creep into the city. The reunion room drips with chandeliers, and its walls are hung with framed portraits of important religious and political figures. Open for short guided tours (Portuguese only) Mondays through Fridays from 8:30 AM to noon and from 2 to 5 PM. No admission charge. Praça do Município (phone: 613371).

Fonte do Pelicano (Pelican Fountain) – The water-spouting pelican at its center is the reason for this lovely baroque fountain's name. Originally in the Archbishops' Palace, it now graces a pleasant park in front of the Town Hall.

Jardim de Santa Bárbara (St. Barbara's Garden) – The 17th-century garden behind the Archbishops' Palace contains over 50 species of flowers, arranged in very original designs that do justice to Portugal's reputation as a nation with a collective green thumb. A 17th-century fountain sits majestically in the midst of this sea of colors, and the medieval wing of the Archbishops' Palace serves as a backdrop. Several stone arches from the interior of the palace, gutted by fire in the last century, have been placed in the garden along with Roman milestones retrieved from nearby archaeological sites. The setting is the most photographed in Braga. Always open; no admission charge. Rua Justino Cruz and Rua Eça de Queirós.

Casa dos Crivos (House of Screens) – The last of its kind in Braga. At one time there were dozens of such houses, with exterior grilles and screens of Moorish design. They were first built in the 16th century, during Dom Diogo's tenure, to allow cloistered nuns to look out onto the street without being seen. The present house dates from the 16th century. Restored inside, it is now open to the public as a gallery for exhibitions by local artists, which normally can be seen from 9:30 AM to 12:30 PM, from 2:30 to 6:30 PM, and from 9 to 11 PM. No admission charge. 45 Rua de São Marcos (phone: 76002).

Casa dos Coimbras (House of the Coimbras) – The handsome house and its chapel, built for Archbishop João Coimbra in 1525, are among the few remnants in Braga of the prolific and highly imaginative Manueline style of early-16th-century Portuguese architecture. Privately owned, they are not open to the public, but they can be admired from the street. The house, which has suffered some unfortunate remodeling, has retained its ornate Manueline windows. Largo de São João de Souto.

Hospital de São Marcos (St. Marcos Hospital) – A functioning hospital known for its lively 18th-century façade by Carlos Amarante. At the top are large granite statues of martyrs and apostles. The figures are standing precariously on the ledge and gesticulating wildly, giving the impression that they are practically floating in mid-air. Largo Carlos Amarante.

Palácio do Raio (Raio Palace) – The 18th-century house was designed by André Soares, and is perhaps the finest example of a *solar,* or mansion, in Braga. Though the building — also called the Casa do Mexicano — is privately owned and cannot be visited inside, its best feature is the façade, an elegant blending of tile and stone, with the unusual shapes of the windows accentuated by the blue tiles surrounding them. Rua do Raio.

Fonte do Idolo (Fountain of the Idol) – Despite the Roman inscriptions, it is generally believed that the fountain dates from pre-Roman times. Some historians have suggested it was an immersion fountain and/or an altar for offerings to the Lusitanian idol Tongenabiago. The structure collapsed at one time; what remains is a high-relief section with a bust of a human over the water spout and a figure beside it holding a child on its lap. The figure is hidden behind a green iron gate, down some steps at 389 Rua do Raio.

ENVIRONS

Bom Jesus do Monte – No visit to Braga is complete without a tour of this spectacular sanctuary set on a densely wooded hill 3 miles (5 km) east of town via N103-3. The complex is composed of a monumental baroque staircase, begun in the early 18th century by order of Archbishop Dom Rodrigo de Moura Teles, leading up to a neo-classical church, begun in the late 18th century and finished in the early 19th. The staircase, decorated with allegorical sculptures, fountains, and chapels, is the pièce de résistance of the sanctuary, and should be climbed in order to appreciate fully its wealth of detail. Those not relishing a hike can take the funicular up (it takes 3 minutes to ascend 380 feet on a 40° incline) and walk back down the stairs. There is also a winding road leading up to the church.

The staircase is divided into three sections. The first part, the Sacred Way, is bordered with chapels presenting scenes from the Passion through the use of life-size terra cotta figures. The second set of stairs, the Stairway of the Five Senses, pays homage to the senses through the use of fountains and figures. Before climbing this section, note the columns on either side of the base, entwined with snakes covered with the water that pours out of their mouths and down their bodies. Stand back and gaze up the stairs: Note how the central granite sculptures blend to form the shape of a chalice. Moving up the stairs, there is Sight, with water gushing from its eyes; Smell, with water dripping from its nose; Taste, with water pouring from its mouth; Touch, with water flowing from its hand; and Hearing, with water coming from its ears. The final section, the Stairway of the Three Virtues, evokes Faith, Hope, and Charity by using more fountains and allegorical figures. It gives way to a lovely circular terraced garden and fountain surrounded by manicured lawns with geometric flower beds. (There is also an equestrian statue of a saint; it is traditionally held that if a woman circles the statue three times, she will be married within the year.) At the top of the stairway, facing the church, are statues of the men who condemned Jesus, fountains dedicated to the Four Apostles, and surrounding the main church, several chapels.

The Igreja do Bom Jesus (Good Jesus Church), designed by Carlos Amarante (who also designed the third staircase) and finished in 1811, contains an altar re-creating the final moments at Calvary with larger-than-life statues. Also of interest inside the church is the Altar das Relíquias (Altar of the Relics), practically buried under modern mementos from devoted pilgrims and tourists. Behind the church are several paths leading through grottoes and fountains to a small lake, where boats can be rented by the hour.

Those who have walked up the stairs may want to take the funicular down. Dating from the late 19th century, it is propelled by gravity and a tank of water — two carriages move in opposite directions at the same time, with the water in the carriage going down providing the weight to pull the other carriage up. It runs every half hour or when its 20 seats are filled and costs $1 for the 3-minute ride. (For about $7, you can rent the carriage between scheduled runs for a private ride.) Bom Jesus is open from 8 AM to 8 PM daily.

Monte Sameiro – The Sanctuary to the Virgin at the summit of this green mountain is the most important center of devotion in Portugal after Fátima. Although the church itself (late 19th to early 20th century) is not particularly interesting, the view of the Minho region from the lantern tower of its cupola is breathtaking, and the size of the sanctuary grounds is also impressive. The courtyard outside the church is larger than a football field, and has held over half a million pilgrims at one time. (The main pilgrimages take place the first week of June and the third week of August.) A larger-than-life statue of Pope Pius XII, at the base of a staircase leading up to the courtyard, commemorates his visit in 1954, but the view up to the church from the stairway is obstructed by a large concrete stage used for outdoor masses. The woods and paths around the church are pleasant, and the *Sameiro* restaurant beside it (see *Eating Out*) is one of the best in the region. Monte Sameiro is located 5½ miles (9 km) east of town, 2½ miles (4 km) past Bom Jesus on N103-3. The sanctuary is open daily from 8 AM to 8 PM; there is a charge to climb the church tower.

Santa Maria Madalena – This granite church, which sits on the wooded heights of the Serra da Falperra, is one of the more unusual examples of baroque work in Portugal. André Soares, the same architect who designed the Raio Palace and the Town Hall in Braga, focused on its façade, playing with curving lines to give the building a sense of depth and movement. The church is normally open only on Sundays between 9 AM and noon (although longer summer hours are contemplated), but even when closed, the interior is visible through a grille in the door at the front entrance. The surrounding woods were once used by a local Robin Hood called Zé de Telhado (and, in fact, there is a Portuguese saint, Santa Marta da Falperra, who is the patron saint of thieves). The church is 3 miles (5 km) east of Braga on N309; it can also be reached from N103-3 by passing Bom Jesus and, less than half a mile before Monte Sameiro, taking the signposted turnoff to Serra da Falperra. Santa Maria Madalena is 2½ miles (4 km) from the turnoff.

Capela de São Frutuoso de Montélios – The chapel of São Frutuoso, believed to have been constructed in the 7th century by Bishop Frutuoso of Dume, was damaged by the Moors in 711 and rebuilt in the 11th century. In the shape of a Greek cross, it is one of the few remaining examples of Byzantine art in Portugal, and despite an advanced state of disrepair — only one of the four naves that made up the cross is still attached to the cupola — it retains the aura and dignity of age. To visit, apply to the priest or sacristan at the adjoining Church of São Francisco. St. Francis itself contains 16th-century stalls that were removed from the cathedral of Braga in the 18th century. To reach São Frutuoso, 2½ miles (4 km) from Braga, take N201 northwest toward Ponte de Lima and turn right at Real.

■ **EXTRA SPECIAL:** As elsewhere in Europe, whiling away the hours in a coffeehouse is an important part of life in Braga. Of the several historic cafés in which to do as the natives do, the most famous is the 19th-century *Café Brasileira.* Its strategic location in the Largo do Barão São Martinho, by the entrance to fashionable Rua do Souto, makes it the city's informal salon. It is here that most of the intellectuals and artists traditionally have met and lingered over the latest news from Lisbon and Porto, and they still do. The marble tables and brass and copper fittings provide an Old World ambience; octogenarian waiters add timeless atmosphere. Patrons sit inside and stare out onto the street through large windows, which slide back in summer. Also recommended are the refurbished *Café Astoria* and *Café Vianna,* in the arcade in front of the tourist office, both with 1930s decor and tables to sit outside in fine weather. The latter is popular with the young, trendy crowd, who are attracted to the café's mix of Art Deco decadence, young waiters and waitresses, and "designer" snack and salad menu. The café doubles as a bar at night with live jazz and folk music.

SOURCES AND RESOURCES

TOURIST INFORMATION: The Municipal Tourism Board located in the center of town (1 Av. Central, at the corner of Av. da Liberdade; phone: 22550) offers advice and assistance in English. It is open daily, from 9 AM to 7 PM (except Saturdays from October through April, when it is open from 9 AM to 12:30 PM and from 2 to 5 PM, and on Sundays during the same months, when it is closed entirely).

Local Coverage – The *Correio do Minho,* the local newspaper with the largest circulation, publishes a daily agenda listing events and other pertinent information, such as exchange rates, the weather forecast, and the schedules of trains and buses departing for major cities in Portugal and elsewhere in Europe. The *Diário do Minho,* another local paper, is also available. Newsstands in the arcade in front of the tourist office sell major European newspapers, and magazines and the European editions of American news magazines, but not the *International Herald Tribune.* A comprehensive English-language pamphlet describing the city, entitled *Braga,* is published by the Municipal Tourism Board and distributed free. Pick it up at the tourist office (address above).

TELEPHONE: The city code for Braga is 53. If calling from within Portugal, dial 053 before the local number.

GETTING AROUND: Most of the major sights of the city are easily accessible by foot. In any case, do everything to avoid driving in town during the rush hours (from 8:30 to 10 AM and from 5 to 7:30 PM), particularly on the Avenida da Liberdade. There is a municipal parking lot on Praça Conde de Agrolongo, on the north side of the Old Town, where a car can be parked for several hours for less than a dollar.

Airport – The local airport (phone: 626530), 2½ miles (4 km) north of Braga at Palmeira, handles neither scheduled domestic nor international flights; it is used mainly by the *Braga Flying Club* (phone: 253530), which leases planes and pilots.

Bus – Service is reasonable, but buses do get crowded during rush hour, and the frequency of their appearance drops off after midnight. Tickets are acquired on the bus (125 escudos — about 80¢ — within the city limits). The main bus station for long-distance arrivals and departures is the Central de Camionagem de Braga (Travessa da Praça do Comércio; phone: 78354). *Abreu,* a travel agency (171 Av. Central; phone: 613100), also handles reservations. The tourist office has lists of bus schedules to all destinations, and the *Correio do Minho* publishes a daily schedule of major runs.

Car Rental – *Avis* has a rental office beside the central bus station (28 Rua Gabriel Pereira de Castro; phone: 72520), and *Hertz* also has a local office (20 Largo Primeiro de Dezembro; phone: 616744).

Taxi – There is a taxi stand in the Largo do Barão São Martinho, near the Municipal Tourism Board. You can also call for a cab (phone: 614019).

Train – The main train station, Estação do Caminho de Ferro (phone: 22166), on the west side of the city at the Largo de Estação, is a central rail hub for northern Portugal. The newspapers publish a daily schedule of trains to and from important destinations; the tourist office also has schedules.

SPECIAL EVENTS: As is to be expected, *Holy Week* is the most important time of the year in Braga, a time when all commercial activity grinds to a halt and the city is transformed into a giant and sumptuous house of worship. Priceless gold and silver ecclesiastical relics are removed from church treasuries and paraded through town by the archbishop and his retinue, themselves clothed in diamonds and pearls. Balconies are decorated with luxurious drapes displaying the coats of arms of ancient families who fought in the Catholic armies to liberate Portugal from the Moors. The streets are festooned with lights and filled with the intoxicating smell of burning wax and incense. Daily processions vent the religious fervor of the populace: In one procession, hundreds of penitents dressed in the black habit of gravediggers carry torches and walk somberly in front of the image of the Lord to the slow, martial cadence of a funerary tune. Hooded men add a dark and mysterious note to the events. At one time, these masked men went around with large torches pointing out the houses of suspected sinners. That practice is a thing of the past, but *Holy Week,* with its grand religious manifestations, is a reminder that the spirit that made Braga the seat of ecclesiastical power and devotion in Portugal is alive and thriving.

From June 23 through 25, the city comes alive once again (and is again lit spectacularly) for the *Festas de São João* (Feast Days of St. John), a Christian holiday with roots in pagan rites celebrating the summer solstice. This is the time of year when the crops are beginning to blossom and the people of the Minho come out and rejoice. Parties go on until all hours of the night, the *vinho verde* flows freely, and the aroma of festive food invades the popular neighborhoods. Young women wear colorful regional dresses and ornate gold filigree, folk groups perform, and medieval dances are staged. Customs such as throwing herbs into large bonfires to make divinations or passing around pots of leeks with carnations attached to them are reminders of the ancient origins of the festivities.

Both *Holy Week* and the *Festas de São João* draw many pilgrims and visitors, so advance hotel reservations are necessary for these periods. At any time of the year, however, Braga is probably playing host to some industrial fair, convention, or congress at the Palácio Municipal de Exposições e Desportos (in the park at the southern end of Av. da Liberdade). The *vinho verde* fair is held in the late spring or early summer (the schedule varies).

MUSEUMS: In addition to those museums mentioned in *Special Places,* the *Museu Pio XII* and the *Museu Medina,* which share the same building, may be of interest. The former is the city's museum of antiquities, housing artifacts dating as far back as the neolithic period (albeit arranged in a haphazard way); the latter consists of a collection of paintings by 20th-century Portuguese artist Henrique Medina, in which his predilection for naturalist settings and young virgins is evident. The remains of a Roman swimming pool are in the courtyard. The museums share the same hours, from 10 AM to noon and from 3 to 6 PM (closed Mondays), but there are separate admission charges. 8 Campo São Tiago (phone: 23370).

SHOPPING: Braga and its environs are known for their fairly large selection of moderately priced handicrafts — lace and embroidery, wicker and straw articles, earthenware goods, and religious artifacts. The best bargains can be obtained at the weekly Tuesday fair in the Palácio Municipal de Exposições e Desportos. For those unable to attend the fair, there is the shop at the tourist office, which carries all the regional goods, including the Minho's famed filigree jewelry, at prices only slightly above those of the manufacturer. Shopping malls, or *centros comerciais,* have made their appearance: They're largely restricted to Avenida da Liberdade, and are especially convenient because they stay open until midnight. Shoppers in search of quality, however, continue to patronize the stores on and around Rua do Souto. Stores are open Mondays through Saturdays, from 9 AM to 1 PM and from 3 to 7 PM.

Casa Eden – A large selection of hand-embroidered linen and bedspreads (a damask bedspread can cost anywhere from $200 to $300). English spoken. 140-144 Rua do Souto (phone: 22756).

Casa Fânzeres – The oldest religious artifacts shop in Braga both sells and restores religious objects. 132-134 Rua do Souto (phone: 22704).

Herdeiros de Francisco José Ferreira – Leather goods of quality — suitcases, briefcases, and ladies' handbags. 124 Rua do Souto (phone: 74574).

Ourivesaria Confiança – Fine silver and gold jewelry and repair work. 1 Rua do Souto (phone: 23187).

Sapataria Teresinha – Good-quality leather shoes made in the region. 84-86 Rua do Souto (phone: 22943).

Vadeca – Typical handmade *viola braguesa,* or *cavaquinho* guitars, from which the ukelele was developed. 15 Largo do Barão São Martinho (phone: 71045).

SPORTS AND FITNESS: Braga has two major public sports facilities. The larger is the municipal sports complex (phone: 616788) that is part of the Parque Municipal de Exposições e Desportos, in the Parque São João da Ponte at the southern end of Avenida da Liberdade. The other is Rodovia Recreation Park (Av. João XXI; phone: 76803). Both have parking facilities and can be reached by public transport.

Boating – Small rowboats can be rented at the manmade lake above the Bom Jesus do Monte sanctuary.

Fishing – Numerous rivers, lakes, and beaches in the vicinity provide diverse fishing opportunities. The huge reservoir at Peneda-Gerês National Park is only 30 miles (48 km) away. The *Braga Amateur Fisherman's Club* (112 Rua dos Chãos; phone: 26060) can be of assistance.

Jogging – The best place to run is the Parque São João da Ponte, which has both green spaces and a track.

Soccer – *Sporting Clube de Braga,* a first-division team, has its own stadium, *Estádio Primeiro de Maio,* in the Parque São João da Ponte. The season runs from September to May, and major league games are played on Sunday afternoons.

Swimming – The Parque São João da Ponte has the largest public pool in town (phone: 24424), with restaurant and café service next door. The Rodovia Recreation Park sports complex has both an indoor pool (phone: 76803) and an outdoor pool (phone: 76703).

Tennis – There is a tennis club at the Rodovia Recreation Park (phone: 611753).

THEATER: The *Cinema São Geraldo* (on Largo Carlos Amarante) and the *Cinema Avenida* (across the square from the tourist office) show films in their original language with Portuguese subtitles. The daily *Correio do Minho* publishes movie listings in its Roteiro section.

MUSIC: The Minho is Portugal's folklore center. On Saturday and Sunday evenings all summer long, regional folk groups, dressed in colorful costumes, take to the stage at the bandstand on Avenida Central, performing ancient songs and lively dances accompanied by small Minho fiddles, small Braga guitars, triangles, and bass drums. Keep an eye out for Braga's most famous group, the *Grupo Folclórico Dr. Gonçalo Sampaio.*

NIGHTCLUBS AND NIGHTLIFE: The list of choices is increasing, and the action all unfolds between 9 PM and 2 AM. Discotheques currently in vogue are the *Discoteca Club 84* (beside the *Turismo* hotel at Praceta João XXI; phone: 76482) and *Coreto* (15 Av. Central; phone: 75814), a disco and pub catering to a younger and wilder set. The *Golden Bar* (in the *Turismo*) serves tropical drinks and late-night snacks, while the *Latino Bar* (in the Old Town, 56 Rua do Anjo; phone: 79127) is a warm and cozy spot with soft music for the romantically inclined. *Café Tuarege* (Rua dos Congregados) exhibits artwork and draws an artsy crowd, and the *Pub John Lennon* (28 Rua do Raio; phone: 26623) provides live music shows for the nostalgia crowd. *O Nosso Café* (Av. da Liberdade; phone: 23930), however, is the latest rave with Braga's chic. The multipurpose complex, housed in a former theater, caters to all the senses. Guests can dine, or sip coffee and tropical drinks in the sleek, pastel-colored coffeehouse, play chess, backgammon, or billiards in the suave "T-Clube," or let loose on the dance floor of "Trignometria." The brain behind this center is a former employee of Régine, the world-renowned socialite and club owner.

BEST IN TOWN

CHECKING IN: Accommodations in the city leave something to be desired, so demanding travelers head for the hills to the more deluxe rooms around the Bom Jesus sanctuary. In Braga, the larger commercial hotels, catering to the business community, are located in the newer part of town, while smaller establishments — of which there are too few for summer demand — are in the quieter and more picturesque historic center. Expect to pay $90 and up for a double room with continental breakfast in the expensive category, between $40 and $80 at a moderate property, and less than $35 at an inexpensive one. Reservations should be made at least a month in advance for summer traveling, and should be double-checked a week before departure. All telephone numbers are in the 53 city code unless otherwise indicated.

Do Elevador – Quite elegant, and tastefully done in classic Portuguese style. On the grounds of the Bom Jesus sanctuary, its plush, Old World decor and efficient service make it a favorite of Lisbon and Porto society. The 25 rooms with bath (which include a TV set on request) face a manicured garden and have a sweeping view of Braga. The posh dining room (see *Eating Out*) commands a similar view and serves fine regional specialties. Parque do Bom Jesus do Monte (phone: 676611; fax: 676679). Expensive.

João XXI – A smaller and more economical variation on the same theme as the *Caranda.* It has 28 rooms with bath, a dining room — and a dimly lit and noisy discotheque in the basement. Its greatest asset is its central location. 849 Av. João XXI (phone: 22146). Expensive.

Do Parque – Also on the grounds of the Bom Jesus sanctuary, it has a turn-of-the-century look that has been retained despite refurbishing and modernization. The large sitting room is fashionably decorated in leather and wood; each of the 49 air conditioned bedrooms has a private bath, radio, and TV set. There is no restaurant, but meals can be taken at the sister *Elevador* hotel a few paces away. Parque do Bom Jesus do Monte (phone: 676607; telex: 33401). Expensive.

Turismo – Modern, with 132 rooms, it is often billed as the city's best. Unfortunately, it's far too flawed to hold that title. It has all the conveniences, but the furniture is already falling apart, and its communications and air conditioning systems are erratic. A lively bar, rooftop pool, and a friendly (but overworked) staff are its greatest assets. Parking is available in front. Av. João XXI (phone: 612200; fax: 612211; telex: 32136). Expensive.

Caranda – It has all the basic conveniences, although it's lacking in local character. There are 100 rooms, a simple restaurant, and a rooftop bar with a view of Bom Jesus. 96 Av. da Liberdade (phone: 614500; fax: 614550; telex: 32293). Moderate.

São Marcos – Friendly service and 13 modern, clean, and simple rooms characterize this *pensão,* which is ideally located in a quiet pedestrian street in the Old Town. As basic sleeping establishments go, it is the best pension in its category in Braga. No restaurant or bar service. 80 Rua de São Marcos (phone: 77177). Moderate.

Sul Americano – On the Bom Jesus grounds, adjacent to the church, this reliable, family-run hotel has 28 clean, simply decorated rooms, and a large dining room (with a fireplace) serving regional fare. Parking nearby. Parque do Bom Jesus do Monte (phone: 676615). Moderate.

Dos Terceiros – Another *pensão* right in town, this one, with 20 rooms, is near the municipal parking lot and close to the Santa Bárbara Garden. No restaurant, but there is bar service. 85 Rua dos Capelistas (phone: 70466; telex: 33228). Moderate.

Inácio Filho – The Portuguese antiques, 8 clean rooms, and perfect location (in the heart of the Old Town) make this *pensão* an attractive bargain. 42 Rua Francisco Sanches (phone: 23849). Inexpensive.

Casa Santa Zita – Run by a lay religious order, it provides functional and pleasant rooms at student rates. 20 Rua São João (phone: 23494). Very inexpensive.

Those wishing to get away from the conventional hotel circuit should note that Portugal's *Tourism in the Country* program — through which private homes take in paying guests — is particularly active in northern Portugal (see *Accommodations,* GETTING READY TO GO) and that many of the participating properties in the area are the very fine stately homes and manor houses belonging to the *Turismo de Habitação* network rather than the simpler houses of the *Turismo Rural* and *Agroturismo* networks. Among the participants in the Braga area is the *Casa dos Lagos,* a terraced house on the wooded hill at the entrance to Bom Jesus. The house has a cozy apartment with 2 double bedrooms, bathroom, sitting room, and kitchen. Contact Senhor Telmo da Silva Barbosa (phone: 676738 or 24563), or write *Casa dos Lagos* (Bom Jesus, Braga 4700). Another participant, the *Casa da Pedra Cavalgada,* a 19th-century home a little over a mile northeast of Braga on N101, offers a pool, a garden, and a self-contained area with 2 spacious bedrooms and individual sitting rooms (but no private bathroom). Contact Dr. José Mariz (phone: 626596), or write *Casa da Pedra Cavalgada* (Lugar do Assento, Palmeira, Braga 4700). Each is in the moderate price category. Reservations for most local *Tourism in the Country* properties — which generally require a minimum stay of 3 nights — can also be made through *Turihab, Associação de Turismo de Habitação* (Praça da República, Ponte de Lima 4990; phone: 58-942729 or 58-741672; fax: 58-741444; telex: 32618).

EATING OUT: The cooking of Braga is rich and heavy, and the portions are generous. Pork, kid, and cod are the staple main dishes, and of the three, pork is the most common. (Until recently, the killing of a pig was accompanied by much fanfare and ritual.) Pork is popular because it can be stored as ham or sausages, and consumed during the cold winter months. Two pork dishes found frequently are *rojões de porco,* or pork dumplings with maize, and *arroz de sarrabulho,* various meats stewed in pig's blood and rice. The *frigideiras de Braga,* flake pies filled with pork or other meat, are the traditional poor man's meal and are ideal for snacks and picnics. Roast *cabrito,* or kid, is in season during the early summer, and *bacalhau,* or dried salt cod, the most prized dish in the Braga repertoire, is consumed throughout the year — including at *Christmas* dinner. There are more than 300 ways to prepare cod — and each restaurant has its own recipe — but oven-baked codfish with cream is one of the better variations on the theme.

Braga is also known for its pastries. Not only are there more than 20 pastry shops — *pastelarias* — from which to choose, but most restaurants (in all categories) make their own pastries. Anyone with a sweet tooth should try the city's *pudim à abade de Priscos,* an extra rich pudding named after a corpulent prelate with a predilection for sweets. The recipe requires 15 egg yolks, in addition to port, lemon, and caramelized sugar.

Dining out in Braga, however, is not as popular as in other major Portuguese cities. Families tend to entertain at home, leaving restaurants for large celebrations, such as weddings and baptisms. The number of good restaurants is, therefore, limited, particularly in the expensive category. There are, however, several establishments on the Praça Conde de Agrolongo, near the municipal parking lot, serving simple, but tasty, dishes at modest prices for the merchant lunch crowd. A two-course meal for two, including regional *vinho verde* (green wine — referring to its age, not its color), brandy, and coffee, will cost $50 or more in any restaurant listed below as expensive, from $25 to $40 in a restaurant listed as moderate, and around $20 in an inexpensive one. All telephone numbers are in the 53 city code unless otherwise indicated.

Do Elevador – In the hotel of the same name, it offers elegant Old World charm, with views of box-hedged gardens and the Bom Jesus sanctuary. The set menu, changed daily, balances regional fare with continental dishes. The typical three courses include fish and meat and may not leave much room for more, although the richly laden dessert cart will still be a temptation. When it arrives, try the homemade almond cake (*bôlo de amêndoa*). Open daily. Reservations advised. Major credit cards accepted. *Hotel do Elevador,* Parque do Bom Jesus do Monte (phone: 676611). Expensive.

Abade de Priscos – A simple, quaint restaurant upstairs, overlooking a tree-lined square beside the Catholic University. Good regional fare is served: Braga specialties and protein-rich dishes for the largely academic crowd that makes up its clientele. Closed Sundays. Reservations advised. No credit cards accepted. 7 Praça Mousinho de Albuquerque (phone: 76650). Moderate.

O Cantinho do Campo das Hortas – Braga's newest temple of culinary delights, lodged in a former townhouse overlooking the Campo das Hortas, has already made a reputation as the best little eating house in town, and attracts a strong and mixed following of city officials, clergy, and businesspeople. The no frills, family-run establishment offers an à la carte menu and daily specials. Try the tender, mouth-watering *cabrito assado* (roast kid). Lunch reservations advised. No credit cards accepted. Largo da Senhora da Boa Luz (phone: 614003). Moderate.

Casa Cruz Sobral – What this ordinary-looking place lacks in decor and atmosphere, it makes up for in food and service. The owner and manager, António Sobral, son of the proprietor of the *Inácio* restaurant (see below), has taken the family recipes to a smaller locale next door, where he offers a traditional, seasonal menu, with special emphasis on roast meat. The *vitela assada à Cruz Sobral,* veal done in a wine-based onion sauce with copious amounts of garlic, parsley, and cumin, and the *sarrabulho com rojões à moda do Minho,* or pork with maize, are both tasty. Closed Mondays. Reservations unnecessary. No credit cards accepted. 7-8 Campo das Hortas (phone: 616648). Moderate.

Inácio – The most popular restaurant in Braga proper. Family-run, it is decorated with regional artifacts, divided into three cozy dining areas, and has stone walls, wooden beams, and an open kitchen to give it a rustic look that goes well with the menu. Cured hams hanging from the ceiling of the bar are consumed as appetizers with dry port. Some dishes worth noting are the *cabrito no forno,* or roast kid, done over a wood fire, and the *lampréia com arroz* (lamprey with rice) — the fish is marinated in wine and its own blood, which is used later to make the rice sauce. (Preparing this dish is time-consuming and labor-intensive, so have your hotel call in advance to order it.) The wine cellar is well stocked with the best alvarinho green wines, as well as more modestly priced varieties such as Casal Garcia. Owner Claudionor Sobral and his very attentive staff oversee it all. Closed Fridays. Reservations advised. Major credit cards accepted. 4 Campo das Hortas (phone: 613235). Moderate.

Palácio de Dona Chica – Though a bit out of town, the trappings of Portugal's patrician past have been preserved in this turn-of-the-century palace. Guests dine in what were once the salons and family quarters, all overlooking a large garden and artificial lake (both open to the public and served by a terrace bar). Their rendition of the local specialty *rojões de porco* (pork dumplings with maize) is superlative. The complex is also called *Investimentos Turísticos,* but the locals know it by its former name, inspired by its erstwhile resident, a diminutive matron. Open daily. Reservations advised. Major credit cards accepted. On the N201 to Monção, 2½ miles (4 km) north of Braga, in Palmeiras (phone: 626679). Moderate.

Sameiro – Pilgrims visiting the shrine next door are not the only ones making tracks to this family-run restaurant beside the Sameiro sanctuary. Food connoisseurs as well are attracted by its excellent dishes and efficient service. The decor is as spartan as a monk's cell, but owner-chef Maria da Conceição has received several culinary awards for her regional cooking. Her wood-fired stoves add extra flavor to the dishes, which include such specialties as lamprey with mayonnaise and a soufflé of cod. The recipe for the squash-based *tarta de chila* is well guarded, but it appears from the taste to have been marinated in caramelized sugar, honey, and port. The house has its own green wine. Closed Mondays. Reservations advised. Major credit cards accepted. Monte Sameiro (phone: 675114). Moderate.

Casa Pimenta – A simple, family-run eating establishment that is a lunchtime favorite among local merchants and other businesspeople. Open daily. Reservations unnecessary. No credit cards accepted. 24 Praça Conde de Agrolongo (phone: 22119). Inexpensive.

Lusitana – Small and bustling, and the best place in town for a snack. Despite its size, it manages to serve as a snack bar, tea shop, and pastry shop. Combination platters include a succulent veal stew, and the Braga *frigideiras* (meat pies) are house specialties. Eat indoors or outdoors on the small esplanade inside the Santa Bárbara Garden, but either way, if you plan to have lunch here, be sure to arrive before 12:30 PM to avoid the crowds. This is also the most popular hangout in town for the tea and pastry set, since the establishment makes its own sweets, including traditional local delicacies such as *fatias de Braga* (square cakes made of almonds, eggs, and sugar) and sweet Romeo and Juliet pastries, not to mention the ultra-rich *pudim à abade de Priscos.* Closed Mondays. No reservations. No credit cards accepted. 127 Rua Justino Cruz (phone: 20690). Inexpensive.

COIMBRA

Sitting on the banks of the Mondego River, halfway between Lisbon and Porto, Coimbra is Portugal's third-largest city — and its most romantic. The greatest Portuguese poets — including Luís de Camões, who wrote the national epic, *The Lusiads,* during the 16th century — lived in Coimbra and immortalized their city, some carving their romantic verses on its very stones. Coimbra is the home of Portugal's oldest university, making the town teem with young people. Indeed, the romantic image of Coimbra is one of students in black capes hurrying through the nearly perpendicular streets around the ancient university as the cathedral bells toll them to class. Or of the same students, armed with guitars, serenading the young women — *tricanas* — of Coimbra under their balconies.

A popular local *fado,* or folk song, from the beginning of the century says that "Coimbra, to be Coimbra, must have three things — guitars, pretty girls, and black-caped students flitting through the streets." Luckily, as the end of the century approaches, the city remains true to itself, even though in a contemporary fashion. Today, the young women bring out their ankle-length mantillas and colorful shawls only on special occasions, preferring jeans and other modern clothes. The black capes worn by the students since the Middle Ages almost disappeared after the end of the Salazar years, when all traditions came to be associated with the nearly half century of ultra-conservative dictatorship, but they are returning. As before, they are pinned with a colored ribbon identifying the student's course of study — dark blue for letters, light blue for science, red for law, yellow for medicine — with a tear at the border for each romantic conquest.

There is no serenading under the balconies today, but Coimbra *fados,* the sweet, nostalgic songs dedicated to love or to the river or to the city itself and sung only by men, are still heard in student cafés and at festivals, or whenever students with guitars gather on the steps by the Old Cathedral at night. Many *fado* singers, among them doctors, lawyers, and judges — graduates of Coimbra University — are better known for their singing than they are in their professions.

Coimbra has witnessed many romantic love stories. Perhaps the greatest of all was that of Dona Inês de Castro, acted out during the 14th century and beautifully told by Camões. Dona Inês, an aristocrat from Aragon, Spain, was loved by Prince Dom Pedro, whose father, King Afonso IV, wanted him to marry someone else. Nevertheless, the pair took up residence in a country house near Coimbra and had several children together. Fearing that her powerful brothers in Spain would usurp the Portuguese throne for her illegitimate children, King Afonso had her murdered. Pedro declared war on his father, but peace was soon established. After his father died, however, Pedro set Inês's body on the throne, forced all of the nobility to pay her obeisance, and executed two of her murderers by cutting out their hearts. In Coimbra, people believed that a spring gushed from the rocks where Inês was murdered, and that its waters were her tears.

Another woman well remembered in Coimbra was not sinner but saint — Isabel of Aragon, celebrated as Santa Isabel or the Rainha Santa (Saintly Queen). Isabel came to Coimbra in 1292 as the wife of Portugal's great King Dinis and devoted her life to good works. She is best known for the "miracle of the roses." In her efforts to help the poor, Queen Isabel often exceeded what the king thought necessary. One day, as she was taking alms to the poor, he angrily questioned her about what she was carrying in her mantle. When she opened it, the alms had turned to roses. Isabel lived out her last years in the Old Santa Clara Convent across the river, and is now buried in the New Santa Clara Convent. When her tomb was opened in 1612 on order of the bishop, her body was found intact, even though she died in 1336.

The university is the dominant force in the life of Coimbra. In 1290, 2 years before Isabel's arrival, her husband-to-be had founded a university — in Lisbon. In 1308, he transferred it to Coimbra. It moved back and forth several times until 1537, when it finally was permanently located in the heart of the city. The university became a renowned center for the study of philosophy, theology, law, and medicine, although it had its periods of stagnation, including one during this century, which prompted the dictator António Salazar, an alumnus and an ex-professor, to take action in the 1940s. Bent on having a really modern university, he tore down part of the historic Alta (Upper Town) surrounding the university — ancient narrow streets lined with 16th- and 17th-century houses and old churches — and to house his New University, erected some of the ugliest utilitarian buildings in Europe. Fortunately, the buildings in the adjoining Old University remain intact.

In the early days, only students, along with their servants, local nobility, and ecclesiastics, were allowed to live in the Alta section. Their lives and study habits were regulated by the ringing of the cathedral bells. There were strict rules for each class, particularly for the freshmen, who were often treated brutally and persecuted by the upperclassmen. Some of the ancient traditions persist. Students still live in repúblicas — houses passed down from one generation of students to another — where they share the household costs and chores. And they still celebrate the ancient ritual of burning their university ribbons at the end of the term in May to symbolize their moving to an upper class. The celebrations go on for a week, and include a famous serenade on the steps of the Old Cathedral.

The other dominant force in Coimbra life is the Mondego River, often called the river of poets because so many poems and songs have been written about it. But the Mondego — born in Portugal and not in Spain, as most Portuguese rivers are — has done more than provide a romantic setting for the city. Long ago it made Coimbra an important port for trade with lands as far away as Phoenicia and Norway. Later, it was the dividing line between Christian and Moorish Portugal. Unfortunately, as it watered the fields and vineyards, it also brought destruction. Over the centuries, nearly 10 feet of silt finally buried a great part of the Baixa (Lower Town), where shopkeepers and artisans lived, and a good part of the Santa Clara area on the opposite bank. Old churches, convents, and other historic buildings disappeared forever before the Aguieira Dam tamed the river during this century.

Coimbra probably began as an Iron Age castro of Lusitanian and Celtic inhabitants on the Alta hilltop several hundred years before Christ. The Romans located their forum on the same hill, at the spot where the Machado de Castro National Museum now stands, and called their settlement Aeminium. The Visigoths brought Christianity, and when the bishopric was moved from the old Roman town of Conímbriga nearby, the name came with it, eventually to be shortened to Coimbra. Then, in 711, the Moors came. During their tenure, they built a set of walls around the hilltop city; one of its gates, the Almedina, still stands. The Christians recaptured the city, but in 987 the Moors again swept through and nearly razed it. The city was taken once more and held for good in 1064, under Ferdinand I, King of León and Castile.

Thus it happened that Coimbra became the capital of all the land between the Douro River to the north and Moorish-held territory to the south. Later, when Dom Afonso Henriques — son of Henry of Burgundy, to whom the Spanish king had given his Portuguese territory — defeated his mother and her Spanish allies and declared himself king of an independent Portugal, he, too, made Coimbra his capital — even though he had been born in Guimarães. In all, three medieval kings were born in Coimbra before Lisbon became the capital in 1260, and three more were born here after the transfer, because Coimbra remained a royal residence.

A good number of Coimbra's monuments date from the 16th and 17th centuries. Besides the permanent establishment of the university, the 16th century saw the arrival of the Jesuits (who remained strong until the mid-18th century) and of many other religious orders, who founded schools and put up notable buildings. A famous school of sculpture was born when the Frenchmen Nicolas Chanterène, Jean de Rouen, and others set up studios and proceeded to produce most of the statues and other stone carvings that now adorn the city's churches. The sculptors were influenced by the new methods and style of the Italian Renaissance, but they owed much of their art to the stone with which they worked — an exceptionally white, solid, granular limestone from the banks of the nearby Ançã River.

The spate of building during the 17th century was brought about by the discovery of gold in Brazil, and it continued into the 18th century. Buildings dating from this time — such as the New Santa Clara Convent, the university library, and the Santo António dos Olivais church — were literally covered with Brazilian gold. Subsequently, Coimbra remained much the same until the 19th century brought a period of turmoil — the sack of the city by Napoleon's army during the Peninsular War and involvement in the War of the Two Brothers. In the latter, Coimbra sided with the liberal Pedro of Brazil, the victor, against his absolutist brother Miguel. There followed the suppression of all religious orders in Portugal, which drastically altered life as it had been on the banks of the Mondego. At the time of their suppression, the city had 33 monasteries, convents, and religious schools. Most became army installations.

The fame of its ancient university and its monuments draws hundreds of thousands of foreign and Portuguese visitors to Coimbra each year. Yet its aura of romance and beautiful buildings are not its only attractions. There are the bohemian student haunts, including the little *tascas* (eating houses) offering all kinds of snacks (from spareribs, ham omelettes, and grilled sardines to boiled pigs' feet). The picturesque, narrow streets in the Baixa, with laundry, bird cages, plants, and balconies hanging over them — and with picturesque names like Terreiro da Erva (Herb Square) and Rua dos Gatos (Street of the Cats) — are fun to explore. Strollers with time to browse may come upon a curio or antiques shop in a cul-de-sac or a little alleyway, or an old workshop where they still make, in the traditional way, the famous guitars — roundish in shape and light in sound — that typify the city. Better yet, those seeking to be at one with the spirit of the place will track down a Coimbra guitar in use, in the hands of a very soulful singer of *fado*.

COIMBRA AT-A-GLANCE

SEEING THE CITY: From the hilltop above the Vale do Inferno (Valley of Hell), off the highway leading into Coimbra from Lisbon — turn left at the Miradouro Vale do Inferno sign about 2½ miles (4 km) before town — there is a panorama of Coimbra with its old churches and university buildings clustered around the Alta hill, modern buildings and green gardens sloping down to the river, and, as a distant backdrop, the peaks of the Serra da Lousã and the pine forests of Buçaco. In town, the patio of the Old University affords an impressive view of the city's rooftops, old buildings, and narrow streets leading down to the river. All of the countryside surrounding the city can be seen from Penedo da Saudade (Place of Nostalgia), a high rocky cliff southeast of the center (take bus No. 3 from the tourist office). An isolated and romantic vantage point at the beginning of the century, it was a favorite haunt of students and poets, who carved verses on its stones. The place is still a nice garden with a view, but it is somewhat spoiled by encroaching modern construction.

SPECIAL PLACES: Coimbra is effectively divided into three districts. The Alta (Upper Town) is the university quarter, as well as the original site of the Iron Age settlement and of the castles and forts of the Romans, Moors, and Portuguese kings. The Baixa (Lower Town) is the part of the city that grew up by the river. Full of narrow streets and crowded with shops, banks, churches, cafés, and hotels, it is shaped roughly like a wedge, with the river on one side, Rua Ferreira Borges, Rua Visconde da Luz, and Rua da Sofia on the other, and Largo da Portagem at its point. Avenida Fernão de Magalhães is its main thoroughfare. The third district is the west bank of the Mondego, or the Santa Clara area, just across the Ponte de Santa Clara. Here, among other things, are the remains of an old convent associated with the saintly Queen Isabel and a newer one built as a replacement after it began to give way to Mondego floodwaters. The Santa Clara Bridge itself is not the first one to cross the Mondego. Parts of an 11th-century stone bridge can be seen from the present one when the water is low. It was torn down when the river silted up and caused the water level to rise too high for boats to pass under it.

The best way to see the sights is to take a taxi to the highest point of the Alta —

the Old University — and walk down through its narrow streets, guided by one of the excellent maps available at the tourist office. To visit places beyond the Alta or the Baixa, it is necessary to use a car, taxi, or bus.

ALTA

Universidade Velha (Old University) – The entrance to the university is through the Porta Férrea (Iron Gate), a 17th-century triumphal arch surmounted by statues of King Dinis, who founded the university — originally in Lisbon — during the 13th century, and King João III, who during the 16th century donated his royal palace to house it. Inside the gate is the enormous University Patio, with a large statue of João III, looking very much like England's Henry VIII. (There is a large statue of King Dinis outside the university entrance in Praça Dom Dinis.) Beside the gate, to the left when entering, is a long, low palace wing that once contained suites for the princes and later served as the Colégio de São Pedro. Now serving as university offices, it has a beautifully carved 18th-century baroque door in its façade.

The baroque Biblioteca Joannina (Joanine Library), the university's — and the town's — pièce de résistance, is in the far left-hand corner of the patio. Its three halls dazzlingly decorated with carved and gilded wood, its precious rosewood and jacaranda tables, and its trompe l'oeil ceilings (to create an illusion of space) qualify it as one of the most beautiful libraries in the world (although the books are not well preserved). A portrait of King João V, who had the library built between 1717 and 1728, hangs at the back. Next to the library, facing the Porta Férrea entrance, is the Capela de São Miguel, the university chapel, with an ornate 16th-century Manueline doorway. The sumptuous interior contains an intricately carved 18th-century baroque organ decorated with gilt panels and Chinese lacquerwork, a Mannerist main altar, rococo altars in the side chapels, and walls covered with beautiful 18th-century tiles. Installed in an annex to the chapel is the *Museum of Sacred Art,* with gold and silver pieces, furniture, vestments, paintings, and sculpture.

The university's 18th-century clock tower stands in the right-hand corner of the patio, dominating the Coimbra skyline. Next to it, on the patio's right side, is the main part of the Manueline palace donated by King João III. An exterior double staircase in stone leads to a colonnade known as the Via Latina (Latin Way), because all who walked there in the Middle Ages, when the university was at its zenith, spoke Latin. From it, another staircase leads to passageways that look down on the Sala dos Capelos (Salon of Cardinals' Hats), which was, and still is, used for the awarding of degrees — it derives its name from the fact that those who presided at such ceremonies in the past were usually cardinals. Portraits of the Kings of Portugal and 17th-century carpet tiles (rectangular panels of tiles that resemble upright rugs) adorn its walls, which rise to a notable 17th-century paneled ceiling. To the right of the Sala dos Capelos is the Sala das Armas (Arms Room), where old arms and standards used in the ceremonies are on display; to the left is a long portico, from which there is a breathtaking view of the Old Cathedral, the Baixa, and the river. Downstairs again, a door at the end of the Via Latina opens to the Gerais, the cloister around which the old lecture rooms were located. The *Museum of Sacred Art* is open from 10 AM to 12:30 PM and from 2 to 5 PM; closed Mondays. The rest of the university opens daily at 9:30 AM. Admission charge to the museum. Praça Dom Dinis (phone: 35410 or 33644).

Aqueduto de São Sebastião (Aqueduct of St. Sebastian) – Though built during the 16th century to bring water to the Alta, it probably stands on the site of a more ancient Roman aqueduct. It originally had 20 arches, but part of it was torn down to make way for the New University. The main arch is topped with images of São Roque and King Sebastião, during whose reign it was built. Arcos do Jardim.

Jardim Botânico (Botanical Garden) – These pleasant gardens next to the aqueduct were begun by Prime Minister Marquês de Pombal during the late 18th century, and work on them continued into this century. Laid out on terraces and divided by tree-lined promenades and staircases, they contain trees and plants from all over the world. The terraces lead down to a large square with a lovely fountain; at the top, near the aqueduct, is an interesting fence of intricate 19th-century ironwork.

Museu Nacional de Machado de Castro (Machado de Castro National Museum) – Named after a major Portuguese sculptor of the 18th century, this is one of the most important museums in the country. It not only contains Portugal's finest collection of sculpture and gold and silver work, but it's housed in the former Paço Episcopal, or Bishop's Palace, which is itself a work of art. Lived in by the Bishops of Coimbra from the 12th century until 1910, when it was transformed into a museum, it is constructed around a large courtyard, with a double-arched verandah on one side affording a good view of the river, the houses of the Alta, and the dome of the Old Cathedral. Underneath it all, forming the foundation of the palace and part of the museum, is the cryptoportico — a series of vaulted underground passages and galleries built by the Romans beneath their forum, probably to serve as storerooms. One of the most interesting constructions of its kind in existence, it holds the museum's collection of Roman sculpture, inscriptions, and other objects found on the spot.

Later sculpture in the collection ranges from 14th-century works from the atelier of Master Pero (who also carved the tomb of Queen Isabel in the New Santa Clara Convent) to 16th-century Renaissance art by Jean de Rouen and his followers of the Coimbra school (including an entire chapel by Jean de Rouen and a *Last Supper* by Philippe Houdart), as well as baroque works by Cipriano da Cruz and Claude Laprade. The museum's gold and silver objects, collected from the cathedral's treasury and other churches, cover all periods from the 12th century to the 19th, including articles that belonged to the saintly Queen Isabel. Flemish and Portuguese paintings of the 16th and 17th centuries (Josefa d'Obidos, a famous female painter of the 17th century, is represented), Oriental and Portuguese carpets, furniture, and a vast collection of faïence from the 16th century to the 19th are also on display. Open from 10 AM to 12:30 PM and from 2 to 4:30 PM; closed Mondays. Admission charge. Largo Dr. José Rodrigues (phone: 24698).

São João de Almedina – This church adjoining the museum once served as a chapel for the bishops. Founded during the 12th century, it was reconstructed during the late 17th and early 18th centuries. Its doorway came from an old west bank convent (Sant'Ana) that was virtually swallowed up by the river. Largo Dr. José Rodrigues.

Sé Nova (New Cathedral) – Begun by the Jesuits during the late 16th century and finished during the mid-17th century, this church became Coimbra's cathedral only after the Jesuits were expelled a century later. It is a severe building, both inside and out, yet a forerunner of the baroque style — note that the façade becomes livelier as it ascends, and the top part, finished last, is rococo. Most impressive inside are the intricately carved and gilded baroque main altarpiece and the choir stalls and baptismal font brought from the Old Cathedral. Also of note are the neo-classical organs and the 17th-century altarpiece in the side chapels. Largo da Feira.

Sé Velha (Old Cathedral) – Looking much like a fortress, festooned with merlons, this is considered the finest Romanesque church in Portugal. Its architects were French — Master Builder Robert and Master Builder Bernard — and its first stone was laid in the 12th century, during the reign of Afonso Henriques, Portugal's first king. The building has been modified since, particularly during the 16th century, and was totally restored during the 19th century. The portal in the west façade, decorated with columns, and the gigantic matching window above show signs of Islamic influence, while the north façade's main portal was, when added in 1530, one of the first signs of the Renaissance in Portugal. One of the most important works of Jean de Rouen, it has a carved medallion of the Virgin and Child over it.

Inside, the cathedral is dominated by the gilded wood altarpiece at the high altar, a beautiful example of Flemish Gothic executed between 1498 and 1508 by the Flemish sculptors Oliver of Ghent and Jean of Ypres. To the right is the spectacular Capela do Sacramento (Chapel of the Sacrament), by Jean de Rouen. His beautifully sculpted life-size figures of Christ with the Apostles, Evangelists, and the Virgin are so filled with personality that they appear almost human. To the left is the Capela do São Pedro, with a retable showing a scene (*Quo Vadis*) attributed to Nicolas Chanterène. The cathedral also contains the tombs of medieval bishops and a Byzantine princess and, via stairs on the south side, a notable Gothic cloister, added during the 13th century. Open from 9 AM to 12:30 PM and from 2 to 5 PM; closed Mondays. Admission charge to the cloister. Praça Sé Velha (phone: 36592).

Torre de Anto (Anto Tower) – This 9th-century tower in the city wall was once the home of the famous 19th-century poet António Nobre. It now houses the nonprofit *Casa de Artesanato da Região de Coimbra* (Coimbra Region House of Handicrafts), displaying and selling a host of local products — ceramics, handwoven rugs, basketwork, wrought-iron objects, woodcarvings, hand embroideries, and starched laces. Open Mondays through Fridays, from 9 AM to 12:30 PM and from 2 to 5:30 PM. 45 Rua de Sobre-Ripas (phone: 36592).

Palácio de Sobre-Ripas (Sub-Ripas Palace) – Some of the city wall is incorporated into the lower part of this palace, which dates from the 16th century. It has a Manueline door and windows and walls covered with bas-reliefs and busts by Jean de Rouen of mythical and biblical figures, noblemen and ladies. Rua de Sobre-Ripas.

Casa da Nau (Ship House) – This house in the shape of a ship, built at the time of Portugal's New World discoveries, is now a students' *república.* Rua Joaquim António de Aguiar.

Arco de Almedina (Almedina Arch) – The Moors built a wall around Coimbra, and this is the only survivor of its three gates (*al-medina* is Arabic for "the city"). It is still the Alta's main entrance and exit, just down the fittingly named "step street," the Escadas de Quebra-Costas (Back Breaker Stairs), so called because of its nearly perpendicular incline.

BAIXA

Praça 8 de Maio (8th of May Square) – At the southern end of Rua da Sofia, the square is named for the date Coimbra was liberated from the absolutist forces of Dom Miguel during the War of the Two Brothers. The eight streets of the Baixa meet in the square, which is lined with well-preserved 17th- and 18th-century buildings. The Câmara Municipal (Town Hall), housed in a wing of the Mosteiro de Santa Cruz (Holy Cross Monastery), is also in the square, its façade adorned with Coimbra's coat of arms.

Igreja de Santa Cruz (Holy Cross Church) – This monastery church is one of the most important monuments in the country, not only because of its historical interest, but also because of the artistic merit of its carvings and tiles. The cornerstone was laid in 1131 under the patronage of Dom Afonso Henriques, Portugal's first king, who is buried here along with his son, Sancho I, Portugal's second king. The church was reconstructed during the 16th century, although traces of the original — by the Frenchman known as Master Builder Robert — can still be seen in the walls near the entrance to the present structure. The Manueline façade that was imposed on the medieval one incorporates statues of the Apostles and churchmen by Nicolas Chanterène and of the Virgin, Isaac, and David by Jean de Rouen.

Inside, the church has a starred dome in its enormous, vaulted ceiling and lovely 18th-century tiles lining the walls (those on the left illustrate the history of the Holy Cross, those on the right the life of Saint Augustine). The intricately carved stone pulpit, in a transitional, Gothic-to-Renaissance style, is one of Chanterène's most important works, and he also sculpted the tombs of the two kings behind the main altar — Afonso Henriques on the left and Sancho on the right. The magnificent 17th-century sacristy, inspired by the architecture of the Vatican, is decorated with paintings by some of Portugal's most famous artists, including Grão Vasco. Beyond are the chapter house, with an interesting Manueline door and 16th-century tiles, and the adjoining 16th-century Manueline Claustro do Silêncio (Silent Cloister), with a lovely Renaissance fountain and bas-reliefs attributed to Chanterène around three of its four sides. Open daily from 9 AM to noon and from 2 to 5 PM. Admission charge to visit the royal tombs, sacristy, chapter house, and cloister, but not for the church itself. Praça 8 de Maio.

Jardim da Manga (Manga Garden) – The garden, behind Santa Cruz and once one of its cloisters, contains a unique Renaissance fountain. Its waters, symbolizing the rivers of Paradise or the word of God spreading to all corners of the world, flow out from a central temple with a pointed dome. (The gargoyles jutting out from the dome represent demons fleeing God's word.) The four chapels surrounding the temple were probably designed by Jean de Rouen, who sculpted the figures in their altarpieces. Rua Olimpio Nicolau Rui Fernandes.

Igreja do Carmo (Carmo Church) – Part of a theological college founded during the 16th century, this church has a single domed nave with a coffered ceiling, an enormous gilt altarpiece in typical Portuguese style, side chapels with rococo altarpieces, and an adjoining cloister paneled in rococo tiles. The college, one of several along a street whose name means Street of Learning, was at one time one of the most prestigious institutions in the city. Rua da Sofia.

Igreja da Graça (Graça Church) – Another church founded during the 16th century as part of a school, it has a sober, classical façade. Inside are a high altar in Mannerist style, with carved, gilt frames surrounding panels depicting the life of the Virgin, and side chapels with rococo altarpieces and interesting 17th-century tiles in carpet designs. The cloister is classic Renaissance. Rua da Sofia.

Praça do Comércio (Commerce Square) – Once known as Praça Velha (Old Square), this was the old marketplace where bullfights, *autos-da-fé,* and festivals were held. It is a large rectangle surrounded by shops and 17th- and 18th-century houses with lovely windows. There is a church at each end of the square and, in the center, a reconstructed pillory.

Igreja de São Tiago (St. James's Church) – People condemned to death by the Inquisition were buried in the cemetery of this early-13th-century church, which has two interesting portals with ornamental molding and intricately carved columns and capitals. The façade was restored during this century. Praça do Comércio.

Igreja de São Bartolomeu (St. Bartholomew's Church) – Probably the oldest church in Coimbra, dating from the 10th century, although the present building was put up during the 18th century; the original church was destroyed by a Moorish invasion, reconstructed during the 12th century, then torn down 6 centuries later to make way for a new one. Archaeological remains can be seen in the floor. The main altar is typical Coimbra rococo. Praça do Comércio.

Largo da Portagem – The large, busy square by the river, in front of the Santa Clara Bridge, is home to the tourist office. The statue is of Joaquim António de Aguiar, a 19th-century statesman born in Coimbra and known as the Mata Frades (Friar Killer), because he signed the proclamation expelling all religious orders from Portugal.

Parque Dr. Manuel Braga – This park is south of Largo da Portagem, with the river running along one side of it and Avenida Emídio Navarro along the other. Besides the gardens, laid out in patterns resembling the emblem and coats of arms of Coimbra, it has a bandstand in ornate ironwork and, at one end, the *Museum of Urban Transport* (open Mondays through Fridays, 9 AM to 12:30 PM and from 1 to 5 PM; admission charge), containing a large collection of old streetcars (phone: 813222).

O Choupal – By the river at the north end of Coimbra, O Choupal was originally a grove of poplar trees (the translation of its name) planted to protect the riverbanks from floods. Most of the poplars have been cut down, but they've been replaced by eucalyptus, acacia, and other trees — as well as joggers. The park is more than a mile long and occupies the junction of the old and new courses of the Mondego — the two have existed since a plan to control floods was put into practice at the end of the 18th century. Inlets of the river cross it, spanned by wooden bridges. At one time, the Choupal was a place for romance, meditation, and serenades, and though less idyllic today, it is still a pleasant place for walking.

SANTA CLARA AREA

Convento de Santa Clara-a-Velha (Old Santa Clara Convent) – A convent for Clarissa nuns once stood here, but all that remains is a church — and not all of it, since the structure is partially buried in silt. When the convent was completed in 1330, floods from the Mondego were already threatening it, and by the 15th century, water had reached the doors. Finally, in 1677, the nuns moved out to their new convent, Santa Clara-a-Nova, on a nearby hill. Both Queen Isabel, the Rainha Santa (Saintly Queen), who spent the last years of her life here, and Inês de Castro, who was murdered nearby, were buried at the convent before their bodies were moved elsewhere, the former to Santa Clara-a-Nova and the latter to the Monastery of Alcobaça, near Nazaré. The old church is a fine example of Gothic architecture, with three very fine rose windows. Rua de Baixo.

Portugal dos Pequenitos (Children's Portugal) – Interesting for adults, too, this is a wooded park containing reproductions of Portuguese houses from all provinces, of all of Coimbra's monuments, and of the principal monuments found throughout the country and its once far-reaching empire (Goa, Macao, Mozambique, Angola, and Guinea-Bissau). They're built on a small scale for children, most of them about 13 feet tall. Open daily, from 9 AM to 7 PM from April through September (to 5:30 PM in winter). Admission charge. Rua António Augusto Gonçalves (phone: 441674).

Convento de Santa Clara-a-Nova (New Santa Clara Convent) – This hillside convent was built during the 17th century — although the cloisters and other buildings were not finished until the 18th century — to keep the Clarissa nuns high and dry as their old convent began to succumb to the continuous flooding of the Mondego. The installation has been likened to a barracks, and in fact, since religious orders were suppressed during the 19th century, most of the convent buildings have been occupied by the army. Only the church and cloister can be visited. The church has a domed, coffered ceiling, sides decorated with ornate false chapels (serving as enormous, intricately carved and gilded frames for portraits), and a sumptuous domed altar flanked with gilded pillars. The remains of St. Isabel lie in the 17th-century silver-and-crystal urn behind the altar, which is also adorned with a statue of the saint and a bas-relief depicting scenes from her life. The most impressive sight in the church, however, is the magnificent 14th-century tomb, carved from a single block of Ançã stone, that the Saintly Queen had made for herself and in which she was originally buried. Located in the *coro baixo* (lower choir), it rests on six stone lions; pink, gold, and green carved statuettes of saints, Franciscans, Clarissa nuns, and other figures occupy niches on its sides; and on top is a reclining statue of the queen dressed in a nun's habit, complete with a pilgrim's staff and an alms bag such as those used by the pious on a pilgrimage to Santiago de Compostela in Spain. The actual pilgrim's staff that belonged to the queen can be seen in the *coro alto* (raised choir), which is a museum of religious objects and silver; the cloister, dating from the 18th century, is impressive for its size and massive architecture. Open from 9 AM to 12:30 PM and from 2 to 5 PM; closed Mondays. Admission charge. Calçada de Santa Isabel.

Quinta das Lágrimas (Estate of Tears) – A 19th-century *palacete* (little palace) stands on the site where Prince Dom Pedro and his beautiful mistress, Dona Inês de Castro, lived and where their tragic love ended in her murder. In the gardens at the back of the estate a spring gushes from the rocks into a wide pool. Local legend holds that the spring's waters are Dona Inês's tears and that the red spots on the plants growing there are her blood, the yellow ferns her hair. Verses by Luís de Camões, who immortalized the love of the unfortunate pair in *The Lusiads,* are carved in stone by the spring in this melancholy and haunted place, where even the tall cedars and their large, entwined roots appear ominous. Although the estate is privately owned, the gardens are open to the public daily (tip the caretaker). Off Estrada das Lages (no phone).

ELSEWHERE

Parque de Santa Cruz – An 18th-century archway off Praça da República (a gathering place for students, especially in the evening) is the entrance to this park. Beyond are fountains, pools, luxuriant vegetation, and paths lined with fragrant bay trees from Goa. An ornate portico with towers on both sides leads to a game area where, during the 17th and 18th centuries, girls played a ball game called *jogo de pela.* Also notable is the fountain, bedecked with statues of Triton and mermaids, at the top of a tall staircase that has pools and tile-backed stone benches on the landings. The park also has a large lake with a small island in its center and a terrace where drinks are served.

Mosteiro de Celas (Celas Monastery) – Founded in 1215 by King Sancho I's daughter, the nunnery was greatly modified later, particularly between the 16th and 18th centuries, and when the last nun died during the late 19th century, it was virtually abandoned. Today, only the church and cloister remain. Inside, the dark oak 16th-century choir stalls and Nicolas Chanterène's cloister door are noteworthy, and the cloister itself is of particular interest: Each of the 13th- and 14th-century capitals on the double pillars supporting the arches is carved with a different story from the lives of Christ and the saints. Largo de Celas (ring the bell at No. 23 for the caretaker).

Igreja de Santo António dos Olivais (Church of St. Anthony of the Olive Grove) – This is the only remnant of a Franciscan monastery that was founded during the 13th century and burned down 600 years later. Its name comes from St. Anthony of Padua, who taught here before going to Italy. Standing on the highest hill above Coimbra, the church, remodeled during the 18th century, is a typical sanctuary reached by a long flight of stairs flanked by chapels and representations of scenes from the Passion of Christ. The interior, covered with tile panels depicting the life of the saint, contains altarpieces from the 18th-century baroque Joanine period, as well as a sacristy richly decorated in gold leaf and finished with a painted, festooned ceiling. In the square at the bottom of the stairs is a small 16th-century chapel containing a Christ on the cross by Jean de Rouen. Rua Brigadeiro Correia Cardoso.

SOURCES AND RESOURCES

TOURIST INFORMATION: The Coimbra Tourist Office (Largo da Portagem, the main square in front of the Santa Clara Bridge; phone: 23886 or 33028) is open weekdays from 9 AM to 7 PM and on Saturdays and Sundays from 9 AM to 12:30 PM and 2 to 6 PM. During the winter, the tourist office is open from 10 AM to 6 PM weekdays, and from 10 AM to 12:30 PM and from 2 to 5 PM Saturdays and Sundays. Attendants offer advice and assistance in English as well as other languages and hand out excellent folders and maps in several languages. They will also make hotel, train, and bus reservations. Multilingual guides are available for about $70 for a half day of sightseeing, about $120 for a full day.

Local Coverage – The local daily newspaper is the *Diário de Coimbra,* published on Sundays as *Domingo.* The *Jornal do Coimbra* is a weekly. The *International Herald Tribune,* along with some of the British dailies and English-language news magazines, is available at newsstands in the better hotels. The newsstand near the *Tivoli* movie theater (Av. Emídio Navarro) is another source of English-language newspapers.

TELEPHONE: The city code for Coimbra is 39. If calling from within Portugal, dial 039 before the local number.

GETTING AROUND: Coimbra is best seen on foot or by public transportation. Travel by car is difficult because of the narrow streets, horrendous traffic jams during rush hours, and limited parking space.

Airport – The very small local airport (phone: 947235) is in Cernache, 5 miles (8 km) southwest of town via the main highway to Lisbon. At present, no regularly scheduled flights land here.

Bus – Getting around by bus is fast and easy. There are no general maps of the routes, but each bus stop has a map. Among the most useful for tourists are bus No. 1, which goes to the Old University and the *Machado de Castro National Museum;* No. 3, to the Botanical Garden and Penedo da Saudade; No. 6, which goes over the river to the Santa Clara area, with the Old and New Santa Clara convents and Portugal dos Pequenitos (from the latter, it is necessary to transfer to another bus to reach Quinta das Lágrimas); and No. 7, to Santa Cruz Park, the Celas Monastery, and the Santo António dos Olivais church. All leave from Largo da Portagem. Tourist passes allowing unlimited travel for 4 days or a week are available. The main bus station for long-distance buses is on Avenida Fernão de Magalhães (phone: 27081).

Car Rental – Six major companies operate here: *Hertz* (133 Av. Fernão de Magalhães and 221 Av. Fernão de Magalhães; phone: 37491); *Avis* (in the Coimbra A train station, Largo das Ameias; phone: 34786); *Beira Centro* (in the *Oslo Hotel,* 23-25 Av. Fernão de Magalhães; phone: 23664); *Hervis* (94 Rua João Machado; phone: 24062 or 33489); and *Auto Turística Central de Coimbra* (23 Rua Dr. Manuel Rodrigues; phone: 29815).

Taxi – Coimbra's metered black-and-green taxis pick up riders anywhere. To call one, dial 28045/9. Rides are inexpensive; one from the tourist office to the Santa Clara area or the Santo António dos Olivais church, for instance, should cost less than $4.

Train – There are two railway stations: Coimbra A (phone: 34998), at Largo das Ameias, beside the *Bragança* hotel, and Coimbra B (phone: 24632), beyond Choupal Park at the junction of the Porto and Figueira da Foz highways. Regional trains to Figueira da Foz and Aveiro on the coast and to Luso and other towns in the mountains leave from the A station. Through trains to Lisbon, Aveiro, and Porto leave from the B station. A special fast train — the *Alpha* — connects Coimbra B with Lisbon (2½ hours), Aveiro, and Porto. Advance reservations are required.

SPECIAL EVENTS: The *Queima das Fitas* (Burning of the Ribbons) is a collective student letting-off-of-steam that goes on for a week at the end of the term in May and culminates when the fourth-year students burn their class ribbons in chamber pots and put on the wider ones of senior class members. (There is a fifth year of university study in Portugal.) The celebration begins at midnight on a Thursday with a serenade of *fado* and guitar music on the steps of the Old Cathedral. Each day thereafter is dedicated to a different faculty and a different class and ends with a musical evening by the riverside. There are balls, theatrical and sports events, and car races, plus a mock bullfight in Figueira da Foz on Sunday. The most colorful day, however, is Tuesday, when the actual burning of the ribbons takes place and the fourth-year students parade through the streets on top of flower-adorned cars. They are followed by freshmen with painted faces and funny clothes, second-year students in black suits and gowns, and upperclassmen in top hats. Coimbra is very crowded, so anyone planning a visit at this time (the exact week varies according to the school calendar) should make hotel reservations far in advance.

Coimbra's other big event, the *Festa da Rainha Santa* (Feast of the Saintly Queen), commemorates the beatification of the saintly Queen Isabel in 1516 and takes place at the beginning of July of even-numbered years. On a Thursday night, the statue of the saint from the altar of Santa Clara-a-Nova is carried to Largo da Portagem by a procession of penitents; all lights in the city are turned off when it arrives, the better to see the spectacular fireworks display over the river. Another procession returns the statue to the church on Sunday afternoon.

MUSEUMS: In addition to those mentioned in *Special Places*, museums of interest include the following:

Bissaya Barreto House Museum – Beautiful furniture and porcelain in a house once owned by the man who built Portugal dos Pequenitos. Open from 3 to 5 PM; closed Mondays and holidays. Admission charge. Arcos do Jardim (phone: 37339).

Museu Militar (Military Museum) – Weapons, uniforms, and photographs from military actions after 1850, housed in a wing of the New Santa Clara Convent. Open daily from 10 AM to noon and from 2 to 5 PM. Admission charge. Convento de Santa-Clara-a-Nova, Calçada de Santa Isabel (phone: 26459).

Museu Nacional da Ciência e da Técnica (Science and Technology Museum) – One part is dedicated to the life and works of Madame Curie and another to Leonardo da Vinci. Open from 10 AM to noon and from 2 to 5 PM; closed Saturdays and Sundays. Admission charge. 23 Rua dos Coutinhos (phone: 24922).

SHOPPING: Coimbra has beautiful handicrafts, examples of which are exhibited and sold in the *Casa de Artesanato da Região de Coimbra* in the historic Torre de Anto (45 Rua de Sobre-Ripas; phone: 23886). Coimbra faïence, made as far back as the 12th century and revived during the 17th and 18th centuries, is being produced once again by several factories. The lovely, hand-painted pieces available in local shops run the gamut of local styles — multicolored Hispano-Arabic designs of the 15th century, Oriental designs of the 16th century, Delft-inspired blue and white designs of the 17th century, and pastel flora and fauna designs of the 18th century. Hand-embroidered bedspreads and tablecloths and wool and linen blankets are also worth buying, as are examples of traditional Coimbra wrought-iron work, artistic tinware, and basketry, still made in the same way they have been for hundreds of years. The tourist office can help to arrange visits to artisans in nearby villages for those with more than a passing interest in the local handiwork. Shops also carry some fine leather goods, footwear, stylish ready-made clothing, and jewelry. Rua Ferreira Borges, which leads north from Largo da Portagem, and Rua Visconde da Luz, its continuation, are the main shopping streets. Stores are open weekdays, from 9 AM to 1 PM and from 3 to 7 PM, and on Saturdays from 9 AM to 1 PM, while shopping centers are open daily from 10 AM to midnight. A big open-air market, selling everything from fish to video equipment, takes place daily from 6 AM to 2 PM at the end of Avenida Sá da Bandeira, near the Jardim da Manga.

Agata Joalharia – Fine jewelry, beautifully mounted at reasonable prices. 2 Escadas de São Tiago (phone: 22361).

Casa das Luvas Camisaria – Elegant fashions for men, one of the best in town. 112 Rua Ferreira Borges (phone: 24369).

Charles – A large selection of Portuguese-made, fashionable shoes for men and women. 113 Rua Ferreira Borges (phone: 23264).

Crislex – Home decorations, porcelain, and good crystal. 187 Rua Ferreira Borges (phone: 26801).

Jorge Mendes – Some of the finest copies of 15th- to 17th-century porcelains and ceramics in Coimbra. At two locations: 19 Praça do Comércio (phone: 22620) and 9 Praça do Comércio (phone: 25646).

Loja das Artes Manuais – A good selection of all regional handicrafts. 1-9 Rua Fernandes Tomás (phone: 33136).

A Nova Paris – Men's and women's fashions. 9 Rua Visconde da Luz (phone: 23642).

Patrão Joalheiros – One of the oldest and most respected jewelers in Coimbra, offering lovely Portuguese filigree, silver salvers, and silver tea and coffee services. 104 Rua Visconde da Luz (phone: 23096).

Renasçença – A big, upscale shop selling fashionable shoes and other leather goods. 104 Rua Visconde da Luz (phone: 35050).

Sociedade de Cerâmica Antiga de Coimbra – A factory making (and selling) reproductions of old Portuguese ceramics, and the only one producing the special, pale flora and fauna designs typical of the 18th century. Open to visitors on weekdays. 2 Quintal do Prior (phone: 23829).

Ultimo Figurino – Ready-made clothing in classic styles. 50 Rua Ferreira Borges (phone: 23489).

SPORTS AND FITNESS: Boating – A popular pastime on the Mondego in the summer, pedal boats and kayaks can be rented in the Choupalinho Park just across the Santa Clara Bridge. A kayak costs about $18 for a whole day including lunch and van transport 10 miles (16 km) up the river to Penacova, from which the person renting the kayak paddles it back down to Coimbra.

Swimming – The municipal swimming pool is on Rua Dom Manuel, next to the *Estádio Municipal.*

MUSIC: Coimbra's music is the *fado* — haunting, sweet ballads sung to the accompaniment of Coimbra guitars. Unlike Lisbon *fado,* which is sung by men and women, *fado de Coimbra* is sung by men only, and by students, lawyers, doctors, and others, rather than by professional entertainers. Coimbra *fado* grew out of the student custom of singing in the streets at night and serenading Coimbra girls; its themes range from unrequited love and homesickness to the city, the river, the university, and social issues. Some songs have become classics, among them the "Balada da Despedida" (Farewell Ballad), sung at graduation by medical students, and the "Balada de Coimbra" (Coimbra Ballad), which closes all serenades, including the beautiful and impressive midnight *serenata* on the steps of the Old Cathedral at the opening of the *Queima das Fitas* celebrations. Although Coimbra *fado* is normally sung only at such special celebrations or for private entertainment, it is possible to hear it in two places in the city. One is the *Diligência,* a very small, characteristic bar (on the narrow Rua Nova, off Rua da Sofia; phone: 27667), where the singing is spontaneous and often catch-as-catch-can. The other is the *Trovador* restaurant (Praça Sé Velha; phone: 25475; see *Eating Out*), which presents *fado* on weekends and is somewhat touristy.

NIGHTCLUBS AND NIGHTLIFE: Neither very lively nor sophisticated, nightlife here tends to center around student activities or nights out with the whole family. There are, however, a number of pubs and discotheques for dancing. The biggest and best dance spot, open only Thursdays, Fridays, and

Saturdays, is *Broadway* (in suburban Pedrulha, about 2 miles/3 km north of town; phone: 36330). It's not much to look at, but it has its own orchestra that plays typical dance music — foxtrot and Sinatra oldies — from 10 PM to midnight; after midnight, the loud disco music takes over. Three others, all closed Sundays, are *Scotch* (Quinta da Insua; phone: 441236), just across the Santa Clara Bridge in a nice old house, with a quiet bar, apart from the disco; *States* (Praça Machado Assis; phone: 27067), decorated in red, white, and blue with stars and catering to young people with lots of loud music; and *Coimbra B* (Monte Formoso; phone: 28919), small, but with two separate floors, a bar, and lots of flashing lights.

Quebra Costas (Escadas de Quebra-Costas; phone: 34724) is a small bar on the stairs in front of Praça Sé Velha; in summer, devotees stand on the stairs with their drinks, some with their guitars. *Sacristia* (phone: 24804), at the top of the stairs, is another small bar; it has live music at times, but people mostly just stand around and talk. Other pubs and bars include *Romisch,* a piano bar (102 Rua dos Combatentes; phone: 72172); *Briosa* (Rua Venancio Rodrigues; phone: 29642), decorated to look like an English pub; and *Café Forte Video Bar* (2nd Floor, 1 Av. Lousã; phone: 721855), a modern bar whose forte is showing videos.

BEST IN TOWN

CHECKING IN: Coimbra suffers from a definite dearth of good hotels, although several new hostelries are being built. Those that exist tend to be very old or purely functional. Most are right downtown, which makes them convenient for sightseeing, but noisy. A number of clean, comfortable pensions supplement the pickings. Expect to pay $70 to $90 for a double room with breakfast in a hotel listed as expensive, from $50 to $70 in the moderate category, and under $50 in an inexpensive place. Reservations for rooms during July and August, or during the *Queima das Fitas* celebrations in May, should be made at least a month in advance. All telephone numbers are in the 39 city code unless otherwise indicated.

Astoria – Built in the 1920s, in the style of that period, it features cupolas, arches, pillars, and wrought-iron balconies. The 64 rooms have baths and telephones; there is a television salon, a bar, and a restaurant serving typical regional dishes. The hotel is shaped like a triangle to fit between two streets that converge at Largo da Portagem, and is consequently a bit noisy (as well as a bit shabby now). 21 Av. Emídio Navarro (phone: 22055; fax: 22057). Expensive.

Dom Luís – This hostelry occupies a high hill by the highway to Lisbon, across the river from Coimbra and a little over a mile (2 km) from the center of town. All of the 105 rooms and suites have private baths, telephones, mini-bars, and TV sets. A panoramic restaurant (food and service are good) and solarium with a terrace on the roof, plus plenty of parking space, help to justify the distance. Banhos Secos (phone: 442510; fax: 813196). Expensive.

Tivoli Coimbra – In the heart of the city, this new and very modern hotel offers 100 air conditioned rooms (including 10 suites) that all feature mini-bars, satellite TV, and telephones. Also on the premises are a restaurant, meeting rooms accommodating up to 100 people, and a health club boasting an indoor pool, a sauna, Turkish baths, a gym, and massage service. Rua João Machado (phone: 26934; fax: 26827). Expensive.

Bragança – Unpretentious and modern, it's on a busy street by the Coimbra A train station and the river. The 83 rooms, all with bath, are simple and functional. A bar, television room, private parking lot, and large restaurant serving Portuguese and French food are among the facilities. 10 Largo das Ameias (phone: 22171). Moderate.

Oslo – This simple, small place (30 rooms) on a busy street in the center of town, not far from the Coimbra A train station, has an upstairs bar and restaurant with a good view. 23-25 Av. Fernão de Magalhães (phone: 29071; fax: 20614). Moderate.

Almedina – A downtown *pensão* with 28 rooms, all with private baths. 203 Av. Fernão de Magalhães (phone: 29161). Inexpensive.

Parque – An excellent *pensão* on the main avenue by Parque Dr. Manuel Braga, near the tourist office and the river. The 15 rooms are large and well furnished, but not all have private baths. 42 Av. Emídio Navarro, 2nd Floor (phone: 29202). Inexpensive.

Among the local participants in Portugal's *Tourism in the Country* program — privately owned homes, even palaces, that take in paying guests (see *Accommodations,* GETTING READY TO GO) — is the *Casa dos Quintais,* a member of *Turismo Rural* set on a hill overlooking Coimbra about 4 miles (6 km) from downtown. The house, endowed with a swimming pool, has 3 double bedrooms with bath for rent and should be considered in the moderate category. To reach it, take the Lisbon highway south and turn left onto N110-2 toward the town of Assafarge. Contact *Casa dos Quintais,* Carvalhais de Cima, Assafarge, Coimbra 3000 (phone: 438305 or 28821; in Lisbon, 01-670321).

EATING OUT: The food in Coimbra's better restaurants is imaginative and delicious, if a bit heavy for some tastes. Some typical dishes include *chanfana,* kid braised in wine; *lampreia à moda de Coimbra,* lamprey (eel) Coimbra-style; *leitão assado,* roast suckling pig; and the very special *boucho* — ox stomach stuffed with meats, sausages, and herbs and then roasted. Restaurants serving international cooking are also easy to find, as are many snack bars. Meals go down best with the fine, fruity bairrada wines that have been made in the region since the 10th century. They tend to be somewhat tannic when very young, so it's best to drink them aged (1980 was a good year). Some names to look for are Frei João, Caves Aliança, Souselas, Porta Férrea, Angelus, and Fundação. Sweets made from old convent recipes are something else to try, though not only in Coimbra. As elsewhere in Portugal, when religious orders were suppressed during the 19th century, the nuns turned to baking in order to support themselves, and many of the confections still eaten today take their names from their convent of origin, such as *pastel de Santa Clara,* made of sugar, eggs, and almonds. Some other favorites are *arrufadas,* arc-shaped puff cakes, and *chilas,* made of squash. Expect to pay $35 and up for a meal for two with wine and coffee at a restaurant listed as expensive, from $25 to $35 in a moderate one, and less than that at an inexpensive one. Note that Coimbra's restaurants tend to be packed with families on Sundays. All telephone numbers are in the 39 city code unless otherwise indicated.

Dom Pedro – Decorated in classic Portuguese style, with interesting tiles on the walls and a fountain splashing in the middle of the room, this place serves well-prepared Portuguese and international dishes. Open daily. Reservations necessary. Visa and MasterCard accepted. 58 Av. Emídio Navarro (phone: 29108). Expensive.

Espelho d'Agua – An elegant, refined restaurant in a beautiful setting — it's in the middle of a garden, with a lovely, glass-enclosed terrace. Excellent Portuguese dinners are served — by candlelight in the evening. Open daily. Reservations necessary. Major credit cards accepted. Parque Dr. Manuel Braga (phone: 20634). Expensive.

Piscinas – Upstairs over the municipal swimming pool, but don't judge this place by its unprepossessing exterior. It has some of the best regional cooking in the city — the *chanfana* and *boucho* are delicious. Closed Mondays. Reservations essential on weekends. Major credit cards accepted. Piscinas Municipais, Rua Dom Manuel (phone: 717013). Expensive.

Trovador – Probably the best dining place in town (or at least the most expensive). The ambience is elegant, the service excellent, the food very good Portuguese and international fare. Near the Old Cathedral, so it's a good place to dine after sightseeing. On weekends, there is *fado* music, and it's possible to drop in after 10 PM and listen to it over a drink. Closed Mondays. Reservations essential. MasterCard and Visa accepted. Praça Sé Velha (phone: 25475). Expensive.

O Alfredo – A typical Portuguese restaurant across the river, always full of people and noise. Good Portuguese food is served. Open daily. Reservations advised. No credit cards accepted. 32 Av. João das Regras (phone: 441522). Moderate.

Crep's Grill Pierrot – Variety reigns here — pizza, plus French, American, and Italian food. The decor is simple (pine furniture and blue sofas); there is a snack bar downstairs. Open daily. No reservations. Visa, MasterCard, and Access accepted. 25 Praça da República (phone: 33569). Moderate.

Jardim da Manga – A self-service eatery, but its location allows diners to eat in a garden, since it is in the beautiful Jardim da Manga. Closed Saturdays. No reservations or credit cards accepted. Rua Olimpio Nicolau Rui Fernandes (phone: 29156). Moderate.

Joaquim dos Leitões – Another specialty spot, serving the typical roast suckling pig of the region. The dining room is also done up in regional style, its walls covered with tiles. Closed Saturday nights and Sundays. Reservations advised. No credit cards accepted. 3 Rua do Arnado (phone: 33935). Moderate.

Lanterns – This large eatery occupying 2 floors in the old part of town serves good Portuguese and international fare. Open daily. Reservations advised. MasterCard and Visa accepted. 6-7 Largo da Sota (phone: 26729). Moderate.

Lung-Wah – A wide variety of Chinese dishes served in Oriental-style surroundings. It's located in a hilltop area in the northern part of town. Open daily. Reservations advised. No credit cards accepted. Monte Formoso (phone: 491743). Moderate.

Real das Canas – Under the same management as *Piscinas,* it's across the river in the Santa Clara area. The decor is simple, but the view of Coimbra from its windows is spectacular, and it serves good Portuguese food. Closed Wednesdays. Reservations advised. Major credit cards accepted. Vila Mendes, Santa Clara (phone: 814877). Moderate.

A Taberna – Very cozy, with a fireplace, it serves good Portuguese food in the main dining room and pizza in the restaurant downstairs. Closed Saturdays. Reservations advised. Major credit cards accepted. 86 Rua dos Combatentes (phone: 716265). Moderate.

O Verde Minho – In the eastern part of town, 10 minutes by car from the city center. Good Portuguese food and some special French dishes are served in a cozy atmosphere. Open daily. Reservations advised. No credit cards accepted. Casal do Lobo (phone: 718163). Moderate.

Calado e Calado – A typical, roomy Portuguese eatery with a large and varied menu, specializing in regional fare with such local favorites as kid in a casserole and rice with shellfish. Open daily. No reservations or credit cards accepted. Rua da Sota (phone: 27348). Inexpensive.

A Pizzaria do André – Italian fare, including pizza. Open daily. No reservations or credit cards accepted. 42 Travessa de Montarroio (phone: 36987). Inexpensive.

EVORA

One of the oldest cities on the Iberian Peninsula, Evora is the Alto Alentejo's traditional capital, the capital of the Evora district, a "museum town," and a work of art all rolled into one. At the very least, it offers ample pleasure simply as a typical, delightful southern Portuguese city. It is untaxingly modest in size (approximately 50,000 inhabitants), and its Old City has pleasing places for strolling, provided visitors are sensibly shod for the cobblestones. All the emblems of the south — the glare of whitewash, bright splashes of geraniums and bougainvillea, tantalizing glimpses of cool, shaded courtyards, the evening air thick with swifts — combine to make it the quintessential Alentejo town. But Evora has another dimension that is not nearly so common, even among the richly endowed towns of this historic region: The number of well-preserved historical buildings — over 30 of them classified as national monuments — is really exceptional for a city of its size.

Evora's earliest origins are lost in time, but all the archaeological clues indicate a city of extreme antiquity. It was already a fortified town of some importance when the Romans captured it from the Lusitanians during the 2nd century BC. Within a couple of centuries, it had become a prosperous imperial outpost, a *municipium* with the right to mint coins and a population that enjoyed most of the privileges of Roman citizenship. Just as it is today, Evora was a center of agriculture during the Roman era, noted for grain production. Pliny the Elder, who for a while held an official post in the region, referred to it, in his *Natural History,* as Ebora Cerealis.

At the beginning of the 5th century, as the Roman Empire crumbled, the city came under Visigothic rule. Then, in 713, it lay in the path of the Muslims sweeping up from North Africa and across the Iberian Peninsula. Under them, Evora grew considerably in military, economic, and cultural importance, so that the city described by the Moorish geographer Idrisi in 1154 is not much different — apart from its size — from the modern one. Evora, he said, is "large and populous, surrounded by walls, and with a strong castle and a mosque. The surrounding territory is of a singular fertility, producing cattle and all kinds of vegetables and fruit."

More than 400 years of Islam left an indelible imprint on the city's architecture and personality, but its most famous legend stems from the time of its recapture by the Christians. Several attempts had been made to win Evora back from the Moors, all of them unsuccessful or, like an assault in 1159, only briefly successful. Then, in October 1165, a Christian warrior chief called Geraldo Sem Pavor (Gerald the Fearless — the epithet was a result of more than one celebrated feat of bravery during the Reconquest) scaled the walls under cover of darkness by driving lances into spaces in the masonry and using them as a ladder. After killing the surprised sentinels, Geraldo let in his men, took the castle, and conquered Evora. He presented his valuable prize to Portugal's first king, Afonso Henriques, who was engaged at the time in driving the Moors from the Alentejo, and in recognition of his feat was appointed *alcaide,* or governor.

Throughout the Middle Ages and the Renaissance, Evora grew steadily in importance and wealth, becoming a center of learning and the arts in the 15th and 16th centuries. It became a bishopric in 1540, and in 1559, Cardinal Henrique, who was later crowned king, founded here one of Europe's oldest universities (which was shut down in 1759 by Portugal's autocratic prime minister, the Marquês de Pombal, but reopened in 1975).

Evora's standing in the political and cultural mainstream had been strengthened by the accession of the House of Avis to the Portuguese throne during the late 14th century. In 1383 and 1384, the townspeople revolted against the Spanish-leaning regency of Queen Leonor, burned down most of the old castle, and proclaimed as Defender of the Realm the head of the Military Order of the Knights of Avis, who had their headquarters here. João I of Avis became king in 1385, and Evora, which had already been a seat of the early kings of the House of Burgundy, became one of the main residences of the new dynasty, remaining prominent for several centuries. João's rise to the throne also marked a turning point for the Portuguese nation. The defeat of Castilian forces at Aljubarrota in August 1385 set the stage for the country's golden age of independence and maritime expansion.

With Portugal poised for its greatest achievements, Evora became the scene of a decisive incident in the struggle for power between the monarchy and the nobility. In 1481, King João II summoned the *cortes* (a representative assembly of nobles) to Evora and extracted a new oath of obedience from this fractious group. When a conspiracy gathered against him, led by his ambitious brother-in-law, the Duke of Bragança, João had the duke arrested and, in 1484, executed — thus consolidating the power of the throne and investing it with an authority that was to be put to advantage in the approaching era. The square that served for Bragança's beheading, now the Praça do Giraldo, was later the arena where heretics and other victims were burned during the Inquisition, one of the skeletons in Evora's historical closet.

In 1637, during the unpopular Spanish monarchy, another grass-roots revolt — the so-called Manuelinho uprising — convulsed Evora and sent shock waves rippling throughout the kingdom. For 5 days, the townspeople ransacked the houses of the Castilian-appointed officials they hated and burned their belongings in a huge bonfire in the main square. This was the first major rebellion in Portugal against the Spanish domination, and just as Evora's ire had been instrumental 250 years earlier in bringing about a change in command, so it was again. Three years later, the Spanish monarchy was ousted; independence from Spain was now permanently secured.

Yet another disaster, the sacking of the city by the French in 1808 during the Peninsular War, left many buildings damaged and a number of works of art lost forever. Then a long period of provincial somnolence ensued, from which Evora seemed to awaken only in 1974, with the April 25 revolution that paved the way for a return to democracy in Portugal. The city became the center of the agrarian reform movement in which the Communist party made a partially successful attempt to create an alternative to the Alentejo's residual feudalism. The university was reopened, attention was paid to promoting the arts and preserving the city's architectural heritage, festivals were organized, and social services and infrastructure were improved. Evora, in short, moved into the 20th century.

But despite this undeniable development, the Alentejo's most famous city still retains a certain isolation from the outside world, afflicted by such trials as drought and an agricultural-social system out of touch with the realities of the European Community to which it now belongs. And Evora, for all its charms, is still no pleasure resort. Good hotel accommodations are limited in quantity; so are restaurants and other entertainment facilities. Nevertheless, advance booking will solve the room problem, and it is certainly true that whatever the city lacks in sophistication, it more than makes up for in other ways. For the native and the visitor alike, Evora is sort of a standing record in stone of the Portuguese nation.

EVORA AT-A-GLANCE

SEEING THE CITY: Early drawings show Evora rising out of the flat Alentejo landscape with the uncluttered simplicity of a child's sandcastle on a beach. Making some allowance for the inevitable urban sprawl, that image is remarkably like the view of the city seen today from the top of the Alto de São Bento, a 1,094-foot hill 2 miles (3 km) out of town on the road to Arraiolos. From this vantage point, the three towers of the cathedral dominate the skyline, and it is apparent that Evora still remains tightly enclosed by its nearly unbroken girdle of 14th-century walls. Legend has it that Evora's Christian reconqueror, Gerald the Fearless, had his castle here on the São Bento hill, but standing on it today is the 13th-century convent of São Bento de Castris, which is thought to be the first nuns' convent founded in Portugal. It has a fine 16th-century cloister, which unfortunately is not normally open to visitors (but you can try ringing the bell). Follow the little road past the convent up to the three ruined windmills for the view.

SPECIAL PLACES: Like all Alentejo towns, Evora is built on a hill. The cathedral occupies the highest point, and the rest of the Old City spreads out from it down to the encircling walls. The cathedral is thus a perfect reference point. It is nearly always visible if you crane your neck a bit, and practically everything there is to see lies within easy strolling distance of it. The old walled city — the "historical nucleus," as it is sometimes called — is divided into three sections: the Judiaria (Jewish Quarter), the Mouraria (Moorish Quarter), and the Zona Residencial dos Nobres (Quarter of the Nobles). Given the small size of Evora as a whole, however, it is easier to divide it into two simple parts: inside the walls and outside. In addition to nearly all the sights, the most worthwhile shops and restaurants are within the inner city.

Besides the sights listed below, several prehistoric sites in the vicinity are worth a short excursion for anyone so inclined. The Alto Alentejo region was a center of the megalithic culture that flourished on the Iberian Peninsula between 4000 and 2000 BC, and there are a number of imposing dolmens and menhirs within easy reach. The tourist office publishes a folder giving the principal sites and their locations. The cromlechs, or religious circles, at Almendres and Xarez are particularly impressive.

IN THE CITY

Templo Romano (Roman Temple) – This structure is something of a trademark for Evora, and with good reason. It wears its age so gracefully that it looks as if it had been built just as it is for a romantic 19th-century stage set. Popularly called the Temple of Diana — although it was probably not dedicated to Diana at all — the temple is Evora's oldest surviving building, dating from the 2nd or 3rd century. It is also one of the best-preserved Roman temples on the Iberian Peninsula, thanks largely to the fact that it was bricked up in the Middle Ages and subsequently used as a storehouse. This practical use may have been inappropriate for such an elegant building, but it saved the structure from almost certain destruction. When the protective shell of bricks and rubble was removed in 1871, 14 of the 26 Corinthian columns that originally formed the peristyle were left standing. Twelve of the granite columns still have their Estremoz marble capitals. A large piece of the architrave remains in place, along with fragments of a frieze, but the rest has disappeared, perhaps incorporated into later construction in the area. Largo Conde de Vila Flor.

Cerca Velha (Old Walls) – The upper part of the city where the Roman temple stands is Evora's acropolis. It was once dominated by an old castle (the one that Gerald the Fearless took and that the angry populace of Evora largely destroyed in 1383–84), and was circled by Roman and Visigothic walls with a circumference of about 3,545 feet. Most of the old wall has disappeared, but some interesting fragments remain, including two of the five original gates: the Arco de Dona Isabel, a Roman archway opening onto Largo Alexandre Herculano, a block west of the Roman temple; and the twin towers that stand in Largo das Portas de Moura, on the southern side of the old perimeter. Bits of the old wall can also be seen incorporated into the façades of two palaces (neither is open to the public) in the former acropolis area: the Palácio dos Duques de Cadaval, across the square from the Roman temple, and the Solar dos Condes de Basto, behind the cathedral and near the old university.

Palácio dos Duques de Cadaval (Palace of the Dukes of Cadaval) – This rather severe, mainly 16th-century building, with two sturdy rectangular towers topped by Moorish-style battlements, was the palace of the Melo family, one of Portugal's oldest noble families. It includes part of a northwest section of the old castle, which King João I awarded to Martim Afonso de Melo in 1390 for his prowess in the Battle of Aljubarrota. The Duke of Bragança was held in the south tower before his execution by João II in 1484. Largo Conde de Vila Flor.

Solar dos Condes de Basto (Manor House of the Counts of Basto) – Originally a Moorish castle, this *solar* is one of Evora's oldest noble residences. It was given to the monks of the order of São Bento de Calatrava by King Afonso Henriques in 1167, after the city's reconquest from the Moors; it became crown property during the 13th century, and thereafter served as a royal residence on several occasions. It's now mainly a 15th- and 16th-century structure, but the base of the outer wall on the north side, facing Largo dos Colegiais, incorporates part of Evora's old wall. Largo dos Colegiais.

Sé (Cathedral) – This very imposing church, dating from the 12th and 13th centuries (consecrated in 1204), is not Evora's most beautiful building, although it is certainly one of its most interesting. Its plan is Romanesque, but in its structure and decorations, the building that rose was already Gothic, and additions made up to the 18th century left it with a mixture of styles. On several occasions the cathedral has lived up to its fortress-like appearance. It was from the terraces of this building that the townspeople supporting João of Avis for king in the late 14th century launched their incendiary assault on the old castle held by the unwanted regent, Queen Leonor. And it was in the cathedral's great naves that the townspeople took refuge during the height of the killing when the French were sacking the city during the early 19th century.

Part of the massive Romanesque-Gothic façade dates from the 12th century, but the two oddly dissimilar towers flanking the deeply recessed Gothic portal — one topped with a tile-covered cone, the other with a series of turrets — are from the 16th century. The Apostles standing guard on either side of the church entrance are 14th-century works, probably southern Portugal's first notable pieces of Christian sculpture. Inside, the three naves are the longest in Portugal. They are early Gothic (though the tasteless white pointing applied to the granite columns is modern), but the side chapels and transept date from the 16th century, and the splendid neo-classical chancel and high altar at the end are from the 18th century, designed by Johann Friedrich Ludwig, the German architect of the great monastery-palace at Mafra. The little polychrome stone statue of the Virgin set in a carved baroque altar at the beginning of the central nave is a 12th-century representation of Our Lady of O, the pregnant Virgin. Be sure to climb the stairs to the *coro alto* (above the west end of the central nave). The 16th-century carved wooden stalls are worth the effort: Panels behind the seats are full of vivid secular scenes of day-to-day country life in the Alentejo, as well as biblical scenes.

The early-14th-century cloister on the south side of the church is a magnificent example of the austere beauties of Evora's transitional Gothic. Its founder, a 14th-century bishop, lies in the carved marble sepulcher in a chapel in the cloister's southeast corner. The cathedral is open daily, from 9 AM to noon and from 2 to 5 PM. Admission charge to the cloister. Largo da Sé.

Museu de Arte Sacra (Museum of Sacred Art) – The collection, installed in the cathedral's south tower, contains fine ecclesiastical paintings, sculpture, vestments, gold, silver, and furniture. The ivory and polychrome stone figures of the 14th and 15th centuries are especially interesting — above all, the rare little ivory statue of the Virgin holding the infant Jesus, which opens up to form a triptych decorated with high-relief scenes from her life. The original head of this nearly unique figure is missing; the present wooden one dates from the 16th century. Open from 9 AM to noon and from 2 to 5 PM; closed Mondays. Admission charge. Largo da Sé (phone: 26910).

Museu Regional (Regional Museum) – In the former Bishop's Palace, a 16th-to-early-18th-century building next door to the cathedral, this museum — also known as the *Museu de Evora* — has an extremely interesting collection of archaeological pieces, paintings, and sculpture. Among several fine works is the series of 13 paintings on the life of the Virgin that once graced the high altar of the cathedral; an anonymous 14th-century Flemish work from the Bruges school, it alone would make the visit worthwhile. Another painting not to be missed is the little 16th-century Limoges enamel triptych of the Crucifixion. The museum's archaeological section contains several exquisite fragments that are tantalizingly evocative of Evora's antiquity. The 3rd-century marble relief of a maenad, her skirt twirling around her as she dances wildly, is particularly haunting. Open from 9 AM to noon and from 2 to 5 PM; closed Mondays. Admission charge. Largo Conde de Vila Flor (phone: 22604).

Biblioteca Pública (Public Library) – Just across from the museum, this is one of Portugal's outstanding libraries, with more than 500,000 manuscripts and 250,000 printed works, including a rare-book section containing over 500 incunabula (books printed before 1501), among other priceless early works. The collection is particularly noted for its codices connected with Portugal's maritime feats of the 15th and 16th centuries. Except for occasional exhibitions, the library's treasures are not on display. Visitors who wish to consult books must show their passports or other credentials to get a reader's card; the process normally takes 24 hours. Open Mondays through Fridays, from 9 AM to 12:30 PM and from 2 to 8 PM. Largo Conde de Vila Flor (phone: 22369).

Igreja e Convento dos Lóios (Lóios Church and Monastery) – The monastery building has become a state-owned inn, or *pousada* (see *Checking In*), but the church, although privately owned, is open to the public and can be visited. Dedicated to São João Evangelista (St. John the Evangelist), it was built in Gothic style between 1485 and 1491, but the main façade, with the exception of the Flamboyant portal, was rebuilt after the 1755 earthquake that destroyed Lisbon. The single Gothic nave is lined with 18th-century *azulejos* depicting the life of St. Lawrence Justinian (a 15th-century patriarch of Venice), some of them signed by Portugal's best-known tile maker, António de Oliveira Bernardes, and dated 1711. The church was founded by the nobleman Rodrigo Afonso de Melo to be his family's mausoleum. The chapterhouse belonging to the church has a particularly beautiful and curious doorway, with Manueline columns supporting two Moorish arches. Open daily, from 9 AM to noon and from 2 to 5 PM. Largo Conde de Vila Flor.

Universidade (University) – At the bottom of the hill, east of the cathedral, the Universidade do Espírito Santo (University of the Holy Ghost), to give it its full name, was founded by Cardinal Henrique for the Jesuits in 1559. The classical-baroque building is a notable piece of architecture with an especially handsome cloister, and it is profusely decorated with 16th-, 17th-, and 18th-century tiles. The university closed in 1759 when the Jesuits were expelled from Portugal by Prime Minister Marquês de Pombal; it reopened in 1975. There are no regular visiting hours, but most parts of the building can be seen upon request. Largo do Cardeal Rei (phone: 25572).

Largo das Portas de Moura – This small, picturesque square is a few blocks south of the university (walk along Rua do Conde da Serra da Tourega, following, more or less, the line of the old Roman wall). The two square towers on its north side mark the site of the south gate through the old wall. The Renaissance fountain in the center, built with funds donated by the people of the neighborhood and by Dom Jaime, Duke of Bragança, was inaugurated with festivities on November 4, 1556. On the square's south side is the verandah of the 16th-century Casa Cordovil. Six slender columns support Moorish arches and a little conical dome, forming a structure that, with its overtones of different cultures, manages to convey the essence of Evora's mixed history.

Igreja Nossa Senhora da Graça (Church of Our Lady of Grace) – The magnificent façade of this semi-ruined 16th-century church, one of the most striking examples of Renaissance architecture on the Iberian Peninsula, inevitably invites comparison with the architecture of Michelangelo because of its dramatic composition of triangles, circles, and columns. It was almost certainly designed by Diogo de Torralva, the architect of the Claustro dos Filipes in Tomar. The four heroically muscular but rather graceless figures supporting the spheres on the corners of the façade actually symbolize the four rivers of faith, but local people call them, ironically, the *meninos da Graça,* the children of Grace. The vault of the church collapsed in 1884, and most of the contents were taken to other churches, including the Church of São Francisco. The adjacent convent building is now occupied by the military. Rua da Graça.

Igreja de São Francisco (Church of St. Francis) – This 16th-century Moorish-Gothic church, about 2 blocks west of Nossa Senhora da Graça, has several outstanding architectural features, including a Gothic vault of unusual proportions over the single nave. But what everybody remembers it for is its curious Capela dos Ossos (Chapel of Bones). The walls of this macabre room are lined with bones and skulls laid out in intricate and sometimes ingenious patterns. The intention was to induce contemplation and instill a proper sense of mortality in the spirit of any Franciscan monk who might feel tempted toward frivolity. "We bones lie waiting here for yours," warns the Latin inscription over the door. The two mummified corpses hanging at the end of the chapel are said to be father and son, victims of an embittered wife's deathbed curse. (The woman's rather unusual malediction was that the flesh should never fall from their bones.) The chapel is open daily, from 9 AM to 12:30 PM and from 2:30 to 6 PM. Admission charge to the chapel. Praça Primeiro de Maio.

Jardim Público – Evora's charming public gardens are just south of the São Francisco church, enclosed by a section of the city wall. In the center is a fine old wrought-iron bandstand, where concerts are given in summer.

Palácio de Dom Manuel (Palace of King Manuel) – What was once a fine late-15th-century palace was sadly allowed to fall into ruin during the last century, and this restored fragment of the structure — the Galeria das Damas (Ladies Gallery) — is all that remains. Several kings lived here: Manuel I, João III, and the Spanish Philips. Many historic ceremonies also took place in the palace, including the momentous investiture of Vasco da Gama as admiral of the fleet that found the sea route to India in 1497. Exhibitions are now staged in its rooms. Jardim Público (phone: 25809).

Praça do Giraldo – A short walk up Rua da República leads to this square, named after the city's Christian liberator. It has been the geographic center and focal point of life in Evora since its beginnings as the forum of the Roman city. Until 1570, a triumphal arch stood at its northern end, where the parish Church of Santo Antão stands today. The Renaissance fountain in front of the church was built in 1571 (and paid for by the Cardinal-King Dom Henrique, the founder of the university), to replace an earlier one that was demolished along with the triumphal arch. The white marble benches ringing the fountain were placed there in 1970.

Igreja de Santo Antão (Church of St. Antão) – This rather sober church, built during the 16th century by the local architect Manuel Pires, is worth a look inside. It has some fine carved and polychromed altars and, on the front of the high altar, a very rare low-relief marble panel of the Apostles, dating from the 14th century. The piece was saved from the Templars Church of Santo Antoninho, the predecessor of the present church. Praça do Giraldo.

Cerca Nova (New Walls) – The approximately 9,840 feet of so-called new walls that once girdled the city are still nearly intact today, although much restored. The new walls were begun during the first half of the 14th century, in the reign of King Afonso IV, and were finished between 1384 and 1433, during the reign of King João I. Originally, there were 40 towers and 10 gates, but most of these have long since fallen prey to time and to cannibalization by stone-hungry builders. One that still remains much as it was during the 14th century is the tower guarding the Porta de Alconchel (Alconchel Gate), at the bottom of Rua Serpa Pinto. A good road, the Estrada da Circunvalação, follows the path of the walls all the way around the city.

OUTSIDE THE WALLS

Ermida de São Brás (Chapel of St. Blaise) – Built during the late 15th century, this is an excellent early example of the battlemented church that is so characteristic of the Alentejo region. Fourteen cylindrical buttress-turrets give the little building its unique, bellicose aspect. Inside, the green-and-white diamond-pattern tiles covering the barrel vault over the nave are from the 16th century. In 1490, a German historian named Munzer described his surprise at finding a huge crocodile hanging over the main door. It had been left there as an offering by Portuguese navigators after a successful voyage of discovery down the coast of Africa. Open daily, from 9 AM to noon and from 2 to 5 PM. Rua da República.

Aqueduto da Prata (Prata Aqueduct) – This outstanding work of engineering was built between 1532 and 1537, during the reign of King João III, to bring water from a spring at Graça do Divor, 11 miles (18 km) away. It cost quite literally a king's fortune at the time (over 700,000 *réis*), but Evora has always suffered a shortage of water, and King João's court spent a lot of time in the city. The road around the walls passes under the aqueduct at the point where it enters the city, but the most monumental section lies between the walls and São Bento de Castris, 2 miles (3 km) away on the road to Arraiolos.

■ **EXTRA SPECIAL:** Wander through the narrow streets and alleys of the Old City with a dictionary in hand, and you will discover wonderfully sonorous and evocative street names everywhere. Some commemorate local "celebrities" or simply local "characters" — Rua do Malbarbado (Street of the Unshaven One), Rua do

Matamouros (Street of the Bully), Rua do Alfaiate da Condessa (Street of the Countesses' Tailor), and Rua da Ama do Cardeal (Street of the Cardinal's Maid). Residence near, or ownership of, an olive grove may have commended Manuel to posterity (Rua Manuel do Olival), and Master Resende de Alvaro (Rua Mestre Resende de Alvaro) may have won renown as a teacher, but the reasons for the immortalization of Beatriz de Vilhena (Rua Beatriz de Vilhena), the Cogominhos family (Travessa dos Cogominhos), or even the Dark Ladies (Rua das Morenas) are less obvious and probably long forgotten. Other names refer to features of the streetscape: Rua da Cozinha de Sua Alteza (Street of His Highnesses' Kitchen); Rua das Pedras Negras (Street of the Black Stones), an old street name often found in southern Portugal and Spain; and Rua das Casas Pintadas (Street of the Painted Houses), where Vasco da Gama's house is located — it has rooms decorated with frescoes of exotic wildlife (but is not open to the public). Some of the names may require a knowledge of Portuguese to appreciate their full flavor, but for beginners, this is a good way to pick up a little of the language, even if some of it might be a bit archaic.

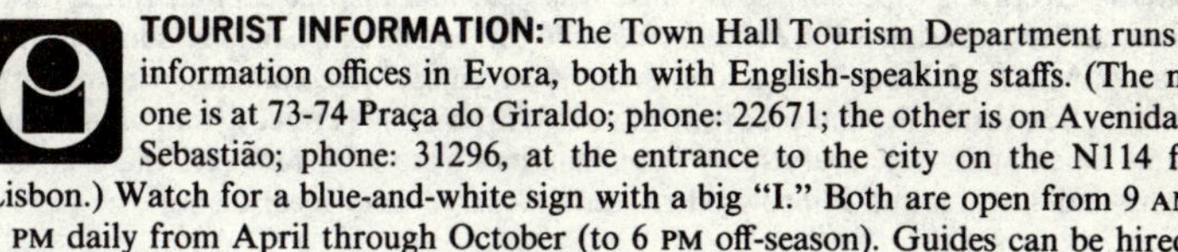

TOURIST INFORMATION: The Town Hall Tourism Department runs two information offices in Evora, both with English-speaking staffs. (The main one is at 73-74 Praça do Giraldo; phone: 22671; the other is on Avenida São Sebastião; phone: 31296, at the entrance to the city on the N114 from Lisbon.) Watch for a blue-and-white sign with a big "I." Both are open from 9 AM to 7 PM daily from April through October (to 6 PM off-season). Guides can be hired by writing in advance to *Evora City Tours* (8 Rua da Corredoura, Evora 7000; phone and fax: 23616). This company can also arrange jeep safaris, hunting and fishing trips, and even hot-air balloon flights over the city and into the surrounding countryside.

Local Coverage – The daily *Diário do Sul* and the weekly *Notícias de Evora* are the leading regional newspapers. English-language newspapers such as the *International Herald Tribune* can be bought at *Tabacaria Paris,* a tobacco and stationery shop (19 Rua da República; phone: 24569). Although two or three locally published guidebooks, written by historians, are in print, their English translations tend to range from quaint to uproariously unintelligible. The best local guidebooks are probably Tulio Espanca's *Evora: Património Mundial* and *Encontro com a Cidade,* but no English versions were available at press time.

TELEPHONE: The city code for Evora is 66. If calling from within Portugal, dial 066 before the local number.

GETTING AROUND: The best way to see Evora is to walk. It is a small city, distances between places of interest are never very great, and the narrow streets make driving difficult if not impossible in the Old City. Parking spaces can usually be found in the squares, for those who do decide to drive across town.

Airport – The nearest commercial airport is Lisbon's Portela de Sacavém (phone: 1-802060). There is a tiny airport for small private charters nearby. Campo de Aviação (phone: 22263).

Bus – There is no inner-city bus service, but the national network, *Rodoviário Nacional,* serves Evora, with daily departures to Lisbon and points south. The buses are reasonably comfortable and inexpensive. Tickets should be bought in advance at the bus station (131 Largo da República; phone: 22121), or from *RN Tours–Viagens e Turismo,* a travel agency (131 Rua da República; phone: 24254).

Car Rental – *Europcar* is at 155 Rua Serpa Pinto (phone: 28815).

Taxi – Taxis are fairly plentiful. The best place to find one is at the city cabstands, especially the centrally located ones at Praça do Giraldo, Largo das Portas de Moura, and Largo Luís de Camões. To call a cab, dial 32220 or 32222. Taxis can be hired by the kilometer for tours in the surrounding area.

Train – The station (phone: 22125) is a little over a half-mile south of the city. There are two or three trains a day to Lisbon (the trip takes about 3 hours) and also connections to Spain, the Lower Alentejo, and the Algarve. Those going to Lisbon should remember that trains do not cross the Tagus River. (The train takes passengers as far as Barreiro, on the south bank of the Tagus, from where they ferry across to the river station on Lisbon's Praça do Comércio; the price of the ride is included with the train ticket.)

SPECIAL EVENTS: Every second Tuesday of the month — June excepted — a market is held in the Rossio de São Brás outside the walls. These monthly markets are important events in all Portuguese country towns, and Evora's is especially so because it is held in a district capital. But Evora's biggest market gathering is the *Feira de São João* (St. John's Fair), held annually during the last 2 weeks of June. This major event is an enjoyable combination of country market, agricultural fair, and folk festival, and it draws huge crowds from all over the district. Open stalls sell everything from handicrafts to hair restorer, there is folk dancing and singing, and improvised restaurants serve tasty local dishes.

MUSEUMS: Evora's major museums, such as the *Museu de Arte Sacra* and the *Museu Regional* (also called the *Museu de Evora*), are discussed in *Special Places.* In addition, the following may be of interest:

Museu de Arte Sacra (Sacred Art Museum) – Not to be confused with the *Museu de Arte Sacra* in the cathedral, this museum of religious art is an annex to the *Museu Regional,* and it's set up in the Igreja das Mercês (Church of Mercy). Open from 9 AM to noon and from 2 to 5 PM; closed Mondays; no admission charge. Rua do Raimundo (phone: 22604).

Museu de Artesanato (Handicrafts Museum) – An excellent collection of local crafts — pottery, textiles, cork work, basketry, and so on — installed in the Celeiro Comun, a magnificent 18th-century building that was formerly a communal granary. Open from 10 AM to noon and from 2 to 5:30 PM; closed Mondays; no admission charge. 7 Praça Primeiro de Maio (phone: 22937).

João Cutileiro – The studio of Evora's internationally known sculptor can be visited in the morning up to 12:30 PM; his works can be purchased or commissioned. 13 Estrada de Viana do Alentejo (phone: 23972).

SHOPPING: This is the sort of provincial city whose inhabitants would probably do their shopping in Lisbon if they could. The local stores are fine for run-of-the-mill household needs; for travelers, the best buys are handicrafts. The main shopping streets are centered around Praça do Giraldo, with many of the most useful shops located on Rua 5 de Outubro and its side streets, as well as in the arcades that run the length of the east side of Praça do Giraldo and continue down Rua João de Deus to Largo Luís de Camões. The *Centro Comercial Eborim,* a modern shopping center (Rua Eborim; phone: 22260), has practically everything under one roof. The *Mercado Municipal* (Municipal Market; on Praça Primeiro de Maio), open every morning except Mondays, is not only the best place for fresh food and delicacies such as the excellent local cheeses and cured sausages, but also a colorful place to visit. Handicrafts, including good, brown-glazed oven pots, are sold from stalls outside, along with the omnipresent plastic goods. Two handicraft shops worth noting:

Casa Silva – Typical painted *alentejano* furniture — one of the best sources for this increasingly rare work. 11 Rua do Cano (phone: 23456).

Teoartis – Hand-painted tiles, original or reproduction, made to order and available from stock. 78 Rua 5 de Outubro (phone: 22736).

SPORTS AND FITNESS: Bullfighting – The *Praça de Touros* is just outside the walls, along the Estrada da Circunvalação. Several bullfights are held during the season, which runs from May to sometime in October, but programming is irregular. Check with the tourist office.

Soccer – The two local teams are not major league, but they have strong support, and, as everywhere in Portugal, soccer is the top spectator sport. The season begins in September and ends in May. Games are played on Sundays in the *Estádio Sanches de Miranda* (phone: 22200).

Swimming – An excellent complex of five municipal swimming pools (*piscinas municipais*) is set among lawns on the edge of town, 1¼ miles (2 km) from the city center. The facilities include an Olympic-size pool, a diving pool, a learners' pool, and two pools for children, plus two restaurants and a bar. The complex (phone: 32324) is open daily, from 9 AM to 8 PM (1 to 8 PM on Mondays, to allow for cleaning).

Tennis – Good clay courts can be rented at either of two sports clubs: *Lusitano Ginásio Clube* (Estrada das Alcaçovas; phone: 22844) and *Juventudes Sport Clube* (*Estádio Sanches de Miranda;* phone: 22200). Bring your own gear.

THEATER: The *Teatro Garcia de Resende* (Praça Joaquim António de Aguiar; phone: 23112) is the biggest theater in the south of Portugal — the only one for miles around, in fact. It was built between 1881 and 1892 and destined rather snootily for opera, recitals, and concerts only, but it was not a great success. In 1975 the theater was handed over to the Centro Cultural de Evora, which since then has operated a theater school in it. Check with the tourist office for possible shows and concerts.

MUSIC: The Câmara Municipal (Town Hall) sponsors classical music, jazz, and pop concerts, but there is no regular program. However, when something is going on, an attempt is made to publish the particulars as far in advance as possible, so check with the tourist office. The concerts take place in the *Teatro Garcia de Resende* (see above) and in other venues such as the Palácio de Dom Manuel, or even in old houses. Brass-band concerts take place in the Jardim Público in summer. Visitors interested in music should also ask about the possibility of taking in a performance of *cantares alentejanos* (Alentejo songs). *Cantares* are folk songs of remote origin, sung (chanted might be a better word) by groups of men. The singers stand together in a tight group or sometimes march along slowly, swaying in unison as they sing. The *Feira de São João* is a good occasion to hear them.

NIGHTCLUBS AND NIGHTLIFE: Evora is the perfect place to enjoy the benefits of early nights without feeling like an old fogey. It has virtually no nightlife worth sampling, other than a few discotheques or the innocent pleasures of sitting on a café terrace or strolling through the town looking at the lighted monuments. Among the most popular discos are *Brown's* (54 Rua Serpa Pinto; phone: 20545) and *Slide* (135 Rua Serpa Pinto; phone: 28272).

BEST IN TOWN

CHECKING IN: Accommodations are limited in quantity, but they range fairly widely in style, from luxury to plain, comfortable economy. At the expensive end of the scale — and there is only one luxury establishment in Evora — expect to pay from $110 to $150, depending on whether it is high season or low, for a double room with breakfast. In the moderate range, expect to pay from $55 to $100, and in the inexpensive range approximately $30 to $40. All telephone numbers are in the 066 city code unless otherwise indicated.

Pousada dos Lóios – This 32-room luxury establishment is one of the best of the state-owned *pousadas.* In the converted and restored Convento dos Lóios, built in 1485 by the nobleman Rodrigo Afonso de Melo, it occupies the site of Evora's old castle. Most of the rooms are in the old monks' cells, with period furnishings, but the essential modern services are adequate. There is an open-air pool and a restaurant serving regional food (see *Eating Out*). The location — next door to the Roman temple and right in the center of everything — is perfect. Largo Conde de Vila Flor (phone: 24051; in the US, 212-686-9213; fax: 27248). Expensive.

Evorahotel – The newest of Evora's lodgings, this hostelry is also the largest, offering guests a choice of 114 rooms, all with private bath, TV sets, and telephones. There's also an outdoor swimming pool and an excellent restaurant (see *Eating Out*). Two miles (3 km) west of town, on the road to Lisbon. Quinta do Cruzeiro, on N114 (phone: 734801; fax: 734806). Moderate.

Monte das Flores – This *estalagem,* or inn, occupies a converted farm 2½ miles (4 km) west of Evora on N114. The 17 rooms are all furnished attractively and comfortably in period rustic, and all have private baths. A pool and tennis courts are among the facilities; there's also horseback riding. The restaurant serves good regional dishes. Monte das Flores (phone: 25018; fax: 27564). Moderate.

Planície – One of Evora's busiest hotels and generally considered the top establishment in its price range, it has 33 well-equipped rooms with baths. Spacious public rooms and a highly regarded restaurant add to the attractions. The location and service are first-rate. 40 Largo de Alvaro Velho (phone: 24026; fax: 29880). Moderate.

Riviera – In line with all establishments in its *pensão residencial* category, it lacks a few of the regular hotel services — no restaurant or bar. But its 22 rooms do all have private baths and color television sets, and it is well located between the cathedral and Praça do Giraldo. 49 Rua 5 de Outubro (phone: 23304; fax: 20467). Moderate.

Santa Clara – An unpretentious but first-rate modern hostelry in the heart of the Old City, west of Praça do Giraldo. The 30 rooms (with bath) are comfortably appointed, the service is attentive, and there is a large and very good restaurant. All things considered, the hotel offers unbeatable value. 19 Travessa da Milheira (phone: 24141; fax: 26544). Moderate.

Vitória – A modern *albergaria* (another category of inn), it's comfortable and very well equipped, although without a restaurant. All 48 rooms have private baths, color TV sets, air conditioning, and phones. The location, about 300 yards outside the city walls to the south, means easy parking. Rua Diana de Lis (phone: 27174; fax: 20974). Moderate.

Diana – A small, 15-room *pensão* in the center of town, modest but well regarded. The rooms are small, but all have baths and phone. No bar or restaurant. 2 Rua Diogo Cão (phone: 22008). Inexpensive.

EATING OUT: Portuguese from regions with more gastronomical cachet tend to look down their noses at Alentejo cooking as lacking variety and finesse. They may be right up to a point, because the spartan character of life on the great, dry, central plains is clearly present in the local food, and the region in general has never been known for the range and refinement of its culinary achievements. This is a virtue at times, but even if it weren't, there are more than enough good things to eat to keep a visitor from feeling homesick for a hamburger.

Bread — the heavy, crusty, delicious kind, with the ash from wood ovens still clinging to the bottoms of the huge loaves — is an important part of all meals, and even finds its way into the soup. The most basic of these, *sopa alentejana,* is in fact mostly bread and water. To make it, water is boiled with a lot of garlic and olive oil, then poured over slices of bread in a bowl. A poached egg is added just before serving.

Pork (*carne de porco*) and lamb or mutton (*borrego*) are the staple meats. In one of the few local dishes that have acquired a wider fame, *carne de porco à alentejana,* small pieces of pork are blended tastily with clams. Pork is also a basic ingredient in popular bean dishes such as the various versions of *feijoada alentejana,* a devastatingly substantial mixture of pork meats, fresh and cured, and white beans. Lamb and kid (*cabrito*) are most commonly eaten in stews (*ensopados*) or roasted in the oven (*assado no forno*). All meat dishes are inclined to be heavy in the Alentejo — and be warned that restaurant servings are never tailored to the needs of weight watchers.

Evora's desserts betray their Moorish and medieval convent background. The people of the Alentejo have inherited a collective sweet tooth, and their traditional sweetmeats (*doçaria*) tend to err in this direction. Most of the favorites, such as *queijo conventual* (convent "cheese") or *toucinho do céu* (bacon from heaven), have an egg base and are flavored with almond. The great alentejo cheese, serpa, made near the town of that name not far from Evora, is increasingly rare and difficult to find. The salty little cheeses made in Evora from cured sheep's milk are good as appetizers.

The best alentejo wines are made in the Borba, Redondo, and Reguengos de Monsaraz areas east of Evora, and in Vidigueira, south of the city. The reds especially are good, rather heavy wines, and are almost always the product of cooperatives. The top wines from each cooperative are sold as *reservas.* Expect to pay from $60 to $90 for a dinner for two with wine at those restaurants listed below as expensive, from $35 to $50 in the moderate range, and under $35 in the inexpensive range. All telephone numbers are in the 66 city code unless otherwise indicated.

Cozinha de Santo Humberto – Humberto is the patron saint of hunters, and this is one of the country's best dining places for game when it is in season (from October into January). At other times, it's famed for its *carne de porco à alentejana* and, for instance, *arroz de pato no forno* (duck casserole with rice). Closed Thursdays. Reservations advised. Major credit cards accepted. 39 Rua da Moeda (phone: 24251). Expensive.

Fialho – Evora's most celebrated restaurant, serving genuinely traditional food — it's not unknown for gastronomes from Lisbon to drive out here for lunch, especially during game season. Little plates of delicious appetizers (*petiscos*) precede the main meal. The *borrego assado* is justifiably renowned, and so is the *favada real da casa,* a monumental bean dish. In the game season, partridge, hare, and wild boar (*perdiz, lebre,* and *javali,* respectively) are specialties. The place is always thronged, and it's not large, so reservations are advised. Closed Mondays, but open throughout the day otherwise, with no break between lunch and dinner; also closed during the first 2 weeks of September. Major credit cards accepted. 16 Travessa das Mascarenhas (phone: 23079). Expensive.

Luar de Janeiro – One of Evora's top dining establishments, it leans less heavily on traditional regional fare than its competitors, concentrating instead on seafood. It also stays open later than most — until 2 AM. Closed Thursdays. Reservations advised. Visa, MasterCard, and Eurocard accepted. 13 Travessa de Janeiro (phone: 24895). Expensive.

Pousada dos Lóios – The food here is not quite up to the standard of others in its price range, but for those in search of something more international, the *pousada,* occupying a 15th-century monastery, could be worthwhile. The dining room itself, once the monks' refectory, is lovely, and in good weather, tables and chairs are set up around the equally lovely cloister. Open daily. Reservations advised. Major credit cards accepted. Largo Conde de Vila Flor (phone: 24051). Expensive.

Evorahotel – This hotel restaurant opened last year with the goal of becoming a gastronomic attraction on its own, rather than just a hotel amenity — an understandable ambition, considering that the celebrated Fialho brothers are part-owners. Comfortably spacious, it features traditional Alentejano furniture and panoramic views of the surrounding countryside. Among the specialties are *bacalhau no formo com tomate,* a massive feast of oven-baked cod, and *feijoada de marisco,* an adventurous variation of the traditional bean dish. It also boasts one of the best regional wine lists in town. Open daily for lunch and dinner. Reservations advised. Major credit cards accepted. Two miles (3 km) west of town, on the road to Lisbon. Quinta do Cruzeiro, on N114 (phone: 734801). Moderate.

Guião – One of Evora's top traditional eateries in the intermediate price range. It's large (3 rooms) and comfortable, with old-fashioned decor. The *borrego no forno* vies with *Fialho*'s. Closed Mondays. Reservations unnecessary. Major credit cards accepted. 81 Rua da República (phone: 23071). Moderate.

1/4 P'ras 9 – The odd-looking name actually means a quarter to nine. A relative newcomer to the Evora scene, it specializes in charcoal grills and seafood. The *açorda de marisco* (a difficult-to-describe mixture of bread and seafood) is excellent. Closed Wednesdays. No reservations. Visa and Eurocard accepted. 9A Rua Pedro Simões (phone: 26774). Moderate to inexpensive.

A Gruta – On the basis of value for money, this has become one of the most popular restaurants in town in recent years. No frills, but the food is good. The specialty is oven-roasted kid. Closed Saturdays. No reservations or credit cards accepted. 2 Av. General Humberto Delgado (phone: 28186). Inexpensive.

Martinho – A good, very popular place, where the specialty is a kid dish called *cabrito na canoa.* Open daily. No reservations or credit cards accepted. 24 Largo Luís de Camões (phone: 23057). Inexpensive.

LISBON

Lisbon is a bit like the heroine of an old movie who faces the gravest of perils in every reel — but emerges in the end still beautiful. During its more than 2,000 years of history, the city has undergone devastating earthquakes, plagues, fires, floods, invasions by barbarians, sackings, revolutions, and, more recently, the incursion of ugly urban development and pollution. But Lisbon remains beautiful, if a trifle faded and disheveled. At certain times of the day, the sun casts a golden reflection so intense that the broad expanse of estuary facing the city seems literally to live up to its popular name, Mar da Palha, or "Sea of Straw." And as the sun moves across the sky, the pastel buildings, tree-lined boulevards, cobblestone streets, and mosaic sidewalks of this city built in tiers on seven hills are bathed again and again in new perspectives of light.

Legend says that Lisbon was founded by Ulysses, who gave it the name Olisipo. Less romantic historians say that the ancient name was Phoenician in origin and that the city grew up gradually as a port town on the estuary of the Tagus River, where traders from many lands drew their boats to shore to sell their wares — or perhaps to raid. Gradually, safety-conscious inhabitants moved to the top of the hill where the old St. George's Castle stands today, and then, little by little, occupied the surrounding hills.

Over the centuries, many people came and went: Celts, Phoenicians, Carthaginians, Romans, Visigoths, and Moors, until the 12th century, when the city was taken by the Christian Portuguese. As Portugal built its vast empire during the 15th and 16th centuries, citizens from many diverse lands came to live in Lisbon. And when decades of dictatorship ended in 1974 and the country dissolved the remnants of its empire, a new wave of immigrants arrived from Angola, Mozambique, Timor, and the Cape Verde Islands.

More than 1.6 million people live in Lisbon and its environs today, and yet, in some ways, this westernmost capital of Europe is still a small town. The *lisboetas,* accustomed to foreigners, are tolerant of their visitors' ways, their dress, and their inability to speak Portuguese. They usually can give directions in English. Sometimes they will even drop what they are doing and take a visitor where he or she wants to go.

Lisbon has known moments of glory. The Romans, who arrived in 205 BC, made it, after Mérida in Spain, the most important city on the Iberian Peninsula, a place with baths, a theater, a 6-mile-long aqueduct (not the one standing today), and roads stretching out in all directions. In their turn, the Moors, whose stay lasted from 714 to 1147, gathered their most brilliant thinkers, scientists, and writers at Aschbouna — as they renamed the city — and made it a renowned center of learning. Lisbon began to come into its own as Portuguese, however, only after its recapture from the Moors during the 12th century (Dom Afonso Henriques, Portugal's first king, and an army of crusaders from northern Europe besieged the castle for 17 weeks to accomplish that), and after King Afonso III's transfer of the court from Coimbra in 1260. By the 14th century, Lisbon had nearly 4 miles of walls, with 77 towers and 38 entranceways.

The city's greatest glory came during the 15th and 16th centuries. At a time when the world's seas were uncharted and darkness and superstition ruled people's imaginations, Lisbon was sending forth Portuguese caravels into the unknown, and her explorers were bringing the world's riches back from Africa, India, Brazil, and China. The Age of Discovery, as it is called, was ushered in by Prince Henry the Navigator (1394–1460), the son of King João I and his English wife, Philippa of Lancaster. During the early 15th century, Prince Henry established a school of navigation at Sagres, in southwest Portugal, and from there ships sailing under his authority explored the coast of Africa, making great strides in the study of geography, map making, and shipbuilding. His contributions to the advancement of exploration led, at the end of the century, not only to the epochal voyage of Christopher Columbus, but also to the voyages of Bartholomeu Dias, who rounded the Cape of Good Hope in 1488, and of Vasco da Gama, who sailed out from Lisbon in 1497 and returned 2 years later after reaching the Indies. Portugal's so-called Spice Age had begun.

Trade with India, and later with Brazil — discovered by Pedro Alvares Cabral in 1500 — made Lisbon immensely rich. By the 16th century, the city had become a great commercial and maritime power, the "Queen of the Tagus," ruling from one of the best harbors in Europe. Churches and palaces were built. In 1502, King Manuel I, wishing to erect a memorial to Portugal's explorers, began construction of one of Lisbon's greatest monuments, the Jerónimos Monastery in Belém, the Lisbon suburb from which Vasco da Gama had set sail. The ropes, anchors, and seaweed carved on this building (and on others of the period) are typical of the uniquely Portuguese decorative style that came to be known as Manueline.

But all was not joyful. Persecution of Jews began during the late 15th century, and the Inquisition was introduced during the early 16th century, to endure some 200 years. Thousands were tortured in the Palace of the Inquisition in the Rossio, and many others died in the autos-da-fé held in the public squares of the city. In 1580, Philip II of Spain annexed the country and became Philip I of Portugal; Spanish rule lasted until 1640, when the Spanish governor of Lisbon was deposed by a group of Portuguese noblemen. Lisbon then revived its profitable trade with the rest of the world, and a spate of new building began. This time, given the discovery of gold in Brazil during the late 17th century, the characteristic decorative element of the period was richly gilded baroque woodwork (it is possible that the name of the baroque style may have come from the Portuguese word *barroco,* meaning "rough pearl"). The reign of João V (1706–50) was known for its magnificence.

Then, on the morning of *All Saints' Day,* November 1, 1755, while most of Lisbon was at mass, one of the worst earthquakes ever known shook the city like a straw in the wind. Within minutes, two-thirds of Lisbon was in ruins. A 40-foot tidal wave rose on the Tagus and slammed into the city. Fires, begun by tapers lighted in the churches for the feast day and fanned by a violent windstorm, burned what the quake had left intact. As many as 40,000 people perished — causing philosophers, among them Voltaire, to conclude that this was not, after all, the most perfect of all worlds.

The prime minister, the Marquês de Pombal, quickly and efficiently set out to rebuild Lisbon on the rubble covering the valley floor between two of its hills. The stately plan of the city's classical squares and boulevards was traced out, and the straight lines and 18th-century proportions of the quarter called the Baixa — lower town — grew up in place of the previous medieval jumble. The Baixa's parallel streets are lined with nearly uniform, 5-story buildings.

Pombal is best remembered for this accomplishment, not for the reign of terror that he instituted against his enemies that made Lisbon a city of fear. Political turmoil marked the rest of the 18th century and the 19th. In 1908, King Carlos I and his son were assassinated in Praça do Comércio; the successor to the throne, King Manuel II, was forced into exile 2 years later, when radical republicans overthrew the monarchy. The political turbulence of the ensuing democratic republic gave way to dictatorship in 1926 and the rise to power of António de Oliveira Salazar, a professor of economics from Coimbra University, who ruled Portugal until 1968. He put the country's finances in order and kept Portugal out of World War II, but during the nearly half century he and his successor, Marcello Caetano, remained in power, Portugal was turned gradually into a police state.

On the 25th of April, 1974, a group of young officers staged a coup in Lisbon and helped set up a democratically elected government. It was a revolution in which few lives were lost, but it altered the face of the capital. As the streets became the scene of demonstrations by newly formed labor unions and political parties, once-pristine buildings and monuments were spray-painted with slogans, and mosaic sidewalks that used to be scoured daily became grubby. Up to this time, Lisbon had been the capital of the world's last colonial empire, but with the breakup of the empire following the revolution, nearly a million refugees poured into the city. The government housed some in hotels; others lived in shanties. Their crated belongings lined the banks of the Tagus.

Within a few years, the situation stabilized. The refugees were miraculously absorbed into the life of the city and helped make Lisbon a more dynamic place. The city's beauty began to reemerge from under the posters and slogans and grime. Many of the old buildings — the greater part of Lisbon's stock is from the late 18th and 19th centuries, with much plain, utilitarian architecture added during this century — are molding away from neglect. But some of the more important ones are getting a facelift and repairs. Post-modernist buildings, in glass and bright colors, mostly the work of architect Tomás Taveira, also have appeared.

Portugal joined the European Economic Community (Common Market) in 1986, bringing in new investment funds and new products for Lisbon's shelves. Anyone who knows the city, but has been absent for a while, will find that Lisbon today is not the same as it was even a few years ago. Many of the streets in the Baixa have been closed to traffic and turned into pedestrian malls paved with cobblestones. Musicians entertain the strollers, and sidewalk artists sketch inexpensive portraits. Artisans offer jewelry, leatherwork, embroidery, and other wares from little stalls. There are many attractive open-air cafés and restaurants. Hotels have been renovated and more new accommodations for visitors seem to be added each year. The delights of Lisbon again are apparent; maybe that's why tourism is flourishing.

LISBON AT-A-GLANCE

SEEING THE CITY: A city built on hills frequently surprises visitors with lovely views that emerge without warning around unexpected corners. Lisbon is such a place. It has 17 natural balconies — called *miradouros* — from which to view the city. Foremost of these is the hilltop on which the ruins of St. George's Castle stand. All of the squares are laid out beneath: Praça do Comércio by the banks of the Tagus; the Rossio with its fountains and flower stalls; Praça da Figueira, the bustling market square; Praça dos Restauradores with its monument to Portugal's independence; the circular Praça Marquês de Pombal at the end of the broad Avenida da Liberdade; and beyond that, the lovely Parque Eduardo VII. On a clear day, it is possible to see the castles of Sintra far to the west. Another vantage point that's worth a pause is Largo de Santa Luzia, in the Alfama district, just downhill from the castle, between it and Lisbon's cathedral. Although the view from here — over the Alfama's red-roofed buildings down to the port — is less broadly panoramic than the one from the castle, the esplanade is charming, lined with *azulejos,* or glazed tiles, and endowed with flower beds and a trellis-topped colonnade. (For those who prefer not to walk, it's reached by one of Lisbon's picturesque, vintage *eléctricos,* or trolleys — the No. 28.) A third *miradouro* is the terrace on Rua de São Pedro de Alcântara, on the opposite hill across the city in the Bairro Alto. From here there is a picture postcard view of the castle, with the Alfama district spread down the slopes below its walls.

Another breathtaking view is from the bridge across the Tagus, known since the 1974 revolution as Ponte 25 de Abril, but previously named for Salazar, who built it in the 1960s. The third-longest suspension bridge in the world, it is particularly spectacular at night, when its cables, the ships in the river, and the city are all brightly lit. On the other side, there is a marvelous panorama of the Tagus estuary from the top of the statue of Cristo Rei (Christ the King), a gift to Portugal from Brazil. (Open daily from 10 AM to 6 PM; there is an admission charge, and an elevator takes visitors up.) Those without a car can cross the river by ferry from Praça do Comércio and take a bus from Cacilhas to the statue.

One excellent way to see the city is to join a 3-hour "Lisbon Walk" sponsored by the *Centro Nacional de Cultura* (National Culture Center; 68 Rua António Maria Cardoso; phone: 346-6722), whose regularly scheduled guided itineraries — in English and Portuguese — take in the Chiado, Alfama, and Belém districts.

SPECIAL PLACES: In ancient times, and later under the Moors, Lisbon was contained within walls that surrounded the hill where St. George's Castle now stands. Today, that area is the Alfama, the oldest part of the city, where traces of the picturesque Judiaria (Jewish Quarter) and Mouraria (Moorish Quarter) still can be seen, along with Roman remains. The Alfama has been destroyed several times by earthquakes, but it always was rebuilt along the same plan, its tortuous, narrow streets spiraling down from the top of the hill to the Baixa below. The Baixa, to the west of the Alfama, is the main shopping and commercial district of Lisbon. Built after the earthquake in a grid fashion, it stretches northward from Praça do Comércio by the river to the top of the Rossio, one of the city's main squares, and includes such aptly named streets as Rua Aurea (its official name — confusingly, it's generally known and shown on most maps as Rua do Ouro, which means the same thing: Gold Street) and Rua da Prata (Silver Street), which are lined with fine jewelers and banks. Up the hill and west of the Rossio is the part of the Baixa known locally as the Chiado — not much more than 10 square blocks. This also is a popular shopping district dotted with coffeehouses and outdoor cafés, but a disastrous fire in September 1988 destroyed a great number of the shops — including two of Europe's oldest department stores — and other landmarks. Happily, most of the façades of the burned buildings remained standing after the flames were put out, even though the interiors were gutted, and rebuilding plans call for restoration of the district, rather than wholesale modernization. The plan, which includes turning the shell of one of the former department stores into an exclusive hotel and the other into a shopping and cultural center, is expected to take at least 5 years to complete.

Higher up is the Bairro Alto, or High Quarter, above and to the west of Praça dos Restauradores and the Rossio. At one time a wealthy (and later a seedy) residential district, it has been taken over by the avant-garde and become the center of nightlife in downtown Lisbon, with fine restaurants, typical *tascas* (taverns or small eating places), and *fado* houses, where sad Portuguese folk songs are sung. West of the Bairro Alto are the Madragoa and Lapa districts, residential areas where restaurants, government buildings, embassies, and several museums and art galleries also can be found. Modern Lisbon, with museums, the zoo, and new quarters, stretches to the north and east of the downtown area.

The Belém quarter is along the riverbank west of all of the above. Because it suffered very little in the 1755 earthquake, many of its fine palaces and monuments are still standing. Belém also is home to several museums, as well as many restaurants.

ST. GEORGE'S CASTLE AND THE ALFAMA

Castelo de São Jorge (St. George's Castle) – Built on one of Lisbon's highest hills, this castle with ten towers is considered the cradle of the city. An Iron Age *castro,* or fortified hilltop town, probably was located here, succeeded by Roman fortifications (Roman walls and other remains are being excavated), a fortress built by the Visigoths during the 5th century, and later, a Moorish fortified town. The present castle was built during the 12th century. Within the grounds are lovely gardens where peacocks roam free, the remains of an Arabian palace where the Kings of Portugal lived from the 14th to the 16th century, and a restaurant, the *Casa do Leão* (locals consider it overpriced for the quality of the food, although the locale is attractive). From the terrace on the south and west sides and from the walk around the towers, the views of Lisbon are extensive. Open daily from 9 AM to 9 PM (7 PM from October through March). No admission charge. Rua Costa do Castelo.

Alfama – This Old Quarter slopes downhill from St. George's Castle. A cobbled labyrinth with some streets so narrow that pedestrians must walk in single file, it is one of the most colorful spots in Europe. Its streets are overhung with balconies ablaze with scarlet geraniums and lined with little taverns decorated with strings of peppers, garlic, and cheese. By day, caged canaries on the balconies sing in the sun; at night, wrought-iron lamps light the scene; and on washdays, the buildings are strung with clotheslines and drying laundry. Although some medieval mansions and Moorish buildings exist, most of the houses date from the late 18th century, after the earthquake. The best times to see the Alfama are in the morning when the markets are open, late in the afternoon when the streets and squares are alive with people, or on a moonlit evening. The quarter stretches north to south from the castle to the banks of the Tagus, and west to east from the cathedral to the vicinity of the church of São Vicente de Fora.

Sé (Cathedral) – Lisbon's oldest church, built just after the Christian Reconquest of the 12th century, suffered enormous earthquake damage in 1755, but was rebuilt during the 18th century and restored during this one. It is a typical fortress-church of solid, massive construction, with battlements and towers. The plain façade is Romanesque, the ambulatory chapels and the cloister are pure Gothic, and the choir is baroque. In the *azulejo*-lined enclosure just inside the door is the baptismal font of St. Anthony of Padua, Portugal's patron saint, who was born here (although he spent much of his life in Italy), and in the chapel to the left is a *presépio* (Nativity scene) by Joaquim Machado de Castro. Relics of St. Vincent, patron saint of Lisbon, also are in the cathedral, but are brought out only on special occasions. There is a collection of religious vestments and ecclesiastical gold, which can be seen only by prior arrangement. The cloister is open from 9 AM to 1 PM and from 2 to 4 PM; closed Mondays (cathedral open Mondays, however). Admission charge to the cloister. Largo da Sé (phone: 866752).

Museu-Escola de Artes Decorativas (Museum-School of Decorative Arts) – Located just around the bend from the Largo de Santa Luzia *miradouro* and housed in a 17th-century palace that survived the earthquake, this museum contains collections of Portuguese porcelain, silver, crystal, paintings, tapestries, and furniture, mostly of the 17th and 18th centuries. They're not arranged museum-style, but much more beguilingly as the furnishings of an aristocratic Lisboan home of yesteryear. The objects once were the property of Dr. Ricardo Espírito Santo Silva, who set up a foundation both to create a museum and to preserve the skills and tools of traditional Portuguese craftsmanship. The foundation runs a school and workshops (phone: 872429) for the reproduction and restoration of antiques — furniture, books, fabrics, and so on — adjacent to the museum, which visitors may tour. An appointment is required for the workshops. The museum is open Tuesdays through Saturdays from 10 AM to 1 PM and 2:30 to 5 PM. Admission charge. 2 Largo das Portas do Sol (phone: 862184).

Igreja de São Vicente de Fora (Church of St. Vincent Outside the Walls) – From Largo das Portas do Sol, follow the *eléctrico* tracks down Escadinhas de São Tomé and then up again to this church, which was built during the late 16th and early 17th centuries by Filippo Terzi and sports a mannerist façade. A remnant of an old monastery, it is notable for its cloisters, lavishly lined with 18th-century *azulejos.* Beyond, set up in the old monastery refectory, is the Panteão Real (Royal Pantheon), the mausoleum of the Bragança family, which ruled Portugal from 1640 to 1910. Most of the Bragança kings and queens, including Portugal's last monarchs, are buried here. Open from 10 AM to 5 PM; closed Mondays. Admission charge to the cloisters and pantheon also gains entrance to an ornate sacristy, lined with inlaid marble. Largo de São Vicente (phone: 876470).

Igreja de Santa Engrácia – Begun during the 17th century but not completed until 1966, when it also was restored, this church gave rise to a Portuguese expression, "*obras de Santa Engrácia,*" used to describe a seemingly never-ending task. The grandiose structure, with a baroque façade and an interior richly decorated in marble, now serves as the Panteão Nacional (National Pantheon), containing the tombs of three Portuguese presidents and three writers, as well as memorials to other famous figures — including Prince Henry the Navigator, Luís de Camões, and Vasco da Gama — who are not buried here. This is within easy walking distance of São Vicente, but on Tuesdays and Saturdays, you may be detained by the flea market that's set up on the street between the two. Open from 10 AM to 5 PM; closed Mondays. Admission charge. Campo de Santa Clara (phone: 871529).

Museu Militar (Military Museum) – Housed in an 18th-century arsenal (the huge, saffron-yellow building in front of the Santa Apolónia train station), it contains cannon, guns, swords, armor, and uniforms, as well as paintings, sculptures, coin collections, and other mementos of Portugal's wars. One room is dedicated to the discoveries of Vasco da Gama. Open Tuesdays through Saturdays from 10 AM to 4 PM; Sundays, from 11 AM to 5 PM. Admission charge. Largo dos Caminhos de Ferro (phone: 867131).

Igreja da Madre de Deus (Church of the Mother of God) – Although the convent complex here was founded in 1501, most of what is seen today was built during the 18th century. The church is resplendent with ornate, gilded baroque woodwork, oil paintings, and *azulejos,* but the church is only part of the attraction, because the *Museu Nacional do Azulejo* is installed in the convent complex, and it's a must-see for tile lovers. Exquisite examples of the art, both Portuguese and foreign, from the 15th century to the present, are displayed in rooms around two cloisters, one of them a small gem. In addition to its other treasures, the museum possesses a long tile frieze dating from approximately 1730 that depicts a panorama of Lisbon before the earthquake. There's also a pleasant cafeteria, decorated with 19th-century kitchen tiles. Open from 10 AM to 1 PM and from 2 to 5 PM; closed Mondays. Admission charge. Bus No. 104 from Praça do Comércio goes to the convent. Rua da Madre de Deus (phone: 814-7747).

Nossa Senhora da Conceição Velha – Built during the early 16th century on the site of Lisbon's ancient synagogue, this was completely devastated in the 1755 earthquake, but its original Manueline portal survived. The beautiful doorway, richly carved with limestone figures, was retained for the new church — which, however, has little of note inside. Rua da Alfândega.

Casa dos Bicos (House of Pointed Stones) – When it was built during the 16th century, this house belonged to the family of Afonso de Albuquerque, a famous Portuguese viceroy to India. The earthquake reduced the 4-story structure to only several feet of foundations, but it was completely rebuilt. The façade is covered with pyramidal stones, similar to the Casa de los Picos in Segovia, Spain, and the Palazzo dei Diamanti in Ferrara, Italy. The house is now used as an art gallery and is open to the public only when there are special exhibitions. Rua dos Bacalhoeiros (phone: 870794).

BAIXA

Praça do Comércio – This impressive riverside square, laid out after the earthquake by the Marquês de Pombal, is edged on three sides by arcaded neo-classical buildings. It's also known as Terreiro do Paço (Palace Square), after the royal palace that stood here in pre-earthquake days, and, to the English, as Black Horse Square, after the bronze equestrian statue of King José I, a design by the 18th-century sculptor Joaquim Machado de Castro, standing in the middle. The triumphal arch on the north side of the square, leading to Rua Augusta and the rest of the Baixa, was finished during the late 19th century. The square was the scene of the assassination of King Carlos I and his son in 1908.

Rossio – Officially called Praça de Dom Pedro IV, after the 18th-century king who is the subject of the statue in the center, this is the heart of the city and the northern limit of the Baixa. As early as the 13th century, this was the city's marketplace, but like Praça do Comércio and the rest of the Baixa, it was destroyed by the earthquake of 1755; the square was then newly laid out by Pombal. On the north side is the 19th-century *Teatro Nacional de Dona Maria II,* standing on the site of a onetime royal palace that during the 16th century became the seat of the Inquisition. The square is much cheerier now, graced with flower stalls, fountains, and open-air cafés.

Elevador de Santa Justa (Santa Justa Elevator) – This lacy gray iron structure reminiscent of the Eiffel Tower — and often erroneously attributed to Alexandre-Gustave Eiffel — was designed by Raoul Mesnier, a Portuguese engineer of French descent, and erected in 1898. It not only spares visitors' feet the climb from Rua do Ouro (Rua Aurea) to Largo do Carmo in the Chiado, but also provides a panoramic view of the city from the top, and as you exit, you pass under a flying buttress of the Igreja do Carmo. The elevator runs from 7 AM to 11 PM (from 9 AM on Sundays).

Igreja do Carmo (Carmo Church) – Built during the 14th century, this was an imposing, majestic structure that overlooked the city until it was largely destroyed by the 1755 earthquake. The shell, with Gothic arches and a Gothic doorway, remains, and is floodlit at night. The ruins were turned into the *Museu Arqueológico do Carmo,* containing prehistoric, Roman, Visigothic, and medieval artifacts, as well as medieval sculpture, *azulejos,* and inscriptions. Open from 10 AM to 1 PM and from 2 to 5 PM (July through September, 10 AM to 6 PM); closed Sundays. Admission charge. Largo do Carmo (phone: 346-0473).

BAIRRO ALTO

Solar do Vinho do Porto – This comfortable bar run by the Port Wine Institute is the best place to sample Portugal's most famous wine — called port in English and *vinho do Porto* in Portuguese — without making a trip to the northern city. It's stocked with all types and vintages of port, which visitors can order by the glass. There are about 160 different kinds, so go early or, better, often. Take the funicular streetcar from Praça dos Restauradores. Open daily from 10 AM to 11:30 PM. 45 Rua de São Pedro de Alcântara (phone: 347-5707).

Igreja de São Roque (Church of St. Roch) – This 16th-century church has a flat wooden ceiling painted to look like a vaulted one, but it's best known for the baroque Capela de São João Baptista, the fourth chapel on the left. The chapel was commissioned during the mid-18th century by King João V, designed in Rome and assembled there, blessed by the pope — and then dismantled, to be shipped to Portugal and rebuilt at its present address. The lapis lazuli, porphyry, marble, alabaster, ivory, and other precious and semi-precious building materials cost the king dearly, but the workmanship was impeccable, as can be seen in the *Baptism of Christ,* which looks like an oil painting but is actually an exquisitely fine mosaic. The *Museu de São Roque* adjoining the church contains paintings and liturgical objects and richly embroidered vestments. Admission charge to the museum, which is open from from 10 AM to 5 PM; closed Mondays. Church remains open after museum closes. Largo Trindade Coelho (phone: 346-0361).

NORTHERN AND WESTERN LISBON

Parque Eduardo VII (Edward VII Park) – Downtown Lisbon's largest green space is this formally landscaped park at the northern end of Avenida da Liberdade, just beyond Praça Marquês de Pombal. From the esplanade at the top of the park, the view extends over the lower town to the Tagus. In the northwest corner is the charming Estufa Fria (Cold Greenhouse), where plants grow in luxuriant abundance among streams, pools, and waterfalls. A slatted roof protects them from the extremes of summer and winter and filters the sun's rays, suffusing the greenhouse with a magically soft light. Within the Estufa Fria is a hothouse, the Estufa Quente. Open daily from 9 AM to 6 PM (5 PM in winter); the Estufa Quente closes a half-hour earlier. Admission charge (phone: 682278).

Museu Calouste Gulbenkian (Gulbenkian Museum) – When the Armenian oil tycoon Calouste Sarkis Gulbenkian died in 1955, he left most of his estate and his enormous art collection to Portugal, the country to which he had fled during World War II and where he spent the last years of his life. The result was the Calouste Gulbenkian Foundation, a modern building that houses not only this museum, but also auditoriums, a library, and exhibition space. Don't miss the museum, a repository of 50 years of astute collecting — 3,000 pieces, including works Gulbenkian bought from the *Hermitage Museum* in the 1920s when the Soviet Union needed foreign currency. The treasures include fine European paintings, sculpture, 18th-century French furniture, Chinese vases, Greek coins, medieval ivories, illuminated manuscripts, Middle Eastern carpets and ceramics, and more. There also is a marvelous collection of small Egyptian pieces and a unique collection of Art Nouveau jewelry by René Lalique. Open June through November from 10 AM to 5 PM; closed Mondays (winter hours are the same except for Wednesdays and Saturdays, when the museum opens at 2 PM and closes at 7 PM). Admission charge. 45 Av. de Berna (phone: 797-4167).

Centro de Arte Moderna (Modern Art Center) – In the gardens behind the *Gulbenkian Museum,* it has an impressive collection of 19th- and 20th-century Portuguese paintings and sculpture, including paintings by José de Almada Negreiros. A cafeteria overlooks the gardens. The hours are the same as those of the *Gulbenkian Museum.* Admission charge. Rua Dr. Nicolau de Bettencourt (phone: 793-5131).

Jardim Zoológico (Zoo) – Set in a 65-acre park, the zoo is home to some 2,000 animals, including an elephant who rings a bell for money. Other distractions include pony rides for children, rowboats, and a small train. Open daily, from 9 AM to 7 PM, from April through October (closes at 6 PM the rest of the year). Admission charge. Parque das Laranjeiras (phone: 726-8041).

Palácio dos Marqueses da Fronteira – West of the zoo, on the edge of the Parque Florestal de Monsanto, is an interesting palace built during the second half of the 17th century and originally used by its aristocratic owners as a hunting lodge. It's notable for the great number of *azulejos* that cover its walls — both inside and outside in the formal gardens — many of them depicting historical events. The palace still is privately owned but open to visitors on Mondays and Wednesdays from 10 AM to noon and on Saturdays from 3 to 6:30 PM. Admission charge. 1 Largo de São Domingos de Benfica (phone: 778-2023).

Aqueduto das Aguas Livres – Built during the first half of the 18th century to bring water from Caneças (11 miles/18 km northwest of Lisbon) to a reservoir near the present-day *Amoreiras Shopping Center,* the Aguas Livres Aqueduct miraculously survived the 1755 earthquake and still supplies the city with drinking water. It consists of 109 stone arches, some of them underground, but an impressive stretch of it (with one arch 214 feet high) runs through the Parque Florestal de Monsanto and the Campolide section of town, and is visible from the road (N7) that leads to Estoril and Sintra. More information about the aqueduct can be obtained by calling the *Museu de Agua* (Water Museum; 12 Rua de Alviela; phone: 835532), itself worthy of interest; it chronicles the history of Lisbon's water supplies, going back to Roman times. The inside of the aqueduct, with its fountains and statuary, is open weekends in the summer only; the museum is open Tuesdays through Saturdays from 10 AM to 12:30 PM and from 2 to 5 PM; admission charge to the museum.

Basílica da Estrela (Basilica of the Star) – Built by Queen Maria I between 1779 and 1790, it fulfilled a vow she had made while petitioning God to grant her a son. The dome is one of Lisbon's landmarks; the tomb of the founder is inside. This church reflects the style of the school of sculpture founded at Mafra by the Italian sculptor Alessandro Giusti, one of whose Portuguese pupils, Joaquim Machado de Castro, was responsible for the manger figures here. Open daily. Praça da Estrela.

Museu Nacional de Arte Antiga (National Museum of Ancient Art) – One of the most important of Lisbon's museums, this is housed partly in a 17th-century palace that once belonged to Pombal and partly in an adjacent 20th-century building. Although it contains numerous foreign works, such as a celebrated Bosch triptych, *The Temptation of St. Anthony,* the museum is most notable for its paintings of the Portuguese school, especially of the 15th and 16th centuries. The prize in this group — perhaps the most famous painting in Portugal — is the six-panel polyptych known as the *Panéis de São Vicente de Fora* (St. Vincent Panels), a masterpiece by Nuno Gonçalves, the most important Portuguese painter of the 15th century. The polyptych is precious not only for its artistic merit (and because it's the only Gonçalves painting still extant), but also because it constitutes a document of Portuguese society of the time. Also in the museum are sculptures; Portuguese, European, and Oriental ceramics; objects in silver and gold; jewelry, furniture, and tapestries; and the entire gilt-and-tile-laden Saint Albert Chapel, an architectural leftover from a Carmelite convent that once occupied the spot. A tea garden overlooking the river is open in summer. Open from 10 AM to 1 PM and from 2:30 to 5 PM; closed Mondays. Admission charge. 95 Rua das Janelas Verdes (phone: 397-2725).

BELÉM

Mosteiro dos Jerónimos (Hieronymite Monastery) – One of Lisbon's great landmarks, this white marble monastery was founded in 1502 by King Manuel I to give thanks for the successful return of Vasco da Gama's fleet from the Indies and to commemorate all the great voyages of Portugal's explorers during the Age of Discovery. Because Vasco da Gama had sailed from Belém in 1497, to return 2 years later, the site of a small mariners' chapel here seemed a fitting one for the memorial, about which it is said that it was "built by pepper," since it was paid for by riches brought by the spice trade. The sea motifs — seashells, ropes, anchors, and other symbols — that are carved throughout in great profusion are the characteristic decorative elements of the Manueline style of architecture, a uniquely Portuguese style that represented a transition from Gothic to Renaissance and eventually took its name from the king, Dom Manuel. The monastery is considered the country's finest example of Manueline architecture: The two portals, the extremely slender columns and characteristic network vaulting of the church, and the richly sculpted 2-story cloister are exceptionally beautiful. King Manuel I and several other monarchs are buried in the church, as is Vasco da Gama, whose tomb, just inside the entrance, is marked by a caravel. Opposite it, marked by a lyre and quill pen, is a monument to Luís de Camões, whose bones may or may not be inside (he died in Africa, and the wrong bones may have been brought back). The long galleries to the west of the monastery, neo-Manueline from the 19th century, contain the *Museu Nacional de Arqueologia e Etnologia* (open from 10 AM to 2 PM and from 2 to 5 PM; closed Mondays; admission charge) and, around the corner, the *Museu de Marinha* (see below). More modern annexes across the courtyard from the entrance to the latter contain its collection of real boats rather than models and the *Planetario Calouste Gulbenkian,* which has presentations several days a week (times are posted outside; admission charge; phone: 362-0002). The monastery is open from 10 AM to 6:30 PM, July through September (to 5 PM the rest of the year); closed Mondays. Admission charge to the cloister. Praça do Império (phone: 362-0034).

Museu de Marinha (Naval Museum) – In the 19th-century galleries attached to the monastery, plus a modern extension to handle the overflow, this museum contains small models of boats from all eras of Portuguese history, from the earliest caravels of the Age of Discovery to warships, trading ships, and submarines — along with naval uniforms and other marine paraphernalia. Real boats are exhibited in the hangar-like extension. Of them, the late-18th-century *galeota,* or galley, built for the wedding of Crown Prince João (who became João VI) to a Spanish princess and rowed by 71 red-coated figures, is the star. Examples of traditional boats from various regions include a *rabelo* boat from the Douro River, a *moliceiro* from the Ria de Aveiro, and fishing boats from the Algarve. Open from 10 AM to 5 PM; closed Mondays. Admission charge. Praça do Império (phone: 362-0010).

Museu Nacional dos Coches (National Coach Museum) – Probably the finest coach collection in the world, housed in a building that was once the riding school of the Palácio de Belém, formerly a royal palace and now the presidential palace. The collection contains coaches ranging from the 16th through 19th centuries, and although a few are simple (such as the first one as you enter, which carried Philip III of Spain when he came to claim the throne as King Philip II of Portugal), most are beautifully carved, gilded works of art suitable for transporting royal personages or their emissaries (note the three Italian-made 18th-century baroque extravaganzas used by the Portuguese Ambassador to the Holy See). Open from 10 AM to 1 PM and from 2:30 to 5 PM; closed Mondays. Admission charge. Praça Afonso de Albuquerque (phone: 363-8022).

Padrão dos Descobrimentos (Monument to the Discoveries) – On the river in front of the monastery, this modern monument was put up in 1960 to commemorate the 500th anniversary of the death of Prince Henry the Navigator. It's shaped like the prow of a Portuguese caravel, with the prince as a figurehead leading a sculptured frieze of the personages of the time seaward. Inside, besides exhibition space, there's an elevator to a belvedere on top, from where the view extends up and down the Tagus and over formally laid-out green lawns to the Mosteiro dos Jerónimos and the rest of Belém. Open Tuesdays through Sundays from 9 AM to 7 PM (to 6 PM October through February); opens at 2 PM on Mondays; admission charge to the belvedere. Praça do Império.

Torre de Belém (Tower of Belém) – This quadrangular, 5-story tower, which looks like a huge chess piece, stands on the banks of the Tagus, west of the Monument to the Discoveries. The Portuguese consider it a symbol of their brave past, and its image often is used on official papers. Built during the 16th century to protect the river from pirates (because land has been reclaimed from the river since then, the tower was at one time farther out, surrounded by water), it later functioned as a prison. This is another example of Manueline architecture, richly decorated with sea motifs, statues, stone tracery, and Moorish balconies. Inside is a permanent exhibition of 15th- and 16th-century armaments and navigational instruments. Visitors may climb to the top for a view of the Tagus from the outside terrace. Open from 10 AM to 6:30 PM (to 5 PM from October through May); closed Mondays. Admission charge. Off Avenida Marginal (phone: 616892).

Palácio Nacional da Ajuda – In the hills behind Belém, this former royal palace was built during the early 19th century and is full of furniture, paintings, sculpture, and objets d'art left much as they were when royalty still occupied the premises. The widow of King Luís, Maria Pia of Savoy, who died in 1911, was its last royal inhabitant, but the palace is still used occasionally by the Portuguese government for state dinners. Open from 10 AM to 5 PM; closed Mondays. Admission charge. Largo da Ajuda (phone: 363-7095).

ENVIRONS

Estoril – This seaside suburb about 15½ miles (25 km) west of Lisbon became internationally famous during World War II when both Allied and Axis spies were tripping over each other, notably at the *Palácio* hotel. Since Portugal was neutral, there was a gentlemen's agreement: Allied diplomats could play golf at the local clubs on certain days, Axis diplomats on others. Immediately after the war, Estoril became home for numerous members of Europe's exiled royalty, giving it a touch of glamour. The crowned heads are gone now, but Estoril, with its bars and cafés and its gambling casino, is still a glamorous place. Its large turn-of-the-century mansions, hidden away behind spacious lawns and gardens flanking winding, hilly streets and wide avenues, lend it a definitely Old World air. The Parque do Estoril, a lovely garden of stately palm trees and purple-red bougainvillea, faces the seaside esplanade and the beach. The modern, elegant *Casino Estoril* sits at the top of the park. The residential district of Monte Estoril is west of the park, tending to merge with Cascais. By train, Estoril can be reached easily from Lisbon's Cais do Sodré station. By car, take either the beach highway (Estrada Marginal) or the new A5 toll highway that links Lisbon with Cascais and the towns in between.

Cascais – Once a simple fishing village whose picturesque, brightly painted boats headed out to sea each morning, Cascais (pronounced Kash-ka-*ish*) evolved during this century into a beach resort and the home of thousands of European — especially British — expatriates and, like Estoril, deposed royalty and dictators. Today, the fast-growing town, just west of Estoril, makes its living largely from tourism, although fishermen remain and the sight of fish being auctioned off at the market (on weekday evenings) by the beach is worth seeing. Cascais has few monuments to detain sightseers:

There is one important church, the Manueline Nossa Senhora da Assunção, notable for its 18th-century *azulejos* and for its paintings by Josefa d'Obidos; the Citadel, a 17th-century military building; and the *Museu-Biblioteca Condes de Castro Guimarães,* with paintings, sculpture, furniture, and objets d'art set up in an old mansion (open 10 AM to 5 PM; closed Tuesdays; no admission charge; Av. Rei Humberto de Italia; phone: 483-0856). The town has plenty of other distractions, however. The bullfights held on summer Sundays at the Monumental de Cascais attract many visitors. Water sports and sailing are available from its beaches; there are also riding stables, tennis courts, and golf courses in the vicinity. The town (and the coast around it) is famous for its seafood restaurants, many of which overlook the bay and the sea. There is no dearth of nightlife, either, as Cascais is full of bars and discos. Along the coast west of town is the Boca do Inferno (Mouth of Hell), a set of rocky cliffs full of caves and smaller cavities through which the sea storms and rages — an awesome sight. Farther along the coast road, 5½ miles (9 km) from Cascais, is Praia do Guincho, an immense stretch of sand between two promontories where the wind howls (*guincho* means "shriek"), the sea is rough, and the undertow dangerous; it is popular with brave surfers. Still farther along is a headland, Cabo da Roca, the westernmost point of continental Europe, where there is a lighthouse. Cascais can be reached by train from Lisbon's Cais do Sodré station.

Queluz – This town 7½ miles (12 km) northwest of Lisbon on the road to Sintra is known for its lovely pink rococo Palácio Nacional, where official guests of the Portuguese government usually are housed. The palace was begun in 1747 by the Infante Dom Pedro, who became Pedro III, consort of Queen Maria I, an unfortunate queen who lived here after going mad following Pedro's death and that of her oldest son. Designed by Mateus Vicente de Oliveira, a pupil of the architect of the Mafra Monastery, the royal residence took decades to finish and was restored after being partially destroyed by fire in this century. Its rooms are filled with Portuguese furnishings and tapestries, Italian glassware and marble, Dutch tiles, Chinese screens, Austrian porcelain, and other exquisite antiques; its gardens are laid out to resemble those of Versailles (Queen Maria had been engaged to Louis XV), with fountains, statuary, and *azulejos.* Among the more striking rooms are the Throne Room, the Hall of Mirrors, the Hall of the Ambassadors, the Music Salon, and the Queen's Dressing Room. In the summer, cultural events intended to re-create the ambience of the 18th-century court of Queen Maria — including costumed dances, chamber music concerts, and even games in which visitors can take part — are staged here. The palace is open from 10 AM to 1 PM and from 2 to 5 PM; closed Tuesdays. Admission charge (phone: 435-0039). Queluz can be reached by train from Lisbon's Rossio station.

■ **EXTRA SPECIAL:** The beauty of Sintra, a town on the north slope of the Serra de Sintra about 17½ miles (28 km) northwest of Lisbon, has been sung through the ages, most notably by Portugal's most famous poet, Camões, in *The Lusiads,* and by Lord Byron, who called it a "glorious Eden" in "Childe Harold's Pilgrimage." The town has an enchanting setting, swathed in towering trees, dense ferns, and plants and flowers of every description brought by the Portuguese from all corners of their once far-flung empire — all kept green by water gushing from the rocks in springs and little waterfalls tumbling everywhere down the mountain. Mists from the nearby Atlantic often envelop its heights and lend it an ethereal and unreal air (as well as give it a pleasant climate in summer while, on occasion, obscuring its majestic views). Among the oldest towns in Portugal, it was occupied by the Moors, who built two castles, one of them winding around the side of the mountain from pinnacle to pinnacle and the other in the center of the present town. After Sintra was taken from the Moors in the 12th century, it became a favorite summer residence of the Portuguese monarchs. Over the centuries, they built the imposing National Palace in town on the site of one of the Moorish castles and the whimsical, *Disneyland*-like Pena Palace on the very peak of the mountain, where it can be seen from as far away as Lisbon and the Arrábida Peninsula.

Sintra is very crowded in summer and on weekends. It can be reached by car on N117 and N249 or by train from the Rossio station. Those who come by train can take a taxi to visit the palaces that are located at some distance from the center; otherwise, the tourist office at Praça da República (phone: 923-3919) provides maps for those who want to walk. There also are horse-drawn carriages that take visitors sightseeing around town. Good restaurants and hotels abound, as do excellent shops selling handicrafts, especially rugs, porcelain, and straw goods. The Feira de São Pedro de Sintra, a market that takes place on the second and fourth Sundays of every month, sells everything imaginable. During the *Sintra Music Festival,* held from mid-June to mid-July, concerts featuring internationally known performers are held in the palaces and other public buildings.

The Palácio Nacional de Sintra, in the main square, was built on the foundations of a Moorish palace by King João I in the late 14th century and added to by King Manuel I in the early 16th century. It received still further additions later, making the enormous structure a survey of styles from Moorish through Mudéjar, Gothic, Manueline, and Renaissance to baroque. Outside, besides the twin conical chimneys that dominate the town, the most notable feature of the palace are the characteristic Manueline windows. Inside, its most important features are the *azulejos* facing its walls throughout, some of the finest to be seen in the country. One of the most interesting rooms is the Sala dos Brazoẽs (Hall of the Coats of Arms), built during Manuel's reign; its ceiling is an octagonal wooden cupola whose painted panels show the coats of arms of the king, his 8 children, and the 72 noble familes of Portugal at the time. (The blue-and-white wall tiles depicting hunting scenes are from the 18th century.) In the Sala das Pêgas (Hall of the Magpies), the ceiling is decorated with 136 magpies — painted, so the story goes, on the orders of João I after his wife, Philippa of Lancaster, caught him kissing one of the ladies-in-waiting. (There were 136 ladies-in-waiting at court, and the idea was to put an end to gossip among them.) The largest room is the Sala dos Cisnes (Hall of Swans), so named because of the ceramic swans decorating it and the painted ones on the ceiling. The palace is open from 10 AM to 1 PM and from 2 to 5 PM; closed Wednesdays. Admission charge (phone: 923-0085).

The Palácio Nacional da Pena, standing on the highest peak above Sintra, is reached up a spectacular road of hairpin curves through beautiful parks and woods. After religious orders were expelled from Portugal in 1832, Ferdinand of Saxe-Coburg-Gotha, consort of Queen Maria II, bought a small 16th-century monastery that stood on this spot and commissioned a German architect, Baron Eschewege, to create a new medieval palace around it. Inspired by the Bavarian castles in his own country, the architect combined their styles with Moorish, Gothic, and Manueline elements to create a fantastic building complete with gold-topped domes, turrets, crenelated walls, parapets, and a drawbridge. The cloister and chapel of the monastery were preserved; the latter has a black alabaster and marble altarpiece executed in the 16th century by Nicolas Chanterène, although its stained glass windows are 19th-century German. The rooms of the palace proper are filled with furniture and ornaments of many different periods and are particularly noteworthy because they have been left much as they were when last occupied by the royal family, which fled into exile in 1910. The views from the palace verandahs are spectacular, and the Parque da Pena surrounding it, planted in the 19th century, also is impressive, containing plants and trees from all over the world. The palace is open from 9 AM to 6 PM (to 5 PM in winter); closed Mondays. Admission charge (phone: 923-0227).

Still another of Sintra's palaces, the *Palácio dos Seteais,* has been turned into a luxury hotel (see *Checking In*), but there are other sights to see, including the Castelo dos Mouros, or Moorish Castle, located off the same road that leads to the Pena Palace, about halfway up the mountain. It was originally built by the Moors in the 8th or 9th century and was restored after the Christian Reconquest of the 12th century and later by King Fernando I. It has five rather dilapidated towers, a keep, and long walls that undulate over a great part of the mountain. Elsewhere is the Quinta de Monserrate, a palace and park built by a 19th-century Englishman, Sir Francis Cook, about 2 miles (3 km) from Sintra via N375. The palace is an odd-looking, three-domed structure, but it is the wonderful gardens, landscaped on a steep slope, that are the prime attraction (open daily, from 9 AM to sunset; admission charge). Another sight is the Convento dos Capuchos, 4 miles (6 km) from town via N247-3. Built in the 16th century, it is a peculiar place in that the monks' cells are carved out of rock and lined with cork to keep out the damp. (Ring the bell and the caretaker will open the door.)

SOURCES AND RESOURCES

TOURIST INFORMATION: Maps, brochures, shopping guides, listings of monthly events, and other information can be obtained from any of the Postos de Turismo (Tourist Posts) run by the Direcção-Geral do Turismo (Directorate General for Tourism), which is headquartered at 86 Avenida António Augusto de Aguiar. A tourist post is located at the same address (phone: 575086), but perhaps the most convenient one in downtown Lisbon is the one at Palácio Foz (Praça dos Restauradores; phone: 346-3624). Other branches are at Lisbon Airport (phone: 893689), at the Santa Apolónia train station (phone: 867848), and at the Alcântara boat dock (phone: 600756). English-speaking staff is available to answer questions and help make hotel reservations. It is possible to hire English-speaking guides through the tourist offices or by calling the guides union, the Sindicato Nacional da Actividade Turística, Tradutores e Intérpretes (phone: 342-3298).

The US Embassy is on Avenida das Forças Armadas (phone: 726-6600).

Local Coverage – The leading daily is the *Diário de Notícias,* a morning paper. *Seminario* and *Expresso* are two of the most prestigious weekly papers. English-language newspapers and magazines are on sale at most newsstands.

TELEPHONE: The city code for Lisbon is 1. If calling from within Portugal, dial 01 before the local number.

GETTING AROUND: Although various sections of the city, such as the Alfama, are ideal for strolling, remember that Lisbon is built on seven hills; visitors probably will want to ride from one section to another. Parking is problematic, so public transportation and taxis are the best bet.

Airport – Lisbon's airport for both domestic and international flights, Portela de Sacavém (phone: 802060), is only 5 miles (8 km) northeast of the center, a 15- to 30-minute drive, depending on traffic. Taxi fare to most Lisbon hotels should come to about $10. The *Linha Verde* (Green Line) express bus runs between the airport and the Santa Apolónia train station, stopping at major downtown points. *TAP Air Portugal* has a local address (3A Praça Marquês de Pombal; phone: 544080 or 575020). For information on *TAP*'s subsidiary, *Linhas Aéreas Regionais* (*LAR*), which has flights to many cities in Portugal, call 848-4754 or 848-7162. The independent company *Portugalia* (170 Rodrigues Sampaio; phone: 352-5336) also has flights to major regional destinations.

Boat – Ferryboats, carrying both passengers and cars, cross the Tagus every few minutes from the Praça do Comércio and Cais do Sodré for Cacilhas, Barreiro, and other points. Short cruises on the Tagus take place from April through October.

Bus – City buses and trams are run by *CARRIS* (*Companhia Carris de Ferro de Lisboa*). Maps and other information can be obtained at the window at the side of the Santa Justa Elevator, just off Rua do Carmo. Bus and tram fares vary according to the zone; the basic fare is about $1. Get on the bus by the front door, buy a ticket from the driver, and cancel it in the machine. Tourist passes for 4 or 7 days of unlimited travel by bus, tram, subway, ferryboat, and the Santa Justa Elevator can be bought at the Praça dos Restauradores and Praça Marquês de Pombal subway stations and at the Santa Justa Elevator. Lisbon's trams are not only vintage vehicles and picturesque in themselves, but many go through the more historic parts of the city, providing a cheap way to take a tour. Long-distance bus service is provided by *Rodoviária Nacional,* the state-owned bus company, whose terminal is at 18 Avenida Casal de Ribeiro (phone: 545439).

Car Rental – Most major firms have offices in Lisbon and at the airport: *Avis* (12C Av. Praia da Vitória; phone: 356-1176; at the airport; phone: 894836; at the Santa Apolónia train station; phone: 876887; and at the *Ritz Inter-Continental* hotel; phone: 692020), *Hertz* (10 Av. 5 de Outubro; phone: 579077; 10 Av. Visconde Seabra; phone: 797-2944; at the *Novotel Hotel,* 1642 Av. José Malhoa; phone: 726-7221; and at the airport; phone: 892722), and *Budget* (6 Av. Fontes Pereira de Melo; phone: 537717; and at the airport; phone: 801785 or 803981).

Elevator – The Elevador de Santa Justa takes passengers from Rua do Ouro (Rua Aurea) in the Baixa to Largo do Carmo in the Chiado. The Portuguese also refer to several streetcars that travel a steep route as "elevators," among them the Glória Elevator, running from Calçada da Glória, on the west side of Praça dos Restauradores, to the Bairro Alto. The unlimited-travel tourist pass is valid on elevators; individual rides cost about 20¢.

Subway – The underground system serving Lisbon is called the *Metropolitano.* A large "M" aboveground designates the stations — Rossio and Restauradores are the most central ones. The fare is about 40¢ — slightly less if bought in a machine — to any point. The unlimited-travel tourist pass is valid underground. Beware of pickpockets.

Taxi – Cabs are metered and inexpensive — a ride to almost any part of the city will cost less than $6. For trips outside Lisbon, a set rate per kilometer is charged beyond the city limits. Taxis can be hailed on the street or picked up at cabstands conveniently scattered around town. (Note that by law, passengers must get in and out on the sidewalk side, not the street side. Also by law, drivers may charge extra for luggage, but the regulation is vague and amounts are sometimes excessive.) To call a cab, dial 825060 or 825422.

Train – Frequent, fast electric trains connecting Lisbon with Belém, Estoril, and Cascais leave from the Estação Cais do Sodré (phone: 347-0181), by the river near Praça do Comércio. Trains to Queluz and Sintra operate from the Estação do Rossio (phone: 877092), just off the Rossio. (It's the 19th-century building with the charming, elaborately carved neo-Manueline façade just across from the side of the *Teatro Nacional.* Confusingly, it's hardly ever referred to by its real name, Estação Central, which is carved in neo-Manueline letters around its circular doors.) Trains for most of the rest of Portugal and elsewhere in Europe leave from Estação Santa Apolónia (phone: 876025), which is located along the river east of the Alfama district, not within walking distance of the center — take a bus or tram. The station for trains to the Algarve is

Estação Sul e Sueste (phone: 877179), on the river at Praça do Comércio. These southbound trains actually leave from Barreiro, on the south bank of the Tagus, but tickets include the price of the ferry ride from the station. Trains between Lisbon, Porto, and Faro have air conditioned coaches with bar and restaurant service.

LOCAL SERVICES: Courier (National/International) – *DHL International,* 37 Av. Marechal Gomes da Costa (phone: 859-9522; for pickups, 859-9017), and at the airport, Rua C, Edifício 124 (phone: 890009).

Dentist (English-Speaking) – The US Embassy has a list of English-speaking practitioners. Av. das Forças Armadas (phone: 726-6600).

Dry Cleaner/Tailor – *Lavandarias AmoreiraSec,* Shop 1003, *Amoreiras Shopping Center,* Av. Eng. Duarte Pacheco (phone: 692384).

Medical Emergency – Lisbon has three hospitals with emergency facilities: *Hospital São José* (phone: 872240); *Hospital de Santa Maria* (phone: 793-2762); and *Hospital São Francisco Xavier* (phone: 301-7351).

Messenger Service – *Pony Express,* 18-1° Av. Marquês de Tomar (phone: 522336).

Office Equipment Rental – *Inforgal,* 321 Av. 5 de Outubro (phone: 793-2650 or 793-4057).

Pharmacy – *The Farmácia Azevedo* is in Lisbon's central square, the Rossio (31 Praça de Dom Pedro IV; phone: 342-7478). Pharmacies take turns for weekend and after-hours service; each one posts the names of the shops on duty on its door.

Photocopies – *Rank Xerox Centre de Copias* (106 Av. António Augusto Aguiar; phone: 577110). Simple facilities also are widely available in stationery shops.

Post Office – There are two main downtown post offices. One (Praça dos Restauradores) is open weekdays from 8 AM to 10 PM, and the other (Praça do Comércio) is open weekdays from 8:30 AM to 6:30 PM.

Secretary/Stenographer (English-Speaking) – *Intess* (62 Rua São Julião; phone: 879947) or *American Typing Services* (phone: 539650). Both companies also can supply translators.

Telex – At two post office locations. One (Praça dos Restauradores) is open weekdays from 9 AM to 7 PM, and the other (in the Forum Center at 48C Av. Fontes Pereira de Melo; phone: 524030) is open from 9 AM to 7 PM daily.

Translator – Lynn de Albuquerque (phone: 419-2383); *Intess* (phone: 879947); and *American Typing Services* (phone: 539650).

Other – Tuxedo rental: *Guarda Roupa Anahory,* Rua Madalena (phone: 872046).

SPECIAL EVENTS: In ancient times, the *Festas dos Santos Populares* (Feasts of the Popular Saints), held in June, were celebrations of the summer solstice, but they are now Christian rites in honor of Santo António (St. Anthony), São João (St. John), and São Pedro (St. Peter). The *Feast of St. Anthony,* June 13 and the night before, is a bit like *New Year's Eve* and *New Year's Day.* Although most people associate St. Anthony (of Padua) with Italy, he actually was born in the Alfama in Lisbon, and people here make much ado about it. The Old Quarter comes alive on the eve: Dances are held in streets festooned with colored lanterns, and throughout the night gallons of good, rough wine are drunk to wash down mountains of sardines roasted on open barbecues. The saint is a powerful matchmaker, so this is the night when the city's young girls hope to meet their future husbands. Street stalls sell little pots of a spicy-smelling variety of sweet basil called *manjericão,* each pot holding a message of advice or consolation for lovers. In the Baixa, neighborhood associations bedecked in traditional costumes parade down Avenida da Liberdade, each attempting to outdo the display of the others. For the *Feast of St. John,* on June 23 and 24, people make bonfires sprinkled with scented herbs and thistles and jump over them to show their daring, an ancient rite connected with fertility. The final celebration is the *Feast of Saint Peter,* on June 29. In little towns around Lisbon, such as Montijo, there is a running of the bulls and a blessing of ships on this day.

MUSEUMS: In addition to those discussed in *Special Places,* the following museums may be of interest. Note that most museums are closed on Mondays, and that many that ordinarily have an admission charge are free on Sundays.

Museu da Cidade (City Museum) – Maps, engravings, and other objects telling Lisbon's history, set up in an 18th-century palace. Open from 10 AM to 1 PM and from 2 to 6 PM; closed Mondays. Admission charge. 245 Campo Grande (phone: 759-1617).

Museu Nacional do Teatro (National Theater Museum) – Costumes, scenery, drawings, programs, posters, and other theatrical memorabilia. Open from 10 AM to 1 PM and from 2:30 to 5 PM; closed Mondays. Admission charge. 10-12 Estrada do Lumiar (phone: 757-2547).

Museu Nacional do Traje (National Costume Museum) – Changing exhibitions of Portuguese and foreign costumes, accessories, and fabric, in a lovely old suburban house located about a mile north of the *City Museum.* Open from 10 AM to 1 PM and from 2:30 to 5 PM; closed Mondays. Admission charge. 5 Largo São João Baptista, Parque de Monteiro-Mor, Lumiar (phone: 759-0318).

Museu Rafael Bordalo Pinheiro – Devoted to the works of the 19th-century caricaturist, ceramist, and painter of the same name. Open from 10 AM to 1 PM and from 2 to 6 PM; closed Mondays. Admission charge. 382 Campo Grande (phone: 795-0816).

SHOPPING: The most important shopping area in Lisbon is the Baixa, the zone between the Rossio and the river, with the mosaic-paved, pedestrian street Rua Augusta as its backbone. Another shop-heavy street, Rua do Carmo, leads from this area to the part of the Baixa known as the Chiado, where many fashionable shops still are located, even though some of the more famous ones, along with two department stores, burned down in 1988, when fire ravaged much of this area. The damaged blocks are being rebuilt, but at present shoppers either take the Santa Justa Elevator to the Chiado or make their way from Rua do Carmo to Rua Garrett, the backbone of the area, via temporary scaffolding erected over the debris. Antiques row also is located in this part of the city: Rua Dom Pedro V, in the Bairro Alto, is the heart of it, but shops also congregate along Rua do Alecrim, Rua da Misericórdia, Rua São Pedro de Alcântara, and Rua da Escola Politécnica. Shops in the downtown area are open Mondays through Fridays, from 9 AM to 1 PM and 3 to 7 PM, Saturdays from 9 AM to 1 PM. Many *centros comerciais* (shopping centers) stay open until midnight, although not all of the shops in the complexes stay open that late. The most famous shopping center, with sophisticated shops of all kinds — more than 300 of them — is the *Centro Comercial das Amoreiras* (Amoreiras Shopping Center), a post-modernist complex (on Av. Engenheiro Duarte Pacheco) with huge towers in pinks and greens and glass, designed by architect Tomás Taveira. At the other extreme is the *Feira da Ladra* (Thieves' Market), a flea market held Tuesdays and Saturdays (on Largo de Santa Clara) at the edge of the Alfama. Among the best buys in Lisbon are gold, silver, and jewelry — it is relatively inexpensive, and the guaranteed content of the gold and silver make many pieces a bargain. There has been a renaissance in painting, tapestry making, and ceramics, with the accompanying opening of many new galleries. A revival in tile making, often in reproduction of 17th- and 18th-century designs, also has taken place, and many of the stores selling these wares will pack and ship. Rugs from Arraiolos and lace from Madeira, beautiful glass and crystal, copperware, fishermen's sweaters, and baskets are other good buys, along with fashionable clothing, shoes, and leather goods. Note that many of the shops below have branches in the *Amoreiras Shopping Center.*

Almorávida – A wide variety of regional crafts, pottery, and filigree jewelry plus an extensive collection of Portuguese-style, custom-made rugs. 10-14 Rua do Milagre de Sto. António (phone: 862261).

Ana Salazar – Clothes by Ana Salazar, Portugal's most famous avant-garde designer for women. 87 Rua do Carmo (phone: 347-2289).

Artesanato Arameiro – A wide variety of regional handicrafts — lace, rugs, ceramics, copperware, and filigree. 62 Praça dos Restauradores (phone: 342-0236).

Atlantis – Crystal tableware from Alcobaça. *Amoreiras Shopping Center* (phone: 693670).

Augustus – Elegant clothes for women. *Amoreiras Shopping Center* (phone: 693479).

Casa dos Bordados da Madeira – Embroidery and lace from Madeira and a wide selection of other Portuguese handicrafts. 135 Rua Primeiro de Dezembro (phone: 342-1447).

Charles – A very wide selection of shoes. 105 Rua do Carmo (phone: 347-7361) and 109 Rua Augusta (phone: 347-7360).

Charlot – Considered a very fashionable boutique, with designer labels from Portugal, Italy, and France. 28 Rua Barata Salgueiro (phone: 573665).

Diadema – Lovely gold and silver jewelry. 166 Rua do Ouro (phone: 342-1362).

Fábrica de Cerâmica Viúva Lamego – Makes and sells reproductions of old tiles; its bird and animal motifs are famous, but it also makes high-quality modern designs. 25 Largo do Intendente Pina Manique (phone: 315-2401).

Galeria Comicos – A good gallery showing avant-garde paintings. 1B Rua Tenente Raul Cascais (phone: 677794).

Galeria Sesimbra – Lisbon's second-oldest art gallery, known for hand-stitched Agulha tapestries, made from designs by leading contemporary Portuguese artists. 77 Rua Castilho (phone: 387-0291).

Galeria 111 – The longest established of Lisbon's art galleries, selling the best of today's Portuguese artists. 111 Campo Grande (phone: 797-7418).

Helio – Top-quality shoes for men and women. 93 Rua do Carmo (phone: 342-3171).

Livraria Bertrand – An enormous selection of books. Corner of Rua Garrett and Rua Anchieta (phone: 346-8646).

Livraria Buchholz – A large stock of foreign books as well as Portuguese ones. 4 Rua do Duque de Palmela (phone: 547358).

Madeira Gobelins – Embroidery, woven tapestries, and carpets from Madeira. 40 Rua Castilho (phone: 356-3708).

Madeira House – Lisbon's oldest shop dealing in genuine Madeira embroidery and lace, it also sells less expensive embroidered linens. 137 Rua Augusta (phone: 342-6813).

New York – A classy shop with the latest in women's clothes. 206 Rua do Ouro (phone: 342-1764).

Ourivesaria Pimenta – Fine jewelry, watches, and silver. 257 Rua Augusta (phone: 342-4564).

Porfirios – For young and trendy dressers. 63 Rua da Vitória (phone: 346-8274).

Quintão – Beautiful handmade Arraiolos rugs that are works of art. 30 Rua Ivens (phone: 346-5837).

Rosa & Teixeira – A highly ranked tailor that sells its own designs for men and women. 204 Av. da Liberdade (phone: 542063).

Sant'Anna – Reproductions of 17th- and 18th-century tiles, made in the shop's own factory. 95 Rua do Alecrim (phone: 342-2537). The factory, at 96 Calçada da Boa Hora, can be visited, but call first (phone: 363-8292).

Vista Alegre – The makers of Portugal's finest porcelain. 52-54 Rua Ivens (phone: 342-8581) and 18 Largo do Chiado (phone: 346-1401).

SPORTS AND FITNESS: Bullfighting – Portuguese bullfighting, quite different from the Spanish version, is more a spectacle of horsemanship than a fight. Bulls are never killed in the ring here, and the fighting is done mostly on horseback, with the *cavaleiros* wearing magnificent 18th-century costumes as they ride against the bulls. After the horseman finishes with a mock kill, the most eagerly awaited part of the bullfight begins: The *forcados* — eight young men dressed in brown pants, white shirts, cummerbunds, and tasseled caps — jump over the barrier and line up to wrestle the bull. Their leader taunts the bull to charge; when it does, he meets it head-on, mounting its head between the horns and grabbing it around the neck. The group then wrestles it to a halt. Although there is a bullfight at *Easter,* the season begins in earnest in June and generally runs through September, with contests usually held on Thursdays, Sundays, and holidays. The most important fights take place in Lisbon at the *Praça de Touros do Campo Pequeno* (Campo Pequeno Bullring), a mosque-like structure with minarets all around its walls (Av. da República; phone: 793-2093), and at the *Monumental de Cascais.*

Fishing – Boats for deep-sea fishing can be rented from local fishermen at Sesimbra, a fishing village 27 miles (43 km) south of Lisbon, or at Cascais.

Fitness Centers – *Health Club Soleil,* a chain, is in the *Lisboa Sheraton* hotel (1 Rua Latino Coelho; phone: 527353); the *Palácio* (in Estoril; phone: 468-8184); the *Estoril-Sol* (in Cascais; phone: 468-8005); and at the *Amoreiras Shopping Center* (Av. Engenheiro Duarte Pacheco; phone: 692907).

Golf – The *Clube de Golfe do Estoril* (on Av. da República in Estoril; phone: 468-0176) has 27 holes; caddies and clubs can be rented, and lessons by professionals are available. Also in the Estoril-Cascais area are the *Estoril-Sol Golf Club* (Estrada da Lagoa Azul; phone: 923-2461), with 9 holes belonging to the *Estoril-Sol* hotel; and the *Clube de Golfe da Marinha,* an 18-hole Robert Trent Jones course (in the Quinta da Marinha tourist development at Cascais; phone: 486-9881). The British *Lisbon Sports Club* has an 18-hole course (at Casal da Carregueira, on the Belas–Sabugo road, about 15½ miles/25 km northwest of Lisbon; phone: 431-0077). The *Aroeira Clube de Campo* (Quinta da Aroeira, Fonte da Telha; phone: 226-3244) has 18 holes on the coast, 9½ miles (15 km) south of Lisbon.

Horseback Riding – Equestrians can be accommodated at the *Clube de Campo de Lisboa* (south of Lisbon; phone: 226-1802 or 226-1060); at the *Clube da Marinha* (at Cascais; phone: 289282); at the *Pony Club Cascais* (Quinta da Bicuda; phone: 284-3233); and at the *Clube de Campo Dom Carlos I* (Estrada Areia, Praia do Guincho; phone: 285-1403).

Jogging – Attractive as it may seem, jogging in Lisbon's central Parque Eduardo VII is not recommended, especially alone or at night. Instead, run along the riverside between the Ponte 25 de Abril and Belém. Another good place is the fitness circuit in the *Estádio Nacional* (National Stadium) area on the outskirts of the city on the way to Estoril, where the track winds through pleasant pine woods. (But do not jog alone.) The park in Estoril and the seafront in Cascais are also good, as is the jog down the median strip of Avenida da Liberdade from the Praça Marquês de Pombal toward the Baixa.

Soccer – This is Portugal's most popular sport by far, and it's ruled by a triumvirate of three top clubs: *Sporting* and *Benfica,* from Lisbon, and *Porto,* from the northern capital of Porto. Any game in which one of these teams takes part should be worth watching, as the rivalries are very intense. (Note that the crowds are not unruly here and there has been no hooliganism, as in some other parts of Europe.) The season runs from August until the end of June, and matches are played on Sundays at various stadiums; tickets can be obtained with the help of the hotel desk.

Swimming – The entire coast west of the city and south of it across the river is banded with sandy beaches, and many hotels have private swimming pools. However, water pollution has become a problem on some of the beaches between Lisbon and Estoril, so check first about possible health hazards. (Don't go in the water unless the blue safety flag is flying.) In Estoril, the *Tamariz* restaurant, on the beach, has changing rooms.

Tennis – Courts are available at Estoril's *Clube de Tênis* (Av. Amaral; phone: 468-6669); at the *Clube de Campo Dom Carlos I* (Estrada Areia, Praia do Guincho; phone: 285-2362); and at the *Lisbon Sports Club* (Casal da Carregueira, 15½ miles/25 km northwest of Lisbon near Belas; phone: 431-0077).

THEATER: Classic and contemporary plays are presented year-round except during July at the *Teatro Nacional de Dona Maria II* (Praça Dom Pedro IV; phone: 347-1078); performances take place in Portuguese. The *revista,* or revue, a popular Lisbon tradition embracing topical sketches, satire, music, and dancing reminiscent of old-fashioned vaudeville, can make for a lively evening even for those who don't understand the language. Many of the best revues are presented in small theaters in the rather ramshackle Parque Mayer theater district, just off Avenida da Liberdade.

MUSIC: Lisbon's opera house, the *Teatro Nacional de São Carlos,* is near the Chiado district downtown (9 Rua Serpa Pinto; phone: 346-5914). Built in the 18th century, it is one of Europe's prettiest, with an apricot-colored interior set off by touches of green and gold. The season runs from mid-December until May. Various ballet companies also perform at the opera house, but the *Gulbenkian Foundation Ballet Company,* sponsored by the foundation, is one of the best ballet companies in Europe at the moment, performing both classical and modern dance. Performances take place at the auditorium of the Gulbenkian Foundation building (45 Av. de Berna; phone: 797-4167). Symphony and chamber music concerts can also be heard here and at the *Teatro Municipal de São Luís* (Rua António Maria Cardoso; phone: 342-7172).

NIGHTCLUBS AND NIGHTLIFE: A good place to begin an evening with a pre-dinner glass of dry, white port is *A Brasileira* (122 Rua Garrett), one of Lisbon's traditional old cafés. Take a seat at one of the tables outdoors and watch the world go by; the gentleman in bronze, occupying the bronze table, flanked by bronze chairs, is the poet Fernando Pessoa (1888–1935) — this statue of him was placed here on the 100th anniversary of his birth. A second old café popular among the old guard is *Café Nicola,* on the Rossio.

Lisbon's popular *fado* houses — restaurants with *fado* music — are scattered throughout the old Alfama and Bairro Alto districts. *Fado,* which means "fate" or "destiny," is the name given to the anecdotal, satirical, sentimental, or occasionally happy songs performed, usually by a woman swathed in black (the *fadista*), to the accompaniment of one or more 12-stringed guitars. Although *fado* has become commercialized and many restaurants beef up their shows with folk dancing and popular music, a visitor may be lucky enough to be on hand some night when the singers and the musicians are in the mood to revive the real thing. Do not make a sound during the singing — neither the singers nor the spectators permit it. Some particularly good spots are *Senhor Vinho* (18 Rua do Meio à Lapa; phone: 397-2681), where the *fado* is pure; *O Faia* (54 Rua da Barroca; phone: 342-1923), one of the best known; *Adega Machado* (91 Rua do Norte; phone: 346-0095), entertaining because it offers spirited folk dancing; *Lisboa à Noite* (69 Rua das Gáveas; phone: 346-8557); and *A Severa* (51-61 Rua das Gáveas; phone: 346-4006). All are in the Bairro Alto, except *Senhor Vinho,* which is in the Lapa district west of the Bairro Alto. Those who are not dining should go after 10 PM. Reservations are essential.

Fado still draws its loyal fans, but over the years discotheques have become the most popular spots for Lisbon's midnight-oil burners. The clientele is cosmopolitan, and the action goes on into the wee hours of the morning. On busy nights, the more conservative top discotheques are sometimes difficult to get into for all but regular customers (they're often frequented by local socialites). Provided there's room, though, a properly dressed (no shorts or jeans) traveler should have no trouble gaining admission. Among the longest-established (and starchiest) of the Lisbon haunts are *Stones* (1 Rua do Olival; phone: 396-4545) and *Ad Lib* (18 Rua Barata Salgueiro; phone: 356-1717). The more relaxed longstanding favorites include *Whispers* (35 Av. Fontes Periera de Melo; phone: 575489), *Fragil* (128 Rua da Atalaia; phone: 346-9587), and *Zona Mais* (formerly *Loucuras;* 37 Av. Pedro Alvares Cabral; phone: 681117). The trendiest of all (and the most crowded) are *Alcântara Mar* (11 Rua da Cozinha Económica; phone: 362-1226) and *Kremlin* (5 Escadinhas da Praia; phone: 608768). In a category of its own, the very fashionable *Bar Bairro Alto* (50 Travessa dos Inglesinhos; phone: 342-2717) features shows and other special events. For fans of African music, *Clave di Nos* (100 Rua do Norte; phone: 346-8420) is a bar-restaurant in the Bairro Alto that has live music from the Cape Verde Islands, with food to match. Good bars for a pre-disco or pre-dinner drink include the antiques- and curio-filled *Pavilhão Chines* (89 Rua Dom Pedro V; phone: 342-4729), on the edge of the Bairro Alto; *Procópio* (21 Rua Alto de São Francisco; phone: 652851), a pub-like hangout for artists, writers, theaterfolk, and politicians; and *Cerca Moura* (4 Largo das Portas do Sol; phone: 874859), in the Alfama, with an outdoor terrace with splendid views of the city.

Bars to try in Estoril include the *Founder's Inn* (11D Rua Dom Afonso Henriques; phone: 468-2221) and the *English Bar* (Estrada Marginal, Monte Estoril; phone: 468-0413). In Estoril, however, don't miss a night at the world-famous *Casino Estoril* (phone: 268-4521), a shiny, modern building in the Parque Estoril. The gambling rooms are open every day (to those over 21 endowed with a passport) from 3 PM to 3 AM, and have all the classic European and American games: roulette, baccarat, chemin de fer, blackjack, French bank, slot machines, and bingo. The roulette stakes are higher than in Portugal's other casinos, and the slot machines sometimes spit out jackpots of more than $200,000. But gambling is only one of the attractions. The glittering restaurant-nightclub resembles the *Lido* in Paris, with balconies and a main floor seating 800 and the only really international show in the country.

Cascais has a spirited nightlife, with many bars and cafés such as the *John Bull,* an English-style pub (32 Praça Costa Pinto; phone: 483-3319); *Tren Velho,* a converted train coach sitting beside the station (Av. Duquesa de Palmela; phone: 486-7355); *Bar 21,* an attractive cocktail lounge (1A Travessa da Misericórdia; phone: 486-7518); and *Cutty Sark* (6 Travessa da Ressureição). The list of popular discos includes *Coconuts* (7 Boca do Inferno; phone: 284-4109), with an outdoor terrace by the sea; *Julianas* (10 Av. 25 de Abril; phone: 486-4052); and the very snooty *Van Gogo* (9 Travessa da Alfarrobeira; phone: 483-3378). For *fado* in Cascais, try *Forte Dom Rodrigo* (Estrada de Birre; phone: 285-1373) or *Picadeiro Maria d'Almeida* (Quinta da Guia, Torre; phone: 486-9982).

BEST IN TOWN

CHECKING IN: A visitor's primary decision will be whether to stay right in Lisbon, to commute (with thousands of *lisboetas*) from Estoril or Cascais via the clean, inexpensive trains that run into the city about every 20 minutes, or even to stay in Sintra. Whichever your choice, a double room with a private bath will cost from $225 to $350 a night in a hotel in the expensive category, from $100 to $200 in the moderate range, and less than $100 in the inexpensive range. Reservations are necessary. All telephone numbers are in the 1 city code unless otherwise indicated.

LISBON

Alfa – A very modern 350-room luxury high-rise near the zoo and the *Gulbenkian Museum.* It has 3 restaurants (one with a panoramic view), a swimming pool, a sauna, shops, and a hairdresser. Business facilities include 24-hour room service, meeting rooms for up to 230, an English-speaking concierge, foreign currency exchange, audiovisual equipment, and photocopiers. Av. Columbano Bordalo Pinheiro (phone: 726-2121 or 726-2626; in the US, 800-843-6664; fax: 726-3031; telex: 18477). Expensive.

Altis – This 9-story ultramodern hotel of steel, glass, and concrete has 307 rooms, a nice view from its rooftop grill, and a heated indoor swimming pool. Business facilities include 24-hour room service, meeting rooms for up to 400, an English-speaking concierge, foreign currency exchange, secretarial services in English by prior arrangement, audiovisual equipment, photocopiers, and translation services. It's located about halfway between the Rossio train station and Parque Eduardo VII. 11 Rua Castilho (phone: 522496; fax: 548696; telex: 13314). Expensive.

Diplomático – Well situated near Parque Eduardo VII, it has 90 rooms equipped with air conditioning, mini-bars, and TV sets, plus a restaurant, bar, and private parking. Business facilities include 24-hour room service, meeting rooms for up to 80, an English-speaking concierge, foreign currency exchange, audiovisual equipment, and photocopiers. 74 Rua Castilho (phone: 356-2041; fax: 522155; telex: 13713). Expensive.

De Lapa – Unquestionably Lisbon's most graciously luxurious lodgings — and possibly the city's priciest. A handsomely converted palace in its own gardens with a harmoniously designed modern annex, it has 102 rooms (including 8 suites), with views over the old Lapa embassy quarter and the Tagus River. All rooms have satellite TV and direct-dial phones; 24 of them have Jacuzzis. Among the pluses are 2 pools, a fitness center, and a good restaurant called the *Embaixada,* with a Swiss chef who specializes in French fare. Business facilities include 24-hour room service, meeting rooms for up to 230, an English-speaking concierge, foreign currency exchange, secretarial services in English, translation services, and fax machines in the rooms on request. 4 Rua Pau da Bandeira (phone: 395-0005; fax: 395-0665). Expensive.

Lisboa Plaza – Centrally located off Avenida da Liberdade, redecorated by a leading Portuguese designer, and elegant, this is family owned and operated. It has 93 air conditioned, soundproofed rooms (with mini-bars, TV sets, and all the rest), in addition to the *Quinta d'Avenida* restaurant; the bar, done in Art Nouveau style, is a popular meeting place. Business facilities include 24-hour room service, an English-speaking concierge, foreign currency exchange, secretarial services in English, photocopiers, and translation services by prior arrangement. 7 Travessa do Salitre (phone: 346-3922; fax: 347-1630; telex: 16402). Expensive.

Lisboa Sheraton – One of the best of the chain in Europe, this 400-room high-rise offers comfortable accommodations, marble bathrooms, and elegant public areas and lounges. All rooms are air conditioned, and there is a heated, open-air swimming pool, plus several restaurants (including the 29th-floor *Panorama*), bars, shops, and a health club. Business facilities include 24-hour room service, meeting rooms for up to 550, an English-speaking concierge, foreign currency exchange, secretarial services in English, audiovisual equipment, photocopiers, computers by previous arrangement, and translation services. It's located a bit away from the city center, a few blocks north of Prâça Marquês de Pombal. 1 Rua Latino Coelho (phone: 575757; in the US, 800-334-8484; fax: 547164; telex: 12774). Expensive.

Meridien – This sparkling modern luxury hotel — offering 350 rooms — overlooks Parque Eduardo VII. The decor runs to chrome, marble, and splashing fountains, and the restaurants feature French cooking, hardly unusual in a hotel run by a subsidiary of *Air France.* Business facilities include 24-hour room service, an English-speaking concierge, foreign currency exchange, secretarial services in English, audiovisual equipment, photocopiers, computers, cable television news, and translation services. 149 Rua Castilho (phone: 690900; in the US, 800-543-4300; fax: 693231; telex: 64315). Expensive.

Penta – Large, modern, and just a short cab ride from the center of town, beyond the *Gulbenkian Museum.* It has restaurants and bars, a disco, shops, a swimming pool on the grounds, and a shuttle service to the city center and the airport; the 592 rooms are fully equipped, with private baths, balconies, color TV sets, video, radio, and direct-dial telephones. Business facilities include meeting rooms for up to 600, an English-speaking concierge, foreign currency exchange, secretarial services in English, audiovisual equipment, photocopiers, cable television news, and translation services. 1600 Av. dos Combatentes (phone: 726-4554; in the US, 800-225-3456; fax: 726-4418; telex: 18437). Expensive.

Ritz Inter-Continental – On a hill overlooking Parque Eduardo VII, next door to the *Meridien,* this luxury establishment is contemporary on the outside (built in the 1950s), but traditional within. The appointments are dazzling — silks, satins, and suedes — and some of its 260 rooms and 40 suites are furnished with reproductions of antiques. It has large public rooms and a lovely piano bar overlooking the park, fine shops, a tearoom, coffee shop, disco, and beauty parlor, as well as the *Ritz Grill Room* (see *Eating Out*), one of the most fashionable restaurants in Lisbon. Bedrooms are air conditioned, soundproofed, and equipped with minibars, TV sets, radio, and in-house movies; some have balconies overlooking the park. Business facilities include 24-hour room service, meeting rooms for up to 700, an English-speaking concierge, foreign currency exchange, secretarial services in English, audiovisual equipment, photocopiers, computers, cable television news, and translation services. 88 Rua Rodrigo da Fonseca (phone: 692020; in the US, 800-327-0200; fax: 691783; telex: 12589). Expensive.

Dom Rodrigo – A centrally located apartment-hotel, it features 9 twin-bed studios, 39 suites, and 9 penthouses. All accommodations are air conditioned and well soundproofed, and have fully equipped kitchenettes and satellite TV. An outdoor pool is an added asset, helping to make this a viable alternative to a standard downtown hotel. For those who prefer to stay out of the kitchen, there is a coffee shop — but no restaurant. Business facilities include an English-speaking concierge; secretarial services in English and translation services can be arranged. 44-50 Rua Rodrigo da Fonseca (phone: 315-4800; fax: 315-4805). Expensive to moderate.

Tivoli – Well situated, with 350 rooms and suites. Because it's so convenient, right on the main avenue downtown, the lobby is a popular meeting place for businesspeople as well as tourists (and the excellent bar just off the lobby is a favorite of local journalists). There is a restaurant, plus a popular rooftop grillroom, a small pool set in a garden, and tennis courts. Business facilities include 24-hour room service, meeting rooms for up to 200, an English-speaking concierge, secretarial services in English, audiovisual equipment, photocopiers, cable television news, and translation services. 185 Av. da Liberdade (phone: 530181; fax: 579461; telex: 12588). Expensive to moderate.

Amazonia – One of a growing number of Portuguese hotels whose strategy is to remain within a moderate price range by sacrificing frills and concentrating instead on convenience. In this case there's no restaurant, but all 192 rooms have satellite TV and direct dial phones. The hotel also boasts a Brazilian-style bar and a heated outdoor swimming pool. Business facilities include 24-hour room service, meeting rooms for up to 200, and an English-speaking concierge; secretarial services in English and translation services can be arranged. Bright and modern, in an old quarter near the *Amorieras Shopping Center.* 12 Travessa Fábrica dos Pentes (phone: 387-7006; fax: 387-9090). Moderate.

Carlton – This small, charming hostelry is only a block away from the *Calouste Gulbenkian Center.* There are 72 rooms, all with satellite TV, safes, mini-bars, hair dryers, and a marble-based decor. No restaurant, but guests may breakfast in the pleasant indoor patio, dominated by a spreading palm tree. English-speaking concierge. 56 Av. Conde Valbom (phone: 795-1157; fax: 795-1166). Moderate.

Dom Carlos – A comfortable place to stay at Praça Marquês de Pombal. The 73 rooms are air conditioned and equipped with private baths, TV sets, and mini-bars. No restaurant, but there is a breakfast room and a bar. Business facilities include 24-hour room service, an English-speaking concierge, foreign currency exchange, and photocopiers. 121 Av. Duque de Loulé (phone: 539071; fax: 352-0728; telex: 16468). Moderate.

Eduardo VII – Not far from Praça Marquês de Pombal, it has 110 air conditioned rooms with private baths and other conveniences. There also is an excellent rooftop restaurant with a view of the city. Business facilities include meeting rooms for up to 40, an English-speaking concierge, foreign currency exchange, secretarial services in English, audiovisual equipment, and photocopiers. 5 Av. Fontes Pereira de Melo (phone: 530141; fax: 533879; telex: 18340). Moderate.

Flórida – It has 120 air conditioned rooms with all the facilities (bath, telephone, TV set, radio); no restaurant, but there's a bar, a gift shop, and a hairdresser. Business facilities include 24-hour room service, meeting rooms for up to 100, an English-speaking concierge, foreign currency exchange, photocopiers, and translation services. Near Praça Marquês de Pombal, at 32 Av. Duque de Palmela (phone: 576145; fax: 543584; telex: 12256). Moderate.

Príncipe – Northeast of Parque Eduardo VII, it has 70 air conditioned rooms, each with a private bath, a TV set, and a telephone, plus a restaurant and bar. 201 Av. Duque de Avila (phone: 536151). Moderate.

Príncipe Real – A small downtown hotel with a traditional flavor, located off Avenida da Liberdade in the vicinity of Parque Mayer and the Botanical Garden. There are 24 rooms, all with air conditioning and a TV set, nearly all with a balcony. The top-floor dining room has a swath of picture window affording a view across the city to St. George's Castle. 53 Rua da Alegria (phone: 346-0116; fax: 342-2104). Moderate.

Rex – Modern, with 70 rooms, and on the edge of Parque Eduardo VII, near the more prestigious *Ritz* and *Meridien* hotels. All rooms have air conditioning, a TV set, and a radio; half have balconies overlooking the park. There are 2 restaurants (one with a panoramic view) and a bar. Business facilities include meeting rooms for up to 200, foreign currency exchange, audiovisual equipment, photocopiers, and translation services. 169 Rua Castilho (phone: 682161; fax: 687581; telex: 18120). Moderate.

Senhora do Monte – This small place is a real find. Located up in the old Graça quarter northeast of St. George's Castle, it has good views of Lisbon from some of its 27 rooms (all with private baths). It's not the best location for access, but old hands swear by it. Business facilities include an English-speaking concierge and foreign currency exchange. 39 Calçada do Monte (phone: 866002; fax: 877783). Moderate.

Tivoli Jardim – On a quieter street behind its sister, the *Tivoli,* and therefore, a much quieter hotel. Modern, it has 120 rooms (each with a private bath and many with balconies), a restaurant, a bar, a snack bar, and a car park. The service is first rate, and guests have access to the *Tivoli*'s pool and tennis courts. Business facilities include 24-hour room service, meeting rooms for up to 200 at the *Tivoli* hotel next door, an English-speaking concierge, foreign currency exchange, secretarial services in English (also at the *Tivoli*), photocopiers, and translation services. 7-9 Rua Júlio César Machado (phone: 539971; fax: 556566; telex: 12172). Moderate.

Veneza – An attractively converted townhouse, with 38 rooms. Though it stands right next to the imposing *Tivoli,* it manages not to be overawed by its neighbor. Its most striking feature is its handsome staircase, thrown into relief by modern murals depicting the city of Lisbon. All the rooms are air conditioned, with satellite TV and direct dial phones. Business facilities include an English-speaking concierge and photocopiers; secretarial services in English and translation services can be arranged. 189 Av. da Liberdade (phone: 352-6700; fax: 352-6678). Moderate.

York House – Like *Senhora do Monte,* this is an insider's inn. One of the most attractive places to stay in Lisbon, although it is some distance west of the heart of the city, close to the *Museu Nacional de Arte Antiga.* Housed in a 17th-century building that was once a convent, this lovely, 45-room, antiques-filled *pensão* has a restaurant, and a nice bar with tables in the garden — a particular favorite of British visitors, writers, and embassy personnel. Across and down the street a bit, in an 18th-century house (No. 47) that once belonged to the writer Eça de Queirós, there's an equally old-fashioned and aristocratic 17-room annex to this small hostelry, making a total of 62 rooms (not all with private bath). Business facilities include an English-speaking concierge, foreign currency exchange, and photocopiers. 32 Rua das Janelas Verdes (phone: 396-2435; fax: 397-2793; telex: 16791). Moderate.

Zurique – In an excellent location, near the *Campo Pequeno* bullring, this modern place has 252 rooms with a full range of services, including a health club, a pool, a restaurant, and a bar. Business facilities include meeting rooms for up to 280 and an English-speaking concierge; secretarial services in English and translation services can be arranged. 18 Rua Ivone Silva (phone: 793-7111; fax: 793-7290). Moderate.

Dom Manuel – Modern and efficient (64 rooms, each with a private bath), and just around the corner from the *Gulbenkian Museum.* The rooms are small but comfortably appointed, with air conditioning, TV sets, and video. There is a breakfast room and a bar, but no restaurant. Business facilities include meeting rooms for up to 12, an English-speaking concierge, foreign currency exchange, and photocopiers. 189 Av. Duque de Avila (phone: 576160; fax: 576985; telex: 43558). Moderate to inexpensive.

Insulana – In the Baixa, this exceedingly central, friendly *albergaria* (inn) has 32 rooms, each with a private bath. Business facilities include an English-speaking concierge and foreign currency exchange. 52 Rua Assunção (phone: 342-3131). Inexpensive.

Torre – This modern, attractive little place is a 15-minute taxi ride from the center of Lisbon, but convenient for sightseeing in Belém, where it's right beside one of Lisbon's best known sights — the Jerónimos Monastery. There are 50 rooms with private baths, a bar, and a restaurant. Business facilities include an English-speaking concierge and foreign currency exchange. 8 Rua dos Jerónimos (phone: 363-7332; fax: 645995). Inexpensive.

ESTORIL

Atlántico – In the pleasant residential district of Monte Estoril, this is a modern spot on the sea (or rather, nearly on the sea, since the electric train tracks run between it and the beach). There are 175 air conditioned rooms (some with balconies overlooking the Atlantic), a terrace with a large saltwater swimming pool, an excellent restaurant, a bar, a nightclub, and a billiards room. Business facilities include meeting rooms for up to 80, an English-speaking concierge, foreign currency exchange, audiovisual equipment, and photocopiers. Estrada Marginal, Monte Estoril (phone: 468-5170; fax: 468-3619; telex: 18125). Expensive.

Lennox Country Club – A hillside *estalagem* (inn) standing in a garden setting overlooking the coast. There are 32 rooms with private baths, some in the main building, which was once a private home, and some in modern additions, plus a very good restaurant with excellent service, a kidney-shape, heated outdoor swimming pool, and a tennis court. The inn emphasizes golf — golfing memorabilia decorate it, there is a putting green, and free transportation is provided to courses in the area, as well as to area riding stables. 5 Rua Engenheiro Alvaro Pedro de Sousa (phone: 468-0424; fax: 467-0859; telex: 13190). Expensive.

Palácio – Imagine Allied and Axis spies peeping around pillars during World War II and the jewels of exiled royalty glinting in the light of crystal chandeliers; that's the essence of this gracious Old World hotel by the park. The public rooms are majestic; the staff is the sort that seems to remember everyone who has ever stayed here; and the 200 rooms and suites, with traditional and contemporary furnishings, are air conditioned. In addition to the dining room, there is the adjoining, superlative *Four Seasons Grill* (see *Eating Out*). A heated swimming pool and cabañas are in the lovely gardens behind the hotel; the beach on the Atlantic is a 5-minute walk away. Temporary membership in the nearby *Estoril Golf Club* is available (hotel guests don't pay greens fees); there are tennis courts next door. Business facilities include 24-hour room service, meeting rooms for up to 300, an English-speaking concierge, foreign currency exchange, secretarial services in English, audiovisual equipment, photocopiers, and translation services. Parque Estoril (phone: 468-0400; fax: 468-4867; telex: 12757). Expensive.

Grande – On a hill overlooking the sea in Monte Estoril, this is a modern establishment with 73 rooms with private baths (some with balconies), a bar, a restaurant, and a covered swimming pool. Business facilities include foreign currency exchange and photocopiers. Av. Sabóia, Monte Estoril (phone: 468-4609; fax: 468-4834; telex: 13807). Expensive to moderate.

Praia – This modern property is near the park in front of the *Palácio.* It has 91 air conditioned rooms, some with balconies, a panoramic restaurant on the seventh floor, a bar, and a swimming pool. Business facilities include 24-hour room service, meeting rooms for up to 40, an English-speaking concierge, foreign currency exchange, and photocopiers. Estrada Marginal (phone: 468-1811; fax: 468-1815; telex: 16007). Expensive to moderate.

Alvorada – Another modern hostelry, near the casino, it has 51 rooms, each with private bath and a balcony. There's no swimming pool, but there is a solarium on top, and the hotel is only 200 yards from the beach. Breakfast room and bar; no restaurant. Business facilities include an English-speaking concierge, foreign currency exchange, and photocopiers. 3 Rua de Lisboa (phone: 468-0070; fax: 468-7250; telex: 13573). Moderate.

Founder's Inn – British-owned and also known as the *Estalagem do Fundador,* it has 14 pleasant rooms with private baths, each furnished differently. The restaurant serves excellent English cooking; there's also a bar, with music, that's a local nightspot. A freshwater pool is on the grounds, which are on a hillside, set back from the beachfront. There is an English-speaking concierge and foreign currency exchange. 11 Rua Dom Afonso Henriques (phone: 468-2221; fax: 468-8779). Moderate.

Inglaterra – A charming, turn-of-the-century private home-turned-hotel, set in gardens near the *Palácio.* Inside, the 45 rooms (each with a private bath) are spare and contemporary, rather than old-fashioned in style; there's a bar, restaurant, and swimming pool, an English-speaking concierge, foreign currency exchange, and photocopiers. 1 Rua do Porto (phone: 468-4461; fax: 468-2108; telex: 65235). Moderate.

Lido – Very comfortable and modern, this hostelry is in a quiet spot on a hillside away from the beach, but not far from the casino and park. The 62 rooms and suites all have private baths and balconies, telephones, and radios; there is a restaurant, a bar, a large swimming pool, a solarium, and a terrace with a view of the ocean. Business facilities include an English-speaking concierge, foreign currency exchange, and photocopiers. 12 Rua do Alentejo (phone: 468-4098). Moderate.

Pica-Pau – A good inn in a nice old white-painted villa with a red tile roof, near the *Lido* and the *Founder's Inn.* The 48 rooms with private baths are completely modern; there is a bar, a restaurant, and a swimming pool. Also, an English-speaking concierge and foreign currency exchange. 48 Rua Dom Afonso Henriques (phone: 468-0803; fax: 467-0664). Inexpensive.

Smart – A *pensão* in a very large old house. It has 16 rooms — most with television sets and private baths (the rest have washbasins) — a breakfast room (no restaurant), and a garden with palm trees. It's not far from the beach. There's also an English-speaking concierge. No credit cards accepted. 3 Rua José Viana (phone: 468-2164). Inexpensive.

CASCAIS

Albatroz – A luxury property perched on the rocks at the water's edge. The location is choice, which is not hard to understand since the core of this hotel was built during the 19th century as a villa for the royal family. Between the original building and a newer balconied addition, there are 40 rooms with bath. An excellent restaurant (see *Eating Out*) and bar, both surrounded by windows overlooking the sea, and a swimming pool with plenty of room for sunbathing are further attractions. Business facilities include meeting rooms for up to 30, an English-speaking concierge, foreign currency exchange, secretarial services in English, audiovisual equipment, photocopiers, and translation services. 100 Rua Frederico Arouca (phone: 483-2821; fax: 284-4827; telex: 16052). Expensive.

Cidadela – Near the center of town, with 140 rooms and some apartments, each with its own seaview balcony. Facilities include a good restaurant, a bar, and a swimming pool set amid attractive gardens. Business facilities include 24-hour room service, meeting rooms for up to 100, an English-speaking concierge, foreign currency exchange, audiovisual equipment, photocopiers, and translation services. Av. 25 de Abril (phone: 483-2921; fax: 486-7226; telex: 66895). Expensive.

Estoril-Sol – The biggest on the coast, with 347 rooms and suites. It's east of town, between the center of Cascais and Monte Estoril, and is separated from the water only by the electric train tracks (an underground passage leads directly to the beach). The hotel is rife with facilities: an Olympic-size swimming pool, a children's pool, 5 bars, a large, panoramic rooftop restaurant, a disco, shops, a health club, a sauna, squash courts, a bowling alley, and its own 9-hole golf course in lovely surroundings nearby. Business facilities include 24-hour room service, meeting rooms for up to 1,200, an English-speaking concierge, foreign currency exchange, secretarial services in English, audiovisual equipment, photocopiers, cable television news, and translation services. Parque Palmela (phone: 483-2831; in the US, 800-843-6664; fax: 483-2280; telex: 15102). Expensive.

Farol – A charming *estalagem* (inn) in a building that was once the private house of an aristocratic family. It's located by the sea, just west of the center along the road to Boca do Inferno and Praia do Guincho. It has 20 rooms with bath, a swimming pool, a tennis court, a bar, a snack bar, and a restaurant that overlooks the water. There's an English-speaking concierge and foreign currency exchange. 7 Estrada da Boca do Inferno (phone: 483-0173; fax: 284-1447; telex: 14658). Expensive.

Guincho – The waves crash on three sides of this restored 17th-century fortress that looks out to sea from a rocky promontory 5½ miles (9 km) northwest of Cascais. The location is spectacular, with beach on both sides, although walking on the beach is recommended more than going in the water, due to the treacherous undertow here, near the westernmost point of continental Europe. The 36 rooms and suites in this elegant establishment all have private baths, old brick-vaulted ceilings, telephones, mini-bars, and TV sets, and some have balconies. There is a bar and a panoramic restaurant (see *Eating Out*). Business facilities include an English-speaking concierge, foreign currency exchange, secretarial services in English, audiovisual equipment, photocopiers, and translation services. Praia do Guincho (phone: 285-0491; in the US, 800-843-6664; fax: 285-0431; telex: 43138). Expensive.

Baia – Right on the beach, in the heart of town, where the local fishermen tie up their painted boats. There are 85 rooms in this modern hotel, most with balconies; restaurant and terrace bar. Business facilities include an English-speaking concierge, foreign currency exchange, and photocopiers. Av. Marginal (phone: 483-1033; fax: 483-1095; telex: 43468). Expensive to moderate.

Dom Carlos – This *pensão* in the center of Cascais occupies a restored house built in 1640, and the breakfast room and chapel maintain the decorations of that period. There are 18 rooms with private baths, a TV salon, and a tree-filled garden. 8 Rua Latino Coelho (phone: 486-8463). Moderate.

Nau – The location is convenient — in front of the train station and only 150 yards or so from the beach. Modern, it has 56 rooms with private baths and balconies, plus a TV room, a bar, and a restaurant with a terrace. An English-speaking concierge and foreign currency exchange are on hand. No credit cards accepted. 14 Rua Dra. Iracy Doyle (phone: 483-2861; telex: 42289). Moderate.

Valbom – An *albergaria* (inn) in the center of Cascais, near the train station, it's better-looking inside than from the outside. There are 40 rooms with private baths; there's a bar, but no restaurant (breakfast is served). There is an English-speaking concierge and a foreign currency exchange. No credit cards accepted. 14 Av. Valbom (phone: 483-2831). Inexpensive.

SINTRA

Palácio dos Seteais – One of the loveliest and most romantic hotels in Europe. Built at the end of the 18th century for the Dutch consul in Lisbon, it was sold to the fifth Marquês de Marialva and was often visited by royalty. Marble gleams underfoot and murals line the walls of the public rooms; the 29 guestrooms and 1 suite are beautifully decorated with antiques, handwoven rugs, and tapestries, but no TV sets and no mini-bars to destroy the neo-classical illusion. Located just outside Sintra, the hotel does have a television lounge, a bar, and a well-known restaurant (see *Eating Out*) overlooking spacious gardens, a formal, windowed salon with views of the Sintra Valley, and a swimming pool and tennis courts. Business facilities include meeting rooms for up to 12, an English-speaking concierge, foreign currency exchange, audiovisual equipment, and photocopiers. 8 Rua Barbosa do Bocage (phone: 923-3200; fax: 923-4277; telex: 14410). Expensive.

Tivoli Sintra – The best in town, this is situated off the main square of Sintra, right by the National Palace. The modern building has all the modern conveniences, along with traditional Portuguese touches in the decor. There are 75 air conditioned rooms with private baths, balconies, TV sets, and telephones. A highly regarded restaurant with a view (see *Eating Out*), lounges, bars, a hairdresser, and a garage are among the facilities. Business facilities include 24-hour room service, meeting rooms for up to 220, an English-speaking concierge, foreign currency exchange, secretarial services in English, audiovisual equipment, photocopiers, cable television news, and translation services. Praça da República (phone: 923-3505; fax: 923-1572; telex: 42314). Expensive.

Central – Short on rooms (only 11, all with private bath), it's long on charm, and it's on the main square, in front of the palace. There is a tearoom, a bar, and a pleasant restaurant with a terrace for lunch in the summer. 35 Praça da República (phone: 923-0063). Moderate.

Sintra – In São Pedro de Sintra, a 10-minute walk from downtown. This *pensão* has 13 rooms (10 with private baths), a swimming pool, a TV room, and a breakfast room (no restaurant). There is an English-speaking concierge and a foreign currency exchange. No credit cards accepted. Travessa dos Avelares, São Pedro de Sintra (phone: 923-0738). Inexpensive.

Portugal's *Tourism in the Country* program — a network of elegant old aristocratic estates and manor houses (categorized as *Turismo de Habitação* properties), simpler but still fine country homes (*Turismo Rural*), and farmhouses (*Agroturismo*) that take in small numbers of paying guests — is most active in the rural north, but travelers interested in this type of accommodation do have some choices in the Lisbon area. Among them is the charming *Casal de São Roque,* by the sea in Estoril. Built at the beginning of the century and furnished accordingly, it has 6 rooms for guests, 4 with private baths; the hosts will serve meals upon request. Contact Casal de São Roque (Av. Marginal, Estoril 2765; phone: 268-0217). In the center of Cascais, there's the *Casa da Pérgola* (13 Av. Valbom, Cascais 2736; phone: 284-0040), set in lovely gardens, offering a luxurious suite and 5 bedrooms with private baths.

Sintra has four properties. The *Quinta de São Tiago* (Sintra 2710; phone: 923-2923) is an imposing noble house several centuries old, surrounded by vast lawns with a swimming pool, near the *Palácio dos Seteais.* There are 7 double bedrooms, luxuriously furnished with antiques; the owners (an Englishman and his Spanish wife) serve meals on request. The *Quinta da Capela* (Estrada de Monserrate, Sintra 2710; phone: 929-0170) is another impressive old noble house surrounded by gardens, located beyond Seteais and the Quinta de Monserrate. One suite and 4 beautifully furnished bedrooms with private baths — or 2 independent apartments — are available. The *Vila das Rosas* (2-4 Rua António Cunha, Sintra 2710; phone: 923-4216) is a large, white 19th-century house with a red tile roof on the northern outskirts of Sintra; 4 double rooms with bath, a suite of 3 rooms with a private bath, and a cottage in the garden are available. In summer, breakfast is served in the cool wine cellar; other meals are served on request. Finally, the *Casa da Tapada* (Sintra 2710; phone and fax: 923-0342) is a 19th-century country mansion situated on a mountaintop, with a view of the Pena and Mouros palaces in front. There are 5 large rooms, all with bath. A buffet breakfast is served in the dining room, and dinner can be arranged upon request. The *Quinta de São Tiago* and the *Quinta da Capella* are in the expensive price category; the remaining two are moderate. Reservations for the above houses can also be made through certain central booking agencies (see *Accommodations,* GETTING READY TO GO).

EATING OUT: Portuguese food offers a surprising variety of tastes. Over the centuries, this seagoing nation's cuisine has come under the influence of far-flung countries in Asia, Africa, and the Americas, as well as neighboring Spain and nearby France. Lisbon's restaurants reflect this heritage (and all its regional permutations). Fish and seafood abound and usually are fresh and delicious. Those who want to splurge should order steamed lobster or grilled prawns, or dishes such as *arroz de marisco* (rice with shellfish). Stuffed crab and boiled sea spider (eaten by cracking it open with a wooden mallet) are flavorful, and codfish is a great local favorite — it's said the Portuguese have as many ways to prepare it as there are days in the year, one of the best being *bacalhau à Gomes de Sá,* named for a Porto restaurant owner. The best restaurants serve delicious smoked swordfish, sliced very thin, with lemon and capers, but for something uniquely Portuguese, sample the charcoal-grilled sardines sold in the street. Although Lisbon's meat is best grilled, typical dishes such as *cozido à portuguesa* (a stew of boiled vegetables, sausages, and different types of meats, popular in the north) and *iscas à portuguesa* (thin slices of calf's liver marinated in wine, garlic, and bay leaves, and cooked in a shallow earthenware dish) are worth trying. Desserts, mostly based on eggs, sugar, and almonds, tend to be too sweet for some palates, but there are good cheeses — *queijo da Serra,* from northeastern Portugal, and Serpa, from the Alentejo, are among the best. Wines from all over the country appear on the city's wine lists. The rule is to choose those that are more than 5 years old (except for northern *vinhos verdes,* which should be less than 2 years old, but which are not often found in Lisbon). Pungent, fruity bairrada wines, mellow, woody dão wines, and flowery douro wines are all good. Bucelas is an excellent white from a small demarcated zone north of Lisbon.

Dinner for two, with a local wine, averages from $90 to $110 at restaurants listed below as expensive, from $50 to $70 at moderate establishments, and from $30 to $50 at inexpensive restaurants. Customary dining time is no earlier than 7:30 PM, but many restaurants close their kitchens at 11 PM. Lunch is served between noon and 2:30 PM. All telephone numbers are in the 1 city code unless otherwise indicated.

LISBON

Alcântara Café – Next door to the very fashionable *Alcântara Mar* discotheque, in a renovated warehouse, this has become one of the city's trendiest eateries. It also boasts some of the tastiest food in Lisbon. The imaginative French-Belgian menu is studded with gems such as duck spiced with rosemary and house pâté with pickled grapes, both nearly legendary among local gastronomes. The wine selection is traditional Portuguese. Closed for lunch weekends and holidays. Reservations necessary. Major credit cards accepted. 11 Rua da Cozinha Económica (phone: 363-7176). Expensive.

Antonio Clara – Located in a 19th-century, Art Nouveau mansion that is now a municipal monument, this dining spot run by the same owners as *Clara* (below) specializes in Portuguese fare and fine fish dishes. It also boasts a good wine cellar. Open Mondays through Saturdays for lunch and dinner. Reservations necessary. Major credit cards accepted. 46 Av. de República (phone: 766380). Expensive.

Aviz – One of the best dining places in town. When the old *Aviz* hotel — where the multimillionaire Calouste Gulbenkian spent the final days of his life in Lisbon — was torn down, Chef Alberto Rapetti and some of his staff opened this restaurant just off Largo do Chiado, bringing with them all the elegance and flair that had made the old hostelry an international favorite. The decor is very Belle Epoque, the food excellent, and the service flawless. Closed Saturdays at lunch and on Sundays. Reservations advised. Major credit cards accepted. 12B Rua Serpa Pinto (phone: 342-8391). Expensive.

Casa da Comida – This discreetly elegant restaurant is in a converted house, with tables set around a charming enclosed garden and an adjoining period bar. The food is delicious and beautifully presented. Closed Saturdays at lunch and Sundays. Reservations advised. Major credit cards accepted. 1 Travessa das Amoreiras (phone: 685376). Expensive.

Chester – Although this attractive little spot near the *Ritz* specializes in steaks, it also has shellfish alive in tanks for the choosing and the fish is always fresh. Closed Sundays. Reservations advised. Major credit cards accepted. 87 Rua Rodrigo da Fonseca (phone: 687811). Expensive.

Clara – Very elegant and spacious, serving excellent regional Portuguese and international food — one of Lisbon's best. It's in an old house with gardens that are illuminated at night. Closed Sundays. Reservations advised. Major credit cards accepted. 49 Campo dos Mártires de Pátria (phone: 355-7341). Expensive.

Escorial – A famous dining place in a district, near Praça dos Restauradores, that's noted for seafood. Elegantly decorated, with a nice bar, and known for good service, it also serves excellent international cuisine. Closed only on the first of May — *Labor Day* in Europe. Reservations advised. Major credit cards accepted. 47 Rua das Portas de Santo Antão (phone: 346-3758). Expensive.

Michel – The owner, a well-known cook on television in Portugal, specializes in nouvelle cuisine, Portuguese-style, although traditional French dishes also are served. Handsomely decorated, this is in the Alfama, just below St. George's Castle. Closed Saturdays at lunch and Sundays. Reservations necessary. Major credit cards accepted. 5 Largo de Santa Cruz do Castelo (phone: 864338). Expensive.

Ritz Grill Room – The restaurant of the *Ritz* hotel prepares unusually good continental food and is a fashionable gathering place for Lisbon businesspeople. Open daily. Reservations advised. Major credit cards accepted. 88 Rua Rodrigo da Fonseca (phone: 692020). Expensive.

Tágide – A beautiful staircase leads from the small dining room on the first floor to a second-floor dining area where picture windows afford a great view of the Tagus, a must for visitors who want to see the city and eat well at the same time. Portuguese and international dishes share the menu; the service is impeccable, yet pleasant. Closed Sundays. Reservations necessary. Major credit cards accepted. 18 Largo da Biblioteca Pública (phone: 342-0720). Expensive.

Tavares – Lisbon's oldest, it began as a café in 1784 and became a luxurious restaurant in 1861. After celebrating its 200th birthday, this city landmark had its gold leaf walls redone, its mirrors replated, its armchairs reupholstered, and more, so the light from its crystal chandeliers shines on a scene that's as opulent as ever, the haunt of businesspeople, government officials, and the like, and the perfect setting for excellent food and fine wine. Closed Saturdays at lunch and on Sundays. Reservations advised. Major credit cards accepted. 37 Rua da Misericórdia (phone: 342-1112). Expensive.

Conventual – The menu is based on old Portuguese convent and monastery recipes, some of which go back to the 17th century, and objects from churches decorate the premises. Typical dishes include *bacalhau com coentros* (cod with coriander) and *ensopado de borrego* (lamb stew). Closed Saturdays at lunch and Sundays. Reservations advised. Major credit cards accepted. 44 Praça das Flores (phone: 609196). Expensive to moderate.

Restaurante 33 – Good food and a pleasant atmosphere prevail in this well-appointed restaurant behind an elegant clapboard façade, not far from the *Ritz.* Closed Sundays. Reservations advised. Major credit cards accepted. 33 Rua Alexandre Herculano (phone: 546079). Expensive to moderate.

Sua Excelência – In the Madragoa quarter, near the embassy residences. Knock on the door to gain entry, and the attentive owner will read out the entire menu in English, if so desired. He serves a very good *açorda* (a sort of "dry" soup, or stew, a combination of seafood, bread, eggs, and coriander) and Mozambique prawns with a peppery sauce. Closed Wednesdays and the month of September. Reservations unnecessary. Major credit cards accepted. 42 Rua do Conde (phone: 603614). Expensive to moderate.

Caseiro – A good restaurant among the many near the Jerónimos Monastery in Belém. It is typically Portuguese, specializing in regional dishes and seafood, and attractively decorated. Closed Mondays. Reservations advised. Major credit cards accepted. 5 Rua de Belém (phone: 363-8803). Moderate.

Faz Figura – Overlooking the Tagus in the Alfama quarter, its wood paneling and leather chairs give it the atmosphere of an exclusive club, but there is also a verandah where diners can sit and watch the ships on the river. Fish and seafood, Portuguese and international dishes, are available. Closed Sundays. Reservations unnecessary. Major credit cards accepted. 15B Rua do Paraíso (phone: 868981). Moderate.

Gondola – A long-established Italian eatery near the *Gulbenkian Museum,* and a favorite with visitors. There's a lovely vine-covered garden for summer dining. Closed Saturday evenings and Sundays. Reservations advised. Major credit cards accepted. 64 Av. de Berna (phone: 797-0426). Moderate.

Laçerda – Also near the *Gulbenkian Museum,* this small place used to be a butcher shop and is still devoted to meat (choose a cut from the hook by the door). Photos of celebrities who have dined here decorate the walls, and strings of garlic and onions hang from the ceiling. Closed Sundays. Reservations unnecessary. No credit cards accepted. 36 Av. de Berna (phone: 797-4057). Moderate.

Pap'Açorda – The entrance to this Bairro Alto bakery-turned-restaurant is through an old wood-paneled bar. Inside, there is a very attractive enclosed patio banked with green plants. The mixed fish grilled on a skewer is very good, but the specialty of the house is the porridgy seafood-bread-eggs-and-coriander mixture known as *açorda.* Closed Saturdays at lunch and Sundays. Reservations advised. Major credit cards accepted. 57 Rua da Atalaia (phone: 346-4811). Moderate.

Varina da Madragoa – An old tavern turned into a blue-and-white tiled restaurant, near Parliament. Good Portuguese food, including excellent *bacalhau,* or codfish. Closed Saturdays at lunch and Mondays. Reservations unnecessary. Major credit cards accepted. 36 Rua das Madres (phone: 396-5533). Moderate.

Bomjardim – Considered tops in preparing *frango na brasa,* chicken that's charcoal-broiled on a rotating spit and, if it's desired, accompanied by a fiery chili sauce (*piri piri*). This is one of Lisbon's most popular — and least expensive — culinary delights. There are two *Bomjardim* restaurants facing each other just off Praça dos Restauradores. Noisy and crowded at lunchtime; open daily. No reservations or credit cards accepted. 10-11 Travessa de Santo Antão (phone: 342-7424). Inexpensive.

Bota Alta – Traditional Portuguese cooking, served in a cheery bistro atmosphere. It's in the midst of all the Bairro Alto nightlife, and usually very busy. Closed Sundays. Reservations advised — or go early. Major credit cards accepted. 35-37 Travessa da Queimada (phone: 342-7959). Inexpensive.

Porto d'Abrigo – Although not imposing in appearance, this tiny eatery is one of Lisbon's culinary landmarks. Famous for its Portuguese specialties, it's usually very crowded at lunchtime. Closed Sundays. Reservations advised. Major credit cards accepted. 16 Rua dos Remolares (phone: 346-0873). Inexpensive.

Xico Carreira – In the picturesque, rather shabby theater district off Avenida da Liberdade, it's off the beaten track for most people and full of local color. A former bullfighter owns it; posters and mementos of the sport decorate it. Try the *bife à cortador* (a big grilled steak) or the *cozido transmontano* (boiled dinner of vegetables, sausages, and meats). Crowded at lunchtime. Closed Sundays. Reservations unnecessary. Major credit cards accepted. Parque Mayer (phone: 346-3805). Inexpensive.

ESTORIL

Casino Estoril – The glittering, balcony-lined restaurant here is known for its international show — at 11:30 PM every night, with stars such as Julio Iglesias and Dionne Warwick — but it's no less recommendable for food and service, both excellent. It has a long menu listing Portuguese and international dishes. Open daily. Reservations advised. Major credit cards accepted. Parque Estoril (phone: 468-4521). Expensive.

Choupana – On a cliff overlooking the sea a bit over a mile (2 km) east of Estoril, this specializes in seafood, but has a varied menu of other dishes as well. The dining room is large, panoramic, and air conditioned. Later at night, there is a show and music until all hours. Open daily. Reservations advised. Major credit cards accepted. Estrada Marginal, São João do Estoril (phone: 468-3099). Expensive.

Four Seasons Grill – A very elegant place for the finest dining in Estoril. The long menu of Portuguese and international dishes changes four times a year, according to the seasons, and when it does, so does the china, the decor, and the waiters' uniforms. It is run by the *Palácio* hotel, which is next door, and can be entered using either its own street entrance or the hotel lobby. Open daily. Reservations advised. Major credit cards accepted. *Hotel Palácio,* Rua do Parque, Estoril (phone: 468-0400). Expensive.

English Bar – This brown-and-white building overlooks the water, with windows all around. It's cozily decorated in the English manner (and has a popular bar), but serves very good Portuguese and international dishes. Closed Sundays. Reservations unnecessary. Major credit cards accepted. Estrada Marginal, Monte Estoril (phone: 468-0413). Expensive to moderate.

A Maré – By the sea with a lovely panoramic view and a varied menu. There is a large air conditioned dining room and, in summer, an outside barbecue. Open daily. Reservations unnecessary. Major credit cards accepted. Estrada Marginal, Monte Estoril (phone: 468-5570). Expensive to moderate.

Ferra Mulinhas – Portuguese and Hungarian cooking. It's open for dinner only and is closed Tuesdays. Reservations unnecessary. Major credit cards accepted. 5A Rua Viveiro (phone: 468-0005). Moderate.

Garrafão – A fish and seafood spot with its own vivarium, on the outskirts of Estoril. Closed Thursdays. Reservations unnecessary. Major credit cards accepted. Amoreira (phone: 468-4195). Inexpensive.

CASCAIS

Albatroz – This outstanding restaurant — the dining room of the hotel of the same name — is set on rocks at the edge of the sea. It's known for a varied menu of well-prepared dishes, including good seafood, and the picture windows that surround it make it exceedingly fine for its views as well. Open daily. Reservations necessary. Major credit cards accepted. 100 Rua Frederico Arouca (phone: 483-2821). Expensive.

Baluarte – By the sea, with 2 air conditioned dining rooms featuring splendid views. It specializes in seafood, but also has a long menu of other Portuguese and international dishes. Open daily. Reservations advised. Major credit cards accepted. 1 Av. Marechal Carmona (phone: 486-5471). Expensive.

Hotel do Guincho – The restaurant here, in a cliff-top hotel that was once a fortress guarding continental Europe's westernmost extremity, is surrounded by windows looking onto the crashing Atlantic. The location alone makes it a wonderful lunch or dinner spot for those on a day's outing along the coast, but the excellence of the food — with emphasis on seafood — and of the service would recommend it even without the view. Located 5½ miles (9 km) northwest of Cascais. Open daily. Reservations advised. Major credit cards accepted. Praia do Guincho (phone: 285-0491). Expensive.

João Padeiro – From its beginnings a number of years ago as a simple eatery, this has become one of the most renowned seafood restaurants in Cascais. Old stone grinding wheels and pieces from windmills decorate the three dining rooms most attractively. Closed Tuesdays. Reservations necessary. Major credit cards accepted. 12 Rua Visconde da Luz (phone: 483-0232). Expensive.

Muchaxo – In an *estalagem* of the same name, this is one of the most famous seafood spots on the Lisbon coast. The inn is by the sea, so there is a marvelous view over the water. Open daily. Reservations unnecessary. Major credit cards accepted. Praia do Guincho (phone: 285-0221). Expensive.

Pescador – A charming place near the fish market, it is decorated with a fishermen's motif. Fish and seafood are very good here. Open daily. Reservations unnecessary. Major credit cards accepted. 10B Rua das Flores (phone: 483-2054). Expensive to moderate.

O Batel – Nicely decorated in a rustic fashion, this is another good seafood restaurant, near the fish market. Open daily. Reservations unnecessary. Major credit cards accepted. 4 Travessa das Flores (phone: 483-0215). Moderate.

Beira Mar – One of the longest established of the seafood eateries near the fish market. Decorated with blue and white tiles, it serves international fare in addition to good seafood. Open daily. Reservations unnecessary. Major credit cards accepted. 6 Rua das Flores (phone: 483-0152). Moderate.

Burladero – By the bullring, it is large and air conditioned, and specializes in grilled meats. Closed for lunch on Wednesdays and Thursdays. Reservations unnecessary. Major credit cards accepted. Praça de Touros (phone: 486-8751). Moderate.

John Bull – A well-known English pub with a good little restaurant attached; international fare is served. Open daily. Reservations unnecessary. Major credit cards accepted. 31 Praça Costa Pinto (phone: 483-3319). Moderate.

O Pipas – A smart seafood spot in the center of town, near the fish market, it consists of a small air conditioned dining room decorated with wine barrels and hanging garlic braids and sausages. Open daily. Reservations unnecessary. Major credit cards accepted. 1B Rua das Flores (phone: 486-4501). Moderate.

A Taverna de Gil Vicente – This cozy little restaurant has a fireplace and features international cooking. Closed Wednesdays. Reservations unnecessary. Major credit cards accepted. 22 Rua dos Navegantes (phone: 483-2032). Moderate.

Galegos – Near the center of town, this simple place serves Portuguese and northern Spanish dishes. Open daily. Reservations unnecessary. Major credit cards accepted. 3 Av. Valbom (phone: 483-2586). Inexpensive.

QUELUZ

Cozinha Velha – The name means "Old Kitchen" — and this is the former royal kitchen of the National Palace at Queluz, now turned into a restaurant with consderable atmosphere. It has high stone arches, a 15-foot-long marble worktable, a walk-in fireplace, enormous spits, and walls lined with copper pots and utensils, many of them originals. Excellent food, combined with the splendor of the setting, make this an experience to remember. Air conditioned; open daily. Reservations necessary. Major credit cards accepted. Palácio Nacional de Queluz (phone: 435-0232). Expensive.

Poço – Large, with 3 air conditioned dining rooms where good Portuguese food is served. Closed Mondays. Reservations unnecessary. Major credit cards accepted. 33 Av. da República (phone: 435-7737). Inexpensive.

SINTRA

Monserrate – The floor-to-ceiling windows of this air conditioned hotel restaurant afford a panoramic view of the valley below Sintra. The menu features international dishes. Open daily. Reservations necessary. Major credit cards accepted. *Hotel Tivoli Sintra,* Praça da República (phone: 923-3505). Expensive.

Palácio dos Seteais – An 18th-century palace makes a lovely setting for lunch on a sunny day, particularly a leisurely Sunday, and especially when the restaurant has an adjoining garden terrace on which to indulge in after-dinner coffee. This very elegant restaurant, serving well-prepared Portuguese and international dishes, is located outside Sintra, in the hotel of the same name. Open daily. Reservations necessary. Major credit cards accepted. 8 Rua Barbosa do Bocage (phone: 923-3200). Expensive.

Cantinho de São Pedro – Also in São Pedro de Sintra, this rustic restaurant has 2 large dining rooms and a wine cellar. Try it for seafood, game, or one of the many French dishes on the menu. Closed Mondays and Thursday evenings. Reservations advised. Major credit cards accepted. 18 Praça Dom Fernando II, São Pedro de Sintra (phone: 923-0267). Moderate.

Dos Arcos – Typical Portuguese dishes are served in an attractive setting that includes a waterfall. In an old part of town, a 10-minute walk from downtown. Open daily. Reservations unnecessary. Major credit cards accepted. 4 Rua Serpa Pinto, São Pedro de Sintra (phone: 923-0264). Moderate.

Galeria Real – Above a gallery of antiques shops in São Pedro de Sintra, this is a lovely dining room, filled with antiques. The menu features Portuguese and French food. Open daily. Reservations unnecessary. Major credit cards accepted. Rua Tude de Sousa, São Pedro de Sintra (phone: 923-1661). Moderate.

Solar de São Pedro – Two large dining rooms with fireplaces and a menu of French and Portuguese selections keep this place busy. Closed Tuesday evenings and Wednesdays. Reservations advised. Major credit cards accepted. 12 Praça Dom Fernando II, São Pedro de Sintra (phone: 923-1860). Moderate.

Tacho Real – Located in what once were the stables and coach house of a mansion in the historic center of town, this place exudes atmosphere. Try the *caldeirada à Tacho Real* (their rendition of the traditional fish stew) or the beefsteak with shrimp sauce. Closed Wednesdays, Thursdays for lunch, and from October 15 to November 15. Reservations unnecessary. Major credit cards accepted. 14 Rua Ferraia, Vila Velha de Sintra (phone: 923-5277). Moderate.

Adega do Saloio – The rustic decor, the strings of onions and garlic hanging from the ceiling, the fireplaces, and the open kitchen tell visitors that this "countryman's winery" is aptly named. Meats, fish, and seafood grilled on the spit are the specialties. Located at the entrance to Sintra from Lisbon or Estoril. Closed Tuesdays. Reservations unnecessary. No credit cards accepted. Chão de Meninos (phone: 923-1422). Moderate to inexpensive.

Portelinho – Small, air conditioned, with a bar, it serves a variety of Portuguese regional dishes at reasonable prices. Open daily. Reservations unnecessary. Major credit cards accepted. 66-70 Av. Movimento das Forças Armadas (phone: 923-3857). Inexpensive.

TEA SHOPS: A tradition almost as hidebound as London's, Lisbon's handsome tea shops provide a firsthand view of one of the city's longstanding ties to England (as well as a relatively inexpensive snacking alternative). Every weekday around 5 PM, the city's tearooms fill up with clerks taking a break from work; families and friends getting together to discuss the latest news; housewives gossiping and nibbling sticky cakes; students doing homework; and shoppers giving their feet a much-needed rest. The tea of choice is a black Mozambican variety known as Licungo, but the shops also serve coffee, soft drinks, and even cocktails. Most of them offer a wide variety of snacks, from chocolate croissants and *pastelaria crema fina* (cream cake) to *pasteis de bacalhau* (codfish balls) and *folhados com salsicha* (sausage bread). The grande dame of the bunch — going strong for more than 60 years — is the high-ceilinged, chandelier-and-mirror-filled *Versailles* (15A Av. da República; phone: 546340), whose formal, immaculately uniformed waiters serve customers from old silver-plated tea services. Even older is *Pastelaria Bénard,* in the Chiado shopping area (104 Rua Garrett; phone: 347-3133). *Pastelaria Ferrari* (2 Calçada Nova de São Francisco; phone: 346-2741) is temporarily located around the corner from its former site (the old building was destroyed in the 1988 fire). Most tea houses are closed on Sundays, except for the *Versailles,* which is open daily from 7:30 AM to 10 PM.

PORTO

Few cities can boast of having a wine, a language, and a country named after them. And many would rest on these laurels alone. But not Porto (Oporto in English). The city is simply too busy doing business. Merchants rule here. The solid gray buildings of Porto's financial district reflect their practical nature, while the sprawl of the city and the industrial belt surrounding it attest to their commercial savvy. But don't let first appearances turn you away. Deep inside the modern jungle is an old city, where Gothic elegance harmonizes with baroque flair, houses cling precariously to terraced slopes like the vines that produce the region's celebrated wine, and the soft pastels of crumbling riverside houses shimmer in the misty morning waters of the golden Douro River.

Portugal's second-largest city, with 500,000 inhabitants, Porto may currently play second fiddle to Lisbon, but it hasn't always. Proud *portuenses* claim their city is the country's hereditary capital, more quintessentially Portuguese than their southern rival. After all, it was the serious, hardworking, and fiercely independent people of Porto who helped give the nation its start, who played a key role in freeing Lisbon from the Moors, and who financed and built the bulk of the Portuguese armadas. In return, the city became known as the *capital do trabalho,* the work capital, and its burghers became the unofficial guardians of the nation's values and traditions. Porto, solid, prosperous, and conservative, makes sure that Lisbon does not step too far out of line. It even allows the flashy and temperamental capital occasional flights of fancy — as long as it doesn't interfere with the important business of making money.

The city's prime location at the estuary of the Douro has always made it attractive to traders and settlers. The Phoenicians, drawn by the region's metal deposits, came to the mouth of the river to trade. By the time the Romans arrived in the 3rd century BC, a city already existed on the north bank of the Douro. The Romans fortified it and called it Portus (port or harbor), and built an urban metropolis on the south bank, which they named Cale. The twin cities became the major military and commercial center of Portus Cale, from which the name, language, and nation of Portugal were later derived.

Porto proved its mettle in the 9th century by being one of the first urban centers in Iberia to shake off the Moorish yoke. At the end of the 11th century, when the daughter of the King of León and Castile married Henry of Burgundy, the city, along with the rest of the county of Portucale, was part of her dowry. She, in turn, handed over the town charter to its powerful bishops. For centuries thereafter, the bishops, aristocrats, and merchants of Porto struggled for control of the city, and in the 14th century, the merchants claimed a major victory: The crown, in return for the merchants' support against powerful rivals, issued a decree in their favor barring the nobility from taking residence in the city's commercial district.

In the 15th century, Porto's most famous son, Prince Henry the Navigator, put the merchants' wealth and shipyards to use: The city built the bulk of the ships used in Portugal's voyages of discovery and reaped many of the profits that came with them. The 16th century was bleak, however. Porto was hit hard by the loss of the country's spice monopoly and the general economic and military decline, which culminated in Portugal's humiliating annexation by Spain in 1580. When the country reclaimed its independence in 1640, João of Bragança was crowned in Porto as King João IV.

By the 18th century, the resilient city was back on top, buoyed by wealth from Portugal's Brazilian colony and a considerable increase in port wine exports following the signing of the Treaty of Methuen with England. Under its terms, English cloth received favored status in Portugal, and Portuguese wine was accorded similar treatment in Britain. British wine merchants set up shop in Porto and went on to play a major role in the success of port wine and the city's subsequent history. Soon, English words such as ruby and tawny were being used to describe the wine, and others, such as the bastardized *chumeco,* for shoemaker, appeared in the popular vocabulary.

But not all went well for the British. In the mid-18th century, to curb their growing influence in the port wine trade, the powerful Marquis of Pombal set up the Alto Douro Company, giving it monopolistic control of wines from the Upper Douro region. But the company's strict rules and pricing policies annoyed producers and British shippers alike and led to violence when a supposedly drunken mob set fire to the company offices in what came to be known as the *revolta dos borrachos,* or "drunkards' revolt." Pombal's reprisal was vicious — public hanging of 25 participants. Eventually, however, the British merchants found ways to work with the Portuguese company, and to this day their descendants flourish in Porto. The British have their own club (where cricket is played), a school, and a church with a cemetery. Today, both the club and school are very international.

In the early 19th century, Porto was occupied twice by Napoleonic armies. The first invasion, in 1808, ended when the British, who were not amused at the prospect of having their coveted supplies of port cut off, sent troops under the command of Sir Arthur Wellesley, later named the Duke of Wellington. Wellesley expelled the French but had to return a year later to repel a second French force, after which Porto's grateful British merchants made him and his officers honorary members of their posh club and opened their wine lodges to the troops.

Soon after, Porto played a major role in the social struggles of the 19th century. In 1820, liberal army officers with merchant connections formed an alliance in Porto to curb the powers of the crown. The movement spread to Lisbon, where, 2 years later, a representative *cortes* drafted a liberal constitution putting an end to feudal rights. King João VI accepted the constitution, but when Miguel I, his son, dismissed it in 1828 and went on to rule like an absolute monarch, Porto rebelled. This caused Miguel's brother, Pedro of Brazil, to abdicate his own throne and return to Portugal to restore the liberal order. Pedro's forces landed north of Porto in 1832 and marched on the city, forcing Miguel to abandon it. Before the War of the Two Brothers, as it came to be known, was over, however, the Miguelites laid siege to Porto for a year — a year in which the populace was reduced to eating cats and dogs. The siege was finally lifted with Miguel's definitive defeat south of Lisbon, and Pedro returned to Porto to thank its citizens for their support. When he died 4 months later, leaving his daughter, Maria da Glória, on the Portuguese throne, he bequeathed his heart (encased in gold) to the city.

With the 20th century and the downfall of the monarchy came the triumph of the republicanism for which Porto's merchants had worked so hard, along with a new era of economic development and public works. Already in the late 19th century, two metal bridges had been built across the Douro gorge, linking Porto with Vila Nova de Gaia (formerly Cale) and the rest of the country. Since 1960, a series of dams have been built on the river for hydroelectric purposes as well as to make it navigable and to control the flow of water in the event of floods. Another headache, a difficult sandbar at the river's mouth, was bypassed by building the new artificial port of Leixões north of the city, between the town of Leça da Palmeira and the onetime fishing village of Matosinhos, now a suburb of Porto. Today, the city's economic emphasis has shifted from the river to this area, where fish canning, oil refining, wood processing, and shipping thrive, and the Exponor exhibition center regularly hosts trade fairs.

The Old City, for better or worse, has been left to age in peace. It is weathered, somewhat tattered, and no stranger to poverty, but it's also teeming with life. Venture into the picturesque Barredo quarter, with its narrow alleyways and stone stairways that meander down to the river, and you will encounter a rich and vibrant world of tiny houses stacked against each other, fanned by the colorful morning wash, and of old women in black leaning over wrought-iron balconies and listening to the laughter of young children echoing off ancient walls. Stroll along the Ribeira, where the sweet smell of flowers emanates from quayside stalls and fish mongers exhibit their wares. Dine at a riverside tavern and gaze out at the south bank, where the city's wine treasure is stored and its handsome *rabelo* boats are docked. This is vintage Porto. Like the venerated wine, it should be savored slowly for its charm to work. And if it doesn't, there are other options: Porto is also the gateway to Portugal's northern lake country and the verdant Minho.

PORTO AT-A-GLANCE

SEEING THE CITY: Porto is built on several hills, so the city offers more than one panoramic vantage point. The best view is from the former Convent of Nossa Senhora da Serra do Pilar, on the south bank of the river in Vila Nova de Gaia, just across one of the city's two 19th-century bridges, the Ponte de Dom Luís I. Here, a tree-lined terrace looks down at the 2-tiered metal bridge and across to the Old City, the remains of the 14th-century Fernandina wall (which at one time encircled Porto but was torn down during 18th-century expansion), and the towers of the cathedral and the Clérigos church. On the north bank, the latter tower, the Torre dos Clérigos, provides an alternative view: Climb its 225 steps and be rewarded with a sweeping panorama that includes the sea to the west and the south bank's wine lodges. (For admission information, see the Igreja dos Clérigos below.)

SPECIAL PLACES: Porto is vast, but monumental Porto — extending roughly from the 20th-century Câmara Municipal (Town Hall) at the northern end of the wide Avenida dos Aliados to the riverfront Praça da Ribeira — is fairly concentrated and can be visited on foot. Within this area is the old, or medieval, city. It begins at the southern end of the Avenida dos Aliados, at Praça da Liberdade, where the old Fernandina wall and an entrance to the city once stood, but which is now the heart of the Baixa, Porto's commercial and shopping district. South of the square is the cathedral — the nucleus of the medieval town — sitting at the crest of the Pena Ventosa, a steep hill or cliff overlooking the Douro and Vila Nova de Gaia on its south bank. The terrain suddenly drops sharply south of the cathedral, forcing houses in the Barredo quarter right below it to cling precariously to the slopes, as narrow cobbled streets and granite stairways make their way down to the quayside Ribeira quarter. Thus, there are two levels to Porto, the upper level stretching northward from the edge of the cliff and the lower level along the river. Be sure to wear comfortable walking shoes.

Four bridges join Porto proper to its Vila Nova de Gaia suburb. The Ponte Dona Maria Pia, the easternmost bridge, was designed by Alexandre-Gustave Eiffel and built in 1877 (a new railway bridge has been built adjacent to it). Not too far to the west is the Ponte de Dom Luís I, built in 1886, a 2-tiered structure that ingeniously joins both the upper and lower parts of the city on both sides, and was the brainchild of an Eiffel disciple. Still farther west is the Ponte da Arrábida, dating from 1963 and also an example of ingenuity in that it stretches 885 feet across the Douro in a single reinforced-concrete span.

DOWNTOWN

Sé (Cathedral) – The twin-towered, fortress-like 12th-century cathedral, with its 17th- and 18th-century modifications, is perched on a hill overlooking the Old Town. Outside, a 13th-century Romanesque rose window stands above the highly stylized baroque doorway. Inside, in the Chapel of the Holy Sacrament, is the church's famous 17th-century silver altar, which was painted over for a period during the French occupation to save it from marauding troops. Also of note are three marble stoups in the nave and a bronze relief of the baptism of Christ in the baptistery to the left of the entrance. The sacristy off the south transept contains a gold-carved retable dating from 1610, as well as the crypt of the Bishops of Porto. A door on the south side of the south transept leads to a 14th-century Gothic cloister decorated with *azulejos* depicting the life of the Virgin and Ovid's *Metamorphoses.* The parents of Prince Henry the Navigator were married at the cathedral in 1387. Open daily from 9 AM to noon and from 2 to 5 PM. Admission charge to the cloister. Terreiro da Sé (phone: 319028).

Terreiro da Sé (Cathedral Square) – Bordering the cathedral is an imposing 14th-century tower; beside it is the Bishop's Palace, an 18th-century building with a flamboyant baroque façade. From the square, you can gaze upon the Douro — or thread your way down to it via a maze of alleys leading to the *cais,* or quay.

Igreja dos Grilos (Grilos Church) – The first building owned by the Jesuits in Porto. The 17th-century structure, laid out in the form of a cross with a vaulted dome, has a handsome baroque wooden altar representing the Presentation of Jesus in the temple. More formally known as São Lourenço, the church is open only for services, weekdays from 7 to 9 AM, Saturdays from 3 to 5 PM, and Sundays from 9:30 to 11 AM. Largo do Colégio (phone: 200-8056).

Casa Museu Guerra Junqueiro (Guerra Junqueiro House Museum) – Currently closed for restoration, the house of the 19th-century Portuguese poet Guerra Junqueiro, on a street behind the cathedral, contains the art objects he collected. Included are fine pieces of 15th-century Hispano-Arabic pottery and a large assortment of 16th-century Portuguese furniture and Flemish tapestries. 32 Rua de Dom Hugo (phone: 313644).

Igreja de Santa Clara (St. Clara Church) – East of the cathedral, this basically Romanesque church was founded in the early 15th century but underwent later transformation. The door is a mix of Gothic, Manueline, and Renaissance stonework, while the interior is covered from top to bottom with gilded woodwork. The ceiling is Mudéjar in style. Open Mondays through Fridays from 9:30 to 11:30 AM and 3 to 7:30 PM; Sundays from 9:30 AM to 12:30 PM; closed Saturdays. No admission charge. Contributions suggested at the small museum inside. Largo Primeiro de Dezembro (phone: 314837).

Estação de São Bento (St. Benedict Station) – The interior walls of Porto's commuter train station are covered with *azulejos* done in 1930 by Jorge Colaço. They depict scenes of the development of the train and other historic events such as the capture of Ceuta by João I in the 15th century. Praça de Almeida Garrett.

Igreja dos Congregados (Congregados Church) – The showy *azulejos* decorating its exterior are the most notable feature of this 17th-century church. Open daily. No admission charge. Beside the São Bento Station, at the corner of Avenida Dom Afonso Henriques.

Igreja dos Clérigos (Church of the Clerics) – This 18th-century baroque church with the unusual, oval shape was designed by the Italian architect Niccolò Nasoni. It is flanked by the Torre dos Clérigos, a 250-foot-high bell tower that dominates the Porto skyline. The 225-step climb to the top of the tower provides a panoramic view of Porto, the Atlantic Ocean, the Douro, and the wine lodges at Vila Nova de Gaia. The church is open daily from 7:30 to 9 AM, 10 AM to noon, and 6 to 8 PM; the tower is open daily (except Wednesdays) from 10 AM to noon and from 2 to 5 PM. Admission charge for the tower. Rua dos Clérigos (phone: 200-1729).

Igreja do Carmo (Carmo Church) – Another 18th-century church, this one designed in an elaborate rococo style and dedicated to Our Lady. The outer eastern wall, covered with 20th-century glazed tiles depicting important events of the age of discovery and expansion, faces the lovely Fountain of the Lions. Open Mondays through Fridays from 7:30 AM to noon and from 2 to 5 PM; Saturdays and Sundays, open mornings only. No admission charge. Rua do Carmo (phone: 200-8113).

Museu Nacional Soares dos Reis (Soares dos Reis National Museum) – The most interesting museum by far in Porto is housed in an 18th-century palace (the Palácio dos Carrancas, a former residence of the Portuguese royal family) and contains art from the 16th century onward. There are paintings by such 16th-century Portuguese masters as Vasco Fernandes, who was known as Grão Vasco (Great Vasco), and Gaspar Vaz; also represented are 19th-century painters Silva Porto, a naturalist, and Henrique Pousão, an Impressionist, as well as Columbano Pinheiro, the 19th- and 20th-century portraitist and still life painter. On display besides paintings are sculptures by António Soares dos Reis, the 19th-century Porto native for whom the museum is named, local pottery, gold and silver liturgical objects, a set of 16th-century Limoges enamels representing the life of Christ, and a sword that belonged to the first King of Portugal, Dom Afonso Henriques. Open from 10 AM to 12:30 PM and from 2 to 5 PM; closed Mondays. Admission charge, except on Sundays. 56 Rua Dom Manuel II (phone: 200-7110).

Museu Romântico (Romantic Museum) – Art objects and furniture from the 19th century make up the contents of this museum lodged in a 19th-century house overlooking the river on the far side of Porto's Pavilhão Rosa Mota exhibition center (formerly the Palácio de Cristal). See the museum and then go down to the basement to the *Solar do Vinho do Porto,* a comfortable wine bar run by the Port Wine Institute, the body that has supervised and certified the quality of port wine since 1935. The museum (phone: 609-1131) is open Tuesdays through Saturdays from 10 AM to 12:30 PM and from 2 to 5:30 PM, Sundays from 2 to 5:30 PM. Admission charge. The bar (phone: 697793) keeps later hours, opening at 10 AM weekdays (at 11 AM on Saturdays) and closing at 11:30 PM (10:30 PM on Saturdays); closed Sundays. 220 Rua de Entre Quintas.

Casa Tait – Next door to the *Romantic Museum,* it is the administrative center for the city's chain of museums. Featured here are changing exhibitions of painting, sculpture, and photography, as well as gardens famous for having the largest tulip trees in Europe. Open Tuesdays through Fridays from 10 AM to noon and from 2 to 5 PM. No admission charge. 219 Rua de Entre Quintas (phone: 606-6207).

Museu de Etnografia e História do Douro Litoral (Museum of Ethnography and History of the Douro Littoral) – Typical costumes, farm implements, pottery, and other objects illustrate the daily life and customs of the people of the Douro region. There are also reconstructions of an old wine cellar and a weaver's workshop. Open Tuesdays through Saturdays from 10 AM to noon and from 2 to 5 PM. No admission charge. 11 Largo de São João Novo (phone: 200-2010).

Palácio da Bolsa (Stock Exchange) – The 19th-century granite building is known for its impressive marble staircase and its dazzling oval Arab Room, whose arabesques and stained glass windows imitate the highly decorative style of the Moorish Alhambra in Granada. Open for guided tours Mondays through Fridays from 9 AM to 11:30 AM and from 2 to 5:30 PM. From May through September, open also on Saturdays and Sundays, from 10 to 11:30 AM and from 2 to 4:30 PM. Admission charge. A statue of Prince Henry the Navigator stands in the square in front of the building. Rua Ferreira Borges (phone: 200-4497).

Igreja de São Francisco (St. Francis Church) – This was originally a Gothic church — and it has a fine rose window at its entrance. Step inside, however, and see the most dramatic and lavish church interior in all of Porto, the result of remodeling in the 17th and 18th centuries. Walls, vaulting, and pillars are generously covered with carved and gilded wood vines, grapes, birds, angels, cherubs; a forest of carved, gilded wood covers the high altar. About the only object not dressed in sumptuous gold is the polychrome granite statue of St. Francis in a 13th-century chapel. Open Mondays through Saturdays from 9 AM to 12:30 PM and from 2 to 5:30 PM. During the months of March through September, open Mondays through Saturdays from 9 AM to 5 PM. Admission charge. Praça Infante Dom Henrique (phone: 200-8441).

Casa do Infante – Prince Henry the Navigator was born in this 14th-century house, or so it is traditionally — and dubiously — thought. The building was a customs house up to the 19th century. Recently restored, it now serves as Porto's *Museu Histórico* (Historical Museum), containing artifacts and documents pertinent to the city's history. Open Mondays through Fridays from 9 AM to noon and from 2 to 5:30 PM. No admission charge. Rua da Alfândega (phone: 316025).

Igreja da Cedofeita (Cedofeita Church) – Porto's oldest church dates from the 12th century. A 5-minute cab ride northwest of the city center, it has a simple and elegant Romanesque exterior; inside, a single-vaulted nave rests on three arches. Open daily from 9 AM to 12:30 PM and from 4 to 7 PM, except Sunday afternoons; Mondays only from 6 to 8 PM. 193 Rua Anibal Cunha (phone: 200-5620).

Museu de Arte Moderna (Museum of Modern Art) – Porto's newest museum, in the Casa Serralves, a former private mansion of the 1930s, is notable for its changing exhibitions of modern art, as well as for its fine, traditional Portuguese garden. Open Tuesdays through Sundays from 2 to 8 PM (gardens open until sunset). Admission charge (except Thursdays). 977 Rua de Serralves (phone: 680057).

PORT WINE CELLARS

No visit to Porto would be complete or entirely satisfying without a tour of one of the wine "lodges," or cellars, where port wine from the Douro Valley is stored and aged. There are some 50 or so wine lodges in the area, located at Vila Nova de Gaia, on the south bank of the Douro. Some say they're kept at this safe distance from the city in order not to interfere with the sober requirements of business. But experts cite more practical reasons: The lodges are on the south side of the river, facing north, to take advantage of the greater humidity and cooler temperatures, which reduce the wine's evaporation in the cellars.

Most of the houses offer free guided tours, in English, which can be arranged through the tourist office (see *Sources and Resources*) or hotels or by calling the lodges directly. Tours generally include a courtesy tasting; bottles can also be purchased. To reach the wine lodges at Vila Nova de Gaia, walk or drive across the lower level of Ponte de Dom Luís I and turn right. A stop at one of the several outdoor cafés on an esplanade by the quay would be in order — from here you can admire Porto proper across the river, as well as the old wine barges docked at the river's edge. These elegant, Egyptian-looking boats, Porto's characteristic *rabelos,* are the last of their kind, remnants of a pre-dam era when wine from the Upper Douro production area traveled downstream to the lodges by boat, rather than by truck and train. The following are some of the better known names that welcome visitors:

Cockburns Smithes – Established in 1815 and now owned by the Allied-Lyons group, this firm maintains a high quality throughout their range of ports. Allow at least 1 hour for the unusually comprehensive and personalized tour, which includes visits to the cooperage (where the casks are made). Of traditional construction, the lodge has high, pine-beamed roofs and earthen floors. The tour also takes in the dust- and cobweb-covered cellars where the wine is stored and aged. Open Mondays through Fridays, from 9:30 to 11 AM and from 2 to 4 PM. Rua D. Leonor de Freitas, Vila Nova de Gaia (phone: 394031).

Ferreira – One of the largest Portuguese port wine companies, it has a long and colorful history. In the early 19th century, its founder, Dona Antónia Adelaide Ferreira, expanded the family holdings from 3 vineyards to 30 large estates stretching all the way up the Douro to the Spanish border. She became the richest woman in Portugal and endeared herself to the local population — who affectionately nicknamed her "Ferreirinha" (little Ferreira) — by building roads, school nurseries, and hospitals. Ferreirinha almost drowned in the Douro in 1861 when the boat on which she and Baron de Forrester, an Englishman, were traveling capsized. He perished, but she managed to survive, apparently buoyed by her voluminous petticoat. Mid-October through mid-April, open Mondays through Fridays from 10 AM to noon and from 3 to 5 PM; from mid-April through mid-October, open Mondays through Fridays from 10 AM to 12:30 PM and from 2 to 5:30 PM, and on Saturdays from 10 AM to noon. 19 Rua da Carvalhosa, Vila Nova de Gaia (phone: 370-0010).

Real Companhia Vinícola do Norte de Portugal – Founded by royal decree in 1756, the company is housed on a large estate on the eastern side of Vila Nova de Gaia, a distance away from most of the other lodges. It produces not only vintage port but also Portuguese champagne, or *espumante,* which is stored and aged in a long tunnel on the premises. To reach the estate, drive across the upper level of the Dom Luís Bridge and follow the signs for Lisbon, turning left at the second intersection. 314 Rua Azevedo Magalhães, Vila Nova de Gaia (phone: 303013).

Sandeman – The lodge is housed, in part, in a former 16th-century convent. It holds about 20 million liters of port in bottles and oak barrels, as well as a small museum of tools and other implements used in the wine industry as early as the 18th century. The oldest section has an interesting floor of soft wood "stilts," placed upright as a cushion to prevent damage to the wine barrels as they are rolled over it. Sandeman was established in 1790 by the Scotsman George Sandeman, and the founder's family continues to supervise the company, although it now is owned by Seagrams of Canada. October through March, open Mondays through Fridays from 9:30 AM to 12:30 PM and from 2 to 5 PM; April through September, open daily from 9:30 AM to 12:30 PM and from 2 to 5 PM. 3 Largo Miguel Bombarda, Vila Nova de Gaia (phone: 304081).

Taylor, Fladgate & Yeatman – One of the last privately owned English wine companies and still considered to produce some of the best ports. The tour is lively and informative; the view over the lodges and river, impressive. Open Mondays through Fridays from 10 AM to 6 PM. 250 Rua do Choupelo, Vila Nova de Gaia (phone: 304505).

Other wine lodges include *Cálem,* open Mondays through Saturdays from 9 AM to 12:30 PM and from 2 to 5 PM (26 Av. Diogo Leite, Vila Nova de Gaia; phone: 394041) and *Dow's, Graham, & Warre,* open Mondays through Fridays from 9 AM to 12:30 PM and from 2 to 5 PM; during the months of April through September, also open on Saturdays from 9 AM to 1 PM (10 Travessa Barão Forrester, Vila Nova de Gaia; phone: 396063). Most wineries are closed on local or national holidays; call in advance to check.

ENVIRONS

Igreja do Bom Jesus (Good Jesus Church) – This church in a secluded, cozy garden alongside a viaduct about 7 miles (12 km) north of the center of Porto is the object of a large pilgrimage every June, because it contains an ancient wooden statue of Christ that was found on a beach several hundred years ago and was, according to legend, carved in biblical times by Nicodemus. The church has a lively, bold 18th-century façade by Niccolò Nasoni; inside, the nave and chancel are covered with a sumptuous coffered ceiling. To reach Bom Jesus, take Avenida da Boavista west out of town and proceed north in the direction of the suburb of Matosinhos. Continue past Matosinhos beach and the docks at Leixões. Open Mondays through Saturdays from 8 AM to noon and from 2:30 to 7 PM; Sundays, from 7 AM to 1 PM and from 5 to 7 PM. Visitors generally have lunch at the beachside fish restaurants at Matosinhos. Av. Dom Afonso Henriques, Matosinhos (phone: 930734).

■ **EXTRA SPECIAL:** For centuries before the arrival of the railroad, roads, and dams, the Douro was the lifeline of the people of Porto and the other towns lining the river. Its quicksilver waters carried the handsome, square-sailed *rabelo* boats with their precious cargos downriver from major wine producing and storage centers such as Régua. It is now possible to cruise up the river and admire the terraced slopes that rise like pyramids from the river's edge and surround the stately *quintas* — farms — of the wine families. The most popular of several options is a 15-mile cruise as far as Crestuma, but longer trips, to Régua, Pinhão, and Barca D'Alva, can also be booked. Prices range from about $100 to $250. Contact *Endouro Turismo* (49 Rua da Reboleira; phone: 324236; fax: 317260). Advance booking is necessary; no cruises from November through most of February. The boats leave from the quay at Praça da Ribeira. Another possibility, for visitors on a tight schedule, is the short cruise under the city's four bridges, which leaves every hour from the quay in front of the Ferreira wine lodge at Vila Nova de Gaia. From mid-April through mid-October, it runs on the hour Mondays through Fridays from 10 AM to 6 PM (except at 2 PM) and on Saturdays to 1 PM (phone: 370-0010).

SOURCES AND RESOURCES

TOURIST INFORMATION: The Porto Tourist Board (25 Rua Clube Fenianos; phone: 312740) is open Mondays through Fridays from 9 AM to 5:30 PM (May to September, open until 7 PM), Saturdays from 9 AM to 4 PM, and Sundays, July through September only, from 10 AM to 1 PM. It provides information on the city and the region, including a monthly booklet (in Portuguese) with information about cultural events in Porto. They also have a handy red pamphlet, in English, called *Oporto/Portugal,* complete with a blue map of the town showing bus routes, a brochure containing pictures of the city's sights, and a guide to port wine and its history. The office will make hotel reservations within Porto for those who require lodging. Lists of manor houses in the area that take in guests also are available. A branch of the national tourist office (43 Praça Dom João I; phone: 317514) also has information on the city and the region. It is open Mondays through Fridays from 9 AM to 7 PM (Saturdays until 2 PM), and on Sundays from 10 AM to 2 PM. The Vila Nova de Gaia Tourist Office (located next to the Sandeman winery, at 242 Av. Diogo Leite; phone: 301902) provides information on the port lodges and other local points of interest. It also features several rooms exhibiting arts and crafts. Open weekdays from 9 AM to 6 PM; Saturdays, from 10 AM to 4 PM.

The US Consulate is open Mondays through Fridays from 8:30 AM to 5 PM and is at 826 Rua Júlio Dinis (phone: 606-3094).

Local Coverage – The *Jornal de Notícias* is one of Portugal's oldest dailies. *Publico,* one of the newest, has the largest circulation. The *International Herald Tribune* can be purchased the day after publication at the airport, at major hotels, and at the larger newsstands around Praça da Liberdade.

TELEPHONE: The city code for Porto is 2. If calling from within Portugal, dial 02 before the local number.

GETTING AROUND: Central Porto can and should be seen on foot, but a car or public transportation is necessary for suburban areas and the environs.

Airport – Porto's newly enlarged Aeroporto Francisco Sá Carneiro (phone: 948-2141; for flight information: 948-2144), 9½ miles (15 km) northwest of the city along N107, handles both domestic and international traffic. A taxi ride into town can cost up to $20; the No. 56 bus provides regular service to Praça da Lisboa in the center of town. *TAP Air Portugal* has a local office (105 Praça Mousinho de Albuquerque; phone: 600-1111) and an office at the airport (phone: 948938); *British Airways* has an office at the airport (phone: 948-6321). The regional shuttle airline, *Linhas Aéreas Regionais (LAR),* flies over the Douro Valley and connects Lisbon to northern tourist spots such as Bragança and Vila Real (phone: 948-3245).

Bus – Buses, trams, and trolleys cover the city. Booklets of discount tickets or unlimited-travel tourist passes (good for 4 or 7 days) can be purchased from the *Serviço de Transportes Coletivos do Porto* (*STCP;* Praça de Almeida Garrett; phone: 606-8226), between 8 AM and 7:30 PM Mondays through Fridays. An interesting trip can be taken aboard the No. 1 tram — from Praça do Infante Dom Henrique (opposite the St. Francis Church) along the river past suburban Foz do Douro and right through to Matosinhos. (On Sundays, the route is covered by bus.) *Rodoviária Nacional* (*RN*), the national bus company (629 Rua Sá da Bandeira; phone: 200-1109), provides sightseeing tours aboard special buses with English-speaking hostesses.

Car Rental – The major international firms represented include *Hertz* (899 Rua de Santa Catarina; phone: 312387; and at the airport; phone: 948-1400); *Avis* (125 Rua Guedes de Azevedo; phone: 315947; and at the airport; phone: 948-1525); and *Europcar* (1158 Rua de Santa Catarina; phone: 317737; and at the airport; phone: 948-2452).

Taxi – Taxis can be hailed on the street or picked up at a cabstand — there is a large stand at Avenida dos Aliados (no phone). Or call *Radio Taxi* (phone: 489898). Meters are not used beyond the city limits, so if you are going a long distance, be sure to ask the hotel concierge for an estimate and discuss the amount with the cab driver before setting off.

Train – There are three train stations. The main one, Estação de Campanhã (Rua da Estação; phone: 564141), on the eastern outskirts of the city, serves most of the country and foreign destinations. (A cab from the center costs under $7.) Estação de São Bento (on Praça de Almeida Garrett in the city center; phone: 200-2722) is a commuter station. The third station, Estação de Trindade (at the end of Rua António Sardinha; phone: 200-5224), near the tourist office, serves the northern part of the country.

SPECIAL EVENTS: The enterprising side of the city can be seen throughout the year at a host of industrial fairs, conventions, and congresses, the largest of which is the *International Industrial Machines Exhibition* in October. But there are also more colorful events, such as the *International Folk Dance Festival,* sponsored by City Hall in August, and the popular festivals of *São João* (St. John) and *São Bartolomeu* (St. Bartholomew). *São João,* which takes place on June 23 and 24, is a mix of pagan and Catholic rituals celebrating the summer solstice and involves curious customs such as passing around leeks and buying small earthenware pots of marjoram. The population stays up all night drinking *vinho verde* and eating roast kid, and lovers leap over huge bonfires. The feast of *São Bartolomeu,* held on the third Sunday in August, has evolved into a *cortejo de papel,* or "paper parade," in which people dress in paper costumes to satirize public personages and politicians. They follow a float carrying Neptune and sirens to the beach, where they battle "pirates" from the sea; the battle ends with all the participants and some of the onlookers rushing into the water for a holy bath, a practice no doubt related to the old superstition that a dip in the sea can cast out the devil.

MUSEUMS: Besides those mentioned in *Special Places,* several other museums in Porto may be of interest:

Casa-Museu Teixeira Lopes (Teixeira Lopes House-Museum) – A collection of this well-known Portuguese artist's work, plus pieces by other contemporary sculptors. Open Tuesdays through Saturdays from 9 AM to 12:30 PM and from 2 to 5 PM. No admission charge. 32 Rua Teixeira Lopes (phone: 301224).

Museu de Arqueologia e Pré-História (Archaeology and Prehistory Museum) – Local artifacts dating as far back as 4,000 years. Open Mondays through Fridays from 9 AM to noon and from 2 to 5 PM. No admission charge. Praça de Gomes Teixeira (phone: 310290).

Museu de Arte Sacra (Museum of Sacred Art) – Religious art, liturgical vestments, old coins, and glass objects. Open Tuesdays through Fridays from 2:30 to 4 PM. No admission charge. 2 Largo de Pedro Vitorino (phone: 200-8056).

Museu Militar (Military Museum) – Small and heavy arms are exhibited here, plus a collection of 10,000 toy soldiers. Open Tuesdays through Sundays from 2 to 5 PM. No admission charge. Rua do Heroismo (phone: 565514).

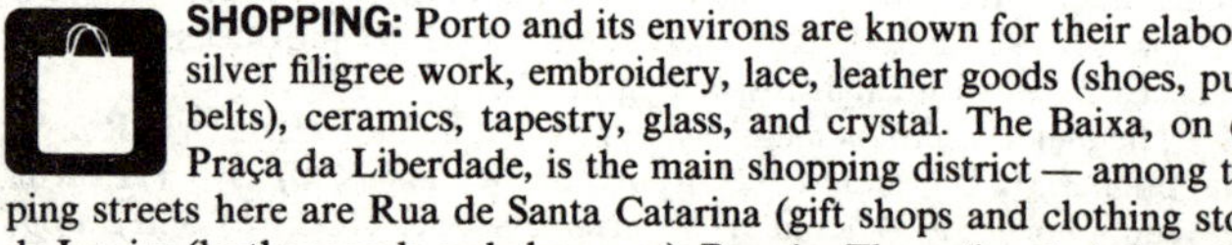

SHOPPING: Porto and its environs are known for their elaborate gold and silver filigree work, embroidery, lace, leather goods (shoes, purses, wallets, belts), ceramics, tapestry, glass, and crystal. The Baixa, on either side of Praça da Liberdade, is the main shopping district — among the best shopping streets here are Rua de Santa Catarina (gift shops and clothing stores), Rua 31 de Janeiro (leather goods and glassware), Rua das Flores (jewelry), Rua das Carmelitas (ceramics and clothing), and Rua dos Clérigos. There are also several popular markets carrying regional handicrafts such as wooden model boats and ox carts, wicker articles, and pottery at bargain prices, as well as clothing and shoes at below store prices. The *Bolhão* market (Rua de Sá da Bandeira) is in the Baixa district, while the more popular *Bom Sucesso* market is in the square of the same name on the western side of town. Both function Mondays through Fridays from 7 AM to 5 PM, and on Saturdays from 7 AM to 1 PM. The outdoor *Vandoma* fair, a small flea market near the cathedral, specializes in antiques and knickknacks and is in operation on Saturdays from 7 AM to 1 PM. Regular shops are open from 9 AM to 12:30 PM and from 2 to 7 PM on weekdays, 9 AM to 1 PM on Saturdays, but some shopping centers stay open on Saturdays and Sundays from 10 AM to 12 PM. The *Centro Comercial Brasília* (113 Praça Mousinho de Albuquerque) is a mini-mall with everything from gift, clothing, and shoe shops to pastry shops and hairdressers. The nearby Rua de Júlio Dinis has a good selection of clothing and shoe stores. Individual shops of note include the following:

Casa dos Linhos – A family-run firm that has specialized in the sale of linen and embroidery for over a century. 660 Rua de Fernandes Tomás (phone: 200-0044).

Crisal – Producers and sellers of fine Atlantis crystal. In the Foco residential complex, at 301 Rua Eugénio Castro (phone: 695805).

Galerias de Vandoma – An antiques shop and auction house. 181 Rua Mouzinho da Silveira (phone: 200-1286).

José Rosas – Antique and modern jewelry. In the Foco residential complex, at 282 Rua Eugénio Castro (phone: 695785).

Rosior – Manufacturers of traditional and modern jewelry. In the Foco residential complex, at 263 Rua Eugénio Castro (phone: 606-8134).

Vista Alegre – Fine handmade porcelain from the town of Vista Alegre; the shop can handle shipping. Open from 9 AM to 7 PM. 18 Rua Cândido dos Reis (phone: 200-4554.)

SPORTS AND FITNESS: Golf – Two golf clubs within easy reach of Porto are the *Clube de Golfe de Miramar* (phone: 762-2067), which has a 9-hole course near the beach at Praia Miramar, 7½ miles (12 km) south of town off N109 (the road to Espinho), and the *Oporto Golf Club* (phone: 722008), with an 18-hole course beside the beach about 3 miles (5 km) south of Espinho and 14 miles (22 km) south of Porto. The latter was opened in 1890 by British wine shippers, and the atmosphere of a British club continues to prevail in its wood-paneled clubhouse. Equipment rental, caddies, and classes are available throughout the year at both clubs; guests of the *Praia do Golfe* hotel in Espinho may use the greens free of charge.

Jogging – Try the gardens (admission charge) of the Pavilhão Rosa Mota, the old exhibition center on Rua Dom Manuel II, or take the No. 18 bus 3 miles (5 km) west to suburban Foz do Douro, at the mouth of the river, and jog along the long esplanade by the beach.

Soccer – The season runs from September through June. Porto's two major clubs are the *Futebol Clube do Porto* (Av. de Fernão de Magalhães; phone: 481738), based at the *Estádio das Antas,* and the *Boavista Futebol Clube* (Rua 1 de Janeiro; phone: 690975), which plays at the *Estádio do Bessa.*

Squash – The *Clube de Squash do Porto* (164 Rua João Branco; phone: 606-6771) is one possibility; the *Sheraton* (1269 Av. da Boavista; phone: 606-8822) also has a squash court.

Swimming – For a tan, go to the Foz do Douro or Matosinhos beaches, but swim farther from the city at Espinho, 10½ miles (17 km) south. An Olympic-size municipal swimming pool, the *Piscina de Campanhã* (Rua Dr. Sousa Avides; phone: 572041), is near the Campanhã train station.

Tennis – The *Clube Tênis do Porto* (Rua Damião Gois; phone: 488506) offers courts and classes.

THEATER: Classic Portuguese plays and *revistas,* lighthearted political and social satires, can be seen at the *Teatro Municipal Rivoli* (Praça Dom João; phone: 200-3782). The *Teatro Experimental do Porto* (134 Rua Duque de Palmela; phone: 569567) offers more modern experimental theater.

MUSIC: The symphony orchestras of both Porto and Lisbon play at the elegant *Auditório Nacional Carlos Alberto* (Rua das Oliveiras; phone: 200-4540) and at the *Teatro Municipal Rivoli* (Praça Dom João; phone: 200-3782).

NIGHTCLUBS AND NIGHTLIFE: Porto has a varied nightlife. *Swing* (766 Praçeta Engenheiro Amaro de Costa; phone: 609-0019) attracts the well-heeled, who like its pub (upstairs) and disco (downstairs) combination. *Twins* (1000 Rua do Passeio Alegre; phone: 685740), in the affluent suburb of Foz, 3 miles (5 km) west of the center, has a similar setup, but it also provides intimate, continental dining. (It's also a members-only club, but this rule is not strictly enforced.) The *Olympia* in the *Meridien* hotel (1466 Av. da Boavista; phone: 600-1913) is a discotheque frequented by the business community, while the younger set flocks to *Griffon's* (*Centro Comercial Brasília;* phone: 606-6091), which is somewhat smaller and noisier.

It is possible to avoid the glitz and fast pace of the disco crowd, however. Although the *fado* tradition did not take hold north of the Douro, the *Taberna São Jorge* (35 Passeio das Virtudes; phone: 318230) is where you can hear them sung from 9:30 PM to 4 AM daily except Sundays (about $85 for two; reservations advised). The *Mal Cozinhado* (13 Rua do Outeirinho; phone: 208-1319) also has *fado* from 9:30 PM daily except Sundays (reservations necessary; see *Eating Out*). Several pubs in the Ribeira district have live music: *Postigo do Carvão* (26-34 Rua da Fonte Taurina; phone: 200-4539), in a refurbished warehouse by the river, is an animated restaurant and piano bar, and *Aniki-Bobo,* next door, offers a jazz and folk repertoire popular with the college crowd. *Bela Cruz* (5458 Av. da Boavista; phone: 680891) is a pub in an old fort, the Castelo do Queijo, by the sea at Foz.

A final option: At Espinho, there's the *Casino Solverde* (phone: 724045), open from 3 PM to 3 AM, with roulette, slot machines, and bingo, as well as dining, dancing, and a floor show. Portuguese law requires foreigners to show their passports at the door; there's a small entrance fee to the gambling room.

BEST IN TOWN

CHECKING IN: Until recently, Porto suffered from a lack of topnotch accommodations. The situation has been remedied with the addition of several new deluxe hotels and the refurbishing of some older establishments, but because the new establishments are in the suburbs (en route to the airport), the supply of recommendable accommodations in the historic part of the city is still limited. It is essential to choose carefully and make reservations well in advance, particularly for the summer months. Expect to pay $180 and up for a double room in the top hotels, listed as expensive; from $130 to $170 in those listed as moderate, and under $115 for those listed as inexpensive. All telephone numbers are in the 2 city code unless otherwise indicated.

Infante de Sagres – Porto's most luxurious hotel — whose guest list has included the British royal family — is tucked away in a small, quiet square near the center of town. It certainly doesn't look its age: It was built during the early 1950s, but has an Old World appearance, a product of decoration in the grand style encompassing several centuries of antiques and a rich assortment of carved wood paneling, stained glass, and wrought iron. The 79 rooms are spacious and plush, the service is efficient and friendly. The hotel has a bar, and its restaurant (see *Eating Out*) is the most elegant eating place in the city. 62 Praça Dona Filipa de Lencastre (phone: 200-8101; in the US, 800-528-1234; fax: 314937). Expensive.

Ipanema Park – Porto's newest multi-star hotel is stylish, with 281 spacious rooms that overlook the estuary. Although the design of the building is ultramodern, antique rugs add a nice classical touch. On the premises are 2 bars, the deluxe *Winter Garden* restaurant and the less formal *Os Rios* (see *Eating Out* for both), the best health club in town, 2 pools, 16 conference rooms, and underground parking accommodating 200 cars. 124 Rua de Serralves (phone: 610-4174; fax: 610-2809). Expensive.

Ipanema Porto – To the west of the city center quite near the Rotunda da Boavista, this modern 150-room hostelry has a good restaurant (*Os Rios;* see *Eating Out*), a piano bar, and its own private parking facility. 156 Rua do Campo Alegre (phone: 668061; fax: 606-3339). Expensive.

Meridien – A modern, luxury, 232-room hotel located in the new commercial zone en route to the airport, about a 10-minute bus or cab ride to the center. A favorite of young executives, who like the spacious conference facilities and the efficient communications system, it has most of the amenities of a chain hotel, including a French restaurant of the same name (see *Eating Out*), a piano bar, a health club (there is a charge), and a discotheque. 1466 Av. da Boavista (phone: 600-1913; in the US, 800-543-4300; fax: 600-2031). Expensive.

Sheraton – Newer than the nearby *Meridien,* this 253-room establishment provides all the familiar comforts of the chain, including a heated indoor swimming pool, a squash court, and a health club that guests may use for an extra charge. There is a piano bar, and the *Madruga* restaurant (see *Eating Out*) offers both regional and continental food. Free parking. 1269 Av. da Boavista (phone: 606-8822; in the US, 800-334-8484; fax: 609-1467). Expensive.

Tivoli Porto Atlântico – This medium-size place (58 rooms) just off the Avenida da Boavista has both outdoor and indoor swimming pools, a sauna, a mini-gym, a bar, and the *Foco* restaurant next door (see *Eating Out*). 66 Rua Afonso Lopes Vieira (phone: 694941; fax: 667452). Expensive.

Batalha – This Best Western affiliate was completely refurbished in 1992. Ideally located in the commercial hub of the city, it has a bar, a restaurant (see *Eating Out*), and 150 rooms. 116 Praça da Batalha (phone: 200-0571; in the US, 800-528-1234; fax: 200-2468). Moderate.

Dom Henrique – A modern, 112-room hotel beside the Trindade train station, up the street from the tourist office. Panoramic views are its best asset. There's a coffee shop on the ground floor, a small bar on the 17th floor, and the *Navegador* restaurant (see *Eating Out*) on the 18th floor. 179 Rua Guedes de Azevedo (phone: 200-5755; fax: 201-9451). Moderate.

Boavista – Small and cozy, and about 3 miles (5 km) west of the center of town in the affluent suburb of Foz do Douro. The building seems a cross between a French château and an English country inn, and most of the 39 rooms, furnished with pine furniture, command views of the Douro estuary and Foz fortress. There's a bar and a dining room (see *Eating Out*), a small patio with a fountain, and terraces for sunning. For an extra payment, guests may use the *Oslo Health Club* in the basement, which has a small indoor swimming pool, a Jacuzzi, a Turkish bath, a sauna, and a massage room. Parking in front. 58 Esplanada do Castelo, Foz do Douro (phone: 680083; fax: 617-3818). Inexpensive.

Grande Hotel do Porto – A classic old hotel on a pedestrian street in the heart of the shopping district. It has a charming *fin de siècle* look to it; the splendor and details of the salons and *Porto,* its dining room (see *Eating Out*), recall past glory. Of the 100 bedrooms, all of which are gradually undergoing redecoration, the ones already refurbished are well worth booking. Another Best Western affiliate; adjacent parking. 197 Rua de Santa Catarina (phone: 200-8176; in the US, 800-528-1234; fax: 311061). Inexpensive.

Ibis – This new establishment, a link in the no-frills European chain, is located next door to the *Novotel,* right on the banks of the Douro River. There are 108 modestly appointed guestrooms and private parking in front. In the lobby is a moderately priced, clean, and bright restaurant serving typical Portuguese dishes. Lugar das Chas, Afurada (phone: 772-0772; fax: 772-0788). Inexpensive.

Novotel – A modern place on the south bank of the river by the Arrábida Bridge, convenient for visiting the port wine lodges. There are 93 rooms (about half with a view of the Douro estuary), a bar adjacent to *Le Grill* restaurant (see *Eating Out*), a small outdoor pool, tennis courts, and parking facilities. Lugar das Chas, Afurada (phone: 781-4242; in the US, 800-221-4542; fax: 781-4573). Inexpensive.

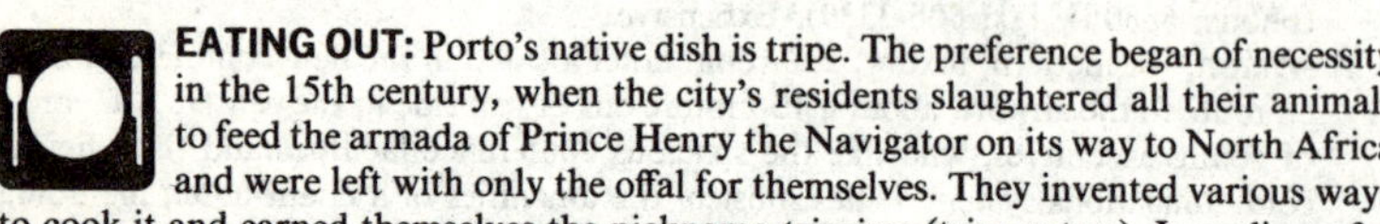

EATING OUT: Porto's native dish is tripe. The preference began of necessity in the 15th century, when the city's residents slaughtered all their animals to feed the armada of Prince Henry the Navigator on its way to North Africa and were left with only the offal for themselves. They invented various ways to cook it and earned themselves the nickname *tripeiros* (tripe eaters). Ingredients for the most typical dish — *tripas à moda do Porto* (tripe, Porto-style) — include tripe, chopped bits of pig's ear and pig's snout, bacon, sausages, white beans, onions, carrots, parsley, bay leaves, cumin seed, salt, and pepper. Served with rice, its advocates swear, it is quite tasty. Before trying the tripe, however, sample the *caldo verde,* or green soup, a northern Portuguese dish made with green cabbage, puréed potatoes, and spicy sausage. Other popular dishes are *bacalhau à Gomes de Sá,* a casserole of salt cod, onions, and potatoes attributed to a Porto restaurant owner, and the local version of *caldeirada,* a steamy stew of many different kinds of fish cooked in a tomato, onion, and herb sauce. Desserts are rich in eggs, almonds, and sugar, and have religious names, such as *barrigas de freira* (nuns' bellies), because they originally were made in convents. A word of caution for shellfish eaters: Lobster and shrimp are prohibitively expensive (up to $65 for a lobster). A delicious, more reasonably priced alternative is *arroz de marisco,* which contains several kinds of shellfish and is Portugal's juicier answer to Spanish paella.

Accompany the meal with the region's *vinho verde* (green wine — but young rather than actually green) or with mature red and white Douro wines. But begin with an extra-dry white port accompanied by a small plate of cheese and cured ham, and finish with a vintage port or an *aguardente velha,* an aged cognac-style brandy that goes well with coffee. Expect to pay anywhere from $70 to $90 for a meal for two (with wine) at a restaurant listed as expensive, from $50 to $65 in a moderate one, and from $30 to $45 in an inexpensive place. It's a good idea to make reservations at the top restaurants, particularly at lunchtime. All telephone numbers are in the 2 city code unless otherwise indicated.

Don Manoel – Housed in a pleasant seaside villa overlooking the Atlantic Ocean. The food is traditionally Portuguese and consistently topnotch, particularly the fish dishes and the multi-fish *caldeirada* stew. Closed Sundays. Reservations advised. Major credit cards accepted. To reach the restaurant, turn left at the end of Avenida da Boavista. 384 Av. de Montevideu (phone: 617-0179). Expensive.

Escondidinho – This popular place serves the best regional food in the city. Tiles, marble, and local crafts decorate it inside, while outside it has been designed to look like a typical country house — which makes it stand out in the otherwise modern urban street. Closed Sundays. Reservations advised. Major credit cards accepted. 144 Rua Passos Manuel (phone: 200-1079). Expensive.

Flor do Castelo – A small and cozy tavern that boasts excellent local dishes, such as freshly caught, grilled *salmão, tamboril,* and *robalo grelhado* (salmon, monkfish, and sea bass, respectively). Closed Sundays. Reservations advised. Major credit cards accepted. In the suburb of Leça da Palmeira, at 102 Rua Santa Catarina (phone: 995-1651). Expensive.

Foco – This place serves a range of both regional and international dishes as well as a buffet lunch on Sundays. Open daily. Reservations advised. Major credit cards accepted. 82 Rua Afonso Lopes Vieira (phone: 606-7248). Expensive.

Infante de Sagres – The poshest place in town, in the hotel of the same name. The game dishes are excellent, the wine cellar large, and the service ultra-professional. The decor — from the crystal chandeliers to the mirrors and wood-paneled walls — is the height of 19th-century elegance. Open daily. Reservations advised. Major credit cards accepted. 62 Praça Dona Filipa de Lencastre (phone: 200-8101). Expensive.

Mal Cozinhado – A fairly large and busy restaurant near the Ribeira, it's also known for *fado* singing. Try their special codfish dishes. Open for dinner only; closed Sundays. Reservations necessary. Major credit cards accepted. 13 Rua do Outeirinho (phone: 381319). Expensive.

Meridien – Another hotel dining room, it offers a choice of traditional French cooking or nouvelle cuisine. Large plants, wicker, and a decor of light greens and browns provide a lively garden-like atmosphere. A businessperson's lunch is served weekdays, a buffet dinner is available on Fridays, and a family buffet is served on Sundays. Open daily. Reservations advised. Major credit cards accepted. In the *Meridien Hotel,* 1466 Av. da Boavista (phone: 600-1913). Expensive.

Porta Nobre – The two dining rooms and bar in this sumptuously renovated waterfront home look out over the river. The fare is mostly international; the white-gloved service, solicitous. Closed Sundays; closed for lunch on Mondays. Reservations advised. Major credit cards accepted. 133 Largo de São Francisco (phone: 200-1101). Expensive.

Portucale – Probably the best restaurant in town, it's favored by executives for its varied menu of Portuguese and continental dishes, attentive service, and sweeping view of the city and countryside. Wood paneling, leather chairs, and colorful modern tapestries make up the simple, lively decor that serves as the background for such house specialties as artichokes au gratin, lobster and rice stew, pheasant stuffed with almonds, chateaubriand with mushroom sauce, and wild boar, as well as tripe, Porto-style. Open daily. Reservations necessary. Major credit cards accepted. 598 Rua da Alegria, 13th Floor (phone: 570717). Expensive.

Winter Garden – Situated in the new, deluxe *Ipanema Park* hotel, it offers superlative international and regional cooking in a sophisticated setting. Among the standouts are *linguado à Ipanema* (oven-baked sole with seafood sauce) and *espetado misto* (mixed grill of meat and sausage). Open daily. Reservations advised. Major credit cards accepted. 124 Rua de Serralves (phone: 610-4174). Expensive.

Madruga – This spacious eating spot, located in the basement of the *Sheraton* hotel, offers both regional and continental food. A buffet lunch is served every day, including brunch on Sundays. A band plays in the evenings. Open daily. Reservations advised. Major credit cards accepted. 1269 Av. da Boavista (phone: 606-8822). Expensive to moderate.

Navegador – An eatery that boasts a beautiful view overlooking the city and serves a wide range of international dishes. Closed Sundays. Reservations unnecessary.

Major credit cards accepted. In the *Dom Henrique Hotel,* 179 Rua Guedes de Azevedo (phone: 200-5755). Expensive to moderate.

Porto Fino – Fairly small, upstairs in a Foz do Douro house. The pleasant atmosphere and the range of fish specialties — try the *linguado grelhado* (grilled sole) or the *lulas gratinadas* (squid gratiné) — have made it popular with the city's social set. A buffet lunch is served weekdays. Closed at lunch on Saturdays. Reservations advised. Major credit cards accepted. 103 Rua do Padrão, Foz do Douro (phone: 617-7339). Expensive to moderate.

Batalha – This place specializes in traditional local dishes including *bacalhau* (cod) and *tripas à moda do Porto* (tripe, Porto-style). It's worth reserving a table near the window for the fine view of old Porto, the cathedral, and the Church of the Clerics. Open daily. Reservations advised. Major credit cards accepted. 116 Praça da Batalha (phone: 200-0571). Moderate.

Churrascão Gaucho – This popular lunch spot specializes in Brazilian food and offer specials daily. Try the *alcatra* (roast beef). Open daily except Sundays and during the month of August. Reservations advised. Major credit cards accepted. 313 Av. da Boavista (phone: 691738). Moderate.

Conde de Leça – On the second floor of an old townhouse, this recently opened restaurant has a light and airy ambience. Specialties include freshly caught fish dishes; try the *caldeirada,* a stew of eel and fish in a tomato sauce. Closed Sundays. Reservations unnecessary. Major credit cards accepted. On the way to the airport, in the suburb of Leça da Palmeira. 110 Rua Pinto Araujo (phone: 995-8963). Moderate.

Downing Street – A pleasant family-run place located in a former warehouse in the Ribeira district. On the street level, there's a bar; for dining, there's an intimate, candlelit, tiled cellar or an upstairs room that's decorated with old photos of Porto and looks out onto a picturesque square of colorful houses. Try the *arroz de tamboril,* or monkfish and rice stew. Open daily. Reservations advised. Major credit cards accepted. 10 Praça da Ribeira (phone: 380-6777). Moderate.

Green's – Elegant dining in a restaurant with the atmosphere of a private club. Try two of its specialties — steak *au poivre* (pepper steak) and *filetes de pescada com camarão* (filets of hake with shrimp). Closed Saturdays at lunch and Sundays. Reservations advised. Major credit cards accepted. 1086 Rua Padre Luís Cabral (phone: 685704). Moderate.

Porto – Elaborate stucco ceilings, crystal chandeliers, and flowers contribute to the turn-of-the-century elegance that endears this hotel dining room to an older, sedate crowd. Grilled ox steaks and the grilled turbot are good menu choices. Open daily. Reservations unnecessary. Major credit cards accepted. *Grande Hotel do Porto,* 197 Rua de Santa Catarina (phone: 200-8176). Moderate.

Os Rios – This hotel eatery offers a good continental menu, with a Portuguese specialty for each day of the week. Open daily. Reservations unnecessary. Major credit cards accepted. In the *Ipanema Porto Hotel,* 156 Rua do Campo Alegre (phone: 668061). Moderate.

Boavista – The greenhouse look of it, the views of the Foz fortress and the Douro estuary, and dinner served by candlelight make this glass-enclosed verandah, the main dining room of the *Boavista* hotel, a good choice for a romantic evening. Fondue and chateaubriand, steak tartare, pepper steaks, and grilled sole are among the specialties. Open daily. Reservations advised. Visa and MasterCard accepted. 58 Esplanada do Castelo, Foz do Douro (phone: 680083). Moderate to inexpensive.

Cervejaria Galiza – Beer on tap and fast, efficient service are the trademarks of this modern, lively fish-and-steak spot. Try the spicy clams *bolhão pato*–style (with garlic and parsley), the *arroz de marisco* (shellfish stew), or the *bife à frigideira,* a butter-fried beefsteak with a fried egg on top, done in an earthenware pot. Open until 2 AM daily. No reservations. Major credit cards accepted. 55 Rua do Campo Alegre (phone: 690059). Moderate to inexpensive.

Le Grill – Ensconced in the *Novotel,* this modern-looking dining spot overlooks the swimming pool and offers an à la carte menu of international fare. Open daily. Reservations unnecessary. Major credit cards accepted. *Novotel,* Lugar das Chas, Afurada (phone: 781-4242). Moderate to inexpensive.

Tripeiro – A popular, no-frills eatery that serves fine regional cooking and fish specialties. Try the *linguado grelhado* (grilled sole) or *filetes de pescada* (hake). Closed Sundays. Reservations unnecessary. Major credit cards accepted. 195 Rua Passos Manuel (phone: 200-5886). Moderate to inexpensive.

A Brazileira – This bustling café-restaurant, built at the turn of the century, is a felicitous marriage of Art Nouveau decor and a flamboyant Brazilian sensibility. The fare is Portuguese, and the adjoining *confeitaria* sells deliciously aromatic blends of coffee. Closed Sundays. Reservations unnecessary. Major credit cards accepted. 61 Rua Sá da Bandeira (phone: 200-7146). Inexpensive.

Chez Lapin – A pleasant, typical Ribeira restaurant lodged in a centuries-old arcade by the river. Walls and ceilings of this tiny but cozy tavern are filled with hunting and kitchen utensils, its busy kitchen is open, and there are two floors for dining. The house specialty is *coelho* (rabbit) in white wine sauce, but for fish lovers, there is tender, black swordfish. Open daily. Reservations advised. Major credit cards accepted. 40 Rua dos Canastreiros (phone: 200-6418). Inexpensive.

Taverna Bebodos – The most authentic of several waterfront taverns serving typical regional dishes. Closed Sundays. Reservations advised. No credit cards accepted. 24 Cais da Ribeira (phone: 313565). Inexpensive.

DIVERSIONS

For the Experience

Quintessential Portugal

Despite its small size and the common and erroneous assumption on the part of some foreigners that it's just an extension of Spain, Portugal boasts a variety of unique and traditional qualities found only here where land meets sea. There is the blend of Mediterranean weather, the variety of its landscapes — where colors can change in the space of a few miles from misty greens to sun-baked ochers — and the abundance of spas and history-packed cities. There is the endless variety of seafood, from the hearty, flavorful *caldeiradas* (fish stews) of the western coast and the aromatic clam dishes prepared in copper *cataplanas* in the Algarve to the sine qua non of a Portuguese summer — charcoal-broiled sardines washed down with rustic red wine. And there is the melodic and melancholy sound of the *fado,* the romance of the Azores and Madeira islands, and the stirring history of the Portuguese explorers.

Portugal's variety comes from its ability to assimilate. The New World sent the old one tomatoes, potatoes, coffee, and the gold that enriched Portugal's churches and made Lisbon one of the most powerful cities in Europe. Over the centuries, Africa, the East, and northern Europe have all contributed to the rich patchwork of Portuguese life. From the Moorish aspect of a southern village and the microtonal strains of a Lisbon *fado* to the ubiquitous café and the evening gathering around the motor scooter in a small town square, this mixed heritage is pervasive and consistently intriguing.

Here are several things that capture the special spirit of this strip of land, hugging the southwest border of Spain, and provide a visitor with an insight into its irresistible personality.

SIPPING THE EARTH'S NECTAR: Port and Madeira: After a long day of sightseeing, nothing goes down more smoothly than a glass of that Portuguese potable, port. Find yourself a comfortable spot in a bar or cozy restaurant and try one of the dryer types such as white or tawny, preferred as an aperitif, and let the inviting aroma and soothing texture wash your worries and sore feet away. If you're at its source in Porto, a trip to one of the lodges to sip the wine first-hand will enhance the experience. As the nectar swirls in your glass, imagine yourself back in the British colonial days when port was the Englishman's wine (it was the British who in the 18th and 19th centuries developed port), and enjoy a chunk of cheese along with your drink.

If it's a still more honeyed wine that suits your fancy, wait until after your meal, and sip the nutty-sweet taste of madeira. The sweeter varieties, such as bual and malmsey, are ideal with dessert — some fresh strawberries or a Portuguese pastry — and the setting sun. Or try the light verdelho and sercial, both good alternatives to a dry sherry — appropriate before or between meals. If you're actually on the eponymous island of Madeira, you might mistakenly think you're in paradise, enjoying the sun and the rich taste of this golden molasses-colored liquid.

FADO FANTÁSTICO, Lisbon: A visit to Portugal would not be complete without an evening listening to the soulful sounds of the Portuguese *fado.* Sit back in a darkened tavern as a black-cloaked singer wails a mournful tale of love and abandonment or an ode to the city of Lisbon. As the musicians strum their guitars, the *fado* fills the room with the sorrowful voices of the singers. If you're in Coimbra, it's the male students from the city's university singing the blues, as *fado* here becomes a ballad of the broken-hearted lover or a paean to the Mondego River, which flows through the city. To hear the pure, unadulterated strains of this melancholy music, book a table at *Senhor Vinho* at Rua do Meio à Lapa in Lisbon and hold someone's hand.

MID-ATLANTIC HONEYMOON, Flores, Azores: Somewhere between Lisbon and New York, the Azores roll like a cluster of billiard balls in the pool-table-green waves of the Atlantic. The island of Flores is the spot to get stranded for a week or two in another century, to kick up your heels or kick off your shoes and wade through the wildflowers that give this remote fleck of land its name. It is the westernmost island of this westernmost outpost of Europe, but still close enough to the New World to have been the site of a battle between Confederate and Union gunboats during the Civil War. Yet this velvet archipelago, brilliantly embroidered with azaleas, hydrangeas, and lemon-yellow 16th-century churches, may be more Portuguese than mainland Portugal itself. Here, where windmills and bell towers still define the skyline, devotion is even stronger, the waterfalls even clearer, the hairpin curves even hairier. While the quaintness of mainland towns may now be somewhat packaged for the benefit of foreigners, the economy of Azorean villages is still tied to the land and sea.

CLIMBING THE BEANSTALK TO SINTRA: After a day spent among the gritty realities of Lisbon, it's just a whoosh up the beanstalk to the mist-shrouded fairyland of Sintra. This town that floats above the mortal world sports a glorious mishmash of extravagant styles, from the time-torn towers of an ancient Moorish castle to the lacy Mudéjar and frilly baroque of the Palácio Nacional de Sintra and the eccentric turrets and domes of the Bavarian-kitsch Palácio Nacional da Pena. You can sleep, dine, or just have a drink in the *Palácio dos Seteais,* once the country retreat of the Dutch consul and later of the fifth Marquês de Marialva; its marbled floors and muraled halls are a fine example of 18th-century Dutch Diplomatic–deco. The eclectic architecture of this medieval town narrates the passing of peoples through Portugal, and, as if the country had also been colonized by a series of foreign plant kingdoms, the Parque da Pena is the meeting place for an international crowd of shrubs, trees, and flowers, all kept moist and luxuriant by the fine spray from the obliging Atlantic down below.

THE EARLY BIRD CATCHES THE FISH, Algarve: Dawn breaks and with the crisp, fresh air the fisherman returns home. In the tiny coastal villages in southern Portugal, there's nothing quite like rising with the sun to witness the weather-worn fishermen bringing in the day's catch. As their brightly colored, sea-beaten boats bob in the surf, the fishermen drag their nets ashore filled with shark, tuna, sardines, and cod (*bacalhau*). The lines on the fishermen's faces hold as many stories as the boats' hulls hold barnacles. Watch as workers on the beach skillfully clean the fish with sharp knives, aware of the awaiting merchants and housewives who are ready to pick and choose for the midday and evening meals. Near the resort areas of Faro, Vilamoura, Lagos, and Portimão, arrangements can be made for visitors to join a fishing boat on its break-of-day outing.

VISIONS OF ALMOND BLOSSOMS, the Algarve and Trás-os-Montes: April showers bring almond flowers, and there's no better land to see and smell the fluffy white and pink blossoms than in the Algarve, in the south, or Trás-os-Montes, in the north. The air is perfumed with their sweet scent. Walking through the almond orchards at blossom time is like walking through a bakery just as a sheet of sugar cookies comes out of the oven. In the Algarve, the trees' fruit is captured in a confectionery delight called *amendoa,* almond and honey candies that come in the shape of vegetables, animals, and flowers. One sugary-sweet bite will bring back the sensation of springtime in bloom. Savor the flavor of this popular nut in a glass of *amendoa amarga,* a liqueur that seems to capture the almond taste and aroma in one delectable swallow. Try it chilled on ice.

EXPLORING THE END OF THE WORLD, Sagres, Algarve: Here, where navigators once thought land ended and the ocean dropped into nothingness, it is worth trying to catch both ends of the day. So get up early, while the lighthouse at the tip of Cabo de São Vicente still beams its comforting nightlight out to exotic pleasure boats and local trawlers. Go sit on the sharp, pointy rocks beneath Henry the Navigator's cliff-top fortress at Sagres, where fishermen cast their lines into the surging froth, and watch the sun's first beams light up the ancient trade routes to the Orient. And when the cool air begins to vibrate with the summer heat, head a few miles north to stretch out on the beach at Carrapateira, wide enough so that there is no need to stake out shoreline turf in meager deck-chair widths even in the highest season. On this wind-cooled coast, your skin may burn before you feel it, so stuff your towels in the trunk, roll back the sunroof, and drive into the wooded hills of Monchique and up to the nearly 3,000-foot peaklet of Fóia, from which, if you squint a little, you can convince yourself your eyes are good enough to see the Moroccan coast. Spend the hottest part of the day napping under a cypress tree, or sipping a glass of *vinho verde* in the shaded main square of Caldas de Monchique. But make it back to the coast in time to curl your toes in the sand and watch the blood-orange sun slip off the edge of the earth. Then end the day with a platter of grilled sardines or tuna in one of the small, smoky restaurants in which the owner is also both waiter and chef.

Pousadas and Manor Houses

No visit to Portugal is complete without a visit or an overnight stay in a *pousada* or a manor house. Imagine sleeping where kings and queens slept, walking corridors and chambers where Franciscan monks walked, and dining in elegant rooms where nobles and aristocrats sat down to countless formal meals over the centuries. The Portuguese people pride themselves on their rich sense of such traditions, and have impeccably restored and converted ancient landmark castles and monasteries into magnificent hotel accommodations, offering travelers a historic return to the past, complete with modern — and often luxurious — facilities.

Many of the *pousadas* in Portugal are restored palaces, castles, and convents; some have retained their original furnishings and antiques. On the way to your room you might pass coats of armor, stone statues, and grand staircases. *Pousadas,* however, may not be for everyone. Some double rooms only have two twin beds — double beds tend to be harder to find, and many of the rooms have neither television sets nor radios. But if you're willing to settle for a bit less luxury (in a contemporary sense), these spots are lovely reprieves from large, impersonal hotels.

The country began its *pousada* program in 1940, and today there are 32 government *pousadas,* including 2 on the island of Madeira; several more are in the planning stage. Nine *pousadas* are restored castles, 16 are modern hotels, and the remainder are small country inns. Their sizes range from 6 to 55 rooms. All are meticulously clean and decorated with attractive furnishings from various centuries. *Pousada* restaurants emphasize regional foods and wines. Rates for a double room, including continental breakfast, range from $50 to $150 per night, depending on category and season. Low season runs from November through March, shoulder seasons are from April through June and all of October, and high season is from July through September. There is a 3-night maximum-stay policy (exceptions are permitted in some cases) throughout the *pousada* network. For more information, contact *Enatur* (10A Av. Santa Joana a Princesa, Lisbon 1100; phone: 01-848-1221; fax: 01-805846; telex: 13609); the *Por-*

tuguese National Tourist Office (590 Fifth Ave., New York, NY 10036; phone: 212-354-4403); or the network's US representative, *Marketing Ahead* (433 Fifth Ave., New York, NY 10016; phone: 212-686-9213).

Another option is to sleep in a manor house, perhaps the *casa, solar,* or *quinta* of one of the country's oldest families. Such aristocratic accommodations are the province of Portugal's *Tourism in the Country* program, a network of privately owned rural properties that take in paying guests. Begun in the 1980s, the program includes three types of properties. Travelers bent on lodgings with recognized architectural merit or a historic past should investigate the manor houses and country estates gathered under the heading of *Turismo de Habitação.* Billing as *Turismo Rural* or *Agroturismo* means less imposing — although equally traditional — houses or rustic farmhouses. Happily, it is the top-of-the-line manor house that is in greatest supply, particularly in northern Portugal. In most cases, the owner lives in the house with his or her family, but can no longer keep up with the large expense of running such an estate. (Some simply enjoy the company of foreign travelers.) Guest quarters are almost always separate and private, sometimes in apartments and adjoining cottages. Some properties have a swimming pool and tennis courts, while others have stables for horseback riding. Many owners help with sightseeing arrangements. The majority of the owners speak English, as well as other languages.

A complete listing of houses is available from the Portuguese National Tourist Office. A 2-month advance notice for booking is usually required. When booking, provide as much information about the intended visit as possible. Prices range from approximately $60 to $125 for two people per night, breakfast included, depending on the type of lodging. The availability of other meals varies from house to house, at the discretion of the owner. A 2- or 3-day minimum stay is usually required. For more information, contact *Direcção-Geral do Turismo* (86 Av. António Augusto de Aguiar, Lisbon 1000; phone: 01-575086). Bookings can be made directly with the houses or through owners' associations. Many houses in the north are represented by the *Associação de Turismo de Habitação* (Praça da República, Ponte de Lima 4990; phone: 058-942729 or 058-741672; fax: 058-741444). Others throughout the country are represented by the *Associação de Casas em Turismo* (*ACT;* Alto da Pampilheira, Torre D2 8A, Cascais 2750; phone: 01-486-7958; fax: 01-284-2901), or by the *Associação Portuguesa de Turismo de Habitação* (*Privetur;* 10 Rua João Penha, Lisbon 1000; for reservations call 01-654953).

POUSADA DO CASTELO, Obidos, Costa de Prata: If Portugal ever had fair maidens scanning the horizons for their returning heroes, surely they sat in the towers of this former castle, located in the picture-perfect village of Obidos. About 60 miles (96 km) north of Lisbon, the town was a traditional wedding gift of the King of Portugal to his bride. An ideal transformation of one wing of the castle has created a 9-room *pousada,* including 3 tower suites. The cobblestone courtyard and thick granite stairways are tasteful reminders of its storybook history. The antique furnishings also tell a tale of age, honor, and strong Portuguese heritage. Outside, the views of the surrounding farmlands are breathtaking. Information: *Pousada do Castelo,* Obidos 2510 (phone: 062-959105).

POUSADA DO INFANTE, Sagres, Algarve: At the western end of the sunny, sandy Algarve coast is this 23-room *pousada* — so popular that rooms must be booked months in advance — named for Prince Henry the Navigator. Balconies overlook a grassy terrace and the sea, often dotted with small fishing boats. On cool winter nights, guests gather in front of the fireplace in the circular lounge, which extends from one end of the bar and into the dining room. The restaurant offers a variety of well-prepared fish dishes, and features an extensive Portuguese and international wine list. Information: *Pousada do Infante,* Sagres 8650 (phone: 082-64222; fax: 082-64225).

POUSADA DOS LÓIOS, Evora, Alto Alentejo: The Portuguese call Evora their "museum city" because of its ancient origins and numerous monuments. The university here dates to the 16th century, and the individual wall tiles depict the subject taught in each room. This 32-room *pousada* in the center of town was once the 15th-century monastery of the Lóios Order. Today's weary and pensive traveler will feel refreshed in the cloisters within the walls. Information: *Pousada dos Lóios,* Evora 7000 (phone: 066-24051; fax: 066-27248).

POUSADA DO PICO DO ARIEIRO, Arieiro, Madeira: Prepare for an ear-popping ride up the mountainside. All 22 rooms here have balconies commanding a view below that combines the pines and woodland on this hilly island and the beautiful expanse of the open sea stretching to the horizon. Comfortable rattan chairs and floral upholstery brighten the rather austere appearance of most of the rooms; the full-service restaurant features regional foods, with a heavy emphasis on fish. Definitely a place for the sports enthusiast, it offers nature hikes with English-speaking guides to Madeira's highest mountains, the nearby Pico do Arieiro and the Pico Ruivo. Information: *Pousada do Pico do Arieiro,* Funchal 9000, Madeira (phone: 091-48188; fax: 091-48119).

POUSADA DE SANTA MARINHA DA COSTA, Guimarães, Costa Verde: The largest of all the *pousadas,* with 51 rooms and 4 suites. Once a 14th-century monastery, it changed owners continuously through the centuries until finally it was sold to a private family. They kept it until the 1940s and, as a game, often rode horses throughout the long hallways. At the end of one hallway was a fountain and a terrace, which still overlooks the entire town. A chapel is next door. Abandoned in the 1940s, and almost destroyed by fire, it was eventually taken over by the government and restored into a *pousada.* The rooms range from spartan cells to baroque suites appointed with furniture from the Ajuda Palace in Lisbon. The *pousada* tends to attract large numbers of tour groups, especially on the weekends. Information: *Pousada de Santa Marinha da Costa,* Estrada da Penha, Guimarães 4800 (phone: 053-514453).

POUSADA DE SÃO BENTO, Caniçada, Costa Verde: The feel of a Swiss chalet and rustic mountain wilderness are what make this *pousada* an excellent diversion. In the Peneda-Gerês National Park, on a hilltop overlooking the Caniçada dam, this modern building has balconies with spectacular views. Bringing its guests close to the nature of Portugal, the 30-room *pousada* offers outdoor sports activities with local campers, hunters, riders, and mountain climbers; daily trips to the surrounding villages and the city of Braga also are available. Information: *Pousada de São Bento,* Caniçada, Vieira do Minho 4850 (phone: 053-647190; fax: 053-647867).

POUSADA DE SÃO FILIPE, Setúbal, near Lisbon: This former 16th-century castle sits atop a hill and overlooks a busy, picturesque waterfront. Inside, the chapel walls boast hand-painted blue tiles depicting scenes from the life of São Filipe and the Virgin Mary. Just a 1-hour drive from Lisbon, this 14-room *pousada* is popular with weekend travelers. The town of Setúbal is itself an attraction worth seeing; it was once an important center of Catholicism, having as many as 13 convents and monasteries. Information: *Pousada de São Filipe,* Setúbal 2900 (phone: 065-523844).

QUINTA DA PONTE, Faia, Beira Alta: An imposing manor house with 3 double rooms and a deluxe suite, all with private baths, is a good base from which to explore the Serra da Estrela. Information: *Mary Alvim, Quinta da Ponte,* Faia, Celorico da Beira 6360 (phone: 071-685597).

QUINTA DE SÃO TIAGO, Sintra, near Lisbon: A Spanish woman and her English husband now own this centuries-old manor house, set in one of Portugal's beauty spots, the verdant Serra de Sintra. The house has 7 luxuriously furnished double rooms and 2 singles, all with private bath. There are also several quaint sitting rooms, a bar, a music room, a swimming pool, and 1 tennis court. Information: *Maria Teresa Bradell, Quinta de São Tiago,* Sintra 2710 (phone: 01-923-2923).

QUINTA DE SANTO ANDRÉ, near Lisbon: Just up the Tagus, outside Vila Franca de Xira, about 20 miles (32 km) from Lisbon, this lovely estate is in the midst of horse and cattle country, where Portugal's fighting bulls are raised. There are 1 single and 4 double rooms, numerous sitting rooms, and a swimming pool. Information: *Karl Gerhard Brumm, Quinta de Santo André,* Estrada de Monte Gordo, Vila Franca de Xira 2600 (phone: 063-22776 or 063-22143).

CASA DO AMEAL, Viana do Castelo, Costa Verde: A manor house whose long aristocratic pedigree explains the almost museum-like display of antiques and memorabilia that it contains, it has 4 double rooms and 2 apartments (each for 4 people) with private baths, sitting rooms, and pleasant gardens and grounds. Information: *Maria Elisa Araújo, Casa do Ameal,* Meadela, Viana do Castelo 4900 (phone: 058-22403).

CASA DO ANTEPAÇO, near Ponte de Lima, Costa Verde: This restored stone house combines the qualities of the past with the comforts of the present and provides a peaceful atmosphere in rural surroundings. There are 4 large double rooms, a living room with a fireplace, a library, a garden, and a terrace offering superb views of the Lima River. Information: *Dr. Francisco de Abreu Lima, Casa do Antepaço,* Ponte de Lima 4990 (phone: 058-941702; reservations 058-942729; fax: 058-741444).

CASA DE CORTEGAÇA, Viana do Castelo, Costa Verde: A historic 16th-century manor house on the left bank of the Lima River, it offers the ultimate in modern comforts, in a setting steeped in tradition. There are 4 double rooms, several sitting and dining rooms, a lovely garden, a farmhouse, and plenty of rippling streams to explore. Information: *Maria Filomena de Abreu Coutinho, Casa de Cortegaça,* Subportela, Viana do Castelo 4900 (phone: 058-971639).

CASA DA PALMEIRA, near Evora, Alto Alentejo: This turn-of-the-century mansion has 8 double rooms, a sitting room, and a dining room, all characteristic of its original architecture. There is also a lovely garden. Information: *Fernando Nunes Gonçalves, Casa da Palmeira,* Praça de Santo António, Reguengos de Monsaraz 7200 (phone: 066-52362).

CASA DO SABUGUEIRO, Sabugueiro, Beira Alta: Situated in the Serra da Estrela, in the highest village in Portugal, this typical *casa* still maintains and operates a *queijaria* (cheese dairy), as well as a traditional oven used to bake corn and rye bread. There is a special "tasting" room, where guests can sample the breads as well as the local serra cheese. The house offers 2 double rooms, a bathroom (shared), and a quaint living room with a fireplace. Information: *Teresa da Graça Trindade, Casa do Sabugueiro,* Sabugueiro, Seia 6270 (phone: 038-22825).

The Best Restaurants of Portugal

When it comes to dining, Portuguese food offers a surprising variety of tastes. Over the centuries, this seagoing nation's cuisine has come under the influence of far-flung countries in Asia, Africa, and the Americas, as well as neighboring Spain and nearby France. The Portuguese love affair with the sea and its bounty is intense. Of all fish, *bacalhau* (codfish) is dearest to the Portuguese palate. *Caldeirada* (fish stew) is another popular seafood dish; its content varies from region to region and with the day's catch, but a good *caldeirada* should include about nine varieties of fish and shellfish, including clams, mussels, squid, and octopus. Carnivores need not despair, as meat dishes and stews, such as *cozido à portuguesa* (made of meats, sausages, and vegetables), are equally abundant.

T CLUB, Almansil: One of the most luxurious culinary spots in the Algarve, set on the grounds of the exclusive, posh *Quinta do Lago* resort. Owner José Manuel Trigo learned his trade from Régine, the queen of clubs, managing her establishments in

Brazil. Marbled wood, velour curtains, impeccably set tables, and soft lighting set the tone in this elegant place, where international nouvelle cuisine and traditional dishes from Portugal and Europe share the menu. A central European flavor is imported in the summer season with the arrival of a Belgian cook. Dinner is served until 1 AM. Guests can dance their calories away in the adjoining boîte, or adjourn to the plush bar for a glass of port. Information: *T Club,* Quinta do Lago, Almansil 8100 (phone: 089-396588).

ALBATROZ, Cascais: Perched on the rocks overlooking the blue waters of Cascais Bay, on the grounds of a manorial home, this luxury hotel harbors one of the most enchanting restaurants on Portugal's mini-Riviera. The impeccable, classical elegance of the wood-paneled piano bar and romantic, candlelit atmosphere of the glass-enclosed dining room with unobstructed sea view make it a favorite haunt of the Estoril coast jet set. Manager Avellos runs the facility with discreet efficiency. White linen and freshly cut flowers add to the decor, enhancing the varied international and Portuguese menu, which includes mouth-watering *arroz de marisco* (rice with shellfish), pheasant, partridge, and the house veal stuffed with cured ham. Highlights among the desserts are flaming crêpes Suzette, sweet *tâmaras* (dates) with hot chocolate sauce, and crusty apple pie topped with warm cream. A select wine list of 12 special vintages, such as rare colares '31 and mouchão '63, is available for appreciative connoisseurs. Dinner reservations are necessary, ties recommended. Information: *Albatroz,* 100 Rua Frederico Arouca, Cascais 2750 (phone: 01-483-2821).

FOUR SEASONS GRILL, Estoril: True to its name, this fancy restaurant on the grounds of Estoril's grand *Palácio* hotel, where many of Europe's exiled royalty and other personages waited out World War II, changes its decor and the uniforms of its staff to suit the season. Its large central table blooms with flowers in the spring and is laden with fruit in the summer. Creative dishes such as *linguado à Four Seasons* (sole stuffed with shrimp and mushrooms and flambéed with whiskey) abound. But the main attraction is its grill. Guests on the ground floor and upper mezzanine can watch the chef at work on a huge, open grill, tending to such savory delectables as *espetada mista* (diced veal and monkfish kebabs bathed in butter sauce). Not to be outdone by the grill captain, the maître d' lights up the room with his flambéed creations or *crêpes de metre* stuffed with almonds and bananas and doused with lemon ice cream. Though the decor is sharp and metallic — copper placemats and bronze columns — the wooden tables, leather-lined chairs, and glowing coals in the fireplace help soften the ambience. The restaurant is open for dinner daily, from 7:30 PM to 1 AM. Information: *Four Seasons Grill, Palácio Hotel,* Ruo do Parque, Estoril 2675 (phone: 01-468-0400).

FIALHO, Evora: The three Fialho brothers have built their temple to Alentejo food in the center of one of Portugal's most beautiful towns. The restaurant's bar and two dining rooms are tastefully decorated with regional copper, pottery, handwoven Arrailos rugs, and paintings; stuffed game mounted on the walls reflect the hunting fervor of the people of the region. Guests can nibble from a cornucopia of *petiscos* (starters), which range from spicy sweet meats to more exotic dishes, such as *cabeça de xara* (pork head). The award-winning restaurant, which is popular among wealthy ranchers of the region, university professors, and politicians, boasts the best and most authentic *carne de porco com amêijoas* (pork and clam stew) in Evora, and *sopa de cação,* a rich, aromatic soup made with shark, bread, garlic, vinegar, and coriander. During the fall hunting season, partridge, wild rabbit, and boar are featured. Egg, almond, and pumpkin desserts provide the sweet touch to the meal, while the region's soft sheep cheeses, the creamy *serpas,* are an equally rewarding finale. Meals can be accompanied by Evora's estate-bottled cartuxa white wine, or other Alentejo greats such as the light, dry white esporão and the heavy red reguengos de monsaraz. Closed Mondays and September 1–15. Information: *Fialho,* 16 Travessa das Mascarenhas, Evora 7000 (phone: 066-23079).

AVIZ, Lisbon: When the elegant, turn-of-the-century *Aviz* hotel closed its doors during the early 1960s, its chef and maître d' joined forces and started a new restaurant — same name, same furnishings — in a former tailor's shop. Legend has it that the Armenian oil millionaire Calouste Sarkis Gulbenkian, a frequent client of the hotel, may have contributed to the venture. Today, the restaurant's clients continue to be captains of industry, who like its subdued intimacy and refined, Belle Epoque look. Guests have a choice of dining rooms: the cozy silk-lined *salão verde* (green room) or the lighter *salão amarelo* (yellow room), decorated with old musical instruments. Parties of 14 to 18 persons can retire to the intimacy of a private salon under the watchful eye of a 19th-century wooden statue of Pocahontas. Other attractions are its wooden pub-like bar and its tile-lined marble staircase. The chef's enticing culinary creations — smoked swordfish, gratinéed cod *Conde de Guarda* style, rack of lamb with ground herbs, and chilled *bôlo de ananás* (pineapple cake) — help make the restaurant one of Portugal's dining landmarks. Closed Saturdays for lunch and Sundays. Information: *Aviz,* 12B Rua Serpa Pinto, Lisbon 1200 (phone: 01-342-8391).

TÁGIDE, Lisbon: Its closeness to Lisbon's financial district makes this restaurant atop one of the city's original seven hills a favorite with businesspeople and government officials, including the president. Other attractions are its large wine list of over 70 vintages, spanning Portugal's eight main wine regions, and its fish delicacies. The house salmon pâté and its *cherne no forno com coentros* (oven-baked stone bass with coriander) reflect the Portuguese penchant for fish. Meat lovers can savor the succulent *churrasco de cabrito* (grilled kid) or *carne de porco à alentejana* (pork Alentejo-style), an ingenious dish of pork and clams prepared with wine, garlic, red pepper, coriander, and oil. The fruit and almond crêpes, topped with vanilla sauce, have been known to seduce the most ardent dieters. Though white walls, leather chairs, and 18th-century tiles depicting mythological characters give the dining room a classical elegance and order, they do not detract from the panoramic view of Lisbon. Closed Saturdays and Sundays. Information: *Tágide,* 18 Largo da Biblioteca Pública, Lisbon 1200 (phone: 01-342-0720).

TAVARES, Lisbon: The grande dame of Lisbon restaurants, opened as a café in 1784, celebrated its 200th birthday with a face-lift. The splendor of the Belle Epoque was restored and Lisbon's old guard flocked to see the doyenne's newly resplendent, gold-painted and paneled walls, large, imperial gilded mirrors, polished silver, and china. Patrons were delighted to find that the old menu was maintained. Maître d' Rodrigo Paia has drilled his black-tied waiters to perform their duties with such finesse that diners are scarcely aware of their presence. House specialties include *santola recheada* (stuffed crab) in Madeira sauce and *cherne à portuguesa* (stone bass Portuguese-style) with a smooth tomato, onion, garlic, and clam sauce. Guests with a predilection for sweets can treat themselves to the *soufflé à Tavares,* with both vanilla and chocolate sauces, or the baked Alaska. Closed Saturday for lunch and on Sundays. Information: *Tavares,* 37 Rua da Misericórdia, Lisbon 1200 (phone: 01-342-1112).

PORTUCALE, Porto: This Porto landmark is favored by executives for its varied menu of Portuguese and continental dishes, attentive service, and sweeping view of the city and countryside. Wood paneling, leather chairs, and colorful modern tapestries make up the simple, lively decor that serves as the background for such house specialties as artichokes au gratin, lobster and rice stew, pheasant stuffed with almonds, chateaubriand with mushroom sauce, and wild boar, as well as tripe, Porto-style. Open daily. Information: *Portucale,* 598 Rua da Alegria, 13th Floor, Porto 4000 (phone: 02-570717).

COZINHA VELHA, Queluz: Guests get the royal treatment at this restaurant housed in the kitchen of the 18th-century palace of the Kings of Portugal, a 15-minute drive west of Lisbon. Remnants of its royal past can be seen in the large copper kitchen utensils bearing the royal seal and displayed on the walls, and in the huge chimney supported by six marble pillars, where whole oxen were once roasted on the spit. Banquets are still held in the antique-tiled *sala dourada* (gold room) for foreign dignitaries who are lodged in the adjoining pink palace. Maître d' José Marinho Carreira has served such distinguished guests as Queen Elizabeth and Ronald and Nancy Reagan, and accompanies Portugal's head of state on his tours. The decor and the food are as refined as the service: Wood-vaulted ceilings, red tile floors, iron lamps, and soft, piped-in music provide an elegant backdrop for such delectables as *terrina de casa* (veal pâté), *linguado suado* (steamed sole) served in a delicate onion, carrot, mushroom, and sour cream sauce, and souffléed, oven-baked *bacalhau espiritual* (codfish). The latter takes 40 minutes to prepare and should be ordered in advance. Guests have a choice of wines from all over the country and neighboring Colares, which produces the light-bodied tavares rodrigues. The restaurant's pièces de résistance are its desserts, fashioned from ancient convent recipes. Very apropos is the *doce real* (royal sweet), which comes stamped with the Portuguese royal seal in confectionery sugar and is made of squash, eggs, and nuts. Information: *Cozinha Velha,* Palácio Nacional de Queluz, Queluz 2745 (phone: 01-435-0232).

Shopping Spree

No matter where the dollar stands relative to the escudo, the temptation of shopping in Portugal is irresistible. Small roadside stalls along the Algarve coast offer a dazzling array of ceramics, and small antiques shops in cities like Lisbon and Porto are like mini-museums, with a fine assortment of items dating back to the 15th century. Although great bargains are now rare, the quality is high and the choice wide: leather goods, embroidery, jewelry, fine porcelain, and fashion ranging from very basic hand-knit sweaters and clothing to haute couture.

The shopping day often begins around 9:30 AM, when shopkeepers are still hosing down the sidewalks in front of their stores. Most owners take pride in their shops; their business is a very personal affair, and they'll no doubt strike up a conversation with curious browsers. It isn't uncommon, either, for those who opt to ship their purchases back to the US to get a handwritten note from shopkeepers.

The Portuguese approach life and shopping with less passion than the neighboring Spaniards. This is not to say, however, that Portuguese shopping should be considered second class. Lisbon is a logical choice, and Porto is worth a visit, particularly for silver. Madeira is known for its embroidery. Portuguese artisans mold earthenware and ceramics into works of art, as do modern Portuguese manufacturing plants, producing whimsical pottery, elegant porcelain, and gleaming crystal befitting any table. Tiles are everywhere: on churches, restaurants, palaces, storefronts, homes, and shops. They capture the bright colors and sunny vistas that are so much a part of Portugal's landscape and heritage. Handwoven rugs, both designer-quality and functional, as well as hand-knit sweaters and intricate embroidery symbolizing a national pride lovingly worked at for centuries, can be found throughout the country.

Portuguese shops are generally open Mondays through Fridays, from 9:30 AM to 1 PM and from 3 to 7 PM; Saturdays, from 9:30 AM to 1 PM (except in December, when they remain open until 7 PM). Shopping malls are open daily, from 10 AM to midnight, though not all shops located in the malls stay open that late. In Porto, shops close at 12:30 PM for the afternoon break and reopen at 2:30 PM. Many shops throughout the country are closed in August. Although store hours are generally observed, shops sometimes close unexpectedly or, when open, leave shoppers waiting for service. Many shopkeepers speak English. Note that many stores in Portugal still *don't* accept credit cards.

WHERE TO SHOP

Travelers can find good buys all over Portugal, provided they know where to look.

POST-CHRISTMAS AND SUMMER SALES: Portugal's *saldos* (sales) are held only twice a year. They begin in January and February and are repeated in September and October. In general, almost everything in Portugal is reasonably priced; in fact, Lisbon remains one of the most reasonably priced of Europe's shopping capitals.

OPEN MARKETS: Never pass up a chance to wander through some of Portugal's bustling open markets. It is here that visitors have the opportunity to see the *real* Lisbon and the *real* Evora come alive — people selling their crafts, friends meeting for a meal or a drink, and curious onlookers taking in the vast array of goods and daily bargains. These open markets are a smorgasbord of vibrant colors, overflowing with the song of the people.

Lisbon – Portuguese Gypsies buy closeout items, discontinued, secondhand, overrun, and leftover stock from many top Portuguese clothing manufacturers and boutiques, then peddle them from stands on street corners throughout the week, especially during lunchtime. Also look for the Gypsies every Tuesday and Saturday at the large flea market in the Alfama district, at Largo de Santa Clara.

Evora – The *Mercado Municipal* on Praça Primeiro de Maio, open every morning except Mondays, is not only the best place for fresh food and delicacies such as the excellent local cheeses and cured sausages, but also a colorful place to visit. Handicrafts, including good, brown-glazed oven pots, are sold from stalls outside, along with the omnipresent plastic goods.

SPECIAL SHOPPING STREETS AND DISTRICTS: The mixture of old and new and the lively sounds of families and couples linked arm in arm make strolling through the streets an inviting experience. Stop and savor both the street scenes and the shops that line them. In addition, department stores generally have anything and everything you desire.

Lisbon – The major shopping area, the Baixa section, consists of about 20 blocks, some for pedestrians only. Up and down the city's hills, small shops are the norm, and they are great places for peeking and poking. The area is anchored by the Praça do Comércio at the water's edge, leading up to the Praça da Figueira. The bordering side streets are Rua do Ouro and Rua da Prata. For pricier shopping, head to the Chiado district, particularly Rua do Carmo and Rua Garrett. Rua Dom Pedro V houses a variety of antiques shops. Gypsies also set up shop on many sidewalks for several hours a day.

Porto – Porto's commercial centers are in the newer part of the city. Rua de Santa Catarina is the main commercial street in the Baixa district, with one portion set aside as an open-air pedestrian mall. There are some good boutiques and shops along Avenida da Boavista, near the *Meridien* hotel. Rua das Flores, near the São Bento train station, is the street for those interested in buying silver. Rua 31 de Janeiro has a fine assortment of clothing boutiques and shoe stores, and nearby Rua da Cedo Feita is also an excellent place to shop for shoes.

CENTROS COMERCIAIS (SHOPPING MALLS): Visitors will feel right at home in the bright lights, chain stores, and fast-food restaurants of a Portuguese shopping mall. Most stay open from 10 AM to midnight 7 days a week, including holidays.

Lisbon – There are about 30 *centros comerciais* in Lisbon, of all sizes and quality. The most famous, with sophisticated shops of all kinds — more than 300 of them — is the *Amoreiras Shopping Center* (Av. Engenheiro Duarte Pacheco; phone: 01-692558), an architecturally controversial post-modernist complex with huge towers in pinks and greens and glass, designed by architect Tomás Taveira. *Centro Comercial Fonte Nova* (497 Estrada de Benfica; phone: 01-714-4654), just outside the city, has 80 shops, including excellent leather goods and home-decoration stores. *Centro Comercial Al-*

valade's 45 shops offer a classy assortment of giftware, clothing, shoes, and general shopping-mall merchandise (Praça de Alvalade; phone: 01-848-0224).

Porto – *Dallas* (1588 Av. da Boavista; no phone), a huge center with 500 stores on 5 levels, is the best place to buy handicrafts and jewelry in Porto. The recently enlarged *Centro Comercial Brasília* (113 Praça Mousinho de Albuquerque) offers a wide range of shops and boutiques; underground parking is provided.

BEST BUYS

ANTIQUES: Portugal is an excellent, if increasingly pricey, hunting ground for antiques, with a wide range of dealers, auction houses, and non-commercial institutions that offer many items at bargain prices.

Lisbon – The city has a fine antiques shop tradition that is broadening into the areas of prints and rare books. Hundreds of shops await the treasure hunter; most are spread along a 1-mile area beginning at Rua da Escola Politécnica, which changes into Rua Dom Pedro V, Rua de São Pedro de Alcântara, Rua da Misericórdia, and, when approaching the Tagus River, Rua do Alecrim. Always be sure to inquire about an item's age, and always request the proper documentation to back it up. *Solar* (68-70 Rua Dom Pedro V; phone: 01-346-5522) has the largest selection of antique Portuguese glazed tiles, arranged by century, beginning with the 15th, as well as a fine collection of pewter and furniture. *Xairel* (3 Rua Dom Pedro V) is another excellent choice. *Sotheby's* is represented in Lisbon by *Frederico Horta Costa* (*Amoreiras Shopping Center,* Av. Eng. Duarte Pacheco; phone: 01-657161). *António Campos Trindade* (18 Rua do Alecrim; phone: 01-342-4660) specializes in Portuguese, English, and French furniture, as well as Chinese porcelain and paintings.

BOOKS AND MAPS: Most visitors may not be able to read many of Portugal's treasured old books, but it's still fun to browse. Many bookstores have dozens of booths and stalls filled with books from around the world, both old and new; some stores specialize in reduced-rate and secondhand books, old editions, and rare titles. Addicted browsers will have to be dragged out of the capital's bookworm haunts.

Lisbon – Original maps and lithographs from the 16th through the 18th centuries can be found at *O Mundo Do Livro* (11 Largo da Trindade; phone: 01-346-9951), one of Lisbon's oldest and most famous bookstores. *Livraria Bertrand* (73 Rua Garrett; phone: 01-342-0081) also has an enormous selection, as well as many English titles. *Livraria Buchholz* (4 Rua do Duque de Palmela; phone: 01-547358) has a large stock of foreign books as well as Portuguese ones.

CERAMICS AND TILES: The diversity of Portugal is highly evident in the country's wide range of ceramics. Arab influence prevails in ceramic designs; wall plates are enameled and trimmed in 24-karat gold. Later, when the English settled in the area, florals and busy scenic designs became the preferred style. Tiles are called *azulejos* in Portuguese, and most of them are the color of the sky. Uniquely Iberian, the tiles can be found throughout the country, and many visitors are tempted to purchase enough to decorate their homes — but are soon discouraged by the shipping costs. Remember, shipping sand is heavy; about 14 fragile tiles packed in sand weigh 10 pounds. The best reminder of any visit could be the many hand-decorated, easily portable tiles, either in blue and white or depicting scenes.

Lisbon – *Fábrica de Cerâmica Viúva Lamego* (25 Largo do Intendente Pina Manique; phone: 01-315-2401) makes and sells hand-painted reproductions of tiles from the 15th to the 18th century; its bird and animal motifs are famous. It also makes high-quality modern designs, as well as a variety of planters, dishes, lamp bases, and pottery. The outside of the store is completely covered with brightly colored tile scenes. Founded in 1741, *Faianças e Azulejos Sant'Anna* (95 Rua do Alecrim; phone: 01-342-2537) carries fabulous reproductions of 17th- and 18th-century tiles, made in the shop's own factory, as well as individual wall tiles, chandeliers, tables with tile inserts, flowerpots, and small kitchen-tile trivets. It will also create tiles for special orders. Even a browse around the store is a shopper's delight. The factory (96 Calçada da Boa Hora; phone: 01-363-8292) also can be visited, but call for an appointment first. *Vista Alegre* (52-54 Rua Ivens; phone: 01-342-8581; and 18 Largo do Chiado; phone: 01-346-1401) is recognized as the maker of Portugal's finest porcelain.

Coimbra – *Jorge Mendes* (19 Praça do Comércio; phone: 039-22620; and 9 Praça do Comércio; phone: 039-25646) sells some of the finest copies of 15th- to 17th-century porcelain and ceramics in town. *Sociedade de Cerâmica Antiga de Coimbra* (2 Quintal do Prior; phone: 039-23829) makes and sells reproductions of old Portuguese ceramics, and is the only factory currently producing the special, pale flora and fauna designs typical of the 18th century. Open to visitors on weekdays.

CURIOSITY SHOPS: A peek into a boutique or specialty shop should provide ample insight into the Portuguese way of life, of both the past and the present. Take a look at *Casa Fânzeres* (132-134 Rua do Souto; Braga, phone: 053-22704), the oldest religious-artifacts shop in town, both selling and restoring religious objects. In the Madeira islands, the commercial center *Bazar do Povo* (1 Rua do Bettencourt, Funchal; phone: 091-22055) has an old shop that features inexpensive odds and ends from another era.

DESIGNER CLOTHING: While Portugal may not be a center for haute couture, it is possible to find some unique styles at good prices. Whatever the latest trend, visitors can rest assured that Portugal's designers are up-to-date.

Lisbon – *Ana Salazar* (87 Rua do Carmo; phone: 01-347-2289) is the forerunner in the capital. She draws artistic inspirations from the turn of the century and the 1940s. Also considered among the best by locals is *Harriet Hubbard Ayer* (12 Rua Manuel de Jesus Coelho; phone: 01-352-0516), where trendy native-born designer José Carlos sells his clothes exclusively. *New York* (206 Rua do Ouro; phone: 01-342-1764) is a classy shop featuring the latest in women's clothes. *Porfirios* (63 Rua da Vitória; phone: 01-346-8274) is popular with young and with-it dressers. *Rosa & Teixeira* (204 Av. da Liberdade; phone: 01-542063) is a highly ranked tailor selling his own lines for men and women.

Porto – *Nanni Strada* (1533 Av. da Boavista; phone: 02-609-2745) is a Milan designer currently designing and manufacturing a hot line of clothes in Porto for men and women. *Pereira da Silva & Araújo* (114 Rua 31 de Janeiro; phone: 02-200-1009) is also a well-respected designer of menswear.

EMBROIDERY AND LACE: In Portugal, embroidery prices are determined by the intricacy of the stitch, not by the size of the item. Look carefully: Stitches made by a human hand cannot duplicate themselves over and over, and will therefore lack consistency; the more perfect the stitch, the more likely that an item was machine made. Lace and embroidery come from Madeira; crocheted items come from the Azores. Regions such as Viana do Castelo produce a coarse, embroidered linen. In order to protect their handicraft industry, the government of Madeira attaches a small lead tag to each piece of Madeira embroidery sold on the island, on mainland Portugal, or anywhere else in the world. Madeira embroidery, while slightly higher in price, is a timeless heirloom.

Lisbon – *Príncipe Real Enxoval* (12 Rua da Escola Politécnica; phone: 01-346-5945) specializes in handmade embroidery shipped in from one of the best factories in Madeira. *Madeira Superbia* (75A Av. Duque de Loulé; phone: 01-537968) carries a fine selection of high-quality linen from Madeira and Viana do Castelo. *Madeira House* (137 Rua Augusta; phone: 01-342-6813), Lisbon's oldest shop dealing in genuine Madeira embroidery and lace, sells less-expensive embroidered linens. *Madeira Gobelins* (40 Rua Castilho; phone: 01-356-3708) also carries fine embroidery, woven tapestries, and carpets from Madeira, as does *Casa dos Bordados da Madeira* (135 Rua Primeiro de Dezembro; phone: 01-342-1447), along with an excellent selection of lace and a wide variety of other Portuguese handicrafts.

Madeira – This tiny island overflows with embroidery shops, located principally in the capital city of Funchal. The British are credited with creating a market for Madeira embroidery and building a reputation for quality that continues to this day, with thousands of Madeiran women carrying on the craft. There is an abundance of embroidered tablecloths, napkins, nightgowns, and other clothing, as Funchal's well-stocked shops reveal. *Oliveiras,* at two adjoining downtown locations (22 Rua dos Murças; phone: 091-29340; and 11 Rua da Alfândega; phone: 091-20245), has one of the widest selections in town. The workroom housed on the floors above is one of 25 such factories in Funchal. Ask to visit, and see what it takes to create a finished tablecloth or negligee (and ask for the 25% factory discount). *Teixeiras* (13 Rua do Aljube; phone: 091-36616) is the place to go for something special; the prices are a bit higher, but the quality is a bit better, too. *Jabara* (59 Rua Dr. Fernão de Ornelas; phone: 091-34318) is another place to shop for embroidery. Opened in 1908, the store is a downtown landmark. *Mima* (298 Estrada Monumental; phone: 091-61901), away from the center in the hotel zone, is an excellent place for smaller items at good prices. Its downstairs shop is well stocked. Also try *Arte Ricamo* (34 Rua dos Murças; phone: 091-20705), specializing in large tablecloths, sheets, and pillowcases. *Agulha d'Ouro* (30 Rua dos Murças; phone: 091-24885) also has a fine selection of hand-embroidered linens at good prices.

Porto – *Casa dos Linhos* (660 Rua de Fernandes Tomás; phone: 02-200-0044) is a 100-year-old family-run firm specializing in the sale of linen and embroidery. *O Sonho* (322 Rua das Flores; phone: 02-200-7827), another family-run store, has a limited selection of fine embroidered baptismal dresses with lace and lace-trimmed bibs, plus hand-knit sweaters.

FOOD AND WINE: Food shopping in Portugal is a pleasure, probably because local customers are so demanding. Everything is fresh — sometimes so fresh that food stores hang unskinned rabbits in their windows. And of course, Portugal is famous for its wines — its *vinhos verdes* and ports.

Lisbon – Some of the country's best pastries are made by *Pastéis de Belém* (84 Rua de Belém; phone: 01-363-7423), an Old World coffeehouse famous for its delicious offerings sprinkled with cinnamon. *Bolachas Nacionais Estrangeira* (23 Rua Garrett) has a wide selection of fine wines as well as excellent cheeses, fruit, and bread.

Madeira – Run by the Madeira Wine Company, the *São Francisco Wine Lodge* in Funchal is the place to go for seven of the better-known labels, including Leacocks, Blandys, and Cossart Gordon. 28 Av. Arriaga, Funchal (phone: 091-20121).

Porto – All major grocery stores carry wide selections of wine and spirits.

GIFTWARE: Travelers can go crazy buying giftware in Portugal. The country is famous for its Atlantis brand crystal, which ranks in quality and design with Waterford and Baccarat. Vista Alegre for porcelain giftware and dinnerware is another safe bet. It is exported worldwide to better stores; New York's *Metropolitan Museum of Art* sells famous reproductions. Portuguese silver products are also well known and range from place settings to elaborately hammered-out soup tureens.

Lisbon – *Almorávida* (10-14 Rua do Milagre de Sto. António; phone: 01-862261) carries a wide variety of regional crafts, pottery, filigree jewelry, and Portuguese rugs. *Atlantis* (*Amoreiras Shopping Center;* phone: 01-693670) has fine crystal tableware from Alcobaça. *Vista Alegre* (18 Largo do Chiado; phone: 01-346-1401) offers a complete line of porcelain, from dinnerware to figurines. Some of the samples and discontinued designs sold downstairs are great values. This is a very sophisticated operation; it will even ship purchases to the US. *A. Chave de Prata* (174 Rua da Prata; phone: 01-877915) features well-stocked shelves of porcelain and glass giftware and some interesting bronze objects. *Vidraria da Marinha Grande* (38 Rua de São Nicolau; phone: 01-342-1840) is a unique store selling glass and crystal exclusively, with one of the largest selections in the country.

HANDICRAFTS: Manual arts are ubiquitous in Portugal.

Lisbon – *Artesanato Arameiro* (62 Praça dos Restauradores; phone: 01-342-0236) offers a wide variety of regional handicrafts including lace, rugs, ceramics, copperware, and filigree. If you happen to be in the city in July, don't miss the international *Feira de Artesanato* (Handicrafts Fair), held for ten days during that month. One of the finest fairs of its kind in all of Europe, it features lace, wicker, pottery, jewelry, hand-knitted items, ceramic and copper dishes, embroidered tablecloths, crystal, the famous Arraiolos rugs, and much more (in the *Feira Internacional de Lisboa* building, Praça das Indústrias; phone: 01-362-0130).

Coimbra – Coimbra has beautiful handicrafts, examples of which are exhibited and sold in the *Casa de Artesanato da Região de Coimbra,* in the historic Torre de Anto (45 Rua de Sobre-Ripas; phone: 039-23886).

Porto – The recently opened *Centro de Artes Tradicionais* (37 Rua de Reboleira; phone: 02-320076) features a permanent exhibition of arts and crafts pieces for sale, including plasterwork, pottery, and woodcarving.

JEWELRY: There are excellent jewelry bargains in Portugal. Silver or gold are the things to buy. Filigree is delicate silver threads made into earrings, necklaces, and bracelets. All Portuguese gold jewelry, by law, must contain at least 19.2 karats. Rua da Prata and Rua Augusta are two of the better streets for jewelry in Lisbon, Rua das Flores in Porto.

Lisbon – *The King of Filigree* (58 Rua da Prata; phone: 01-877441) sells silver filigree items made in Porto. Some are dipped in gold. Also try *W.A. Sarmento* (251 Rua do Ouro; phone: 01-342-6774) for gold pieces. *Ourivesaria Diadema* (166 Rua do Ouro; phone: 01-342-1362) sells gold, filigree, and souvenirs. Another shop worth a try is *Ourivesaria Pimenta* (257 Rua Augusta; phone: 01-342-4564), offering fine jewelry, watches, and silver.

Coimbra – *Patrão Joalheiros* (104 Rua Visconde da Luz; phone: 039-23096) is one of the oldest and most respected jewelers in Coimbra, selling lovely Portuguese filigree, silver salvers, and silver tea and coffee services. *Agata Joalharia* (2 Escadas de São Tiago; phone: 039-22361) sells fine jewelry, beautifully mounted at reasonable prices.

Porto – *Luiz Ferreira & Filhos* (9 Rua Trindade Coelho; phone: 02-316146) is a small shop featuring chic and expensive jewelry and giftware. Its own designs mix sterling silver with quartz, marble, and other interesting stones. *Cândido José Rodrigues* (275 Rua das Flores; phone: 02-200-1840) has many antique jewelry pieces, as well as the shop's own creations, including some interesting silver animal figurines, all of superior quality. *David Rosas* (1471 Av. da Boavista; phone: 02-606-8464) is a sleek shop carrying expensive pieces. It is Portugal's largest manufacturer of silver animals, many life-size! It also specializes in custom silver frames. *Rosior* (263 Rua Eugénio Castro; phone: 02-606-8134) also carries a fine line of traditional and modern jewelry.

LEATHER GOODS: Most leather in Portugal comes from sheep and lambs; cows produce a heavier-quality skin that's made into jackets and coats. There are hundreds of stores selling leather jackets, coats, gloves, pocketbooks, wallets, and other items. Generally speaking, shoppers can tell the quality of the leather by the feel. The softer it is, the more expensive. Portugal's selection concentrates on leather accessories and shoes.

Lisbon – *Luvaria Ulisses* (87 Rua do Carmo; phone: 01-342-0295) specializes in leather gloves. *Escondipel* (9 Rua Ramalho Ortigão; phone: 01-542275) has fine leather goods and is well known for its fur creations.

Braga – *Herdeiros de Francisco José Ferreira* (124 Rua do Souto; phone: 053-74574) is the place for high-quality leather goods, including suitcases, briefcases, and ladies' handbags. Try *Sapataria Teresinha* (84-86 Rua do Souto; phone: 053-22943) for top-quality leather shoes made in the region.

Porto – *Vincent* (174 Rua 31 de Janeiro; phone: 02-200-2478) has a wonderful antique interior and sells top-quality leather jackets, pants, and coats.

MUSICAL INSTRUMENTS: Who can resist listening to the haunting sounds of Portuguese music? If you want to take the music home with you, check out a store in Braga called *Vadeca* (15 Largo do Barão São Martinho; phone: 053-71045) that sells the typical handmade *viola braguesa,* or *cavaquinho* guitar, from which the ukelele was developed.

RUGS AND TAPESTRIES: Rugs from Arraiolos, a small town near Evora, are reminders of the Moorish occupation of the Iberian Peninsula centuries ago. Today, local women still do needlepoint on these rugs in small workshops. They use 100% wool in the small petit point and the larger *ponto largo* stitch to create animals, birds, or more elaborate scenes. Depending upon the design and its intricacy, prices vary per square foot. Most establishments welcome special orders. The rugs can be found in stores all over the country, even tourist souvenir shops, and (surprise!) there are many suppliers in Arraiolos itself. Prices in the US, in some cases, are three to four times higher.

Lisbon – *Casa Quintão* (30 Rua Ivens; phone: 01-346-5847) is one of Lisbon's finest Arraiolos rug stores. Several other shops selling Arraiolos rugs are *Casa dos Tapetes de Arraiolos* (116 Rua da Imprensa Nacional; phone: 01-396-8246); *Tapetes Trevo* (33 Av. Oscar Monteiro Torres; phone: 01-797-8415); and *Casa Regional da Ilha Verde* (4 Rua Paiva de Andrade; phone: 01-325974). *Galeria Sesimbra* (77 Rua Castilho; phone: 01-387-0291), Lisbon's second-oldest gallery, commissions well-known Portuguese artists to create designs that are transferred onto needlepoint canvases. The gallery stocks a huge supply of Agulha tapestries, which are 100% wool, hand-stitched, limited editions in three-dimensional motifs.

Arraiolos – *Kalifa* (44-46 Rua Alexandre Herculano; phone: 066-42117) is the oldest workshop, as well as one of the most highly regarded. *Tapetes Calantica* (20 Rua Alexandre Herculano; phone: 066-42356) has a wide variety of tapestries and rugs. *Fracoop* (Praça Lima Brito; phone: 066-42277), a cooperative, carries items from a number of different workshops. The long-established firm *Condestavel* (Av. Bombeiros Voluntarios; phone: 066-42423) offers many designs, as does its store in Evora (66 Rua 5 de Outubro; phone: 066-42219).

SHOES: Portuguese styles are fashionable, and the leathers used are soft and durable. Women's shoes rarely come in half sizes, but men's do. Many shoe stores also carry leather accessories.

Lisbon – *Charles* (109 Rua Augusta; phone: 01-347-7358; and 105 Rua do Carmo; phone: 01-347-7361) is a national chain store that has its own factory. It's the only store in Portugal that makes women's half sizes. It also specializes in Italian designer brands. *Helio* (93 Rua do Carmo; phone: 01-342-2725) sells top-quality shoes for both men and women.

SPORTING GOODS: Department stores are usually the best bet, carrying everything including equipment and clothing for hunting, camping, surfing, tennis, golf, fishing, and aerobic workouts.

Most Visitable Vineyards

Portugal has a long-standing wine making tradition, but the practice of opening wineries to the visiting public is still relatively new here. Because of this, and the vast profusion of small vineyards, it is advisable to make arrangements in advance. In Roman times, when Portugal was known as Lusitania, its wines were shipped to Italy. During the middle of the 13th century, the

Portuguese monarchy ordained that all wine growing be submitted to royal protection and regulation, and that vineyards be planted on all arable lands not suited to growing grain.

Wine grapes are grown almost everywhere today in Portugal; approximately 8% of its arable land is devoted to vineyards. Production, however, is concentrated in the central and northern parts of the country.

Portugal's northern Minho district is famed for its *vinho verde,* or "green wine," so named not for its color (there is also a red *vinho verde*), but because the grapes are gathered before they are quite ripe and are then allowed to ferment for a very brief period, to produce a light, dry wine that is often slightly effervescent and has a low alcohol content. The special grapes used are such unfamiliar varieties as loureiro, pedernã azal, espadeiro, verdelho, trajadura, and borraçal. A few of the better *vinhos verdes* come from just north of the Douro in the Amarante region, but the finest, made from the alvarinho grape, hail from the area between the Lima and the Minho rivers, in the far north of the country. *Vinhos verdes* account for one-quarter of Portugal's total wine production.

From the granite and schist slopes along the Dão, Mondego, and Alva rivers in the north come the traditionally prestigious dão wines. They are no longer Portugal's prize wines, but the reds from this region can still be excellent if they are well aged, and the whites, at their best, are delicately dry and flowery. Farther to the west, north of the city of Coimbra, the Bairrada region produces robust, aromatic red wines and crisply dry whites.

Although the great vineyards of the Douro Valley are best known as the producers of port, the region has also come into prominence in recent years as the home of some of the country's finest table wines. Nowadays, aristocratic douro wines such as the famed barca velha from the Quinta do Vale de Meão vineyards, and the Quinta do Cotto's Grande Escolha labels, have become collector's items for oenophiles.

The introduction of modern techniques has begun to revolutionize wine production in the south. Vineyards such as the Herdade do Esporão in the Reguengos region near Evora are now producing wines that vie in quality with the great classic wines of the northern and central regions.

But Portugal's particular vinicultural strength is in its port and madeira wines. Fortified with vinous spirits, moderately sweet, and with a high alcohol content, these are wines for drinking before or after meals. Port wines come from the hillside vineyards of the Upper Douro Valley, but they take their name from the city of Porto, at the mouth of the river, where they are blended, aged, and bottled. Madeira wine is produced on the island of the same name. Both are blended wines produced by the *solera* system: a combination of the produce of several different years. Vintage ports or madeiras occur when the wine of a particular year is considered to be of especially high quality and the producer sets it apart to be aged alone.

Though the wine dealers in the Porto suburb of Vila Nova de Gaia offer winery visits and tastings at their lodges (where the port is stored before shipment), this most often includes just a brief explanation — with mock-ups — of the port wine making process and a meager sampling of the more mediocre wares. This is an opportunity, however, to taste the sherry-like white port, which is not exported. Beyond this, winery visits are by no means a touristic event in Portugal. Those interested in learning more about the wines of the country can write ahead to the port wine and dão wine associations, whose experts will provide literature and opportunities to observe the wine making process. The port wine organization is the *Instituto do Vinho do Porto* (Rua Ferreira Borges, Porto 4000). The dão wine producers are at *Federação dos Vinicultores do Dão* (102 Rua Dr. Duarte, Viseu 3500). For more information about Portuguese wine dealers that conduct public tours and wine tasting visits, see *Porto,* THE CITIES, and *Madeira,* DIRECTIONS.

Spas

The spas of Portugal are a slightly different breed from those of the US. Unlike their American counterparts, which are predominantly exercise- and fitness-oriented, Portuguese spas take more of a therapeutic approach. They are health resorts in a purer sense, and are monitored by the country's National Health Association.

The spas are generally more primitive and don't offer much in the way of facilities. Most have been built around the many mineral and thermal springs of the northern and central regions of the country. Their charm lies in the fact that they aren't overcommercialized commodities, but places where one can bathe in soothing waters and find peace with nature. Full details are available from the *Associação Nacional dos Indústrias de Aguas Minero-Medicinais e de Mesa* (93 Rua de São José, Lisbon 1100; phone: 01-347-5623) and from the *Direcção-Geral de Turismo* (86 Av. António Augusto Aguiar, Lisbon 1000; phone: 01-575086). Additionally, many US travel agencies specialize in spa vacations. Two of the best are *Spa-Finders Travel Arrangements* (91 Fifth Ave., New York, NY 10003; phone: 212-924-6800; elsewhere in the US, 800-255-7727) and *Spa Trek International* (475 Park Ave. S., New York, NY 10016; phone: in New York City, 212-779-3480; elsewhere in the US, 800-272-3480).

CALDAS DO GERÊS, near Braga, Costa Verde: One of Portugal's most picturesque spas, it's situated in an unspoiled valley on the left bank of the Gerês River and inside the Peneda-Gerês National Park. The spa features immersion baths, bubble baths, and underwater massages, to aid in curing liver and kidney ailments and hypertension. The water here supposedly has the highest fluoride content in Europe. In addition to the natural springs, guests can enjoy swimming, tennis, fishing, boating, and hiking. Information: *Empresa das Aguas do Gerês,* 114 Praça da Liberdade, Sala E, Porto 4000 (phone: 02-313584 or 02-313587).

CURIA, near Coimbra, Costa de Prata: Portugal's most famous and most recommended spa. Located in the Bairrada region amid the freshness, peace, and shade of the forest of Buçaco, this spa is well known for its medicinal waters and its treatments for rheumatism, hypertension, gout, kidney ailments, gastric disturbances, and stress, including immersion baths and massages. There is also a gymnasium, a sauna, a swimming pool, tennis courts, fishing, boating, and a beach. Accommodations are available at the nearby *Curia Palace, Hotel das Termas, Grande Hotel da Curia,* and the *Estalagem Sangalhos.* For a truly memorable experience, stay at the *Palace Hotel do Buçaco,* a former 19th-century palace. The old-fashioned spa town of Luso and the glittering nightlife of Figueira da Foz are nearby. Information: *Sociedade das Aguas da Curia,* Anadia 3780 (phone: 031-521856 or 031-521857).

LUSO, near Buçaco, Costa de Prata: Like Curia, the Luso spa is set near the secular purity of the Buçaco woods and is one of the most renowned spas in Portugal. The mild climate and natural conditions of the region make for excellent physical and mental recuperation. The famous Luso waters rise in the São João spring in the center of town. Treatments include immersion baths, mud applications, and underwater massages. There is also a swimming pool, tennis courts, a sauna, a gymnasium, and ample opportunities for hiking. Accommodations are available at the nearby *Eden* hotel, *Grande Hotel das Termas,* and the luxurious *Palace Hotel do Buçaco.* Information: *Sociedade das Aguas do Luso,* Rua Alvaro de Castelões, Mealhada 3050 (phone: 031-93201).

MONTE REAL, near Leiria, Costa de Prata: Near the coast, halfway between Lisbon and Porto, Monte Real features some of Portugal's most famous ruins, as well as some of its most varied activities. There are nearby beaches at São Pedro de Muel,

Pedrogão, and Vieira. There is also a swimming pool, tennis courts, and fishing on the premises. The spa features Old World charm and a wonderful view of the poetic green fields of the Lis and Lena valleys. Information: *Termas de Monte Real,* Monte Real 2425 (phone: 044-62151).

SÃO PEDRO DO SUL, north of Viseu: The waters here — one of Portugal's most popular spa areas — lay claim to a variety of curative powers, effective in treating such ailments as asthma, bronchitis, a variety of other respiratory infections, and rheumatism. The ultramodern, 64-room *Hotel das Termas,* which overlooks the Vouga River, offers all sorts of amenities, including its own health club with a gymnasium, sauna, massage, solarium, and beauty center. A swimming pool, tennis, archery, and canoeing also are available to guests. Information: *Hotel das Termas,* Termas São Pedro do Sul 3660 (phone: 032-72333; in the US, 800-528-1234; fax: 032-71011; telex: 53595).

VIDAGO, near Chaves, northern Portugal: A cosmopolitan resort that produces most of the fresh water consumed in the country. Treatments include intramuscular injections of mineral water and medicinal baths. Located in a peaceful forest, the resort also has a swimming pool, sauna, horseback riding, tennis courts, golf, hunting, fishing, and a nightclub. Information: *SOVIPE, Vidago, Melgaço, and Pedras Salgadas,* 463 Rua de Santo António do Telheiro, São Mamaede de Infesta 4465 (phone: 02-901-4729).

VIMEIRO, Torres Vedras, Costa de Prata: The Vimeiro village, which dates back to the first French invasion in 1808, is today a much-frequented spa, known for its perfect climate. Activities include horseback riding, golf, fishing, swimming, and tennis. Vimeiro's famous waters are recommended for liver, kidney, and skin ailments. Information: *1876 Empresa das Aguas do Vimeiro,* Av. Conselheiro Fernando de Sousa, Lisbon 1000 (phone: 01-680568 or 01-651445).

For the Body

Great Golf

The British brought golf to Portugal around the turn of the century, but it was another 50 years before the game acquired any degree of popularity — and then it remained an activity of only the very social or the very rich. Today, an increasing number of foreign golfers have discovered that Portugal's 30 or so courses offer the perfect formula for a golfing vacation: a beautiful natural setting, ideal climate almost year-round, and some rather challenging layouts. American visitors will find little problem adjusting to Portuguese course configurations, which tend to be designed in the American mold — target golf, with fairly narrow fairways leading to greens surrounded by bunkers and trees.

Most trips to Portugal begin in the capital, and championship courses surround Lisbon. The most popular courses, however, are found in the south. There are some 20 courses scattered across the mainland and the islands of Madeira and the Azores. Among them are the championship courses in the southern Algarve — some of the finest playing places on the continent — where perfect climate and increasing numbers of courses have made the region a magnet for golfers. Some of the best are listed below.

Golf fees vary at most resorts. For guests staying at a golf hotel, greens fees usually are included. Expect to pay at least $40. Club rentals start at $20 per half-set, handcarts at $5, gas or electric carts at $35. Lesson costs vary according to the reputation of the pro and the price level of the resort. Some courses require a valid US handicap certificate. Information: *Direcção-Geral do Turismo,* 86 Av. António Augusto de Aguiar, Lisbon 1000 (phone: 01-575086), or the *Federação Portuguesa de Golfe,* 39 Rua Almeida Brandão, Lisbon 1300 (phone: 01-397-4658).

QUINTA DO LAGO, Almansil, Algarve: Three different 18-hole combinations are possible on these 27 holes, featuring several doglegs and lakeside tees. The holes are spread over some 300 acres, and were designed by the late American golf course architect William Mitchell. The three 9-hole layouts (A, B, and C) are considered among the best courses in Europe by *Golf Digest* and are most popular with British golfers, which makes English the prevalent language. The surrounding resort is a city within a city, featuring a shopping complex, a nightclub, and various restaurants, as well as other non-golf activities including horseback riding, swimming, and tennis. Some of the finest hotels in Portugal are nearby, including the deluxe *Four Seasons* and the elegant *T Club,* which is situated on the grounds of the resort. Information: *Quinta do Lago,* Almansil 8100, Algarve (phone: 089-396562; fax: 089-396574).

PALMARES GOLF COURSE, Lagos, Algarve: Not only is this 18-hole course, designed by Frank Pennink, an Algarve attraction, but it is also the only championship course in southern Europe offering anything remotely similar to links golf. The first 5 holes are strategically placed on dunes along an immense Atlantic beach of white sand. Then the course takes on a different character, namely high hills and deep valleys. Palmares is also the site of the Portuguese championship, *Amendoeiras em Flor,* and hosted the European Zone qualifying competition for the *1985 World Cup.* Facilities include a clubhouse with a restaurant and bar, pro shop, beach, and water sports. Accommodations are available at the nearby *Hotel de Lagos* or at *Meia Prata,* about 2 miles east of Lagos. Information: *Palmares Golf Course,* Lagos 8600, Algarve (phone: 082-762953 or 082-762961).

PENINA GOLF CLUB, Penina, Algarve: In the heart of the Algarve, 3 courses surround the large *Penina Golf* hotel. Designed by three-time *British Open* champion Henry Cotton, the courses have managed to overcome the disadvantage of being set on very flat terrain. Literally hundreds of thousands of trees and shrubs were planted to provide a frame for the golf holes, and this former rice field is now a fine test of golfing skill. The south course has been a frequent venue for championships and tournaments, with 18 holes ranging from easy to difficult. The 13th hole, a 190-yard par 3 that doglegs to the right around a lake to a tightly guarded green, requires a tee shot of 190 yards in order to avoid the aquatic wildlife. There also are two 9-hole courses, which are said to "separate the men from the boys." Information: *Penina Golf Club,* PO Box 146, Penina, Portimão 8500, Algarve (phone: 082-415415; in the US, 800-225-5843 or 800-223-6800; fax: 082-415000).

PARQUE DA FLORESTA, Salema, Algarve: This development, just inland from the little coastal fishing village of Salema (15 minutes from Lagos), provides the ideal environment for golfers yearning to get away from it all. The unspoiled 318-acre estate features an 18-hole course designed by Pepe Gancedo, the Spanish architect responsible for the *Torrequebrada* course on Spain's Costa del Sol. The 564-yard-long 1st hole curves gracefully into the horizon, while the short 5th hole is a mere 120 yards, with no place to go except on or over the green. The 17th hole, surrounded by lakes, gives way to the 18th, which climbs past a magnificent pine to the green set in an amphitheater below the clubhouse terrace. Information: *Parque da Floresta,* Vale do Poco, Budens, Vila do Bispo 8650, Algarve (phone: 082-65333, 082-65334, or 082-65335).

CLUBE DE GOLF, Vale do Lobo, Algarve: Rugged and beautiful, this is perhaps Portugal's most scenic course. Located 20 minutes from Faro, the 27 holes here were designed by three-time *British Open* champion Henry Cotton. The famous 7th hole, perched atop sandstone cliffs at the edge of the ocean, is among the most photographed in Europe. There is also a driving range. This self-contained resort also offers the *Roger Taylor Tennis Clinic* (see *Tennis,* in this section) and a full range of water sports. Information: *Clube de Golfe,* Vale do Lobo, Almansil 8100, Algarve (phone: 089-393939).

VILAMOURA GOLF CLUB, Vilamoura, Algarve: Three courses set among umbrella pines and gentle slopes in sight of the sea. *Vilamoura I,* designed by Frank Pennink, plays to par 73, and its 6,923 yards add up to one of the best courses in the Algarve. The 6th hole is by far the most spectacular: an excellent par 3 with a narrow fairway cut through wild pine trees. Another feature favored by golfers is that the 5th, 9th, and 15th greens are close to the clubhouse, making for frequent stops at the "19th hole." *Vilamoura II* is a newer course, designed by Robert Trent Jones, Sr. In addition, the resort features tennis, horseback riding, shopping, water sports, and excellent restaurants. *Vilamoura III,* the club's latest layout, has 18 holes and a barrage of water hazards. The resort complex is in the midst of an ambitious expansion to include new villas, hotels, restaurants, and sports facilities, and is fast becoming one of the country's centers for golf and tennis enthusiasts. Numerous international tournaments are already held here, and it is one of the most popular resorts in the Algarve. Accommodations are available at the nearby *Dom Pedro Vilamoura* hotel, the *Vilamoura Marinotel,* or at the new *Ampalius* hotel; all offer special packages, reduced greens fees, and other golf specials. Information: *Vilamoura Golf Club,* Vilamoura, Almansil 8100, Algarve (phone: 089-389988).

QUINTA DA MARINHA GOLF, Cascais: Carved out of a thick umbrella pine forest, this 18-hole, par 72 course designed by Robert Trent Jones, Sr. is the centerpiece of a deluxe 330-acre residential resort complex. Sea-washed rock outcroppings and wind-blown dunes are visible along its 6,684 yards. The 14th hole features both the sea and a deep rocky gorge, which separates the tee and the plateau including the green. The 10th hole presents two large lakes joined in a figure eight by a narrow isthmus of land. Information: *Quinta da Marinha Golf,* Cascais 2750 (phone: 01-486-9881).

ESTORIL-SOL GOLF CLUB, Sintra: In the Sintra mountains 20 miles (32 km) from Lisbon, this course moves through pines, eucalyptus, and acacias, with the fairy-tale Pena Palace perched above. Although it is a short course (4,644 yards), offering 9 holes with 18 tees, it presents numerous challenges — among them the second green, which lies 33 feet above a sheer drop. Information: *Estoril-Sol Golf Club,* Sintra 2710 (phone: 01-923-2461).

ESTORIL GOLF CLUB, Estoril: Opened in 1928 and expanded in 1945, the club features 27 holes in a compact layout that winds through pines, eucalyptus, and mimosa, and offers wonderful views of the sea, the rolling countryside, and the Sintra mountains. To score low on this course, players must drive the ball well. The accent here is on accuracy rather than distance. The well-trapped greens offer plenty of birdie opportunities. For unusual play, take note of the 9th hole, which has to be seen to be believed — a highway runs between the tee and the green. The course is administered by the elegant *Palácio* hotel, which includes a swimming pool among its facilities. On the weekends, only 9 holes are open to non-members. Information: *Estoril Golf Club,* Estoril 2765 (phone: 01-468-0176).

LISBON SPORTS CLUB, Queluz: This relaxing 18-hole, par 72 course is set amid green hills, about 15 miles (24 km) from Lisbon on the Belas–Sabugo road. Other facilities include a clubhouse, swimming pool, tennis courts, and a restaurant. Although the club is private, non-members may play during the week; they must book a starting time with the club secretary or the caddy master. Information: *Lisbon Sports Club,* Queluz 2745 (phone: club secretary, 01-431-2482; caddy master, 01-432-1474).

AROEIRA CLUB DE CAMPO DE PORTUGAL, Monte de Caparica: Located 11 miles (18 km) from Lisbon on the Setúbal Peninsula, this 18-hole course, designed by Frank Pennink, stretches across rolling hills. Highlights are the 11th and 14th greens, both surrounded by seemingly unavoidable lakes and bunkers. Information: *Lisboa Country Club,* Monte de Caparica 2825 (phone: 01-226-3244; fax: 01-226-1358).

TRÓIA GOLF CLUB, Setúbal: This club is on the Tróia Peninsula, about 20 minutes from Setúbal by ferry, and a 30-mile (48-km) drive from Lisbon. A challenging Robert Trent Jones, Sr. creation, it offers fine views of the sea, sand dunes, and pines. Be careful of the 3rd hole, a long par 4 that runs along the beach, and the 14th, where a sharp dogleg to the left demands a good drive. Other amenities include a bar and restaurant, private beach, swimming pool, tennis courts, and a variety of water sports. Accommodations are available nearby. Information: *Tróia Golf Club,* Setúbal 2900 (phone: 065-44112; fax: 065-44162).

Tennis

In Portugal, tennis usually takes a back seat to golf. But many hotels and resorts have tennis facilities, and beginners and experts alike will find plenty of places to play. Racquets, balls, and courts are easily rented, and a single player can find a partner easily. The actual tennis-oriented resorts and clubs, however, are concentrated mainly in the Algarve, which is in the midst of rapid expansion, with more and more emphasis being placed on residential developments —

small communities of villas and townhouses clustered around sports facilities and the sea. So far, only the British and wise Americans have truly "discovered" this area, and thanks in part to their inroads, almost everyone speaks English. There are a number of exclusive areas where the tennis enthusiast can enjoy a vacation amid sandy beaches and warm waters.

Most Portuguese tennis courts have either an asphalt or clay surface, and traditional tennis whites are preferred — often required. Expect to pay about $7 per hour for court time. In most cases, court time must be reserved in advance. There is also an emphasis on the social aspects of tennis, and visitors will find that many hotels sponsor weekly tournaments and "get acquainted" parties where tennis enthusiasts can meet and mingle. In addition, there are a variety of members-only tennis clubs spread among the major cities and resort areas where, for a small additional fee, guests are permitted to play. Also keep in mind that tennis can be fun to watch, and despite its slow start, tennis as a spectator sport is catching on in Portugal. The country hosted its first tournament sponsored by the ATP (Association of Tennis Professionals) in 1989, in Estoril. For more information on tennis tournaments in Portugal, contact the *ATP,* 200 ATP Tour Blvd., Ponte Vedra Beach, FL 32082 (phone: 904-285-8000).

CARVOEIRO CLUBE DE TÊNIS, Praia do Carvoeiro, Algarve: Perched atop a mountain development overlooking the small fishing village of Carvoeiro, this private resort community and racquet club commands one of the most breathtaking views of the Atlantic and the whitewashed town below. Five of the 10 hard courts are floodlit for night play, and there is a half-size children's court — all adjacent to the racket-shaped swimming pool. The tennis center can provide as much (or as little) tennis activity as is desired. There is also a pro shop, various social activities, and occasional tournaments. Guest accommodations range from small apartments and townhouses to villas, complete with fireplaces, terraces, and gardens. Information: *Carvoeiro Clube de Tênis,* Apartado 231, Lagoa Codex 8400, Algarve (phone: 082-357847).

ROGER TAYLOR TENNIS CLINIC, Vale do Lobo, Algarve: Roger Taylor is to the Algarve what Lew Hoad is to Spain's Costa del Sol. Built amid the very planned, very developed, and very neatly organized Vale do Lobo complex, this 12-court (6 floodlit) facility has earned a reputation as one of Europe's top tennis centers. The club hosts special amateur tennis weeks twice a year, in June and November. Facilities include a pro shop, a swimming pool, a restaurant, and 6 squash courts. Accommodations surrounding the club range from standard and deluxe rooms at the *Dona Filipa* hotel to exclusive villas. Information: *Roger Taylor Tennis Holidays,* 85 High St., Wimbledon SW19 5EG, England (phone in Portugal: 089-394779; in England, 081-947-9727).

VILAMOURATÊNIS, Vilamoura, Algarve: Although it does not have the name of a *Wimbledon* champion behind it, this tennis resort has the push of a young up-and-comer, Victor Gonçalves, who is determined to put Vilamoura on the map as a premier tennis resort and host to international events. Currently, guests stay at the nearby *Dom Pedro Vilamoura* hotel, the *Vilamoura Marinotel,* or the new *Ampalius,* all of which offer plenty of opportunity for windsurfing, fishing, sailing, scuba diving, and golf. Completed so far are about 100 luxurious villas with private pools, terraces, fireplaces, and landscaped gardens. At press time, the resort was completing the addition of 17 courts to its existing 12 (all hard), bringing its total to 29; 4 will be in competition stadiums — one seating 3,000, another seating 10,000. Information: *Vilamouratênis,* Vilamoura 8125, Algarve (phone: 089-312125).

QUINTA DA MARINHA, Cascais: Also within view of the Atlantic on the aristocratic Estoril coast west of Lisbon, this golf and country club development offers privacy amid splendid, pine-studded surroundings. Villas and townhouses blend in with the landscape. Three of the 6 tennis courts are floodlit, and the estate also has a swimming pool and horseback riding, as well as golf. Information: *Quinta da Marinha,* Cascais 2750 (phone: 01-486-9881).

Horsing Around: Post Trekking/Trail Riding

There's nothing quite as delightful as seeing the countryside from the back of a horse or sure-footed native pony, heading through narrow trails, along abandoned train beds, and down wide sandy beaches — and staying away from the trekking center for up to a week at a time. Post trekking, or trail riding, as this activity is called, is not generally recommended for riders without experience, as it usually involves good horses and a fast enough pace to cover about 25 miles (40 km) a day. Usually a warm camaraderie develops among riders en route, as they traverse the rural miles. Post trekking is also a practically worry-free holiday: There are guides to keep riders going at a reasonable pace, to make sure the group doesn't get lost, and to arrange for the rider's luggage to be transported from one hostelry to the next.

ALGARVE: Southern Portugal's cork forests and beaches are within easy access of the Quinto do Lago estate, where Englishwoman Beverly Gibbons takes groups of riders out on elegant Lusitano steeds to tour the dunes and lagoons of the Algarve. Information: *Centro Hípico,* Quinto do Lago, Almansil 8100, Algarve (phone: 089-394369 or 089-396468).

ESTORIL AND CASCAIS: There is year-round riding along the sandy paths and beaches of Estoril and through the Marinha pine woods in Cascais. *Clube da Marinha* has its own stable, which offers lessons and an English-style pub. Information: *Clube da Marinha,* Quinta da Marinha, Cascais 2750 (phone: 01-486-9084). Nuno Veloso, in Cascais, organizes riding circuits and can provide details on watching horse-jumping competitions. Call him at 01-486-9084.

The *Portuguese National Tourist Office* (590 Fifth Ave., New York, NY 10036; phone: 212-354-4403) can provide further details on horseback riding.

Best Beaches

Bordering the southwest corner of Spain, with nearly 50% of its periphery surrounded by water, Portugal's shoreline has been a source of attraction as well as a gateway to the rest of the world for hundreds of years. The variety of sea, sand, and landscape range from the shivering shocks of the Atlantic surf, to the wild isolation of the Azores, to the lively excitement of the Algarve.

One way to choose a beach is by its lack of recognition. Since many of Portugal's most popular beach resorts are now being overrun by tourists, visiting them is as much of a return to nature as going to lunch at a salad bar. Many visitors, therefore, carefully take the time to seek out remote and undiscovered ocean paradises, far removed from the sands of mass tourism. Many others, however, head straight for the crowds. For those unable to avoid the large resorts, but wishing to escape the masses, try a visit in late August or September. The less-than-torrid Costa Verde is rather quiet during May — the tradeoff is paler tans and cooler waters for the luxury of a private beach.

ALGARVE, Tavira: It was in the Algarve, in this nether corner of Europe, that the end of the world was thought to begin. The lighthouse at Cabo de São Vicente still beams out over the horizon to keep ships from falling off the disk of the earth. The white stucco town of Tavira is still untouched by tourism. Fishing boats depart daily and return loaded with tuna and sardines for the evening's grill. The spacious beach is on the long, sandy island of Tavira, where shoreline turf is abundant, so much so that on Sundays in July, there's even room for an oceanside game of touch football. The pallid be warned — the water is warm and the waves gentle, but the Algarvian sun is deceptively wind-cooled and burningly fierce. Information: *Região de Turismo do Algarve,* 100 Rua Ataide de Oliveira, Faro 8000 (phone: 089-803672); in Tavira, at the tourist office on Praça da República (phone: 089-22511).

ESTORIL AND CASCAIS, Lisbon: As the countries of Europe found democracy, their exiled monarchs came here, turning this slice of coast into a retirement community for kings and queens, with even a tiny, turreted castle on the beach at Estoril. The villas have faded some, and many of the beaches are polluted, but the casino and the nightlife still gleam. And if this isn't temptation enough, outside Cascais awaits the Boca do Inferno (Mouth of Hell), a large hole bitten out of rock by the angry Atlantic. A little farther out, the ocean spits white spray and hammers at the chiseled cliffs of the Cabo da Roca, the westernmost point of the mass of land that stretches from here east to the Bering Straits. Ideal for windsurfing, the beach at Guincho at sunset has a perfect view of the Cabo, as well as the last drops of daylight in Europe. Information: *Junta de Turismo da Costa do Estoril,* Arcadas do Parque, Estoril 2765 (phone: 01-468-0113).

NAZARÉ, Costa de Prata: In some respects a typical tourist beach town, it nonetheless retains some of its ancient customs and traditional garb. Men typically wear plaid pants rolled up to their knees and stock their tobacco, matches, and lighters in their black caps. Women often wear seven petticoats and clean and salt the fish along with the men. The Praia quarter, the area near the beach, affords glimpses of colorful fishing boats and fishermen mending nets. Perhaps more interesting is the Sítio — the Old Town, on a cliff far above the beach — where the church of Nossa Senhora da Nazaré is located. The church's small black image of the Virgin is carried down to the sea during the town's annual *romaria,* in September. At night, when the fishing boats return, head over to the port to watch the local restaurateurs bid for the best-looking catches of the day. Information: *Pôsto de Turismo,* 23 Rua Mouzinho de Albuquerque, Nazaré 2450 (phone: 062-561194).

Gone Fishing

With mile after mile of sun-soaked Atlantic coastline, over 150 varieties of fish, and mostly unpolluted waters, Portugal is truly an angler's paradise. Deep-sea enthusiasts can wrestle year-round with swordfish, ray, tuna, shark, trout, and snapper, while freshwater anglers can cast for tench, salmon, carp, trout, pike, bass, barbel, and chub. Although there are numerous lakes and rivers for fishing, it is not a wide-open free-for-all. In order to protect and maintain their fish populations, Portugal has instituted numerous restrictions for visiting anglers, as well as for locals. There are no restrictions for deep-sea fishing, but freshwater fishing has its share. There are limits on where and when fishing is permitted, as well as various catch limits. These laws are often so dizzying that the effort to obtain permits and satisfy restrictions may not be worth the day spent at sea. Consequently, many of the best — and most convenient — outings are organized through marinas and the various resorts along the water.

Nearly all game-fishing waters in Portugal are tightly controlled by the various local and regional governments. Some regions do not allow foreigners to fish in their waters, period! Those that do require the appropriate licenses and permits, but bear in mind that these documents do not grant fishing enthusiasts the right to clean out the ocean, lakes, rivers, or streams. There are strongly enforced catch limits, as well as strict rules regulating minimum sizes, bait and tackle, and Sunday fishing. Sea angling in Portugal is very common, and no license is required.

Because of Portugal's mild climate, fishing tends to be good year-round. There is an awesome variety of over 200 species; some such as the scabbard fish, which averages 6 feet in length, are unique to Portuguese waters. There are three species of trout native to Portuguese waters: rainbow trout, *fareo* trout, and sea trout. The rainbow can be found only in lagoons and dams in the northern and central regions of the country, the *fareo* is common in almost every river and stream, and the sea trout is found in the Minho and Lima rivers. Black bass is best found in lagoons and dams throughout the country, especially in the Algarve, as well as the natural lagoon in Pateia de Fermentelos, near Agueda, about 25 miles (40 km) north of Coimbra. Salmon appears only in the Minho and Lima rivers. The best spot to catch it is in the north end of the Gadanha, a Minho tributary, near Monção. Portugal also boasts a variety of shellfish, namely dog whelks, rock and giant lobsters, crabs, and spider crabs. Sports fishermen divide the Portuguese coastline into two distinct zones, with the frontier between the two lying more or less at Peniche (regarded as the center of Portuguese big-game fishing), in the center of the coastal area. The northern zone tends to be richer in cold-water fish, such as skate, grouper, tope, shark, and bass. The coast between Moledo and Porto (encompassing Vila Praia de Ancora, Esposende, Ofir, Póvoa de Varzim, Viana do Castelo, Vila do Conde, and Espinho), Figueira da Foz, and the towns of Nazaré and São Martinho do Porto are among the best areas, and are especially good for visitors because of the abundance of fishing boats.

ALGARVE: It is truly an experience of a lifetime to hook and finally bring in a mako or a hammerhead shark. The warm southeastern currents provide this area with a prolific and varied marine life. For many years, only fishing villages existed along Portugal's southern coast. Today, the extreme ends of the Algarve remain much as they were. The sun-roughed skin of fishermen, their hands tough and calloused, their character lines smooth and telling, will greet visitors who decide to venture out on their own. In between, near the resort areas of Faro, Vilamoura, Lagos, and Portimão, visitors are better off taking an organized tour out to sea. Big-game fishing is the sport here. Spectators are invited as well, and there are sun decks and bar service to keep them occupied. Information: *Surfpesca,* 35 Rua Santa Isabel, Portimão 8500 (phone: 082-25450). Other big-game fishing is available through the Algarve's *Big-Game Fishing Center,* Cepemar, 24A Praça da República, Portimao 8500 (phone: 082-25866).

AZORES: The nine-island Azorean archipelago, called the stepping-stones between the Old and New worlds, offers astounding results for big game anglers. Much of the sea surrounding the islands, especially the islands of São Miguel, Faial, and Terceira, are truly virgin waters, virtually untouched and undiscovered. From May through July, millions of large fish such as Allison tuna roam the surface, feeding on smaller fish. White and blue marlin, broadbill swordfish, and bluefin tuna have also been spotted here on a regular basis. For the light caster, the Azores present a fascinating array of amberjack, bluefish, barracuda, tuna, mackerel, and jack crevalle. Information: *Pescatur,* 1 Largo Francisco Tavares, Ponta Delgada, São Miguel, Azores 9500 (phone: 096-24757), or *World Wide Sportsman, Inc.,* PO Drawer 787, Islamorada, FL 33036 (phone: in Florida, 305-664-4615 or 305-238-9252; elsewhere in the US, 800-327-2880).

COSTA VERDE: The Minho River and its tributaries, particularly the area between Valença and Melgaço, are ideal for game fishing. The Lima and Homen rivers near Gerês, and the rivers near Trás-os-Montes, are excellent spots for trout and bass. A good base for a Costa Verde fishing trip is Viana do Castelo. Once a Roman outpost, this small, pleasant town offers easy access to the bucolic Lima River and the coast. Information: *Pôsto de Turismo,* Rua do Hospital Velho, Viana do Castelo 4900 (phone: 058-822620).

NAZARÉ, Costa de Prata: This little village lives for the sea. Its people spend the day either on the water, cleaning and salting fish, or preparing bait. Once known only to diehard fishermen, Nazaré has become a very popular, rather touristy beach resort, but its fishing tradition remains intact. Information: *Pôsto de Turismo,* 23 Rua Mouzinho de Albuquerque, Nazaré 2450 (phone: 062-561194).

PENICHE AND THE BERLENGA ISLANDS, Costa de Prata: Long dependent on the fishing industry, the city of Peniche, some 30 miles (48 km) from Obidos, is a working town often ignored by tourists on their way to the Ilhas Berlengas (Berlenga Islands). This is a bustling fishing port whose colorful fleet can be seen unloading the daily catch by the tons and where seafood restaurants are plentiful (the local version of *caldeirada* is famous). Information: *Pôsto de Turismo,* Rua Alexandre Herculano, Peniche, Leiria 2520 (phone: 062-79571).

TOMAR, Ribatejo: Mix with the locals at Tomar's *Clube dos Amadores de Pesca* and hook up with a fisherman familiar with the ways of the famous Nabão River, which crosses through the town. The Alva River and the Ribeira de Alge, north of Tomar, are also good spots for catching trout and bass, among other fish. Information: *Pôsto de Turismo,* Av. Dr. Cândido Madureira, Tomar 2300 (phone: 049-313237).

Freewheeling by Two-Wheeler

Because of the mild climate in Portugal, touring by bicycle is easy and the itinerary possibilities are nearly inexhaustible. Visitors who pedal through the Portuguese countryside will get to know parts of the country that most people never see. These are the real sights, the hidden enclaves still untouched by tourism. Leisurely bicycle rides pass through tiny fishing villages and medieval towns occasionally dotted with Moorish ruins. A variety of terrain exists in Portugal, although there is much flat land and the roads tend to be narrow, and cyclists almost always share them with farmers riding their mules, a sack of feed draped over each side. It is not uncommon for riders to have to stop to let shepherds, with crooked walking sticks in their hands and toothy grins on their faces, cross the road with their flocks.

Those who have traveled around Europe by bicycle before will find that a cycling vacation in Portugal is slightly more primitive than in most other Western European countries. There is hardly an abundance of sophisticated repair shops, nor even the guarantee of well-surfaced secondary roads. Bicycle rentals are available, but not omnipresent. Intermediate and diehard cyclists will want to bring their own bicycles and gear. Airlines will generally transport bikes as part of passengers' personal baggage, but they may insist that the entire bike be crated; check with the airline before departure. Also be sure to confirm insurance coverage.

Some cyclists choose to travel alone through Portugal. Others, however, team up with fellow cyclists and soon become fast friends. The natives are so friendly, they will practically apologize if they cannot accompany a rider to his or her destination (many riders often wind up staying in one place longer than they had planned). It does help, however, to have a rudimentary understanding of Portuguese, especially when touring the rural routes, as most people in the countryside do not speak English. A pocket dictionary is heartily recommended. As usual, taking along a basic set of tools and spares, including a tire pump, puncture repair kit, tire levers, spoke key, oil can, batteries and bulbs, rag, extra spokes, inner tubes and tires, pliers, and odd nuts and bolts, is also a good idea. Traveling with a minimal amount of cash and a credit card is also advised. In addition, take along a good map; Michelin generally has the best.

If the thought of biking alone is less than a satisfactory vacation idea, there are numerous organized bicycle tours in Portugal. For information on bicycle tours, see *Camping and Caravanning, Hiking and Biking,* GETTING READY TO GO.

When cycling in Portugal, always remember that it is more relaxing and enjoyable to take it slowly and enjoy the country's sights and sounds. After choosing a region, consult the local tourist literature. Then plot out the tour on a large-scale highway map of the country. Base daily mileage on what usually is covered on the road at home, but be sure to allot time for en route dawdling — chats with the locals, walks through ruined castles, wine and cheese at the local bar.

ALGARVE: Portugal's coastal resort area provides some of the country's best cycling. The roads are fairly flat, the temperatures remain moderate year-round, the towns are very attractive and well spaced, and the landscape is a lyrical mixture of blue sky, fine golden sand, and crystalline water. This circuit begins in Vale do Lobo or the Quinta do Lago area, the center of activity in the Algarve and the point from which cyclists can choose to ride either east or west. Ride out to Sagres, the southwesternmost point of Europe, and watch the sun set like a ball falling off the edge of the earth. The region between Faro and the Spanish border is the least developed and most undiscovered, and makes for a very tranquil and leisurely ride. Information: *Pôsto de Turismo,* 8-12 Rua da Misericórdia, Faro 8000 (phone: 089-803604).

ALTO ALENTEJO: This is the northern part of Portugal's plains region, flat and largely unpopulated. For cyclists looking to escape the city, this is a perfect route. Begin in the walled town of Elvas, conveniently situated some 20 miles (32 km) west of the Spanish border, and known throughout Portugal for its sugarplums. The tour passes through large farms and whitewashed hamlets, where olive and cork trees dot the countryside, to Evora, a medieval university town filled with reminders of the 15th and 16th centuries. The entire city is practically a living museum. Information: *Pôsto de Turismo,* 73-74 Praça do Giraldo, Evora 7000 (phone: 066-22671).

COSTA VERDE: This very green region in the northwestern corner of the country extends from the Douro River to Porto and up to the Minho River near the Spanish frontier. The route offers a close look at Porto, home of Portugal's famous port wines, and continues into the rolling hills and elegant parks of Braga, as well as the wine region of Viseu. The terrain here is challenging, but the roads are in good condition and very quiet. Information: *Pôsto de Turismo,* 25 Rua Clube Fenianos, Porto 4000 (phone: 02-312740).

Great Walks and Mountain Rambles

Almost any walker will say that it is the footpaths of a country — not its roadways — that show off the local landscape to best advantage. Closer to earth than when driving or even biking, those on foot notice details that might not otherwise come to their attention: valleys perfumed with almond blossoms, for instance, or hillsides dotted with villages; sheep gambol in the shade of fig and cork oak trees, and the friendly company of the sun makes the leaves shine and the hilltops glisten.

Portugal's topography makes walking here a pleasurable pastime. There is agreeable terrain for walkers and hikers of all abilities. The hills of northern and central Portugal and the sandy beaches of the Algarve all make for peaceful, pleasant strolls or climbs. There are a number of national parks to explore, while visitors less attracted to wilderness will find villages perched on high, with cobblestone streets, mansions, churches, ruins, and shops that are guaranteed to hold their interest and challenge their feet. Add to this a climate that is generally benign (Portugal is often referred to as the California of Europe), friendly natives, and good food — all the ingredients of a perfect expedition.

Before choosing a specific area of the country for hiking, look at a general road map of Portugal that shows physical characteristics, so as not to opt for terrain that is too demanding for one's level of fitness. For those who are sedentary, the choice of a rugged region would be foolhardy. To make the outing safe and pleasant, it is imperative for hikers to know their own limits. Unless they are very experienced, hikers always should stick to the defined areas — and *always* let someone know the planned destination and time of expected return (leave a note on the car if hiking alone). Those who prefer going as part of an organized tour should contact a local hiking club, a travel agent, or one of the many tour packagers specializing in hiking tours. For information on Portuguese hikes, see *Camping and Caravanning, Hiking and Biking,* GETTING READY TO GO.

Since hot weather is not necessarily a welcome companion on a walk, it's best to avoid the southern regions in midsummer. And since it can get warm almost anywhere in Portugal between May and September, the wise walker will get most of a day's journey done before midday. Basic hiking essentials should include a sturdy pair of shoes and socks, long pants if headed into heavily wooded areas, a canteen, a hat, sunblock, rainwear, and something warm, just in case. It is always best to dress in layers. Also make sure to wear clothes with pockets, or bring along a pack so that both hands can remain free. Some useful but often overlooked tools include a jackknife, waterproof matches, a map, a compass, and snacks. In the more remote areas, a backpack, sleeping bag and pad, cookstove, food, and other gear are required.

Portugal's best treks are not quite as varied as those of its Iberian neighbor. The country is generally flat, with its highest peak, the Malhão da Estrela (also called Torre, or "Tower"), rising only 6,532 feet. Still, there are numerous enjoyable walks to be had — rambles through countrysides laden with natural beauty and the occasional Moorish ruin. Best bets include the Algarve, the Costa Verde, and the Costa de Prata.

ALGARVE: This is one of the most ideal places for hiking, because the temperature is always just right — visitors are practically guaranteed clear skies all summer and steady breezes that keep the temperatures bearable. One of the most interesting places to walk along Portugal's southern coast is in the vicinity of Sagres, at the extreme southwestern corner of the country, and once considered the end of the world. The sunsets here alone are worthy of a visit. Some 40 miles (64 km) inland to the east is Porto de Lagos, on the road to Monchique. The town of Silves is 6 miles (10 km) east of Porto de Lagos, and between the two is a circular hiking route that skirts groves of orange trees and an irrigation ditch as it follows the course of the Arade River and Ribeira de Odelouca. Where the two meet, the Arade estuary, islands, and rice fields are visible. The village of Monchique and the hills surrounding it are also worthy hiking country. After perusing the village streets, follow a track of stone pavement that leads through the woods to an old convent, from where there is a wonderful view over the valley. The route begins at Monchique's main square, then rises up the slope along Rua do Porto Fundo, located at the top of the square. Upon reaching Rua Dr. Bernardino Moreira, turn right and continue to follow the road up, along Rua da Igreja, through Praça Alexandre Herculano, and along Rua Costa Gerdo, until finally reaching the Largo de São Gonçalo de Lagos, a small square. The street becomes steep here, but the reward is the scenic old convent in the distance. There are many walking tours of this region, and most can be found with the help of each individual area's tourist office. Ask for the book called *The Algarve Guide to Walks* (in English), which provides complete instructions on transportation, levels of difficulty, cafés along the way, length of tours, and more. Information: *Pôsto de Turismo,* 8-12 Rua da Misericórdia, Faro 8000 (phone: 089-803604).

ALTO ALENTEJO: Lonely little villages set between olive and cork trees are the treasures that await hikers in Portugal's plains region. The city of Portalegre, in the northern part of the region, lies in the foothills of the Serra de São Mamede, a mere 30 miles (48 km) from the Spanish border. This is a charming area, full of history. Sights include homes emblazoned with ageless family crests, as well as Moorish ruins, remnants of another era that ironically fit right in today. There are numerous footpaths between the villages surrounding Portalegre, and this is an idyllic place to escape the tourist traps of the coastal areas and truly savor the traditions of the Portuguese. Information: *Pôsto de Turismo,* Convento de Santa Clara, 25 Estrada de Sant'ana, Portalegre 7300 (phone: 045-21815).

COSTA VERDE, near Porto: This region has been called the cradle of the Portuguese nation throughout its vast history. Originally inhabited by the Celts some 3,000 years ago, it remains rich in tradition, natural beauty, and wonder. Along with the historical monuments dotting the countryside, the tour passes vineyards where the famous port and *vinho verde* wines are produced. Begin in Braga, one of Portugal's oldest Christian towns, surrounded by rolling green hills and elegant parks. Nearby is the Peneda-Gerês National Park, a splendidly unspoiled expanse of mountains, lakes, vegetation, and wildlife. Hiking routes between the main village of Gerês and Pedro Bela pass crashing waterfalls and natural pools. Information: *Pôsto de Turismo,* Av. Manuel Francisco da Costa, Gerês 4845 (phone: 053-65133).

COSTA DE PRATA, near Coimbra: The Silver Coast of Portugal offers hikers some of the country's most diverse terrain. Among the region's many scenic towns is a wide variety of magnificent mountain ranges, poetic green valleys, and high dunes. Among the must-sees is the Buçaco Forest, situated just outside the university town of Coimbra. Rocky paths shaded by luxurious foliage have drawn solitary hikers to this enchanted forest for centuries. The forest contains over 700 varieties of flora, including exotic plants from Asia and the Far East, brought by the first Portuguese explorers. What makes the area even more endearing is the lovely *Palace Hotel do Buçaco,* a former palace and hunting lodge. Wandering freely among the forest's many paths can be confusing, so pick up a map at the refreshment stand, located next to the palace. Information: *Pôsto de Turismo,* Largo da Portagem, Coimbra 3000 (phone: 039-23886 or 039-33028).

TRÁS-OS-MONTES: The Marão and Alvão ranges are among the mountains separating Portugal's northern coastal area from the more remote reaches of the Trás-os-Montes region. While difficult to reach, the fertile fields and rocky slopes of this zone are both challenging and rewarding to the dedicated and experienced hiker. Start off in Vila Real. Information: *Região de Turismo da Serra do Marão,* 94 Av. Carvalho Araújo, Vila Real 5000 (phone: 059-22819).

For the Mind

Museums, Monuments, and Ruins

A series of conquests, losses, and clever marriages left Roman ruins, Moorish castles, medieval turrets, and sinuous spires sculpted out of the land all over Portugal. Preserved and renovated, or ruined and crumbling, they stand as reminders of a turbulent and fascinating past.

Portugal has fostered the development of some of the most original artists in Europe. Such influential painters as Jan van Eyck and Nuno Gonçalves both made their greatest impact while working in Portugal, and native sons Alvaro de Pires and Luís de Portugal were also well known throughout Europe. Coimbra was the main center for sculptors, who produced the majority of religious sculpture still found in churches, cathedrals, and art museums today. While some of the works have made their way to various museums and art galleries in the US, the bulk of the masters' works remain where they originated, and you'll be able to see the paintings of Jorge Afonso displayed in Lisbon's *Igreja da Madre de Deus.*

A museum can be all the more pleasurable if a few simple guidelines are kept in mind. Rather than one long visit to a large museum, plan several short ones, staying for an hour and taking in no more than a dozen fine works each time. There's no fatigue quite like aching, yawning museum fatigue — which has been described as the dread "museum foot" — and when it has set in, merely sitting in front of a masterpiece for 3 minutes will not effect a cure.

MUSEU CALOUSTE GULBENKIAN E CENTRO DE ARTE MODERNA, Lisbon: Calouste Gulbenkian was an Armenian who lived in France and later in Portugal, invested in Iraqi oil, and bought Dutch paintings, Egyptian sculptures, Persian tapestries, and Oriental ivories, which now form the core of Portugal's artistic patrimony. The addition of the *Center of Modern Art* in the elegant, sprawling complex of the Gulbenkian Foundation brings this collection of 4,000 years of ancient art and exquisite bric-a-brac up to the minute with the latest in Op and Pop Art. A sinuous sculpture by Henry Moore and the oversize tapestries of the Portuguese Modernist José de Almada Negreiros are among the permanent fixtures, while thousands of other works play an ongoing game of musical walls. Information: *Museu Calouste Gulbenkian,* 45 Av. de Berna, Lisbon 1000 (phone: 01-797-4167).

MUSEU NACIONAL DE ARTE ANTIGA, Lisbon: Established in 1833 in the former palace of the Counts of Alvor, this is the best place to see Portuguese painting, dating back to its 15th-century origins. Since there is not much Portuguese painting abroad, the museum is worth a special visit, especially to see the works of Domingos António Sequeira and Nuno Gonçalves. The most prized possession is the six-panel *Panéis de São Vicente de Fora* (St. Vincent Panels), depicting Lisbon's patron saint — the only Gonçalves painting still extant and the one that launched him to fame. The museum also has a superb collection of early Oriental ceramics. Worthy of special attention are the Japanese painted screens portraying the first Portuguese visitors to Japan. Information: *Museu Nacional de Arte Antiga,* 95 Rua das Janelas Verdes, Lisbon 1100 (phone: 01-397-2725).

MUSEU NACIONAL DOS COCHES, Belém, Lisbon: Whether by curricle, chaise, litter, or tilbury, royalty travels in style. And of the stylish coaches that came from other courts, some of the most ornate, gilded, garnished, and tooled now sit in Lisbon's western suburb of Belém. Decorated with painted myths and sculpted cherubs, they carried princess brides from Paris or Vienna, paraded monarchs through Portugal, and simply wheeled nobles around gardens. Opened in 1905, the museum is housed in what was originally the 18th-century *Royal Riding Academy.* Connected to the Belém Royal Palace, it also houses an important collection of livery, harnesses, and bullfighting costumes. Information: *Museu Nacional dos Coches,* Praça Afonso de Albuquerque, Belém, Lisbon 1100 (phone: 01-363-8022).

TORRE DE BELÉM, Belém, Lisbon: This majestic, quadrangular, 5-story tower stands along the banks of the Tagus River, defying anyone to enter. Built between 1515 and 1520 to protect the seaward entrance of the Portuguese capital from pirates (it was originally situated farther out, surrounded by water, but land has since been reclaimed from the river), it later functioned as a prison. The Portuguese consider it a symbol of their brave past, and its image is often used on official papers. An excellent example of typically Portuguese Manueline architecture, it is richly decorated with sea motifs, statues, stone tracery, and Moorish balconies. Inside is a permanent exhibition of 15th- and 16th-century armaments and navigational instruments. Information: *Torre de Belém,* Av. Marginal, Belém, Lisbon 1100 (phone: 01-301-6892).

PALÁCIO NACIONAL DA PENA, Sintra: High atop one of the highest peaks in the Sintra range sits the Pena Palace, a fairy-tale castle that inspired Lord Byron to dub Sintra a "glorious Eden" in his autobiographical poem "Childe Harold's Pilgrimage." Built in 1840 by Ferdinand of Saxe-Coburg-Gotha, Queen Maria II's consort, who had bought a 16th-century monastery on the spot, this was the royal summer residence through 1910, when a republic was proclaimed in Portugal. The rooms inside are a delightful mixture of Indo-Portuguese and Sino-Portuguese furnishings, a fantasy in which only the eccentric would choose to live. The original cloister and chapel of the monastery were preserved; the latter has a black alabaster and marble altarpiece executed during the 16th century by Nicolas Chanterène, although its stained glass windows are 19th-century German. A short distance away sits the Moorish-style, 14th- to 16th-century Sintra Palace, erected over the remains of an 8th-century Arab structure. Most noticeable is the Hall of Swans, featuring paintings of swans with crown-shaped collars of gold. Information: *Palácio Nacional da Pena,* Parque da Pena, Sintra 2710 (phone: 01-923-0227), or *Pôsto de Turismo,* Praça da República, Sintra 2710 (phone: 01-923-1157 or 01-923-3919).

TOMAR, Ribatejo: The striking monuments of the medieval town of Tomar attest to its former status as the headquarters of the Knights Templars. These warrior-monks first set up residence here during the 12th century, but their fierce determination was passed down over generations to the villagers. The town's imposing fortress-palace, the Convento de Cristo, was built by the templars and their successors, the Knights of Christ, from the 12th to the 17th century. It is richly designed and decorated to express a triumphant Christianity during a time of exploration and conquest when Portuguese explorers set their sails and opened up the East for commerce and adventure. The exotic oceanic iconography associated with that era is displayed here. Tomar also was the home of a thriving Jewish community during the 15th century; its remains can be seen at the *Luso-Hebraic Museum of Abraham Zacuto* (73 Rua Dr. Joaquim Jacinto). This small museum, set up in the old Synagogue of Tomar, contains an assortment of tombstones with Hebrew inscriptions, collected from various sites. Information: *Pôsto de Turismo,* Av. Dr. Cândido Madureira, Tomar 2300 (phone: 049-313237).

PALÁCIO NACIONAL DE MAFRA, Mafra: This enormous monastery-palace is one of the largest historic monuments in Europe. Work on the imposing structure began in 1717, after Franciscan monks pursuaded King João V that if he built the monastery his wife would produce a long-awaited heir. When the first of his children was born soon after, the king spared no expense in showing his gratitude. Johann Friedrich Ludwig, an Italian-trained German architect, was commissioned to build a monastery for 13 friars, as well as a palace for the entire royal family and court. Completed in 1735, the structure includes a palace, the monastery, and a church, with an imposing façade containing some 4,500 doors and windows. Information: *Pôsto de Turismo,* Av. 25 de Abril, Mafra 2640 (phone: 061-52023).

The Performing Arts

In Portugal, much cultural activity centers around the *fado* (literally meaning "fate"), a style of singing and the country's unofficial national ballad. Its nostalgic strains pour out of numerous city and village nightspots through the early-morning hours. Equally important to the Portuguese is the variety of opera, ballet, and theater possibilities increasingly available to them. A complete listing of concerts, movies, plays, and exhibits appears in the Portuguese newspaper *Sete.* The *Gulbenkian Foundation* in Lisbon (45 Av. de Berna; phone: 01-797-4167 or 01-795-0241) sponsors classical music concerts throughout the year, in addition to a full program of art exhibits and ballet. During the summer, the foundation sponsors jazz concerts, Nordic festivals, and theatrical, music, and dance events in its gardens and salons. Also in the summer, there are regularly scheduled folk concerts and dance performances in the *Congress Palace* in Estoril. The Portuguese opera season begins in late September and lasts through mid-June.

GRANDE AUDITORIUM DE FUNDAÇÃO CALOUSTE GULBENKIAN, Lisbon: This performing arts center presents orchestral, choral, and solo works next to the museum that houses the formidable art collection of the late Armenian financier Calouste Gulbenkian. The foundation also supports its own ballet, orchestra, and choir. Information: *Grande Auditorium de Fundação Calouste Gulbenkian,* 45 Av. de Berna, Lisbon 1000 (phone: 01-793-5131).

PARQUE MAYER, Lisbon: Located in the center of the city off Avenida da Liberdade, Lisbon's dilapidated theater district hosts plays and *revistas* (revues) that combine satirical sketches, music, and dancing. They're performed in Portuguese, but that shouldn't stop anyone from enjoying the spectacle. Two Parque Mayer theaters are *Teatro ABC* (phone: 01-346-6745) and *Teatro Maria Vitoria* (phone: 01-347-8556).

TEATRO MUNICIPAL DE SÃO LUÍS, Lisbon: Located in the Chiado district, this is where the *National Ballet Company* performs with the *Portuguese National Broadcasting Station Orchestra.* Plays are also staged here. Information: *Teatro Municipal de São Luís,* Rua António Maria Cardoso, Lisbon 1000 (phone: 01-342-7172).

TEATRO NACIONAL DE DONA MARIA II, Lisbon: Some of the most important classical and contemporary plays are staged here year-round (except during July). All performances are in Portuguese. The theater stands on the site of a onetime royal palace that, during the 16th century, became the seat of the Inquisition. The square is much cheerier now, graced with many flower stalls, fountains, and open-air cafés. Information: *Teatro Nacional de Dona Maria II,* Praça Dom Pedro IV, Lisbon 1200 (phone: 01-342-2210).

TEATRO NACIONAL DE SÃO CARLOS, Lisbon: Ensconced in the Chiado district, this is the city's principal concert hall and opera house, an 18th-century jewel adorned in apricot, green, and gold. Performances include operas by such greats as Verdi, Rossini, and Mozart. The *National Ballet Company* also performs here, along with the theater's own symphony orchestra and choir. Information: *Teatro Nacional de São Carlos,* 9 Rua Serpa Pinto, Lisbon 1000 (phone: 01-346-5914).

TEATRO TRINDADE, Lisbon: Musicals and ballet are the fare in this theater. Information: *Teatro Trindade,* 9 Rua Nova da Trindade, Lisbon 1200 (phone: 01-342-0000).

ADEGA MACHADO, Lisbon: Fine examples of spirited folk dancing in addition to its moving renditions of the *fado* can be found here. 91 Rua do Norte (phone: 01-346-0095).

SENHOR VINHO, Lisbon: No gimmicks, no tourist tricks, this is the spot to hear *fado* as it's meant to be — pure and lyrical. 18 Rua do Meio à Lapa (phone: 01-397-2681).

Best Festivals

Festivals, direct descendants of the Greek drama marathons and the first *Olympic* games, are annual celebrations of the pleasures of creating, competing, or just plain existing. They let a visitor cram the best and most of any given experience into the shortest possible time — whether it's auto racing or chamber music, wine tasting or bullfighting.

In Portugal, the calendar year is a kaleidoscope of celebration, a constant whirl of dancing, drinking, and devotion. There are festivals to honor saints, bulls, horses, flowers, grapes, and shellfish. There are symphony orchestras and blaring local bands, dancers in ballet slippers and on stilts, and evenings lit by chandeliers or fireworks. Each festival bears the trademark of its town, and most fall on Catholic holidays — *Carnaval, Corpus Christi,* and *Holy Week* before *Easter* are celebrated everywhere — but many still show traces of their pagan roots. For the Portuguese *Feast of St. Bartholomew* (April 21–23) in Esposende, women dressed in white bathe in the ocean, then sacrifice a black chicken to exorcise the devil. For a complete listing of events, contact the *Portuguese National Tourist Office,* 590 Fifth Ave., New York, NY 10036 (phone: 212-354-4403).

A word of caution to those planning to hurl themselves into the merriment at one of Portugal's frothiest celebrations: Everyone loves a party, so be prepared for crowded hotels, crowded restaurants, crowded streets, and crowded auditoriums. Advance planning will mitigate much of the discomfort — so reserve rooms ahead of time — but it's still necessary to be prepared for being jostled, for waiting in line, and for paying $2 or more for a can of warm cola — all part and parcel of festival-going.

FÁTIMA, near Tomar, Ribatejo: Twice a year, the desolate land around Fátima teems with pilgrims who ride, walk, and drag themselves to where three children said they saw the Virgin Mary in 1917. Unlike most pilgrims, however, these worshipers come in modern clothes, without pomp or pageants or flowered carts, unorganized by any festival committee. This *romaria* (pilgrimage) is not swanky but sincere, not a folksy celebration of a shrouded local myth but a mass veneration of a 20th-century front-page story. Up to 1 million people converge on this tiny town on the eves of May 13 and October 13 to commemorate the reported appearances of the Virgin; the first witnessed only by the three young shepherds, the last by a crowd of 70,000 people. Information: *Direcção-Geral do Turismo,* 86 Av. António Augusto de Aguiar, Lisbon 1000 (phone: 01-575086), *Pôsto de Turismo,* Av. Dr. Cândido Madureira, 2300 Tomar (phone 049-313237), or *Pôsto de Turismo,* Av. Dom José Alves Correia da Silva, Fátima 2495 (phone: 049-531139).

NOSSA SENHORA DA AGONIA, Viana do Castelo, Costa Verde: A dawn serenade of bursting rockets and pounding drums awakens this seaside town for the joyous *Feast of Our Lady of Suffering.* For 3 days in August, there's a bustle of pilgrims and a burble of pouring wine. The holy statue of the Virgin is followed along a carpet of flowers by reverent revelers wearing giant heads with shiny red noses and toothy grins. The women deck themselves in golden heirlooms and the men strut in waistcoats, vests, and colored cummerbunds worn once a year for generations. At the conclusion, the statue is carried to the harbor to bless the fishing fleet, where the festival culminates in a blaze of fireworks. The festival may be named for the agony of indecision visitors will go through to select from the pottery and porcelain for sale at the outdoor market. Information: *Pôsto de Turismo,* Rua do Hospital Velho, Viana do Castelo 4900 (phone: 058-822620).

FEAST OF ST. ANTHONY, Lisbon: Although most people associate St. Anthony (of Padua) with Italy, he was actually born in the Alfama in Lisbon, and people here make much ado about it. The *Feast of St. Anthony,* held June 13 and the night before, is a bit like *New Year's Eve* and *New Year's Day.* Lisbon's Old Quarter comes alive on the eve: Dances are held in streets festooned with colored lanterns, and throughout the night gallons of good, rough wine are drunk to wash down mountains of sardines roasted on open barbecues. The saint is a powerful matchmaker. This is the night when the city's young girls hope to meet their future husbands and street stalls sell little pots of a spicy-smelling green herb called *manjericão* (a variety of sweet basil), each pot holding a message of advice or consolation for lovers. Information: *Direcção-Geral do Turismo,* 86 Av. António Augusto de Aguiar, Lisbon 1000 (phone: 01-575086).

HOLY WEEK, Braga, Costa Verde: Braga is famous for its religious processions, and though the crowds may be smaller than those that gather for *Holy Week* in Seville, Spain, the enthusiasm is no less fervent. Held annually a week before *Easter Sunday,* a day that also marks the start of Portugal's bullfighting season. Information: *Pôsto de Turismo,* 1 Av. Central, Braga 4700 (phone: 053-22550).

Antiques and Auctions

Antiques bargains abound in Portugal for the careful, tireless shopper. The country is particularly notable for its antique jewelry (especially filigree), old books, and ceramics, although much that is antique has already been sold. Although Portugal remains one of the least expensive European destinations, antiques prices have skyrocketed as their supply has dwindled. Nevertheless, the ardent antiques hunter will still find a variety of pleasures in Lisbon and, to a lesser extent, in other cities. Rua Dom Pedro V and Rua São Bento are the best browsing grounds in the capital. Portugal is famous for its needlepoint rugs, glazed ceramic tiles, and pottery.

The Fundação Ricardo Espírito Santo Silva in Lisbon is dedicated to Portugal's decorative arts. It features a museum full of antique furniture, silver, tapestries, paintings, rugs, and ceramics, as well as a school complete with a workshop, where artisans are trained to restore antiques and make accurate reproductions. The foundation is also a good source of information on Portuguese auctions. 2 Largo das Portas do Sol (phone: 01-862184).

A REPERTOIRE OF ANTIQUES SOURCES

SHOPS AND ANTIQUES CENTERS: There are basically three different types of places in Portugal to hunt for antiques. At the low end of the scale are the flea markets, where those willing to sift through piles of miscellanea may uncover a true gem, or at least a good bargain. Auction houses are another option that can often yield a good find or two. Antiques shops, however, are usually the best bet. They are convenient; the dealer already has made the rounds through the markets and has purchased the cream of the crop. These shops do tend to be on the expensive side, but the quality is excellent and the selection can't be beat. Antiques hunters are practically guaranteed to find something of interest in one of these shops.

Lisbon – Portuguese antiques dealers tend to congregate in certain areas. Most of the best Lisbon shops are spread along a 1-mile stretch, including Rua Dom Pedro V and Rua do Alecrim, that winds its way from the Bairro Alto to the Tagus River. Most are open Mondays through Fridays, from 9 AM to 1 PM and from 3 to 7 PM; Saturdays from 9 AM to 1 PM. For *azulejos* (antique tiles), go to *Solar* (68-70 Rua Dom Pedro V; phone: 01-346-5522), where stacks of glazed tiles from monasteries and palaces date back to the 15th century. Visitors also can find old pewter plates and oversize candlesticks. *Xairel* (3 Rua Dom Pedro V) is another winner. *Sotheby's* is represented by *Frederico Horta Costa* (*Amoreiras Shopping Center,* Av. Eng. Duarte Pacheco; phone: 01-657161). Portugal is also noted for its beautiful hand-stitched wool Arraiolos rugs. Antique rugs can be found at *Jalco* (44 Rua Ivens; phone: 01-342-8095). *Ourivesaria Aliança* (50 Rua Garrett; phone: 01-342-3419) has a selection of silver trays and tea service sets. At *Ana,* the tiny shop at the *Ritz Inter-Continental* hotel (88 Rua Rodrigo da Fonesca; phone: 01-658767), visitors can find tiles and small 18th-century plaques. For antique as well as modern jewelry, the place to shop is *W. A. Sarmento* (251 Rua do Ouro; phone: 01-342-6774). A family business begun in 1870, it has a collection of antique gold jewelry in its back room.

Anyone heading for Lisbon's antiques row should prepare for possible disappointment. One day there may be a stunning assortment; the next day, not much at all. Note that current regulations make it hard for foreigners to ship antique furniture home from Portugal, so make the proper inquiries before buying. To send purchases by air mail, parcel post, or freight, go to the American Visitors Bureau at 61 Rua Castilho (phone: 01-534879).

Outside Lisbon, there are some interesting buys in small villages around Porto, or in the Alentejo area east of Lisbon. The towns of Borba, Estremoz, and Evora are also good for antiques hunting.

FLEA MARKETS AND OTHER SPECTACLES: The heady mixture of rubbish and relic affords collectors the chance to find that special, unrecognized rarity. Try to arrive early, as markets quickly get crowded with other people who have the same idea.

Lisbon – The best bazaar is the flea market in the Alfama, the old Moorish part of town, Saturdays and Tuesdays on Largo de Santa Clara. Bargaining begins at sunrise. Though the market is open until noon, the best buys are gone long before that, so come early. Outside Lisbon, in São Pedro, near Sintra, antiques shops are open all day at the market on Largo Primeiro de Dezembro.

AUCTIONS: As any auction addict knows, this is a sport that combines the fanaticism of the stock market, gambling casino, and living theater. The Portuguese word for auction is *leilão,* and unlike auctions in New York, which usually are quite specialized, a Portuguese *leilão* offers an assortment of many kinds of objects. There are none held on any regular basis in Lisbon, although *Sotheby's* is represented by *Frederico Horta Costa* (*Amoreiras Shopping Center,* Av. Eng. Duarte Pacheco; phone: 01-657161); to find auctions in other areas of Portugal, inquire among antiques dealers and hotel concierges. Also check newspapers. Auctions are the perfect answer to rainy day blues, provided newcomers pay attention to these notes:

Don't expect to make a killing. Even Chinese peasant children are hip to the art market today, it seems. But chances of unearthing a real find are better for those who shop at smaller auctions.

Buy the catalogue before bidding. Catalogues often include a list of estimated prices. Those prices are not a contractual commitment, but they do act as a guide for prospective buyers. An elaborate stylistic code hints at the conviction the house may have about the age or authenticity of an item. The use of capital letters, of artists' full names, and of words like "fine," "rare," and "important" all carry positive connotations. The use of a last name only and of words like "style" and "attributed" should serve as warnings.

Visit the pre-sale exhibition carefully, thoroughly, and even repeatedly. There is the pleasure of browsing in a store without a hovering clerk. Even more important is the prospective buyer's chance to examine the offerings. *Caveat emptor* is the prevailing rule at any auction. Serious buyers should have paintings taken down from the wall and ask to handle objects under lock and key. Those who can't be at the sale can leave a commission bid with the auctioneer, or even place a bid by telephone, but if they can't be at the exhibition they should be wary of buying.

Decide on a top bid before the auction begins, and don't go beyond it. Bidding has its own rhythm and tension. The auctioneer becomes a Pied Piper, with buyers winking, blinking, and nodding in time to his or her music. This situation arouses unusual behavior in some people. Suddenly their self-worth is at stake, and they'll bid far beyond what the item is worth — or even what they can afford. A bid may be canceled by promptly calling out "Withdrawn." *Note:* In determining their top price, bidders should remember to add the house commission, which is generally 10% but can be more, plus any value added tax.

RULES OF THE ROAD FOR AN ODYSSEY OF THE OLD

Buy for sheer pleasure and not for investment. Treasure seekers should forget about the supposed resale value that dealers habitually dangle in front of amateur clients. If you love an object, you'll never part with it. If you don't love it, let someone else adopt it.

Don't be timid about haggling. That's as true at a posh Lisbon shop in the Chiado district as at a market. You'll be surprised at how much is negotiable — and the higher the price the more it has to fall.

Buy the finest example you can afford of any item, in as close to mint condition as possible. Chipped or tarnished "bargains" will haunt you later with their shabbiness.

Train your eye in museums. Museums that specialize in items you collect are the best of all. In Lisbon, take a close look at the furniture and clocks in the *Gulbenkian Museum* and the paintings and sculptures in the *National Museum of Ancient Art.*

Peruse art books and periodicals — preferably before you go auction hunting. Unfortunately, however, there is a lack of English-language reading material available.

Get advice from a specialist when contemplating a major acquisition. Major auction houses like *Sotheby's* have fleets of resident specialists available for consultation. The Portuguese tourist offices may also be able to offer some assistance.

Sacred Portugal

All over Portugal, every invasion, migration, and wave of conversion left its signature in stone, much of which has been all but erased by time and the furor of the Reconquest. With each new upheaval, remnants of previous rulers were destroyed, leaving new edifices in their place.

In Portugal, the Roman Temple of Diana at Evora and the Shrine at Fátima are just two of the entries in the guestbook of religions.

TEMPLO DE DIANA, Evora, Alto Alentejo: Just the sight of the sleek Corinthian columns stretching toward the sky here is in itself inspiring. When gazing at the heavens, it is easy to envision the generations of people who have stood at this spot in prayer and meditation for hundreds of years. The temple dates back to the 2nd or 3rd century, when the city of Evora, then called Liberalitas Julia, was one of the most important Roman towns on the Iberian Peninsula. Information: *Pôsto de Turismo,* 73-74 Praça do Giraldo, Evora 7000 (phone: 066-22671).

FÁTIMA, near Tomar, Ribatejo: Even in this skeptical century, we have become used to the idea that miracles take place in desolate or remote spots like the sweaty flatness of Cape Canaveral, the laboratories of Silicon Valley — or this arid Portuguese plateau. But while we know the sites of manmade miracles mostly as newspaper headlines, every year millions of pilgrims, riding everything from hired buses to tired donkeys, converge on this land of shrubs and goats and sheep. On May 13, 1917, the Virgin Mary, it is said, appeared before three shepherd children, preaching peace and anti-communism, and telling them to wait at the same spot, on the same day, each month for a new manifestation. The news quickly spread, and more and more people came for each new vigil until, 6 months later, many in a crowd of 70,000 believers, journalists, and curious skeptics saw the sun "spinning out of its axis," descending toward earth, and filling the sky with a sensational light. Soon after, a modern church was erected, as was a square bigger than Rome's St. Peter's, along with flocks of souvenir stands and hotels. The site received the official approval of a papal visit in 1967. Information: *Direcção-Geral do Turismo,* 86 Av. António Augusto de Aguiar, Lisbon 1000 (phone: 01-575086), or *Pôsto de Turismo,* Av. Dom José Alves Correia da Silva, Fátima 2495 (phone: 049-531139).

Parks and Plazas

Regardless of a visitor's touristic fervor, fatigue will eventually slow the maddest rush from site to sight, forcing a periodic stop for a stretch, a drink, or a snack. Fortunately, in this part of the world, the snack is an institution and the stroll a national pastime. The Portuguese have turned musty quays and dusty castles into sleek spaces specifically for lazing, lounging, and loafing. So when planning a trip, be sure to include a dollop of idleness on the list of musts, and a glass of port and a *passeio* (stroll) at the top of the vocabulary list. Here are some of the lushest parks, the most languid plazas, and the most luxurious *passeios* in Portugal.

ESTUFA FRIA AND ESTUFA QUENTE, Lisbon: In these botanical gardens, as in a state dinner in the plant kingdom, a Mexican cactus is seated near a Balinese banana tree, and a Korean date palm swaps yarns with an African flower. In these circles, the common language is still Latin, and the placards read *Australis alsophila* and *Brunfelsia hopeana.* Thorny shrubs, lanky ferns, filigreed buds, and wide, flopping leaves mill among the pathways, tunnels, and bridges over goldfish ponds. Come sit in the year-round gentle warmth and read, woo, or mull in the nooks colored a million shades of green, with exotic splashes of scarlet, turquoise, and magenta. If a visitor gets some heavenly idea, it may be thanks to the tree called "Muse of Paradise." Open daily from 9 AM to 6 PM (5 PM in winter). Information: *Direcção-Geral do Turismo,* 86 Av. António Augusto de Aguiar, Lisbon 1000 (phone: 01-575086).

PRAÇA DO COMÉRCIO, Lisbon: This impressive riverside square in the Baixa section (the major shoping area) of Lisbon is bordered on three sides by arcaded neo-classical buildings. The triumphal arch on the north side of the square, leading to

Rua Augusta and the rest of the Baixa, was finished in the 19th century. It's also known to locals as Terreiro do Paço (Palace Square), after the royal palace that stood here in pre-earhquake days, and to the English as Black Horse Square, after the bronze equestrian statue of King José I. So get a cool drink at a nearby café, sit down on the wall facing the Tagus, and try to block out the ballyhoo of the begging children and vehicular traffic that unfortunately have taken over part of the square.

SLIDING INTO TOWN, Funchal, Madeira: The most dramatic way to reach Funchal is to toboggan into town in a wicker chair. Entrust your life to two men in white who run alongside and brake and steer the open, wheelless carriage of straw. Relax while clattering down a cobblestone hill from the village of Monte, perhaps holding a cocktail in one hand and crossing two fingers of the other. As you whiz by, remember to admire the islandful of orchids and fuschia, of passion fruit and papaw. Information: *Direcção-Geral do Turismo,* 86 Av. António Augusto de Aguiar, Lisbon 1000 (phone: 01-575086), or *Companhia de Caminhos de Ferro do Monte,* 2 Caminho do Comboio, Funchal, Madeira 9000 (phone: 091-25636).

DIRECTIONS

Introduction

All too often, people mistake Portugal for a mere extension of its imposing neighbor Spain, since it is attached to its western border before the land reaches the sea. It is not until you actually land on Portuguese soil that the unique and varied qualities of this small but diverse country can truly be appreciated. In many ways Portugal still represents — in its unspoiled hills and pristine shores — the final frontier of Europe, and although prices are rising, it remains one of the few Western European countries that is still affordable.

This is a country rich in history and grounded in tradition and culture. As small as Portugal may be, it played an enormous role in man's discovery of the world. Portugal's native sons — Prince Henry the Navigator, Bartolomeu Dias, Magellan, and Vasco de Gama — helped to widen the world's scope and usher in the Age of Discovery.

As you travel from one end of Portugal to the other, you will be delighted with the ever-changing landscape and the wealth of folklore and customs. Cities like Lisbon and Porto, situated on the Atlantic Ocean, are centers of business and industry. Lisbon is the gateway to the New World, and Porto gives us its fine port wine. Inland regions such as the Alentejo are agricultural areas filled with the lovely green of olive trees and sweet aroma of almond orchards. Visitors who head south will find the Algarve, now a popular tourist destination, drawing crowds to its beaches, golf courses, and nightlife. If a mainland holiday isn't for you, islands of the Azores and Madeira, situated hundreds of miles offshore in the Atlantic, remain rustic and unspoiled — the perfect escape for a traveler in search of peace, solitude, and natural beauty.

On the following pages, we have outlined what we think are the best driving routes throughout the country. We have chosen roads and paths that best show off what Portugal has to offer, taking you through small villages and farmlands, to the bigger cities, and along the coast. The *Checking In* and *Eating Out* sections at the end of each tour offer suggestions for the best hotels, *pousadas,* small *pensões,* and restaurants along the way where you can refresh yourself (hotels are listed first, in order of expense, followed by restaurants). In this section, we also have included detailed information on the islands of Madeira and the Azores, recommending the best places to lay your head, please your palate, or satisfy your yen for art, music, and culture.

The new highways in Portugal are excellent, and more new roads are being built and improved all the time. Some of the smaller roads are slow-going and in less than good repair, but they will take you through some of the less-often-seen parts of the country. Each route is planned to last for approximately 3 days. Depending on your timetable and interests, however, each traveler can mix and match the routes to fit his or her own needs. We have included in a single itinerary what we think best represents each area, so if time limits you to only one or two routes, you'll be certain to see the best that there is.

Lisbon to Porto

The road from Lisbon to Portugal's second-largest city — about a 197-mile (315-km) trip if approached in a direct, no-distractions-permitted fashion — proves that there is more to Portugal than the 500 miles of beaches that customarily take pride of place in the tourist brochures. Beaches are certainly not lacking here; in fact, the Costa de Prata (Silver Coast), which bridges the gap between the Lisbon and Estoril coasts and northern Portugal's Costa Verde (Green Coast), is one long succession of them. But the two Portuguese provinces that this coastline borders — Estremadura and Beira Litoral — contain much more than distractions for the aquatic sports enthusiast and the person who merely wants to lie in the sun.

For the historian, there are the remains of *castros* — ancient, fortified hilltop towns — from the Bronze and Iron Ages, as well as old Roman roads, bridges, and a whole Roman city, Conímbriga, to be seen. There are fortresses — which have repelled attacks by everyone from the Moors to the troops of Napoleon — and Portugal's first capital, Coimbra, to be explored. Students will be fascinated by Coimbra's old university, a contemporary of those at Oxford and Cambridge, and probably more so by its students, who hurry to class wearing traditional black capes.

Lovers of art and architecture will be impressed by the profusion of fine Romanesque, Gothic, and baroque buildings, not to mention structures carved with the entwined ropes, seashells, nets, waves, and anchors characteristic of Portugal's own Manueline style. Three of Europe's greatest buildings — the monasteries at Mafra, Alcobaça, and Batalha — are here, and everywhere there are carvings in marble and golden Ançã stone by sculptors of the Mafra and Coimbra schools. Intricate gilt carvings and beautiful 17th- and 18th-century tiles adorn churches, as do some fine paintings, such as those by the 17th-century artist Josefa d'Obidos.

Numerous visitors are less interested in landmarks than they are in the features of Portugal's landscape. Nature lovers will feel in tune with their surroundings in the vast pine forest between Leiria and the sea and in the wildlife preserve in the sand dunes by the Ria lagoon at Aveiro. In fact, the entire misty, rather eerie Ria is a restful place outside the summer season — only the birds and high-prowed, painted fishing boats seem to disturb the peace. Nature lovers who also happen to be concerned about health may want to spend time in one or more of the spas of Vimeiro, Luso, and Curia, reputed to cure all manner of complaints.

And then there are the beaches. Those who would like to sun themselves on a deserted strand or in a secluded cove between high cliffs have only to follow one of the many little roads that lead off the main route down to just such private worlds by the sea. Those who prefer something more domesticated can head for one of the area's numerous popular beach resorts, such as Figueira da Foz, which has a casino in addition to a beach that is more than 1,500 feet wide — it feels as if you're crossing the Sahara just to get your toes wet. Scuba divers might be lucky enough to discover one of the old treasure ships said to be sunk here, and enthusiasts of other water sports will find plenty to keep them busy. But the less adventuresome who prefer pools to the sea will find them at most hotels and, because the surf can be rough along this Atlantic coast, in some of the beach towns themselves.

The giant lobsters and crabs that abound in the chilly coastal waters are a delight for food connoisseurs. (Such treats can be washed down with the fine wines of the Bairrada region around Coimbra and Aveiro or the not-quite-so-high-caste, but very good, wines of Torres Vedras.) Visual pleasures of the seashore with universal appeal include the brightly painted boats in the harbors and on the beaches at Ericeira, Peniche, Nazaré, and Aveiro; the sturdy white windmills twirling on the hilltops; and the scenery in the mountains that climb up from the coast.

Finally, a vast number of visitors who come this way are the devout, drawn by the miracle that is believed to have occurred at Fátima early in this century. The spot where three shepherd children in 1917 claimed to have seen the Virgin Mary several times and to have spoken with her is now a shrine attracting hundreds of thousands of worshipers from all over the world every year.

The history of this region is that of all of northern Portugal. Lusitanians, probably Celtic in origin, were the first inhabitants of whom there is historical evidence; they were succeeded by Romans, waves of barbarians, Moors, and, during the 11th century, conquering Christian kings. In 1385, the famous battle of Aljubarrota, between a Portuguese and a Spanish pretender to the Portuguese throne, led to a Portuguese victory and to the building of the beautiful monastery at Batalha (Battle) — a monumental token of thanksgiving. From 1580 to 1640, however, the area — along with the rest of Portugal — *was* ruled by Spanish kings. Napoleon's armies invaded during the early 19th century; the two lines of fortifications built from the Tagus to the sea in the vicinity of Torres Vedras and Mafra were paramount in expelling the French. Before that happened, however, the invasion caused King João VI to flee to Brazil, taking most of the portable riches of the Palace of Mafra with him.

Political chaos characterized the rest of the 19th century and the beginning of this one. In 1910, 2 years after King Carlos and his heir were assassinated in Lisbon, the inhabitants of the Estremaduran fishing port of Ericeira saw Portugal's last king, Manuel II, leave for exile in England. Later, economics students at Coimbra University saw a former professor, António de Oliveira Salazar, become Prime Minister of Portugal and install a dictatorship that lasted until a coup by the armed forces in 1974 led to the present democratic regime.

Today, the people of Estremadura and the Beira Litoral live by a variety of means. There are increasing numbers of chemical, cellulose, textile, and shoe factories, but many of the old professions, such as fishing, seaweed gathering, wine making, and cattle raising, persist. Tourism is growing rapidly, although this coastal region can still be considered underexplored and its people remain hospitable. Almost every town has a well-signposted tourist office with a multilingual staff.

The route outlined below begins in Lisbon and runs north, zigzagging between inland and coastal towns all the way to Porto. The first major monument, the monastery-palace in the inland town of Mafra, is encountered almost immediately, followed by the first of the Costa de Prata beach towns, Ericeira. The route then takes in Torres Vedras en route to the ancient fishing village of Peniche, from which an excursion to the island of Berlenga can be made. The lovely walled town of Obidos comes next, then Caldas da Rainha and its hot springs, the fishing port and beach resort of Nazaré, and Alcobaça and Batalha, each of which can claim a monastery ranking among the most impressive buildings in Europe. After visits to Fátima, to Leiria (which has an impressive hilltop castle), and to the popular beach resort of Figueira da Foz, the itinerary leads the traveler into the ancient university town of Coimbra, where those who won't be going all the way to Porto can break the trip if desired. (Our driving route through the mountains to the east begins and ends in Coimbra — see *The Beiras,* DIRECTIONS.) The final leg of the route detours to the Roman ruins of Conímbriga and then proceeds to explore Aveiro and its misty lagoon, before pulling into Portugal's northern capital, Porto.

Towns are very close together, so more than one can be visited in a day. However, some, such as Obidos, Nazaré, and Aveiro, are each worth an entire day or more, and Coimbra is so rich in history and monuments that 2 or 3 days are needed to see it all. The area's beach resorts and spas can be pleasant places for rest and relaxation or, since they are close to the historical sites, convenient headquarters for touring. But be warned that with the exception of the new toll highway between Lisbon and Porto, the roads in this area are not very good — narrow, potholed, and full of trucks — and Portuguese drivers can be a menace.

Hotels are scarce in some places, so visitors should make reservations far in advance — sometimes as much as 6 months. Compared with Lisbon and the Algarve, however, hotel prices are reasonable. For a double room with bath and breakfast in a hotel listed as expensive, expect to pay $70 and up in summer (generally no higher than $90, although the *Pousada do Castelo* in Obidos costs as much as $110 for a double in summer); the cost is from $40 to $60 in a hotel listed as moderate, and less than $40 in an inexpensive one. Rates can drop by as much as 25% off-season. Given the proximity of the sea and many rivers, most of the restaurants encountered specialize in fish and seafood; happily, lobster and other such delicacies cost less on this rocky coast than they do in the Lisbon and Algarve areas. Expect to pay $35 and up for a meal for two with wine at a restaurant listed as expensive, from $20 to $35 at a moderate one, and less than $20 in an inexpensive one.

En Route from Lisbon – Leave the city on the A7 highway west toward Estoril, turning right onto N117 toward Sintra and Queluz. After 2½ miles (4 km), turn right again at the signposts for Sintra and Queluz (avoid continuing to Amadora, which is an ugly, sprawling dormitory town). In Queluz (see *Lisbon,* THE CITIES), follow the signs leading to the Palácio Nacional (National Palace). At the end of the highway, turn left into the (unsignposted) street; after a block, turn right onto Avenida Elias Garcia. The turnoff for Belas will be on the left. Continue north through Pero Pinheiro (where N117 becomes N9) to Mafra, 25 miles (40 km) from Lisbon. The road passes marble quarries and factories where stone and marble are turned into ornaments, tables, and fireplaces; some have showrooms and will arrange to ship purchases.

An alternative, more commonly used route to Mafra is to continue to Sintra (see *Lisbon,* THE CITIES) from Queluz; Mafra is 14½ miles (23 km) from Sintra via N9.

MAFRA: The Palácio Nacional de Mafra, an enormous monastery-palace that is one of the largest historic monuments in Europe, rises up without preamble. Work on the imposing structure, often compared to the Escorial in Spain, began in 1717, after Franciscan monks convinced King João V that his wife would produce a long-awaited heir if he built them a monastery. The first of the royal brood was soon born, and with gold pouring in from Brazil, the king spared no expense in showing his appreciation. An Italian-trained German architect, Johann Friedrich Ludwig, was commissioned to build a monastery for 13 friars (a number that quickly grew to 300), as well as a palace for the entire royal family and the court. At one time, more than 50,000 workers were engaged in the construction, which was completed in 1735.

The resulting edifice, consisting of the palace, the monastery, and a church, or basilica, covers 10 acres, with a main façade 725 feet long and, all told, some 4,500 doors and windows. Rife with pink, white, and black marble from the nearby quarries of Pero Pinheiro and with exotic woods from Brazil, the embellishments caused so many foreign artists to gather here that the project became a training ground for an entire generation of Portuguese artists. It eventually gave rise to the famous Mafra school of sculpture, founded in mid-century under the Italian master Alessandro Giusti.

The basilica, predominantly Italian neo-classic and German baroque in design, occupies the middle of the façade, flanked by two majestic bell towers. Together, the towers contain 100 Flemish-made bells — the carillon of Mafra — which are considered among the finest in Europe. Inside, the church is noted for its elegant proportions and its breathtakingly high, richly carved dome, as well as for the side chapels, which contain beautiful Carrara marble altarpieces with bas-reliefs carved by artists of the Mafra school. Note also the six great early-19th-century organs and the plethora of brass chandeliers, candlesticks, crosses, and beautiful wrought-iron work.

The remainder of the building is an overwhelming maze of interminable corridors, vast staircases, and living quarters for the royal family and the monks. Most worthwhile are the Throne Room, with 19th-century paintings, and the marble-vaulted Benediction Room, with its beautifully patterned mosaic floor and, in the center, a bust of João V by Giusti. From the windows of this austere but impressive space, the royal family looked down into the church to hear mass. Other rooms have richly painted ceilings and murals, and there is an odd dining room with furniture made of the antlers and skins of deer from the palace's royal preserve. Gamerooms, a pharmacy, the kitchen, monks' cells, and a rich collection of religious art and vestments are also worth seeing, as is the largest single library room in Europe — 290 feet long. The walls are covered with shelves and intricately carved balconies of white-painted wood; the coffered wood ceiling also is white; and tall windows fill the space with light. In all, there are some 40,000 16th- to 18th-century volumes, covered in white leather and gold.

The monastery-palace (phone: 061-52332) is open from 10 AM to 1 PM and from 2 to 5 PM; closed Tuesdays and national holidays. Admission charge. (The basilica, visited separately at no charge, is open daily.) Given the probable absence of English-speaking guides, the vast size of the building, and the enormous amount of artwork (even though João VI stripped it of a good deal of its paintings, tapestries, furniture, and china when he fled the French invasion during the early 19th century), it is best to buy a map and guidebook at the entrance. The tourist office (Av. 25 de Abril; phone: 061-812023) can supply information on other sights in Mafra, although the town — which was at one time a hilltop *castro* inhabited by Celts and Lusitanians and later occupied by Romans and Moors — is overwhelmed by its single monument and has little else to see except for a church or two. Pottery — off-white and trimmed in pale blue — is made in the region and is for sale in local shops.

CHECKING IN: *Castelão* – A modern hotel on the main street, not far from the monastery-palace; it has 27 rooms with bath and a glassed-in restaurant and bar. Av. 25 de Abril, Mafra (phone: 061-812050). Moderate.

EATING OUT: *Frederico* – Good Portuguese dishes are served in this modest restaurant, whose windows look out on the monastery. Open daily. No reservations. No credit cards accepted. Av. 25 de Abril, Mafra (phone: 061-52089). Inexpensive.

Pátio – Built around an interior courtyard — hence its name — this new eatery serves up fine renditions of local specialties. Open daily. No reservations. No credit cards accepted. Rua Serpa Pinto, Mafra (no phone). Inexpensive.

ERICEIRA: A simple fishing village that has become popular with the Portuguese as a summer resort, Ericeira sits on cliffs above the Atlantic 7 miles (11 km) northwest of Mafra via N116. There is a small beach in town, where colorful fishing boats are drawn ashore, and another larger beach outside town, where the water can be rough. Small restaurants, bars, and shops abound. Among the sights is the chapel of Santo António, which has tiles portraying the royal family's departure into exile from the port of Ericeira in 1910. North of town is the ruined São Isidro fort, built to protect the coast against pirates. About three-quarters of a mile (1 km) south of town, on the road to Sintra, is a big new flashy disco called *Sociedade Anônima,* which features an esplanade, a gameroom, and several bars (Foz do Lizandro; phone: 061-62325). The Ericeira Tourist Office is at 33 Rua Dr. Eduardo Burnay (phone: 061-63122).

CHECKING IN: *Pedro o Pescador* – A pretty place with pointed dormer windows, on the main street. White marble floors and blue-and-white decorations everywhere make it seem light and airy. Besides its 25 rooms, it has a small garden patio off the bar, air conditioned lounges, and a dining room. 22 Rua Dr. Eduardo Burnay, Ericeira (phone: 061-864302; fax: 061-62321). Expensive.

Turismo – A sprawling white building roofed in green tiles and set in gardens atop the cliff, it has 250 rooms with bath and telephone. What it lacks in decorative taste, it makes up for with views of the sea, as well as its 3 seaside swimming pools, private beach, restaurants, bar, and disco. Rua Porto de Rezés, Ericeira (phone: 061-864045 or 061-864498). Expensive.

Vilazul – A charming blue and white inn in the center of town, only 5 minutes from the sea. It has 21 rooms with baths and TV sets, 2 bars, and a restaurant, *Posso.* Major credit cards accepted. 10 Calçada da Baleia, Ericeira (phone: 061-864101; fax: 061-62927). Expensive.

Morais – This blue-trimmed hotel on a quiet side street has a lovely inner garden graced with trees, flowers, and a swimming pool (around which lunch is served in summer). It also has 40 modern, clean rooms with bath. Reserve far in advance. 3 Rua Dr. Miguel Bombarda, Ericeira (phone: 061-864200; fax: 061-864308). Moderate.

Vinos – A restored old mansion featuring 10 rooms (all with bath). No restaurant, but there is a bar on the premises. 25 Rua Prudêncio Franco de Trindade, Ericeira (phone: 061-63830). Inexpensive.

EATING OUT: ***O Cantinho do Madeirense*** – English-owned, it specializes in meats done on a spit, Madeira-style. The red tile floor, gold-and-blue tablecloths, and mats on the wall make up the decor, and there is a patio in front. Open daily. Reservations advised. Major credit cards accepted. Praça dos Navegantes, Ericeira (phone: 061-864101). Expensive.

César – An enormous panoramic restaurant on the cliffs north of town. Lobsters swim in an indoor fountain, and beneath the restaurant is a huge vivarium filled with baroque-decorated tanks of shellfish. There is a bar and music for dancing, and *fado* singing on Saturday nights. Closed Tuesdays. Reservations advised. American Express, Diners Club, and Visa accepted. On N247, Km 1 (phone: 061-62926). Expensive to moderate.

O Barco – A highly recommended dining place on a narrow, cobbled street, down the stone steps that lead to the fishing harbor. Try the *arroz de marisco* (rice with seafood), the *arroz de polvo* (rice with octopus), the *caldeirada de enguias* (eel stew), or the curried shellfish. Windows have views of the sea. Closed Thursdays in winter. Reservations advised. Rua Capitão João Lopes, Ericeira (phone: 061-62759). Moderate.

Parque dos Mariscos – In a big, white building on the main street, it has green tables and green lattices and plants decorating its red brick walls. As expected, *arroz de marisco* is a specialty; so is *linguado à Parque* (sole, house-style). Open daily. Reservations advised. Major credit cards accepted. 28 Rua Dr. Eduardo Burnay, Ericeira (phone: 061-62162). Moderate.

Pátio das Marialvas – A small seafood restaurant with a terrace on the main street. Try the *mariscadas* (a variety of fried seafood), the fricassee of octopus, or the *arroz de marisco.* Closed in November. No reservations. No credit cards accepted. 29 Rua Dr. Eduardo Burnay, Ericeira (phone: 061-62549). Moderate to inexpensive.

En Route from Ericeira – A good road, N247, leads north into the Costa de Prata. It runs along the tops of cliffs, with spectacular views of rough seas smashing onto rocks below, and little roads lead down from it to inlets and indented beaches — Praia de São Sebastião, Praia de São Lourenço, and Porto da Calada. A number of windmills — some billed as "working windmills" — can be visited. The road then meets N9 and turns eastward across a flat plain beside the Sizandro River to Torres Vedras, 16½ miles (27 km) from Ericeira. Before town, there's a turnoff to the right (over an unpaved road) for the ruins of an important fortified hilltop town of the Iron and Bronze Ages — Castro do Zambujal — which has walls and towers still standing from 2500 BC. The many artifacts discovered here are in the *Municipal Museum* in Torres Vedras.

CHECKING IN/EATING OUT: ***Dom Fernando*** – This *pensão* sits dramatically on a cliff in solitary splendor above the Atlantic 7 miles (11 km) north of Ericeira on N247. Originally a private house, it has a lovely garden and terrace over the sea, access to the beach below as well as a pool, a restaurant, and 14 rooms and suites, all with lovely views and furnished with elegant reproductions of antiques. Quinta da Calada, Talefe (phone: 061-855204). Moderate.

TORRES VEDRAS: An old town that has been inhabited by Celts, Visigoths, Romans, and Moors, Torres Vedras is most famous as the headquarters for the defense of Lisbon from Napoleon's troops during the early 19th century. The Linhas de Torres Vedras were two lines of earthen battlements incorporating fortresses and castles that English and Portuguese troops under the command of Arthur Wellesley (later to become the Duke of Wellington) raised clear across the peninsula jutting from the coast to the Tagus River. The more northerly line began at the mouth of the Sizandro on the Atlantic and ended just south of Vila Franca de Xira, passing through Torres Vedras. The southern line crossed the peninsula at a point just north of Mafra. To see the remains of the lines, turn left at the entrance to town, where the sign points upward. The ruins of the São Vicente fort, built as part of the lines (many of its round towers were disguised as windmills to fool the French), stand at the top of a nearly perpendicular hill commanding a wide view of the countryside. Inside the courtyard there are reconstructions of the earthen battlements, but nothing of the original fort remains except the walls and an empty dome.

Torres Vedras today is a modern town with little of its ancient character, except for the Old Quarter, which has narrow, cobblestone streets winding steeply up to the old castle on the hill opposite the São Vicente fort. The castle was badly damaged when it was wrested from the Moors during the 12th century, and again in the earthquake of 1755, but it, too, became part of Wellington's lines. The Church of Santa Maria do Castelo, within its walls, has two Romanesque portals, numerous paintings, and 17th-century *azulejos,* but São Pedro, with its Manueline portal, opulent gilt work, and baroque tiles, is the most important of the town's churches — of which there are many more, including the 16th-century Graça with lovely 18th-century tiles, the flood-damaged Santiago, and the Misericórdia. Also to be seen are a Gothic fountain (the Chafariz dos Canos) and the *Museu Municipal* (7 Rua Serpa Pinto; phone: 061-25319), where, in addition to items dug up at the prehistoric Castro do Zambujal site, silver crowns, coins, paintings, and ceramics are on display (open from 10 AM to noon and from 2 to 6 PM; closed Mondays and, from October through June, national holidays; no admission charge). The tourist office is on Rua 9 de Abril (phone: 061-312777).

CHECKING IN: ***Império*** **–** Built in post-modernist style, it is in the center of town and is charming, light, and cheerful. Some of the 26 rooms have balconies with views of the town and the Graça church; there is a restaurant, a bar, and a café. Praça 25 de Abril, Torres Vedras (phone: 061-25232). Inexpensive.

EATING OUT: ***Barrete Preto*** **–** The most elegant restaurant in town, with 3 dining rooms — one of them wood-paneled and carpeted, another done up in regional style, with decorative tiles and antique lanterns. The menu is long, but codfish, eel stew, roast kid, and *cozido à portuguesa* (Portuguese boiled dinner — a one-dish meal containing a variety of meats and vegetables) are specialties. Closed Thursdays and the month of September. Reservations advised. Visa accepted. 25 Rua Paiva de Andrade, Torres Vedras (phone: 061-22063). Moderate.

O Diamante **–** A charming dining place, it provides light music as an accompaniment to meals. Closed Mondays. Reservations advised. Visa accepted. 32A Rua António Leal da Assunção, Torres Vedras (phone 061-25988). Moderate.

Pateo **–** An old house has been turned into a modern restaurant, and with its white walls and pale pink and green decor, it's very attractive. Mixed grills, *porco recheado* (loin of pork stuffed with cheese and ham), Portuguese boiled dinner, and other well-cooked dishes are on the menu. Closed Sundays. Reservations advised. Visa accepted. 1B Rua José Eduardo César, Torres Vedras (phone: 061-311496). Moderate.

En Route from Torres Vedras – Take N8-2 north through high hills covered with vineyards and pine woods. Proceed directly to Lourinhã or, after about 4½ miles (7 km), turn left to the spa town of Vimeiro (another 4 miles/17 km along a not-so-good road) and the wide sandy beach of Praia do Porto Novo (still another 2½ miles — 4 km — west); then backtrack through Vimeiro to rejoin N8-2 north. Lourinhã, a flat and medieval-looking town beside the sea, is the gateway to many of the region's beaches, and it has several interesting monuments in its own right, such as the 14th-century Gothic Igreja Matriz (Parish Church);

the Church of Nossa Senhora da Annunciação, which is part of a Franciscan monastery founded in 1598; and the Misericórdia church, with a Manueline door. North of town about 2½ miles (4 km) is the shell-shaped beach of Praia da Areia Branca, with several hotels and restaurants, and still farther along is the fishing port of Peniche, at the tip of a peninsula jutting out to sea 12 miles (19 km) from Lourinhã. The tourist office is located at Praia da Areia Branca (phone: 061-422167).

CHECKING IN: ***Golf Mar*** – Its beautiful, dramatic, solitary setting amid landscaped gardens very high above the rocky coast at Praia do Porto Novo gives guests the feeling of being suspended between the sky and the sea. Half of the nearly 300 rooms have terraces overlooking the water, and the hotel has a 9-hole golf course, a heated indoor pool in addition to an outdoor pool, a panoramic restaurant and bar, shops, a discotheque, a gameroom, a hairdresser, and lounges. Praia do Porto Novo (phone: 061-984157). Expensive.

Areia Branca – Modern and near the beach, this *estalagem* (inn) has 29 rooms and a good restaurant. Praia da Areia Branca (phone: 061-412491). Moderate.

Apartamentos Turísticos São João – This modern complex of 18 well-furnished tourist apartments has a swimming pool, a bar, a discotheque, and a mini-market. Praia da Areia Branca (phone: 061-422491). Inexpensive.

Do Rossio – A contemporary *pensão* with 15 rooms (with bath), and use of the swimming pool at the *São João* apartments (see above) near Praia da Areia Branca. No restaurant. Rua dos Bombeiros Voluntarios, Lourinhã (phone: 061-432049). Inexpensive.

EATING OUT: ***O Chalé*** – French fare is the specialty here. Open daily. No reservations or cards accepted. Largo Mestre Anacleto Marcos da Silva, Lourinhã (phone: 061-423003). Moderate.

Frutos do Mar – At Porto das Barcas, south of Lourinhã, this eatery specializes in lobster — in fact, it has the largest vivarium in Portugal. Closed Tuesdays. No reservations. Visa and American Express accepted. Agua Doce, Porto das Barcas (phone: 061-422774). Moderate.

PENICHE: This is a bustling fishing port whose colorful fleet can be seen unloading the daily catch by the tons and whose seafood restaurants are plentiful. (The local version of *caldeirada,* fish stew, is famous.) On a mile-long peninsula jutting out to sea, Peniche was once an island — silt deposited over the centuries built up the sand isthmus that now joins it to the mainland. In earlier times, the island was the last refuge of Lusitanian warriors fleeing Roman invaders and a port of call for Phoenicians, Crusaders, and pirates.

The massive, sprawling fortress that dominates the harbor was built during the 16th century and later enlarged until its moats, walls, bastions, cisterns, and towers occupied 5 acres. Used as a political prison during the Salazar regime and later as a camp for refugees from Angola, it now houses the *Museu Municipal* (Campo da República; phone: 062-781848), a repository of prehistoric artifacts and articles pertaining to ships, fishing, and lace making (the ancient art of *bilros,* or bobbin lace, still flourishes in Peniche), as well as relics from its past as a prison (open from 10 AM to noon and from 2 to 7 PM, July through September; closes at 5 PM the rest of the year; closed Mondays; admission charge). Several of the town's churches are also worth a visit, among them the Misericórdia, where the walls are covered with beautiful 17th-century tiles and the ceiling is painted with New Testament scenes — in all there are about 100 paintings in the church, five of them by Josefa d'Obidos. The Church of Nossa Senhora do Socorro (Our Lady of Succor) has paintings attributed to Josefa's father, as well as interesting glazed tiles and gilt carving; São Pedro has an enormous baroque altarpiece and paintings of the life of the saint; and Nossa Senhora da Conceição is completely covered with 18th-century tiles. Peniche's Tourist Office is on Rua Alexandre Herculano (phone: 062-789571).

The coast of the Peniche Peninsula is lined with giant rock formations in the sea, many in fantastic, surreal shapes, as well as with caves, grottoes, and wide sandy beaches. At the tip of the peninsula is Cabo Carvoeiro, with another church, the tiny sanctuary of Nossa Senhora dos Remédios, which is completely covered with tiles attributed to the 18th-century master António de Oliveira Bernardes; nearby is an 18th-century lighthouse. The church is the focal point of one of Peniche's traditional festivals, the *Romaria da Nossa Senhora dos Remédios,* held in October, when the image of the Virgin is carried from the church down to the sea. Another local festival, also sea-related, is the *Festas da Senhora da Boa Viagem* (Festival of Our Lady of the Good Voyage), held the first week in August in Peniche and marked by a procession of boats. Cabo Carvoeiro provides smashing views of the surf-pounded coast and, in the distance, of Berlenga, the main island of an archipelago (the Ilhas Berlengas) whose rocks, caves, and coves are home to migratory birds and rare flora and fauna. From June through September, boats run from Peniche to Berlenga (for schedules, call *Empresa Víamar;* phone: 062-782153), making the trip in about an hour. During the 16th century, the island was inhabited by monks, who abandoned it after constant attacks by pirates. Today, a few fishermen and lighthouse keepers live here. The lighthouse stands on the highest point of the island, above the 17th-century São João Baptista fort, which is set on an islet connected to Berlenga by a winding stone bridge.

CHECKING IN: ***Praia Norte*** **–** This modern place at the entrance to town has 103 rooms and suites, a swimming pool, a discotheque, and a restaurant and grillroom. On N114, Praia Norte, Peniche (phone: 062-781161; fax: 062-781165). Expensive.

Felita **–** A small *pensão* with 9 rooms (each with private bath), near the town gardens. 12 Largo Professor Franco Freire, Peniche (phone: 062-782190). Inexpensive.

Pavilhão Mar e Sol **–** On Berlenga Island, this comfortable, 5-room residence is run by the Peniche municipal government. Open from June through mid-September, it has a pleasant restaurant — the only one on the island, in fact. Ilha Berlenga (phone: 062-782031). Very inexpensive.

EATING OUT: ***Praia Mar*** **–** On the beach, this place specializes in fish and seafood and has windows looking out to sea. Open daily. No reservations. No credit cards accepted. Molhe Leste, Peniche (phone: 062-782523). Moderate.

Marisqueira Mili **–** A typical restaurant near the fishing port, it, too, specializes in seafood. Open daily. No reservations. No credit cards accepted. Rua José Estevão, Peniche (phone: 062-782278). Inexpensive.

En Route from Peniche – Head east on N114, passing through Atouguia da Baleia, an interesting little town with a 13th-century Romanesque-Gothic church and, in front of the church, a Manueline pillory. In the square in front of another church — a massive baroque one — are the rough stone remains of a bull stall built by King Pedro I during the 14th century — evidence that bullfighting is very old in Portugal. Continue east on N114, turning north onto N8 to the beautiful walled town of Obidos, 15 miles (24 km) from Peniche.

OBIDOS: This small town set on a high hill is rightly called a "museum town." Its medieval atmosphere remains intact, and so many of its houses and other buildings are of historic or artistic significance that it has been declared a national monument. A picture-postcard town today, with flower-covered balconies, whitewashed houses, and narrow cobblestone streets — all surrounded by Moorish walls and dominated by an equally old castle — it was evidently just as pretty during the Middle Ages. The Saintly

Isabel admired it so much during a 13th-century visit with her new husband, King Dinis, that he gave it to her as a wedding present. Obidos later became the property of Leonor Teles, wife of King Fernando; Philippa of Lancaster, the English wife of King João I; Leonor of Portugal, wife of João II; and Catherine, wife of King João III. Thus it became known as the Casa das Rainhas (House of Queens).

Pass through the double-arched gateway to the town (Porta da Vila) and follow the narrow main street, Rua Direita, to the Praça de Santa Maria, where there are a few tree-shaded parking spaces. The Igreja de Santa Maria is a beautiful 17th-century church (on the foundations of a Visigothic temple that later became a Moorish mosque), virtually paved with blue-and-white *azulejos* inside. The paintings over the main altar are by João da Costa, while those of St. Catherine over the altar in a chapel to the south (right) were signed by Josefa·d'Obidos in 1661 (the great 17th-century painter, born in Seville, Spain, lived most of her life in Obidos and is buried in another town church, São Pedro). Note, too, the large paintings of biblical scenes, attributed to her father, Baltazar Gomes Figueira, as well as the exquisitely carved Renaissance tomb of a Governor of Obidos. More works by Josefa d'Obidos are in the *Museu Municipal,* in the same square (open from 9 AM to 12:30 PM and from 2 to 6 PM; admission charge, except on Wednesdays; phone: 062-959263), along with other paintings, sculpture, furniture, archaeological artifacts, and exhibits devoted to the Peninsular War. In the center of the square is a 15th-century pillory donated by Queen Leonor, the wife of João II. It bears the royal coat of arms and the *camaroeiro* (shrimp net) that became her symbol after her son drowned in Santarém and his body was recovered in a fisherman's net.

Proceed on foot to the Igreja de São Tiago, where a path on the left leads to the ramparts. Built by the Moors, the walls enclosing the town are nearly a mile in circumference, with a wide walkway along the top that makes it possible to circumnavigate the crenelated battlements and take in a spectacular view of both the town and the countryside. There are only two interruptions in the circuit: one at the town gateway, the other at the castle, which began as a fortress, was turned into a royal palace during the 16th century, and has now been transformed, in part, into a *pousada,* or government-run inn (see *Checking In*).

Outside the walls, there are several churches and chapels, but the most noteworthy is the unfinished hexagonal church of Senhor da Pedra, which sits alone in a field to the north of town via N8, inside the 17th-century baroque building is an early Christian stone cross. To the south of town is the 16th-century aqueduct, a nearly 2-mile structure of double arches ordered built by Queen Catherine to feed water into the town's various fountains. The tourist office is on Rua Direita (phone: 062-959296).

CHECKING IN: ***Pousada do Castelo*** – A rustically elegant, government-owned inn in the castle of Obidos, complete with medieval armor in the decor. There are only 9 rooms and suites, some of them in the towers, plus an excellent restaurant and a bar. Given its size, advance reservations are essential. Paço Real, Obidos (phone: 062-959105; in the US, 212-686-9213; fax: 062-959148). Very expensive.

Do Convento – Just outside the walls, it was built during the early 19th century to cloister nuns, and it has been delightfully converted into an *estalagem* offering every modern convenience while maintaining its character. There are 24 rooms, a bar, and a beamed restaurant with a stone fireplace (and a garden patio for summer dining). Rua Dom João de Ornelas, Obidos (phone: 062-959217; fax: 062-959159). Expensive.

Josefa d'Obidos – An *albergaria* (inn) in an old house just outside the walls at the entrance to town, it has 42 nicely furnished rooms with bath, a typical restaurant, a bar, and a weekend discotheque. Rua Dom João de Ornelas, Obidos (phone: 062-959228; fax: 062-959533). Moderate.

Rainha Santa Isabel – Another *albergaria,* on the main street of Obidos. Formerly a private home, it's decorated with tiles and has 20 rooms with bath, as well as a bar and several lounges. Rua Direita, Obidos (phone and fax: 062-959115). Moderate.

EATING OUT: ***A Ilustre Casa de Ramiro*** – The shell of this building outside the walls is very old, but the interior was designed with an Arabic motif by the contemporary architect José Fernando Teixeira. Among the specialties on the extensive menu are *arroz de pato* (rice with duck) and grilled codfish; wines are from the Obidos region. Closed Wednesdays. Reservations advised. Visa and American Express accepted. Rua Porta do Vale, Obidos (phone: 062-959194). Expensive to moderate.

Alcaide – On the main street in the center of town, with lovely views of the countryside. Try the tuna, Azores-style. Closed Mondays and the month of November. Reservations advised. Major credit cards accepted. Rua Direita, Obidos (phone: 062-959220). Moderate.

CALDAS DA RAINHA: This sprawling agricultural town, 4 miles (6 km) north of Obidos on N8, has two claims to fame: hot springs and ceramics. The town's name means "the Queen's hot springs" — referring, in this case, to the 15th-century Queen Leonor, wife of João II. Passing through on her way to Batalha, she noticed peasants bathing in some local pools and, upon learning that the waters were good for rheumatism, did the same. So effective was the therapy for her own ailments that the queen pawned her jewels to establish a hospital and lay out a park, both of which still bear her name (and it's still possible for visitors to steep themselves in the sulfurous waters at the Rainha Dona Leonor Hospital Spa). The Church of Nossa Senhora do Pópulo, which was the chapel of the hospital, is a Gothic and Manueline structure noted for its *azulejos* and a fine 16th-century triptych.

Caldas has been a pottery-making center since ancient times. The ceramics fair that takes place here each July draws thousands of visitors, but for those who miss it, the local pottery (the cabbage leaf bowls are a typical item) and other crafts can be seen at the Saturday market on Praça da República, the main square. One of the most famous Caldas potters was Rafael Bordalo Pinheiro, a 19th-century ceramist, cartoonist, and painter who established a studio here and created brightly colored caricatures of people that are still copied today. The *Museu José Malhoa* (open from 10 AM to 12:30 PM and from 2 to 5 PM; closed Mondays and holidays; admission charge, except on Sunday mornings; in the park; phone: 062-24821) displays a fine collection of ceramics by Bordalo Pinheiro, along with paintings by the late-19th- and early-20th-century artist after whom the museum is named. More ceramics can be seen at the far end of the park in the *Museu da Cerâmica* (open from 10 AM to noon and from 2 to 5 PM; closed Mondays and holidays; admission charge, except on Sunday mornings; phone: 062-23157), which has a tiled garden, and more of Bordalo Pinheiro's work can be seen nearby at the Faianças Artísticas Bordalo Pinheiro (Bordalo Pinheiro Faïence Factory), which maintains a small museum (closed Saturdays and Sundays). For more information on Caldas da Rainha, contact the tourist office (Praça da República; phone: 062-34511).

CHECKING IN: ***Malhoa*** – There are 113 rooms with bath in this modern hostelry, whose amenities also include a swimming pool, a sauna, a restaurant, and a discotheque. 31 Rua António Sérgio, Caldas da Rainha (phone: 062-842180). Moderate.

Europeia Pension – This very modern place has 50 double rooms and 2 suites with private bath, phone, refrigerator/bar, and TV sets. Rua Almirante Cândido dos Reis, Caldas da Rainha (phone: 062-34781; fax: 062-832680). Moderate to inexpensive.

Dona Leonor – A *pensão* with 30 rooms, each of which has a private bath, TV set, and telephone. There is a bar, but no restaurant. 6 Hemiciclo João Paulo II, Caldas da Rainha (phone: 062-842171; fax: 062-842172). Inexpensive.

EATING OUT: *Pateo da Rainha* – Good regional cooking and attentive service prevail. Specialties of the house are rice with monkfish, codfish, and *cozido à portuguesa,* or Portuguese boiled dinner. Open daily. No reservations. Visa accepted. 39 Rua de Camões, Caldas da Rainha (phone: 062-35658). Moderate.

En Route from Caldas da Rainha – Take N8 north 7½ miles (12 km) to Alfeizerão and then turn west onto N242. São Martinho do Porto, on a quiet bay, with some interesting 19th-century buildings among the more modern ones of a beach resort, is only 3 miles (5 km) from the turnoff. After São Martinho, N242 heads north to Nazaré, 18 miles (29 km) from Caldas da Rainha.

CHECKING IN: *São Pedro* – This is a small *albergaria* (inn) with 24 rooms and a bar, located near the beach. 7 Largo Vitorino Frois, São Martinho do Porto (phone: 062-989327). Expensive.

Apartamentos Turísticos São Martinho – A tourist complex offering 160 apartments with kitchenettes, plus a restaurant, a bar, a swimming pool, and a discotheque that's open from March to October. It's near the beach, with water sports available. 31 Rua Dr. Rafael Garcia, São Martinho do Porto (phone: 062-989335; fax: 062-989343). Moderate.

EATING OUT: *O Viveiro* – A good seafood restaurant near the quay. Open daily. No reservations. Visa accepted. Rua Cândido dos Reis, São Martinho do Porto (phone: 062-989691). Moderate.

NAZARÉ: This fishing village has recently become a very popular, rather touristy beach resort, but some of its quaint customs remain, including the wearing of traditional costumes — full skirts with up to seven petticoats for the women, and long, black, plaid-lined capes and black stocking caps for the men. There are two parts to Nazaré. The Praia quarter, along the beach, is the lower, newer part of town, while the older Sítio, or Upper Town, is atop a cliff to the north, reachable by car or by an old funicular. The sea once covered what is now the Lower Town, but it suddenly receded during the 17th century, after which fishermen from Sítio built huts on the beach and eventually made Nazaré the premier fishing town along the coast — an impressive feat, since it has no natural harbor and, until very recently, had no real port facilities. The fishermen launched their boats from the beach and used oxen and, later, tractors to pull the nets back to shore. Given the strong currents, it was a dangerous occupation, but today there is a new sheltered port for the boats — which are long and narrow, with bright eyes painted on the pointed prows, highly suggestive of the Phoenicians from whom it is believed the people of Nazaré are descended. The Praia area is now full of hotels and restaurants and the other trappings of a seaside resort, but visitors can still see women drying fish and men mending nets, even though only a few fishermen remain on the beach.

Before the fishermen spread to the Lower Town and before the advent of tourists, the Sítio quarter was all there was to Nazaré. There is a spectacular view from the belvedere here; it takes in all the town below, the beach tents and umbrellas, the boat shelter at the far end of the beach, and the distant coastline. On the main square is the Nossa Senhora da Nazaré church, rich in marble and gilt carving; the church's little black image of the Virgin, said to have been brought from the Holy Land after the death of Emperor Constantine, is carried down to the sea during the annual *Romaria da Nossa Senhora de Nazaré,* a festival held in early September. The tiny white Capela da Memória, built into the side of the cliff by the square, commemorates a 12th-century miracle performed by the Virgin. According to the legend, Dom Fuas Roupinho, a very religious man, was hunting on the cliffs when his horse jumped over the edge after a deer. Dom Fuas prayed to the Virgin, who miraculously set him and his horse back on terra firma, after which he built the chapel on the very spot. The present chapel, dating from the 17th century, is covered with 17th-century *azulejos.* A remaining Sítio landmark is the São Miguel fort, built during the 16th century to protect the town from pirates and now turned into a lighthouse. The tourist office in Nazaré (23 Rua Mouzinho de Albuquerque; phone: 062-561194) is in the Praia section of town.

CHECKING IN: ***Dom Fuas*** – This hotel has 32 well-furnished rooms, all with TV sets, as well as a restaurant, a bar, and a snack bar. It's at the southern end of the Praia section, open from April to mid-October. Av. Manuel Remígio, Nazaré (phone: 062-551351). Expensive.

Praia – Modern, with 40 rooms with bath, air conditioning, and TV sets, this is on a main street near the beach. It has no restaurant, but there is a breakfast room, a bar, and a disco. 39 Av. Vieira Guimarães, Nazaré (phone: 062-561423). Expensive.

Maré – Small (36 rooms) and convenient, it's in the heart of the Praia, about a block from the beach, with a restaurant and a bar. 8 Rua Mouzinho de Albuquerque, Nazaré (phone: 062-561122). Moderate.

Da Nazaré – In a little square several blocks back from the beach in the Praia quarter, it has 52 rooms with bath, a bar, a restaurant, and a nightclub, and there is a place next door — *Mar Alto* — to take in some folk music and dancing. Largo Afonso Zuquete, Nazaré (phone: 062-561311; fax: 062-561238). Moderate.

EATING OUT: ***Paulo Caetano*** – Named after a famous Portuguese bullfighter and decorated with bullfighting pictures and posters, this Sítio restaurant specializes in seafood. Open daily. No reservations. Visa and MasterCard accepted. Largo Reitor Baptista, Nazaré (phone: 062-552011). Expensive to moderate.

Ribamar – In a *pensão* on the beach in the center of town — a white building with yellow balconies and windows — it has a lovely view of the sea. Fish, seafood, and typical regional dishes are the specialties. Open daily. No reservations. Major credit cards accepted. Av. da República, Nazaré (phone: 062-551158). Expensive to moderate.

O Caselinho – Comfortable and traditional, this famous local culinary veteran specializes in grilled fish and seafood. The decor is typically Portuguese-provincial, with a nautical motif. Open daily. No reservations. Major credit cards accepted. 7 Praça Sousa Oliveira, Nazaré (phone: 062-551328). Moderate.

A Petisqueira – Run by three brothers, this yellow, glassed-in restaurant, at the far end of the beach by the fishing boat shelter, serves nine different variations of *caldeirada da Nazaré* (fish stew). Open daily. No reservations. Visa accepted. Av. Manuel Remígio, Nazaré (phone: 062-551594). Moderate.

ALCOBAÇA: Only 8½ miles (14 km) southeast of Nazaré via N8-4, this small town at the confluence of the Alcoa and Baça rivers is completely dominated by the enormous white limestone Cistercian abbey — the Mosteiro de Santa Maria — in its midst, once the home of Portugal's most prosperous religious community and still one of the country's most important architectural landmarks. In thanks for his victory over the Moors at Santarém in 1149, King Afonso Henriques granted land to St. Bernard of Clairvaux, the influential French Cistercian who had championed the Portuguese cause against the Moors. The monks began to build in 1178 and, on the Cistercian model, set to work farming their vast domain, recruiting lay brothers to help them and introducing new agricultural techniques (which accounts for the superior quality of the Alcobaça vineyards and wines).

The style of the monastery church, the largest church in Portugal, marks the transition from Romanesque to Gothic, although the façade, with its rose window and two bell towers, is a result of 17th- and 18th-century baroque alterations. Inside, the spacious church is, in accordance with Cistercian austerity, devoid of adornment, with two notable exceptions: the exquisite, intricately carved 14th-century Flamboyant Gothic tombs of King Pedro I and his beloved mistress, Dona Inês de Castro, the most famous lovers in Portuguese history. As a prince, Pedro had fallen in love with the beautiful Spanish aristocrat, but his father, fearing Spanish interference with the Portuguese throne, ordered her murder (which took place in Coimbra in 1355). Dom Pedro had his revenge when he ascended the throne. Besides executing some of Inês's murderers, he exhumed her body, dressed her in royal robes and a crown, and forced all of the nobility to kiss her hand. Whether the monastery church at Alcobaça was the scene of this "coronation" is open to question, but both Pedro and Inês are buried here, in tombs placed on opposite sides of the transept, so that their first sight upon opening their eyes on Judgment Day will be of each other.

Behind the ambulatory of the church is the sacristy, preceded by an ornate, 16th-century Manueline doorway, and just off the church nave is the beautiful 14th-century Claustro do Silêncio (its upper story, added later, is Manueline). Around the cloister range other monastic spaces, including the Sala dos Reis (Kings' Hall), an 18th-century addition with terra cotta statues of the Kings of Portugal surmounting an *azulejo* frieze, and the impressive kitchen, totally covered in pale tiles. Not only does the kitchen have a huge fireplace and chimney big enough to roast several oxen at once, it also has a branch of the Alcoa running through it — an early labor-saving device that allowed the monks to catch fish for their dinner and to wash the dishes, too. The monastery (phone: 062-43469) is open daily from 9 AM to 7 PM (to 5 PM from October through March; closed *Christmas* and *New Year's Day*). Admission charge, except on Sunday mornings. The Alcobaça Tourist Office is in Praça 25 de Abril (phone: 062-42377).

CHECKING IN: ***Santa Maria*** – This modern white building with a tiled roof sits in gardens directly in front of the monastery. There are 31 rooms with bath (some of the rooms have balconies), plus a nice, wood-paneled bar. Rua Dr. Francisco Zagalo, Alcobaça (phone: 062-597395; fax: 062-596715). Moderate.

EATING OUT: ***Frei Bernardo*** – Behind the Art Nouveau exterior is a nice bar and a very large dining room specializing in *frango na púcara* (chicken in a pot), *chanfana de borrego* (lamb stew), grilled fish, and *açorda de marisco,* a stew or "dry" soup made of seafood and other ingredients. Entertainment is a show of folk dancing and singing and a band that plays Portuguese music on request for groups. Open daily. Reservations advised. Major credit cards accepted. 17-19 Rua Dom Pedro V, Alcobaça (phone: 062-42227). Moderate.

Trindade – The region's most typical dishes are the specialties — *frango na púcara, açorda de marisco,* and fish. Besides the restaurant, there's also a snack bar and a small bar; original 18th-century tiles are part of the decor. Closed Saturdays in winter and from mid-September through the first week in October. No reservations. Visa accepted. 22 Praça Dom Afonso Henriques, Alcobaça (phone: 062-42397). Moderate.

En Route from Alcobaça – The town of Aljubarrota is 4 miles (6 km) north along N8, not far from the place where the armies of two pretenders to the Portuguese throne — one Portuguese and one Castilian — faced each other on August 14, 1385. The Portuguese pretender, whose forces were vastly outnumbered, vowed he would build a great monastery if he defeated the Spaniards. The battle was brief and won by the Portuguese, thereby assuring the country's independence and the right of João I to occupy its throne. The enduring monument he constructed is farther up the road, 6 miles (10 km) along N8 and then 2½ miles (4 km) along N1, in Batalha.

CHECKING IN: ***Casa da Padeira (House of the Baker)*** – Named after a baker woman who fought the Spaniards with a wooden shovel and pushed them into her oven, this modern manor house has 8 rooms with bath, swimming pool, and a bar set in ample gardens. Estrada N8, Aljubarrota, Alcobaça (phone: 061-48272). Moderate.

BATALHA: The monastery that João I raised to the Virgin Mary in thanks for his decisive victory at Aljubarrota is probably the most beautiful monument in Portugal, despite the discoloration and pollution damage inflicted by passing traffic. Begun in 1388, worked on by several architects throughout the 15th century, and left unfinished early in the 16th century, the Mosteiro de Santa Maria da Vitória (Monastery of Our Lady of Victory) is a masterpiece of Portuguese Gothic, often cited as an example of how the country's builders were able to absorb various foreign influences to forge their own national style. Outside, it's trimmed with gargoyles, flying buttresses, pinnacles, and lacy balustrades (the west front is particularly suggestive of the English Perpendicular style, which is not surprising since the founder's wife, Philippa of Lancaster, was English). Inside, while the church nave is stark and soaring, cloisters and chapels are richly decorated with the delicate curves of Flamboyant Gothic and the florid details of the transitional, Gothic-to-Renaissance, Manueline style.

Be sure to see the Capela do Fundador (Founder's Chapel), off an aisle to the right, where King João I, Queen Philippa, and their children (including Prince Henry the Navigator) are buried beneath a star-shaped vault. The tomb of the king and queen is topped with reclining figures of the pair, their hands joined. The Claustro Real (Royal Cloister), on the other side of the church, mixes Gothic with Manueline (note the pearls, shells, and coils carved on the columns). Just off it is the Sala do Capítulo (Chapterhouse), which has a vaulted ceiling without intermediate supports — its construction was such a dangerous engineering feat that condemned criminals did the actual work. Another cloister, the Claustro de Dom Afonso V, is beyond the Royal Cloister, after which the visitor can walk around to the Capelas Imperfeitas (Unfinished Chapels): seven chapels radiating around a rotunda that was meant to be topped with a dome. The incomplete pillars, which serve no purpose now, are nevertheless encrusted with Manueline carving, and the doorway to the chapels is a Manueline tour de force. The Batalha monastery (phone: 044-96497) is open daily from 9 AM to 6 PM (to 5 PM from October through May; closed *Christmas* and *New Year's Day*). Admission charge. Batalha's Tourist Office is on Largo Paulo VI (phone: 044-96180).

CHECKING IN: ***Pousada do Mestre Afonso Domingues*** – Formerly a privately owned *estalagem,* it's now a government-owned *pousada,* although unlike most of the chain it's of modern construction. In the square by the monastery and named after the first of the monastery's architects, it has 20 rooms with bath, a small bar, and a good restaurant. Largo Mestre Afonso Domingues, Batalha (phone: 044-96260; in the US, 212-686-9213). Expensive.

Quinta do Fidalgo – This totally restored 17th-century house in front of a monastery is surrounded by acres of woods and gardens. It has 26 rooms with private bath. In 1744, it hosted two princes who later became Kings of Portugal — Dom José I and Dom Pedro. Breakfast only is served. Reservations necessary. In front of the monastery, Batalha (phone: 044-96114). Moderate.

São Jorge – A motel up the hill on the road to Lisbon. Besides the 10 rooms, there are tennis courts, a large swimming pool amid lawns and trees, and a regional-style restaurant. On N1, Batalha (phone: 044-96210 or 044-96186; fax: 044-96313). Moderate.

EATING OUT: ***Mestre de Avis*** – A large restaurant upstairs above a café near the monastery square. Decorated in blue and white, it has bay windows offering a good view of the monastery, as well as a terrace for summer dining. Open daily. No reservations. Largo Dom João I, Batalha (phone: 044-96427). Moderate.

En Route from Batalha – Leiria is only 7 miles (11 km) north on N1, but for those with time to spare and an interest in the phenomenon that made it famous, Fátima — in the mountains 12½ miles (20 km) east of Batalha along the A1 toll road — is worth a side trip.

FÁTIMA: On May 13, 1917, a vision of the Virgin Mary, standing above a small oak tree, appeared to three peasant children who were tending their sheep here. The apparition returned five more times — on the 13th of each succeeding month — and by the time of the last appearance, a crowd of 70,000 people had gathered at the spot. They saw the sun break through a stormy day and appear to spin toward earth, but only the children saw the Virgin. Fátima has since become a world-famous Roman Catholic shrine, and to this day, pilgrims arrive — some crawling on their knees for miles — to hear mass on the 13th of each month from May through October. On the anniversaries of the first and final apparitions, the crowds are particularly large, and on special occasions they have been known to number a million. The visitor sees a huge esplanade, where the mass is celebrated and torch-lit processions take place, edged by a neo-classical basilica containing the tombs of two of the children, Francisco and Jacinta Marto, who died of influenza in 1919 and 1920 (the third child, Lúcia dos Santos, still lives as a Carmelite nun in Coimbra). The Chapel of the Apparitions, marking the spot where the oak tree stood and the Virgin appeared, is at the far end of the esplanade.

Those who decide to visit Fátima should note that roads leading to it are jammed to capacity on the 12th and 13th of pilgrimage months, and that while hotels are not in short supply, they are equally jammed on those days, since they cater mainly to pilgrims who make reservations months in advance. The Fátima Tourist Office is located on Avenida Dom José Alves Correia da Silva (phone: 049-531139).

CHECKING IN: ***Dom Gonçalo*** – A 43-room *estalagem,* with a TV set in each room, a good restaurant and bar, and gift shops. 100 Rua Jacinta Marto, Fátima (phone: 049-532262; fax: 049-532088). Moderate.

EATING OUT: ***Grelha*** – One of the very few independent restaurants in Fátima, it specializes in Portuguese cooking, especially grilled meats. The dining room has a fireplace, and there's a good bar. Closed Thursdays. Reservations unnecessary. Major credit cards accepted. 76 Rua Jacinta Marto, Fátima (phone: 049-531633). Moderate.

En Route from Fátima – Backtrack to Batalha and from there take the road north to Leiria or the A1 toll road. Alternatively, return to Batalha by making a circuit southwest of Fátima via N360 and N243 and the towns of Mira de Aire and Porto de Mós. Several caves — *grutas* — are located in this area, among them the São Mamede, Moinhos Velhos, Santo António, and Alvados caves. Of these, the last two — the Grutas de Santo António and the Grutas de Alvados — are probably the most interesting. At the former (phone: 049-84876), there is an enormous chamber of nearly 5,000 square yards, plus rooms of dramatically lighted stalactites and stalagmites. A restaurant and snack bar are also at the site. The latter contain a succession of halls with giant columns and lakes, all well lighted. The caves are open daily year-round. Admission charge (a combined ticket can be bought for both caves).

LEIRIA: An attractive, clean town at the confluence of the Liz and the Lena rivers, Leiria consists of an old medieval quarter and a new town of pleasant gardens and wide avenues. Crowning the whole is a dramatic hilltop castle, which was wrested from the Moors during the 12th century. An Iron Age *castro* and a Roman fortress preceded the castle, whose Moorish foundations are still visible, even though the structure was rebuilt by King Sancho II during the 13th century and later by King Dinis, who, with Saintly Queen Isabel, used it as a residence. Inside the castle walls are the ruins of the Gothic chapel of Nossa Senhora da Pena, roofless but with tall arches; the royal palace of King Dinis, which has an arched loggia with a good view; and the keep of the castle, built by the same king and affording an even better view (open daily from 9 AM to 7 PM, 6 PM in winter; admission charge). Other monuments in the town include the 12th-century Romanesque Church of São Pedro and the Sé (Cathedral), a large, 16th-century building in pale stone.

On the hill opposite the castle's is the Santuário de Nossa Senhora da Encarnação, built during the 17th century and full of tiles from that period. Dedicated to the patron saint of Leiria, it is approached by a staircase of 172 steps. Leiria's Tourist Office (phone: 044-823773) is in the Jardim Luís de Camões, a large park in the center of town graced with cafés and beer gardens. Here, too, is a statue of a man and a woman, representing the two rivers that meet and fall in love in Leiria and continue as one. An open-air market takes place in Leiria on Tuesday and Saturday mornings.

CHECKING IN: ***Dom João III*** – Modern, comfortable, and conveniently located, with 64 rooms (with TV sets and telephones), a bar, a restaurant, and gift shops. Av. Heróis de Angola, Leiria (phone: 044-812500; in the US, 800-528-1234; fax: 044-812235). Expensive.

Euro-sol – A modern high-rise, nicely landscaped. Together with its sister hotel next door, the *Euro-sol Jardim,* it offers 134 rooms with TV sets, mini-bars, and air conditioning, an enticing outdoor swimming pool on a terrace, a top-floor bar and restaurant with a view, a discotheque, and a shopping center. 1 Rua Dr. José Alves Correia da Silva, Leiria (phone: 044-812201; fax: 044-811205). Expensive.

São Luís – A simple, cozy place in a modern building located in the town center, it has 46 rooms with private baths and TV sets; its 8 suites have mini-bars. There is a pleasant bar and breakfast room. Breakfast is not included in the price of the room. At the corner of Rua Henrique Sommer and Rua Beatris Machado (phone: 044-813197; fax: 044-813897). Moderate.

Lis – Attractive and in a renovated building, it has 42 rooms with bath and a bar. Largo Alexandre Herculano, Leiria (phone: 044-31017; fax: 044-25099). Inexpensive.

EATING OUT: ***Tromba Rija*** – An eatery in regional style, typically decorated with onions and garlic hanging from the ceiling and located in a village three-quarters of a mile (1 km) north of town. The codfish and steak dishes are delicious. Try one of the homemade desserts and an almond liqueur. Closed Sundays, holidays, and Saturday nights. Reservations advised. Visa and American Express accepted. Marrazes (phone: 044-32421). Expensive to moderate.

O Casarão – Located 3 miles (5 km) southwest of town via the road to Nazaré (N1), this is an excellent regional restaurant with a cozy fireplace. There's a garden for summer dining. Closed Mondays. Reservations advised. Visa accepted. Cruzamento de Azóia (phone: 044-871080). Moderate.

Tia Elvira – Regional food is served in this rustic place — to the accompaniment of *fado* music on Saturdays. It's about 2 miles (3 km) from the center of town. Open daily. No reservations or credit cards accepted. 14 Rua do Pinhal Grosso, Marinheiros (phone: 044-31171). Moderate to inexpensive.

Jardim – A good, modern place, in the large garden in the center of town by the tourist office, it is especially recommended for outdoor dining in summer. Closed

Fridays. Reservations advised. Major credit cards accepted. Jardim Luís de Camões, Leiria (phone: 044-840444). Inexpensive.

En Route from Leiria – Figueira da Foz is 34 miles (54 km) north on N109 or A1, but a side trip to the coast from Leiria (a 15-mile/24-km round trip) is worthwhile to visit the famous old glassmaking town of Marinha Grande and the beach resort of São Pedro de Moel. Take N242 west, passing through the Pinhal do Rei, the pine forest that King Dinis planted almost 700 years ago to control the shifting sands; it later provided timber to build Portugal's fleet. Marinha Grande, 7½ miles (12 km) from Leiria, has more than 40 crystal and glass factories, but the oldest is the Fabrica Escola Irmãos Stephens, formerly the Real Fábrica de Marinha Grande, established in 1748 by an Englishman, John Beare, and taken over later in the century by two more Englishmen, the Stephens brothers, who willed it to the state. It became one of the most prestigious glassworks in the world and still uses traditional methods demanding a high degree of skill on the part of its craftsmen. São Pedro de Moel, an ancient fishing village turned charming resort, is another 6 miles (10 km) west. It boasts a wide, sandy beach set between cliffs below the pine woods and an enormous saltwater swimming pool by the sea (which is fairly rough here).

Return to Leiria and head north on N109 or the toll road A1 to Figueira da Foz. Just to the west about 8½ miles (14 km) up the road is Monte Real, a spa with a ruined castle and Belle Epoque houses set in shady gardens. Beyond, the road continues north through beautiful pine forests, skirting Atlantic beaches, only 6 or 7 miles (10 or 11 km) away.

FIGUEIRA DA FOZ: The most popular bathing resort and one of the most important fishing ports on the Portuguese Atlantic is endowed with an exceedingly long, wide sandy beach, plus a full complement of hotels, restaurants, and discos, a Belle Epoque gambling casino, a bullring, and facilities for golf, tennis, and water sports. The town is on a flat plain at the mouth of the Mondego River (which flows into the sea here from Coimbra), its estuary forming a wide inland lagoon. Rice paddies and salt pans are nearby. Cross the soaring bridge, turn left, and follow the Centro (Center) and Praias (Beaches) signs to the tree-lined esplanade along the seafront. Here there are modern hotels and shops facing the beach and turn-of-the-century houses decorated with tiles and wrought-iron balconies; the old Santa Catarina Fort (with a lighthouse on top) guards the river's mouth.

Most visitors to Figueira spend their time on the 2-mile-long, approximately 1,600-foot-wide beach; indeed, the town has little to detain sightseers, but the enormous *Casa do Paço* (Rua 5 de Outubro), built by a bishop during the 17th century, is well worth the time spent away from the sun. The walls of this old house, now a museum, are decorated with several thousand tiles, many of them Delft, constituting the largest collection in Portugal (open from 9 AM to noon and from 2 to 5 PM; closed Mondays; admission charge; phone: 033-22159). Another museum, the *Museu Municipal Dr. Santos Rocha* (Av. Calouste Gulbenkian; phone: 033-24509), contains archaeological artifacts, ceramics, coins, furniture, sculpture (religious and African), and contemporary Portuguese and other paintings (open from 9 AM to 12:30 PM and from 2 to 5:30 PM; closed Mondays and holidays; no admission charge). Figueira's Tourist Office (Av. 25 de Abril; phone: 033-22610 or 033-22126) has information on other sights, which include the parish church of São Julião and the Misericórdia and Santo António churches. The fish auction, held in the port in the morning when the fleet comes in, is worth getting up early to see. As in other fishing towns, seafood of all kinds is on local restaurant menus, and Figueira has its own typical *caldeirada,* or fish stew.

The old fishing village of Buarcos, 1¼ miles (2 km) along the coast northwest of

Figueira (in the direction of Cabo Mondego), represents a change of pace from its larger, more worldly neighbor. Very rich during the 17th century, but always subject to attacks by pirates, the town has a ruined castle and long, sandy beaches with colorful *bateiras* (flat-bottomed fishing boats) drawn up on shore.

CHECKING IN: ***Atlântico*** – This very tall tower is an apartment-hotel with 70 fully equipped units with living room, bedroom, bath, kitchen, telephone, and radio, as well as a bar, TV lounge, and shopping center. The rooms have spectacular views of the beach and the Mondego. Av. 25 de Abril, Figueira da Foz (phone: 033-20245; fax: 033-22420). Expensive.

Clube Vale do Leão – A luxurious tourist complex on a hill above Buarcos, on the road to Vaís. It has 24 apartments and villas furnished with antiques and endowed with lovely views, in addition to a host of amenities such as a pool by the sea, a restaurant serving international and regional food, a health center, a piano bar, a cinema, a pub, a tearoom, a boutique, and a hairdresser. Vaís, Serra da Boa Viagem (phone: 033-33057). Expensive.

Estalagem da Piscina – Named for the Olympic-size swimming pool that's next door and shared with the *Grande Hotel da Figueira* (see below), this 20-room inn is modern and comfortable, with a restaurant overlooking the pool and the beach. Closed from November through April. 7 Rua de Santa Catarina, Figueira da Foz (phone: 033-22146). Expensive.

Grande Hotel da Figueira – The best in Figueira da Foz, situated on the seafront, next door to the Olympic-size swimming pool it shares with the *Estalagem da Piscina.* There are 91 rooms with bath (those on the front have balconies), an excellent restaurant, and a piano bar. Guests enjoy free admission to the casino's international floor show. Av. 25 de Abril, Figueira da Foz (phone: 033-22146; fax: 033-22420). Expensive.

Costa de Prata – There are two modern hotels by this name, *Costa de Prata I* and *Costa de Prata II,* with 66 and 120 rooms respectively, close to each other and both close to the beach. No restaurant. 1 Largo Coronel Galhardo, Figueira da Foz (phone: 033-26610), and 59 Rua Miguel Bombarda, Figueira da Foz (phone and fax: 033-266100). Moderate.

Tamargueira – Modern and functional, with 87 rooms and suites, and a panoramic restaurant and bar. It's on the harbor in the village of Buarcos. Marginal do Cabo Mondego, Buarcos (phone: 033-32514; fax: 033-21067). Moderate.

EATING OUT: ***Sereia do Mar*** – Good seafood complements this modern place, decorated in blue and white, on the esplanade near the sea. Open daily. Reservations advised. No credit cards accepted. 59 Av. do Brasil, Figueira da Foz (phone: 033-26190). Expensive to moderate.

Teimoso – Though the owners also rent rooms, this place is better known as a fish restaurant. It's located just outside Buarcos, on the road to Cabo Mondego, and is as good a place as any to try the *caldeirada.* Open daily. Reservations advised. Visa and MasterCard accepted. Estrada do Cabo Mondego, Buarcos (phone: 033-32785). Expensive to moderate.

Caçarola II – Right in front of the casino, with a snack bar downstairs and a restaurant upstairs. The seafood is especially good. Open daily. No reservations. Major credit cards accepted. 85 Rua Bernardo Lopes, Figueira da Foz (phone: 033-24861 or 033-26930). Moderate.

O Pateo – Decorated in typical regional style, this eatery is in an old part of town above the beach and specializes in grilled meat and fish dishes. There is a patio with fruit trees for summer dining. Closed Mondays. No reservations. No credit cards accepted. 31 Rua Dr. Santos Rocha, Figueira da Foz (phone: 033-26657). Moderate.

Quinta da Santa Catarina **–** On the edge of town, in a tree-filled garden with a pool. The food is good, specializing in seafood — the *açorda* (shrimp and rice with shellfish) is a standout. Closed Mondays. No reservations. Major credit cards accepted. Rua Joaquim Sotto Maior, Figueira da Foz (phone: 033-22178). Moderate.

En Route from Figueira da Foz – Take N111 east along the Mondego. The road descends into a valley and then climbs through forests of pine, chestnut, and oak trees, passing water mills and little white churches. After 10 miles (16 km), one of the biggest and most beautiful castles in Portugal is seen standing dramatically above the little town of Montemor-o-Velho. Although the site has been fortified for more than 4,000 years, the castle dates mainly from the 14th century; the church within, Santa Maria da Alcaçova, built during the 11th century, is now mostly Manueline in style. Continue along N111 the remaining 18 miles (29 km) to Coimbra.

COIMBRA: Portugal's most romantic city came into its own during the 12th and 13th centuries as the newly independent country's first capital. Though the capital moved to Lisbon in 1260, the famed *universidade* that King Dinis founded here in 1290 assured the city's continued importance as a cultural and artistic center. Coimbra is still known for its university and for the special brand of Coimbra *fado* that grew out of the student custom of serenading the local girls and singing on the steps of the Old Cathedral at night. For a detailed report of the city, its sights, hotels, and restaurants, see *Coimbra,* THE CITIES.

En Route from Coimbra – Before continuing north toward Aveiro, take a short detour to visit the Roman ruins of Conímbriga, 9½ miles (15 km) southwest of town. Cross the bridge over the Mondego and take N1 south to Condeixa, then follow the signs.

CONÍMBRIGA: The most important Roman site in Portugal, Conímbriga was probably inhabited as far back as the Iron Age, but it was the Romans who made it a monumental city, with an aqueduct, forum, temple, public baths, shops, and houses with beautiful mosaic floors. Situated along the Roman highway between Olisipo (Lisbon) and Bracara Augusta (Braga), the city was at its height during the first part of the 3rd century. Unfortunately, barbarian invasions began during the latter part of the century, forcing the inhabitants to build a new defensive wall, which encompassed only half of the city (stones from buildings outside, funerary stones, bits of statuary, and the old wall were used to construct the new one). The Suevians captured it during the mid-5th century, and the Visigoths later moved to the nearby, more easily protected Aeminium, also Roman in origin. Aeminium grew at Conímbriga's expense and eventually took its new name — Coimbra — from Conímbriga.

Visitors can see remains of the old wall and the aqueduct before entering the site via the main gate in the new defensive wall. On the right are the ruins of the 3rd-century House of Fountains, which was partially destroyed to make way for the wall and in which the layout of the rooms, several with mosaic pavements, is clearly visible. Beyond are other houses, shops, and public baths; the 5th-century House of Cantaber, with private baths beside it; and the forum, including the temple, market, and tribunal. The *Museu Monográfico* at the site (phone: 039-941474) displays objects unearthed here — coins, pottery, cloth, lamps, games, jewelry, sculpture, murals, and mosaics. The museum is open from 10 AM to 1 PM and from 2 to 6 PM, June through September (to 5 PM the rest of the year); closed Mondays and holidays. The site itself is open daily from 9 AM to 1 PM and from 2 to 8 PM, June through September (to 6 PM the rest of the year). There are admission charges to both the ruins and the museum; there also is a restaurant with a panoramic terrace.

En Route from Conímbriga – Return to Condeixa and take the A1 toll highway 37½ miles (60 km) north (bypassing Coimbra) to the junction with N235, which leads to Aveiro. Along the way, watch for turnoffs to points of interest such as Luso, a very ancient spa town on a mountainside (for a description of Luso and its hotels, see *The Beiras* in DIRECTIONS), and Curia, another spa town, famous not only for its waters, but also for its bairrada wines, among the best in Portugal. The bairrada wine producing area extends all the way north from Coimbra to Aveiro.

CHECKING IN/EATING OUT: ***Palace Hotel da Curia*** – This was the most elegant and fashionable hotel in Portugal when it opened in 1922, and it's still a beautifully kept, Old World hostelry, surrounded by lovely woods and formal gardens. Besides 114 rooms, it has an Olympic-size swimming pool, tennis courts, a deer park, a bar, and a restaurant. A stay here among the stained glass windows, marble statues, and Art Nouveau tables will be memorable. Closed from October to *Easter.* Parque da Curia, Anadia, Curia (phone: 031-52131; fax: 031-55531). Expensive.

AVEIRO: Intersected by several canals, Aveiro was once a port on the Atlantic, at the mouth of the Vouga River. But ocean currents built up a coastal sandbar and the river deposited silt in the estuary, so that by the time a giant storm in 1575 closed the natural channel through the sandbar, Aveiro was left occupying the eastern side of an enclosed lagoon. The ancient port that had traded with the Phoenicians, and from which only a short time before ships had set sail on voyages of discovery and on fishing expeditions to the cod banks of Newfoundland, was left without an outlet to the sea. Only early in the 19th century was a canal cut through the sandbar (stones from the town's 15th-century walls were used in the construction), restoring a measure of prosperity.

Aveiro's shallow saltwater lagoon — the Ria de Aveiro — stretches nearly 30 miles from north to south, though it is only a few miles wide. The lagoon is productive, providing fish, salt, seaweed for fertilizer, and, in the parts above sea level, fertile farmland. It is picturesque, too, dotted with islands, bordered by salt flats, and full of impressive conical mountains of white salt, as well as a variety of boats. Of these, the most beautiful are the seaweed gatherers' flat-bottomed, square-sailed *moliceiros,* their high, curved prows brightly painted with Ria scenes. Their numbers have dwindled, but they can still be spotted throughout the lagoon or gathered together on special occasions, such as Aveiro's *Festa da Ria,* which takes place in late July and early August. A *moliceiro* regatta (departing from Torreira, a fishing village to the north, and arriving in Aveiro 2 days later) and a race of *moliceiros* and other boats are part of the festivities.

Aveiro itself is a lovely town, with more to see than many cities farther south, because the devastating earthquake of 1755 did not reach here. Its canals are crossed by interesting bridges, and in the middle of town, the Central Canal is lined with charming, colorful houses. The former Convento de Jesus, at Praça do Milenário, now the *Museu de Aveiro* (phone: 034-23297), is the first stop for most sightseers. Founded during the 15th century, but mainly baroque following later remodeling, the convent was for almost 2 decades the home of the daughter of King Afonso V, Infanta Dona Joana, who entered it to lead a saintly life after having refused marriage to several kings. She died here in 1490, and her marble tomb, supported by angels, can be seen in the convent church, which is decorated with 18th-century baroque woodwork so intricately carved and gilded it looks like filigree. As a museum, the convent contains valuable collections of sculpture, gold and silver work, vestments, and paintings (the most famous is one of Princesa Santa Joana in 15th-century court dress) — works of art gathered from churches and monasteries throughout the region after the expulsion of religious orders during the 19th century, as well as works originally made for use here. The museum is open from 10 AM to 12:30 PM and from 2 to 5 PM; closed Mondays and holidays. Admission charge, except on Sunday mornings.

Across from the convent is the Church of São Domingos, founded during the 15th century as a monastery church but now serving as the Sé (Cathedral) of Aveiro; its baroque door is the result of an 18th-century renovation. Not far away, in Praça da República, is the Misericórdia, a 16th-century church covered with *azulejos* inside (from the 17th century) and out (19th century). The 17th-century Igreja das Carmelitas, to the south (near the post office), is worth a stop to see more *azulejos,* as is, beyond it, the 16th-century Santo Antônio, known for its interesting barrel-vaulted ceiling and carved gilt work. On the north side of the Central Canal, near the fish market, is the Chapel of São Gonçalinho, the patron saint of salt workers. Still farther north, not far from the railroad station, is the 18th-century chapel of Senhor Jesus das Barrocas, an octagonal building with a rectangular chancel; magnificent woodcarvings adorn the interior, along with modern paintings of the lives of the saints, commissioned by the devout fishermen of Aveiro.

A variety of water sports — sailing, windsurfing, water skiing, and swimming — can be practiced in the Aveiro area, and there are several excursions that can be made in the vicinity. From mid-June to mid-September, a boat tour of the Ria leaves from Aveiro daily at 10 AM, stopping for lunch at Torreira, and returning to Aveiro at 5 PM. The tourist office (Praça da República in Aveiro; phone: 034-23680) can supply information. Some suggested driving routes taking in more of the colorful Ria towns are given below. Visitors should also make an effort to visit Vista Alegre, about 4½ miles (7 km) south of Aveiro via N109. The world-famous Vista Alegre porcelain factory (Fábrica de Porcelana da Vista Alegre), founded in 1824, is located here, with the *Museu Histórico da Vista Alegre* on its grounds (open from 9 AM to 12:30 PM and from 2 to 5:30 PM; closed Mondays and holidays; no admission charge; phone: 034-322365). The museum has a large collection of the stoneware and crystal that the factory produced in its early years, plus vases, lamps, and porcelain dinnerware from all periods, including examples of valuable pieces made for European royalty. A further attraction is the showrooms, where porcelain can be purchased.

CHECKING IN: ***Afonso V*** – In a quiet residential district not far from the canals and monuments, it has 80 rooms with private bath and all the modern comforts, a pub-style bar, a discotheque, and the *Cozinha do Rei,* one of the best restaurants in town (see *Eating Out*). 65 Rua Dr. Manuel das Neves, Aveiro (phone: 034-25191; fax: 034-38111). Moderate.

Imperial – A big, modern hotel (107 rooms) in the center of town, with views over the canals and river. There are 3 bars, a solarium, and a very good, very big restaurant, with windows all around. Rua Dr. Nascimento Leitão, Aveiro (phone: 034-22141; fax: 034-24148). Moderate.

Arcada – This lovely old hotel is right in the center of town, on the Central Canal. All 52 rooms have TV sets and telephones; 48 of them have private baths. There is a good bar. 4 Rua Viana do Castelo, Aveiro (phone: 034-23001). Moderate to inexpensive.

EATING OUT: ***Cozinha do Rei*** – In the *Afonso V* hotel and unquestionably the best restaurant in town. Fountains, plants, and the pink-and-white decor make the large dining room a pleasant place, and the *sopa do rei* (king's soup), with fish and lobster, really is fit for a king. Open daily. Reservations advised. Major credit cards accepted. 65 Rua Dr. Manuel das Neves, Aveiro (phone: 034-25191). Expensive to moderate.

Cozinha Velha – Typically Portuguese, with blue-and white tiles on the walls, long tables with benches, and an open kitchen. The specialties are grilled meats and regional dishes such as eel stew. Closed Sundays. No reservations. Visa accepted. 7 Travessa da Rua Direita, Aveiro (phone: 034-20392). Moderate.

Taverna Dom Carlos – Attractive, oak-beamed, with old bairrada wine bottles around the walls and even old wine bottling machinery on the premises, it serves good grilled meats and seafood. There is *fado* music after 10:30 PM Thursdays, Fridays, and Saturdays. Closed Sundays. No reservations. Visa and MasterCard accepted. 46-48 Rua Dr. Nascimento Leitão, Aveiro (phone: 034-22061). Moderate.

En Route from Aveiro – Porto is 42 miles (67 km) north of Aveiro via the A1 toll highway, but for a closer look at the Ria, the salt pans, and the *moliceiro* boats, take N109-7 west 5 miles (8 km) to Barra. The canal through the sandbar is located here, as are two beaches and houses with pointed roofs, tiled fronts, and brightly painted doors. Turn left and drive south along the Ria to Costa Nova, where there are rows of houses with red-and-white, green-and-white, or blue-and-white stripes, as well as little beaches, cafés, and restaurants. Farther south, at Vagueira, travelers may see trawlers launching their boats into the Atlantic and pulling back the nets with yoked oxen. Retrace the route to Aveiro or return by way of the opposite margin of the Ria.

To visit the northern part of the Ria, take N16 east out of Aveiro, turn onto N109 toward Estarreja, and then onto N109-5 to Murtosa. (The roads are not very good and full of trucks.) Murtosa has an interesting 18th-century parish church, but its port — Cais do Bico — with *moliceiros* gathering or unloading seaweed is what should be seen. Continue on N109-5 and, at the end of the causeway, turn onto N327 to Torreira, where a *moliceiro* race is part of a local festival, the *Romaria de São Paio da Torreira,* held from June 15 to August 15. Still on N327, continue south through sand dunes and pine forests to São Jacinto. On the right is the Reserva Natural de São Jacinto nas Dunas, a nature and wildlife preserve in pine-wooded dunes. Paths, elevated walks, and observation towers have been built so visitors can see the birds and animals, and there are two marked trails, one beginning by the preserve headquarters (phone: 034-331282) at its southern end.

Return north 14 miles (22 km) to the turnoff for Ovar, a town famous for its *pão de ló* (sponge cake); its yearly carnival enlivened by masked revelers, flower battles, and allegorical floats; and its *Holy Week* processions. The tile-faced parish church and two chapels (Calvário and Nossa Senhora da Graça) are worth a visit.

Ovar is at the northern tip of the Ria, about 28 miles (45 km), via the A1 toll highway, from Porto, Portugal's second-largest city. To reach the highway, take N327 east for 4 miles (6 km). Or, if one last dip in the sea is desired, take N109 to Porto, passing through the popular, modern Costa Verde beach resort of Espinho.

CHECKING IN/EATING OUT: ***Pousada da Ria*** – This beautiful, waterside state-owned *pousada* has verandahs where guests can sit and watch the Ria boats, and its 19 rooms have private balconies overlooking the water, too. There is also a pool set in lawns and a restaurant with a terrace and a panoramic view. Fish and seafood are served — fishermen deliver the catch to the *pousada* at 8 every morning. Open all year, but very full from April through September; make reservations at least a month in advance. On N327 between Torreira and São Jacinto (phone: 034-48332; in the US, 212-686-9213; fax: 034-48333). Expensive.

Riabela – A modern, 35-room *estalagem* at the water's edge. It has a very good restaurant, glassed in on three sides with views of the Ria, as well as a swimming pool, tennis courts, and a bar. Torreira (phone and fax: 034-48147). Moderate.

The Minho

The Minho — the northwest corner of Portugal, bordered by the Minho River and Spain to the north, the Douro region to the south, the Atlantic Ocean to the west, and high mountains to the east — is the emerald in Portugal's crown. Of all the Portuguese regions, Mother Nature was most generous with the Minho, gracing it with an eternally green and varied landscape, dense forests, fertile valleys, rolling hills, majestic peaks, golden beaches, and thermal springs. People, in turn, went on to decorate it with picturesque granite villages, fortified castles, elegant manor houses, and a green mantle of vines. With time, this fair land came into its own and gave birth to the Portuguese nation.

This is a fairy-tale land shrouded in mist. Lush and verdant, the Minho has the highest level of rainfall in Portugal during the winter. Clouds coming in from the Atlantic are blocked from the interior by mountain ranges, or *serras,* such as Peneda, Gerês, and Padrela, and are forced to unload their precious cargoes before reaching the high plains of the neighboring Trás-os-Montes region. The temperature is mild, the air somewhat humid, the light soothing to the eye.

Signs of human habitation have been found dating as far back as 5,000 years. Vestiges of fortified granite hamlets (*castros*), built on high ground by Celtic tribes who settled here about 3000 BC, still dot the landscape. The Phoenicians and Greeks, attracted by the area's rich metal deposits, traded actively with the inhabitants during the Bronze and Iron Ages. The Romans encountered stiff resistance during the 3rd century BC and never totally subjugated the Minho, but they did manage to introduce vine growing techniques and an extensive road system. The Suevians, a Germanic farming tribe, replaced the Romans and introduced the iron plow and the practice of cultivating small land holdings detached from villages. The Visigoths, who arrived next, embraced Catholicism. The Moors invaded from North Africa during the 8th century, but they, like the Romans before them, encountered resistance and were forced out — after several generations.

The region claimed its independence during the 12th century when Afonso Henriques of Guimarães, ruler of an entity known as the county of Portucale and as such a vassal of the King of León and Castile, broke away from his feudal lord and had himself crowned King of Portucale. The Portuguese nation was thus born in the Minho, which continued to provide leadership until Portugal's New World discoveries shifted the political focus south to Lisbon. Even then, it continued to play a large economic role, and today, it is one of the principal cattle raising, wine making, and textile manufacturing areas of the country.

Modernity has made inroads into the Minho, with some ugly results; but a large part of it, particularly the rural interior, retains much of its original beauty and charm and many of its age-old traditions, including a strong community spirit. During the harvest, for example, neighbors help each other husk the corn, singing elaborate traditional songs and drinking wine liberally as they work. This is also an occasion for the young to meet prospective partners, and for maidens who find a rare red ear, the *milho rei* (king corn), to kiss their young suitors. The *minhotos* are friendly, hardworking, and devoutly religious. Unlike most northern workaholics, however, they also know how to play — witness their lively folk dances, the *viras* and the *malhão,* and their colorful traditional clothing. The character of the region is best summed up by its symbol, the heart — a symbol that is as warm and hospitable as its people.

The food in the Minho is diverse. There are game, kid, and pork dishes in the mountain areas, lamprey and trout in the river valleys, fish stews, shellfish, cod, and sardines in the coastal areas, and steaks in major livestock centers around Braga and Guimarães. Meals are accompanied by *pão de milho,* delicious, rich corn bread, and the region's *vinho verde,* or green wine. The wine, drunk chilled, takes its name from its relative youth and the Minho's verdant vegetation rather than its own color (which is usually white). The British, who began importing green wines during the 16th century, called them "eager wines" because of their natural effervescence. The best are the whites from estates such as Palácio de Brejoeira and Solar das Bouças, which have a slightly higher alcohol content than the more common wines such as casal garcia and gaitão. The vines are trained aboveground on concrete *pérgulas* (trellises) and *cruzetas* (or crosses) and cling to wires strung over roadways and telephone poles — sometimes at heights of 30 to 40 feet. This frees the land for other crops and keeps the grapes from overripening on the warm soil. The result is a wine that is low in alcohol, not too sweet, and extremely refreshing, but one that doesn't age well. Green wines should be drunk within the first 2 years after bottling.

Allow 9 to 10 days for the leisurely tour outlined below. The route begins in Guimarães, the cradle of the nation, and moves on to Braga, the religious capital of Portugal, famous for its *Holy Week* processions and pilgrimages. It then proceeds north into the heart of the Minho to Ponte de Lima and from there follows the bucolic Lima River past monasteries, Roman bridges, manor houses, and rustic farms, crossing paths with oxen whose highly decorated yokes are carved with Celtic inscriptions. The itinerary includes a visit to the Peneda-Gerês National Park before cutting across an impressive mountain pass into the spa-haven of Monção. From there, it makes its way west along the picturesque left bank of the Minho River, past a string of fortresses guarding Portugal's border with Spain. The region's Atlantic coast is explored during the final leg of the journey, as the route moves south past multicolored fishing villages, stops off at Viana do Castelo (known as the capital of Portuguese folklore), detours briefly inland to Barcelos for a dazzling display of pottery, then returns coastward for a final swing through the beach resorts of Póvoa de Varzim and neighboring Vila do Conde.

During July and August, the main roads become congested with tourists and Portuguese workers on vacation from jobs in northern Europe. Try to avoid traveling on weekends, and move from town to town between 1 and 3

PM, when most of the population is eating, working, or at the beach. Better yet, schedule a visit for late May and early June, or mid-September and the first 2 weeks of October, to catch the grain and grape harvests. At all times, try to avoid driving at night, particularly on mountain roads. They tend to be winding and not well marked.

Whenever possible, reserve rooms in advance for the summer season, which runs from June through September. In addition to choosing from among hotels, *pousadas,* and other types of accommodations, travelers in the Minho can opt to stay in a variety of private houses that take in paying guests as part of Portugal's *Tourism in the Country* program (see *Accommodations,* GETTING READY TO GO), which is particularly active in the area. A great many of the participating properties along the route are the manor houses and other stately homes of *Turismo de Habitação,* while a few are the simpler rural houses and farmhouses of *Turismo Rural* and *Agroturismo.* Reservations can be made by contacting the houses directly or, in most cases, by contacting *Turihab, Associação de Turismo de Habitação* (Praça da República, Ponte de Lima 4990; phone: 058-942729 or 058-741672; fax: 058-741444; telex: 32618). *Promoções e Ideias Turisticas* (*PIT*) also handles bookings for a limited number of the Minho's manor houses. Reservations can be made by contacting *PIT* (Alto da Pampilheira, Torre D2, 8A, Cascais 2750; phone: 01-486-7958; fax: 01-284-2901; telex: 43304).

Expect to pay from $90 to $140 for a double room in a hotel listed below as expensive, approximately $45 to $80 for one in the moderate category, and $35 or less for one in the inexpensive category. A meal for two with house wine will cost $50 and up in restaurants listed as expensive, from $25 to $40 in moderate ones, and less than $20 in inexpensive ones.

GUIMARÃES: The birthplace of the first Portuguese king and the cradle of the nation lies at the foot of a mountain range 32 miles (51 km) northeast of Porto via N105-2 and N105. Founded during the 10th century, the city came into prominence in 1095, when the King of León and Castile awarded the hand of his daughter, Teresa, to a French nobleman, Henry of Burgundy, who had assisted the Spanish king in driving the Moors out of northern Iberia. The county of Portucale (roughly, the land between the Minho and the Douro, including the city of Porto) was part of Teresa's dowry, and the couple chose Guimarães as their court. Teresa bore Henry a son, Afonso Henriques, and 2 years later, when Henry died, she became regent for the child. She soon incurred the wrath of her subjects, however, by taking up with a Galician count and allying herself with the Spanish overlords. When Afonso came of age, he revolted against Teresa's forces outside Guimarães, in 1128, and in 1139 dealt the Moors a severe blow near Santarém. As a result of these victories, Afonso broke his ties with León and Castile and crowned himself King of Portucale in 1139. Spain recognized the new kingdom in 1143.

Guimarães was also the birthplace of Gil Vicente (1470?–1540?), the founder of Portuguese theater. A goldsmith by trade, he nevertheless found time to entertain the courts of João II and Manuel I with his farces and tragicomedies, and he also wrote religious dramas. Gold- and silver-smithing continue to thrive today, as do other crafts such as embroidery and linen weaving, but they are less important than the manufacture of textiles, shoes, and kitchenware. The new industries keep Guimarães prosperous, but take their aesthetic toll. The medieval quarter, however, has been rediscovered and is being slowly restored — for the full medieval treatment, be here for the *Festas*

Gualterianas, the first Sunday in August, when the townspeople dress in medieval attire, a large folk fair with singing and dancing takes place, and all Guimarães returns to the 15th century.

Begin a tour of the city at Largo da Oliveira, a square in the heart of the medieval quarter. On the northwestern side is the Antigo Paço do Conselho (Old Town Hall), an arcaded and crenelated 16th-century building now serving as a public library. On the eastern side is the former convent of Nossa Senhora da Oliveira (Our Lady of the Olive Tree). The convent church marks the spot where the 6th-century Visigothic warrior Wamba was confirmed as king. (According to legend, he said he would accept the charge if his staff sprouted olive leaves when he drove it into the ground, and it did.) During the 10th century, a primitive church was built on the site; virtually nothing remains of the original, but the church's main entrance, where a 14th-century doorway is surmounted by a Gothic pediment, is amusing (it looks like another doorway on top), and the Gothic porch in front is impressive. The convent's 13th-century Romanesque cloister and grounds house the *Museu Regional de Alberto Sampaio* (phone: 053-412465), with a collection of priceless 14th- to 17th-century works from various churches and convents — tiles, paintings by Portuguese masters, tapestries, statues, and a treasure in ecclesiastical plate. Note the Manueline monstrance attributed to Gil Vicente and the magnificent 35-pound silver cross. Open for guided tours from 10 AM to 12:30 PM and from 2 to 5:30 PM; closed Monday and Tuesday mornings. Admission charge. A tour of the square and museum can be topped off with a visit to the *Garrefeira Santa Maria* wine shop on the western end of the square, where an impressive array of Portuguese and regional wines are exhibited and sold to the public. Open Mondays through Fridays, from 9 AM to 1 PM and 3 to 7 PM; Saturdays, from 9 AM to 1 PM.

Walk west along Rua da Rainha to the *Museu Arqueológico da Sociedade Martins Sarmento* (Rua Paio Galvão; phone: 053-415969), housed partly in the cloister of the Church of St. Dominic (São Domingos). Named for the 19th-century archaeologist who excavated the Iron Age cities of Briteiros and Sabroso near Guimarães, the museum contains items from these sites and elsewhere. Most impressive are the stone finds from Briteiros — the Pedra Formosa, a huge carved granite slab that could have been the entrance to a Celtic crematorium, and the Colossus of Pedralva, a 10-foot-high granite idol that took 24 pairs of oxen to drag to its present home. Open for guided tours from 9:30 AM to noon and from 2 to 5 PM; closed Mondays. Admission charge.

Return to Largo da Oliveira and walk north along the cobbled Rua de Santa Maria, lined with handsome 14th- to 17th-century aristocratic residences decorated with coats-of-arms, iron grilles, and statuary. The road slopes upward to the 15th-century Paço dos Duques de Bragança (Palace of the Dukes of Bragança). The massive complex was built by the first duke, Dom Afonso, who was the bastard son of King João I — his status mandated the tilt to the left of the family coat of arms at the entrance to the palace courtyard. The third duke was beheaded by King João II, but the resilient and Machiavellian family returned in style in 1640, when the Duke of Bragança was crowned King João IV, the beginning of a dynasty that furnished Portugal with kings until the country became a republic in 1910. In more recent times, the palace was restored by the late dictator António de Oliveira Salazar, who turned it into an official northern residence for the Portuguese president as well as a museum. To be seen inside are a collection of 15th- to 17th-century Persian carpets, copies of French and Flemish tapestries, Portuguese furniture, Chinese porcelain, paintings by Portuguese, Italian, and Dutch masters, and an armory with 15th-century chain mail. Note the chestnut wood ceilings of the dining and banquet halls, shaped like the hull of a Portuguese caravel in honor of the country's maritime exploits. Guided tours (in Portuguese only) take place from 10 AM to 5:15 PM, except on holidays. Admission charge, except on Sunday mornings until 2 PM (phone: 053-412273).

At the top of the hill overlooking the town is the 10th-century castle, with its eight flanking towers and large central keep, the inspiration for the country's coat of arms. Afonso Henriques, Portugal's first king, was born in the castle, which is restored and can be visited (open from 9 AM to 9 PM; closed Mondays; no admission charge); he was baptized, it is said, in the lovely, tiny 12th-century Igreja São Miguel do Castelo, set on the green between the castle and the ducal palace. Besides the baptismal font, the church contains a stone basin where parishioners placed offerings of grain; the floor is covered with the graves of Portuguese grandees.

The Guimarães Tourist Office is in the southern part of town (83 Largo 28 de Maio; phone: 053-412450). Nearby, and worth a visit if time permits, is the Igreja de São Francisco (Church of St. Francis), a collage of 15th-, 17th-, and 18th-century architecture, rich in gilt and *azulejos* (open from 10 AM to noon and from 3 to 5 PM; closed Mondays; no admission charge; phone: 053-412228); ask the sacristan for permission to see the fine coffered ceiling in the sacristy. The surrounding countryside is also worthwhile, especially the forested Serra de Santa Catarina southeast of town. The road winds up the mountain to the 20th-century pilgrimage Church of Nossa Senhora da Penha (the patron saint of travelers) at the summit, where there are also restaurants, cafés, a simple hotel, and a breathtaking view of the region. Leave the city via N101 east and turn right after Mesão Frio; return to Guimarães via N101-2 by bearing left at the esplanade by the sanctuary.

CHECKING IN: ***Casa dos Pombais*** – High walls and a large wooden gate protect this handsome 17th-century manor house from encroaching urban development in the western corner of Guimarães. Its 2 spacious double rooms are decorated with antique family heirlooms and have fine views of a manicured garden. The patrician home is frequently rented out on weekends for weddings and other formal functions to which lodgers often are invited. Closed the month of September. Av. de Londres, Guimarães (phone: 053-412917). Expensive.

Casa do Ribeiro – This large Minho estate with its own woods and streams is a *Turismo de Habitação* participant. About 3 miles (5 km) west of town off N206, it has 2 double bedrooms, 1 suite, and a single with bath for rent, but no central heating. Guests are served breakfast in a 15th-century stone kitchen. Open March to November. Contact Dona Maria do Carmo Ferras Pinto, *Casa do Ribeiro,* São Cristovão do Selho (phone: 053-532881). Expensive.

Fundador Dom Pedro – A modern high-rise hotel, with 63 rooms and suites and a bar. 760 Av. Dom Afonso Henriques, Guimarães (phone: 053-513781; fax: 053-513786; telex: 32866). Expensive.

Paço de São Cipriano – An elegant country manor house with a crenelated tower and a swimming pool, 6 miles (4 km) south of town off N105. Another *Turismo de Habitação* participant, it has 5 double bedrooms. Closed in winter. Contact Dr. João Santiago Sottomayor, *Paço de São Cipriano,* Taboadelo (phone: 053-481337). Expensive.

Pousada de Santa Maria da Oliveira – On a quaint narrow street in the heart of the medieval town beside the church of the same name, this is ideal for travelers in search of the service and elegance of old Portugal. Made up of converted townhouses, it has 16 rooms, a cozy bar, and a fine restaurant. Known for its succulent *rojões à minhota* (pork stew). Rua de Santa Maria, Guimarães (phone: 053-514157; in the US, 212-686-9213; telex: 32875). Expensive.

Pousada de Santa Marinha da Costa – One of Portugal's most luxurious *pousadas,* a favorite of those looking for peace and quiet, it is about 1¼ miles (2 km) out of Guimarães via N101-2. It's housed in a former Augustinian convent on a mountain overlooking the city. Guests have a choice of 50 rooms, ranging from monastic cells to suites furnished with objects from the former royal palace of Ajuda in Lisbon. They can dine in the former kitchen, lined with pillars and arches (see *Eating Out*), and explore the huge garden, which stretches endlessly. Estrada da Penha, Guimarães (phone: 053-514453; in the US, 212-686-9213; telex: 32686). Expensive.

Palmeiras – This modern bed and breakfast inn (*albergaria*) with 22 rooms, a pub, a bar, and a small terrace is located in a shopping center in the newer part of town. *Centro Comercial das Palmeiras,* Guimarães (phone: 053-410324). Moderate.

EATING OUT: ***Pousada de Santa Marinha da Costa*** – Simple medieval decor and fine Portuguese cooking, served in the splendor of a former monastic kitchen. Located about 1¼ miles (2 km) from town via N101-2. Open daily. Reservations advised. Major credit cards accepted. Estrada da Penha, Guimarães (phone: 053-514453). Expensive to moderate.

Jordão – A lively and popular restaurant with regional decor and some of the best food in town. Closed Monday evenings and all day Tuesdays. Reservations unnecessary. Visa accepted. 55 Av. Dom Afonso Henriques, Guimarães (phone: 053-516498). Moderate.

Solar da Rainha – This typical family-run establishment is ideal for a simple, unpretentious lunch. Closed Mondays. Reservations unnecessary. Visa accepted. 133 Rua da Rainha, Guimarães (phone: 053-413519). Moderate.

El Rei – A comfortable, romantic little bistro in the medieval quarter, facing the back of the former Town Hall and the *Pousada de Santa Maria da Oliveira.* Gracing the walls are local works of art for sale. Closed Sundays. Reservations unnecessary. Visa accepted. 20 Praça de São Tiago, Guimarães (phone: 053-419096). Moderate to inexpensive.

Castelo – No frills and home-style cooking make this place a bargain worth the short walk north from the castle. Closed Saturdays. Reservations unnecessary. No credit cards accepted. 47A Rua Dona Teresa, Guimarães (phone: 053-412218). Inexpensive.

En Route from Guimarães – Head 4 miles (6 km) north on N101 to the town of Taipas, renowned at one time for its Roman baths. From here, continue directly to Braga, 10 miles (16 km) away, or take a more scenic and historic route — an extra 8 miles (13 km) or so — and visit the ruins of an Iron Age settlement, Citânia de Briteiros, perched on a 1,112-foot hillock overlooking the valley of the Rio Ave. To reach Briteiros, turn right onto N310 toward Póvoa de Lanhoso, then turn left onto N309 toward Braga. The road climbs to the archaeological site, which is the largest and most important pre-Roman hill town discovered in Portugal, with remains of some 200 granite huts, streets, sewers, and a subterranean cistern. Two of the huts were reconstructed by Dr. Francisco Martins Sarmento, the 19th-century archaeologist who excavated the site. On the southwestern corner of the town is a carved granite slab believed to have been part of a Celtic reincarnation ritual. Open from 9 AM to sunset; admission charge; small objects unearthed here can be seen in the *Museu Arqueológico da Sociedade Martins Sarmento* in Guimarães.

Continue climbing north on N309 through a forest of pine, oak, and eucalyptus trees. As the road ascends, the lantern tower of the Sanctuary of the Virgin at the crest of Monte Sameiro comes into view through the treetops; after Sobreposta, the road becomes N103-3 and leads to the sanctuary, which commands a sweeping view of the Minho, over a 1,881-foot mountain pass. Continue on the eastern side of the mountain to the sanctuary of Bom Jesus do Monte (see *Braga,* THE CITIES), shaded by trees, surrounded by fountains, and known for its magnificent staircase. Braga is 3 miles (5 km) away via N203, but be advised that the hotels around Bom Jesus are superior to those in Braga, and the *Sameiro* restaurant (phone: 053-675114) at the Monte Sameiro sanctuary is one of the region's best.

BRAGA: The Minho provincial capital is set in a valley at the junction of three mountain ranges. During the Roman era, it was the intersection of five military roads that crisscrossed northern Portugal and led to Rome. With the establishment of the nation during the 12th century, it became the seat of Portugal's archbishops, who maintained their title, Lords of Braga, into the 18th century, accounting for the city's valuable religious treasures and the unusually large number of its churches. Braga is also the center of baroque art in Portugal, the result of an 18th-century building boom largely directed by two of its prelates and financed by wealth flowing in from the New World. For a detailed report of the city, its sights, hotels, and restaurants, see *Braga,* THE CITIES.

En Route from Braga – Take N201 north and stop at Real to inspect the neo-Byzantine Chapel of São Frutuoso de Montélios, 2½ miles (4 km) from Braga. Farther along, at Prado, the Cávado River is crossed on an elegant 17th-century bridge, said to have been built by a rich Spanish grandee to allow him to visit his Portuguese lover. The road then begins to climb and, after cresting the pass at Queijada, enters the heart of the Minho. Tiny wood and stone villages and large manor houses dot the landscape, and grape vines on granite crosses follow the contours of the road as it winds down to the valley of the Lima River and the town of Ponte de Lima.

PONTE DE LIMA: When the Roman legions first came upon the Lima, they were so enchanted by its beauty that they mistook it for the Lethe, the mythical river of forgetfulness, and refused to budge until one of their braver generals swam across. Eventually they built a bridge and included the Celtic town on its south bank in the network of roads between Braga and Rome. During the 12th century, the town was an important stronghold against the Moorish-dominated south and provided many of the men who backed young Afonso Henriques when he revolted against León and Castile to establish the Portuguese nation. Today, the river is as enchanting as ever, as is the Roman bridge that has been closed off to cars for the bucolic benefit of pedestrians. The charming medieval town's martial bent is gone — one of the two medieval towers that used to be a prison is now the town archives, and the 15th-century fortress-palace of the Marquis of Ponte de Lima serves as the Town Hall. The Igreja Matriz (Parish Church), a 14th-century building with 18th-century additions, has an interesting Romanesque doorway, while the 18th-century church of São Francisco, at the eastern end of town facing the river, has been turned into the *Museu dos Terceiros,* a museum of sacred art, containing beautifully carved wood pulpits and altarpieces (open from 10 AM to noon and from 2 to 6 PM; closed Tuesdays; no admission charge).

The main square, with its ornate baroque fountain, is the town's sitting room, a good place from which to admire the river, the bridge, and the church and tower of Santo António da Torre Velha on the opposite bank. (The tiny chapel of São Miguel beside it was used as a stopover by pilgrims on their way to the shrine of Santiago de Compostela in Spain.) Every other Monday, the riverbanks are transformed into the most picturesque of markets, selling farm produce, animals, and local crafts such as linen, wooden furniture, wickerwork, tin lamps, rugs, pottery, and colorful wool blankets. Another good time to be here is during the *Festas de São João* (Feast of St. John), June 23 and 24, or during the *Feiras Novas* (New Fairs), the third weekend (Saturday through Monday) in September. The town's monuments shimmer in the sparkle of thousands of decorative lights, while the night sky is streaked by lavish firework displays. Several parades provide medieval pageantry and costumes, and gigantic floats display the wares and crafts of the region. Other attractions are folk dancing and singing by the river, and nocturnal cornhusking parties at nearby manor houses. Many of these private properties in the vicinity take in guests, and the headquarters of *Turihab,* the owners' association (phone: 058-942729 or 058-741672; fax: 058-741444), is in the same building as the local tourist office (Praça da República; phone: 058-942335).

CHECKING IN: *Paço de Calheiros* – An impressive 18th-century manor house (a member of *Turismo de Habitação*) perched high amid vineyards a few miles northeast of Ponte de Lima. In the main house, 4 bedrooms face a courtyard and garden; 6 apartments with kitchenettes are in a newer addition. A new tennis court and a sleek pool with sweeping views of the valley are added attractions. The Count of Calheiros, whose family traces its ancestry back to the founding of the nation, is a charming host who may invite guests to dinner or to visit his textile factory. Contact *Paço de Calheiros,* Calheiros (phone: 058-941432). Expensive.

Casa do Arrabalde – A spacious townhouse with 4 sizable bedrooms and a large lounge, complete with a fireplace. Ask for a room that faces the courtyard, which is graced by the family chapel and ablaze with camellias. On a quiet residential street across from the handsome Roman pedestrian bridge. Arcozelo, Ponte de Lima (phone: 058-941702). Moderate.

Casa do Crasto – A pleasant 17th-century manor house (a *Turismo de Habitação* participant) ideally located on a hill to the west of the town center. The property includes a vineyard, a rose garden, and a long verandah with sweeping views of Ponte de Lima and the valley. Its 5 double rooms are spacious and decorated with all the proper patrician trimmings, including fresh flowers from the garden. Guests are given the run of the newly restored house, including the baronial kitchen with its huge granite chimney, where whole oxen once were roasted. Ribeira, Ponte de Lima (phone: 058-941156). Moderate.

Casa do Outeiro – A baronial 16th-century manor house (member of *Turismo de Habitação*) with appropriately aristocratic touches, including a crenelated entrance, a ceremonial, tree-lined courtyard, rich family heirlooms, and stately dining room and parlors. Eating breakfast in the huge Renaissance kitchen with wood-fired stoves and a large granite chimney is like taking a trip back to a grander era. It has 2 double bedrooms with views of the courtyard and fountain. Arcozelo, Ponte de Lima (phone: 058-941206). Moderate.

Casa do Pomarchão – Guests can look at the manor house, but they stay in a more modest 2-story house surrounded by orchards and vines. The upper floor (2 double bedrooms, a fireplace, and a kitchen) is ideal for a family; downstairs is more rustic and suitable for a couple. A *Turismo Rural* participant, it's located 1¼ miles (2 km) north of town on N201. Contact Dona Carmen Bernar y Real de Asua, *Casa do Pomarchão,* Arcozelo, Ponte de Lima (phone: 058-941139). Moderate.

Moinho de Estorãos – Another participant in the *Turismo Rural* program, this is a converted 17th-century water mill beside a Roman bridge on a peaceful river nearly 4 miles (6 km) west of Ponte de Lima. It has a double bedroom, a small kitchen, and a living room with a fireplace. Contact Ernesto Martins Pereira, *Moinho de Estorãos,* Estorãos (phone: 058-942372). Moderate.

Quinta de Sabadão – A typical Minho manor house (a *Turismo de Habitação* participant) with an impressive crenelated entrance bearing the family crest. It's just short of a mile (1.6 km) northeast of Ponte de Lima, with 3 large double rooms in the main house. Contact Dona Maria Eulália Abreu Lima e Fonseca, *Quinta de Sabadão,* Arcozelo, Ponte de Lima (phone: 058-941963). Moderate.

Solar de Cortegaça – A member of the *Promoções e Ideias Turisticas* (*PIT*) program, this stately manor provides all the comforts enjoyed by the rural aristocracy. The 3 guestrooms (all with bath) are tastefully appointed with family heirlooms; romantic, candlelit meals can be arranged in the sumptuous family dining room. The best views of the estate are from the tower suite. Closed November through February. Situated on the right bank of the river, 5½ miles (9 km) east of Ponte de Lima on EN202. Subportela, Viana do Castelo (phone: 058-971639). Moderate.

EATING OUT: ***Churrasqueria Tulha*** – Pleasant and welcoming, it specializes in grilled meats and fish. It's set up in a former grain storage barn, and guests can see the food cooking over a wood fire in the open kitchen. Try the paço do cardido, a fine estate-bottled *vinho verde* from the area. Closed Tuesdays. Reservations unnecessary. Visa accepted. Rua Formosa, Ponte de Lima (phone: 058-942879). Moderate.

Monte da Madalena – A great view, classical elegance, gracious service, and well-prepared regional dishes make this a favorite with local dignitaries and aristocrats. Trout with ham and *coelho à caçador* (wine-stewed rabbit) are specialties. It's located on N307 about 2½ miles (4 km) south of town at the summit of a hill overlooking the Lima Valley. Closed Wednesdays. Reservations unnecessary. Visa accepted. Monte de Santa Maria Madalena (phone: 058-941239). Moderate.

En Route from Ponte de Lima – Take N203 east toward Ponte da Barca, 10½ miles (17 km) away, passing impressive Minho estates, old water mills, rococo monasteries, Romanesque churches, and typical granite farmhouses. At Bravães, 9½ miles (15 km) from Ponte de Lima, is the lovely São Salvador, an intriguing church in a mixture of Romanesque, Moorish, Gothic, and local styles (although the predominant note is 12th- to 13th-century Romanesque). Human and animal motifs are carved in its doorways, and the interior walls show vestiges of Renaissance frescoes.

CHECKING IN: ***Casa do Barreiro*** – This participant in the *Turismo de Habitação* program, a lovely estate overlooking the Lima 3 miles (5 km) east of Ponte de Lima on N203, is a particularly fine example of a traditional Minho *solar.* It's replete with a colonnaded courtyard, a quaint garden with tiles, flowerpots, roses, and geese, and an adjoining terraced vineyard. There are 7 bedrooms, common rooms, a small bar furnished with Portuguese antiques, and a swimming pool. Contact Gaspar Malheiro, *Casa do Barreiro,* Gemieira (phone: 058-941937). Moderate.

PONTE DA BARCA: The town where the explorer Fernão de Magalhães — more commonly known as Ferdinand Magellan — is said to have been born lies on both banks of the Lima. At the entrance to the town, beside an 18th-century bridge, is a pleasant square with a covered market and a *pelourinho* (pillory — a decorative column that served, from the Middle Ages to about the 18th century, as both a symbol of municipal power and a place of punishment). Nearby is the Garden of the Poets, paying tribute to two of the region's most famous men of letters, Diogo Bernardes and Father Agostinho da Cruz. It's said that baptisms used to be performed at midnight under the bridge, with the first passerby acting as the godparent. The tourist information office (Largo de Misericórdia; phone: 058-42899) hands out maps with detailed walking tours of the region. Every other Wednesday, the town holds a large crafts fair (on the remaining Wednesdays, the fair takes place in Arcos de Valdevez, a few miles north — see below). The *Festas de São Bartolomeu,* August 23 and 24, is a lively event with music, dancing, and fireworks.

CHECKING IN: ***Paço Vedro de Magalhães*** – This baronial 18th-century manor house (a member of *Turismo de Habitação*) belongs to one of Portugal's oldest families. The sprawling grounds — 1¼ miles (2 km) southeast of town off N101 — have views of the surrounding mountains, and the 3 double rooms and 2 suites are furnished with antiques. The imposing baronial hall of the estate is lined with heraldic standards and portraits of family members, among them famous Portuguese explorers and statesmen. Contact Dona Maria Constança Corte-Real e Lima, *Paço Vedro de Magalhães,* Ponte da Barca (phone: 058-42117). Expensive.

Casa da Agrela – Another handsome 18th-century manor house, this one has a garden and panoramic views of the Amarela mountains. (A *Turismo de Habitação* property.) One suite and 2 double bedrooms are available. Located 4 miles (6 km) south of Ponte da Barca off N101. Contact Antonio Calheiros Fernandes de Oliveira, *Casa da Agrela,* São Pedro do Vade (phone: 058-42313). Expensive to moderate.

EATING OUT: ***Varanda do Lima*** – A pleasant spot near the bridge over the Lima, it's very popular during the summer. Regional specialties include *rojões com arroz de sarrabulho,* a pork and rice dish. Open daily. Reservations advised. Largo do Corro, Ponte da Barca (phone: 058-43469). Moderate.

En Route from Ponte da Barca – Travelers in a hurry should take N101 north 24¼ miles (39 km) to the spa town of Monção. Otherwise, take a 50-mile (80-km) day tour through the Parque Nacional da Peneda-Gerês. The national park, hard by the Spanish border and roughly horseshoe-shaped as it follows the outlines of the Serra da Peneda to the north and the Serra do Gerês to the south, with the Lima River between, contains some of the wildest mountain country in Portugal. Head east out of Ponte da Barca along N203, which accompanies the wooded banks of the Lima, and in 10 miles (16 km) arrive at the park entrance at Entre Ambos-os-Rios. (Since there are no recommendable restaurants along the park route, it's a good idea to pack a picnic lunch for the trip; also, although the road is being widened, night driving should be avoided.) Take the river road into the park toward Lindoso; as it climbs, the terrain becomes rockier — all available land, which is not much, is planted with corn, and cattle graze along the steep slopes.

LINDOSO: The 13th-century castle of this tiny frontier village guards a pass where the Lima River enters Portugal from Spain. Its moat, walls, and towers are well preserved, and some of the original soldiers' quarters have been restored (open May through September, from 10 AM to sunset; generally closed the rest of the year; no admission charge). Look down from the southern end of the castle walls toward the village to see a large concentration of granite *espigueiros* (grain storage huts) on stilts. In the fall, villagers help each other husk corn, and the mountain echoes with their singing.

En Route from Lindoso – To cross the Lima, backtrack 7 miles (11 km) to Parada do Monte, cross the river, and take the N304 2 miles (3 km) to Soajo. The tiny village of Soajo sits at the edge of the park atop a mountain overlooking the barren peaks of the Serra da Peneda as they stretch northeast to form a natural border with Spain. Its inhabitants, called *monteiros* (hunters), are known for their independent character, derived from centuries of earning their living by hunting for themselves and the royal house. In turn, they were allowed to govern themselves. King Dinis (1261–1325) went so far as to prohibit the nobility from living here, by ruling that they could not spend more time in the village than it took for a piece of bread to cool down on a spear. This may explain the unusual pillory in the main square, shaped like a spear with a triangle, presumably bread, perched on top. At the eastern end of town, on a large, smooth granite rock, is a large group of *espigueiros.* Cornhusking parties, with singing and dancing, take place on the spot during the fall harvest.

Leave Soajo and the park by heading for Arcos de Valdevez, either by taking N202 directly west or by taking the more scenic route along the Lima. For the latter, leave Soajo by the same road used to reach it and turn toward Ermelo. The cluster of crude, round stone houses seen at the edge of the mountain along the way are *brando* (soft) houses — improvised rock shelters used by shepherds in the summer months. Ermelo itself is a quaint village perched on the steep banks of the river, with a pretty Romanesque church. (To visit the town, park the car on the road and walk several hundred yards on a narrow stone path.) Continue to São Jorge, where the road curves north to Vale and Arcos de Valdevez, leaving the river behind.

CHECKING IN/EATING OUT: ***Casa do Adro*** **–** A participant in the *Turismo Rural* program, it is in a renovated 18th-century townhouse beside the town square. There are singles, doubles, and suites sleeping 4 to 6 people. Guests have breakfast in the old, rustic kitchen; two cafés next door serve simple meals. Contact Maria or António Enes, *Casa do Adro,* Soajo (phone: 058-67327). Moderate to inexpensive.

ARCOS DE VALDEVEZ: The town, dating from the 10th century, takes its name from the calm Rio Vez, whose banks it graces. It has known better days, but there are several monuments of note, including a Romanesque chapel and a Manueline pillory in the center and the Paço de Giela, a fine example of a medieval baronial house with crenelated tower, about 1¼ miles (2 km) northeast. Arcos de Valdevez can be used as a base to explore the river valley or the mountains (short hikes will turn up a variety of rustic farmhouses, water mills, and *canastros* — wicker containers with thatch covers used to store and dry corn). The tourist office, located at the southern end of town (Av. Tilias; phone: 058-66001), provides maps and tour information. A crafts fair takes place every other Wednesday in Arcos, alternating with the one in Ponte da Barca, a few miles south.

CHECKING IN: ***Casa de Requeijo*** **–** The terraced gardens of this 17th-century manor house (a *Turismo de Habitação* property) have been replaced by a concrete tennis court, a swimming pool, and an outdoor grill, and all available space in the house has been turned into guest quarters, furnished in less than baronial style. The riverside location and sports facilities (including several rowboats and bicycles), however, are an attraction. There are 2 apartments with kitchenettes and 2 suites with double bedrooms on the main floor, plus 2 rustic and slightly cramped suites in the garden. A minimum stay of 5 days may be required from mid-June through September. Contact Alberto and Catherine Pereira, *Casa de Requeijo,* Arcos de Valdevez (phone: 058-656530). Expensive.

EATING OUT: ***Adega Regional*** **–** A converted farmhouse in the northern outskirts of town beside the Rio Vez. Dine in a rustic courtyard covered with vines or in a pleasant room decorated with farm implements. The restaurant's grill draws a large clientele — meats and fish are brought in fresh from nearby farms and the river. Closed Mondays. Reservations advised. Major credit cards accepted. Located off N101 toward Monção. Silvares (phone: 058-66122). Moderate.

En Route from Arcos de Valdevez – About 9½ miles (15 km) north (N101), the winding but well-paved road begins to climb the Serra de Boulhosa, via a spectacular pass onto whose slopes villages, churches, and vines cling precariously. Once over the top, the valley of the Minho suddenly comes in view and the road descends into the Pinheiros district. It is here that alvarinho, the king of *vinho verde* grapes, grows best, particularly on the estate surrounding the sumptuous 19th-century Palácio de Brejoeira, whose *vinho verde* is the most famous and most expensive of "green wines." (The estate's *aguardentes* — rough brandies — are also coveted.) Peer through the wrought-iron gate into the sprawling grounds; the last King of Portugal spent his final night before exile here, and Britain's Prince Andrew has been a guest.

MONÇÃO: The Minho forms Portugal's northwestern border with Spain, and this small town on the river's south bank — a spa noted for its hot mineral springs — is one of a string of fortified towns that have for centuries guarded the Portuguese frontier. Legend has it that during the 14th century, a young noblewoman, Deu-la-Deu Martins, saved Monção from a Castilian siege by throwing what was left of the town's bread over the walls, to make the Spanish believe there was bread enough to last a long time. The invaders swallowed the ruse and lifted their siege, and today, a statue of the heroine stands in the town square. Some of Monção's medieval walls and parts of a 17th-century fortress are still standing, and the Romanesque parish church has an elegant 12th-century door. In May or June, *Corpus Christi* is celebrated with a colorful bout between a dragon and a brilliantly clad St. George mounted on a white steed. The tourist office is in the center at Largo do Loreto (phone: 051-652757).

CHECKING IN/EATING OUT: *Casa de Rodas* – This elegant 18th-century manor house (a member of *Turismo de Habitação*) surrounded by woods and vineyards is about 1¼ miles (2 km) southeast of Monção. Guests have access to most of the house, which has several drawing rooms furnished with Portuguese antiques, a turn-of-the-century billiards room, and a dining room dripping with chandeliers. There are 4 bedrooms with views. Contact Dona Maria Luísa Tavora, *Casa de Rodas,* Lugar de Rodas, Monção (phone: 051-52105). Moderate.

Mané – A simple, clean, 8-room *pensão* in the historic center near the river, suitable for an overnight stay. There is a modern restaurant and snack bar serving tasty food. Open April through September. 5 Rua General Pimenta de Castro, Monção (phone: 051-652490; fax: 051-652376). Moderate.

En Route from Monção – The road southwest (N101) meanders through hills and farm country, playing hide-and-seek with the river. Before entering Valença do Minho, 12 miles (19 km) from Monção, turn left onto N101-1 for a short detour to Monte do Faro, whose 1,865-foot summit provides an impressive view. The Minho Valley and Spain stretch to the north and west, coastal towns and the Minho estuary to the southwest, and the mountains of the Peneda-Gerês National Park to the east.

CHECKING IN/EATING OUT: *Monte do Faro* – A pleasant *pensão* at Monte do Faro, with sweeping views of the surrounding countryside and a fine restaurant. Monte do Faro (phone: 051-22411). Moderate to inexpensive.

VALENÇA DO MINHO: Perched on a hillock overlooking the Minho and, on the opposite bank, the Galician town of Túy, this walled fortress town is another in the series of fortified settlements that have guarded Portugal's northern border from past invasion. Today, the impregnable garrison has become a bazaar, which the Spanish are welcome to plunder as long as they leave their valuable pesetas behind. The old fortified town consists of two 17th-century double-walled forts that are linked to each other by a bridge and a manmade vaulted passage and are lined with two sets of walls, a moat, and trenches. Inside are two quaint quarters with narrow, cobbled streets, whitewashed churches, crenelated townhouses, and loads of shops selling linens, leatherware, pottery, wicker, and Portuguese scarves and sweaters. From the ramparts on the northern side of one of the forts, a 19th-century bridge across the Minho, designed by Alexandre-Gustave Eiffel, is visible.

Outside the walls, to the south, is the new town of Valença, devoid of the charm of the old one except for the vintage train museum in the railroad station. On display are a British steam engine built in Manchester in 1875 and an elegant salon car built in France for the Portuguese royal family. (Ask permission from the stationmaster to visit.)

A word of caution: Plan a trip to this area carefully. Valença is on the main road (N103) between Porto and Santiago de Compostela in Spain — a road that becomes congested during the high summer season and on weekends, particularly during July and August. The tourist office (Av. Espanha; phone: 051-23374) is at the border post by the bridge.

CHECKING IN: ***Pousada de São Teotónio*** – An elegant inn at the northern end of Valença's fortifications, with a gorgeous view of the Minho and Spain. Although this is a contemporary structure, the architects cleverly incorporated its courtyard and garden into one of the bastions and ramparts of the fortress. There are 16 bedrooms, a bar, and a restaurant (see *Eating Out*). Baluarte Socorro, Valença do Minho (phone: 051-824242 or 051-824252; in the US, 212-686-9213; telex: 32837). Expensive.

Lara – Modern, with 54 rooms and a reasonable restaurant. Outside the old fortified town, it's suitable for a night if the *pousada* is booked. Rua São Sebastião, Valença do Minho (phone: 051-824348 or 051-824349; telex: 33363). Moderate.

EATING OUT: ***Pousada de São Teotónio*** – The most luxurious restaurant in town is lodged in the *pousada* overlooking the river and Spain. Tasty regional dishes and Portuguese nouvelle cuisine are served by a courteous staff. Open daily. Reservations advised. Major credit cards accepted. Valença do Minho (phone: 051-824242). Expensive.

Parque – A cozy, family-run establishment in the Old Town, decorated with tiles and peasant pottery and offering a view of the western battlements. Grilled dishes, particularly chicken, are its forte. Closed Fridays. Reservations unnecessary. Rua Oliveira, Valença do Minho (phone: 051-23131). Moderate.

Monumental – A typical, bustling Minho bistro housed inside the stone walls of the fortress, in the former guardhouse that overlooks the town's main entrance. Surrounded by pine, stone, and folk art, customers dine informally on grilled specialties. No reservations. No credit cards accepted. Valença do Minho (phone: 051-23557). Inexpensive.

En Route from Valença – As N13 leads southwest 17 miles (27 km) to Caminha, the rough forested terrain softens. The river begins to widen and a patchwork of orchards and fields of grain, vines, and vegetables spreads quilt-like along its flat embankment. Two tiny islands, Boega and Amores, appear in front of the ancient town of Vila Nova de Cerveira. This is an ideal place to stop and explore the river and surrounding hills, which abound in legends of hidden Moorish treasures and echo with the romantic song of nightingales. Patrician northerners — and wealth from Portugal's colonies — built splendid estates on the banks of this section of the Lima.

CHECKING IN: ***Pousada de Dom Dinis*** – Built within the ruins of a 14th-century castle overlooking the Minho, it has 29 rooms and apartments with kitchenettes, terraces and patios, several bars, and a glass-enclosed restaurant. Praça da Liberdade, Vila Nova de Cerveira (phone: 051-795601, 051-795602, or 051-795603; in the US, 212-686-9213; fax: 051-795604; telex: 32821). Expensive.

Da Boega – An *estalagem* (inn) of 48 rooms perched on terraced slopes above the quaint town of Vila Nova de Cerveira. Guests have a choice of motel-style accommodations or more gentrified rooms in the main ivy-covered house. There is a good restaurant (see *Eating Out*), a swimming pool fed by spring water, a garden, and a tennis court. Quinta do Outeiral, Gondarém (phone: 051-95231). Moderate.

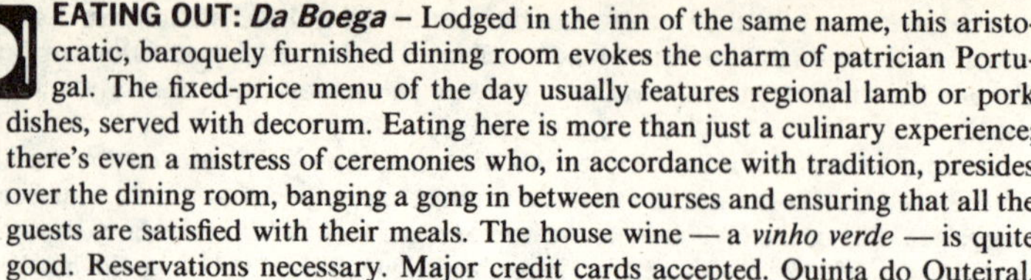

EATING OUT: ***Da Boega*** – Lodged in the inn of the same name, this aristocratic, baroquely furnished dining room evokes the charm of patrician Portugal. The fixed-price menu of the day usually features regional lamb or pork dishes, served with decorum. Eating here is more than just a culinary experience; there's even a mistress of ceremonies who, in accordance with tradition, presides over the dining room, banging a gong in between courses and ensuring that all the guests are satisfied with their meals. The house wine — a *vinho verde* — is quite good. Reservations necessary. Major credit cards accepted. Quinta do Outeiral, Gondarém (phone: 051-95231). Expensive to moderate.

Kalunga – Perched on the crest of the mountain above *Da Boega,* this homey place boasts the best views of the region's vineyards and tiny farms, as well as of the Minho River. Guests can dine in the pub-like indoor area or alfresco on the terrace. No reservations. No credit cards accepted. The signposted restaurant is off the road to Gondarém, on a cobbled lane across from a diminutive country chapel. Calvar, Gondarém (phone: 051-795886). Moderate.

CAMINHA: This ancient fortified town guards Portugal's northern border at the mouth of the Minho, at a point where a lesser river, the Coura, flows into the larger one. The tiny Portuguese fortress island of Insua and the Spanish town of Santa Tecla face it. Caminha's whitewashed town square still retains some of its medieval flavor: Of interest here are the loggia and coffered ceilings of the 17th-century Town Hall; the crenelated clock tower; the 15th-century Gothic Pitas Palace, with its neo-Manueline windows; and the parish church, with its beautifully carved Mudéjar ceiling. Inspect the northern exterior of the church to see an amusing gargoyle of a man relieving himself, with his backside facing Spain.

CHECKING IN: ***Casa do Esteiro*** – This pleasant country house, a *Turismo Rural* property, is surrounded by gardens and vineyards in the southeastern suburbs of Caminha. Guests can choose a double room or a suite. Contact Dona Maria do Patrocinio de Vilas Boas, *Casa do Esteiro,* Caminha (phone: 058-921356). Moderate.

Quinta da Graça – A member of *Promoções e Ideias Turisticas,* this blue-blooded estate occupies the slopes to the southeast of Caminha, offering breathtaking views of the Atlantic Ocean and the Minho and Coura rivers. There are 3 antiques-filled double rooms (with private bath) in the main house, plus 3 apartments with kitchenettes and terraces. Guests can lounge beside the tree-lined pool or meander down to the bucolic Coura river. Vilarinho, Caminha (phone: 058-828637). Moderate.

Ideal – A clean and simple, 30-room *pensão* on a hill overlooking Caminha, about 2 miles (3 km) from town. 125 Rua Engenheiro Sousa Rego, Moledo do Minho (phone: 058-922605). Moderate to inexpensive.

EATING OUT: ***Adega Machado*** – The coziest and most hospitable restaurant in town, on a secluded street southwest of the main square. Discreetly decorated with tiles and wood, it offers a wide selection of typical regional dishes, including *tainha assada no forno* (oven-baked mullet), cold and pickled *sável* (shad), and shellfish. Closed Monday evenings. Reservations unnecessary. 85 Rua Visconde Sousa Rego, Caminha (phone: 058-922794). Moderate.

Remo – A modern restaurant sitting on stilts on the wharf of the Caminha sailing club, facing Spain. Although its decor has seen better days, its view of Spain and the river, and its food, have secured a loyal clientele. Both Spanish and Portuguese dishes are served; *arroz de marisco,* Portugal's version of Spain's paella, is a specialty. Closed Tuesdays. Reservations advised. Major credit cards accepted. *Pôsto Náutico do Sporting Clube Caminhense,* Caminha (phone: 058-921459). Moderate.

Confeitaria Docelandia – This immaculate Old World sweet shop is the area's best. Cakes, cookies, deli sandwiches, and port and tea are all served; they also do a respectable take-out business. No reservations. No credit cards accepted. 32 Rua de São João, Caminha (phone: 058-921144). Moderate to inexpensive.

En Route from Caminha – The road (N13) to Viana do Castelo, 15 miles (24 km) from Caminha, heads south along the Atlantic coast past fishing villages and tourist resorts. The crème de la crème of northern Portugal's elite own homes in the pine woods here, about 1 mile (1.6 km) south of Caminha, where wide, uncluttered Modelo beach stretches south from where the Minho meets the Atlantic. Vila Praia de Ancora, set at the mouth of the Rio Ancora, has a small castle, secluded beaches, and good fish restaurants. The river and town apparently received their name after the wife of a local patrician ran away with a Moorish emir, was brought back in chains, and was dropped into the river strapped to an anchor (*âncora*). Afife, nearby, is another small beach resort, with a strange *Lenten* custom: The townspeople burn one of the town's older women in effigy as part of a cleansing ritual. After Afife, the road crosses a flat, windswept marshland and enters Viana do Castelo.

VIANA DO CASTELO: This holiday resort lies at the mouth of the Lima River, with a basilica-topped hill, Monte de Santa Luzia, looming behind it. Legend has it that Viana takes its name from a beautiful woman, Ana, who lived here. Her fiancé, a boatman on the Lima, was so persistent in asking acquaintances encountered on his run whether they had seen Ana — to which they would answer "Vi Ana" ("I saw Ana") — that the name stuck. (Others say the name has something to do with the Greek goddess Diana.) The small city's Manueline and Renaissance houses attest to its prominence during the 16th century, when it played a major role in Portugal's maritime discoveries, providing boats, seamen, and explorers such as Alvares Fagundes, who charted the waters of Newfoundland for Portuguese fishermen. Gold from Brazil and an early prominence in the port wine trade with England contributed to a baroque building boom in the 18th century.

The Praça da República and its environs hold some of the city's most impressive architecture. An ornate 16th-century fountain by Viana's master stonemason, João Lopes the Elder, stands in the middle of the cobbled square. Facing it, to the east, is the crenelated Paços do Conselho, the former town hall, a late-16th-century Gothic structure. Next door is one of Viana's most delightful buildings, the Misericórdia; the façade of this 16th-century Renaissance hospice, designed by João Lopes the Younger, is alive with nubile atlantes and caryatids. The adjoining church contains important 18th-century *azulejos* by António de Oliveira Bernardes and his son, Policarpo. South of the square, medieval tradesmen and merchants can be seen resting on the shoulders of the Apostles in the carved portal of the Gothic parish church, which faces a lovely Renaissance house reputed to have belonged to João Lopes the Elder. More contemporary artwork created by regional and city artists can be appreciated and purchased nearby at the *Instituto da Juventude Viana do Castelo* (Rua do Poço). The center's café-bar is open at night and is a popular haunt of Viana's artistic community. On the west side of town, the *Museu Municipal* (Largo de São Domingos; phone: 058-24223), housed in an 18th-century palace, contains many treasures, including a valuable collection of 18th-century glazed pottery from Coimbra and a handsome, pre-Roman statue of a Lusitanian warrior. The museum is open for guided tours from 9:30 AM to noon and from 2 to 5:30 PM; closed Mondays and holidays. Admission charge.

Walking tours (Portuguese only) of Viana depart from the tourist office, lodged in a handsome 15th-century palace (Rua do Hospital Velho; phone: 058-822620). Regional crafts are on display here, as well as in several shops around the colonnaded courtyard. Viana is known for its blue-and-white ceramics, table linen, copper goods, gold and silver filigree work, regional costumes and dolls, peasant scarves, and sprays of artificial flowers called *palmitos.* Most conspicuous are the handkerchiefs decorated with hearts that young maidens traditionally give to their boyfriends.

Tradition is indeed strong in this city, which has been called the capital of Portuguese folklore because of the flair and the sheer number of the *festas* (feast days) and *romarias* (pilgrimages) that occur in and around it. The tiny baroque Igreja Nossa Senhora da Agonia (Church of Our Lady of Suffering) is famous throughout Portugal for its annual pilgrimage, probably the most spectacular and lively event of its kind in the north. For 3 days at the end of the third week in August, the city is transformed, with thousands of lights glowing, food and *vinho verde* sold at hundreds of small stalls, and the sounds of singing and dancing echoing through the night. Young women parade in colorful traditional dress, weighed down by intricately carved gold filigree. Mythical giants of the forest — *gigantones* — roam, and a sumptuous procession carries a statue of the Virgin through streets paved with flower petals to bless the fishing fleet. It all ends in a blaze of fireworks at the harbor.

Other events include the *Festas de Santa Cristina,* the first weekend (Friday through Sunday) in August, in the suburb of Meadela, featuring lively folk music and dancing, floats, and religious pageantry — the regional costumes worn by the women are a big part of the attraction. In May there are also lavish flower festivals in Viana and its environs. The *Festas da Senhora das Rosas* (Festival of Our Lady of the Roses), early May in Vila Franca do Lima, has young women carrying large baskets woven with intricate rose petal designs of their own making; in the *Festa dos Andores Floridos,* late May in Alvarães, floats covered with roses ride over a carpet of flowers.

Before leaving Viana, don't forget to visit the Basílica de Santa Luzia, on Monte de Santa Luzia (Mount St. Lucy), roughly 2½ miles (4 km) north of town on a well-marked road (or reachable by funicular from Av. 25 de Abril — it runs from 9 AM to 6 PM, every hour until noon, then at 12:30 PM, 1:30 PM, and every half hour thereafter; from April through September, it also runs at 6:30 and 7 PM). In times of plague or invasion, the people of Viana have always taken refuge in the woods here, and the neo-Byzantine basilica on top of the mountain — a 20th-century copy of the Sacré-Coeur in Paris — is an important pilgrimage church. Those who don't mind narrow passages and a climb of 142 steps will be rewarded at the top of the lantern tower with a panoramic view of the city and its environs. Those interested in exploring the region by rail should inquire at the tourist office (address above) about the 19th-century train that travels from Viana up the dreamscape coast to the fortress town of Valença. Pulled by a steam engine and manned by "conductors" in period dress, the train re-creates the slower, more genteel ambience of a bygone era. The 1-day tour, offered sporadically throughout the year, includes lunch in a Minho manor.

CHECKING IN: ***Do Parque*** – A modern, 123-room hotel in a small park on the eastern side of the city, a 5-minute drive from the center. It has a view of the river, a rooftop restaurant, a swimming pool, and a discotheque. Praça da Galiza, Viana do Castelo (phone: 058-828605; telex: 32511). Expensive.

Paço d'Anha – One of the most attractive manor houses in the north of Portugal, it's part of the *Agroturismo* program and is located in a large *vinho verde*-producing estate near the beach 3 miles (5 km) south of town. Guests stay in farm buildings converted into apartments (2 double bedrooms, living room, bath, and kitchen). Horseback riding and meals can be arranged; the estate wine is highly recommended. It was as a guest here, in 1580, that the Prior of Crato received the news that he had been proclaimed King of Portugal. Contact António Júlio Alpuim, *Paço d'Anha,* Anha (phone: 058-322459). Expensive.

Santa Luzia – A turn-of-the-century luxury hotel on Monte de Santa Luzia, with a sweeping view of the region. Refurbished in a 1930s style, it has an elegant dining room, salon, and terrace, plus 44 rooms and 3 suites, an outdoor swimming pool, and a tennis court. Monte de Santa Luzia (phone: 058-828889; telex: 32420). Expensive.

Casa do Ameal – This *Turismo Rural* program participant is a pleasant townhouse on the Lima River in suburban Meadela; it has 4 double rooms and 2 apartments sleeping four people. Contact Dona Maria Elisa Araújo, *Casa do Ameal,* Meadela (phone: 058-22403). Moderate.

Casa Grande da Bandeira – A *Turismo de Habitação* property, it offers 2 double bedrooms in a large 18th-century townhouse near the center. Contact Dona Maria Mayer de Faria, *Casa Grande da Bandeira,* 488 Rua da Bandeira, Viana do Castelo (phone: 058-823169). Moderate.

Jardim – This quaint inn faces the river and an esplanade near the center of town. There are 20 tastefully furnished rooms. 68 Largo 5 de Outubro, Viana do Castelo (phone: 058-828915). Moderate.

Viana Sol – Pleasant and hospitable, it's near the city center, with 72 rooms, a cozy bar, discotheque, sauna, a squash court, and an indoor pool. The only weak point is a rather staid indoor restaurant. Largo Vasco da Gama, Viana do Castelo (phone: 058-828995; telex: 32790). Moderate.

Calatrava – This tiny *albergaria* (inn) offers guests plenty of rustic charm. The 15 bedrooms feature pine wood decor and colorful folkloric pottery and handicrafts; ask for one with a view of the Lima River. An intimate bar and lounge (no restaurant) with soft lighting provide a romantic touch. In the east part of town, at 157 Rua M. Fiúza Junior, Viana do Castelo (phone: 058-828911 or 058-828912; fax: 058-828637). Moderate to inexpensive.

Alambique – A simple *pensão* of 24 rooms on a quiet side street near the center, it has an adjoining restaurant serving good traditional fare (see *Eating Out*). 86 Rua Manuel Espregueira, Viana do Castelo (phone: 058-823894). Inexpensive.

Dolce Vita – Another little *pensão,* in the center of town across from the tourist office. The 7 rooms are basic and clean (some look out onto medieval streets and Renaissance houses), and there is an adjoining restaurant (see *Eating Out*). This is only for those who don't mind kitchen sounds and don't need parking in the immediate vicinity. 44 Rua do Poço, Viana do Castelo (phone: 058-24860). Inexpensive.

EATING OUT: ***Cozinha das Malheiras*** – The fanciest restaurant in Viana has a nouvelle Portuguese look to it and its food has earned it two Michelin stars. *Arroz de marisco* (shellfish stew) is a house specialty. It is lodged in the stable of an adjoining palace behind the former Town Hall. Try the Paço d'Anha, a white *vinho verde* from a neighboring estate. Open daily. Reservations advised. Major credit cards accepted. 19 Rua Gago Coutinho, Viana do Castelo (phone: 058-823680). Expensive.

Casa d'Armas – A waterfront restaurant in an old armory. The medieval decor may be slightly stiff, but the food is good and served by a courteous staff. Try the river salmon or the veal with mushrooms for a main course, and the rich *torta de amêndoa* (almond tart) for dessert. Closed Mondays. Reservations advised. Major credit cards accepted. 30 Largo 5 de Outubro, Viana do Castelo (phone: 058-24999). Expensive to moderate.

Alambique – This bistro has good regional food and lively decor. The *carro de caranguejo* (crab stuffed with onions, olives, and egg), lobster with rice, and *cabrito no forno* (roast kid) are recommended. Closed Tuesdays. Reservations unnecessary. Major credit cards accepted. 86 Rua Manuel Espregueira, Viana do Castelo (phone: 058-823894). Moderate.

O Espigueiro – A regional restaurant 3 miles (5 km) out of Viana, off the road to Porto. The place has built up a large, regular clientele, who keep coming back for the fine cooking and the outdoor vine-covered courtyard. Open daily. Reservations necessary. Major credit cards accepted. Lugar do Santoinho, Darque (phone: 058-322156). Moderate.

Os Tres Portes – The city's most typical Minho restaurant, in an old bakery near the town center, features soft lighting, rustic decor, waitresses in traditional dress, and regional cooking. It's also the place to see and hear folk dancing and singing on Friday and Saturday nights from June through September (Saturdays only during the rest of the year). A fixed-price menu gives guests a sample of various dishes, including such tasty meat dishes as baked kid and *rojões* (pork cooked with pigs' blood). The English owner makes sure the Irish coffee is up to par. Closed Mondays. Reservations are necessary in summer. Major credit cards accepted. 7 Beco dos Fornos, Viana do Castelo (phone: 058-829928). Moderate.

Dolce Vita – This rustic Italian restaurant done up with checkered tablecloths is across from the tourist office. The Italian specialties, including pizza baked in a large adobe oven, are a nice change of pace from the sometimes heavy Minho diet — and they go well with white *vinho verde.* Open daily. Reservations unnecessary. No credit cards accepted. 44 Rua do Poço, Viana do Castelo (phone: 058-24860). Inexpensive.

Quinta do Santoinho – To experience an *arraial,* the Minho's version of a barn party, head for this lively and colorful barn-like locale where the folk music and dancing go on till the wee hours, with fireworks and *gigantones* to fuel the excitement. For a fixed price, guests feast on grilled pork, sardines, and chicken, and drink to their heart's content out of barrels of wine. Those who last until morning are served a *champorreão* — a powerful punch. The *arraial* takes place at 8 PM on Tuesdays, Thursdays, and Saturdays in August; on Thursdays and Saturdays in July and September (the last two Thursdays of September excluded); and on Saturdays in May, June, and October. The location is 3 miles (5 km) out of town, at Lugar do Santoinho, Darque, but the necessary reservations can be made in Viana at the *AVIC* travel agency, 206 Av. dos Combatentes (phone: 058-829705). Inexpensive.

En Route from Viana do Castelo – The main road (N13) toward Porto crosses the Lima on a bridge designed by Alexandre-Gustave Eiffel. Stay on the road for 6 miles (10 km), then turn left onto N103 to Barcelos.

BARCELOS: The home of the Portuguese symbol of good luck, the rooster, lies inland 19 miles (30 km) southeast of Viana do Castelo on the Rio Cávado. According to the story, a Galician on his way to Santiago de Compostela was accused of stealing from a wealthy landowner and was sentenced to death by hanging. As his last wish, he requested an audience with the judge, who happened to be sitting down to a meal of roast cockerel when the condemned man was brought before him. The accused pointed to the bird and cried out that as proof of his innocence the cock would get up and crow. The judge laughed and sent the Galician off to his death, but did not touch his meal. Just as the man was being hanged, the cock stood, crowed, then fell back dead again. The judge rushed to the gallows and found the man alive because the knot around the noose had not tightened. A 15th-century monumental cross documenting the miracle, the Cruzeiro do Senhor do Galo (Cross of the Gentleman of the Cock), can be seen in the ruins of the 15th-century Paço dos Duques de Bragança (Palace of the Dukes of Bragança), which have been turned into an open-air archaeological museum (open daily from 9:30 AM to 5:30 PM; no admission charge). The Solar dos Pinheiros, a 15th-century mansion facing the palace on the northeast of the square, is also known as Casa do Barbadão (bearded one). The nickname comes from a Jewish occupant who vowed never to shave following his daughter's shameful affair with a gentile. The gentile happened to be King João I, who later rewarded his lover by making the son she bore him out of wedlock the first Duke of Bragança. Up the street from the house, on Largo do Município, is the parish church, which has some interesting capitals and rich interiors, while the Igreja do Terço (Av. dos Combatentes da Grande Guerra), to the east, is covered with 18th-century *azulejos.*

Most visitors to Barcelos, however, are drawn by its weekly fair, one of the biggest and most colorful in the country, held on Thursdays in Campo da República. Hand-loomed rugs, colorful straw bags and hats, lace, and other regional crafts are sold, but the main attraction is the pottery — literally tons of it, decorative and utilitarian, in every size and color, made in small cottages and factories in the surrounding countryside. The anthropomorphic animals and large-headed devils playing musical instruments are amusing buys, holdovers of an earlier pagan tradition. The foremost artist of this genre, Rosa Ramalho, who made delightful pregnant goat figures that are said to have inspired Picasso, is no longer living, but her granddaughter continues the family trade. Those who miss the fair can take heart, because many of the goods can be purchased at the *Centro de Artesanato* (phone: 053-812135), the handicrafts shop in the same building as the tourist office (Largo da Porta Nova; phone: 053-811882). Barcelos is also known for its elegant sweets. The top tasting establishment is the *Confeitaria Salvação,* which sits on the pedestrian mall just a few minutes' walk west of the tourist office. A front parlor exhibits award-winning pastries fashioned by its fifth-generation owner and master confectioner, Dona Alice, while a more intimate tearoom in the back exhibits her trophies and antique pastry shop wares. Dona Alice's creations include the rich *Barca Cellus,* an almond, egg, and pumpkin treat named after the original river boat that ferried people across the town's Cavado River and from which Barcelos derived its name. Dona Alice also runs a tiny curio shop that stocks Barcelos pottery and other regional crafts (137-43 Rua Dom António Barroso; phone: 053-811305).

CHECKING IN: ***Casa do Monte*** – An *Agroturismo* participant, it is a large, 2-story house with ivy-covered walls and manicured lawns overlooking a valley, a pool, and a tennis court, about 2 miles (3 km) north of Barcelos off N103. There are 2 double bedrooms, 1 single, 1 large suite with 2 adjoining bedrooms, and another smaller suite with a parlor in the main house. The look and feel fits the gentrified country background of its owners. Contact Dona Maria Duarte de Sousa Coutinho, *Casa do Monte,* Abade de Neiva, Barcelos (phone: 053-811519). Moderate.

Quinta do Convento da Franqueira – A former 16th-century Franciscan monastery, now the residence of an Englishman, it stands on 35 acres of pines and vineyards. A participant in *Turismo de Habitação,* it's 2½ miles (4 km) southwest of town off N205, has a swimming pool, and offers a suite and 2 double bedrooms looking onto attractive gardens. Meals can be arranged (the *quinta* produces its own estate-bottled *vinho verde*). Contact Piers Gallie, *Quinta do Convento da Franqueira,* Lugar de Pedrego, Barcelos (phone: 053-815606). Moderate.

Arantes – Clean and simple, this 12-room bed and breakfast *pensão* is in the center of town, across from the park where the weekly crafts fair is held. 35 Av. da Liberdade, Barcelos (phone: 053-811326). Inexpensive.

Dom Nuno – Another small bed and breakfast *pensão,* with 27 rooms near the center of town. 76 Av. Dom Nuno Alvares Pereira, Barcelos (phone: 053-815084). Inexpensive.

EATING OUT: ***Bagoeira*** – One of the oldest eating places in town. Wholesome traditional cooking and good service make it a favorite of the old guard. Open daily. Reservations unnecessary. Major credit cards accepted. 53 Av. Dr. Sidónio Pais, Barcelos (phone: 053-811236). Moderate.

Casa dos Arcos – It's cozy and charming, with tasty, authentic Minho cuisine. Ancient stone walls, wood beams, and soft lights provide a medieval touch. Closed

Saturdays. Reservations unnecessary. Major credit cards accepted. 185 Rua Duques de Bragança, Barcelos (phone: 053-811975). Moderate.

Pérola da Avenida – A modern Portuguese bistro with fine regional cooking and a gracious staff. It faces the park where the weekly crafts fair is held. Open daily. Reservations unnecessary. Major credit cards accepted. 66 Av. dos Combatentes da Grande Guerra, Barcelos (phone: 053-821363). Moderate.

Muralha – Basic regional fare served in a simple, rustic setting beside the tourist office. Open daily. Reservations unnecessary. No credit cards accepted. 1 Largo da Porta Nova, Barcelos (phone: 053-812042). Inexpensive.

En Route from Barcelos – Take N205 southwest 12½ miles (20 km) to the beach town of Póvoa de Varzim and then N13 another 2 miles (3 km) south to the neighboring resort of Vila do Conde. Anyone in a hurry to return to Porto, however, and intending to skip Póvoa and Vila do Conde, should note the existence of a bypass, which begins about 3 miles (5 km) north of Póvoa and continues for 11 miles (18 km) before connecting again with the main road south (N13).

PÓVOA DE VARZIM: One of the more popular northern beach resorts and the largest fishing town north of Porto is really two towns. The northern side is devoted to pampering visitors, with long, sandy beaches, a casino, tennis courts, water slides, pools, discos, beachside restaurants, boats for hire, and a marina. The southern side contains the fishing port and the picturesque fishermen's *bairro,* where women mend the nets and sell fish while the men tend to the colorfully painted wooden sailboats, or *barcos poveiros.* During the *Festas da Senhora da Assunção* (Feast of Our Lady of the Assumption), August 14 and 15, a large procession of fishermen carries a life-size statue of their patron saint to bless the boats. The event is followed by a lively beachside *arraial,* with music, dancing, fireworks, and a bullfight. The *Museu Municipal de Etnografia e História* (17 Rua do Visconde de Azevedo; phone: 052-622200) has an interesting collection of relics relating to the town's fishing history (open from 10 AM to 12:30 PM and from 2:30 to 6 PM; closed Mondays; admission charge, except on Thursdays).

Póvoa de Varzim is known for its gold- and silver-smithing. Watch the silversmiths at work on household items such as ornate candelabras at the famous *Gomes* shop (68 Rua da Junqueira; phone: 052-624638), behind the casino. Less pricey but equally beautiful purchases are the hand-embroidered wool fishermen's sweaters sold at shops lining the beachfront Avenida dos Banhos. The beachfront casino (passport identification required for entry to the gambling rooms) is not only a place to try your luck, but also a cultural center where art and crafts exhibits are held.

Several excursions can be made in the area. At A-Ver-o-Mar, 2 miles (3 km) north, seaweed harvesters have built huts on the beach. At Rates, about 9½ miles (15 km) from Póvoa off N206 toward Guimarães, the elegant 12th-century São Pedro church is one of the better-preserved examples of Romanesque architecture in the region. For exact driving instructions, contact Póvoa's Tourist Office (160 Av. Mouzinho de Albuquerque; phone: 052-624609); the numbering of the buildings along this avenue is confusing, so look for the tourist office near the beach. Another option in the vicinity is the 18-hole course at the *Estela Golf Club* (phone: 052-685567), located beside the beach at Estela, 5 miles (8 km) north of Póvoa and 2½ miles (4 km) off the main road (N13). Equipment rental and lessons are available throughout the year, and the clubhouse has a restaurant and bar overlooking the sea. The Sopete group, which owns the club, also owns hotels in Póvoa; hotel guests receive discounts on greens fees.

CHECKING IN: *Vermar* – A modern hotel beside the beach, it has 208 rooms, a fine restaurant, grill, bar, sauna, discotheque, and 2 heated pools as an alternative to the cool Atlantic. The service, professional and efficient, doesn't spare the small touches that add up to a hospitable environment. Part of the Sopete group, which also owns the *Estela Golf Club;* guests receive a discount on greens fees. Av. dos Banhos, Póvoa de Varzim (phone: 052-615566; telex: 25261). Expensive.

Costa Verde – This upgraded hotel has 50 rooms, a small garden, and parking space. 56 Av. Vasco da Gama, Póvoa de Varzim (phone: 052-681531; telex: 27698). Moderate.

Grande – Near the beach and the casino, with 99 rooms and a restaurant. This was the forerunner of the hotels on the beach strip and, though it has faded somewhat, it still retains some of its Old World charm and elegance. Because it's part of the Sopete group, guests receive a discount on the greens fee at the *Estela Golf Club.* Largo do Passeio Alegre, Póvoa de Varzim (phone: 052-622061; telex: 22406). Moderate.

Santo André – A pleasant *estalagem* (inn) with 49 rooms right on the beach 2 miles (3 km) north of town at A-Ver-o-Mar. The pool and a restaurant overlooking the water are added attractions. Also a member of the Sopete group. A-Ver-o-Mar (phone: 052-615766). Moderate.

Gett – Simple but welcoming decor and service recommend this 22-room *pensão* near the tourist office. 54 Av. Mouzinho de Albuquerque, Póvoa de Varzim (phone: 052-683206). Moderate to inexpensive.

EATING OUT: *Casino Monumental* – The most luxurious dining in the area is in the casino. Both Portuguese and international dishes are served, but the *caldeirada de peixe* (fish stew) — Portugal's answer to bouillabaisse — and the *lagosta suada* (steamed lobster) go especially well with the marine decor. There is dancing and a floor show at the cabaret. Open daily. Reservations are essential in summer, advised at other times. Major credit cards accepted. Av. de Braga, Póvoa de Varzim (phone: 052-615151). Expensive.

Eurocini – Tiny and romantic, this bistro, also near the tourist office, has a good French menu. Open daily. Reservations advised. Major credit cards accepted. 29 Av. Mouzinho de Albuquerque, Póvoa de Varzim (phone: 052-627136). Expensive.

Marinheiro – At the northern entrance of the town on the main road to A-Ver-o-Mar, is this elegant eating establishment for serious fish and shellfish lovers. Its ship-shaped design, the maritime decor, the waiters' sailor uniforms, and the large tanks filled with fish and shellfish complement its seafaring name and menu. *Caldeirada dos Póveiros,* a rich fish chowder invented by the area fishermen, can be savored here. Open daily. Reservations unnecessary. Major credit cards accepted. Fontes Novas, A-Ver-o-Mar (phone: 052-682151). Expensive to moderate.

Chez Tomaz – A warm and relaxed beachside bistro with traditional Portuguese hospitality and menu, efficient and discreet service, and a mix of nautical and bucolic decor. Stone-paved floors with fish motifs, cork and wood walls and ceilings, and soft lighting add to its charm, making it one of the more pleasant dining experiences on the strip. Closed during the month of October. Reservations advised. Major credit cards accepted. 116 Largo do Passeio Alegre, Póvoa de Varzim (phone: 052-620117). Moderate.

Costa – Unpretentious Portuguese cooking and a rustic decor. Closed Mondays. 104 Rua Dr. Caetano de Oliveira, Póvoa de Varzim (phone: 052-684139). Moderate to inexpensive.

VILA DO CONDE: Only 2 miles (3 km) south of Póvoa de Varzim via N13 is another resort and fishing town. Its picturesque Old Quarter retains some of its earlier flavor and architectural beauty. Set on the north bank of the Rio Ave, Vila do Conde was one of Portugal's major shipbuilding and commercial centers during the voyages of discovery, and the shipyards continue to make handsome wooden boats for the country's cod fleet. The cod is still dried in the traditional way on stilts by the river. A tradition of lace making going back to the 17th century also endures. Visitors are welcome at the Escola de Rendas (Lace School; 70 Rua Joaquim Maria de Melo), where they can buy bobbin lace — *rendas de bilros* — on the spot. The town's annual crafts fair, beginning on the Saturday of the third week of July and running through the first weekend in August, is another attraction. One of the largest of its kind in Portugal, it features artisans at work, along with folk singing and dancing. The *Festas de São João* (Feast of St. John) on June 23 and 24, another occasion for singing, dancing, feasting, and fireworks, ends with a floodlit procession to the beach.

The Praça Vasco da Gama is the heart and architectural pearl of the Old Quarter. At the center of the square is an unusual carved *picota* (pillory), where the hand of justice is personified by a sword pointed menacingly at several heads above it. On the eastern end of the square lies the handsome 16th-century Igreja Matriz (Parish Church) with a sumptuous Plateresque doorway carved by Biscayan stonemasons. The elegant Manueline carvings of some of the houses and windows of the tiny, stone-paved Rua da Igreja, running north from the square, echo some of the Renaissance wealth of the town. The Mosteiro de Santa Clara (Convent of St. Clare), founded during the 14th century but rebuilt during the 18th, has a Gothic church with beautifully carved Renaissance tombs. Note the 18th-century fountain in the cloister — it's fed by an aqueduct that runs from Póvoa de Varzim and was built with 999 arches. (The builders thought that 1,000 would have been too grandiose and might have offended God!) Apply at the convent (it is now a juvenile rehabilitation center) to visit the church and climb the parvis before the church for a view of Vila do Conde and the surrounding countryside. From the southwestern corner of the monastary, you can gaze down at the river at low tide and see the top half of a manmade tunnel stretching across the Ave River to a watermill on the left bank. This was the escape hatch for the nuns in times of trouble. The tourist office (103 Rua 25 de Abril; phone: 052-642700) can provide further information on the town and its environs, and when the tourist office is closed, the *Centro de Artesanato* (Handicrafts Shop; 207 Rua 5 de Outubro; phone: 052-642700) provides information.

CHECKING IN/EATING OUT: ***Do Brasão*** **–** A comfortable, centrally located *estalagem* (inn) with 30 rooms, with a lived-in feeling and small-town touch to it. It is ideally located in the center of the old town, a few paces away from the Vasco da Gama square. The restaurant serves good fish dishes such as river trout and shad. Order the *doce de ovos* for a final dose of eggs and sugar. Restaurant closed during the month of September. Major credit cards accepted. 144 Av. Dr. João Canavarro, Vila do Conde (phone: 052-642016; fax: 052-632028). Moderate.

En Route from Vila do Conde – Stop off at Azurara, across the river from Vila do Conde, to inspect the Manueline parish church or do some last-minute shopping. (Azurara is known for its wool fishermen's garments — shirts, hats, and socks.) The view of Vila do Conde and the monastery from the restaurant at the *Sant'Ana* motel make it a favorite dining venue in the area, as do the aroma and sizzling sounds of its dining room grill (Monte de Sant'Ana, Azurara; phone: 052-631994; telex: 27695). Then continue down N13 to Porto, 17 miles (27 km) from Vila do Conde. For a full report on Portugal's second-largest city, the home of port wine, see *Porto,* THE CITIES.

Douro and Trás-os-Montes

Until recently, the spectacular, rugged scenery of the Douro and Trás-os-Montes regions of northern Portugal eluded most visitors. The natural urge to peer behind the massive mountain ranges east of the country's northern coastal areas was tempered by a lack of suitable accommodations and other facilities for tourists. The situation has improved lately, and now intrepid travelers in search of a scenic vacation free of crowds and noise can venture into this remote hinterland. The reward is a pioneering look at Portugal's last frontier.

The Douro River flows from Spain clear across the north of Portugal into the Atlantic Ocean at Porto. For some 70 miles, the river is the natural border between the two countries. Its namesake region consists of the Douro Litoral (Coastal, or Lower, Douro), which stretches from Porto and its industrial environs east to the Marão mountain range, and, farther upriver, the Alto Douro (Upper Douro), a dramatic, vine-covered river valley hemmed in by mountains. The river is the backbone of the region, and, before roads, railroad tracks, and dams, it was the region's major highway — called the Rio do Ouro, or River of Gold, because of its golden complexion in certain kinds of light. The real gold mine, however, consists of the grapes that grow on its banks and those of its tributaries — the substance that produces Portugal's famous port wine.

The port wine gold mine begins at Peso da Régua, 75 miles upstream from Porto, and fans out from there to the richest veins in the vicinity of Pinhão, 20 miles farther east. The countryside here is one huge mantle of green and yellow leaves, punctuated occasionally by the white manor house of a grower or shipper. The vines are cultivated on terraces that follow the contours of granite and schist hills, making the riverbanks appear to be edged by gigantic pyramids. There are 85,000 vineyards and 25,000 growers in the port wine zone, the limits of which were set in 1756, making it the world's oldest demarcated zone for wine production. Thanks to the mountains that keep out cold Atlantic winds and rains, this part of the Douro Valley enjoys a semi-Mediterranean climate that is heaven for grapes. (The colder, wetter climate in the coastal areas just over the mountains produces Portugal's lighter, less alcoholic *vinho verde* wine.) It also allows the cultivation of olive, almond, and fruit trees wherever the terrain permits.

In the summer, the Alto Douro is scorched by temperatures up to 104F (40C). A good time to visit, therefore, is during the *vindima* (vintage, or grape harvest) in September and October, when the region bustles with life and the songs of grape pickers echo throughout the valley. The sheer bravado of the men, women, and children who carry heavy baskets up and down steep slopes can make a visitor not only dizzy, but also fully appreciative of the labor behind a glass of port.

The Alto Douro and the port wine zone are actually part of Portugal's Trás-os-Montes province, which, however, stretches far beyond the river into the northeastern corner of the country. Its name means "behind the mountains," and much of this land — a plateau sloping up to Spain, surmounted by rocky heights and cut through by deep river valleys — is indeed remote. Only recently have roads and electricity reached some of the tiny villages tucked away in its fertile valleys, so its air remains pure, its waters fresh and clean. Cold, blistering winters and blazing hot summers are the norm, but oases can be found in the valleys where corn, almonds, olives, and citrus fruits thrive. On its high pasturelands, sheep and cattle graze, producing some of the country's best meat.

The area has been inhabited for thousands of years. There are vestiges of Celtic and pre-Celtic habitation in stone *castros* (fortified hamlets) and dolmens, and in the customs and dances of the people. Ancient beliefs such as devil worship persist, and *bruxas* (witches) and *curandeiros* (medicine men) are consulted regularly. Some villages continue to be self-sufficient, leading a communal life. Their inhabitants are friendly and may invite visitors into their granite houses for a taste of rich corn bread, smoked ham, and homemade wine. Don't be surprised to find modern conveniences such as television sets, refrigerators, and gas or electric ovens inside these ancient dwellings, however. They are usually paid for by emigrant members of the family working elsewhere in Europe or overseas. Village elders complain that the appliances are eroding their way of life and that foreign-style houses and modern additions to ancestral homes are altering the harmony of the landscape.

Today, Trás-os-Montes and the Douro Valley are maturing like an ancient bottle of port. A major highway linking Porto and Spain is under construction, and part of it is already in use. There are also large iron and coal deposits under the soil of Trás-os-Montes, waiting to be exploited. The Douro Valley has been transformed by hydroelectric dams and the river is now navigable to the Spanish border, using a system of locks at each dam.

The route outlined below takes travelers east from the Douro capital of Porto, Portugal's second-largest city, to the picturesque town of Amarante. From there, it dips south to Lamego and follows the south bank of the Douro through the port wine region. It returns to the river's north bank at Pinhão and climbs vine-covered mountains to Vila Real, the capital of southwestern Trás-os-Montes. Some 50 miles (80 km) east of Vila Real, a decision must be made either to continue directly to the fortified town of Bragança, at the northeastern tip of Portugal, or to reach the same goal via a less direct swing through the rarely visited southeastern part of Trás-os-Montes, which offers almond-studded valleys, a final view of the Douro before it turns into Spain, and tiny border towns such as Miranda do Douro, renowned for its ancient stick dances and unique dialect. After Bragança, the route perforce turns west, skirting the Montezinho Natural Park on its way to the spa town of Chaves, graced with a Roman bridge and picturesque wood-balconied houses.

Several short excursions are suggested as the route continues west to the spectacular lake region in and around the Peneda-Gerês National Park and into the spa town of Caldas do Gerês. The itinerary ends in Portugal's Minho region, at Braga.

Along the way, look forward to dining heartily on veal, lamb, kid, ham, and sausages, on dairy products such as goat cheese, and on thick vegetable soups such as *caldo verde.* Fish lovers can order trout stuffed with ham in Lamego and Chaves. Wine drinkers will savor real port — now officially known as Porto to distinguish it from port-like wines made elsewhere. Port is laced with brandy to stop its fermentation and allow it to retain some of its sweetness, but note that the Douro Valley also produces dry red wines. Rosés from the Vila Real area and reds from Valpaços in central Trás-os-Montes are other popular choices.

Hotels and good restaurants in the area are limited, but the dearth of accommodations is relieved by the existence of private homes taking in paying guests under the auspices of Portugal's *Tourism in the Country* program, whose participants range from the manor houses of *Turismo de Habitação* to the simpler houses of *Turismo Rural and Agroturismo* (see *Accommodations,* GETTING READY TO GO). Reservations for all accommodations in summer (June through September) should be made well in advance. Expect to pay $70 and up for a double room in hotels listed below as expensive ($100 and higher for a *pousada*), between $50 and $65 for accommodations in the moderate category, and less than $45 in inexpensive ones. A dinner for two runs from about $45 to $50 and up in restaurants listed as expensive, from $25 to $40 in those listed as moderate, and less than $25 in those listed as inexpensive.

AMARANTE: This old town lies on the banks of the Tâmega River at the foot of the Serra do Marão, 45 miles (72 km) east of Porto via the IP4 highway. At sundown or in the morning mist, with the wooden balconies of its picturesque houses leaning over the river, there is a dreamy enchantment to the scene. The town is known for its patron saint, São Gonçalo, a 13th century priest who gained a reputation for helping old maids to marry. Several stories explain the origin of his reputation; in one, he is a frolicsome soul who organized parties for women of dubious repute in order to find them husbands. The party tradition has been revived as the *Arraiais de São Gonçalo,* open-air parties held Thursdays and Saturdays from June through October. For a small fee, guests eat and drink to their heart's content, dance, and enjoy a lavish fireworks display. The colorful saint is also remembered on June 1 and 2, when, for the semi-religious *Romaria de São Gonçalo* (St. Gonçalo Pilgrimage), single women take red carnations to the Church of São Gonçalo, kiss the statue of him there, pull the red cord of his habit, and pray for a good husband. The lovely 16th-century church, part of the Convento de São Gonçalo, stands by the 18th-century São Gonçalo bridge and contains, besides the remains of the saint, an attractive 17th-century organ case. The *Museu Municipal Amadeu de Sousa Cardoso,* the museum in the cloister of the church (open from 10 AM to 12:30 PM and from 2 to 5:30 PM; closed Mondays; no admission charge; phone: 055-423663), contains an extensive art gallery, as well as the town's *demônios,* a pair of devils that are holdovers from the devil worship that once was practiced in the area. A Bishop of Braga took a dim view of this practice and sold the pair to England — causing such a furor that they had to be returned.

Also to be seen in the town is the 18th-century Igreja de São Pedro, which has a baroque façade and an unusual nave decorated with 17th-century *azulejos.* Leisurely repasts on the balconies of the tea houses overlooking the river, scenic walks on paths in the wooded park above the town, and swimming, trout fishing, and boating on the Tâmega are popular local pastimes.

Ask at the Amarante Tourist Office, located in the museum, for information on excursions in the vicinity (open October through June, Mondays through Saturdays from 9:30 AM to 12:30 PM and from 2 to 5 PM; closed Sundays; July through September open daily from 9:30 AM to 7 PM; Alameda Teixeira Pascoais; phone: 055-424259). The area is rich in *solares* (manor houses), Romanesque churches, dolmens, Iron Age *castros,* and strange rock formations called *pedras baloiçantes* (balancing rocks). By driving north along N210 and the banks of the Tâmega for 14½ miles (23 km), it's possible to visit Celorico de Basto, a medieval earldom with fine country houses and an 18th-century castle.

CHECKING IN: ***Casa Zé da Calçada*** – This is a pleasant townhouse overlooking the Tâmega, a short walk from the town center. A participant in *Turismo de Habitação,* it offers 7 double bedrooms, and the owner runs the town's best restaurant, opposite the townhouse (see *Eating Out,* below). Contact José da Fonseca Herdeiros, *Casa Zé da Calçada,* 83 Rua 31 de Janeiro, Amarante (phone: 055-422023). Expensive.

Amaranto – Modest, it has 35 rooms, a panoramic view of the town monuments, and a restaurant serving regional fare. Major credit cards accepted. Rua Madalena, Amarante (phone: 055-422106). Moderate.

Navarras – A few minutes' drive from the center, this place is modern, with 61 air conditioned rooms, a heated indoor pool, and a large restaurant with a verandah. Major credit cards accepted. Rua António Carneiro, Amarante (phone: 055-424036). Moderate.

EATING OUT: ***Zé da Calçada*** – The town's best restaurant has an old-fashioned look and serves tasty local dishes. House specialties include cod *Zé da Calçada* style, *cabrito assado no forno* (roast kid), and a variety of fancifully named sweets — *pinhas de ovos* ("egg cones"), for example, and *pinhas de chocolate amarantinos* made with eggs, sugar, and almonds. Several local *vinho verde* wines, such as caves moura bastos and quinta do outeiro, are on the wine list. Open daily. Reservations advised. No credit cards accepted. 72 Rua 31 de Janeiro, Amarante (phone: 055-422023). Expensive.

Adega Regional de Amarante – A picturesque *tasca* (tavern) in a manmade cave near the river. This is a favorite pre-dinner haunt for tasting regional snacks such as the hams and spicy sausages hanging from the ceiling. The *salpicão,* a sausage cured in red wine and smoked, is a favorite with locals. Open daily. Reservations unnecessary. No credit cards accepted. 57 Rua António Carneiro, Amarante (phone: 055-424581). Inexpensive.

A Taberna – Situated in an old cottage, this traditional *tasca* features a rustic ambience — farming tools hang on the walls, and diners sit on wooden benches. Hearty regional fare is prepared in the wood-burning oven; try the local red wine, which is served in white china tankards. Open daily. No reservations. No credit cards accepted. Campo de Feira, Amarante (phone: 055-422450). Inexpensive.

En Route from Amarante – Head southeast toward Lamego on N15 and N101, stopping at Mesão Frio, 14½ miles (23 km) from Amarante, to admire the elegant churches and manor houses in its tree-lined center. At Mesão Frio, take N108 8½ miles (14 km) east to Peso da Régua, at the confluence of the Douro and Corgo rivers. The best port wine vineyards begin here and spread eastward along the Douro and its tributaries. Peso da Régua, also known simply as Régua, is the industry's main administrative and storage center in the Alto Douro, and although the town lacks charm, the surrounding countryside is starkly beautiful. In fact,

Régua is the junction of several scenic train routes, including the "Linha do Douro," which runs from Porto up to Pocinho, about 19 miles (30 km) short of Barca d'Alva on the Spanish border. For more information, contact the tourist office opposite the Régua train station, Largo da Estação (open from November through April, Mondays through Fridays 9 AM to 12:30 PM and 2 to 6 PM, closed Saturdays and Sundays; from May through October, open daily 9 AM to 7 PM; phone: 054-22846).

Cross the Douro at Régua; just past the bridge is *Garrafeira e Artesanato Duriense,* an interesting shop that carries a wide variety of local wines and handicrafts (phone: 054-23504). Drive south on the N2 8 miles (13 km) to Lamego. The well-paved but winding road climbs mountain slopes covered with terraced vineyards and whitewashed manor houses.

LAMEGO: The location of this attractive and peaceful agricultural town — at the edge of a valley surrounded by mountains, vineyards, and orchards — made it an important commercial center in the Middle Ages. Portugal's first *cortes,* a representative assembly of nobles, met here in 1143 to recognize Dom Afonso Henriques as the country's first king. On a hill northeast of town are the partially restored ruins of a 12th-century castle, while the baroque Santuário da Nossa Senhora dos Remédios (Sanctuary of Our Lady of the Remedies) occupies a hill to the south of town. The sanctuary can be reached by car, 2½ miles (4 km) through a lovely wooded forest, or, more dramatically, by climbing an impressive granite staircase decorated with *azulejos* and bristling with pinnacles. During the *Festas da Nossa Senhora dos Remédios,* the largest cultural and religious event in the region and one of the country's biggest fairs, pilgrims can be seen crawling up the steps on their knees. Held from late August to mid-September, the fair also features folk dancing and singing and religious processions with dazzling floats pulled by oxen.

In town, the Sé (Cathedral) has a fine Gothic entrance in which an amusing scene of animal eroticism appears to have eluded the censors of the time. The 18th-century Bishop's Palace next door now houses the *Museu de Lamego* (Largo de Camões; phone: 054-62008), where priceless 16th-century tapestries from Brussels and an early-16th-century painting of the Visitation by the Portuguese master Grão Vasco can be seen (open from 10 AM to 12:30 PM and from 2 to 5 PM; closed Mondays; admission charge, except on Sundays from 10 AM to 12:30 PM). Also of interest is the Igreja do Dêsterro (Church of the Exile), with its sumptuous coffered ceiling depicting scenes from the life of Christ. (Ask at 126 Rua da Calçada for the key to visit.) Lamego produces Raposeira, one of Portugal's best sparkling wines. For a taste, visit the Raposeira company's cool cellars carved into the mountainside south of town, reachable via N2 (tours Mondays through Fridays at 10 AM, 11 AM, 2 PM, 3 PM, and 4 PM, but it's best to call *Caves de Raposeira* for an appointment first; phone: 054-62003).

Among the sights in the vicinity of Lamego is the 7th-century Visigothic Church of São Pedro de Balsemão, 9 miles (14 km) east on the banks of the Balsemão River. Besides the elaborate granite tomb of the bishop who remodeled it during the 14th century, it contains a 15th-century stone statue of Nossa Senhora de O (Our Lady of O), depicting a pregnant Virgin. To reach the church, leave Lamego via the popular Bairro da Fonte quarter, where women still bake bread in old-fashioned ovens and blacksmiths still work at open forges. Turn left at the bridge and follow a narrow, unmarked road running north along the banks of the river. The last 100 yards or so is on a dirt road, so begin early enough to avoid driving in the dark.

Another sight is southeast of Lamego. The 12th-century Mosteiro de São João de Tarouca, a former Cistercian monastery (Portugal's first), lies 10 miles (16 km) from town off N226. The impressive church, which was later given a baroque interior, contains exquisite paintings by the 16th-century master Gaspar Vaz, as well as the granite tomb of Dom Pedro, Count of Barcelos and bastard son of King Dinis. (His wife's tomb was taken by a local farmer and used as a wine press before it was recovered and put in the museum in Lamego.) The sacristy has 4,709 tiles, no two alike, and its ceiling has a series of paintings depicting the life of St. Bernard. To visit, apply at the house on the right facing the square. For information on still other sights, contact Lamego's Tourist Office, Avenida Visconde Guedes Teixeira (phone: 054-62005).

CHECKING IN: ***Do Cerrado*** – This pleasant *albergaria* (inn) at the entrance to Lamego has 30 air conditioned, balconied rooms. Regional furniture and handmade rugs decorate the common room. Breakfast and snacks are served on a terrace with views of the town and the surrounding countryside. Major credit cards accepted. Lugar do Cerrado, Lamego (phone: 054-63164). Expensive.

Vila Hostilina – This restored farmhouse, a *Turismo Rural* participant, sits on a hill overlooking the town and the valley, surrounded by gardens and vineyards. Guests are invited to help with the *vindima* (grape harvest) in the fall and to crush grapes the old-fashioned way — by foot. There are 7 rooms with private bath, a rustic bar, a tennis court, and a large swimming pool, plus a health club with a gym, exercise machines, and a sauna. Meals are served on request; reservations are a must in summer. Contact Joaquim Brandão dos Santos, *Vila Hostilina,* Lamego (phone: 054-62394). Expensive.

Parque – A simple, turn-of-the-century hotel of 40 bedrooms, known for its fine restaurant (see *Eating Out*) and ideal location in the gardens beside the Nossa Senhora dos Remédios sanctuary. Nossa Senhora dos Remédios, Lamego (phone: 054-62105). Moderate.

Solar do Espírito Santo – Lamego's newest hotel — with 28 rooms — offers comfort, dependable service, and a central location. There is private parking, plus a good restaurant that's just across the road (see *Eating Out*). Rua Alexandre Herculano, Lamego (phone: 054-63450). Moderate.

Solar – A small, comfortable, and newly refurbished *pensão* with 25 rooms (with bath), in front of the tourist office. 9 Av. Visconde Guedes Teixeira, Lamego (phone: 054-62060). Moderate to inexpensive.

Império – A simple but quaint *pensão,* beside the town's main street and monuments. The look is small-town Portugal; 14 rooms with bath. 6 Travessa dos Loureiros, Lamego (phone: 054-62742). Inexpensive.

Silva – The accommodations are clean but extremely spartan at this 16-room *pensão* on a quiet side street near the cathedral. No private baths. 26 Rua Detrás da Sé, Lamego (phone: 054-62929). Inexpensive.

EATING OUT: ***Parque*** – By far the best place to eat in Lamego, it has a varied regional menu that includes river trout baked with ham and the chef's award-winning cod dish. Courteous service, an austere old Portugal ambience, and garden views enhance the repast. Raposeira sparkling wines are stocked; have a *bruto* (brut) with the meal and a *meio-seco* (semisweet) with dessert. Open daily. Reservations advised. Major credit cards accepted. *Hotel Parque,* Nossa Senhora dos Remédios, Lamego (phone: 054-62105). Moderate.

Solar do Espírito Santo – This new, wood-paneled eatery has been getting high marks for its renditions of local specialties such as *vitela assado* (roast veal) and *cozida portuguesa* (pork stew). Open daily. Reservations unnecessary. Major credit cards accepted. Across the road from the hotel of the same name. Rua Alexandre Herculano, Lamego (phone: 054-64470). Moderate.

Turiserra – The reward for a 20-minute drive into the mountains north of Lamego is a modern restaurant at an altitude of 2,970 feet, with a spectacular view of the Douro Valley and the atmosphere of a mountain lodge. To reach it, take Avenida 5 de Outubro, turn left onto Avenida Marquês de Pombal, and follow the signs for the Parque de Campismo Turiserra. Closed Mondays and 1 month each year.

Reservations necessary only on Sundays. Major credit cards accepted. Serra das Meadas (phone: 054-63380). Moderate.

Mina – A rustic, family-run restaurant with a wholesome regional menu, near the town center, beside the charming Capela do Espírito Santo (Holy Spirit Chapel). The specialty, *cordeiro assado* (roast lamb), is cooked and served in unglazed black pottery from the region. This is also a good place to try *bôlo de Lamego* (ham pie). Closed Mondays. Reservations unnecessary. Major credit cards accepted. 5 Rua Alexandre Herculano, Lamego (phone: 054-63353). Moderate to inexpensive.

En Route from Lamego – To reach Vila Real by the shortest route — 23½ miles (38 km) — return to Peso da Régua and cut north through the impressive gorge of the Corgo River. To reach the city by a longer, more scenic route — 43½ miles (73 km) — through the epicenter of the port wine zone, return to the Douro and take N222 east along its south bank, crossing to the north bank at Pinhão. The road passes some of the larger wine estates along the way, and in Pinhão itself there is a lovely train station with *azulejos* depicting the history of wine making in the area. From Pinhão, take N323 north, climbing steep mountain slopes streaked with terraces and vines and punctuated only occasionally by a lone tree or a white manor house. At Sabrosa, a suitable watering hole with a Luso-Roman cemetery, head west on N322.

About 1¼ miles (2 km) short of Vila Real, the 18th-century Palace of Mateus appears on the left. To many, it will be a familiar sight, because the façade graces the label of the famous Mateus rosé wine. The palace is one of the most elegant examples of the baroque style in Portugal, and although it is a private residence, parts of it, along with the grounds, are open to the public (daily from 9 AM to 1 PM and from 2 to 6 PM from April through September, and from 10 AM to 1 PM and 2 to 5 PM the rest of the year; admission charge). A museum in the palace contains, among other things, a precious collection of fans and letters from 19th-century personalities. Classical music concerts and opera, guitar, and other music courses are given on the premises in August and September. For information, contact the Fundação da Casa de Mateus (Vila Real; phone: 059-23121). Wine tasting takes place at the Sogrape bottling plant nearby, which is open Mondays through Fridays from 9 AM to noon and from 2 to 5:30 PM. An appointment is required. Contact *Sogrape-Vinhos de Portugal* (1159 Av. da Boavista, Porto; phone: 02-695751).

VILA REAL: The administrative capital of the southwest Trás-os-Montes is a thriving agricultural town on a plateau at the foot of the Marão and Alvão mountain ranges and at the confluence of the Cabril and Corgo rivers. The major road from Porto to the northeast Trás-os-Montes capital of Bragança passes through here, and the scenic "Linha do Corgo" train line arrives here from Peso da Régua. There are also air links with Porto and Lisbon. The main sights are in the town center along the Avenida Carvalho Araújo, where the tourist office (phone: 059-22819) is located (at No. 94). The cathedral, a former Dominican monastery with Romanesque and Gothic touches, has an interesting statue of the Virgin. Beside the church, at No. 19, is the Renaissance façade of the house of Diogo Cão, the Portuguese explorer of the Congo basin. Just off Avenida Carvalho Araújo, on Rua Central, is the lovely baroque 17th-century Capela Nova (New Chapel), which features beautiful tilework. At the western end of the avenue is the monumental double staircase of the 19th-century Câmara Municipal (Town Hall). The Old Town behind it has an esplanade encircling the 14th-century Church of São Dinis and a commanding view of the Corgo ravine. Vila Real is a good base from which to explore the Parque Nacional do Alvão, which lies to the northwest and is endowed with stone and shale houses, ancient water mills, tumbling waterfalls, ravines, and valleys carpeted with flowers. To reach the park, take the 1P4 west for 6 miles (10 km); then turn right onto the N304 for Mondim de Basto and Campeã. Along this stretch, the Alto do Velão pass affords a breathtaking view of the environs.

CHECKING IN: *Casa das Quartas* – A handsome, 16th-century manor house (a *Turismo de Habitação* property), it is surrounded by orchards and flower beds in a southeastern suburb. The sprawling estate, which even has its own private chapel, offers 3 double rooms with private baths and mountain views. Contact José Mourão, *Casa das Quartas,* Abambres (phone: 059-22976). Expensive.

Mira Corgo – Modern, it has 76 air conditioned rooms, a bar, an indoor swimming pool, and a disco. It overlooks the Corgo River gorge. 76-78 Av. 1 de Maio, Vila Real (phone: 059-25001). Expensive.

Casa da Cruz – Near the Alvão National Park, this typical 18th-century Trás-os-Montes house (a *Turismo Rural* property) offers 3 guestrooms. Contact Hilario Oliveira, *Casa da Cruz,* Campeã, Vila Real (phone: 059-979422). Moderate.

Tocaio – This aging hostelry in the center of town has 52 rooms and simple country charm. 45 Av. Carvalho Araújo, Vila Real (phone: 059-23106). Moderate.

EATING OUT: *Maranus* – Light, airy, and modern, this new establishment boasts regional specialties — try the *bife à Maranus,* a mouthwatering beefsteak. Open daily. Reservations unnecessary. Major credit cards accepted. In the suburb of Quinta do Seixo, Lote 2, Loja 5 (phone: 059-321521). Expensive.

Espadeiro – There's a classic dining room, endowed with a fireplace, and in summer an adjacent smaller room with a terrace overlooking the Corgo River. This is a sophisticated restaurant, well known for regional dishes such as *truta com presunto* (grilled trout with ham) and *cabrito assado com arroz* (roast kid with rice). Open daily. Reservations unnecessary. Major credit cards accepted. Av. Almeida Lucena, Vila Real (phone: 059-22302). Moderate.

Nevada – The regional menu here features Vila Real's very own *bôlo de carne,* a spicy meat loaf. Modern, with a relaxed atmosphere and simple decor, it's beside the *Mira Corgo* hotel. Try a table wine from the Adega Cooperativa de Vila Real. Open daily. Reservations unnecessary. Major credit cards accepted. Av. 1 de Maio, Vila Real (phone: 059-71828). Moderate.

Churrasco – A medium-size eatery decorated in local traditional style. Grilled meats are the specialty. Closed Sunday evenings. Reservations unnecessary. No credit cards accepted. 24 Rua António Azevedo, Vila Real (phone: 059-22313). Moderate to inexpensive.

En Route from Vila Real – As N15 leads northeast toward Bragança, pine trees begin to alternate with vineyards, olive groves, and fields of grain. The town of Murça, on high slopes above the Tinhela River 25 miles (40 km) out of Vila Real, has an interesting Iron Age granite boar (Porca de Murça) in its main square, one of many such peculiar statues found throughout the region. The agricultural town of Mirandela, known for its 16th-century bridge and a lively fair that runs from the end of July to early August, lies another 19 miles (31 km) east on the banks of the Tua River. Nearby, the rolling hills around Jerusalem do Romeu, 7 miles (11 km) farther east, are covered with olive and cork oak trees as far as the eye can see. Turn right at Jerusalem do Romeu and go about 2 miles (3 km) to Romeu, a typical Trás-os-Montes village that has been restored. The tiny hamlet and its *Maria Rita* restaurant (see *Eating Out*) are owned by a patrician Portuguese family, as is the interesting *Museu das Curiosidades* (Museum of Curiosities), which contains family memorabilia such as old sewing machines, photographic and musical equipment, four model Ts, and 19th-century fire trucks (open daily — the keeper lives on the premises; admission charge).

Return to N15 and continue east 5½ miles (9 km) to the junction with N216. Here a decision must be made. Either continue on N15 28½ miles (46 km) directly to Bragança (through some of the most barren and thinly populated countryside in southern Europe), or take a more circuitous route via a string of old fortress towns running along the Douro and the Spanish border. To follow the latter course, turn southeast onto N216 and drive the few miles to Macedo de Cavaleiros, a neat farming town and favorite hunting spot for northern aristocrats. Continue on N216 toward Mogadouro; in about 7 miles (12 km), take a short detour left to the Santuário Nossa Senhora de Balsamão. Perched atop a small hill, the hermitage is now run by Polish Marianist brothers; the structure dates back to the early 13th century. The chapel, added in the 18th century, features a beautiful painted ceiling and a statue representing the Immaculate Conception.

Return to the N216 to Mogadouro, 26 miles (44 km) away, known for its woodcrafts and silk, wool, and leather goods, as well as for a ruined 12th-century fortress. The town also is the home of the 17th-century Igreja de São Francisco (Church of St. Francis), which has one of the finest carved and gilded-wood altars in the region. Near the Old Town center is a small new archaeological museum (open Tuesdays through Fridays from 10 AM to 12:30 PM and from 2 to 5 PM; no admission; no phone) that displays recently excavated artifacts from the area's *castros* (fortified villages). If it's spring, take the time to drive up to the nearby Serra da Castanheira and see the countryside covered by a mantle of white from thousands of blossoming almond trees. Seventeen miles (27 km) east of Mogadouro on N221 is the tiny town of Sendim, whose main square is the site of a well-preserved 17th-century church in which traditional *capas de honra* are still made. (These "capes of honor," made from a local coarse woven-wool fabric, are worn by landowners and farmers on market days and special occasions. The degree of elaboration of the front of the cape denotes the wealth of the owner; capes are often passed down in families for generations.) Surprisingly, Sendim also boasts one of the better restaurants in Trás-os-Montes (see *Gabriela's* in *Eating Out*). The border town of Miranda do Douro is another 13 miles (20 km) beyond Sendim.

CHECKING IN: ***Do Caçador*** – A splendid *estalagem* (inn) and hunting lodge in the former Town Hall of Macedo de Cavaleiros. The 25 rooms are furnished with antiques, the public rooms are rife with wood and leather, and the bar, filled with wicker furniture and hunting trophies, looks like a set out of colonial Africa. Specialties in the dining room include steaks stuffed with ham and, during hunting season (mid-October through December), game dishes such as partridge and hare. Guests can stroll around a tiny rose garden and swim in a marble-lined pool. Major credit cards accepted. Largo Manuel Pinto de Azevedo, Macedo de Cavaleiros (phone: 078-421354). Expensive.

EATING OUT: ***Gabriela's*** – This 80-year-old restaurant is the culinary pride and joy of Trás-os-Montes. Adelaide Gabriela, the third-generation owner, has maintained the traditions and famous dishes for which her late mother won many awards. The decor is rustic and pure country, as are the smells from the open kitchen, where guests can see Alice in action at a wood fire. Try the *posta à mirandesa à Gabriela,* a large veal steak cooked over a fire of grape vines or olive branches. The sauces are a professional secret. Open daily. Reservations advised. Major credit cards accepted. 28 Largo da Praça, Sendim (phone: 073-73180). Moderate to inexpensive.

Maria Rita – One of the best restaurants in the region, lodged in a typical Trás-os-Montes house in a tiny village. The large stone fireplaces, antiques, and heavy oak tables set with china and silver add up to an elegantly rustic setting. The regional food features such items as a thick and spicy garlic soup, and *espargos bravos,* wild asparagus — not to mention whole turkeys, baby pigs, and lambs for parties calling in advance. Closed Mondays. Reservations advised. No credit cards accepted. Rua da Capela, Romeu (phone: 078-93134). Moderate to inexpensive.

MIRANDA DO DOURO: This ancient town perches atop the narrow rocky canyon of the Douro that here forms a natural border between Portugal and Spain. It is remote enough to have its own dialect, Mirandes, a mixture of Galician Spanish, Portuguese, and Hebrew, yet during the 16th century it was the cultural center of Trás-os-Montes and the seat of an important bishopric. After several military catastrophes and the loss of its bishop's seat, the town fell into obscurity during the 18th century and is only now coming out of its isolation with the construction of a dam (the northernmost of five on the Douro) and the opening of a border road with Spain. Among the sights to see is the former cathedral, a 16th-century building rich in carved and gilded wood and graced with an unusual little statue — Menino Jesus da Cartolinha — of the baby Jesus sporting a top hat. (It's said to represent a boy who appeared miraculously to help the townspeople resist a Spanish invasion in the 18th century.) The *Museu da Terra de Miranda* (Museum of the Land of Miranda, Plaza Dom João III; phone: 073-42164) has costumes of the area, rustic furniture, archaeological artifacts, and carved stones from an old synagogue (open from 10 AM to 12:15 PM and from 2 to 4:45 PM; closed Mondays; admission charge).

A treat is in store for anyone who visits Miranda during the *Festas de Santa Bárbara,* on the third Sunday in August, or the *Romaria de Nossa Senhora de Nazaré,* in early September. These are two occasions to see the town's *pauliteiros,* or stick dancers, perform. Although other ancient and colorful folk dances, such as the *pingacho* (rough ballet), the *geribalda* (a round dance), and the *mira-me-Miguel* (a square dance), are still performed here, the stick dance is the one for which the town is best known. What's involved is a sort of ritual sword dance performed by men in white flannel skirts, aprons, and flower-covered hats, who clash their *paulitos* (sticks) to the tune of a bagpipe, cymbals, and drums. Other components of the local folklore are the coarse wool capes and waistcoats worn by the people of the region and the *facas de palacoulo* — knives with forks attached to them — used traditionally by the shepherds of the area.

CHECKING IN: ***Pousada de Santa Catarina*** **–** This simple, modern, 12-room *pousada* sits on a hill overlooking a dam on the Douro about 2 miles (3 km) east of town. The restaurant, which has a fine view of the water and the Spanish plain of Zamora, serves regional dishes such as wood-fired *posta à mirandesa* (veal steaks), *fumeiro* (smoked sausage), river trout, and small game. Major credit cards accepted. Estrada da Barragem, Miranda do Douro (phone: 073-42755; in the US, 212-686-9213). Expensive.

Santa Cruz **–** A family-run *pensão* on a quiet street off the Praça do Castelo. There are 17 simple rooms, plus a restaurant offering typical local fare like *posta à mirandesa* and *bacalhão à sargento* (oven-baked salt cod). Major credit cards accepted. 61 Rua Abade de Baçal, Miranda do Douro (phone: 073-42474). Inexpensive.

EATING OUT: ***Buteko*** **–** This air conditioned eatery affords diners a nice view of the main square, and serves dishes typical of the region. Open daily. Reservations unnecessary. Major credit cards accepted. Largo Dom João III, Miranda do Douro (phone: 073-42150). Moderate.

Mirandes **–** A rustic, family-run restaurant in the heart of town, offering a range of local specialties. The *folares de Páscoa,* or sweet *Easter* cakes, are a local dessert. Closed Mondays. Reservations unnecessary. Major credit cards accepted. Largo da Moagem, Miranda do Douro (phone: 073-42418). Moderate to inexpensive.

En Route from Miranda do Douro – Head north on N218 toward Bragança, 52½ miles (84 km) away. Outeiro, 32½ miles (52 km) up the road, has a large church with an ornate Manueline doorway and a Gothic rose window. Bragança is another 20½ miles (33 km) ahead.

BRAGANÇA: The medieval walls and castle that dominate this fortified town at Portugal's extreme northeastern corner are the best preserved in the country. Bragança, which occupies a high hill in the Serra da Nogueira, was known to the Celts as Brigantia and to the Romans as Juliobriga. During the 15th century, it was made a fiefdom of the powerful Dukes of Bragança, who became Portugal's royal family in 1640 and ruled until the end of the monarchy in 1910. The town was a major silk center during the 15th century, thanks largely to a thriving Jewish merchant community (which dispersed with the Inquisition, although the area's remoteness allowed some Jews to stay and practice their religion in secret). Today, copper and leather goods and baskets replace silks in the shops around the main square, Praça da Sé, which is outside the walls in the newer (but still old) part of town — Bragança had already begun to expand beyond its medieval walls during the 15th century.

The old walled town contains the 12th-century castle and its tall, square keep, which serves as a military museum. The Torre da Princesa (Princess Tower) beside it was the scene of tragedy when the fourth duke locked up his lovely wife, Dona Leonor, to keep men from laying eyes on her; later, when he moved his court south, he murdered her. In front of the castle is a medieval *pelourinho* (pillory), its shaft driven through a granite statue of a boar said to date (as does the boar in Murça) back to the Iron Age. The 12th-century Domus Municipalis (Town Hall) is one of the few remaining Romanesque civic buildings in Portugal (to visit, apply at the house in front); it stands next to the 16th-century church of Santa Maria. An interesting museum, the *Museu do Abade de Baçal* (27 Rua Conselheiro Abilio Beça; phone: 073-23242), is outside the walls in the 18th-century Bishop's Palace. Named for the Abbot of Baçal (1865–1945), who spent years recording the history and customs of the region in an 11-volume series, it houses archaeological artifacts, furniture, tools, ancient coins, church plate and vestments, and paintings. The museum (open from 10 AM to 12:30 PM and from 2 to 5 PM; closed Mondays; admission charge, except on Sunday mornings) is on the street that leads to the cathedral, an unimpressive church that was elevated to cathedral status when the seat of the bishop moved here from Miranda do Douro during the 18th century.

Bragança is the ideal spot from which to explore the Parque Natural de Montezinho, whose high plateaus and mountains stretch northeast and northwest of town and contain some of the wildest country in Portugal. Populated with wild boar, wolves, foxes, and other small game, the park is also dotted with tiny, self-sufficient villages where communal life and pre-Christian rituals endure and people still believe in the evil eye, fairies, and witches. The town of Rio de Onor, straddling the border 16½ miles (26 km) northeast of Bragança, has a communal system of ownership and a democratic electoral system that sociologists have studied. Half of the village lies in Portugal and the other in Spain, and the inhabitants, who cross freely from one to the other, have intermarried for centuries. For further information and a map of the park, visit the tourist office (open Mondays through Fridays from 9 AM to 12:30 PM and 2 to 5:30 PM; in the Edificio do Principal; phone: 073-23078); the small tourism booth at the entrance to town from N218; or the park's administrative office in Bragança (past the entrance to town from N218, take a right into the signposted housing estate; phone: 073-28734).

CHECKING IN: ***Bragança*** – Simple, near the town center, with 42 rooms facing the battlements and castle. There is a restaurant serving a range of regional dishes. Major credit cards accepted. Av. Dr. Francisco Sá Carneiro, Bragança (phone: 073-22579). Expensive.

Pousada de São Bartolomeu – A modern, 16-room inn, perched on a hill facing the walled town, its castle, and the surrounding mountains. Guests have a choice of regional or international dishes in the posh restaurant. Major credit cards accepted. Estrada do Turismo, Bragança (phone: 073-22493; in the US, 212-686-9213). Expensive.

Tulipa – A modern *residencia* with 33 rooms and a good restaurant, conveniently close to the center of town. Major credit cards accepted. 8-10 Rua Dr. Francisco Felgueiras, Bragança (phone: 073-23675; fax: 073-27814). Moderate.

Cruzeiro – A no-frills *pensão* with 31 rooms near the town center. Travessa do Hospital, Bragança (phone: 073-22634). Inexpensive.

EATING OUT: *O Geadas* – A new, air conditioned dining spot specializing in local fare. Highlights of the unusually extensive menu include *butelo com feijão* (smoked sausage with beans) and *arroz de lebre* (hare with rice). Open daily. Major credit cards accepted. Reservations unnecessary. 4 Rua do Laureto, Bragança (phone: 073-24413). Expensive.

Solar Bragançano – This pleasant, old-fashioned restaurant occupies a palatial townhouse in the main square. A tiled entrance and staircase lead to the formal dining room with wood ceilings, chandeliers, and handwoven rugs. Specialties of the house are *cabrito branco à Montezinho* (white Montezinho kid), cod, and veal steaks *Solar* style. Try the semisweet favaios wine as an aperitif, with *alheiras* (spiced sausages) or some goat cheese. Open daily. Reservations unnecessary. Major credit cards accepted. 34 Praça da Sé, Bragança (phone: 073-23875). Moderate.

Lá em Casa – A modern, airy restaurant with pine-paneled walls and rustic regional decor and food. Open daily. Reservations unnecessary. Major credit cards accepted. 7 Rua Marquês de Pombal, Bragança (phone: 073-22111). Moderate to inexpensive.

En Route from Bragança – The road (N103) to Chaves, 60 miles (96 km) west, sets out running along the edge of and sometimes into the Montezinho Natural Park. Only 3 miles (5 km) beyond Bragança, the Benedictine Monastery of Castro de Avelãs, a handsome building with Romanesque and Moorish touches, sits beside the road; once flourishing, it was abandoned when religious orders were banned during the 19th century. Moving westward, as the high peaks of the Serra de Montezinho and the Serra da Coroa begin to loom majestically, the traveler passes chestnut and oak trees, whitewashed *pombaias* (pigeon houses), trout farms, and grazing cattle. Vinhais, overlooking a valley 19½ miles (31 km) from Bragança, has a castle, a monastery, and churches in a bad state of repair, but its large market is worth attending on the 9th and 23rd days of the month, to see the villagers gather from the surrounding countryside. If the car can endure the bumpy dirt road, take the turnoff, 8½ miles (14 km) short of Chaves, to the Castelo de Montorte, about half a mile (1 km) away. The impressive 14th-century castle sits on a high, windswept hill with views of Spain to the north. Surrounding it are the remains of what is believed to be a Lusitanian *castro* (fortified village) with Roman additions. The castle can be visited daily from 3 to 6 PM (tip the guard).

CHAVES: The spa capital of Portugal, Chaves is on the banks of the Tâmega River in the center of a fertile valley near the Spanish border. The Romans took advantage of this breach in Portugal's northern mountains during the 1st century, when they captured the site, exploited its rich gold and mineral deposits, and built a town called Aquae Flaviae — so named for its warm thermal springs, which are said to cure rheumatism and liver and stomach disorders. When they built Trajan's Bridge over the Tâmega, the town became an important stopover on the Roman road between Braga and Astorga, Spain. The bridge is still in use, but most of the Roman town lies beneath the newer medieval and modern town. Agriculture and textiles are the economic mainstays today, and Chaves is particularly known for its *presunto* (ham).

Most of the sights are found in and around Praça de Camões, the main square. The *Museu da Região Flaviense* (Museum of the Flaviae Region), housed in the former palace of the Dukes of Bragança, contains archaeological and ethnographic exhibits, including Roman and pre-Roman relics and old coins. The *Museu Militar* (Military Museum), in the adjacent 12th-century keep, has 4 floors of uniforms and weapons from various periods of Portuguese history, while the view from the platform at the top embraces the town and the surrounding countryside. Both museums (phone: 076-21965) are open from 9:30 AM to 12:30 PM and from 2 to 5 PM, Tuesdays through Fridays; Saturdays and Sundays, open 2 to 5 PM; closed Mondays; admission charge. The manicured keep gardens contain archaeological remains, and its ramparts provide a sweeping view of the river.

Also on the Praça de Camões is the baroque Misericórdia church, its interior embellished with 18th-century *azulejos* depicting the life of Christ; the parish church with a lovely Romanesque doorway; and an ornate Manueline pillory. Note the houses on the eastern side of the square and on the neighboring Rua Direita — they have lovely painted wood verandahs. Nearby, on Rua General Sousa Machado, is the former Jewish Quarter (the chapel at No. 63 is thought to have been a synagogue). Other points of interest in town are two 17th-century fortresses, São Francisco and São Neutal; the 13th-century Romanesque chapel of Nossa Senhora de Azinheira; and the train museum at the railroad station (open weekdays, from 2:30 to 5 PM).

For further information and maps of the Chaves area, contact the tourist office (open daily October through May from 9 AM to 6:30 PM; June through September, open daily from 9 AM to 7 PM; Terreiro da Cavalaria; phone: 076-21029). Two neighboring spa towns, Vidago and Pedras Salgadas, respectively 10½ miles (17 km) and 18½ miles (30 km) south of Chaves on N2 toward Vila Real, provide most of the region's recreation (swimming, golf, and other sports).

CHECKING IN: ***Aquae Flaviae*** – A relatively new hostelry with 170 rooms, 3 restaurants, a bar, a health club, a swimming pool, tennis courts, miniature golf, and conference facilities. It's located near the 12th-century keep, overlooking the Tâmega. Major credit cards accepted. Praça do Brasil, Chaves (phone: 076-26496; fax: 076-26497). Expensive.

Vidago Palace – Set in a lush park and surrounded by gardens, ponds, and fountains, this pink Belle Epoque building in a spa town south of Chaves offers guests a taste of royal Portugal. The hotel was inaugurated by King Dom Luís in 1910. Although the "palace" has lost some luster over the years, a portion of its original splendor is still visible in the carved double staircase and in the large dining room with a white and gold ceiling, marble columns, and ornate lighting fixtures. (The chef cooks a daily fixed-price meal with a choice of regional and international dishes.) There are newer apartments, a swimming pool, and a discotheque behind the hotel; tennis and rowing on a manmade lake are also available on the sprawling grounds. A picturesque 9-hole golf course nearby may be expanded to 18 holes by next year. All told, there are 126 rooms. During the months of October through May, only 50 rooms are available and at a reduced rate. Major credit cards accepted. Parque, Vidago (phone: 076-97356; fax: 076-97359). Expensive.

Trajano – This 39-room hostelry stands on top of a Roman bathhouse, discovered while the newer foundations were being laid. It's on a quiet cobbled street near the center of town and is decorated in dark wood and tiles. The dining room is somewhat dim, but the food, particularly the desserts, brightens things up. Travessa Cândido dos Reis, Chaves (phone: 076-22415). Moderate.

São Neutel – A modern, family-run *residencia* near the stadium, with 31 rooms but no restaurant. Av. 5 de Outubro, Chaves (phone: 076-25632; fax: 076-27620). Moderate to inexpensive.

EATING OUT: ***Cubata II*** – This small, recently opened restaurant specializes in seafood. Especially good: the *bacalhãu à Cubata* (salt cod with Chaves ham). Open daily. Reservations necessary. Major credit cards accepted. Av. Nuno Alvares, Chaves (phone: 076-25499). Moderate.

Campismo – Homey, family-run, and simply decorated, it has excellent food, including ham-stuffed river trout, *posta de vitela na brasa* (braised veal), and *cabrito de churrasco* (barbecued kid). Try the house white or the wine from the cooperative in neighboring Valpaços. To reach the restaurant, cross Trajan's Bridge to the left bank of the Tâmega and take the first left past the campground. Closed Thursdays. Reservations unnecessary. Major credit cards accepted. Largo de São Roque, Chaves (phone: 076-22912). Moderate to inexpensive.

O Pote – Busy and popular, on the outskirts of town on the road to Spain. A large regional menu is offered. Closed Mondays. Reservations unnecessary. No credit cards accepted. Casa Azul, Av. Duarte Pacheco, Chaves (phone: 076-21226). Moderate to inexpensive.

En route from Chaves – The goal is Caldas do Gerês, 71 miles (114 km) away in the Peneda-Gerês National Park. Take N103 west into countryside littered with ancient *castros* and dolmens, as well as primitive granite villages known for their dairy products and handsome, long-horned oxen. At Sapiãos, 12 miles (19 km) from Chaves, a short side trip beckons via N312 to Boticas, 2½ miles (4 km) away, and then via N311 to Carvalhelhos, another 5 miles (8 km) away. Carvalhelhos is known for its spa waters and solitude, Boticas for its wine, which is buried for a year before it is drunk. The practice developed during the Napoleonic invasions, when the villagers hid their wine from French soldiers. Later, when the bottles were dug up, the wine was found to be much improved — and wine bottles ever after have been called *mortos* (dead ones). In summer, tiny villages around Boticas pit their best bulls against each other in the *Chegas de Touros.* The bull that manages to kill its opponent or force it to retreat is led away triumphantly, a source of great pride to its village. At the end of the season, the champion is rewarded by being put to pasture with the region's cows.

Return to N103 and, some 10½ miles (17 km) farther along, make another short detour, to the town of Montalegre, 5½ miles (9 km) away on N308. The small town is crowned by a 14th-century castle facing the peaks of the Serra do Larouco and an ancient *castro* to the north. To return to the route, follow signs to Vila Nova da Chá and then, back on N103, continue westward along the rocky north bank of the huge manmade lake formed by the Barragem do Alto Rabagão, a dam on the Rabagão River. Beyond the dam, the road crosses the river itself and proceeds along its south bank to another lake, the reservoir of the Barragem de Venda Nova, an ideal place for picnics and swimming.

After the Venda Nova Dam, the Rabagão River flows into the Rio Cávado, and the road weaves along the steep slopes above the latter, passing stone houses, water mills, and churches, with the majestic peaks of the Serra do Gerês looming to the north. About 15 miles (24 km) west of Venda Nova, just before Cerdeirinhas, turn right onto N304; as the road descends past heather and pine trees, the steep Cávado gorge appears, offering one of the most spectacular natural sights in Portugal. (Farther to the west, the power of the Cávado and its tributary, the Caldo, have been harnessed by the Barragem da Caniçada.) After passing Caniçada itself (really only a cluster of houses) and crossing a bridge, turn right onto N308-1, cross a second bridge, and drive along the wooded banks of the Caldo River past the village of Vilar de Veigas and into the spa town of Caldas do Gerês, in the Peneda-Gerês National Park.

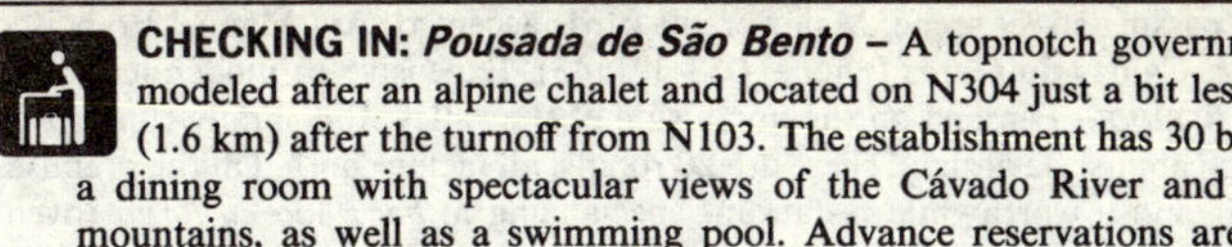

CHECKING IN: ***Pousada de São Bento*** – A topnotch government-run inn modeled after an alpine chalet and located on N304 just a bit less than a mile (1.6 km) after the turnoff from N103. The establishment has 30 bedrooms and a dining room with spectacular views of the Cávado River and surrounding mountains, as well as a swimming pool. Advance reservations are required in summer. Major credit cards accepted. Caniçada (phone: 053-647190; in the US, 212-686-9213; fax: 053-647867). Expensive.

De Carvalhelhos – This simply decorated 19-room *estalagem* (inn) surrounded by gardens and forested hills is a pleasant retreat for those in search of something quiet and away from the beaten track. Other attributes are the courteous service and the tasty regional and international dishes available in the dining room. Carvalhelhos (phone: 076-42116). Moderate.

São Cristovão – A modern motel beside the Rabagão just before the town of Venda Nova. The 18 rooms are decorated in pine and marble, and have balconies overlooking a small artificial pond. There are 2 dining rooms, one with a terrace. Major credit cards accepted. Venda Nova (phone: 053-659387). Moderate to inexpensive.

EATING OUT: ***Santa Cruz*** – A typical regional restaurant, family-run and enclosed in glass, where guests can watch their meals being prepared in the large kitchen or gaze down at the Beça River. Dine heartily on stick-to-the-ribs beef, kid, game, and mountain trout, and wash it all down with one of the village's *mortos.* Closed Sundays. Reservations unnecessary. No credit cards accepted. Boticas (phone: 076-42157). Inexpensive.

CALDAS DO GERÊS: This small resort town, whose mineral springs were known to the Romans, was a fashionable spa in the 18th century and still has several quaint, turn-of-the-century hotels, many of which have been restored, thanks to a recent EEC grant. Tennis, lake and pool swimming, boating, and horseback riding are all available in the area, but since the town lies at the base of a deep wooded gorge just inside the boundary of the Parque Nacional da Peneda-Gerês, it is an important base for park excursions. The 178,000-acre park, shaped like a horseshoe to encompass the Serra do Gerês on its southeastern side and the Serra da Peneda on its northwestern side, runs beyond Caldas up to the Spanish border and contains a wealth of archaeological vestiges — such as milestones and sections of Roman road — as well as waterfalls, wild ponies, rare birds, and 18 species of plants unique to the area. Hiking on marked trails, alone or with a guide, camping, fishing for trout in rivers and lakes, and going on organized day-long or week-long tours by bus or horseback are all possible. The *Museu Etnológico* (Museum of Ethnology; phone: 053-35888), outside São João do Campo, offers a look at the area's crafts, home furnishings, and farm implements. (Open October through April, Mondays through Fridays from 8 AM to noon and 1 to 5 PM; Saturdays and Sundays from 9 AM to 12:30 PM and 1:30 to 6 PM; May through September, Mondays through Fridays from 8 AM to noon and 1 to 7 PM; Saturdays and Sundays from 9 AM to 12:30 PM and 1:30 to 6:30 PM; admission charge.)

Maps of the park are available at the park's cabin (phone: 053-391181) at the entrance to town or at the local tourist office (open daily May through October from 9:30 AM to 12:30 PM and from 2 to 5:30 PM; closed November through April; Av. Manuel Francisco da Costa; phone: 053-391133). For advance tour reservations and brochures, contact Paulo Pires, *Trote-Gerês* (Cavalos Cabril, Borralha 5495; phone: 053-659292). The park headquarters, Sede do Parque Nacional (Quinta de Parretas, Braga 4700; phone: 053-613166), or their branch office (29 Rua de São Geraldo, Braga 4700; no phone) also can mail information on the park.

CHECKING IN: ***Termas*** – A recently refurbished fin de siècle establishment on the main street. Here, marble baths and the antique common room with fireplace recall a more luxurious era. The dining room of this 31-room hotel faces the Caldo River and the gorge, and the outdoor tables of the busy bar-café face the passing street scene. Major credit cards accepted. Av. Manuel Francisco da Costa, Caldas do Gerês (phone: 053-391143). Expensive to moderate.

Carvalho Araujo – Perched on the north side of the valley, this family-run *pensão* has a log-cabin-style design. There are 20 rooms, all facing south. On the premises are a bar and a worthwhile restaurant specializing in *bacalhão no forno* (oven-baked salt cod). Open year-round. Termas do Gerês (phone: 053-391185; fax: 053-391225). Moderate.

Jardim – A *pensão* popular with travelers in search of modest accommodations (some of the recently redecorated 57 rooms have TV sets and VCRs, however) and wholesome home cooking. Open year-round. Av. Manuel Francisco da Costa, Caldas do Gerês (phone and fax: 053-391132). Moderate.

Universal – These nicely restored turn-of-the century lodgings are right on the tree-lined main street. There are 50 air conditioned rooms with TV sets and radios, plus a quiet restaurant, a bar (with a fireplace) in the glass-enclosed patio, and a café that opens onto the street. Open year-round. Av. Manuel Francisco da Costa, Caldas do Gerês (phone: 053-391135). Moderate.

En Route from Caldas do Gerês – Return to N103 and head southwest toward Braga, 26½ miles (43 km) from Caldas. Beyond Cerdeirinhas, the landscape becomes barren, with round boulders, smoothed by time, teetering precariously on rocky crests. If you have time, take the dirt road that begins about 4 miles (6 km) beyond Cerdeirinhas, barely a mile (1 km) up to the sanctuary of São Mamede. At the summit, there's a tiny chapel and a panoramic view of the region that extends, on a clear day, as far as the Sanctuary of the Virgin on Monte Sameiro, outside Braga. Return to N103; soon the barren landscape gives way to the fertile valley of the Ave River, rich in vines and dotted with tiny hamlets. At Pinheiro, turn left to visit the castle at Póvoa de Lanhoso, about 1¼ miles (2 km) off N103. It was here that the first King of Portugal, Afonso Henriques, imprisoned his mother after defeating her forces in 1128, and here that the wife and father confessor/lover of an enraged Póvoa mayor were later burned. Póvoa de Lanhoso is also known for its goldsmiths and silversmiths, who fashion some of Portugal's famous filigree.

Braga is 10 miles (16 km) beyond Pinheiro on N103, and Porto is 33 miles (54 km) beyond Braga. To get to Porto, leave Braga via the old N14; after about 6 miles (10 km) change to the A3, a much newer (and infinitely quicker) toll road that will get you to Porto in half an hour. For full details on those cities, see *Braga* and *Porto,* THE CITIES.

The Beiras

Occupying a roughly horizontal strip of Portugal slightly north of the center, between the Douro River and the Tagus, the Beiras region unfolds before visitors like the pages of an age-old romance. In timeworn inns, travelers enjoy the warmth of kindly people and roaring log fires. Ancient crafts endure in picturesque villages that reverberate with the clang of smithies' anvils and the whir of potters' wheels. Shepherds draped in long woolen blankets as protection from the mist and cold move their flocks from pasture to pasture. Medieval castles wreathed in legend cling to the mountains, where visitors can experience the exhilaration of tobogganing down a sunlit, snow-covered slope or hooking a trout from a tumbling river. Unexpected pleasures, like catching the white underbelly of a swooping owl in a car's headlights or the fragrance of almond blossoms on the evening breeze, reawaken a childhood sense of wonder.

The region's inspiring beauty and historical fascination have not yet been undone by mass tourism. Yet the traditional country cooking and fine local wines found in its pleasant hotels and restaurants often rival those of more sophisticated locations, and the friendly welcome surpasses them. Visitors from abroad are usually surprised by the low prices and happy to find themselves far from the madding crowd — although hotels are often fully booked during the peak *Christmas, New Year, Easter,* and summer holiday weeks.

The name Beira, meaning "edge," is thought to derive from the region's position on the edge of the central Spanish mountain range that spills over into Portugal as the Serra da Estrela. There are three Beiras. Beira Alta (Upper Beira), in the northeast, is a high plateau capped by the Serra da Estrela range, which forms the country's highest peaks. Beira Baixa (Lower Beira) drops in altitude as it slopes southward to the highlands of the Alentejo. Beira Litoral (Coastal Beira), to the west of both of these, is a lower-lying region reaching down past the city of Coimbra to the Atlantic coast.

The mountains of the Beiras ripple throughout the region. Their granite and schist rocks can be seen in the sturdy village houses and monuments that have withstood the weathering of centuries. Two main rivers, the Mondego and the Zêzere, rise in the Serra da Estrela, cutting deep valleys in the mountains on their way to the sea. High in the *serra,* gorges, glacial basins, and manmade lakes spreading out behind hydroelectric dams provide dramatic vistas; lower down, the contrast between fertile, green river valleys and craggy uplands is striking. The region's climate is relatively temperate. Winter temperatures in the Serra da Estrela are the lowest in Portugal, dropping to between 23 and 59F; in summer, they range from 50 to 68F. Elsewhere in the Beiras, winters are milder and summers hotter, but there are always cooling breezes from the river valleys. Rainfall is considerable in the mountains.

Castles, ramparts, forts, and city walls scattered across the Beiras attest to a history of invasion. Viriatus (Viriato in Portuguese), a shepherd-warrior from the Serra da Estrela, valiantly led a Celtic people known as the Lusitanians in fighting off Roman domination until his assassination (ca. 140 BC). Barbarian tribes — the Suevians and the Visigoths — later overran the province, and the Moorish invasion of Portugal and the subsequent Christian Reconquest also brought heavy fighting. The next wave of invaders came from across the border, when Philip II of Spain seized Portugal in 1580; an uprising in Lisbon in 1640 restored the country's independence, but before Spain formally recognized it in 1668, Portuguese troops had made several stands along the frontier.

Portugal's alliance with Britain against revolutionary, Napoleonic France led to the Peninsular War of 1807–10, during which the French invaded three times. They were finally expelled by an Anglo-Portuguese army led by the brilliant military tactician Sir Arthur Wellesley, who later became the Duke of Wellington. Although Portugal emerged the winner, the war ravaged the country, and many treasures were lost to pillaging by both the French and the British. Traces of the military campaigns abound in the region, particularly around the ancient forest of Buçaco, where Wellington achieved his most significant victory.

Like the invasions of the past, the traditional culture of the region weaves through its history in an unbroken thread. In such a rural world, where the earth is often tilled by hand and where donkeys and oxen have not yet been totally replaced by mechanical beasts of burden, life is still dominated by the seasons. Many of the local festivals, while related to the Roman Catholic calendar, have their roots in more primitive beliefs. Spring flower festivals echo pagan fertility rites, and some *Christmas* customs, such as dances around burning *Yule* logs, hark back to the winter solstice. Almost every town and village has its patron saint, and the pilgrimage festivals, or *romarias,* held every year in the saint's honor provide one of the more congenial ways of discovering the region's heart. After the flower-decked statue of the saint or the Virgin is carried in procession, the town is given over to merrymaking. Under a sky brightened by carnival lights and fireworks, couples dance into the night to the sounds of brass bands and local pop groups. Stalls selling crafts and sweetmeats fill the streets, as everyone dines out on chicken and pork, grilled sardines, and flagons of wine.

Beiras farmers cultivate corn and rye in the arable land of the valleys; orchards and olive groves occupy the lower slopes and spill over onto terraces supported by granite stones as the hillsides grow steeper. Livestock is reared in the rich upper valley of the Zêzere. But the true wealth of the region is trees. One-third of Portugal is covered with trees, with the Beiras among the most prominent of the forested areas. The scents of pine, eucalyptus, resin, and wood smoke are pervasive. Forests, from productive extents of oaks and Aleppo and umbrella pines to the hundreds of exotic varieties at Buçaco, form the backdrop to all the area's breathtaking panoramas. Timber products include resin, pitch, turpentine, and railway sleepers, and the country also has a sizable furniture industry. But wood pulp, used to make paper and cardboard, is the main product of the forests, as well as Portugal's biggest foreign currency earner after tourism and textiles.

Above the forests rise the mountains, the other key to the soul of the Beiras. Where the craggy terrain can no longer support crops, sheep and goats become the mainstay of Portugal's mountain communities, as they have been since time immemorial. The animals provide wool, milk, and *queijo da serra,* one of Portugal's most sought after delicacies. For hundreds of years, between December and May, this oozy ewe's milk cheese has been made by hand in the farmhouse dairies of the Serra da Estrela — an area of production that is now strictly limited by law. Although an industrially manufactured *queijo do tipo serra* is available more cheaply, it is no match for the real thing. The ewes are milked before dawn and again in the evening. The milk is poured through a cloth bag filled with powdered thistle flowers — a natural coagulant — and a little salt, and is heated over pine logs and broom twigs until it coagulates. It is then patiently squeezed by hand into a wooden press. The round cheeses, bound with a cloth, are cured for 2 weeks to a month until the butter-yellow rind forms; the cheese itself is pale, with a subtle sharp edge to its creaminess. Every restaurant in the region serves *queijo da serra,* and shopkeepers will be happy to help buyers choose a properly ripe one.

The Beiras also produce what many consider to be Portugal's finest wines — the smooth, strong dão reds and crisp dão whites, which take their name from the Dão River, a tributary of the Mondego. The demarcated zone centers on the town of Viseu and includes some 1,200 square miles, although vines can be grown on little more than 5% of the land. The zone's high, forested terrain, rocky granite soil, and climate of hot summers and cold, wet winters are an unlikely combination for wine production, but it is precisely these elements that give dão reds their distinctive flavor — silky with a slight earthy tang — and their strength, averaging 12% alcohol. The whites have a clean, fresh taste. The best age for a good dão red is 7 to 10 years, but whites get no better after 3 years, the experts say.

This route, focusing on the heart of the region where the three Beiras meet, begins in the historic university city of Coimbra and winds eastward into the Serra da Estrela mountains (encompassed since 1976 by the Serra da Estrela Natural Park, which seeks to protect the plant and animal life, as well as the environment, culture, and traditions of Portugal's most extensive and highest mountain range). It dips south across the *serra* — detouring to the summit of the 6,532-foot-high Torre, Portugal's highest peak, if desired — to the wool town of Covilhã and then travels along the verdant valley of the Zêzere River to the *serra*'s northeastern tip at Guarda, the country's highest town. A modern highway leads westward to Viseu in the heart of the Dão wine region, from where the route descends through the forested *serras* of Caramulo and Buçaco back to Coimbra.

The round-trip distance, about 500 miles (800 km), can be covered comfortably in 5 to 7 days. Distances between possible overnight stops are short, which allows for leisurely detours to villages and other sights along the way, since many attractions lie off the principal roads and are reached by branching off along the main route or traveling out from the towns. Nevertheless, drivers should be cautious and allow plenty of time for traveling; driving in the Beiras is enjoyable, but it can be taxing. Many of the roads are steep and narrow, twisting up hillsides in sharp hairpin bends, often with a precipice falling away to one side, and some are in poor repair. Allowances should be made for unexpected maneuvers by other drivers — Portugal, unfortunately, has the worst accident rate in Europe. Resist the temptation to enjoy the magnificent views from behind the wheel; instead, use the designated viewing points (signposted *miradouros*). Special care has to be taken in winter, when roads can be treacherously icy and snow occasionally makes it impossible to cross the Serra da Estrela.

Although the region has not been commercialized by tourism, it does not lack comfortable accommodations, which include the luxury of the *Palace Hotel do Buçaco* — among the finest in Europe — and other pleasant hotels, plus government-owned *pousadas* and small, welcoming inns and *pensões*. Also available, under Portugal's *Tourism in the Country* program (see *Accommodations*, GETTING READY TO GO), are rooms in privately owned houses, including the manor houses and other stately country homes that are part of the *Turismo de Habitação* network and the simpler rural houses and farmhouses categorized as *Turismo Rural* and *Agroturismo*. Most hotels are small, and booking ahead is essential for the peak summer and winter seasons, particularly at the *pousadas*. Expect to pay $100 and up for a double room in establishments listed below as expensive, $50 to $100 in moderate places, and less than $50 in inexpensive ones.

Excellent country fare — such as roast mountain kid, trout, and a delicious variety of sausages — is offered at even the simplest of restaurants, accompanied by wines that hold their own against the more famous labels of France and Italy. The majority of the best restaurants belong to hotels or pensions, leaving relatively few independent places in the listings. Most restaurant meals, including wine, will be in the moderate range, meaning from $30 to $50 for two, but there are many small places serving inexpensive meals for under $25.

COIMBRA: For a detailed report on the city, its sights, hotels, and restaurants, see *Coimbra*, THE CITIES.

En Route from Coimbra – Take N17, which leads northeast out of the city to the edge of the Serra da Estrela. You'll soon be climbing steep hills clothed in tall pine trees. Black-clad women balancing baskets on their heads, heavily laden donkey carts (often unlit at night), and terraced plots of vines and fruit trees high on the hillsides are an indication of how the people of the Beiras earn their livelihoods. After about 9½ miles (15 km), turn right onto N236 to Lousã, crossing a small river, the Arouce, which was named after an early king, Arunce, whose court was at Conímbriga. Arouce Castle, with an imposing square watchtower, dominates a nearby hillside. Historians date the fortress to the 11th century, but according to legend, it was built during the 1st century BC, when King Arunce fled to the forests to escape pirate attacks. Most of the present structure is from the 14th century, although it has been heavily damaged by hunters searching for the treasure the king reputedly buried somewhere inside. Ancient hermitages lie on a ridge below.

LOUSÃ: This small, busy town is deep in the Arouce Valley, 5 miles (8 km) from the turnoff from N17. Here, wood from the dense forests of the Beiras is still turned into paper at the country's oldest paper mill, founded in 1718. The town has some fine 18th-century houses of aristocrats, including the white-walled Casa da Viscondessa (Rua do Visconde), whose neo-classical frontage and door were added in 1818. The green wooded hills and bare purple crests of the Serra da Lousã sweep southeast from the town, with small villages and farms dotting the forests. At the western end of the range, not far outside Lousã, is its highest peak, the 3,942-foot-high Alto do Trevim, which rewards climbers with spectacular views over much of central Portugal. Close by the peak are the Real Neveiro, or "royal snow caves," where ice used to be dug out for the court in Lisbon, and the Chapel of Santo António da Neve (St. Anthony of the Snow).

En Route from Lousã – One road from Lousã leads south across the Serra da Lousã to Castelo Branco. But it is a long haul over difficult mountain roads and, despite breathtaking views, offers too few interesting stopping places to make the journey worthwhile. Instead, return to N17, turn right, and continue eastward toward Seia. After about 25 miles (40 km), a turn to the right leads to Lourosa, an ancient village noted for its pre-Romanesque church; built in the form of a basilica in 912, it is one of the rare religious monuments of its era to survive in Portugal. Continue on N17 another few miles to Venda de Galizes, turning right there onto N230 to visit some particularly picturesque Beiras villages. Follow the narrow road as it winds through terraced orchards and vineyards amid magnificent mountain views and turn right at the first crossroads, where the tiered granite houses of the village of Avô, rising from the far side of the banks of the Alva River, can be glimpsed below.

AVÔ: One of the most attractive of the Beiras' many pleasant villages, Avô has a quiet rural charm that belies its somewhat turbulent past. The village, dating back to the 12th century, was part of a line of defense during the reconquest of Portugal from the Moors, and in the early years of this century, when the country became a republic, it was at the center of a short-lived effort to restore the monarchy. Before crossing the narrow bridge that leads into the village, stop in the courtyard beside the Igreja Matriz (Parish Church). The restored 18th-century church, of medieval origin, has a distinctive entrance with round bell towers rising on each side, linked by a crowning arch; inside is a precious baroque altarpiece. Across the bridge, narrow cobblestone steets, steep alleys, and mossy stone steps weave around Avô's ancient houses, some dating from the 15th and 16th centuries. The sadly dilapidated house of Brás Garcia de Mascarenhas, an early-17th-century poet and adventurer, stands by the water (to the left of the bridge when leaving the village). Modified during the 18th century, it has a beautiful Manueline window at the rear.

En Route from Avô – Return to the crossroads and N230, taking it east a mile or so to the curious Ponte das Três Entradas (Bridge of the Three Entrances), where three roads meet, simultaneously crossing the Alvoco and Alva rivers at their junction. Turn right from the bridge to climb the Serra do Colcorinho to Aldeia das Dez. (In driving these steep narrow roads with their tight hairpin bends, it is not surprising to learn that one of the toughest stages of the *Portuguese Motor Rally,* considered one of the most grueling rallies in the world, is held at Arganil, less than 15 miles — 24 km — away.) Just before reaching the village, stop at the Miradouro Penedo da Saudade to take in the exhilarating view.

ALDEIA DAS DEZ: The name, meaning Village of the Ten, derives from the ten houses that gave the settlement its start during the 12th century. Clustered in the folds of the *serra,* Aldeia das Dez is banked too steeply to be traversed easily by streets and is consequently threaded through with cobblestone steps. The stone pillory, a symbol of municipal authority found in towns throughout Portugal, is dated 1661. Most of the village's dwellings are in traditional Beiras style, the lower part built solidly of granite, with wooden balconies sheltered by the roof eaves. Similarly, the lifestyle here is typical of a Beiras farming village — witness the goatskins hung out to dry, the stacks of pine logs dotted about the streets, and the men returning from the fields with hoes on their shoulders.

En Route from Aldeia das Dez – Return to N17 at Venda de Galizes and, about 3 miles (5 km) farther east, turn left onto the northern stretch of N230, leading to Oliveira do Hospital. In 1120, Queen Teresa gave this small town to the crusading Order of the Hospitalers of St. John of Jerusalem, and several important figures of the order were born here. Today, a statue in homage to Beiras shepherds stands in the tree-lined square. The parish church, built from the 13th to the 14th centuries and reconstructed during the 17th, is noted for the 13th-century funerary chapel of a local nobleman and his wife, whose figures, sculpted in Ançã stone, lie above their tombs below a painted altar carved in the same stone.

Return to N17 and continue northeast 10½ miles (17 km), skirting the edge of the Parque Natural da Serra da Estrela (Serra da Estrela Natural Park). Turn right onto N231 at the crossroads signposted Seia. The town is 2 miles (3 km) farther along, inside the park at the foot of the mountains.

CHECKING IN: ***Pousada de Santa Bárbara*** – This modern member of the government-run *pousada* chain was built in the 1970s. It's set among pines on the western edge of the Serra da Estrela, 2 miles (3 km) along N17 from the Oliveira do Hospital turnoff. There are 16 secluded rooms, plus tennis courts and a swimming pool. Visitors can warm themselves in front of a log fire in the wood-paneled interior and enjoy the view across the hills from the excellent restaurant. Regional specialties include roast kid and trout. Major credit cards accepted. Póvoa das Quartas (phone: 038-52252; in the US, 212-686-9213; fax: 038-50545). Expensive.

Casa do Boco – A participant in *Turismo Rural,* this is a large Beiras house in the village of Meruge, on the Cobral River 5 miles (8 km) north of Oliveira do Hospital. Two apartments with double bedrooms are available, for a minimum of 2 nights. Contact Dona Maria da Conceição Antunes, *Casa do Boco,* Meruge, Lagares da Beira (phone: 038-54118). Moderate.

São Paulo – This comfortable, newly renovated hostelry in the center of town has 44 rooms, all with bath, as well as a restaurant. Visa and MasterCard accepted. Rua Professor Antunes Varela, Oliveira do Hospital (phone: 038-52361 or 038-52393; fax: 038-52094). Moderate.

SEIA: Set at the foot of the Serra da Estrela, Seia (pop. 5,700) is light and airy, with broad streets. The parish church, of Romanesque origin but rebuilt after the Napoleonic wars of the early 19th century, dominates it from a hilltop. The ancient town was captured from the Moors in 1057 and officially recognized as a municipality in 1136. An imposing 18th-century palace, the Casa das Obras, also known as the Solar dos Albuquerques, houses the Town Hall; the future Duke of Wellington used it as his headquarters during the French invasions. Other landmarks nearby are the Solar dos Botelhos, a restored 16th-century granite manor house with three Manueline windows; the 18th-century Misericórdia church; and the pillory. Many of Seia's residents work in the dairy plant in the southern part of the town, and the shops in the streets around the main square are a good place to buy *queijo da serra,* the ewe's-milk cheese that is justly famed among Portugal's cheeses. There are also several handicraft shops here selling sheepskin, pottery, and copper products.

CHECKING IN/EATING OUT: ***Camelo*** – Highly regarded and decorated with antiques, this hostelry replaced a hotel that had been destroyed by fire. The 66 rooms and suites have wood-paneled ceilings, pink marble-fitted bathrooms, and TV sets. The restaurant is one of only five in the country distinguished by an award by the Portuguese government; specialties include *sopa à nossa moda* (a vegetable and veal soup), *bacalhau com broa* (codfish with corn bread and almonds), and *requeijão,* a farmer cheese served as dessert. *Bacalhau* is served at Thursday and Sunday lunch; at other times it has to be ordered in advance. Major credit cards accepted. 86 Largo Marquês da Silva, Seia (phone: 038-22530; fax: 038-23031). Moderate.

Seia – This extensively renovated old granite *estalagem* (inn) has 35 rooms and a restaurant. Visa accepted. Av. Afonso Costa, Seia (phone: 038-22666; telex: 52863). Moderate.

Serra da Estrela – A pleasant *pensão* with 21 rooms and a good restaurant specializing in regional fare. Rua Dr. Simões Pereira, Seia (phone: 038-22573). Inexpensive.

En Route from Seia – Before penetrating the Serra da Estrela, check the large blue board beside the Misericórdia church. It indicates whether the roads across the mountain — which are sometimes blocked by snow for short periods from November to May — are passable (marked white) or closed (red). If the route is clear, take N339 and climb 7 miles (11 km) for a look at Sabugueiro, the highest village in Portugal, now crowded with souvenir stalls and shops. Then double back toward Seia and turn right at the first crossroads onto N339-1. (There is a more direct route from Sabugueiro to N339-1, along 3 miles — 5 km — of dirt road, but it is recommended only for the adventurous.)

At the next junction, with N232, a right turn leads to Manteigas, but those with time to spare may want to take the left turn to Gouveia, an attractive, ancient town in the hills rising from the Mondego valley. Either way, the road climbs into a desolate landscape where granite crags are strewn with massive boulders, some whipped into strange shapes by the wind and snow. One such boulder, on the right on the way to Gouveia, has been sculpted by the elements into the perfect picture of a toothless old man and is known, fittingly, as the Cabeça do Velho (Old Man's Head). Mountain flowers blossom among the scrub of grass, heather, and juniper — the latter (*zimbro* in Portuguese) used to brew the fiery white brandy, *aguardente de zimbro,* found all over the Beiras.

CHECKING IN: ***Casa do Sabugueiro*** – Part of the *Turismo Rural* program, it offers the chance to stay in a traditional village house, complete with *queijaria* (cheese dairy) and bread oven. The apartment available has 2 double bedrooms, a living room, a kitchen, and a bathroom. A horse and cart are available for guest use, as are boats on the river in summer. Contact Dona Teresa da Graça Trindade, *Casa do Sabugueiro,* Sabugueiro (phone: 038-22825). Moderate.

O Abrigo da Montanha – This is a modern *pensão* with 25 rooms, a restaurant, a bar, and its own discotheque. Local handicrafts are on sale and ski equipment can be rented. The restaurant specializes in regional dishes, notably *mocela de tia Madalena,* a black sausage dish, and *borrego,* roast lamb. Visa and MasterCard accepted. Sabugueiro (phone: 038-22394). Inexpensive.

GOUVEIA: The town (pop. 600) reputedly dates back to the 6th century BC. Just outside of town, it's possible to climb to a pre-Roman fortification, the *castro* of Alfátima, where Julius Caesar is said to have stayed in 38 BC. (The *castro* takes its name from a later time when Christians and Moors battled over Gouveia, and Fatima, the beautiful daughter of an Arab emir, is supposed to have fled to the mountain with her jewels.) One of the most attractive buildings in town is the Casa da Torre, a late-17th-century manor house with the sculpted ropes of the Manueline style wreathing its windows. The exterior of the 18th-century parish church of São Pedro was renovated in 1940 with blue-and-white tiles depicting religious scenes. The imposing *paço* (palace) was also built during the 18th century, originally as a Jesuit school, although the Jesuits were able to use it for only a few years before they were expelled from Portugal by the Marquês de Pombal. The building became a military hospital during the Peninsular War and later a barracks. An esplanade leading off the small baroque Calvário chapel affords splendid views.

In March, a fair dedicated to *queijo da serra* takes place in Gouveia, but all of the rural trades and crafts around which local life revolves are on display during the *Festas do Senhor do Calvário,* a summer festival held during the second or third week of August. A religious procession and folk dances are the highlights of the festival, but part of the event is devoted to the dark honey of the Beiras — which owes its special flavor to the mountain flowers the bees feed on — and to a competition for Serra da Estrela sheepdogs. As they did in pre-Roman times, these fine dogs still protect their flocks from foxes, wild boar, and, it is said, wolves; a kennel that raises them — the Canil dos Montes — can be visited in the vicinity. It's located at Algueiro, on the southern edge of Gouveia, and welcomes visitors during working hours. (But don't fall in love with the puppies. There usually are waiting lists for all litters. On the other hand, specialists advise smitten visitors not to buy dogs from shops and roadside stands, where they may not be purebreds. All pure sheepdogs should have proof of pedigree.)

CHECKING IN/EATING OUT: ***Casa Grande*** – Three apartments with double bedrooms are available in the 16th-century manor and adjoining 18th-century house at this *Turismo Rural* participant in Paços da Serra, 5 miles (8 km) south of Gouveia on N232. All the apartments have log fireplaces. Extra rooms can be provided for larger families. Breakfast and firewood in the winter are included. Contact Dona Maria Amelia Ribeiro Saraiva, *Casa Grande,* Paços da Serra (phone: 038-43341; for reservations in Lisbon: 01-668676; for reservations in Porto: 02-816587). Moderate.

Gouveia – In the center of town, this hostelry has 27 rooms, all with central heating, radio, television sets, telephones, and private baths (4 additional suites also have living rooms). Guests have access to the municipal swimming pool and tennis courts. The restaurant serves regional dishes including trout, roast kid, and *fritada serrana,* a fried dish featuring several kinds of local sausage. Av. Primeiro de Maio, Gouveia (phone: 038-42890; telex: 53789). Moderate.

Estrela do Parque – A 25-room *pensão* with a pretty restaurant that serves regional food. 36 Av. da República, Gouveia (phone: 038-42171). Inexpensive.

En Route from Gouveia – Retrace the route south on N232, following signs for Manteigas. Not too far after the road bends east, in the vicinity of the junction with N339-1 from Sabugueiro, a signpost indicates the Nascente do Mondego to the right. It is from this spring, at an altitude of 4,462 feet, that the most important of the Portuguese rivers that begin within the country descends, to flow eventually through Coimbra and out to the sea at Figueira da Foz.

Back on N232 to Manteigas, another turn to the right climbs for 2 miles (3 km) to a magnificent view of the Penhas Douradas, a line of three peaks called "golden crests" because they glow in the setting sun. They rise up to 5,471 feet and, like other Serra da Estrela summits, remain capped with snow for all but the three hottest summer months. Continuing to Manteigas, the road begins to descend through 9 miles (14 km) of tortuous bends to the town, which lies at an altitude of 2,362 feet. The scenery is superb: Small waterfalls cascade down the mossy rocks, tumbling through tunnels under the road or freezing into a wild filigree of ice in winter. Tall pines provide green, leafy shade, while ferns, golden and red in the fall, light up the slopes.

MANTEIGAS: This picturesque town of 3,000 is deep in the valley of the Zêzere River. Its white, pink, and beige houses reflect the bright mountain light; the air is crisp and invigorating, the tranquillity refreshing. Viriatus and his Lusitanian warriors are reputed to have used it as one of their last refuges from the Romans during the 2nd century BC. The parish church, with twin bell towers, is of Roman origin, although it betrays no evidence of its beginnings, presenting instead a baroque structure that has been considerably altered over the centuries. The square beside the church has a charming bandstand and offers engaging views over the town's steep, tiled rooftops.

CHECKING IN/EATING OUT: ***Pousada de São Lourenço*** – An 11-room *pousada* of modern vintage, but built of granite high in the hills along the descent to Manteigas from the Penhas Douradas, 8 miles (13 km) north of town. It has wooden paneling, roaring fireplaces, and marvelous views from its balconies and terraces. The restaurant serves a wealth of excellent regional dishes such as *batatas à caçoila,* a tasty pork and potatoes dish, and regional wines. Estrada de Gouveia, Manteigas (phone: 075-981321; in the US, 212-686-9213; fax: 075-981664). Expensive.

Casa de São Roque – At this 3-story townhouse, a *Turismo Rural* participant, visitors can walk out onto the terrace overlooking the valley. A suite and 5 double bedrooms, together with several living rooms, are available; there's also a bar and a restaurant on the premises. Contact Dona Maria Capelo Ramos, *Casa de São Roque,* 67 Rua de António, Manteigas (phone: 075-981125 or 075-981476). Moderate.

De Manteigas – This is a comfortable, restful hotel offering fine views from the mountainside at Caldas de Manteigas, a small spa 2 miles (3 km) south of town. There are 26 rooms in the hotel, plus two annexes with 13 and 15 rooms each, tennis courts, and a good restaurant. Visa and MasterCard accepted. Caldas de Manteigas (phone: 075-981514). Moderate.

En Route from Manteigas – Leave town heading south on N338, passing through Caldas de Manteigas, a small spa town with Alpine-style houses, where visitors can take a sauna during the summer months. Cross the bridge over the Zêzere, whose waters splash over the rocks below and operate a nearby water mill. Here it's possible to visit a fish farm, the Pôsto Aquícola da Fonte Santa (open daily from 9:30 to 11 AM and from 1 to 5 PM; no admission charge), to see trout gleaming in the clear water before they are released into mountain lakes and rivers. A narrow, poorly surfaced road turns off to the left, leading about 4 miles (6 km) up through stirring views to the Poço de Inferno (Well of Hell), where a cataract crashes from wooded heights into a limpid pool below. (In winter, it freezes into a wild weave of ice.)

Continue on N338 as it follows the upper valley of the Zêzere — actually a deep trough formed by an Ice Age glacier. Springs and waterfalls tumble down the slopes into the river, and cabins of rough stone, some built in crevices beneath huge boulders, dot the hillsides. As the route climbs toward Torre, the highest point in Portugal (its name, in fact, means tower), snow-covered peaks emerge. At the first crossroads, with N339, a left turn leads to Covilhã; but turn to the right, if there's time, to reach the Torre summit. Pale green moss and lichen lend the strangely shaped rocks an otherworldly appearance as the road rises higher and higher, with the lake of the Covão do Ferro dam below on the left. A little farther on, to the right, a statue of Nossa Senhora da Boa Estrela (Our Lady of the Holy Star) has been carved in relief in the black granite. Stone steps lead up to this sanctuary, where a religious festival marked by a long procession is held each year on the second Sunday in August.

The road continues, well surfaced, sufficiently broad, and not too steep; drivers who branch off left at the signpost can drive half a mile right onto the Torre summit, 6,532 feet above sea level. A stone tower was built to take the peak up to the round figure of 2,000 meters, or 6,560 feet, but this has since been topped by the higher domes of two meteorological observatories. Also known as the Malhão da Estrela (which could be loosely translated as the "High Shot" of the Estrela), Torre is a favorite destination for excursions — the circular road around the top is ringed with cafés and stalls selling regional food, crafts, and souvenirs. The views are magnificent.

Return to N339 and head east for the steep descent to Covilhã, a town tucked into the folds of the mountains at the southeastern edge of the Serra da Estrela Natural Park. The road passes through pine, oak, and chestnut woods along the way, and through Penhas da Saúde, a base for skiers that's in full swing from December to May. There are two ski runs with lifts: the 1,246-foot slope at Piornos, between Penhas da Saúde and Torre (although for the past several years there hasn't been enough snow for this one to be used), and the 2,590-foot Covão de Loriga slope, which falls away westward from the summit of Torre itself. Ski lessons are available, equipment can be rented, and other activities, such as hiking, climbing, fishing, and camping, are also possible. For further information, contact the *Clube Nacional de Montanhismo* (5 Rua Pedro Alvares Cabral, Covilhã; phone: 075-23364), the *Sede da Região de Turismo da Serra da Estrela* (Praça do Município, Covilhã; phone: 075-22151), or *Turiestrela,* the company that runs the ski lifts (phone: 075-24933).

CHECKING IN/EATING OUT: ***O Pastor*** – A small, 8-room *estalagem* with ski equipment and toboggans for rent, and a log fire in the lounge for warmth and atmosphere; there's also central heating. Specialties of the restaurant include both the traditional Portuguese bean-and-pork stew known as *feijoada* and *bacalhau à Pastor,* a dried codfish dish made with grated cheese and cream. Restaurant open daily in the winter and summer peak seasons and closed 1 day weekly (variable) the rest of the year. Major credit cards accepted. Penhas da Saúde (phone: 075-22810). Moderate.

COVILHÃ: From Torre to this congenial town (pop. 22,000) on the southeastern slopes of the *serra,* the road drops from 6,532 feet to 2,296 feet in only 12½ miles (20 km). Don't drive too fast or your ears might pop! Covilhã is an ancient town, thought to have been founded by the Romans in 41 BC. For centuries, its life has revolved around the flocks of sheep that graze on the mountains, providing raw materials for the town's main industries: dairy products such as *queijo da serra* and wool. But today, much of its livelihood also derives from the winter sports enthusiasts who flock to the area. The intimate relationship with the Serra da Estrela comes as no surprise — almost every street in town offers a stirring panorama of the mountains above and the plains to the south and east.

Covilhã became the center of Portugal's cloth-making industry during the 15th century, famed not only for its wool but also for silk, cotton, and linen. From the beginning, the industry struggled against competition from imported fabrics, particularly from Britain. Foreign textiles were outlawed in 1677, but only 26 years later, in 1703, Portugal and Britain signed the Methuen Treaty, which facilitated the entry of British cloth into Portugal while providing a boost for Portuguese exports of port wine to Britain. The agreement dealt a heavy blow to the cloth makers of Covilhã, despite King João V's support in 1710, when he awarded the town a contract to supply his army with uniforms.

Half a century later, in 1755, nature dealt the town a second blow. The earthquake that devastated Lisbon also destroyed many of Covilhã's houses and most of the town walls, with their five gates. The Marquês de Pombal, the prime minister who oversaw the rebuilding of the capital, ordered a textile factory built in Covilhã, using stones from the fallen walls. (The Fábrica Real, on Avenida Marquês d'Avila Bolama, now houses the Beira Interior University Institute.) By the mid-1800s, as many as 7,000 workers were employed in the town's cloth mills; more recently, local cloth makers have again suffered the effects of less expensive foreign imports and the massive artificial fiber industry.

Despite its history, Covilhã, with its trees and gardens, has little of the appearance of an industrial town. The main square, Praça do Município, features a statue of Pero de Covilhã, a 15th-century explorer and adventurer who was born here. The Palacete-Jardim (Av. Frei Heitor Pinto) affords an attractive example of *azulejos,* or painted tiles, and architecture from the turn-of-the-century Art Nouveau period. (The building now houses a regional delegation of the Labor Ministry.) The Capela de São Martinho e Calvário, in the lower part of town, is a simple Romanesque chapel of rough stone housing an 18th-century painting of the Crucifixion and two primitive representations of saints.

CHECKING IN: ***Montalto*** – A small *pensão* on the main square, it has 15 rooms, all with bath, television set, telephone, and heating. No restaurant, but breakfast is served. Praça do Município, Covilhã (phone: 075-25091). Moderate.

Solneve – This 36-room hotel, in an old (but modernized) building, is in the town center. It has a noted restaurant that specializes in regional dishes, including *truta do paul,* a trout dish, and roast mountain kid. Visa and MasterCard accepted. 126 Av. Visconde da Coriscada, Covilhã (phone: 075-23001; fax: 075-314773). Moderate.

EATING OUT: ***Café Regional*** – Although this is a good, modest *pensão* in the center, with 20 rooms, it is especially recommended for its restaurant, which serves regional specialties such as *panela no forno,* a rice dish made with pork. The restaurant is closed Sunday evenings, Mondays, and the first 2 weeks of September. Reservations unnecessary. Major credit cards accepted. 4-6 Rua das Flores, Covilhã (phone: 075-22596). Inexpensive.

En route from Covilhã – Take N18 north out of town. The road winds through the green, fertile valley of the Zêzere — the river basin here is a rich farming region known as the Cova da Beira — up to Guarda, 24 miles (38 km) from Covilhã. About halfway to Guarda, make a short detour to the right onto N345, signposted Belmonte. This hilltop town, commanded by a medieval castle, was the birthplace of Pedro Alvares Cabral, who discovered Brazil in 1500; the Romanesque São Tiago church, where he is buried, can be seen. Back on N18, the next right turn, the road to Comeal da Torre, leads to the impressive ruins of what was probably a Roman-Lusitanian inn, known as the Centum Cellas.

GUARDA: High on an exposed hilltop overlooking Spain (the border is only 29½ miles — 47 km — away), this town (pop. 15,000) of granite buildings, lantern-lit alleys, and pillared balconies breathes a medieval atmosphere that brings its history vividly to life. Buffeted by rough winds and winter snow, Guarda, at 3,281 feet, is the highest town in Portugal, and its hardy, hearty character reflects its historic role as the first stronghold against successive invasions from across the frontier. To the Portuguese, the town is known as *feia, forte, farta, e fria,* meaning "ugly, strong, plentiful, and cold." Visitors enjoying its traditional hospitality today are likely to take issue only with the adjective "ugly."

Guarda has been inhabited since prehistoric times, and Julius Caesar is thought to have used it as a military base. The Visigoths and then the Moors took it; after Afonso Henriques, the first King of Portugal, recaptured it, the town was enlarged, fortified, and officially founded by King Sancho I, in 1199. A statue of Sancho stands in the main square, the Praça da Sé (also known as Praça Luís de Camões), to the north of which stands the Sé itself, a magnificent cathedral whose granite stones look almost as pristine as the day they were cut from the surrounding hills more than 500 years ago. To the right is the Paço de Concelho, the Town Hall, and to the left is the charming building housing the tourist office (phone: 071-22251). On the south side is a gallery of shops and houses.

The cathedral was begun in 1390 and completed in 1540, a passage of time that resulted in a mixture of Renaissance and Manueline styles with the original Gothic. The flying buttresses, pinnacles, and gargoyles of the exterior are reminiscent of the monastery at Batalha, a masterpiece of Portuguese architecture that similarly mixes Gothic with Manueline. (The two buildings both feature work by the master architect Boytac and the Mateus Fernandes family.) The cathedral's main doorway, flanked by two octagonal bell towers, is Manueline; inside is a vaulted interior containing a Renaissance altarpiece by Jean de Rouen. It consists of more than 100 figures, sculpted in high relief and painted in gold and white, depicting scenes from the life of Christ on panels that rise to the arched windows. Also of note, through a magnificent Renaissance doorway, is the Capela dos Pinas, which holds the late Gothic tomb of a cathedral founder. He is said to have thrown himself from the roof after he asked the people if the building had any defects — and an old lady replied that the door was too small! The cathedral is open to visitors from 10 AM to 12:30 PM and from 2 to 5:30 PM; closed Mondays. There is a charge to climb to the top of the towers.

From the Praça da Sé, walk through an ancient alleyway to the Torre dos Ferreiros (Blacksmiths' Tower), one of three of the original six gates still standing amid the ruins of the 12th- and 13th-century town walls. (The other two are the Porta da Estrela and the Porta do Rei; the castle keep, or Torre de Menagem, also remains from the original fortifications.) Cross the tree-lined street to the restored 17th-century Misericórdia church, with its attractive white pediment between two pinnacled bell towers; it has a carved wooden ceiling and a baroque altar and pulpits. Farther along the same street is the *Museu da Guarda* (phone: 071-23460), housed in the 17th-century Bishop's Palace, which has been elegantly modernized and extended. Primitive paintings, sculptures, and ancient town manuscripts are on the ground floor; upstairs are examples of the timeless trades and handicrafts of the region, ranging from linen weaving and silk making to basketry, pottery, and ironwork (open from 10 AM to 12:30 PM and from 2 PM to 5:30 PM year-round; closed Mondays; admission charge).

CHECKING IN: *Solar de Alarcão* – Spending a night at this 17th-century manor house, within yards of the cathedral, is a delightful way to experience Guarda. A *Turismo de Habitação* property, it has a covered terrace, a private chapel, and a garden with a belvedere offering views over the Spanish plains. The 3 double bedrooms and suite for 4 people are beautifully decorated with antiques and tapestries. President Mário Soares inaugurated this place as an accommodation for tourists in 1986, when he spent 8 days in the suite during a presidential visit to the town. Contact *Solar de Alarcão,* 25-27 Largo Dom Miguel Alarcão, Guarda (phone: 071-21275). Expensive.

Aliança – Another central *pensão,* almost next door to the *Filipe* (see below), with 31 rooms, all with private bath. The specialties of the restaurant include kid and *cozido à portuguesa,* the national stew made with beef, pork, sausages, cabbage, and potatoes. All major credit cards accepted. 8A Rua Vasco da Gama, Guarda (phone: 071-22135; fax: 071-26451). Moderate.

De Turismo – A sprawling, imposing building with views across the plains, it has 105 rooms and suites, all with private bath, TV sets, and mini-bars. There are 3 bars, a private discotheque, a swimming pool, a sizable conference room, and a garage. The large restaurant serves Portuguese and international food. Major credit cards accepted. Av. Coronel Orlindo de Carvalho, Guarda (phone: 071-22205; in the US, 800-528-1234; fax: 071-22204). Moderate.

Filipe – In the town center, this is a comfortable *pensão* with 40 rooms (not all with private bath) and a restaurant. Major credit cards accepted. 9 Rua Vasco da Gama, Guarda (phone: 071-22658; fax: 071-26402). Moderate.

EATING OUT: *A Mexicana* – Less than a mile (1 km) out of town on the road to Spain, this is a good restaurant whose specialties include *tornedós à mexicana,* or tournedos of beef, *lombinho à Beira Alta,* a pork loin dish, *garoupa com môlho de camarão,* or grouper with shrimp sauce, and shellfish. Open for lunch and dinner daily, except for 2 weeks' annual vacation (variable), and every other Wednesday (market day) at lunch. Reservations unnecessary except for large parties. Visa and MasterCard accepted. Estrada Nacional 16, Guarda (phone: 071-21512). Moderate.

O Telheiro – A bit farther (about a mile/1 km) from the town center on the road to Spain, this large dining room offers panoramic views and good regional cooking, as well as French and Italian dishes. Meals can be served on the terrace in fine weather, or visitors can recover from the winter cold in a bar with deep leather armchairs and a log fire. Open for lunch and dinner daily. Reservations unnecessary. Visa and MasterCard accepted. Estrada Nacional 16, Guarda (phone: 071-21356). Moderate.

Casa Reduto – Good home cooking in a small friendly place in the town center. Specialties include kid and *chouriçada,* based on a variety of homemade sausages. It's open for lunch and dinner daily but sometimes closes for a month in summer. Reservations unnecessary. No credit cards accepted. 36 Rua Francisco de Passos, Guarda (phone: 071-21879). Inexpensive.

En Route from Guarda – Following signs out of Guarda for Viseu will lead the traveler to the modern highway, IP5, that cuts across the northern tip of the Serra da Estrela some 55 miles (88 km) west to Viseu. About halfway there, in the town of Mangualde, just off the highway to the left, is a 17th-century aristocratic estate, the Palácio dos Condes de Anadia, with some fine 17th- and 18th-century *azulejos* (open daily, from 2 to 6 PM, and occasionally also in the morning; admission charge).

VISEU: A fresh-faced country town set among vineyards, orchards, and pine-forested hills, Viseu (pop. 22,000) exudes life and a long, cultured history. Every Tuesday, crowds jostle amid the colorful stalls of the weekly market on the narrow, medieval streets of the old town. In August and September, people from across the Beiras flock to the annual *São Mateus* fair (black pottery, lace, and carpets are among the traditional crafts to look for). And every June 24, a procession of horseback riders and floats from outlying Vil de Moinhos (Village of the Water Mills) winds through town to the chapel of São João de Carreira. According to tradition, the annual procession began in 1652 as a gesture of thanks from the millers of Vil de Moinhos to their patron saint, John the Baptist, after a dispute with local farmers over the use of water from the Paiva River was decided in their favor. Rich corn bread, or *broa,* baked from flour milled in Vil de Moinhos can still be bought in Viseu's market, while the cakes and sweetmeats found in the local cafés — *ovos moles* (soft eggs), *papos de anjo* (angel's cheeks), and *bolos d'amor* (love cakes), made from eggs, almonds, and lots of sugar — come from old convent recipes.

Walk up the hill from the tree-lined main square, Praça da República, or Rossio, through the Porta do Soar, a 15th-century gate that leads into the old town, and turn right to the Adro da Sé (Cathedral Square), the historical heart of Viseu. On the left, strikingly silhouetted against the sky, is the white façade of the Igreja da Misericórdia, a pure baroque church with twin bell towers and a delicate doorway topped by a balcony. Built during the late 18th century, it now holds a magnificent organ. Across the square are the weathered granite towers of the Sé (Cathedral), which dates from the 13th century but was extensively restored between the 16th and 18th centuries. Inside, its graceful vaulting of knotted ropes reflects the seafaring themes of the 16th-century Manueline style, while its gilded wood altarpiece is baroque. The sacristy has 16th-century tiled walls and a wooden ceiling painted with plants and animals; from the Renaissance cloister, a beautiful late Gothic doorway leads back into the church.

The *Museu de Grão Vasco,* perhaps Viseu's greatest treasure, is housed in the former 16th-century Bishop's Palace next door to the cathedral. Grão Vasco — the Great Vasco — is the name given to Vasco Fernandes (1480–ca. 1543), the founder of a notable school of painting that flourished in Viseu during the 16th century. Two of his masterpieces, a *Calvary* and *St. Peter on His Throne,* are on display in the museum, along with a series of 14 panels, originally from the cathedral altarpiece, painted by him and his collaborators. (One of the kings in the *Adoration of the Magi* from this series is represented in the form of an Indian from newly discovered Brazil.) The collection also contains two paintings — *The Last Supper* and *Christ in the House of Martha* — by Gaspar Vaz, another master of the Viseu school. The museum (phone: 032-26249) is open from 9:30 AM to 12:30 PM and 2 to 5:30 PM all year; closed Mondays and some bank holidays; admission charge.

The remains of the enormous trenches of a Roman encampment can be visited in a park in the northern outskirts of town. The camp, known as the Cava de Viriato (Pit of Viriatus), was originally octagonal, but only two sides remain. It was dug for imperial Roman legions during a campaign against the Galicians in 138 BC, and although it was not used by Viriatus, the Serra da Estrela shepherd-warrior who led the Lusitanians against Portugal's Roman invaders, a bronze monument to him and his warriors stands in the park.

CHECKING IN: ***Avenida*** – Comfortable and just off the main square, it has 40 rooms. The restaurant serves regional dishes. 1 Av. Alberto Sampaio, Viseu (phone: 032-423432). Moderate.

Grão Vasco – Set in attractive gardens in the town center, this spacious hostelry has 110 rooms, an outdoor swimming pool, a discotheque, and central heating. The restaurant serves meals on the garden terrace in good weather. Rua Gaspar Barreiros, Viseu (phone: 032-423511; in the US, 800-528-1234; fax: 032-27047). Moderate.

Maná – Less than 2½ miles (4 km) from the center, along N16 to the east, this air conditioned hotel offers television sets, radios, and telephones in its 47 rooms. It also has a restaurant, a garden, a swimming pool, squash courts, an amphitheater seating 1,500, and a car park. Major credit cards accepted. Via Caçador, Viseu (phone: 032-479243; fax: 032-28744). Moderate.

Moinho de Vento – Here there are 30 modern rooms, with television sets, radios, and telephones, near the main square (Rossio). Breakfast is served, but there's no restaurant. 13 Rua Paulo Emílio, Viseu (phone: 032-424116). Moderate.

Quinta do Vale do Chão – This fine 17th-century house, a *Turismo Rural* participant, offers a double bedroom, bathroom, and large living room — and the freedom of the rest of the house. A second double suite without a private bathroom also is available. Children are welcome. It's located 10 miles (16 km) south of Viseu on N231 at Santar, the birthplace of Dom Duarte de Bragança, the man who would be king if Portugal were still a monarchy. The small village has many attractive 18th-century houses. Contact Dona Berta Bebiano Coimbra, *Quinta do Vale do Chão,* Santar, Nelas (phone in Lisbon: 01-765974). Moderate.

EATING OUT: ***O Cortiço*** – An excellent restaurant in the medieval part of town, it serves dishes based on old local recipes, whose details are kept secret. Some of the many specialties include *arroz caqueirado,* a veal-and-rice dish; *coelho bêbado,* made from wine-fed ("drunken") rabbits; and *bacalhau podre,* a tasty dish worthy of a better name than this, which means "rotten codfish"! Open for lunch and dinner daily except *Christmas.* Reservations unnecessary. Major credit cards accepted. 43 Rua Augusto Hilário, Viseu (phone: 032-23853). Moderate.

Trave Negra – Also in the old part of town, it specializes in traditional dishes, including kid and *espetadas* — kebab-style meat or fish on a skewer. Closed Mondays. Reservations advised. Major credit cards accepted. 40 Rua dos Loureiros, Viseu (phone: 032-423853). Moderate.

En Route from Viseu – Take N2 south 15 miles (24 km) through wooded hills to Tondela, then turn right onto N230, following signs for Caramulo, another 12 miles (19 km) away. The N230 highway winds up through the wild pine, oak, and chestnut woods of the Serra do Caramulo, dense with ferns and brambles and interspersed with terraces of olive and other fruit trees and vines.

CARAMULO: This small, well-groomed health resort (pop. 1,500) full of cypress trees and box hedges stands at an altitude of 2,500 feet, basking in crisp air and exhilarating views. The *Museu de Caramulo* (also named after its founder, Abel de Lacerda) features an unexpected mixture of vintage cars and fine art. The automobiles, all in pristine condition, include a 1911 Rolls-Royce, classic 1930s Bugattis, a 1924 Hispano-Suiza, and the suitably sober 1937 armored Mercedes used by António de Oliveira Salazar, Portugal's former dictator. Upstairs, the art collection includes a few lesser-known works by Picasso, Dalí, and Chagall, some fine Portuguese primitives, and 16th-century tapestries. The museum (phone: 032-861270) is open daily from 10 AM to 6 PM; admission charge.

Several imposing panoramas are within easy reach of Caramulo. Drive 5 miles (8 km) west along Avenida Abel de Lacerda, which becomes N230-3, to reach the foot of Caramulinho, the highest peak of the Serra do Caramulo. It's possible to climb a steep, rocky path to the summit, 3,527 feet high, for an impressive view. Returning toward Caramulo, branch right to Cabeço da Neve, a 3,264-foot-high peak with a view south over the villages of the Mondego River Valley. Pinoucas, a 3,481-foot-high peak offering a magnificent panorama over the *serra,* is 2 miles (3 km) north of Caramulo, via N230 and then a dirt road.

CHECKING IN/EATING OUT. ***Pousada de São Jerónimo*** – A modern, government-owned inn with spectacular views from the 6 guestrooms and the dining room. Roaring fires, wooden beams, and an elegant restaurant make this an excellent setting in which to enjoy mountain walks, trout fishing, and seclusion. There also is a badminton court and an outdoor swimming pool. Major credit cards accepted. Estrada Nacional 230, Caramulo (phone: 032-861291; in the US, 212-686-9213). Expensive.

En Route from Caramulo – Follow N230 back toward Tondela and turn right onto N2. Santa Comba Dão, a pretty village where the Dão flows into the Mondego, is 10 miles (16 km) farther south. It is best known as Salazar's birthplace, but no statue remains of the dictator, and his abandoned family house has fallen into disrepair. Turn right at Santa Comba Dão onto N234, passing the lovely village of Mortágua on the 16-mile (26-km) journey to the Mata do Buçaco — the ancient forest of Buçaco — and the famed spa of Luso.

BUÇACO: A secluded forest that was tended by monks for more than 1,000 years, the stirring history of a decisive battle, and a romantic summer palace built by a king are all woven into the magic of Buçaco (Bussaco in English), a 2-square-mile national park atop the northernmost peak of the Serra do Buçaco. Benedictine monks first built a refuge in the primitive forest during the 6th century, and priests from Coimbra cared for the woodland from the 11th to the early 17th century. In 1628, barefoot Carmelite monks began erecting a monastery, ringing the forest with a wall to keep the outside world at bay. The monks carefully tended their domain, adding maples, laurels, Mexican cedars, and many exotic varieties from seeds gathered by their missions around the globe. Earlier, in 1622, a papal bull banned women from the forest, and in 1643, a second bull prohibited damage to the trees — punishment for either offense was excommunication. (Inscriptions bearing the texts of the bulls can be seen on the walls of the Portas de Coimbra, one of the seven gates in the ancient walls.) Even after religious orders were suppressed in Portugal in 1834 and the care of Buçaco passed to the state, the forest has continued to grow — there are now some 400 native tree varieties and 300 exotic ones, from eucalyptus and oaks to sequoias and evergreen thujas.

In 1888, King Carlos commissioned Luigi Manini, an Italian architect and a set painter at the São Carlos opera house in Lisbon, to build a summer palace and hunting lodge in the midst of the forest. Much of the Carmelite monastery, including the library, was demolished to make way for it, leaving only a small church and a cloister. The building that emerged is a marvelously extravagant pastiche of the Manueline style, with pinnacles, battlements, towers, arched windows, and a magnificent gallery of 12 double arches in the style of the cloister at the Jerónimos monastery in Lisbon. Panels of *azulejos* by renowned Portuguese artists depict scenes from the 16th-century epic *Os Lusíadas,* by Portugal's national poet Luís de Camões, on the outside walls and famous battle scenes in the interior. The palace was completed in 1907, but King Carlos, who was assassinated in 1908, never occupied it, although his son and successor, King Manuel II, stayed in Buçaco in 1910 — reputedly with a mistress — before seeking exile in England. The palace then became a hotel (see *Checking In*), which is well worth a visit as a charming monument in its own right.

Buçaco was the scene of a decisive battle of the Peninsular War, when in 1810 the British general Sir Arthur Wellesley, the future Duke of Wellington, commanding 50,000 Portuguese and British troops, faced the third invasion of Napoleon's army from Spain. As the French, led by Marshal André Masséna, advanced westward via Viseu, Wellesley concealed his troops along the ridge at Buçaco, spending the eve of the battle in one of the cork-lined monks' cells. (The olive tree where the general is said to have tethered his horse can still be seen.) The French attacked through thick mist on the morning of September 27 and were repulsed during 2 hours of artillery fire, cavalry charges, and bayonet fighting. They lost 4,600 men, while the British and Portuguese lost only 626. Although Masséna's army later captured Coimbra, the French defeat at Buçaco prepared the way for the end of the war. Processions on the anniversary of the battle are still held today.

A walk anywhere in Buçaco is enjoyable, particularly if crowded weekends and holidays are avoided. Among the loveliest features is the Fonte Fria (Cold Fountain), where waters that spring from a cave cascade down 144 stone steps into a pool. The path from here leads past a small lake to the Rua dos Fetos (Fern Lane), a 250-yard pathway lined with tall cypresses. The Via Sacra, or Way of the Cross, is a series of 20 small 18th-century chapels in which scenes leading up to the Crucifixion are depicted by terra cotta figures (fashioned in 1938 — sadly, many of them have since been damaged). A few hundred yards outside the Portas de Sula, at the park's southeastern corner, an obelisk topped by a glass star commemorates the Battle of Buçaco and other engagements of the Luso-Britannic campaigns, and offers magnificent views of the Estrela and Caramulo *serras.* Down the hill toward the Portas da Rainha is the interesting *Museu Militar do Buçaco* (phone: 031-93310), a military museum featuring maps, weapons, uniforms, and models from the battle and related campaigns (open Tuesdays through Saturdays from 9 AM to 5:30 PM; Sundays and holidays from 10 AM to 5 PM; closed Mondays; the museum keeper, who lives next door, will open the museum to after-hours visitors; admission charge). One of the trees in Buçaco is an olive tree, the symbol of peace, planted by Wellington after the heavy fighting that led to his victory.

CHECKING IN/EATING OUT: ***Palace Hotel do Buçaco*** – Now one of the finest hotels in Portugal, it really was built by a king as his summer palace, and it immerses present-day guests in an atmosphere of turn-of-the-century romance and royal luxury. Many of the 68 sumptuous rooms open onto broad terraces, from which guests can watch the stars over the deep green forest. Fine international cooking and local dishes are served under a vaulted, Renaissance-style cupola in good weather, with wine from the hotel's famed cellars, which guests can visit on request. The elegant period charm of the palace and its wonderful setting make it one of the most pleasurable places to stay in the entire country. Major credit cards accepted. Mata do Buçaco, Buçaco (phone: 031-93101; Lisbon reservations: 01-7931024; fax: 031-93609). Very expensive.

LUSO: This attractive, bustling spa town of 2,700 on the northwest slope of the Serra do Buçaco is only 2 miles (3 km) from the gate at the northern tip of Buçaco National Park. It's famed for the curative properties of its waters, which rise at a temperature of 80F from a spring in the town center. One of the country's most famous mineral waters, bottled Luso is sold all over Portugal. Here, a pavilion given over to physiotherapy has a heated swimming pool, gyms, mud baths, and other specialized installations, where treatment is given under medical supervision. But Luso is a relaxing and enjoyable place to visit even for those not "taking the waters," and it's a less expensive base for visiting Buçaco than the *Palace* hotel. The town has a splendid outdoor swimming pool and visitors can row on a lake, play tennis, or jog around a special circuit; in addition, there's a cinema, nightclub, and discotheque, as well as several hotels and small pensions.

CHECKING IN: ***Eden*** – Modern, with 57 rooms next to the Fonte de São João, the spring from which the spa waters rise. There are TV sets in every room, a restaurant, and a disco. Rua Emídio Navarro, Luso (phone: 031-930191). Moderate.

Grande Hotel das Termas – Large and comfortable, it adjoins the thermal baths and is run by the same company that operates them. It offers 173 rooms, a restaurant, indoor and outdoor swimming pools, tennis, squash, miniature golf, and a disco. Some rooms have satellite television sets. Rua dos Banhos, Luso (phone: 031-93450; fax: 031-93668). Moderate.

Vila Duparchy – On a hill above Luso, this large 19th-century house was built by a French engineer engaged in the construction of the Beiras railroad. A *Turismo de Habitação* participant, it has 6 comfortable bedrooms with modern bathrooms, central heating, 4 living rooms, and a dining room. There is a swimming pool in the spacious garden, which offers a view over the town. Contact *Vila Duparchy,* Estrada Nacional 234, Luso (phone: 031-930120). Moderate.

Alegre – This *pensão* of 21 rooms, all with baths, is a former noble's house and offers a splendid view over the town. It has a good restaurant. No credit cards accepted. Rua Emídio Navarro, Luso (phone: 031-93251). Inexpensive.

Astória – A pleasant 12-room *pensão,* with an English country touch. The amenities include a pub and a restaurant, which closes from November to March. Major credit cards accepted. Rua Emídio Navarro, Luso (phone: 031-93182). Inexpensive.

EATING OUT: ***O Cesteiro*** **–** This modern eatery offers regional cooking including *chanfana,* kid cooked with red wine, and *leitão,* roast suckling pig — one of the delicacies of this part of the Beiras. Open for lunch and dinner daily. Reservations unnecessary. No credit cards accepted. Rua José Duarte Figueredo, Luso (phone: 031-92360). Inexpensive.

En Route from Luso – Drive west 4½ miles (7 km) along N234, a mountain road, past Mealhada to join the main N1, which leads south another 13 miles (21 km) to Coimbra or north 60½ miles (97 km) to Porto. Alternatively, return to Coimbra via the smaller N336. Remember to always drive cautiously and be patient on Portuguese roads, where passing is often difficult and inadvisable.

Central Portugal

The Tagus River is Portugal's Mason-Dixon Line. For the sake of convenience, everything above it is lumped together as "The North" and everything below it as "The South." The division, though a fairly sweeping generalization, is remarkably valid. Crossing Portugal's biggest river heading south is indeed like crossing a frontier of some kind. In the space of a few miles the granite of the Beiras fades and a radically different landscape takes its place: terra cotta in color, brilliantly lit, studded with olive, cork, and holm oak trees — unmistakably the landscape of southern Europe. The transformation from North into South is so total, it is as if the curtain had gone up on another set.

The two Portuguese provinces where this intriguing transformation occurs are the Ribatejo and its eastern neighbor, the Alto, or Upper, Alentejo. The latter is the northern half of a region that is not only by far the largest in the country, but also the least densely populated, the hottest, and the driest. It also produces more cork than anywhere else in the world and has what must be the most readily recognized landscape in Portugal. Apart from the São Mamede range in the northeast, reaching up to 3,382 feet high, and the Ossa range near Evora, with peaks up to 2,154 feet, there are few outcrops in the Alentejo high enough or rocky enough to be called mountains. The whole region unfolds southward from the Tagus River to the Algarve in a practically unbroken succession of low, rolling hills, bright with wildflowers in the spring, ocher in summer. Providing the car's suspension is youthful enough to handle the sometimes rough roads, it is good driving country — the landscape uncluttered, the roads relatively uncrowded, and the little white towns a constant lure on the horizon.

Even though the existence of the Ribatejo has been a geographic and historical fact since medieval times, cartographers have always had trouble drawing its exact limits. That technicality aside, near the town of Santarém the Tagus spreads out and threads through wide alluvial flats before finally flowing into the estuary above Lisbon. This is the quintessential Ribatejo — lonely expanses of grassland where egrets and other wild fowl congregate and where horsemen with long wooden lances herd black fighting bulls. The area has an almost mystical appeal for romantics and aficionados of Portuguese bullfighting and the equestrian arts, but it also has a more prosaic side, as Lisbon's breadbasket and kitchen garden. When the Tagus overflows its banks in winter, the low-lying parts are afflicted by heavy flooding, but the big riverside fields, the *lezirias,* produce large quantities of grain and vegetables when they are not under water, and vineyards in the drier zones away from the river produce much of the country's staple table wine.

Both the Alentejo and the Ribatejo are legendary places: lands of giants, heroic deeds, battles, and chivalry. Very few towns are without a castle or some other reminder of Portugal's long history, and in places the traces of occupation reach back to the Stone Age. During the Iron Age, various Indo-European tribes, probably mostly Celts, drifted across the *mesetas* from Spain, some of them — the ones who were later to become known as Lusitanians — settling the highlands north of the Tagus and elbowing their way into a position of dominance over the whole of the central region. When the Romans turned up during the 2nd century BC, these hillsmen put up fierce resistance under the leadership of Portugal's first truly national hero, the Lusitanian chieftain Viriatus. His death in 139 BC opened the way for the Roman troops and marked the beginning of an occupation of the Ribatejo and Alentejo that lasted some 400 years.

Towns grew up along the Roman roads that crossed the Alentejo plain from Emerita Augusta (Mérida) in Spain and led northward through the Ribatejo. Several of these, notably Ebora (now Evora) and Scallabis (presumed to have been near Santarém, but now lost), were of considerable provincial importance. Archaeological remains from the Roman period are fragmentary but widespread, and most local museums have a collection of Roman pieces.

The Roman period was followed by centuries of invasion and settlement by tribes from northern Europe and ultimately by the Visigoths, who ruled until the arrival of the Moors during the 8th century. Little is left of the Visigothic presence, apart from architectural traces in fortifications, but the influence of their Muslim successors, while almost as fugitive in terms of architecture, was more pervasive, and it is detectable today in such things as place-names (many that begin with "al" are Moorish in origin), language, and local tradition.

Moorish dominance lasted until nearly the end of the 12th century. By that time, the Muslims had become weakened by internal power struggles and by frequent raids from the Christian-held north. In 1139, Portugal's first king, Afonso Henriques, won a decisive victory at Oric, which may or may not have been the present-day Chã de Ourique, near Santarém; later, he took Santarém itself and, in 1159, the Muslim strongholds of Evora and Beja. By 1190, the area was in Christian hands, its defense largely entrusted to military orders — the Knights Templars in the Ribatejo and the Knights of Avis in the Alentejo — and the Portuguese turned their attention toward their Spanish neighbors. Both the Ribatejo and the Alentejo lay in the path of any army bent on Lisbon, so fortifications became a major preoccupation. One of the legendary figures of the new nation, King Dinis, who ruled from 1279 to 1325, was prodigious in this respect: He had a hand in building most of the castles encountered along this route.

Marching armies remained a familiar sight until well into the 19th century, as the Spaniards, the French, the British, and, of course, the Portuguese themselves played out their martial chess games with strategically placed Lisbon as the prize. But less bellicose pursuits also managed to flourish, and towns such as Evora, Santarém, and Tomar grew into centers of learning and the arts.

Throughout the military maneuvering, the Alentejo retained the distinctive social structure it had acquired from the Romans and the Moors. North of the Tagus, inheritance laws and custom turned the countryside into a mosaic of tiny properties. The Alentejo is the land of the *latifúndio:* the big landed estate where workers are hired (and fired) seasonally and conditions are sometimes close to feudal. Dispossession of the religious orders and royalty during the 19th-century growth of liberalism merely caused the properties to change hands, but a somewhat successful attempt to change the system was made after the April 25 revolution in 1974. Nearly 3 million acres were confiscated in an agrarian reform program, and many of the big estates were turned into collective farms.

However, don't let this whiff of revolution — tenuous now, in any case — be a deterrent. The people here are as hospitable as any in this hospitable country, and they welcome foreign visitors — for example, at local fairs and festivals, of which there are many. They are skilled in crafts such as pottery, iron working, and weaving, turning out a number of attractive handmade products. Among these, two that have attained international renown and become correspondingly costly are carpets from Arraiolos and woven tapestries from Portalegre, but there are many other hand-crafted articles to buy that carry more modest price tags.

The route outlined below, beginning at Lisbon, follows the Tagus up through the Ribatejo, passing through two towns of great touristic interest: Santarém and Tomar. It then turns inland in the direction of the Spanish border, crossing into the Upper Alentejo. At the spa town of Castelo de Vide, it turns south into the heart of the region, visiting Portalegre, Estremoz, and Evora, one of the most picturesque old cities in Portugal. The return to Lisbon begins as the route proceeds due west from Evora to Setúbal and the Arrábida Peninsula, which actually fall within the boundaries of a third region, Estremadura, although its cultural and geographic affinity with the Alentejo is so close that travelers will hardly note a difference. After a Setúbal-to-Sesimbra-to-Palmela loop around the peninsula, the route heads back to Lisbon via the A2, crossing the Tagus into the city by the impressive suspension bridge.

Apart from two stretches of toll highway, the route follows the regular main highway system, and the roads are good, with two lanes in either direction. Leave the highway to take one of the secondary roads, however, and be prepared for rougher conditions. Even on main roads, in addition to such rustic hazards as slow-moving tractors, herds of animals, and horse-drawn carts, watch out for locals rattling along at night on little motorcycles. Quite often they don't bother about lights — particularly tail-lights. Last, try to avoid approaching Lisbon from the south on a Saturday or Sunday evening in summer. That is precisely when everybody else will be trying to get back after a day at the beach, and the lineup before the bridge sometimes stretches for miles.

Standard international cooking is usually served in the hotels and better restaurants on this itinerary — probably just as well for weight watchers, as the regional cooking is on the heavy side. Meat dishes such as the typical *ensopado de cabrito* or *ensopado de borrego,* kid or lamb stew, are more prevalent than fish dishes in these inland areas, although the rare and pricey *lampréia* (lamprey eel) and *sável,* a river shad, are Ribatejo delicacies. Even in the dry Alentejo, *bacalhau* (dried salt cod) dishes are popular, and one of the Alentejo's better-known dishes is *carne de porco à alentejana,* a mixture of clams and pork. A superb ewes' milk cheese is made at Serpa, in the Alentejo, and another at Azeitão on the Arrábida Peninsula. Both are becoming regrettably hard to find, but they are worth the search — try them with fresh bread cut from one of the huge, crusty *alentejano* loaves and some of the strong-bodied wine made in the Reguengos or Borba areas.

As predominantly agricultural regions, neither the Ribatejo nor the Alentejo has a highly developed tourist industry. This means that their paths are still relatively untrodden; but it also makes advance planning advisable, because good hotels are not plentiful. That said, it must be added that some of the most interesting accommodations in Portugal are to be found precisely along this route. Expect to pay from $100 to $150 for a double room with bath in hotels listed below as expensive, such as the *pousadas* in Estremoz, Setúbal, and Palmela; from $60 to $100 in hotels listed as moderate; and less than $60 in the inexpensive ones. Dinner for two with wine and coffee will cost $70 and up in one of the few expensive restaurants listed, from $45 to $60 in the more common regional type listed as moderate, and less than $40 in the inexpensive ones.

En Route from Lisbon – Pick up the A1 toll highway on the northern outskirts of town, just past the airport (from downtown, follow signs for the *aeroporto* and the city of Porto). The exit for Santarém, the first major sightseeing stop on this route, is at Km 65. However, if you don't feel like an extended amount of uninterrupted motorway driving, an attractive alternative is to drive to Santarém on EN118 on the other side of the river. EN118 is a secondary road, but provides a closer look at the Ribatejo region than does the A1. Instead of continuing on A1, turn off at the Vila Franca de Xira exit (follow signs for *Espanha* — Spain), drive across the bridge, and turn onto EN118 6 miles (10 km) down the road at Porto Alto. The road passes through typical Ribatejo wine and cattle country all the way to Almeirim, where you cross the river again into Santarém. Several of the little towns along the way are worth stopping in, perhaps to sample some of the full-bodied red cartaxo wines from this region, found at their simple best in the local tavern, or stop just for a stroll. The whole area was once a preserve of royalty and the Lisbon aristocracy. At Salvaterra de Magos, for instance, there are the remnants of the once famed palace of the Bragança dynasty. At the height of its glory in the 17th and 18th centuries, the palace boasted its own opera house. Today, all that remains are the Capela Royal (Royal Chapel) and an interesting *falcoaria* (falcon house) with perches for over 300 hawks; both are worth seeing.

SANTARÉM: The administrative capital of the Ribatejo and an important market town, Santarém hosts one of Europe's leading agricultural fairs, the *Feira Nacional de Agricultura* (10 days in June, beginning the first Friday of the month), which is accompanied by bullfights and other festivities, and the *Festival Nacional de Gastronomia,* a national culinary and handicrafts fair held every November. The city is assumed to stand on or close to the site of the Roman city of Scallabis, an important provincial capital in ancient times that has since disappeared without leaving a physical trace. Its present name comes from Santa Iria (St. Irene), a 7th-century nun who was martyred in Tomar — according to tradition, her body was thrown into the river and washed ashore here. A statue of the saint stands in a riverside shrine on the edge of town, and it is said that if the river ever rises to touch her feet, the final deluge will have come. Winter flooding is a common scourge here and may even have accounted for the disappearance of Scallabis.

Santarém was conquered by the Moors during the 8th century and reconquered by Portugal's first king, Afonso Henriques, during the 12th century. After that, it grew into a town of considerable strategic importance. King Dinis died here in 1325, and it was here, in 1360, that King Pedro I staged the final act in one of history's great tragic love stories by exacting bloodthirsty revenge on the murderers of his former mistress, Inês de Castro. Several monarchs held court in the city at one time or another, a fact that contributed to its architectural heritage.

In the oldest part of the city, which was once walled and fortified, is the 14th-century Graça church. It has an ornate Portuguese Gothic doorway, but its outstanding feature is a superb rose window above the door, with tracery carved out of a single piece of stone — possibly the finest example of this work in Portugal. Inside is a plain tomb said to hold the remains of the discoverer of Brazil, Pedro Alvares de Cabral. The charming little 13th-century Church of São João de Alporão nearby functions as a somewhat disorganized *Museu Arqueológico* (open from 9 AM to noon and from 2 to 5 PM; closed Mondays; no admission charge). Its collection includes several Roman pieces, Moorish architectural fragments, and, notably, the beautiful Gothic tomb of Dom Duarte de Meneses, a knight who died in battle against the Moors in 1465. The tomb contains just one tooth — all that could be found after the ferocious contest. The church's original Romanesque bell tower was knocked down to make way for the royal coach of Queen Maria during a visit in 1815, but standing opposite is another tower, the 15th-century Torre das Cabaças, so called because of the gourd-shaped pots (*cabaças*) placed around the bell on top to give it greater resonance.

A short distance beyond is the little tree-lined Avenida 5 de Outubro, which leads to an ornamental garden, Portas do Sol, set within the old castle walls. From here, there are panoramic views of the Ribatejo countryside, with the Tagus River and the 4,000-foot-long 19th-century Dom Luís Bridge in the foreground. On the way back to the center, stop in at the Igreja da Marvila, founded by the Knights Templars during the 12th century after Afonso Henriques retook the city from the Moors. This church has a wonderfully ornate Portuguese Gothic porch and, inside, three lofty aisles covered with fine 16th-century *azulejos.* Two more churches, Santa Clara and Santa Cruz, can be seen as the road winds down to the river on the way out of Santarém. Santa Clara, its interior stripped down to its 13th-century bones, is a fine example of early Gothic, with another superb rose window. The early Gothic doorway of Santa Cruz, also founded during the 13th century (by King Dinis), was uncovered during restoration work in the 1960s.

EATING OUT: ***Pateo d'Al-Meirim*** **–** This restaurant, in an old Ribatejo house on the outskirts of the town of Almeirim, 4½ miles (7 km) southeast of Santarém, is famed for its *borrego assado no forno de lenha* (lamb roasted in a wood oven), but it's also the place to try any of the regional specialties. Closed Mondays. Reservations advised. Major credit cards accepted. 10 Rua das Cancelas, Almeirim (phone: 043-52836). Moderate.

Castiço **–** A popular regional-style restaurant at the cattle fairground on the outskirts of Santarém. The decor is heavily rustic — the chairs are tree trunks — but the food is good. Try the *caldeiradas* (fish stews) and the grilled steaks. Closed Sundays. Reservations advised. No credit cards accepted. Campo da Feira, Santarém (phone: 043-23891). Inexpensive.

O Mal Cozinhado **–** One of Santarém's most popular eateries, and the one with perhaps the strongest regional flavor. It has wooden walls, bullfight posters, a bull's head over the bar, and a husband-and-wife team running a kitchen that produces some of the best dishes in town, including *lombinho com coentros* (pork tenderloin with coriander) and *magosto de bacalhau,* the house codfish dish. Open daily. No reservations. Major credit cards accepted. Campo da Feira, Santarém (phone: 043-23584). Inexpensive.

Portas do Sol **–** Unpretentious but good regional cooking is served in this small place, which has an outdoor terrace for summer dining. It's inside the Portas do Sol garden, so the surroundings and view are attractive. Closed Mondays. Reservations advised. No credit cards accepted. Jardim das Portas do Sol, Santarém (phone: 043-29520). Inexpensive.

Toucinho – A favorite of Ribatejo cooking fans in search of authenticity rather than comfort. Helia, the owner, presides over her open country kitchen and the brick oven where the restaurant's famed bread is baked. Try the various grills or the local specialty, *sopa de pedra* — stone soup, literally — a soup made of beans and a variety of meats and vegetables, and served with a small stone in the bowl. (It doesn't taste the same without it, they say.) Closed Wednesdays and the month of August. No reservations. No credit cards accepted. Rua Macau, Almeirim (phone: 043-52237). Inexpensive.

En Route from Santarém – Those who haven't already driven over to Almeirim should take N114 across the Dom Luís Bridge and, about 1¼ miles (2 km) beyond it, turn left onto N368 for Alpiarça. (Those already in Almeirim should take N118 to Alpiarça.) Both Almeirim and Alpiarça are little towns that have been favorite country haunts of Portuguese royalty at one time or another — an abundance of game and excellent wines were the attractions. In Alpiarça, stop at the *Casa dos Patudos,* on the left side of the road as you enter the town. This was once the country residence of José Relvas, a prominent political figure and patron of the arts at the beginning of the century. When he died in 1929, he left his house and his sizable art collection to the town as a museum. The Oriental rugs, porcelains, and tiles are outstanding (open Wednesdays through Sundays from 10 AM to 12:30 PM and 2 PM to 5 PM; admission charge; phone: 043-54516). After the visit, take N118 north 11 miles (18 km) to Chamusca, which is worth a stop, then continue north about 2½ miles (4 km) and take N243 across the river — those with an eye for engineering will like the iron bridge the French built in 1905 — another 3 miles (5 km) into Golegã.

CHAMUSCA: Scarcely anything remains from medieval times, when Chamusca was an important port on the busy thoroughfare of the Tagus, but the town still has a few sights to see, and the old part, with its typical Ribatejo houses, is a pleasant place to stroll. Those who appreciate early Portuguese tiles should not miss the 17th-century interior of the parish church of São Brás or the charming little church of Nossa Senhora do Pranto, from which there is also a magnificent view of the surrounding countryside. The *Casa Rural Tradicional,* a museum (Largo 25 do Abril; no admission charge), is an interesting reconstruction of a typical Ribatejo farmhouse of 50 years ago, with some fine pieces of rustic furniture and other household items. (To visit, ask for the keys at the tourist office, on the same square.)

GOLEGÃ: For the first 2 weeks of November each year, when one of Europe's most important horse fairs, the *Feira Nacional do Cavalo* (also known as the *Feira de São Martinho*), takes place here, this town becomes horse lovers' heaven. The event attracts breeders and dealers from all over the world, principally because of the high-stepping Lusitanian and Andalusian breeds for which the Ribatejo is famous. (If you happen to come here during the fair, be prepared for jam-packed, narrow streets; it's advisable to leave your car on the outskirts of town.) At other times of the year, the main attraction is the Igreja Matriz (Parish Church), toward the center of town on the road from Chamusca. Founded by King Manuel I during the 16th century, the church has a magnificent doorway in the Manueline style (the Gothic-to-Renaissance transitional style named after the king himself). In front of it stands the town's *pelourinho,* or pillory (in the old days, both a symbol of municipal power and a whipping post). A block away, off Largo Dom Manuel I, is the *Museu Municipal de Fotografia Carlos Relvas,* which is well worth a visit even for those who are not photography buffs. Carlos Relvas, the father of José Relvas (responsible for the *Casa dos Patudos* in Alpiarça), was a wealthy landowner, art collector, and statesman, as well as a passionate amateur photographer, and his studio and splendid Victorian house have been preserved as a museum (open from 11 AM to 12:30 PM and from 2:30 to 6 PM; closed Mondays; admission charge).

EATING OUT: ***Central*** – This restaurant is in the restored house of one of Portugal's best-known bullfighters, Manuel dos Santos. No great flights of fancy, but the regional fare is good, including the specialty, *açorda de sável,* a sort of "dry" shad soup in which the river fish is mixed with bread and other ingredients. Open daily. Reservations advised. No credit cards accepted. Largo da Imaculada Conceição, Golegã (phone: 049-94345). Inexpensive.

En Route from Golegã – Take N365 north to the junction with N3, 4½ miles (7 km) away, then turn onto N110, following signs for Tomar, 12 miles (19 km) from the crossing. About 1¼ miles (2 km) along, the road passes the church of Nossa Senhora da Assunção (Our Lady of the Assumption) in Atalaia. The church is an interesting example of Renaissance architecture, with an impressive portal at the center of a very imposing but oddly shaped façade; its most beautiful feature, though, is the yellow-and-blue-tiled interior — a must-see for tile fans. Another 4 miles (6 km) along, off the road to the right, is the village of Asseiceira, the center of a once-important earthenware pottery industry. Though the use of these traditional pots has declined, some of the family potteries are still in business after 200 years or more. Asseiceira is also known for its cast-metal cowbells, *chocalhos,* considered by some collectors to be the best in the country.

TOMAR: Founded during the early 12th century on the Nabão River, near the site of a Roman town and a later Visigothic and Moorish settlement, Tomar is intimately linked with what is often termed the heroic period in Portuguese history — encompassing the founding of the nation during the 12th century, the Christian Reconquest, and then the great maritime expansion of the 15th century. The first sight to see is the Convento de Cristo (Convent of Christ), the extraordinary convent-castle of the two military orders that made Tomar their headquarters. Begun by the Knights Templars on a hilltop overlooking the town during the 12th century, it was continued by the Knights of Christ, who replaced the disbanded Templars during the 14th century, and was finished only during the 17th century. The Templars had been entrusted with the defense of the Tagus Valley after the recapture of Lisbon from the Moors in 1147, and they used their crusaders' knowledge of the military architecture of the Holy Land to build a state-of-the-art castle, with double walls protecting a towering keep. The design proved its value in 1190, when Moors attacking the castle breached the south gate, only to be trapped between the two lines of defense and massacred. To commemorate the carnage, the gate became known as the Porta do Sangue (Gate of Blood).

Besides the fortifications, the Charola — a circular oratory, or temple, modeled after the Holy Sepulcher in Jerusalem — is also part of the convent's 12th-century nucleus (the painted decorations and figures in it are from a later period, however). From the outside, this too looks fortress-like, and it is said that when the knights were at prayer, they would leave their horses standing behind them in the passage surrounding the altar. The early-16th-century Manueline nave attached to the oratory is one of many additions to the original convent. Its exterior is decorated with splendidly ornate tracery full of allusions to Portugal's seafaring past — not surprising, since the Convento de Cristo had been closely linked to the epic voyages of the 15th century, and the square cross that Prince Henry the Navigator's caravels bore on their sails was in fact the emblem of the Order of Christ, of which Prince Henry himself was a Grand

Master. Among other buildings, the labyrinthine complex contains seven cloisters, including a magnificent mid-16th-century Palladian structure, the Claustro dos Filipes (Cloister of the Philips), in which King Philip II of Spain is supposed to have been proclaimed King Philip I of Portugal. The convent was sacked and pillaged by the French during the 19th-century Peninsular War, but just for the buildings alone it remains one of Europe's great historical sites (open daily from 9:30 AM to 12:30 PM and from 2 to 6 PM, 5 PM in winter; admission charge).

Also to be seen in Tomar is the little church of Nossa Senhora da Conceição, perhaps the best example of early Renaissance architecture in Portugal. It's on the way down the hill from the convent, but arrange the visit with the tourist office in town (address and phone below), because the church has been stripped practically bare by thieves and is now kept locked. In the Old Town between the foot of the hill and the river is the country's oldest surviving synagogue (open from 9:30 AM to 12:30 PM and from 2 to 6 PM, 5 PM in winter; closed Wednesdays; 73 Rua Dr. Joaquim Jacinto). Built during the 15th century and square in plan like a mosque, it was probably used only briefly before the Inquisition was introduced into Portugal — by a monk named Baltazar de Faria, who happens to be entombed in one of the cloisters in the convent.

Just across the river is the lovely and historic Santa Maria do Olival (St. Mary of the Olive Grove), once the mother church for all of Portugal's churches overseas. Historians date it to the mid-13th century, but popular tradition holds that it was founded a century earlier by the celebrated Grand Master of Portuguese Templars, Gualdim Pais, whose bones are interred here along with those of other Templar worthies. Restoration has ruthlessly stripped away the decorative accretion of centuries, but two little stone images of the Virgin and some very pretty tiles relieve the starkness inside. Another church worth a visit is São João Baptista, the parish church that dominates the main square in the center of town, Praça da República, with its imposing bell tower and Manueline doorway. The pulpit in the central nave is a masterpiece of Gothic stone carving.

Near the weir in the town's riverside gardens is a huge waterwheel, of the sort once used for irrigation purposes in the Tomar region. Another water-related sight, the Aqueduto dos Pegões, built between 1593 and 1616 to bring water to the convent, is about 3 miles (5 km) out of town (almost 2 miles — 3 km — on the N113 in the direction of Fátima and Leiria, then left onto the road for Pegões). Over 3 miles long, with 180 arches, the structure was a remarkable piece of engineering for its time and is impressive even now. It is also fairly close to one of Tomar's best restaurants, *Chico Elias* (see *Eating Out*), so a visit to both can be combined.

One of Portugal's most spectacular traditional festivals, the *Festa dos Tabuleiros,* takes place in Tomar. During the festivities, which were probably pagan in origin but later became associated with the alms-giving activities of the saintly Queen Isabel, young girls in white parade through the streets, balancing on their heads enormous crown-like contraptions, the *tabuleiros,* made of loaves of bread interwoven with flowers. The celebration takes place 50 days after *Easter,* but it is not a regular event (at one time it was held more or less biennially), so it should be confirmed first at the tourist office, on Avenida Dr. Cândido Madureira (phone: 049-313237).

CHECKING IN: *Ilha do Lombo* – This exceptionally pretty *estalagem,* or inn, is located about 10 miles (16 km) east of Tomar, on an island in the reservoir upstream from the Castelo de Bode dam (Portugal's biggest dam). There are 17 rooms with tiled terraces looking onto the water. There is also an outdoor pool, and boating and fishing are available. To reach the inn, take N110 north for about half a mile (1 km), then turn right onto the road to Serra and Barreira for the remaining 9½ miles (15 km). The road is narrow and poorly paved, but it winds through pleasant scenery; from Barreira, a small, closed cabin boat called the *Zêzere* ferries guests out to the island — about a 5-minute trip. Bookings for the summer should be made at least 2 months in advance. Ilha do Lombo, Serra de Tomar (phone: 049-371128). Moderate.

Lago Azul – Handsome and modern, this *estalagem* boasts 20 air conditioned rooms with telephones, radios, and panoramic views of the Zêzere River. The management also runs *Templários* (see below). The restaurant focuses on regional fare; when it's in season, order the *lampréia* (eel). Major credit cards accepted. Located 12½ miles (20 km) northeast of Tomar in Lago Azul, Ferreira do Zêzere (phone: 049-361445). Moderate.

Pousada de São Pedro – A quiet and comfortable government-run inn, with genuine antique furnishings and old prints on the walls, it has 8 rooms in the main building and another 7 in an annex. The picture window in the air conditioned restaurant looks out onto the dam. Major credit cards accepted. On the Zêzere River, right beside the Castelo de Bode dam, 8 miles (13 km) southeast of Tomar. Take N110 south for 4½ miles (7 km), then turn left onto N358. Castelo de Bode (phone: 049-381159; in the US, 212-686-9213). Moderate.

Santa Iria – This recently opened riverside *estalagem* (inn) successfully combines rustic charm with modern amenities like air conditioning, TV sets, and tennis facilities. The restaurant serves good regional dishes and wines. There are 13 rooms, plus 1 elegant suite. Right in the center of town, in delightful Mouchão Park. Major credit cards accepted. Parque do Mouchão, Tomar (phone: 049-313326; fax: 049-321082). Moderate.

Templários – A regional favorite combining modern comforts with small-town tranquillity, it's set in a pleasant garden by the river and has 84 rooms, an excellent restaurant, an outdoor pool, and tennis courts. From the balconies of many of the upper rooms, guests can look across to the convent on the hill. Major credit cards accepted. 1 Largo Cândido dos Reis, Tomar (phone: 049-321730; fax: 049-322191). Moderate.

Trovador – The best of Tomar's economical hostelries, it's modern, clean, and located in the newer part of town, near the bus station. The 30 rooms all have private baths and TV sets. No restaurant, but there is a breakfast room and a small bar that's open at night. Rua Dr. Joaquim Ribeiro, Tomar (phone: 049-311567; fax: 049-316194). Inexpensive.

EATING OUT: ***Bela Vista*** – One of the oldest restaurants in Tomar and regarded as the most traditional in culinary terms. The combination of old-fashioned decor and good home cooking — including *cabrito no forno* (roast kid) and *caldeirada* (a stew prepared with different kinds of fish) — plus a nice riverside location have turned it into an obligatory port of call. Closed Mondays at lunch and all day Tuesdays. Reservations advised. No credit cards accepted. 6 Fonte do Choupo, Tomar (phone: 049-312870). Moderate.

Chez Nous – It has a French bias, but it's also noted for excellent local fare — *bacalhau com natas* (dried cod with a cream sauce), for example. In the old part of town, with an agreeably cozy ambience, it's a popular place and seats only 30, so reserve before going. Closed Saturdays. Reservations advised. Major credit cards accepted. 31 Rua Dr. Joaquim Jacinto, Tomar (phone: 049-314743). Moderate.

Chico Elias – This stands apart among the handful of top restaurants in Tomar not only because of its food, but also because it cooks only to order. Phone first and tell them what you want to eat. Among the choices — prepared by Dona Ceu, wife of the owner — are *coelho na abóbora* (rabbit served in a pumpkin), *bacalhau assado com carne de porco* (dried cod baked with pork), *couves a Dom Prior* (a spicy cabbage dish), and *leite creme* (a creamy milk-based dessert that Dona Ceu is reputed to make better than anyone else). The decor is not entirely successful pseudo-rustic, but the food makes up for it. Closed Tuesdays. Reservations essential. No credit cards accepted. The restaurant is in a small village about 1¼ miles (2 km) beyond Tomar. Estrada de Torres Novas, Algarvias (phone: 049-311067). Moderate.

Marisqueira de Tomar – Large, air conditioned, and pleasantly decorated with rural scenes painted on glass, this is the place to sample the famous Nabão River lamprey. Try the *arroz de lampréia,* a Ribatejo specialty in which the eel is cooked with rice, wine, and garlic and served in a black earthenware pot. The restaurant also has a good seafood bar next door. Closed Mondays. Reservations unnecessary. Major credit cards accepted. 9 Av. Norton de Matos, Tomar (phone: 049-313903). Moderate.

En Route from Tomar – Take N110 south 4½ miles (7 km) and turn left onto N358. The pleasant country road winds through hills and woods for 10 miles (16 km), crossing the Zêzere River via Portugal's biggest dam, at Castelo de Bode, until it reaches Constância. A pretty, quiet little town nowadays, Constância has known busier times, thanks to its strategic position at the confluence of the Tagus and Zêzere rivers. During the Peninsular War in the early 19th century, the future Duke of Wellington mustered his troops here before marching against the French at Talavera, Spain. The town can even boast the not very impressive ruins of a house where Portugal's greatest poet, Luís de Camões, is said to have written some of his verses in 1546. The steps beside the ruined house afford views of Constância's narrow, whitewashed streets as they climb up to the 18th-century parish church that sits atop everything.

Almost 3 miles (5 km) west of town, and definitely worth the short backtrack, is the Castelo de Almourol. The castle hasn't seen much real action since the Knights Templars built it on top of earlier fortifications in 1171, but it has made up for that by accumulating legend — a process to which its remarkably romantic appearance on an island in the Tagus has contributed enormously. A boatman will row travelers across during visiting hours, daily from 9:30 AM to 5 PM (no admission charge, but pay the boatman). East of town, N3 leads away from the river through wooded countryside and then back to it again at the old town of Abrantes, 10 miles (16 km) from Constância.

ABRANTES: The town stands on the north bank of the Tagus, and its castle, which commands a wide circle of the surrounding land, is worth visiting. Abrantes has been fought over repeatedly during its long history. King Afonso Henriques took it from the Moors in 1148 and then successfully fought off a recapture attempt in 1179. The castle was restored and enlarged, most notably by King Dinis, who finished the walls in 1279; afterward, it was frequently used as a royal residence; several Portuguese princes were born in it. (Some of the halls that once formed part of the residential quarters have been restored to reveal their fine brickwork vaults.) It was here, too, that King João I assembled the army that won the celebrated battle of Aljubarrota against the forces of Castile on August 14, 1385, thus assuring Portugal's continued independence. Later on, in 1807, during the Peninsular War, the French took Abrantes for Napoleon, only to be chased out shortly after by the British. (The French general was named Duke of Abrantes for his pains, however.)

On the hilltop with the castle is the 13th-century Church of Santa Maria do Castelo, inside which is installed the *Museu Regional de Dom Lopo de Almeida* (open from 10 AM to 12:30 PM and from 2 to 5 PM; closed Mondays; no admission charge). It contains an interesting collection of Roman statuary, 15th- and 16th-century church carvings, and some very fine early Mozarabic tiles from Seville, Spain. The church was badly damaged by an earthquake in 1492 and was then reconstructed as the pantheon of the Almeida family, Counts of Abrantes, whose elegant Gothic tombs are part of the collection. Information on other sights in town is available at the tourist office on Largo da Feira (phone: 041-22555).

CHECKING IN: ***Turismo*** – A modern, comfortable hostelry of a standard not usually found in the provinces, it has a privileged and convenient hilltop site on the edge of town, gardens, a pool, and tennis courts, as well as a good restaurant (see *Eating Out*). Most of the 50 rooms and suites are air conditioned. Major credit cards accepted. Largo de Santo António, Abrantes (phone: 041-21261 or 041-21271; in the US, 800-528-1234; fax: 041-25218). Moderate.

EATING OUT: ***Casa do Pastor*** – This is a 7½-mile (12-km) drive away, but worth considering for its rustic lodge decor and classic regional dishes such as *ensopado de borrego* (lamb stew), as well as more international standbys such as steaks. Before noon it doubles as a cafeteria for snacks, and after 10 PM as a pub-style bar. Closed Mondays. Reservations advised. Take N244-3 north 5 miles (8 km), then turn right onto N358 for Mouriscas. The restaurant is about 2 miles (about 3 km) down this road on the right, between Cabeça das Mos and Mouriscas (phone: 041-95255). Moderate.

Turismo – The best choice in town, serving very good local and regional dishes in addition to more standard hotel fare. The dining room is large, with pleasantly panoramic views from its big picture windows. Reservations advised. Major credit cards accepted. Largo de Santo António, Abrantes (phone: 041-21261 or 041-21271). Moderate.

En Route from Abrantes – At Rossio, just after crossing the bridge going south (there are ruins of an old Roman bridge over the Tagus), turn east at the signposted crossing onto N118 for Portalegre. The road climbs away from the river as it moves toward the Alto Alentejo. At Alpalhão, 37 miles (59 km) from Abrantes, turn left onto N246 in the direction of the Spanish frontier and drive the 10 miles (16 km) to Castelo de Vide. After a visit, continue on N246 another 5½ miles (9 km) to the turnoff (left) to Marvão, which is another 2½ miles (4 km) up a winding road.

CASTELO DE VIDE: This spa town on the slopes of the Serra de São Mamede is of considerable historical interest and one of the prettiest towns in the region. Its waters are said to do wonders for sluggish digestive systems, and for this reason, as well as because it escapes the fierce Alentejo heat, Castelo de Vide has long been a popular summer resort for the Portuguese middle classes. Like virtually all Alentejo border towns of any size, it grew up around a castle — 60 families, in fact, still live within the walls of this one. Portuguese occupation of the site, originally fortified by the Romans, dates to the beginning of the 13th century; early in the following century, King Dinis strengthened it. Since then, the castle has been the object of numerous sieges, during one of the last of which, in 1704, it was badly damaged when the Spanish tried to wrest it from its Portuguese and English defenders.

Most of this small town can be seen on a morning's stroll. Begin in the central square, Praça Dom Pedro V, which is bordered by two fine 18th-century buildings — the Town Hall and the big Church of Santa Maria da Devesa — and by several handsome 17th-century mansions. Head down from the northwest corner of the square to the 16th-century *fonte da vila* (village fountain), in a square at the foot of the oldest part of town. The fountain, one of the prettiest in Portugal, consists of four marble columns supporting a pyramidal roof set over basins that have been worn into undulating curves by centuries of use. From the square, walk up to the castle through the enchanting medieval alleys of the old Jewish Quarter. On the way up, on Rua da Judiaria, don't miss the tiny 16th-century synagogue, which is partly restored and open to the public daily; and note the original medieval details, such as doorways and windows, on the houses on the same street. Not to be missed in the castle itself are the superbly vaulted Gothic hall in the tower and the fine main hall with its brick tunnel vault ceiling. There are stunning views of the surrounding countryside from the ramparts. The castle can be visited at any time — a caretaker will open sections that are closed off. Castelo de Vide's Tourist Office is at 81 Rua Bartolomeu Alvares da Santa (phone: 045-91361).

CHECKING IN: ***Jardim*** – This 20-room *albergaria* (inn) doesn't have the spaciousness or the modern sophistication of the town's main hotel, the *Sol e Serra,* but it makes up for it by being more homey. Old hands sometimes prefer it to its smarter competitor. 6 Rua Sequeira Sameiro, Castelo de Vide (phone: 045-91217). Moderate.

Sol e Serra – Modern, comfortable, and conveniently situated near a park at the edge of town, it has 51 rooms with balconies, most with an agreeable view. The restaurant specializes in Alentejo dishes (try the *cachafrito de cabrito,* a casserole of kid), and, in keeping with the town's Jewish heritage, kosher fare is offered as well. The hotel has its own game reserve across the border in Spain, where guests can hunt partridge, pheasant, deer, and wild boar in season; fishing and tennis can also be arranged. Major credit cards accepted. Estrada de São Vicente, Castelo de Vide (phone: 045-91301 or 045-91337; fax: 045-91337). Moderate.

EATING OUT: ***Dom Pedro V*** – On the central square, it serves excellent, classic Portuguese dishes, as well as some regional ones. Apart from those attached to hotels, it's considered the best restaurant in the area. Closed Mondays. Reservations advised. Visa and MasterCard accepted. Praça Dom Pedro V, Castelo de Vide (phone: 045-91236). Moderate.

Casa do Parque – This cheery, attractive restaurant attached to a *pensão* of the same name serves good regional fare without putting on any airs. On the menu are *ensopado de cabrito* (kid stew), a regional and house specialty, and *pezinhos coentradas* (pigs' trotters cooked with fresh coriander). Closed Tuesdays. Reservations advised. Visa accepted. Av. da Aramanhã, Castelo de Vide (phone: 045-91250). Inexpensive.

MARVÃO: This beautiful little walled town 8 miles (12.5 km) east of Castelo de Vide perches on a mountaintop overlooking the Spanish border, only 5 miles (8 km) away. After the turn from N246, the road winds up into the mountains right to the town walls; squeeze through the gate and find a parking space — driving is naturally limited in these tortuous cobbled streets. Because of its strategic position, Marvão has played a part in a great many wars. Afonso Henriques captured the town in 1116, and at the end of the 13th century King Dinis fortified it, building up the walls and the tall castle keep. From then on, it became a vital piece in the military chess game played out on the Iberian Peninsula. The views from the castle, which can be visited at any time, are surely the most impressive in the Alentejo — the only place where "you can look down on eagles," as one Portuguese poet put it. The tourist office is on Rua Dr. Matos Magalhães (phone: 045-95236).

CHECKING IN/EATING OUT: ***Pousada de Santa Maria*** – A state-owned inn in a converted 17th-century mansion. Very comfortable and very popular, it's in a beautiful spot; because it has only 9 rooms, it's necessary to book well ahead. The excellent restaurant (reservations necessary), which has a spectacular view of the surrounding countryside, is the best eating place in town. The house specialties are regional ones such as *sopa de sarapatel,* a richly flavored, heavy, gruel-like soup of giblets, almost a meal in itself, and *robalo com amêijoas* (turbot cooked with clams and flavored with fresh coriander). Major credit cards accepted. 7 Rua 24 de Janeiro, Marvão (phone: 045-93201; in the US, 212-686-9213). Moderate.

Dom Dinis – The rooms are tiny in this *pensão,* but they're attractive; some have delightful views, and all have private bathrooms. The restaurant (reservations necessary) serves plain, regional home cooking. Rua Dr. Matos Magalhães, Marvão (phone: 045-95236). Inexpensive.

En route from Marvão – Heading 13 miles (20.5 km) south to Portalegre, N359 crosses the Serra de São Mamede, which contains the highest peak (3,382 feet) in the Alentejo plain. The landscape is pretty, with cork and olive trees beginning to predominate and small farms disappearing as the route enters the domain of the large estate.

PORTALEGRE: The capital of the Alto Alentejo is a busy city and one of the few centers of industry in the region. The cathedral, in the old part of town, is an impressively large edifice, mostly from the 18th century, although it was founded 200 years earlier. It has three vast naves, a wonderfully elegant dome crowning the transept crossing, and some fine 17th-century *azulejos.* Also worth visiting is the church of the Convento de São Bernardo. Founded for the St. Bernard sisters in 1530, the convent is now a barracks, but visitors are escorted in to see the church. Worth noting are the fountain in the courtyard and the superb 16th-century carved doorway, in marble quarried in nearby Estremoz. The history of the order up to its dissolution by the Marquês de Pombal during the 18th century has been poignantly recorded by the nuns on the backs of the stalls in the upper choir.

Portalegre has a famous tapestry factory, located in the center of town in a 16th-century Jesuit convent on Rua Guilherme Gomes Fernandes. Founded in 1947, it specializes in tapestries designed by Portugal's leading artists. All are handwoven, by girls who sit at two long looms running the length of the workshop, surrounded by beautifully dyed wools. The factory can be visited on weekdays from 9 to 11 AM and from 2 to 4:30 PM. Information on other sights in town can be obtained from the tourist office, in the Convento de Santa Clara, near the cathedral on Rua de Elvas (phone: 045-21815).

En Route from Portalegre – Take N18 south through a characteristic Alentejo landscape of dry, open expanses, cork trees, and distant clusters of low, white houses. About halfway to Estremoz, which is 36 miles (58 km) from Portalegre, is the village of Monforte, with Roman excavations nearby and several fine old country houses.

ESTREMOZ: A magnificent 13th-century fortified tower, surrounded by battlements and 18th-century palace buildings, looms majestically over the medieval summit of this attractive and interesting old town. A full 89 feet high, with corner balconies from which boiling oil could be conveniently poured on attackers, the tower was the main defensive feature of what was once one of the Alentejo's most formidable castles, and it is generally considered to be among the finest surviving pieces of medieval military architecture on the Iberian Peninsula. The imposing structure is known as the Torre das Tres Coroas (Tower of the Three Crowns), because three kings are said to have had a hand in its construction. However, it seems to have been mostly the work of King Dinis, who finished it shortly before the end of the 13th century. Dinis also added a royal palace to the fortifications, and this became one of the favorite residences of his wife, Queen Isabel. Unfortunately, most of the original palace was destroyed in 1698 in the explosion of a powder magazine. The present palace, which adjoins Dinis's tower and is now a state *pousada* (see *Checking In*), was built on the same site during the 18th century by King João V. All that is left of the royal residence of Dinis and Isabel is a lovely little arcade of Gothic arches, known as the Gallery of the Audience Hall, as well as the room where the sainted queen died in 1336, which was later turned into a chapel decorated with scenes from her life. Access to the chapel, the tower, and the gallery is through the *pousada* (all three are open to non-guests).

In the Lower Town, which is partially enclosed by a second set of walls (17th-century this time), the focal point is the great central square, the Rossio (in full, the Rossio do Marquês de Pombal). Among the interesting buildings surrounding it is the Câmara Municipal (Town Hall), built during the 17th century as a convent; inside is a superb marble staircase decorated with 18th-century tiled panels depicting the life of St. Philip Neri. Another is the Misericórdia Church, with lovely Gothic cloisters. The *Museu Rural da Casa do Povo de Santa Maria,* also on the square, contains a small but extremely interesting collection of local crafts and costumes (open from 9:30 AM to 12:30 PM and from 2:30 to 5:30 PM; closed Mondays; admission charge). The market held on the Rossio every Saturday is a good opportunity to see the earthenware pottery for which Estremoz has been famous for centuries. The traditionally shaped jugs and cooking pots and the charming little painted figures are becoming collectors' items, although they remain inexpensively priced here. Estremoz's Tourist Office is on Largo da República, south of the Rossio (phone: 068-22538).

CHECKING IN: ***Pousada da Rainha Santa Isabel*** – One of the most highly rated of Portugal's string of state-owned *pousadas,* it's installed in the former palace of King João V, adjoining the Tower of the Three Crowns, and the views are spectacular. The 23 rooms are beautifully furnished with genuine 17th- and 18th-century antiques, and there is a restaurant specializing in regional cooking (see *Eating Out*). Major credit cards accepted. Largo Dom Dinis, Estremoz (phone: 068-22618 or 068-23982; in the US, 212-686-9213). Expensive.

Alentejano – For all its enchantments, Estremoz is lamentably poor in accommodations, and the gap between the *pousada* and this rickety old commercial hotel is abysmal as far as modern comforts go. Nevertheless, the place has a certain character, and for those who don't mind walking down the hall to the bathroom, it is worth considering. Breakfast is the only meal served. 50 Rossio do Marquês de Pombal, Estremoz (phone: 068-22717). Inexpensive.

EATING OUT: ***Pousada da Rainha Santa Isabel*** – The best choice in town — in addition to the food (regional cooking, with particularly noteworthy game dishes in season), there are panoramic views from the dining room windows. Try the various lamb (*borrego*) dishes or, during hunting season, the *javali assado* (roast wild boar) or *coelho ao caçador* (a richly flavored rabbit casserole). Open daily. Reservations necessary. Major credit cards accepted. Largo Dom Dinis, Estremoz (phone: 068-22618). Expensive.

Aguias d'Ouro – A comfortable, air conditioned restaurant on the main square. The *borrego assado no forno* (roast lamb with onions and bay leaves) is reputed to be the best in the area. Open daily. Reservations advised. Major credit cards accepted. 27 Rossio do Marquês de Pombal, Estremoz (phone: 068-22196). Moderate to inexpensive.

En Route from Estremoz – Go directly to Evora, 28½ miles (46 km) from Estremoz, by driving west on N4 for about 4 miles (6 km) and then picking up the southbound N18. Or first make a short but worthwhile detour to the lovely royal town of Vila Viçosa, 11 miles (18 km) from Estremoz, by taking N4 east for 9 miles (14 km) and then turning right onto N255.

VILA VIÇOSA: During the 15th and 16th centuries, this town was the seat of the Dukes of Bragança, who continued to maintain a residence here even after the family became Portugal's last ruling dynasty — in 1640, when the eighth duke became King João IV. Be sure to visit the Paço Ducal (Ducal Palace), whose gorgeous marble façade fills one side of the Terreiro do Paço, the spacious main square. Begun during the 16th century, although dating mainly from the 17th century, the palace has been turned into a museum — the *Museu Biblioteca da Casa de Bragança* — containing furniture, tapestries, paintings, ceramics, and other works of art, as well as many of the possessions of the last Portuguese king, Manuel II, who died in exile in England in 1932 and left behind an important library of 15th- and 16th-century Portuguese books. There is also a small *Museu dos Coches* (Coach Museum). The palace is open from 9:30 AM to 1 PM and from 2 to 6 PM (5 PM in winter); closed Mondays. Admission charge.

In the same square is another good 16th-century Renaissance building, the Convento das Chagas, where the Duchesses of Bragança are buried. The Bragança dukes are buried apart from the ladies, in the church of Santo Agostinho nearby. The *tapada,* the family's walled hunting preserve, the largest in Portugal, has remained intact and is now a nature reserve. For additional information, contact the tourist office on Praça da República (phone: 068-98584).

EVORA: The encircling walls of this remarkable and lovely old city have evidently protected it very well over the centuries. Few cities of Evora's age can boast a standing record of their past quite so neatly encapsulated. Evora was a Roman town of some importance in Julius Caesar's days and became one of the foremost cities on the peninsula during the Moorish occupation from the 8th to the 12th centuries. After the Moors, it was at various times the seat of Portuguese monarchs and was the object of numerous sieges and battles. Today, the city is an important agricultural and university center with a burgeoning tourist industry. For a full description, see *Evora,* THE CITIES.

En Route from Evora – Heading west, N114 leads back to the N4 at Montemor-o-Novo, 20 miles (32 km) from Evora. Anyone who has admired the Arraiolos carpets seen in shops, museums, and some of the better hotels throughout Portugal, however, is advised to take a short detour to the town where they are made, 10 miles (16 km) north of Evora on N370. Arraiolos has been producing these famed woolen carpets since the beginning of the 18th century, and while there is actually no price advantage in buying straight from one of the factories, it is possible to ask to see the workshops and watch the carpets being made. The oldest established of the factories is *Kalifa,* 44-46 Rua Alexandre Herculano (phone: 066-42117)

Montemor-o-Novo, 15½ miles (25 km) west of Arraiolos on N4, has the picturesque remains of a Moorish castle at the top of the Old Town, but it's notable mainly as the birthplace of João de Deus (John of God), the founder of the Order of Charity, who was declared patron saint of hospitals throughout the Christian world 350 years after his death in 1550. Continue 23 miles (37 km) west of Montemor to Pegões, where there is a crossroads with two possible routes to Lisbon. Be sure to take the one going left, toward Setúbal.

SETÚBAL: This busy, ancient port town sits on the estuary of the Sado River, at the edge of the range of hills known as the Serra da Arrábida. Hans Christian Andersen, who visited Setúbal in 1866, called it a terrestrial paradise. It is now the hub of the most important industrial area in the south of Portugal, with shipbuilding, chemicals, automobile assembly, and fishing its major activities, but it has nevertheless retained a lot of the charm that delighted Andersen over a century ago. On Praça Miguel de Bombarda is the late-15th-century Igreja de Jesus, "one of the prettiest little churches" Andersen had ever seen and the earliest example of the Manueline style of architecture, which was to reach its zenith in the Jerónimos monastery in Lisbon and in Tomar (open until 5 PM). Across the river on the Tróia Peninsula — a dune- and pine-backed sandbar blocking the estuary — is the big Torralta tourism development, with apartment-hotels, a golf course, and miles of good white sand. In a quiet creek near the apartment complex are the excavated ruins of a Roman fish processing factory (which may have been part of the once important Roman town of Cetóbriga) and a fascinating little 8th-century Christian church. The site is open to visitors daily from 9:30 AM to 5:30 PM, from June through September; no admission charge. A regular car ferry service connects Setúbal to Tróia. Information is available from the tourist office on Largo do Corpo Santo (phone: 065-24284) in Setúbal.

CHECKING IN: ***Pousada de São Filipe*** – This government-run inn is about half a mile (1 km) west of town, overlooking the Sado estuary. It's installed in a fortress built during the late 16th century by King Philip I (Philip II of Spain) to defend the "invincible" armada he had assembled in Portugal against a possible English attack. There are 14 rooms (ask for one on the waterfront) and a panoramic restaurant (see *Eating Out*). Major credit cards accepted. Castelo de São Filipe, Setúbal (phone: 065-523844; in the US, 212-686-9213). Expensive.

Apartamentos Turísticos Torralta – There are three high-rise apartment-hotels in this development: the *Magnóliamar,* the *Rosamar,* and the *Tulipamar.* On the Tróia Peninsula, a 20-minute ferry ride across the Sado River estuary from Setúbal, they're worth considering as an alternative to something in town, because guests have access to all the facilities of the residential resort complex — a golf course, tennis courts, seawater pools, a supermarket, restaurants, and a disco. The three buildings, each with 129 spacious rooms and suites with kitchenettes, stand close to the beach, surrounded by lawns and flowerbeds; views from the upper-floor balconies are superb. Each hotel has its own telephone number (*Magnóliamar:* 065-44361; fax: 065-44162; *Rosamar:* 065-44151; *Tulipamar:* 065-44201). There also is a central booking office for information and reservations (phone: 065-44221). Expensive to moderate, depending on the season.

Esperança – A comfortable, no-frills hostelry conveniently situated in town. It has 76 small but well-furnished rooms with private baths, plus a restaurant of some repute. 220 Av. Luísa Todi, Setúbal (phone: 065-25151). Moderate.

Novotel – With 105 rooms and relatively extensive facilities, including swimming pools and tennis courts, this hostelry is a good roadside stopover. It offers guests private baths, air conditioning, telephones, and satellite TV. The decor is simple, bright, and modern; there's also a restaurant. Just east of Setúbal, on N10 (phone: 065-522809; in the US, 800-221-4542; fax: 065-522912). Moderate.

Ibis – This 102-room hotel, a member of the international chain, makes a point of providing a full range of basic amenities — private baths, satellite TV, telephones, air conditioning, automatic wake-up service — at extremely reasonable rates. The convenient location for travelers is another plus. Located 2½ miles (4 km) east of Setúbal, on N10 (phone: 065-772927; in the US, 800-221-4542; fax: 065-772447). Inexpensive.

Solaris – A centrally located *albergaria* (inn) lodged in a converted 18th-century home. There are 24 nicely furnished, air conditioned rooms, all with private baths, TV sets, and telephones. The restaurant features hearty regional fare; the 18th-century pillory in the square on which the inn is situated is a national monument. Visa and MasterCard accepted. Praça Marquês de Pombal, Setúbal (phone: 065-525914; fax: 065-522070). Inexpensive.

EATING OUT: ***Pousada de São Filipe*** – The inn's dining room serves very good regional dishes, along with a good view. The fish is especially recommended: Try the *cherne grelhado com frutas do mar* (grilled turbot with a seafood sauce) or *amêijoas na cataplana* (clams with tomatoes and onions, steamed quickly in a covered copper pan — the *cataplana*). Reservations necessary. Major credit cards accepted. Castelo de São Filipe, Setúbal (phone: 065-523844). Expensive.

Rio Azul – Big, with an open kitchen, this is a prime place for lovers of seafood —

fresh crab, lobster, shrimp, and prawns. Remember, however, that seafood can be astronomically expensive by local standards (although it's sold by weight, so diners can control what they spend). Try the sea spider (*sapateira*) — it's cheaper than crab or lobster, and just as good. Closed Wednesdays. Reservations advised. Major credit cards accepted. 44 Rua Guilherme Fernandes, Setúbal (phone: 065-522828). Expensive to moderate.

A Roda **–** This small place produces some of the best regional cooking in Setúbal and serves it up with a certain amount of cosmopolitan dash. Like most of the local restaurants, it specializes in fish dishes, but the *lombinho de vaca ao moscatel* (filets of beef braised in wine from nearby Azeitão) is a non-fish specialty. Or try the *espadarte na cataplana,* swordfish cooked in a covered copper pan. The house wine is the local pedras negras. Closed Sundays. Reservations advised. Major credit cards accepted. Near the ferryboat station for Tróia. 7 Travessa Postigo do Cais, Setúbal (phone: 065-29264). Moderate.

Retiro da Algodeia **–** No frills, and they aren't needed. Big, informal, noisy, and very enjoyable, this is the destination of fish lovers for miles around. *Caldeiradas,* or fish stews, and open-fire grills are the specialty. Try the *salmonete* (red mullet) or the *peixe espada* (blade, or scabbard fish), both of which lend themselves wonderfully to grilling. The local pedras negras wine is a good accompaniment. Closed Mondays. Reservations advised. No credit cards accepted. 30 Estrada de Algodeia, Setúbal (phone: 065-527090). Moderate to inexpensive.

Bocage **–** A popular dining spot where the traditional regional food is prepared simply but well. The establishment doesn't aspire to gastronomic heights or surprises, but it does offer good value. The *costeletas de vitela ao moscatel* (veal cutlets braised in wine with potatoes and onions) are a good choice. Closed Monday evenings and Tuesdays. Reservations advised. Major credit cards accepted. 5-8 Rua Marquesa de Faial, Setúbal (phone: 065-522513). Inexpensive.

En Route from Setúbal – The Serra da Arrábida, on the Arrábida (or Setúbal) Peninsula, is one of Portugal's loveliest and most distinctive regions. This range of hills rises out of the Sado River estuary west of Setúbal and forms a high ridge of limestone along the peninsula's southern coast. The whole area, comprising the *serra* itself, which is a national park, and the region around it, has a character of its own, with its own wines, its own cheeses, its own microclimate, and its own flora and fauna. Because of its geographic situation, plants survive here that long ago disappeared from the rest of the Iberian Peninsula. Two roads lead west from Setúbal through the range: N10-4 follows the coastline, while N379-1, more spectacular, traverses the spine of the hills, offering stunning views along the way. About 7½ miles (12 km) from Setúbal along N379-1, a signposted left turn winds down to a little harbor, Portinho da Arrábida, where there is a marvelous, crescent-shaped beach protected by a high escarpment. (Lack of space makes parking problems formidable in summer.) High on the mountainside above the harbor is the Convento de Arrábida, a Franciscan monastery founded in 1542. A close view of the lovely old monastic building, rising in cellular form like a terraced wasp's nest, can be had by driving a little way along N10-4 from the road leading down into Portinho. About 4½ miles (7 km) beyond the Portinho turnoff from N379-1, the road branches left to the fishing town of Sesimbra.

SESIMBRA: A popular holiday resort and consequently very crowded in summer, Sesimbra is a center for big-game fishing. Tuna, shark, and swordfish are all caught here. Unfortunately, uncontrolled development has blighted the outskirts of what was once an attractive little fishing village, but there is some charm left in the old village core. The remains of a fine 13th-century castle stand guard over the town from a high hilltop (the castle is empty now, but visitors can walk around it for the superb view). Sesimbra has plenty of fish restaurants where it is easy to get a good meal — although, oddly enough, given all the fish available, no really outstanding restaurant has emerged. The meal to try here is swordfish, because it's difficult to find on menus elsewhere; it's usually prepared as a steak (*bife de espadarte*). Also a delicacy is *peixe espada,* which translates literally as "swordfish" but is, in fact, blade, or scabbard, fish. Sesimbra's *caldeiradas,* fish stews made with six or seven varieties of fish, are also particularly good.

CHECKING IN: ***Villas de Sesimbra*** **–** An apartment-hotel complex set back in the hills, it boasts a full complement of resort-type facilities, including heated outdoor pools, a health club (with a gym and a sauna), tennis and squash courts, bars, restaurants, and even a children's play area. The 207 units — all equipped with kitchenettes, telephones, satellite TV, 4-channel video, and private baths — range in size from studios to penthouse suites, and are set around gardens and panoramic terraces. About 1¼ miles (2 km) from the ocean, on Altinho de São João, Sesimbra (phone: 01-223-2775; fax: 01-223-1533). Expensive to moderate, depending on the type of apartment.

Mar **–** In a good position overlooking the sea, this is an excellent, modern hostelry offering 120 rooms with private baths and balconies, as well as a restaurant, a disco, and a swimming pool. Major credit cards accepted. 10 Rua General Humberto Delgado, Sesimbra (phone: 01-223-3326; fax: 01-223-3888). Moderate.

EATING OUT: ***Ribamar*** **–** There is no "best" seafood restaurant in town, but this is typical of the better eateries. Try any of the Sesimbra specialties. Closed Mondays. Reservations advised. No credit cards accepted. 29 Av. dos Naufragos, Sesimbra (phone: 01-223-4853). Moderate to inexpensive.

En Route from Sesimbra – Returning eastward, an 9-mile (14-km) drive along N379 leads to Vila Nogueira de Azeitão, at the foot of the Serra da Arrábida. The most notable of several fine buildings in this attractive old village is the early-16th-century palace of the Dukes of Aveiro, still used as a family residence. Here also are two wineries that should be visited. On the main street of town are the old cellars of *José Maria da Fonseca* (phone: 01-208-0002), where the once widely appreciated moscatel de Setúbal is made. Little known outside of Portugal, it is nevertheless a superb dessert wine that many experts place among the finest of Europe's sweet wines. The cellars are open Mondays through Fridays, from 9 AM to noon and from 2 to 5 PM, and members of small groups can ask to see the small wine museum that the firm maintains here. Around the corner, on the main Lisbon–Setúbal road, is the big, ultramodern winery belonging to *J. M. da Fonseca International* (phone: 01-208-0227), which makes several classic table wines that are highly regarded in Portugal but is best-known abroad for Lancers Rosé. Visiting hours are the same as those of the old cellars.

Continue eastward from Azeitão, taking N10 in the direction of Setúbal for about 1¼ miles (about 2 km); then branch left onto N379 and follow the signs for Cabanas, Quinta do Anjo, and Palmela.

CHECKING IN/EATING OUT: ***Quinta das Torres*** **–** This very comfortable 12-room *estalagem* is in a 16th-century mansion, approached by a tree-lined driveway and surrounded by delightful gardens. A natural pool for swimming graces the grounds, as does a fine ornamental irrigation pond with a little classical pavilion in its center. The style of an old country house extends to the dining room, which serves simple but good Portuguese fare, and to the service. Two dishes to try are the *bacalhau dourado,* fried dried cod, and the *carril de gambas,* curried shrimp. This is also one of the few places where the exquisite and increasingly rare azeitão cheeses — small, creamy sheep's milk cheese with a flavor rather like good brie — can still be found. (The restaurant is closed Saturdays; reservations necessary.) The entrance to the inn's driveway is on the right side of N10 just after leaving Vila Nogueira de Azeitão in the direction of Setúbal. Visa and MasterCard accepted. Quinta das Torres (phone: 01-208-0001). Moderate.

PALMELA: The massive castle towering over this little town, at the northeastern end of the Serra da Arrábida, is worth the climb for the views alone. Constructed by the Moors, it was reconstructed after the 12th-century Reconquest, but was partially demolished by the 1755 earthquake that laid waste to Lisbon. Many of the 18th-century houses in the narrow streets below the walls were built with stones salvaged from the disaster.

CHECKING IN/EATING OUT: ***Pousada de Palmela*** – This 27-room, air conditioned inn is installed in a monastery (Convento de São Tiago) that was built within the castle precincts during the 15th century. The marvelous location and handsome appointments make it one of the flagships of the state-owned *pousada* chain, and the restaurant, occupying the old refectory, offers not only delightful decor, but also the best cooking to be found around Palmela. When game is in season in the fall and around *Christmas,* this is a good place to try partridge or quail casseroles in red wine (*perdiz* or *codorniz estufado*). At other times, try the various lamb dishes, especially *borrego assado no forno,* an oven roast with onions, garlic, and bay leaves. This is also another of the few remaining places where azeitão cheeses can be found. The restaurant is open daily; reservations necessary. Major credit cards accepted. Castelo de Palmela, Palmela (phone: 01-235-1395; in the US, 212-686-9213; fax: 065-235-0410). Expensive.

En Route from Palmela – The signposted access to the A2 toll highway is about 1¼ miles (2 km) away. From there, it is a 20-mile (32-km) drive to the Tagus bridge — the Ponte 25 de Abril — which leads into Lisbon. The world's third-longest suspension bridge, it offers what is probably the finest view of the capital, as a reward for homecoming travelers.

The Algarve

From the wild and windy headlands of Cabo de São Vicente (Cape St. Vincent) to the tranquil estuary of the Guadiana River on the Spanish border, Portugal's Algarve coast is as replete with history as it is with the good things of modern living. Like many southern European coasts, the Algarve has been marred by over-commercialization, but anyone with a spark of imagination who explores beyond the resort condominiums will find rich treasures, products of an exotic mix of Europe with Africa. Sipping an aperitif at sunset on a chalky-white poolside terrace facing Africa, a visitor won't quite be able to see the Moroccan coast, but as the red disk of the sun slips down to the horizon, the spiritual affinity is evident. And if the African heat of the coast seems too harsh, there is the traditional option of Algarve-dwellers — taking to the hills of the Monchique mountain range, which offers the best of both worlds.

In 1927, a Portuguese travel writer lamented the fact that the Algarve women's custom of wearing veils — a last trace of pure Arab influence — had almost given way to Paris fashions. But he noted that in some parts of the region the women — described as "healthy, full-fleshed women with red mouths and great, dark eyes . . . veiled by long, silky eyelashes" — still bore traces of their heritage, bringing to mind "the purest of Arab types." The young Algarve woman of today is more likely to be wearing a bikini than a veil, but the writer reminds us of how culturally different the Moorish-influenced Algarve is from the rest of Portugal, a point borne out by a glimpse of the white rectangular houses with flat roof terraces characteristic of the region and the many Arab waterwheels that can still be seen here.

The Algarve's natural setting is also different from that of the rest of Portugal. While the Alentejo region, just to the north, shares the Algarve's sunny disposition, its undulating landscape is sparsely vegetated and spotted with cork oaks and olive trees. By contrast, the Algarve has distinctive vegetation, its roads and byways lined with almond trees (a delight when they blossom in early spring), lush spreading fig trees, olive trees, and the carob bean tree (*alfarrobeira*), which is the basis of a thriving local industry. Unfortunately, development for the tourism industry has destroyed much of this natural growth on the main highway that traverses the coast for about 100 miles, but the back roads of the Algarve open up another world. Here the traveler may share the road with only a plodding mule cart and breathe in the beauty of a landscape uncorrupted by neon signs.

And there are wide variations in the landscape, even within this relatively small coastal province of Portugal. The area between Sagres and Lagos — known as the Costa Vicentina, at the western end of the Algarve — is characterized by dramatic bluffs and promontories and has been declared a protected zone because of the special value of its flora and fauna. To the east, near Faro, is the Ria Formosa marshland, where the coast is paralleled by long sandbanks enclosing seawater lagoons. This is quite a different kind of geography, teeming with interesting birds and marine creatures and considered unique in Europe.

The marked Moorish character of the Algarve derives from the sheer duration of the Islamic occupation, which lasted longer here than it did elsewhere in the country. Before the Moors and Christian crusaders fought their final battles, however, the Algarve shared with the rest of Portugal a history of invasion by Phoenicians, Romans, and barbarians. The original inhabitants of the area — known to the ancient Greeks as the Cunete tribe — played host first to the Phoenicians, a Semitic seagoing people from the eastern Mediterranean who, around 1300 BC, founded cities at Tavira, Faro, Portimão, and Lagos. The most obvious trace they left was the exotic form of the local fishing boats, which are graced with sweeping Oriental prows and sometimes have a mystical-looking eye painted on either side. (They can still be seen in Albufeira, Portimão, and Faro.)

The Romans then had their turn. Their road system on the Portuguese side of the Iberian Peninsula ran south from Lisbon through Alcácer do Sal to Beja (which was their southern capital) in the Alentejo, then on through Mértola to emerge in the Algarve at Castro Marim, just north of Vila Real de Santo António on the Spanish border. Castro Marim, a fortress town of humble, whitewashed houses that commands a view into Spain over the Guadiana River, imparts a sense of this long, long history. The salt pans that lie below the battlements were worked by the Romans, too.

The Moors conquered the Iberian Peninsula in 711. The Portuguese nation was forged and founded in the Christian crusaders' struggles to oust them, which began in earnest with the reconquest of Porto during the mid-9th century and was broadly won at the Battle of Ourique, near Santarém, in 1139. However, the Algarve did not come back into the fold until 1249. The inland city of Silves, on the Arade River, was then known as Xelb and was the capital of Moorish Algarve. At its apogee, it was considered an Arab city of great luxury and nobility, a place where fleets loaded oranges, figs, and olives for export to distant lands. The river has long since silted up, but the rich orange groves and an imposing castle with subterranean cisterns testify to its role in this period. Many Algarve towns still retain their Moorish names — Faro, Tunes, Odeleite, Odeceixe, Odeáxere, Odelouca, Alcoutim, Aljezur, Alvor — as does the name of the Algarve itself, which comes from the Arabic *Al-Gharb,* meaning "the West," referring to the land west of their territory in Andalusia.

The Algarve has been attracting European vacationers for years, but only recently have Americans begun to discover its beaches — fine, pale sand in long stretches, as well as tiny coves — and year-round sunshine (the best time to visit is from the end of January through October, however, or from mid-May to the beginning of October for swimming). Luxury and lesser hotels and resort complexes abound in the more developed parts of the coast, offering excellent opportunities for fishing, boating, water skiing, windsurfing, golf, tennis, and riding. Yet development notwithstanding, there are also simple towns and small fishing villages.

Seafood is, naturally, the basis of traditional Algarve cooking. Clams (*amêijoas*) are the prize coastal produce, and they are presented at their best as *amêijoas na cataplana,* a dish named after the sort of Moorish copper pressure cooker in which it is prepared, using, in addition to clams, ham, local salami, garlic, and coriander — a taste sensation. Lobster, crayfish, and crab (*lavagante, lagosta,* and *caranguejo,* respectively) are also featured, as is squid (*lulas*), cooked in a variety of local styles. No visit to Portugal would be complete without trying the humble but tasty sardine, and the recommended place to do this in the Algarve is at the *Portimão Sardine Festival,* held in August on the waterfront, under the town's picturesque iron bridge. Umbrella-shaded tables are set out in the blazing sun, and the sardines are served from the charcoal grill accompanied by boiled potatoes and fresh green salad. They can be washed down with sparkling *vinho verde* — "green," or young, wine — or a cold beer.

The town of Sagres, at Portugal's southwesternmost point, is a logical starting place for a visit to the Algarve, although reaching it may involve retracing steps, because the main road from Lisbon meets the coast's trunk road (N125) at Ferreiras, near Albufeira, 50 miles (80 km) east. An alternative is to use the poorer-quality coastal road from Lisbon, passing through Odemira and Aljezur and picking up N125 at Vila do Bispo, a few miles north of Sagres. Those arriving by plane at Faro, toward the Spanish border, can work their way east or west, but they, too, will have to cover some ground twice, since there is only one main road along the Algarve coast. And note that it is not a coastal route — it's necessary to turn off it to reach beach destinations. Because the entire road is little more than 100 miles (160 km) long, repeating part of it is easily done; one journey can be slow and exploratory, the other a more rapid return, checking on sights missed along the way. One suggested alternative, for those working their way west from Faro with the intention of then following the route west to east as outlined below, would be to take the back road to Silves from Faro, through the Algarve's rural hinterland. Leave the main highway 5 miles (8 km) west of Faro and go to Loulé, turning left at the main city square, near the bus terminal, and heading north to Salir, 9½ miles (15 km) away. Turn left there and go another 9½ miles (15 km) to the delightful town of Alte, immortalized by James Michener in his book *The Drifters.* Continue in the same direction, through São Bartolomeu de Messines, to Silves. When returning east from Sagres, proceed straight on N125, dispensing with the need to detour to Silves and Loulé as described below.

Expect to pay $100 and up for a double room in a hotel listed below as expensive — up to $250 a night at places commanding oil-sheik rents, such as the deluxe resorts of Vale do Lobo and Quinta do Lago. Medium-quality establishments, such as the *Baleeira* at Sagres, are listed as moderate and run from about $50 to $75. Inexpensive hotels and pensions can cost less than $50 — much less in the low season — but none have been included below, because such establishments are generally not up to the standards of the foreign pleasure traveler. All hotels listed have air conditioning and are open year-round; for accommodations in July and August, it is advisable to book well in advance. Eating out needn't be costly. With resourcefulness, it is possible to have a good meal for two with wine for $20 to $30, marking the inexpensive end of the spectrum. Moderate means from $30 to $70 for two; at restaurants listed as expensive, allow $70 to $100.

SAGRES: This dramatic promontory (Ponta de Sagres in Portuguese) and Cape St. Vincent (Cabo de São Vicente), 4 miles (6 km) away, form the southwestern tip of Europe, a wild landscape where rugged cliffs plunge down to clear blue waters alive with sea life — as the many local fishermen who perch precariously on the rocks bear witness. A popular belief stemming from prehistoric times held that the gods met here, and to the ancients, this was the end of the known world, beyond which the setting sun fell off the face of the earth. The gods aside, the area has played an important role in Portuguese history. It was here during the early 15th century that Prince Henry the Navigator, son of João I of Portugal and his English wife, Philippa of Lancaster, established a school of geography and navigation — a community of scholars who pooled their knowledge of mapmaking, shipbuilding, and mathematics. Under his leadership, Portugal's first voyages of discovery were planned and undertaken, preparing the way for the epic voyages of later men such as Vasco da Gama, Bartholomeu Dias, and Christopher Columbus (the latter — an Italian — sailed under the Spanish flag after being snubbed by the Portuguese). Although Prince Henry, known in Portuguese as Infante Dom Henrique, did not sail himself, the contributions he made to the advancement of navigation and exploration in the area for 40 years (he died in 1460) provided the basis for the rise of the Portuguese colonial empire and allowed the country to maintain naval supremacy for almost 2 centuries.

The village of Sagres, set on the cliffs, came into the news again in 1597, when it was razed by the British fleet under Sir Francis Drake, then at war with the Spanish (Portugal was subordinated to the Spanish throne at this time). Today it is a bit of an eyesore, but redeemed by the area's spectacular views. Within walking distance of the village is Cabo de São Vicente, where the lighthouse can be inspected at the keeper's discretion daily, between 10 AM and noon and 2 and 5:30 PM (a tip is expected). Between the two villages, on a windswept bluff, is the Fortaleza do Beliche, dating from the 15th century, but largely reconstructed during the 18th century. An enormous mariner's compass etched into the ground here was presumably designed by Prince Henry. The fort (always open; no admission charge) has climbable ramparts, and its main building houses a youth hostel. Also within the walls is the Sagres Tourist Office (phone: 082-64125).

CHECKING IN: ***Pousada do Infante*** **–** This government-owned inn has a stylish setting on the cliff top; there are 23 rooms, with private terraces overlooking the sea. Sagres (phone: 082-64222; in the US, 212-686-9213; fax: 082-64225). Expensive.

Baleeira **–** Also on the cliffs, it offers quality service and a tasteful, well-maintained interior. Dining here at sunset as migratory swallows swoop around the bluff is an experience in itself; the 120-room hotel also has its own tennis court, swimming pool, and bicycles for hire. Fishing excursions can be arranged. Sagres (phone: 082-64212). Moderate.

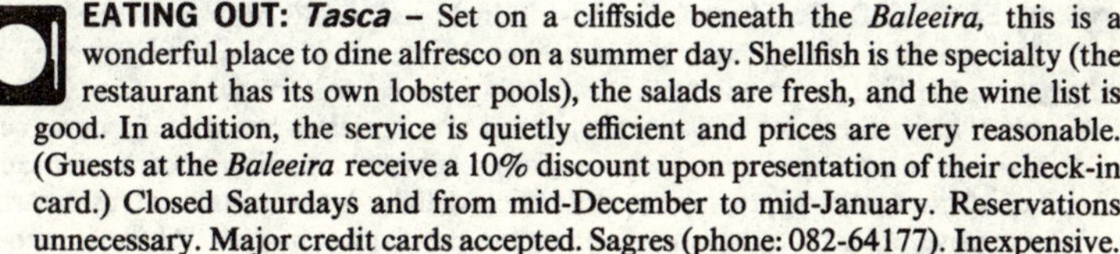

EATING OUT: ***Tasca*** **–** Set on a cliffside beneath the *Baleeira,* this is a wonderful place to dine alfresco on a summer day. Shellfish is the specialty (the restaurant has its own lobster pools), the salads are fresh, and the wine list is good. In addition, the service is quietly efficient and prices are very reasonable. (Guests at the *Baleeira* receive a 10% discount upon presentation of their check-in card.) Closed Saturdays and from mid-December to mid-January. Reservations unnecessary. Major credit cards accepted. Sagres (phone: 082-64177). Inexpensive.

En Route from Sagres – The road to Lagos (N125), 20½ miles (33 km) away, is in poor condition and has little traffic, heightening the feeling of otherworldliness at the Algarve's western tip. The road runs inland from the coast — here called the Costa Vicentina — but a series of good beaches (*praias*) can be reached by turning off N125. All signposted, they include Praia do Martinhal (the sign reads *Martinhal Motel Restaurant*), Praia da Salema, Praia do Burgau, and Praia da Luz, which is a popular resort center.

LAGOS: An attractive harbor town, this, too, holds memories of Henry the Navigator. It was from this port in the mid-15th century that the ships sailing under Prince Henry's authority actually embarked, setting their course south to explore the west coast of Africa. It was also from Lagos that the doomed, fanatically religious King Sebastian sailed in 1578 to fight the Moors at the historic battle of Alcázarquivir in Morocco. He died on the battlefield, leaving the throne to his elderly uncle, the childless Cardinal-King Henrique, who reigned for 2 years. An illegitimate member of the royal family, the Prior of Crato, claimed the throne next but was bested by the superior force of another claimant, Philip of Spain. Because Sebastian's death in North Africa had not been confirmed, his subjects persisted in the belief that he would one day return to rule again. Thus, a legend was born. In the centuries since, fake Sebastians have "returned" to Portugal — even today claimants show up in small villages — and the term Sebastianism came to be used to describe the belief in a returning redeemer. The legend is commemorated in Lagos with a controversial statue by modern sculptor João Cutileiro, who depicts Sebastian as a visionary adolescent gazing out to sea. The statue is in the central Praça de Gil Eanes (named after one of Prince Henry's explorers, born in Lagos), where young travelers with backpacks congregate nowadays, as a starting place to explore the town.

As a result of the voyages to Africa, Lagos had the dubious privilege of being the site of Europe's first slave auctions. The arcaded building where they were held, the Mercado de Escravos (Slave Market), still stands near the waterfront in the Praça da República, opposite the Church of Santa Maria, although there is no plaque to mark its significance. Another of the town's highlights is the 18th-century baroque Igreja de Santo António (Rua General Alberto da Silveira), with a breathtaking ornate altarpiece, gilt cherubs, and antique tiled surfaces. The *Museu Regional* (open from 9:30 AM to 12:30 PM and from 2 to 5 PM; closed Mondays; admission charge), adjoining the church, contains a strange mix of works, from local handicrafts to Roman statuary and a mid-16th century diptych showing the Annunciation and the Presentation in the Temple, attributed to Francisco de Campos. Parts of the Old City walls remain; built by the Moors and fortified by their Christian successors, they were largely destroyed by the 1755 earthquake that devastated most of Lagos. Outside the walls is the 17th-century Forte do Pau da Bandeira, built as a defense against pirates. For more information on this historic city, capital of the Algarve from the late 16th to the mid-18th century, stop in at the Lagos Tourist Office (Largo Marquês de Pombal; phone: 082-763031).

CHECKING IN: ***Meia Praia*** – Located a bit over 2½ miles (4 km) to the east of Lagos, it has 66 rooms and its own pool, gardens, and tennis courts facing a good swimming beach. Meia Praia (phone: 082-762001). Moderate.

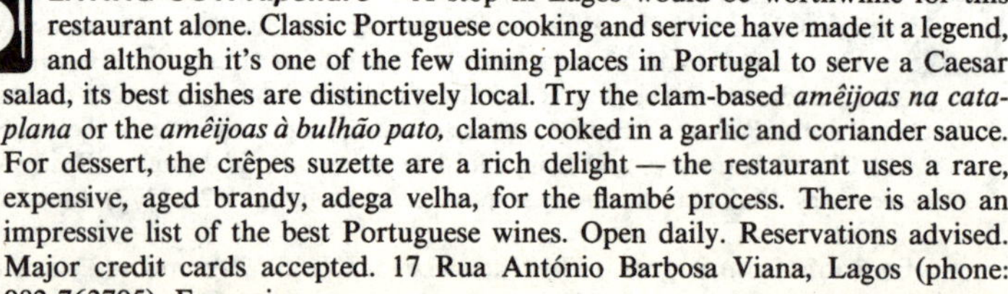

EATING OUT: ***Alpendre*** – A stop in Lagos would be worthwhile for this restaurant alone. Classic Portuguese cooking and service have made it a legend, and although it's one of the few dining places in Portugal to serve a Caesar salad, its best dishes are distinctively local. Try the clam-based *amêijoas na cataplana* or the *amêijoas à bulhão pato,* clams cooked in a garlic and coriander sauce. For dessert, the crêpes suzette are a rich delight — the restaurant uses a rare, expensive, aged brandy, adega velha, for the flambé process. There is also an impressive list of the best Portuguese wines. Open daily. Reservations advised. Major credit cards accepted. 17 Rua António Barbosa Viana, Lagos (phone: 082-762705). Expensive.

En Route from Lagos – The road improves between Lagos and Portimão, 11 miles (18 km) away. Between the two, off the main road, are several good beaches and rocky coves, among them Praia da Dona Ana and Praia dos Três Irmãos, besides Meia Praia. Browse through Portimão, then turn north (N124 and N266) to the Monchique mountain range.

PORTIMÃO: This is one of the fishing capitals of the Algarve — a modern commercial fishing center rather than a picturesque village, however. Set on the estuary of the Arade River, Portimão was largely destroyed by the 1755 earthquake, but after rebuilding, it has grown into the second-largest town along the coast (after Faro). It has a relaxed Mediterranean atmosphere and a host of sidewalk cafés, bars, restaurants, and shops; its August sardine festival is an optimal occasion to sample the Algarve's *sardinha assada* straight from the charcoal grill. A little over a mile south of town, on the western side of the river's mouth, is Praia da Rocha, a seaside resort on one of the best (but unfortunately overcommercialized) beaches on the coast, noted for its majestic rock formations. On the opposite side of the river is Ferragudo, a small waterfront hamlet with a ruined 16th-century castle.

CHECKING IN: ***Bela Vista*** – At Praia da Rocha, this is an oasis of quality in a desert of tourist hype. An old-fashioned, privately managed, 14-room hotel, installed in a former mansion, it is something of a Victorian folly, with spires, dark woodwork, and stained glass windows. There is direct access to the beach. Av. Marginal, Praia da Rocha (phone: 082-24055; fax: 082-240556). Expensive.

EATING OUT: ***A Lanterna*** – This simple place on the outskirts of Portimão, near the bridge over the Arade, serves fish and seafood, as well as other basic but tasty Portuguese dishes. Closed Sundays and from early December through late January. Reservations unnecessary. Visa and MasterCard accepted. Estrada N125, Cruzamento de Ferragudo, Portimão (phone: 082-23948). Moderate.

Safari – An unpretentious place with good, fresh seafood and a beachfront view. Open daily, except for a few weeks in January or February. Reservations unnecessary. Major credit cards accepted. Rua António Feu, Praia da Rocha (phone: 082-23540). Moderate.

MONCHIQUE: The eucalyptus-scented and lushly wooded heights of the Monchique Mountains are a pleasant change from the landscape of the coast. The Serra de Monchique, along with the Serra do Caldeirão to the east, forms a natural barrier between the Algarve and the rest of Portugal — which explains not only the coastline's flawless weather, but also why the Moors were able to hold out longer here than elsewhere in the face of advancing Christian armies. In bygone days, the Monchique hills were also a fashionable retreat from the Algarve's searing heat, the medicinal springs bursting from volcanic rock deemed beneficial for a variety of ailments. The springs, located at Caldas de Monchique, a leafy spa town about 11 miles (18 km) north of Portimão, were known to the Romans; King João II, who reigned from 1481 to 1495, was said to have been treated for dropsy here (to no avail — he died soon after). The spa's more recent heyday was around the turn of this century, when the *Grand* hotel and its casino were in full swing. Today, the charm of Caldas still lies in its old-fashioned cafés banked with potted palms, its walks and views, and the cool town square, where the old hotel (but not the casino) has been restored. The town of Monchique proper, 4 miles (6 km) north of Caldas, has a parish church with a Manueline doorway, but the town itself is less an attraction than the drive to the summit of the nearly 3,000-foot Fóia, the highest point of the Serra de Monchique. Take N266-3 west out of Monchique, and in a few miles the view opens up to the coast and the sea and seems to stretch almost to Africa. The whole Monchique area is known for its handicrafts, including colorful rugs and furniture — the folding wooden Monchique stools are derived from a Roman design and are a good bargain (quite portable, too).

CHECKING IN: ***Abrigo da Montanha*** – A recently enlarged *estalagem* (inn) of 11 rooms and 5 suites, it sits a mile or so southwest of Monchique, along the way to Fóia. Given its size, it's advisable to book well in advance, but even those not staying here can sit under the umbrellas amid the cool hydrangeas of the terrace restaurant and enhance the famous Fóia view with good food and wine. Estrada de Fóia, Monchique (phone: 082-92131). Moderate.

Do Lageado – This is a pleasant *albergaria* (another category of inn) with 21 rooms and its own swimming pool, in the main square of Caldas. It's open only from May through October, and note that it doesn't take credit cards. Caldas de Monchique (phone: 082-92616). Moderate.

EATING OUT: ***1692*** – The restaurant's name comes from the date the stone building it occupies was constructed. At first owned by the Catholic church, then converted into a hotel — the *Grand* — the building has been restored (the *Grand* is now the *Albergaria Velha,* but it's fairly spartan and unattractive). Local dishes are served in a wonderfully green, shady setting. Be sure to try the traditional hot bread, baked with *chouriço,* the spicy Portuguese sausage; it comes from the village's restored bread oven. Open daily. Reservations unnecessary. Major credit cards accepted. Caldas de Monchique (phone: 082-92205). Inexpensive.

En Route from Monchique – Return to Portimão and take N125 east 5 miles (8 km) to Lagoa, a market town of some charm that is the junction for the road to Silves, 4½ miles (7 km) north, and Carvoeiro, 3 miles (5 km) south.

SILVES: The sleepy, sunny inland town gives few clues to its former importance as the capital of the Moorish kingdom of the Algarve, although its combination of cypresses, orange groves, and the red stone Moorish castle do impart the flavor of an Arab city. Known as Xelb in Moorish times, Silves sits on the north bank of the Arade River, which is now silted up but at one time made the town a flourishing river port. The castle (open daily from 8 AM to 5:30 PM; no admission charge) has enormous underground cisterns and provides a sweeping view of the Algarve coast. Next to it is the 13th-century Gothic cathedral, the Sé, built on the site of the former mosque. With its gargoyles and cleft windows offset by the same rich, reddish local stone as the castle, the church holds considerable architectural interest. The Cruz de Portugal, an unusual 15th-century limestone sculpture about 10 feet high showing Christ crucified on one side and in the arms of the Virgin Mary on the other, is at the town's eastern exit (on N124 toward São Bartolomeu de Messines). The tourist office in Silves is on Rua 25 de Abril (phone: 082-442255).

CARVOEIRO: This little fishing village has become the favored Algarve playground of northern Europeans — Germans, Dutch, and Scandinavians (and British, too, although their stamping ground tends to be the zone farther east, from Albufeira to Faro). Fishermen's white houses on the cliff tops set the tone, and Carvoeiro remains picturesque, despite the modern resort villa complexes that encircle it, with tennis courts, pools, and their own bar and restaurant facilities. The town has a small but pretty beach.

En route from Carvoeiro – Pick up N125 east once again and continue to Ferreiras, where a right turn onto N395 leads to Albufeira, 16 miles (26 km) from Lagoa. A few miles beyond Lagoa, on the right side of the road, is *Porches Pottery,* just before the village of the same name. Founded by the late Irish artist Patrick Swift, who was well known in Portugal as an illustrator, the pottery sells hand-painted ceramics, many bearing his distinctive designs. The pieces are not as authentically Portuguese as other local products — they have a style of their own — but traditional Portuguese techniques have been used in making them, along with superior glazes, which makes them chip less easily in everyday use. A book on Portuguese birds, with illustrations by Swift, is also available at the shop.

ALBUFEIRA: This large resort town was the last Moorish stronghold in the Algarve. At one time, it was a picturesque fishing village, but in recent years it has suffered from the onslaught of development and become the heart of the tourist's Algarve. Set on a cliff, it has steep, cobbled streets that are thronged in summer, and its main beach, reached via a tunnel carved through rock, is wall-to-wall flesh at the height of the season. (There are beaches nearby where it is possible to find space, however — just walk along in either direction.) Little of historical value remains in Albufeira, but a walk through town is a pleasant experience, since there are multitudes of shops, small bars, and restaurants to suit every taste. Albufeira's Tourist Office is on Rua 5 de Outubro (phone: 089-512144), the main street.

CHECKING IN: ***Boa Vista*** – A cut above average in the Albufeira area, mainly because of its tasteful decor and its site on the cliff, which faces a little away from the center of town. It has 93 rooms and a swimming pool, plus a restaurant. 20 Rua Samora Barros, Albufeira (phone: 089-589175; fax: 089-588836). Expensive.

EATING OUT: ***A Ruína*** – Good fish and seafood are served in the pleasant setting of an old fort overlooking the main beach. Open daily. Reservations unnecessary. No credit cards accepted. Cais Herculano, Albufeira (phone: 089-512094). Moderate.

En Route from Albufeira – Return to N125 and continue east to Almansil, where roads lead north to the town of Loulé and south to the hotel, resort villa, and golf course complexes of Vale do Lobo and Quinta do Lago, while the main road presses on to Faro. A must stop in the vicinity is the Igreja de São Lourenço, in the village of São Lourenço, a mile (1.6 km) beyond Almansil. A small church, this is nevertheless one of the most noteworthy in the Algarve, because its walls and barrel-vaulted ceiling — even the underside of the dome — are entirely covered with blue-and-white 18th-century *azulejos* depicting the life of St. Lawrence. The nearby *Centro Cultural São Lourenço,* set up in restored, 200-year-old buildings, is a privately run establishment that maintains its own art gallery and sponsors classical music concerts in summer. Among the regular exhibitors at the gallery are Portuguese artists José Guimarães and João Cutileiro (creator of the statue of King Sebastian in Lagos), whose works can be bought here for prices that are reasonable by the standards of the international art market.

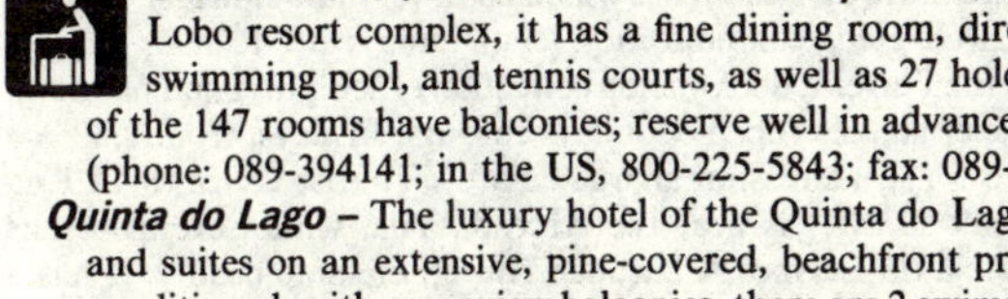

CHECKING IN/EATING OUT: ***Dona Filipa*** – A luxury hotel in the Vale do Lobo resort complex, it has a fine dining room, direct access to the beach, a swimming pool, and tennis courts, as well as 27 holes of golf next door. Most of the 147 rooms have balconies; reserve well in advance. Vale do Lobo, Almansil (phone: 089-394141; in the US, 800-225-5843; fax: 089-394288). Very expensive.

Quinta do Lago – The luxury hotel of the Quinta do Lago resort offers 150 rooms and suites on an extensive, pine-covered, beachfront property. All rooms are air conditioned, with oceanview balconies; there are 2 swimming pools (3 if you count the private pool that goes with the presidential suite), 2 tennis courts, and a health club, in addition to the resort's 27 superb holes of golf nearby. There's also the *T Club,* one of the best restaurants in the Algarve. Quinta do Lago, Almansil (phone: 089-396666; in New York City, 212-838-3110; elsewhere in the US, 800-223-6800; fax: 089-396393). Very expensive.

LOULÉ: This old market center with tree-lined streets is in the hills only 3 miles (5 km) up a back road from Almansil. The market, in the center of town and open mornings only, daily except Sundays, used to be the place to buy traditional, hand-crafted wooden toys. Alas, they've given way to the plastic variety, but there are other bargains to be had: rough terra cotta plates hand-painted with exuberant peasant designs in the pottery section; figs, almonds, mountain cheeses, and juicy local oranges in the produce section; and, in the surrounding shops, excellent baskets and raffia hats at ridiculously low prices. Decorative bridles and cattle bells that make good wall hangings can also be bought at local saddleries.

CHECKING IN: ***Loulé Jardim*** – Charming small hostelry in Loulé's town center, set on an old-fashioned square. It has 52 rooms and a rooftop swimming pool, but no restaurant. Praça Manuel de Arriaga, Loulé (phone: 089-413094 or 089-413095; fax: 089-63177). Moderate.

En Route from Loulé – Take the road to Faro, 10 miles (16 km) southeast of Loulé in a direct line.

CHECKING IN/EATING OUT: ***La Réserve*** – Off the road between Loulé and Faro, this is an elegant, modern, and luxurious establishment (a member of the prestigious Relais & Châteaux group — the only one in Portugal). It offers 8 suites (all with bedroom, bath, and living room, plus a verandah with a sea view) and 12 rooms; grounds that include a swimming pool and a tennis court; and a highly praised restaurant that has earned a Michelin star. Open year-round (restaurant closed Tuesdays; reservations advised). Note that credit cards are not accepted and that this hostelry is not on the coast, which is 6 miles (10 km) away. Santa Bárbara de Nexe (phone: 089-90234; in the US, 800-677-3524; fax: 089-90402). Expensive.

FARO: Although the airport for the Algarve is located here and the city teems with tourists, there is nevertheless a very attractive quality about Faro, which is the modern-day capital of the Algarve and, with about 29,000 inhabitants, the largest town on the coast. It has streets paved with white cobblestones, cafés set in parkland, and, despite having been reduced to nearly total rubble in the earthquakes of 1722 and 1755, an Old Town partly enclosed by defensive walls. Enter the old section through the 18th-century Arco da Vila, an archway just south of the Manuel Bivar Gardens bordering the harbor (*doca*). Not far away is the Sé (Cathedral), in Largo da Sé, a square noteworthy in itself for its harmonious lines. The cathedral, first built during the 13th century at the time of the Christian victory over the Moors, was rather clumsily restored during the 18th century after the earthquakes. Little of the original remains — just a 13th-century Gothic tower — but its main body is lined with 17th-century *azulejos.* The *Museu Municipal* (Municipal Museum), near the cathedral in the 16th-century Convent of Nossa Senhora da Assunção (which has a very fine cloister), is made up of two sections: an archaeological collection containing rare Roman objects unearthed in the area, and the Ferreira do Almeida collection of sculpture and painting, including 14th-century jasper statues (open Mondays through Fridays, from 9:30 AM to 12:30 PM and from 2 to 5 PM; admission charge). Faro's Tourist Office (8-12 Rua da Misericórdia; phone: 089-803604) is near the Arco da Vila, while several blocks north is the interesting Igreja do Carmo. A baroque church of some beauty, it has a gruesome Capela dos Ossos — a chapel paneled in bones and skulls dug up in the adjacent cemetery.

A completely different Faro can be discovered by taking a boat excursion through the rare Ria Formosa marshlands, which form a sort of coastal apron south of the city. As planes drone regularly overhead to and from the airport runway nearby, it is possible to see — with the help of a guide — fiddler crabs, gray herons, egrets, storks, gannets, plover, terns, oystercatchers, and, on a good day, the rare purple gallinule. The day trips, available from *Animarus* (Urbanização Horta do Peres, Lote 21-8A, Faro; phone: 089-21376), include a simple Portuguese lunch on a deserted island; bird-watching books and binoculars are provided. Faro's beach, Praia de Faro, also occupies an island, Ilha de Faro; this long and narrow coastal sandbank, about 3 miles (5 km) south of the center, is connected to the mainland by a bridge and also by a ferry from the harbor.

EATING OUT: ***Roque*** – Popular with the locals for its fresh sea fare and low prices, it is on the Ilha de Faro, a short drive from town on the airport road and then across a long, low bridge. The restaurant faces the beach on the marshland side of the island, with a large area for dining outside. Closed Wednesdays in winter. Reservations unnecessary. Major credit cards accepted. Ilha de Faro, Faro (phone: 089-817868). Inexpensive.

En Route from Faro – From here to the east, almost to the Spanish border, the coast is paralleled by a series of sandbars. Like the Costa Vicentina of the western Algarve, the eastern extremity has special charms. Nature has not been spoiled by development, and it is less crowded in summer. Take N125 about 5 miles (8 km) to Olhão and then another 14 miles (22 km) to Tavira.

OLHÃO: A pretty fishing port, Olhão is known as the "Cubist" village, because of its cube-shape white houses with terraced roofs. The peculiarity of its architecture gives it a Moorish appearance, although the town was founded during the 18th century, long after the Moors departed the Algarve. A good local market sells fresh produce and some handicrafts.

TAVIRA: A leading Portuguese weekly has described this as "one of the few places in the Algarve that tourism hasn't corrupted and urban development hasn't disfigured." Happily, the town council has banned construction that might affect the historic qualities of the old town center, which is well worth a stroll. Another fishing port, straddling the Gilão River, Tavira is of ancient origin — the foundations of the bridge across the river date from Roman times. There are remains of an old Moorish castle, and the houses have an Eastern touch to them, with Moorish-influenced roofs. Tavira's Tourist Office is located at the Praça da República (phone: 081-22511).

CHECKING IN: ***Eurotel Tavira*** – This sprawling 80-room hotel is among the better places to stay in the eastern Algarve. It's set in a tourist complex with its own sports facilities and pools, along the main highway almost 2 miles (3 km) east of town. Quinta das Oliveiras, Tavira (phone: 081-22041). Moderate.

En Route from Tavira – Continue east on N125; after Conceição there is a turnoff for Cacela Velha, a small village reconquered by the Moors in 1240 and featuring an 18th-century fort. Another tiny coastal settlement, almost within sight of Cacela Velha, is Fabrica, reached from a road leading off from the Cacela Velha turnoff. Both places have restaurants — little more than local taverns — that make a good stop for a meal. Or stop for a swim or a meal at Praia da Manta Rota (reached by another turnoff from N125), a beach offering a long stretch of white sand (although it is pretty packed in summer). Alternatively, press on along N125 past Monte Gordo — a fishing village turned resort, with pale blue houses and a wide, pine-backed beach — to Vila Real de Santo António, where the Algarve coast comes to an end at the Spanish border.

EATING OUT: ***O Estábulo*** – On Manta Rota beach, it offers a cross-section of traditional Algarve seafood dishes and a good wine list. Reservations unnecessary. Major credit cards accepted. Praia da Manta Rota (no phone). Moderate.

Cacela Velha – A simple, pleasant place catering to a very local clientele (don't expect anything but Portuguese to be spoken). Chicken, pork, and fresh fish cooked on the charcoal grill are the stock in trade, and the fresh oysters are a bargain. No reservations or credit cards accepted. Cacela Velha (no phone). Inexpensive.

Costa da Fabrica – Another very simple place, with a large rush verandah providing an outdoor dining area facing a lagoon-like strip of water busy with swimmers, boaters, and windsurfers. The menu includes *caldeirada* (seafood stew), *frango com amêijoas* (chicken with clams), *ensopado de enguia* (stewed eels), and *arroz de marisco* (rice with shellfish), as well as more fresh, steamed oysters. No reservations or credit cards accepted. Fabrica (no phone). Inexpensive.

VILA REAL DE SANTO ANTÓNIO: This town provides a fitting farewell to the Algarve. When Lisbon was destroyed by an earthquake in 1755, much of the Algarve was also affected, and Vila Real de Santo António was razed. It benefited from the national reconstruction plan drawn up by the Marquês de Pombal, whose classical buildings with minimal exterior decoration were laid out in an austere grid pattern. The old center, an example of a pure Pombaline town, imparts the sense of harmony inherent in this style, but the town's unique flavor also comes from the strong Gypsy influence here. Vila Real looks out on the great expanse of the Guadiana River, across which is Ayamonte, Spain, reached by a recently constructed bridge. A whimsical but interesting museum, the *Museu Manuel Cabanas,* in Praça Marquês de Pombal, the main square, specializes in wood engravings, but it also has material on the history of the town (open from July through September, from 4 to 6 PM and from 9 to 11 PM; the rest of the year, from 11:30 AM to 12:30 PM and from 2 to 7 PM; closed Mondays; no admission charge). The Vila Real de Santo António Tourist Office is on the riverside Avenida da República (phone: 081-43272).

CHECKING IN/EATING OUT: ***Vasco da Gama*** – One of the better places to stay at this far eastern end of the Algarve, it's set among pine trees in the seaside resort of Monte Gordo, a bit less than 2 miles (3 km) west of Vila Real. It has 164 rooms, a restaurant, bar, tennis courts, and its own swimming pool, as well as access to a long strip of sandy beach. Major credit cards accepted. Av. Infante Dom Henrique, Monte Gordo (phone: 081-511321). Moderate.

En Route from Vila Real de Santo António – Travelers can either cut roughly 125 miles (200 km) north across the Alentejo via Beja to Evora (see *Evora,* THE CITIES) and from there return to Lisbon, or they can retrace their path along the Algarve coast to Albufeira and pick up the trunk road back to Lisbon. Before leaving Vila Real, however, one last Algarve excursion can be made to the historic fortress town of Castro Marim, 2½ miles (4 km) north on N122.

CASTRO MARIM: Possibly Portugal's oldest town, it has an unbroken history of settlement going back many centuries before the birth of Christ — neolithic implements found here are believed to have been hewn by the original Portuguese tribes. The Phoenicians arrived during the 9th century BC, and the Romans and the Moors followed centuries later, until the Christian reconquest in 1242. Most of the walls of the original castle-fortress, an accretion of centuries of building, have collapsed, but the whitewashed houses that now constitute the town once all nestled within it. The remaining castle nucleus houses a small historical museum run by the same government agency that administers a nature reserve in the triangle formed by Monte Gordo, Vila Real de Santo António, and Castro Marim. Postcards and posters of the protected wildlife, which includes the white stork and the black-winged stilt, are on sale in the museum (open Mondays through Fridays, from 9:30 AM to 12:30 PM and from 2:30 to 5:30 PM; admission charge). The castle ramparts provide a wonderful view of the Guadiana and the Spanish town of Ayamonte, as well as the Castro Marim salt pans (worked since Roman times) and Vila Real de Santo António.

The Azores

Dreamers and rebels quickly appreciate places like the Azores, which continue to resist the inevitability of progress as the civilized world has come to know it. Rising from the depths of the mid-Atlantic (Lisbon lies about 900 miles to the east, New York 2,300 miles to the west), they are a land apart in pace and setting. Although there has been substantial economic evolution during the past decade, the nine volcanic islands of the archipelago retain a simplicity and cohesiveness that have been erased elsewhere by the frantic tempo and complex demands of modern times. Anyone despairing of finding a place of escape as "unspoiled" as the travel brochures claim it is will find that, in the case of the Azores, the word is apt.

Of the nine islands in the Azores chain, São Miguel, the largest, and neighboring Santa Maria are easternmost. Between 90 and 160 miles to the west are Terceira, Graciosa, São Jorge, Pico, and Faial, clustered in a central island grouping. Flores and its tiny companion, Corvo, are approximately another 150 miles to the west. That they are today an autonomous region of Portugal (linked to the mainland, but fiscally and operationally independent) is a result of settlements established soon after Portuguese explorers came upon them in 1427 or 1431, 8 decades or so after the islands first appeared, misplaced by several hundred miles, on a Genoese map of 1351. While 14th-century Italians (or Italians sailing for Portugal) may have preceded the 15th-century Portuguese, it is also thought that the Carthaginians, consummate seafarers of ancient times, may have preceded them both by nearly 2,000 years, although no remains of Carthaginian settlements have been found.

The Portuguese, who named the islands after the goshawks (*açores*) seen here, proved more committed to these mid-ocean outposts than their possible Carthaginian predecessors. In the century following the Azores' discovery, the Portuguese empire extended to Africa, Asia, and South America, and the islands provided an anchorage and resupply point for voyages of exploration, settlement, trade, plunder, and conquest. Colonization of the Azores themselves began almost immediately, in 1439, with farmers and herdsmen the first settlers. Where soil was ample, large pastures soon replaced the native forest. Where the land was more rock than soil, rock removal followed the cutting away of trees and brush, and the rocks became the walls that today etch the landscape with thin lines of black. Towns developed both in the countryside and along the coasts. Wealth flowed through the ports, where merchants reprovisioned ships or exported barley and maize. By the 18th century, Ponta Delgada (on São Miguel), Angra do Heroísmo (on Terceira), and Horta (on Faial) were large and architecturally distinguished townships, a factor that still weighs in their favor.

Land grants provided a basis of wealth for missions established by Jesuits, Franciscans, and other Catholic religious orders. Beautiful churches and chapels were built in thanks for safe passage or for profits anticipated or gained. Their interiors were gilded and richly detailed, their treasuries stocked with valuable gifts. Although the religious orders are long gone (expelled during the 18th century for religious, political, and economic reasons), the churches they left behind are still in use. Easily accessible and remarkably well preserved, they are a fundamental element of the Azorean lifestyle.

In the late 1700s, after the fortunes of empire had waned, a new armada — American whaling ships — discovered the Azores. Many of the thousands of Azorean men who signed aboard American vessels during the better part of the following century ultimately settled in the United States, forming sizable communities in New England, California, and Hawaii. Others headed to Canada, South Africa, and South America. By local reckoning, today's quarter million Azoreans are outnumbered by emigrants and their descendants four to one.

During World War II, the islands served as a staging area for Europe-bound American forces, a factor that strengthened the already existing commercial and family links to the United States. (The American presence continues in the form of the American-run NATO airfield maintained at Lajes, Terceira.) After the war, but before the advent of the jet plane, the Azores served as a refueling point for airplanes crossing the Atlantic. Otherwise, in the 20th century, with whaling, treasure seeking, and the discovery of new worlds all in the past, the islands settled into the time warp that today is their greatest asset. Outside of Ponta Delgada on São Miguel, the largest city in the islands, there are no traffic jams in the Azores, no contemporary chic, no franchised homogeneity. There is also no mass tourism to thwart authenticity and clutter the landscape with high-rise hotels (though some building projects have recently been undertaken). Few cruise ships come to call, although several hundred sailboats in transatlantic runs between the Caribbean and the Mediterranean do drop anchor off Faial and Flores.

In the villages, where donkeys and horses share the road with cars and pickup trucks, it is the former that set the pace, moving to the rhythm of a pre-industrial clock that ticks in concert to the rise and fall of a temperate sun. Even in Ponta Delgada, and in the other large town, Angra do Heroísmo, on the island of Terceira, the scale remains human, with buildings rarely more than 4 stories high, and even on these two most heavily populated islands, windmills and church towers still dominate the rural skyline. Surrounding them is an intricate web of fields that provide most Azoreans with a livelihood. Farmland — maize is the main crop — and pasture — mostly for dairy cows — occupy the lowlands and the foothills. Only higher up on the mountains are there remnants of the original forests.

The landscape attests to the volcanic origin of the Azores, although once-fiery craters and cinder cones are now dressed in a carpet of green. On most of the islands the largest craters house lovely, steep-walled lakes that reflect the passing clouds and a nightly display of moonglow and shooting stars. Steam vents and hot springs evince the molten fires that still burn beneath the surface calm. Almost all of the islands have experienced either volcanic eruptions or major earthquakes within the past half-decade or so.

Wrestling with nature in mid-ocean isolation has made pioneering self-reliance a definitive part of the Azorean temperament. The climate may be benevolent, avoiding extremes of hot and cold and the worst of the earth's storms, but life still exacts its toll, as the weatherworn features of the old reveal. Homes must be built and kept in good repair. Vineyards must be planted and tended, their grapes turned into wine. Cows must be herded and milked, the milk carted to cooperatives that make flavorful Azorean butter and cheese. Boats must be built and repaired, nets woven and mended for fish to be caught.

Yet because many Azoreans have spent time overseas or have family settled elsewhere, there's a casual sophistication, an awareness of the world beyond that seems incongruous with their rural isolation. English is widely spoken, even in remote villages. Something like "Yeah, I spent 12 years in the States" usually explains it. Some expatriates return to the islands at retirement, when there's an American pension or savings to bankroll land, a house, and the good life. Like mainland Portugal, the Azores are relatively inexpensive, a feature attractive to visitors, too.

The Catholic church plays a crucial role in communal life, dominating the spiritual as well as the terrestrial landscape, as can be seen in the baroque façades on the churches that grace every village, their bells chiming the passing hours to those at home or in the field. The full measure of belief surfaces during the long festival season that runs from spring through early fall, with the largest, most impressive processions and displays held soon after *Easter.* Week after week, different villages celebrate and affirm family bonds and religious fraternity, some villages creating giant street tapestries made of countless flower petals in extravagant design. On Terceira, the festival season ends with the running of rope-tethered bulls through the narrow streets of the larger towns.

Some people believe the Azores are all that remain of the lost continent of Atlantis (Spain's Canary Islands are also a contender for that distinction). Certainly few places offer such easy access to their magic, which makes them both wonderful to explore and vulnerable to the impact of discovery. Winding two-lane roads circle the islands and challenge their volcanic heights. Sometimes views are panoramas, encompassing the mountains, cliffs, and sea. At other times, the attention is drawn by details: the sweet smell of native cedar, the pink brilliance of roadside lilies, the harmony of forest birds. Island to island, nature runs rampant, providing justification for hyperbole and the real opportunity to get away from it all.

SOURCES AND RESOURCES

TOURIST INFORMATION: The Regional Tourism Board for the Azores is headquartered on the island of Faial (Rua Marcelino Lima, Horta; phone: 92-23801). Branch tourist offices are found in Horta, Faial (Rua Vasco da Gama; phone: 92-22237); in Ponta Delgada, São Miguel (Av. Infante Dom Henrique; phone: 96-25743); in Angra do Heroísmo, Terceira (47A Rua Rio de Janeiro; phone:

95-23393); and at Santa Maria Airport (on the island of Santa Maria; phone: 96-82155). There is also a tourist office representative at the *Aparthotel Caravelas* (Rua Conselheiro Terra Pinheiro, Madalena, Pico; phone: 92-92500).

Local Coverage – An English-language booklet, *Azores: Guide for Tourists,* revised annually and distributed free at tourist offices, provides excellent information on all the islands. Also worth reading and available in English editions are pamphlets on the individual islands, each containing useful maps of the island and its main town. The Azorean Emigration Center (11 Praça 5 de Outubro, Ponta Delgada, São Miguel; phone: 96-27486) produces a monthly tabloid that includes some features in English. It is available at the center or at the tourist office in Ponta Delgada.

TELEPHONE: The area code for the islands of São Miguel and Santa Maria is 96; for Terceira, Graciosa, and São Jorge, 95; for Pico, Faial, Flores, and Corvo, 92. If calling from a different area code within the Azores, or from mainland Portugal, dial 0 plus the appropriate area code before the local number. Remember that time in the islands is 1 hour earlier than on mainland Portugal all year long.

CLIMATE: The Azores are not tropical isles. Palm trees are not abundant, and beaches are almost nonexistent. The waters of the Gulf Stream modify the islands' maritime climate, and temperatures average a very comfortable 55 to 77F from the coldest to the hottest months. There are, nevertheless, four distinct seasons, with a change of flowers from spring through autumn. At times, the air can be quite humid, exaggerating summer's warmth or winter's chill. Because the islands lie beneath a mid-ocean convergence of high altitude winds, they have earned a reputation for quickly changing weather and frequent rains. The rainfall that keeps them green occurs mostly from October to April, but weather can be changeable in any season. Frequently heard advice: "Get out there when the sun's out; you never know when it'll change on you."

GETTING THERE: To serve the numerous Azoreans who have settled in New England, *TAP Air Portugal* flies nonstop (once a week) between Boston and Ponta Delgada (São Miguel) and Terceira. Most inbound traffic arrives aboard *TAP* flights from Lisbon to Terceira, Ponta Delgada, and Horta (Faial). Once a week, a *TAP* flight departs from Porto to Ponta Delgada. *TAP* also flies to Ponta Delgada from Madeira.

Inter-island service for all islands except Corvo (which is reached by boat from Flores) is provided by *Serviço Açoreano de Transportes Aéreos* (*SATA*). Local weather conditions may result in flight delays or cancellations, and it is advisable to travel to remote islands such as Flores and Corvo only if there's time to absorb a possible delay of several days or longer. Advance reservations and early arrival at the airport are suggested as flights are often sold out, particularly during winter, when frequency is reduced substantially. *TAP* offices can provide ticketing and information for *SATA* flights.

No ferries connect mainland Portugal with the islands, and there is inter-island ferry service only among the islands of the central group (Terceira, Graciosa, São Jorge, Pico, and Faial). The service is operated by *Transmaçor* (29 Rua Nova das Angústias, Horta, Faial; phone: 92-23334), and if the ferry schedule fits your itinerary, it's a relaxing, scenic, and inexpensive way to travel. The shortest run links Faial to Pico in about a half hour. Faial to São Jorge takes about 2 hours, São Jorge to Terceira about 4 hours, and Terceira to Graciosa about 3 hours. For travel between Flores and Corvo, it's possible to rent a boat, with or without a captain.

SPECIAL EVENTS: Religious festivals held in one village or another fill the calendar year, but are most concentrated from *Easter* through August, so it's worth planning an itinerary to include one. The largest include elaborate processions and tapestries, or mosaics, of flowers laid down in the streets. Particularly noteworthy are the *Festas do Senhor Santo Cristo* (Lord Christ Festivities), the largest religious festival in the islands, held on São Miguel the weekend of the fifth Sunday after *Easter,* in honor of a 16th-century image of Christ in a local church. Two weeks later, on *Whitsunday* (7 Sundays after *Easter*), all the islands begin to hold *festas* in honor of the Holy Spirit, which go on for successive Sundays as village after village puts on its own version of a celebration that goes back to the Middle Ages. The festival lasts throughout the summer on Terceira, where offerings are collected in little chapels called *impérios* and where *touradas à corda* — bullfights in which the bull is tied to a rope and teased but not killed — and the running of bulls through the streets mark the end of the season. The same bullfights, along with folk singing and dancing, are part of the colorful *Festas de São Joaninhos* (St. John's Festivals), held in June on Terceira. From the first to the second Sunday in August, the island of Faial celebrates *Semana do Mar* (Sea Week), a secular event stressing water sports and other water-related activities, with accompanying folk music, band concerts, and parades. Another water-related event is the *Festa dos Baleeiros* (Whalers' Festival), the last week in August on Pico; although whaling is a thing of the past in the Azores, this religious procession, followed by music and dancing, still fulfills a vow made by local whalers in the 19th century. Also during August, Santa Maria holds the *Maré do Agosto* (August Tide), a music festival of contemporary artists that often features international names.

SPORTS AND FITNESS: In addition to the options below, tours with a focus on sports (fishing, golfing, hunting, and others) can be arranged through *Freitas Martins,* 14 Rua Açoreano Oriental, Ponta Delgada, São Miguel (phone: 96-26415).

Deep-Sea Fishing – Local waters provide not just sustenance but big-game sport fishing and some world records. From August through October, the catch is marlin; from September through November, swordfish and tuna; shark, barracuda, bonito, and others are in season all year. Contact *Pescatur* (1 Largo Francisco Tavares, Ponta Delgada, São Miguel; phone: 96-24757). Inland waters on São Miguel and Flores offer a limited season on black bass, pike, perch, and trout. The required licenses can be obtained from *Direcção dos Serviços Florestais* (38 Largo de Camões, Ponta Delgada, São Miguel; phone: 96-26288).

Diving – On Terceira, contact the *Clube Náutico de Angra do Heroísmo* (Estrada Gaspar Côrte Real, Angra do Heroísmo; phone: 95-23300) and rent a boat and driver for a run to the nearest reefs. On Faial, contact *Clube Naval da Horta* (Cais de Santa Cruz, Horta; phone: 92-22331). The *Estalagem de Santa Cruz* (Rua Vasco da Gama, Horta; phone: 92-23021) also handles water sports equipment rentals. On São Miguel, the *Caloura* hotel (Agua de Pau, Lagoa; phone: 96-93240) can provide information regarding equipment, rentals, and locations, as can *H. Moriera* (73 Engenheiro José Cordeiro; phone: 96-35047). Wet suits prevail for much of the year.

Golf – The *Clube de Golfe da Ilha Terceira* (Terceira Island Golf Club; Fajãs Agualva; phone: 95-25847) has an 18-hole course, clubs and caddies for hire, a clubhouse bar and snack shop, and 2 tennis courts. It's closed Mondays except those that fall on holidays (including American holidays, thanks to the air base nearby). São Miguel has a beautiful 9-hole course at the *São Miguel Golf Club* (phone: 96-54141) near Furnas, 45 minutes to an hour from Ponta Delgada. Both offer a setting that emphasizes the relaxation of the game.

Hiking – Hikers can set out on scores of walks in the countryside with no cause for concern. Information about sightseeing hikes can be obtained at the local tourist offices. On Pico, the hike to the summit comes with some precautions (see *Pico,* "Special Places").

Swimming – Rocky coasts make swimming difficult. Among the few beaches are Praia Pim, a half-mile stretch of sand on the outskirts of Horta, Faial; the Praia do Populo, near São Roque, and the Praia da Agua d'Alto, both some miles east of Ponta

Delgada, São Miguel; and a nice carpet of white sand at São Lourenço Bay, on Santa Maria. In addition, swimming is possible in the freshwater crater lakes of São Miguel, particularly the easily accessible Sete Cidades, although the shoreline entry is muddy and coastal waters shallow. Other natural pools created by volcanic rock formations are popular swimming spots for the locals. Cool winters usually make swimming a summer-only sport.

Tennis – There are courts at the *São Miguel Clube de Tênis* (Av. Cecília Meireles, Fajã de Cima, São Miguel; phone: 96-33647). On Terceira, visitors can play at municipal courts or at the tennis courts of the *Terceira Island Golf Club* (see above). There are 2 courts at Horta's *Clube de Tênis* (at the *Fayal* hotel; phone: 92-22181), and another 2 at Pico's *Clube de Tênis* (Externato da Madalena; phone: 92-92145).

SÃO MIGUEL

The largest island of the archipelago and the most heavily populated, São Miguel extends approximately 38 miles from east to west and 10 miles from north to south. It is also widely considered to be the most beautiful island, thanks to luxuriant vegetation, a series of magnificent crater lakes, and a landscape that seems to glow with vibrant color. In the eastern part of the island, at Furnas, the still-active volcanic depths surface in sulfur-fumed steam and boiling water. Not the first of the islands to be discovered, it was, with Santa Maria, one of the first to be colonized, and it has maintained its importance ever since. Ponta Delgada, on the south coast, is the island's capital, the capital of the Ponta Delgada district (one of the three political districts into which the archipelago is divided), and the largest city in the Azores. It's a lively town, with much of architectural note, shops that add a touch of unexpected sophistication, and a distinctive charm. Ribeira Grande, Vila Franca do Campo, and Povoação (the first settlement on the island) are other towns of historical and architectural merit.

It takes a day in the countryside to understand why São Miguel is also called the *ilha verde* (green island). The landscape is a rock-veined patchwork of greens, amply accented with blue-purple hydrangeas, azaleas, and other flowers that scent the air for 8 months of the year. Gently sloping lowlands are punctuated by rows of graceful cinder cones, and dark patches of forest crown the heights. From lookouts atop its tallest mountains, the views are spectacular — but the same could be said about almost any drive on the island.

GETTING AROUND: It takes 2 to 3 days to begin to do justice to São Miguel. Excellent roads circle the island, cutting through the mountains at several places.

Airport – *TAP Air Portugal* arrives daily from Lisbon and weekly from Boston, Porto, and Funchal, Madeira. *SATA* flies in from the other islands. São Miguel's Aeroporto de Ponta Delgada (also called Nordela) is 3 miles (5 km) from the heart of town. Rental cars are available, and a taxi ride into town costs about $3. Offices of both *TAP Air Portugal* (phone: 96-26201) and *SATA* (phone: 96-27221 for information, 96-22311 for reservations) are on Avenida Infante Dom Henrique in Ponta Delgada.

Bicycle – The countryside provides some excellent biking possibilities, although flat, open stretches alternate with hilly terrain that can prove tiring on cross-country rides. Contact *Logo* (Av. Kopke, Ponta Delgada; phone: 96-25795) for bicycle and motorbike rentals.

Bus – Local bus service is available around the island. Sightseeing tours by bus are offered by *Agência de Viagens Ornelas* (Av. Infante Dom Henrique, Ponta Delgada; phone: 96-25379) and by *Agência de Viagens e Turismo Melo* (24 Rua Santa Lucia, Ponta Delgada; phone: 96-25314).

Car Rental – The local Avis affiliate, *Ilha Verde Rent-a-Car* (19 Praça 5 de Outubro, Ponta Delgada; phone: 96-25200; and at the airport; phone: 96-27301), has the largest fleet. You also can find vehicles at *Autoatlantis* (65 Largo de Santo Andre; phone: 96-23465; and at the airport; phone: 96-22491). As a rule of thumb, here and elsewhere in the archipelago, expect a rental car to cost anywhere from $65 to $100 a day, including gas and taxes. Watch out for traffic jams in Ponta Delgada around 9 AM and between 5:30 and 7 PM. Azoreans can be aggressive drivers, so stay alert on the road.

Taxi – Taxis are available, and most offer car-and-driver day rates. As on other islands, hiring a car and driver for a day of touring usually costs less than a rental car, with most taxis available at $50 to $65 for an 8- to 10-hour day. Hotel personnel are usually helpful in securing a car and driver if a taxi is not readily at hand. Be on the lookout for newer, plusher Mercedeses (like the one driven by Vasco Guadencio; phone: 96-97119), if you're going to spend the day touring. They're not necessarily more expensive than some of the more basic models seen around town.

SPECIAL PLACES: Ponta Delgada – Capital of São Miguel since 1546, Ponta Delgada (pop. 63,000) is a flat town that stretches nearly 2 miles along a bay on the island's south coast. The seafront promenade — the Avenida Infante Dom Henrique — is fed by narrow streets that invite wandering. Highlights of any tour of the town are several old churches, including the parish Church of São Sebastião, built in the 16th century, altered in the 18th century, and noted for a Manueline façade and two baroque doorways as well as for a high altar of carved cedar; the Igreja do Colégio, or former Jesuit church, founded in the 15th century, although the present building, an exercise in baroque geometry, dates from later; and the Church of São José, decorated with blue-and white 18th-century *azulejos* (glazed tiles). Also of note are the 18th-century town gates and the Santa Ana Palace, a 19th-century building decorated with intricate woodcarvings and tilework. The *Museu Carlos Machado* (Rua João Moreira) is the city's museum of ethnographic interest, art, and natural history; it's open Tuesdays through Fridays from 10 AM to 12:30 PM and from 2 to 5:30 PM, Saturdays and Sundays from 2 to 5:30 PM; no admission charge. Ponta Delgada began as a fishing village, and boats still unload their catches at sunrise at the western end of the harbor. For those who like sleeping past dawn, an equally colorful sight is the open-air market near Largo São João, open weekdays until 5 PM. The best days for market lovers, however, are Fridays and Saturdays before 1 PM. The market is closed Sundays and holidays.

Caldeira das Sete Cidades – About 20 minutes by car northwest of Ponta Delgada, this is perhaps the single most spectacular sight in the Azores. In the crater of an extinct volcano lie two lakes, separated by a land bridge only a few yards wide. One lake is green, the other blue, and the panorama from the crater rim is worthy of several visits, since it shifts dramatically with the quickly changing Azorean weather. Two roads lead to the crater rim and the charming lakeside village of Sete Cidades. According to legend, one of the seven cities of Atlantis is buried in the crater, thus the name.

Vale das Furnas – The volcanic past comes to life in the steam vents, hot springs, thermal pools, and boiling mud of the Furnas Valley, about an hour east of Ponta Delgada. Also here are a lake (Lagoa das Furnas), a botanical garden (Parque Terra

Nostra), and the spa town of Furnas, whose waters are reputedly effective cures for rheumatism, lumbago, sciatica, skin conditions, and other ailments. For those with adventuresome palates, there are local folk who can help prepare stews or corn on the cob cooked or steamed in the hot thermal springs. Ask at the *Terra Nostra* hotel, Rua Padre José Jacinto Botelho (phone: 96-54304).

Ribeira Grande – Granted a charter in 1507, this town of 27,000 on São Miguel's north coast has many fine 16th- and 17th-century buildings. The church of Nossa Senhora da Estrela, consecrated in 1517, is the oldest; inside, the Santos Reis Magos chapel contains various paintings, including a 16th-century Flemish triptych.

SHOPPING: Ponta Delgada is the island's shopping center. Some very high-style European fashions can be found, but on the whole, the town caters to the local population, meaning more basic clothing, housewares, and other necessary items.

Caleche Design – High-fashion leather goods, some made regionally. Largo da Matriz, Ponta Delgada (phone: 96-22523).

A Central dos Moveis – The furniture may not be worth considering, but the imported Chinese porcelain and bric-a-brac are another matter. 47 Largo Manuel da Ponte, Ponta Delgada (phone: 96-22403).

Jamé – The place to head for camping gear. 42 Largo de Camões, Ponta Delgada (phone: 96-27309).

Radiante – An interesting collection of small gold charms. 46-51 Rua Machado dos Santos, Ponta Delgada (phone: 96-24696).

Xandi – Antiques and contemporary local craftwork. 22 Largo da Matriz, Ponta Delgada (phone: 96-22410).

NIGHTCLUBS AND NIGHTLIFE: Nightlife is scarce in the Azores, and what action there is can be found mostly in São Miguel. The *Nautilus* (1A Praça Velha, Povoção; phone: 96-65481) is a relatively new pub on the island's far southeastern end, with an *esplanada* (patio) and snack bar, plus a discotheque that opens at 11 PM. Closed Mondays. *Cheers* (2 Rocha Quebrada, Atalhada, Lagoa; phone: 96-92662) is a refurbished disco that attracts rowdy locals and is open daily from 10 PM to 4 AM; *Populo's Inn* (Villa Pann, Livramento, Ponta Delgada; phone: 96-31680) is one of São Miguel's most popular dance floors. Closed Mondays. *A Taverna* (42 Rua de São Miguel, Ponta Delgada; phone: 96-24727) is a quiet place with live music nightly, and *fado* on Friday and Saturday evenings.

CHECKING IN: Hotels, pensions, and the occasional inn (*albergaria* and *estalagem*) provide accommodations for visitors. On the whole, on all the islands, even modest rooms are clean and comfortable; at better hotels, they generally come with private baths, telephones, and television sets. As on the Portuguese mainland, breakfast is almost always included in the price. Advance reservations are suggested, particularly during the summer, when limited space may well sell out. Rates are anywhere from 20% to 30% lower in low season, from November through April, but even at their highest, they are quite reasonable compared with mainland Portugal or other tourist destinations. For that reason, almost all of the hotels below fall into one of only two categories, moderate or inexpensive. Expect to pay $75 and up for a double room in the rare hotel listed below as expensive, from $50 to $70 for a double room at hotels listed as moderate, and from $25 to $45 at those listed as inexpensive.

Açores Atlântico – A pink marble hostelry on Ponta Delgada's main seafront avenue. Outside, it's an exercise in island-style architecture with modern flair; inside, there are 140 air conditioned rooms and suites with private balconies, plus a restaurant, a heated indoor pool, a sauna, and a gymnasium. Av. Infante Dom Henrique, Ponta Delgada (phone: 96-629300; fax: 96-629380). Expensive.

Avenida – A modern, 80-room hotel in the heart of town, it's clean and well kept, with such up-to-date facilities as a bar, a restaurant, satellite TV, and gift shops.

Rua Dr. José Bruno Tavares Carreiro, Ponta Delgada (phone: 96-27331; fax: 96-27698). Moderate.

Caloura – On the southern coast of São Miguel, about a 20-minute drive from Ponta Delgada, this contemporary resort offers 40 rooms, a sauna, and a workout room, as well as a swimming pool and an oceanfront setting. Boating, scuba diving, and horseback riding are other options for guests. Agua de Pau, Lagoa (phone: 96-93240). Moderate.

Gaivota – An apartment hotel, its rooms (27) with kitchen facilities are a prime asset; another is a harborfront setting that offers panoramic views from flower-decked balconies. 103 Av. Marginal, Ponta Delgada (phone: 96-23286; fax: 96-27209). Moderate.

São Pedro – This would be a find anywhere in the world, which makes it all the more exceptional in as unexpected a place as Ponta Delgada. An elegant, early-19th-century private home — it originally belonged to Thomas Hickling, first American consul in the Azores — has been turned into the finest hotel in the archipelago, with 26 spacious rooms, antique furnishings, excellent service, and a quiet setting just on the edge of downtown. Advance bookings are heartily recommended. It also has a good restaurant (see *Eating Out*). Largo Almirante Dunn, Ponta Delgada (phone: 96-22223). Moderate.

Solar do Conde – A renovated nobleman's mansion, this apartment hotel has 27 rooms with a traditional atmosphere. Situated a half hour from Ponta Delgada on the north side of the island, it's just yards away from the ocean. There is a restaurant, a bar, a swimming pool, and 2 tennis courts, one of which is covered. 36 Rua do Rosário, Capelas (phone: 96-98887; fax: 96-98623). Moderate.

Terra Nostra – Adjacent to the hot springs in the spa town of Furnas, and permeated with the spirit of the 1930s, when it was built. Staying here is a good idea for those who want to explore the eastern part of the island without the hour's drive from Ponta Delgada. Guests can play golf nearby, stroll in the lovely botanical gardens, dine at the restaurant, soak in the outdoor thermal pool or the newer indoor pool, or otherwise take the waters. There are 74 rooms, including 40 in the wing that contains a gymnasium. Advance reservations are necessary. Rua Padre José Jacinto Botelho, Furnas (phone: 96-54304). Moderate.

Vinha da Areia – An *estalagem* (inn) of 38 rooms, 2 of which are suites facing the sea. Located in Vila Franca do Campo, some 20 miles east of Ponta Delgada, this property has a restaurant, a small private beach, and a natural bathing pool. Vila Franca do Campo (phone: 96-53133; fax: 96-52501). Moderate.

América – This modern, 22-room residential *pensão* is centrally located and well maintained. Friendly service adds a personal touch; no restaurant, but there is a small bar. 58 Rua Manuel Inácio Correia, Ponta Delgada (phone: 96-24351). Inexpensive.

Canadiano – There are 50 rooms in this modern hostelry not far from the *Museu Carlos Machado.* There's no restaurant, but there is a comfortable bar and video room. 24A Rua do Contador, Ponta Delgada (phone: 96-27421). Inexpensive.

Central – The oldest residential pension in Ponta Delgada benefits from charm, a friendly atmosphere, and a central location. No restaurant. 82 Rua Machado dos Santos, Ponta Delgada (phone: 96-24491). Inexpensive.

EATING OUT: On São Miguel and the other islands, restaurant fare tends to be grilled fish or meat rather than local specialties such as *caldo de nabos* (turnip soup) or *linguiça com inhames* (spiced sausage with yams). Dorado is the most common catch of the day; squid, octopus, shrimp, lobster, and crab may all be on the menu of the better restaurants of Ponta Delgada or Angra do Heroísmo. Cheeses, usually tangy, are made in many rural districts; those of São Jorge are the best known. São Miguel's pineapples, grown in greenhouses, are prized. Verdelho wines from Pico are the islands' finest; those of Graciosa and Terceira are also highly rated. The Azores are not the place for haute cuisine, although a few of the better restaurants come close. Happily, the cost of dining in such restaurants is not a great deal higher than eating in more modest establishments, and because the span from most to least is not great, the restaurant listings below dispense with an expensive category. Expect to pay anywhere from $20 to $35 for dinner for two, with light drinks or fairly good wine, in restaurants listed as moderate, and less than $20 in those listed as inexpensive.

London – The place where many local VIPs like to have dinner, it has good service and a varied menu. The location is central. Closed Sundays. Reservations advised. Major credit cards accepted. 21 Rua Ernesto do Canto, Ponta Delgada (phone: 96-22500). Moderate.

São Pedro – The dining room of the best hotel in the islands. Tables are elegantly laid with linen, the waiters are equally well attired, and the food matches the setting. Grilled dorado, shrimp, and spider crab are all worth a mention. Open daily. Reservations unnecessary. Major credit cards accepted. Largo Almirante Dunn, Ponta Delgada (phone: 96-22223). Moderate.

Tropicália – This dining spot created by the owner of the *London,* just a few steps from the *São Pedro* hotel, serves seafood specialties. Open daily for lunch and dinner until 11 PM. Reservations advised. Major credit cards accepted. Largo Almirante Dunn, Ponta Delgada (phone: 96-27100). Moderate.

Arcturus – Nice atmosphere with seafood and meat specialties, located on the west side of town. Open daily except Mondays from noon to 3 PM and from 7 to 11 PM. Reservations unnecessary. Visa accepted. 49C Rua João Francisco Cabral, Ponta Delgada (phone: 96-24990). Moderate to inexpensive.

Boavista – Seafood specialties range from lobster to barnacles, all prepared to taste. This is in the residential part of the city, above the downtown area. Closed for lunch on Saturdays and all day Sundays. Reservations unnecessary. Visa accepted. 12 Rua Ilha São Miguel (upstairs), Ponta Delgada (phone: 96-24272). Moderate to inexpensive.

O Fervedouro – Regional dishes include *caldeirada de peixe* (fish chowder) and *polvo guisado em vinho* (octopus cooked in wine sauce). This is a good lunch stop for those touring the island. Closed Mondays. Reservations unnecessary. Visa accepted. 3 Rua do Passal, Ribeira Grande (phone: 96-72820). Moderate to inexpensive.

White Shark – A small place with interesting maritime decor on the west side of town, it's run by Paul and Mary, a German couple who specialize in shark and beef steaks cooked over a lava stone grill. Open from 6 PM to midnight. Closed Sundays. Reservations advised. Major credit cards accepted. 95 Rua de Tavares Resendes, Ponta Delgada (phone: 96-27663). Moderate to inexpensive.

O Corisco – Casual and in the heart of town, it offers regional specialties and seafood. Closed Mondays. Reservations unnecessary. No credit cards accepted. 28 Rua Manuel da Ponte, Ponta Delgada (phone: 96-24444). Inexpensive.

John's Pub – Piano, guitar, and violins provide the mood for sandwiches or cocktails. Closed Sundays. Reservations unnecessary. No credit cards accepted. Rua Diário dos Açores, Ponta Delgada (phone: 96-24741). Inexpensive.

A Lota – Fresh seafood is the specialty, with a sea view the bonus. Open daily. Reservations unnecessary. No credit cards accepted. 13 Largo do Porto, Lagoa (phone: 96-92595). Inexpensive.

São Miguel – A typical *restaurante da terra* (local eatery) where you'll often see hardy farmers and noisy fishermen having lunch after a trip to Ponta Delgada. Very good fish, and some good, though basic, meat dishes. Near the *Mercado da Graça.* Open from 10 AM to 3 PM and from 6 to 10 PM. Reservations unnecessary. No credit cards accepted. 45 Rua do Mercado (phone: 96-25603). Inexpensive.

SANTA MARIA

Probably the first of the Azores sighted by Portuguese explorers, Santa Maria is 55 miles south of São Miguel and is the southernmost island in the archipelago. Along with São Miguel, it was also one of the first to be settled, and by 1472 its main town, Vila do Porto — but then known simply as Porto — became the first town in the islands to receive a charter. Christopher Columbus dropped anchor here in 1493 on his return from the West Indies; members of his crew are said to have prayed in a tiny church that still stands at Anjos, on the north coast. The island measures approximately 11 miles from east to west and 6 to 7 miles from north to south, yet its terrain ranges from hilly in the northeast to flat in the southwest and encompasses sheer coastal cliffs, deeply indented bays, and pastoral villages. The large airport outside Vila do Porto is a still-used reminder of the role the Azores played during World War II as a forward base for American troops and in Allied antisubmarine efforts. Today, jets make use of its long runway on flights linking the islands with South America.

GETTING AROUND: Airport – *SATA* flies between São Miguel and Santa Maria (*SATA*'s phone in Vila do Porto: 96-82497). The island's Aeroporto de Santa Maria is just short of 2 miles (3 km) northwest of Vila do Porto.

Car Rental – Rental cars are available from *Rent-a-Car Mariense,* at the airport (phone: 96-82880). Two-lane roads crisscross the island, which can easily be seen in a day. More time can be utilized by slowing down to appreciate things at an Azorean pace.

SPECIAL PLACES: Vila do Porto – Whitewashed walls and red tile roofs define Santa Maria's main town (pop. 5,800), located on a bay in the southwestern corner of the island. Among its landmarks is the 19th-century parish church, built on the site of a ruined 15th-century church, of which a chapel with a Manueline ceiling remains. The Convent of São Francisco, built in the 17th century, then destroyed by pirates and rebuilt in the 18th century, has lovely chapels, including one decorated with 17th-century glazed Portuguese tiles.

Pico Alto – Santa Maria's highest peak (almost 1,950 feet), in the center of the island, provides wide-angle views.

Baia de São Lourenço – On the northeast coast, São Lourenço has, besides the bay itself, a beach of white sand — a rarity in the Azores. Off the beach is an islet, the Ilhéu do Romeiro, which has an interesting cave and can be reached by boat.

Anjos Chapel – This small chapel on the north coast is a beautifully detailed 15th-century gem that is probably the oldest church in the islands. It has associations with Columbus, some of whose crew gave thanks here in 1493 for their safe return from the voyage that resulted in the European discovery of America.

NIGHTCLUBS AND NIGHTLIFE: *Paradise* is Santa Maria's only nightclub, open daily from 11 PM to 4 AM. Rua São José, Vila do Porto (phone: 96-84229).

CHECKING IN: *Aeroporto* – The only choice. Luckily, this 73-room hotel at the airport is clean and well run, and has a pretty good restaurant (see below). Estrada do Aeroporto, Vila do Porto (phone: 96-82211 or 96-86215). Inexpensive.

EATING OUT: ***Praia*** – A simple place in a village on a south coast beach; the menu leans toward fish and seafood. Open daily. Reservations unnecessary. Major credit cards accepted. Praia Formosa (phone: 96-82635). Moderate.

Aeroporto – This comfortable restaurant with fish, seafood, beef, and chicken specialties is at the *Aeroporto* hotel. Open daily. Reservations unnecessary. Visa accepted. Estrada do Aeroporto, Vila do Porto (phone: 96-82211). Moderate to inexpensive.

Atlântida – A small eatery that serves good local dishes. Open daily. Reservations unnecessary. No credit cards accepted. Rua Teófilo Braga, Vila do Porto (phone: 96-82330). Inexpensive.

TERCEIRA

The most heavily populated island in the Azores' central group is 90 miles northwest of São Miguel. Measuring approximately 19 miles by 11 miles, it received its name as the third of the islands to be discovered. The first settlers, who arrived in 1450, were Flemish rather than Portuguese — Flanders was linked by marriage to the Portuguese crown. Vasco da Gama made Terceira a port of call on his return from India and buried his brother on the grounds of the Franciscan friary. Thanks to a central location, the port at Angra (the word means "bay"), in the middle of the island's south coast, soon became the largest in the Azores. Raised to the status of town in 1534, it prospered from the 16th to the 18th centuries and was embellished with beautiful churches, mansions, and government buildings. In the 19th century, Queen Maria II added the honorific *heroísmo* to its name in recognition of the role the island played on behalf of the liberal Regency during the Portuguese civil war. The city is the island's capital and the capital of the Angra do Heroísmo district, the second of the political districts into which the islands are divided.

The Terceiran landscape ranges from starkly volcanic to lushly pastured to meticulously divided into walled fields known as *cerrados.* In contrast to Angra's relative sophistication — and despite the presence of a US-manned NATO air base that also serves as the island's commercial airport — the countryside remains remarkably rural and untouched, much as on the more remote islands.

GETTING AROUND: Airport – *TAP Air Portugal* (25-27 Rua Rio de Janeiro, Angra; phone: 95-24489) flies in once a week from Boston and several times weekly from Lisbon; *SATA* (2 Rua da Esperança, Angra; phone: 95-22013 for information, 95-22016 for reservations) flies in from the other islands. Lajes Airport is 15 miles (24 km) northeast of Angra, about 30 minutes by car (rental cars are available). The local buses that stop near the airport entrance take about an hour.

Bus – Public buses provide scheduled, though infrequent, service to outlying villages. Sightseeing tours by bus are arranged by *Empresa de Viação Terceirense* (*EVT*), 15 Rua Dr. Sousa Meneses, Angra (phone: 95-24101).

Car Rental – Several firms operate, including *Rent-a-Car Angrauto* (14-16 Rua Frei Diogo das Chagas, Angra; phone: 95-25585); *AçorAuto* (27B Rua Gervásio Lima, Praia da Vitória; phone: 95-52305), which also has an office at the airport; and *Ilha 3*

Rent-a-Car (22 Rua Direita, Angra; phone: 95-23115), which picks up and delivers anywhere on the island.

Ferry – Ferry service connects Terceira with the other islands of the central group: Graciosa, São Jorge, Pico, and Faial.

Taxi – Taxis are available for full-day and half-day touring, as well as for point-to-point service.

SPECIAL PLACES: Angra do Heroísmo – Named for the sheltered bay that made it a commercial port, Angra was planned in the 16th century but built largely in the 17th and 18th centuries. Although it grew to be one of the two largest cities in the Azores (pop. 36,000), the mansions, churches, and residential and commercial core retain their architectural integrity, and the old part of town has been recognized by UNESCO as a historic monument of international significance. Unfortunately, many of the city's oldest buildings collapsed and many others were badly damaged in 1980, when an earthquake struck. Much has been restored, but there still are signs of the quake's damage.

Among Angra's old buildings, which line narrow streets that wind their way uphill from the port, are the 16th-to-17th-century Colégio church, which has an elaborately carved and gilded altar and a collection of 17th-century Dutch glazed tiles; the 16th-century church of São Gonçalo, also with a carved and gilded altar; and the 17th-century Palácio Bettencourt, a baroque mansion now the repository of extensive archives. The *Angra Museum* (Ladeira de São Francisco; phone: 95-23147), housed in the former Convento de São Francisco (where the remains of Vasco da Gama's brother are supposed to lie), contains paintings, ceramics, coins, and weaponry (open Mondays through Fridays from 9 AM to 12:30 PM and from 2 to 5 PM; no admission charge). The 16th-century castle of São João Baptista, at the western edge of town, is still used by the Portuguese military; it stands at the foot of Monte Brasil, an extinct cinder cone that guards the approach to the port and provides panoramic views of the city and surrounding countryside — it's a favorite picnic spot.

Biscoitos – On the island's north coast, this coastal plain is dotted with unusual formations of black volcanic rock. Walls of lava rock enclose fields of black soil planted with grapes, the harvest used to make the local Biscoitos wines.

Mata da Serrata – These forested hillsides on Terceira's west coast, 45 minutes to an hour from Angra, offer expansive views that take in the neighboring islands of São Jorge and Pico. The sight is particularly impressive at sunset.

Algar do Carvão and Furnas do Enxofre – Ten miles (16 km) and approximately 25 minutes from Angra, in the island's central highlands, are caves with stalactites and stalagmites, usually open on weekends only (more frequently during the summer). Nearby are the steam vents known as the Furnas do Enxofre.

SHOPPING: The best buys are island crafts, particularly embroidered items.

Casa Ilha Lilas – Hand-embroidered goods and other regional handicrafts. 40A Rua de Santo Espírito, Angra (phone: 95-22436).

Direcção Regional dos Assuntos Culturais – The best selection of crafts in the Azores — handwoven wools, appliquéd wall hangings, embroidery — all reasonably priced. Palácio dos Capitões Gerais, Largo Prior do Crato, Angra (phone: 95-25024).

João Pimental e Companhia – Another source of handmade embroidered items and other handicrafts. 107 Rua de Jesus, Angra (phone: 95-24968).

Luís Brandão – A well-priced selection of handmade embroidery, including appealing children's clothing and high-quality table linen. 84A Rua Rego, Angra (phone: 95-23284).

NIGHTCLUBS AND NIGHTLIFE: *Twin's* (54 Rua Dioga Teive, Angra do Heroísmo; phone: 95-32999) is one of the best-known dance spots in the islands, closed Mondays. *Charlie Crown* (138 Estrada 25 de Abril, Praia da Vitória; phone: 95-52570) is a disco near the American air base, open daily.

CHECKING IN: ***Angra*** – A popular 86-room hotel in the heart of the Old City — which means both a central location and a noisy stay if your room faces the busy Praça Velha (formerly Praca da Restauração), the city's main square. Praça Velha, Angra (phone: 95-24041 or 95-24044; fax: 95-24041). Inexpensive.

Beira Mar – This 15-room *pensão* in the Old City looks out on the harbor and Monte Brasil. Rooms are comfortable and quiet, with small balconies and modern facilities, while the restaurant on the ground floor (see *Eating Out*) is one of the best in the Azores. 1 Rua São João, Angra (phone: 95-25189). Inexpensive.

Cruzeiro – A modern *albergaria* (inn) with 47 rooms in a quiet setting only a short walk from the heart of town; no restaurant. Praça Dr. Sousa Júnior, Angra (phone: 95-24071). Inexpensive.

Monte Brasil – In a lovely setting overlooking the harbor in the Monte Brasil residential section of Angra, this *pensão* has 32 modern rooms (but those facing the street tend to be noisy on weekends). The dining room offers wide-angle views. 8-10 Alto das Covas, Angra (phone: 95-22440). Inexpensive.

Teresinha – A best bet for those who want to stay outside Angra, in smaller Praia da Vitória on the island's east coast, about 10 minutes south of the airport. A residential *pensão* with no restaurant, it offers a homey atmosphere and 27 rooms with private bath. 45 Praçeta Dr. Teotónio Machado Pires, Praia da Vitória (phone: 95-53032). Very inexpensive.

EATING OUT: ***Adega Lusitânia*** – Regional dishes are served in a setting reminiscent of a candlelit wine cellar. This is a favorite with local cognoscenti. Closed Sundays. Reservations unnecessary. Major credit cards accepted. 63 Rua de São Pedro, Angra (phone: 95-22301). Moderate.

Beira Mar – A restaurant that is better known than the *pensão* to which it belongs and is considered one of the best in the islands. Both continental and regional specialties — fish, seafood, beef, chicken, and pork — appear on the menu. The interior is contemporary Portuguese, with plenty of tile to add to the decibel level of a convivial mix of natives and visitors. Closed Mondays. Reservations unnecessary. Major credit cards accepted. 1 Rua São João, Angra (phone: 95-25188). Moderate.

A Ilha – In a village east of Angra, steaks are the specialty of the house. Closed Tuesdays. Reservations unnecessary. Major credit cards accepted. 49 Rua da Igreja, São Sebastião (phone: 95-94166). Moderate.

Bomina – A very popular pastry shop and ice cream parlor. Open daily, throughout the day. Reservations unnecessary. No credit cards accepted. 3 Alto das Covas, Angra (phone: 95-25611). Inexpensive.

Café-Pastelaria Athanasio – The best sandwiches and pastries in town. Open for breakfast and lunch only. Reservations unnecessary. No credit cards accepted. 130 Rua da Sé, Angra (phone: 95-23702). Inexpensive.

GRACIOSA

Only 10 miles by 4 miles in size, this island 60 miles northwest of Terceira is the smallest of the central group. Its proper name means "gracious" or "graceful" in Portuguese; it is also often called the *ilha branca,* or "white island," because of numerous place-names derived from that color, from Barro Branco to Serra Branca. Among its first settlers was Pedro da Cunha, brother-in-law of Christopher Columbus. By 1486 a charter had been granted to Santa Cruz da Graciosa, which is today the island's main town. Given its isolation from the other islands of the group to the south, Graciosa attracted few ships and developed a predominantly agricultural economy, exporting barley, wine, and brandy to Portugal via markets on Terceira. It retains its agricultural focus, as is evident in the lowland pastures and fields surrounding centrally located Pico Timão, only about 1,320 feet high but still the highest point on this least mountainous of all the Azores. Windmills, added in the 19th century to grind grain and draw water from subterranean depths, dot the landscape. Some are still in use, for this is also the driest of the Azores.

GETTING AROUND: Airport – *SATA* (phone in Santa Cruz: 95-72456) flies in several times a week, more frequently in summer than in winter. Ferry service links the island with Terceira. Taxis can be hired for island touring. There is also public bus service on the island.

Car Rental – Rental cars are available from *Auto Turístico Escobar* (*Pensão Santa Cruz,* Largo Barão de Guadalupe, Santa Cruz; phone: 95-72345), and from *Quedina e Filhos Limitada* (Rua Visconde Almeida Garrett, Santa Cruz; phone: 95-72278).

SPECIAL PLACES: Santa Cruz da Graciosa – Set on the northeast coast of the island, this picturesque town (pop. 5,200) of red-roofed white houses is Graciosa's chief port, but it feels like no more than a rural village. The 16th-century parish church and the three small 18th-century chapels at Monte da Ajuda are typically Azorean in style and detail, containing Flemish paintings, carved wood altars, and glazed tiles. The *Ethnographic Museum* (Rua Alexandre Herculano) is a typical old residence displaying artifacts of Graciosa's agricultural past (open from 10:30 AM to 12:30 PM and from 2 to 5:30 PM; closed Mondays; no admission charge).

Praia – Narrow streets lined with 16th- and 17th-century homes make for interesting browsing in this small port and fishing village 5 miles (8 km) south of Santa Cruz. A boat takes visitors to nearby Praia islet for views of the town and surrounding countryside.

Furna do Enxofre – This sulfur cave, also called the Furna da Caldeira, since it's located inside the island's summit crater, is a rare volcanic phenomenon in the southern part of the island. A 300-foot natural tunnel burrows through rocks into a 250-foot high underground cavern, the roof of which is covered with stalactites that hang over a lake of sulfurous water. A stone stairway leads to the lakeshore. Visit between 11 AM and 2 PM, when the sun enters the cave from a narrow opening above and creates dazzling visual effects. Outside, a trail following the crater rim offers sweeping views of the island and, on a clear day, of neighboring, but distant, Terceira, São Jorge, and Pico.

CHECKING IN: *Ilha Graciosa* – An adaptation of a historic old home, this residential *pensão* has 15 rooms with private bath. There is a snack bar, but no restaurant. Av. Moniz Albuquerque, Santa Cruz (phone: 95-72675). Moderate.

Santa Cruz – A centrally located *pensão* with 19 comfortable rooms (with private bath) and an at-home ambience. There is a restaurant (see *Eating Out*). Largo Barão de Guadalupe, Santa Cruz (phone: 95-72345). Inexpensive.

EATING OUT: *Santa Cruz* – The dinner menu at this pension dining room includes fish chowder, parrot fish (when available), and chicken and beef dishes. Open daily. Reservations unnecessary. Major credit cards accepted. Largo Barão de Guadalupe, Santa Cruz (phone: 95-72345). Moderate to inexpensive.

SÃO JORGE

This island is, in fact, a long, narrow, steep mountain range surrounded by the sea: 33 miles long from end to end, but only 5 miles across at its widest point. Despite its central location, 60 miles west of Terceira, 20 miles north of Pico, and 30 miles east of Faial, it is more often seen from a distance than visited. As was the case with most of the other islands in the archipelago, its fertile lowlands were first settled in the middle of the 15th century; subsequently, aside from an invasion (repelled) of French corsairs in the early 18th century, its history has been uneventful. While farms dominate the lowlands, pasture covers much of a central plateau — São Jorge is particularly noted for its dairy products, especially cheese. The island peaks at the nearly 3,500-foot Pico da Esperança. Up-country views are memorable, encompassing not only broad vistas, but also the sight of blue and purple hydrangeas lining the roads in summer. There are several nature preserves, including the small lagoon of the Caldeira do Santo Cristo and the tiny Ilhéu do Topo, an islet off the village of Topo that attracts masses of seabirds. Topo, at the far southeastern tip of São Jorge, was the island's first settlement, but its two main towns today are Velas (pop. 5,500) and Calheta (pop. 4,800), two ports farther up the south coast.

GETTING AROUND: Airport – *SATA* (Rua de Santo André, Velas; phone: 95-42125) flies into the airport outside Velas. Ferry service links the island with others in the central group.

Car Rental – Rental cars and cars with drivers are available from *J. N. Moura* (Av. do Livramento, Velas; phone: 95-42292). A single road runs the length of the island, with several roads climbing upward from it to the central plateau.

SPECIAL PLACES: Velas – Houses with whitewashed walls and red tile roofs make up São Jorge's largest village. The church of São Jorge, built in 1460 with funds donated by Prince Henry the Navigator (but rebuilt in the 17th century), was one of the earliest in the Azores. Also of interest are the 17th-century town hall and small museums dedicated to religious art and island ethnography.

Urzelina – Several miles along the coast south of Velas, at Urzelina, is an isolated bell tower, all that remains of a church destroyed when Pico da Esperança last erupted in 1808.

Belvederes – The lookouts at Ribeira do Almeida and Fajã das Almas, both southeast of Velas on the road to Calheta, provide impressive views of Faial and Pico. The lookout at Fajã dos Cubres, on the north coast near Norte Pequeno, takes in the small lakes of the island's summit crater.

NIGHTCLUBS AND NIGHTLIFE: *Zodiac* is a discreet pub with live music on Tuesdays, Wednesdays, and Thursdays; open from 8 PM to 4 AM, closed Mondays. Av. do Livramento, Velas (phone: 95-42677).

CHECKING IN: *Solmar* – The best bet for those staying in Calheta, it has 9 clean, comfortable rooms with private baths. No restaurant, but there's a bar. Rua Domingos Oliveira, Calheta (phone: 95-46120). Moderate.

Das Velas – The island's largest hostelry is an *estalagem* (inn) of 24 rooms, featuring private baths and verandahs with views of Velas and of neighboring islands. A restaurant and lounge are on the property. Rua Machado Pires, Velas (phone: 95-42632). Inexpensive.

Neto – A *pensão residencial* offering 16 rooms with private bath and a seawater swimming pool. No restaurant. Largo Conselheiro Dr. João Pereira, Velas (phone: 95-42403). Inexpensive.

EATING OUT: *Beira Mar* – Seafood specialties include octopus and the catch of the day. Open daily in summer; closed Sundays the rest of the year. Reservations unnecessary. Visa accepted. Largo Conselheiro Dr. João Pereira, Velas (phone: 95-42342). Moderate.

Continental – The menu ranges from seafood to beef, pork, and veal. Closed Mondays. Reservations unnecessary. Visa accepted. Rua Padre Joaquim Moreira, Calheta (phone: 95-46200). Moderate.

Café Central – Regional dishes are the menu, with *cozido à portuguesa* (a potluck of various meats and vegetables) topping of the list of specialties. Reservations unnecessary. No credit cards accepted. Travessas, Ribeira Seca, Calheta (phone: 95-46178). Inexpensive.

PICO

The volcanic peak that dominates the landscape also gives Pico (peak) its name. At just over 7,750 feet, cloud-shrouded Pico Grande is the tallest not only in the Azores, but in all of Portugal. The island is the second-largest in the chain (measuring approximately 30 miles from east to west and 9 miles from north to south). Its northern coast falls to the sea in a series of steep cliffs; its southern coast, where the descent to the sea is more gradual, hosts numerous fishing and farm villages. Pastureland exists, but most of the farming done on rugged Pico is fruit growing and the cultivation of the vine, particularly on the fertile volcanic soil of the western part of the island. Several small lakes are also found on the western side, and throughout there are unusual formations of lava rock, called *mistérios,* caused by 18th-century volcanic eruptions, as well as several caves. Native laurel and cedar line the roads.

Settlement began in 1460 on the island's southern coast, near the village of Lajes do Pico. By the 19th century, Lajes had emerged as a major whaling port, and today the town has a small museum, the *Museu dos Baleeiros* (Rua da Pesqueira), documenting its whaling history (open daily from 10:30 AM to 12:30 PM and from 2 to 5:30 PM, Sundays from 2 to 5:30 PM; no admission charge). The *Festa dos Baleeiros* (Whalers Festival), which takes place the last week in August, continues to fulfill a vow made by local whalers in the late 19th century, even though whaling is now a thing of the past in the Azores. Besides Lajes, Pico has two other main towns: São Roque do Pico, on the island's northern coast, and Madalena, on its northwestern coast, directly across from Horta, Faial. Either Lajes or Madalena can make a good base for touring, although Madalena is better prepared to serve visitors.

GETTING AROUND: Airport – *SATA* (phone in Madalena: 92-92411) has daily flights to and from Terceira in summer, less frequently in winter. Ferries connect the island with others in the central group.

Bus – Public buses circle the island.

Car Rental – Cars can be rented from *Manuel Pereira do Amaral Rent-a-Car* (Largo Cardeal Costa Nunes, Madalena; phone: 92-92253), and from *Colômbis Rent-a-Car* (Av. Machado Serpa, Madalena; phone: 92-92601). The island can be seen in 1 day, although side trips to explore all its villages and caves and perhaps to hike to the summit can easily absorb 3 days.

Taxi – Taxis are available for car-and-driver hires.

SPECIAL PLACES: Pico Grande – Pico's summit caldera can be reached by trail. While the hike is not too demanding, it can be dangerous if bad weather suddenly sets in, which frequently happens. During the winter, hiking is complicated by snows that cover the upper slopes. Guides are recommended (check with the tourist office representative at the *Aparthotel Caravelas* in Madalena). The ample reward is a 360° perspective that includes Pico and neighboring Faial, São Jorge, and Terceira.

CHECKING IN: ***Açor*** – A 13-room *pensão residencial* in a private garden setting, on a quiet street within easy walking distance of both the port and the center of town. Rooms have private baths, and there are wonderful views of the sea; no restaurant. 5A Rua D. João Paulino, Lajes (phone: 92-97243). Inexpensive.

Aparthotel Caravelas – This modern 67-unit hotel, including 17 apartments with kitchens, is within walking distance of Madalena's small harbor. Rooms have balconies and views of the coast; the hotel has a restaurant, a gymnasium, a sauna, and a solarium. Rua Conselheiro Terra Pinheiro, Madalena (phone: 92-92500). Inexpensive.

Montanha – A *pensão residencial* in a scenic wooded area that offers a panoramic view over Pico to the island of São Jorge. There are 16 rooms with bath; no restaurant, but there is a snack bar. Rua do Capitão-Mor, São Roque do Pico (phone: 92-94699). Inexpensive.

Pico – Conveniently located on the outskirts of town, this *pensão* has 32 modern, comfortable, quiet rooms and a friendly and helpful staff. The restaurant is perhaps the best on the island (see *Eating Out*). Biscoitos, Madalena (phone: 92-92392). Inexpensive.

EATING OUT: ***Pico*** – The dining room of the *Pensão Pico* offers an extensive menu of well-prepared fish and meat specialties, as well as alfresco dining in summer. Open daily. Reservations unnecessary. Major credit cards accepted. Biscoitos, Madalena (phone: 92-92392). Moderate.

O Moinho – Fresh catch of the day is the specialty of the house. Just outside Lajes, with spectacular coastal views from the outdoor patio. Open daily. Reservations unnecessary. Major credit cards accepted. Miradouro do Arrife, Terras (phone: 92-97292). Moderate to inexpensive.

O Cadete – Regional dishes and specialties fresh from the sea are served here. Open daily. Reservations unnecessary. No credit cards accepted. Poço, São Roque do Pico (phone 92-94595). Inexpensive.

FAIAL

The westernmost island in the central group, measuring 15 miles by 10 miles, Faial is in part scarred by the eruption of an offshore volcano that took place in 1957, lasted a year, and left the island slightly larger than it had been. Elsewhere, typically flourishing green pastures dominate the landscape, providing a foreground for magnificent views of the towering summit on neighboring Pico, 5 miles away across the Canal do Faial. The island takes its proper name from the forests of beech that once covered it, although it is the ubiquitous blue hydrangeas that grow here today that have earned it the nickname "blue island." Horta, in the southeast corner of the island, is an important port, the island capital, and capital of the third of the Azores' three political districts.

The earliest settlers on Faial were Flemish farmers and herdsmen who arrived in the mid-15th century under the auspices of a Flemish nobleman, Josse de Hurtere. The parish of Flamengos, which lies in a picturesque valley, is a reminder of those times, as is the name of the town of Horta itself. Several centuries later, with the island heavily settled by Portuguese, Faial became a popular port of call for American whalers, who took advantage of Horta's sheltered waters to reprovision their ships. During World War II, the Allies used it as a way station for troops en route to the invasion of Normandy. In 1919, Horta also served as a stopover for the first airplane flight across the Atlantic, and at one time it was the relay point for every cablegram sent across the ocean floor. Today, particularly in April, May, September, and October, it provides refuge for yachts in transit between the Mediterranean and the Caribbean.

GETTING AROUND: Airport – *TAP Air Portugal* (28 Rua Vasco da Gama, Horta; phone: 92-22665) flies nonstop from Lisbon 3 days a week year-round. *SATA* (Rua Serpa Pinto, Horta; phone: 92-23911) flies in from the other islands. The island airport, Aeroporto da Horta, is about 6 miles (10 km) west of town, at Castelo Branco.

Bus – Local bus service links Horta with other island villages.

Car Rental – Contact *Auto Turística Faialense* (12 Rua Conselheiro Medeiros, Horta; phone: 92-22308), or *Ilha Azul* (14 Rua Conselheiro Medeiros, Horta; phone: 92-31150).

Ferry – There is direct ferry service between Horta and Madalena, Pico, and between Horta and Velas, São Jorge; service to Terceira and Graciosa is indirect.

Taxi – Island taxis are available for touring as well as for individual trips. Try *Fraga* (phone: 92-25575), *João Duarte* (phone: 92-98270), or *Gilberto Dutra* (phone: 92-23921).

SPECIAL PLACES: Horta – This is a tranquil town of 15,300, set on gently sloping land surrounding a sheltered harbor and still graced with the scale and architectural detail of its 16th- and 17th-century origins. It is hard to imagine it as a battleground, but that is indeed what it became in 1583, when the Spanish fleet attacked the Portuguese garrison at the Fort of Santa Cruz; in 1597, Sir Walter Raleigh attacked the same fortress. Horta's harborside jetties are most interesting: They're covered with graffiti — that is, signatures, dedications, and hand-painted murals done by sailors throughout the years, their artistic efforts memorializing long journeys and adventures shared. Also see the 17th-century parish Church of São Salvador, with carved choir stalls and two notable panels of tiles, and the 17th-century São Francisco convent, which has a magnificent gilded altar, paintings, and more glazed tiles. The *Horta Museum* (Largo Duque d'Avila e Bolama; phone: 92-23348) includes religious art, wood sculptures, and a collection of intricately carved figwood miniatures that are something of a local tradition (open weekdays from 9 AM to 12:30 PM and from 2 to 5 PM, weekends from 2 to 5:30 PM; no admission charge). The *Café Sport* (see *Eating Out*) houses an interesting scrimshaw museum. Just outside Horta is the Jardim Botânico do Faial (Botanical Garden of Faial; Rua São Lourenço, Flamengos; phone: 92-31119), which features over 100 species of flora. Open daily from 9 AM to noon and from 2 to 3:30 PM; no admission charge.

Ponta dos Capelinhos – The lava- and cinder-scarred landscape here at the westernmost point of the island is a result of the Azores' last major volcanic eruption, which took place in 1957 when a submarine volcano emerged from the sea. Multicolored cinder cones add beauty to a scene of silent devastation, with half-buried houses protruding from hardened ash and the burned-out skeleton of the towering lighthouse that once stood on a coastal cliff now several hundred feet inland.

Caldeira – In the center of the island, Faial's summit caldera is more than a mile in diameter and filled with a crater lake. The highest point is reached at 3,500-foot-high

Cabeço Gordo, and the road leading up to it provides magnificent views of the islands of São Jorge and Pico. En route, some of the few remaining windmills on the island can also be seen.

CHECKING IN: ***Fayal*** – Set on a hillside overlooking Horta, this is as close as Faial gets to a resort hotel. It offers modern conveniences, 84 comfortable rooms, a nightclub, a restaurant (see *Eating Out*), and a bar, as well as quiet, landscaped grounds that include a swimming pool and tennis courts. Rua Consul Dabney, Horta (phone: 92-22181). Moderate.

Santa Cruz – A contemporary 25-room *estalagem* (inn) built atop the 16th-century fortress of Santa Cruz. It's graced with a historic setting, a central location, Portuguese decor, and across-the-harbor views of the summit on Pico. Facilities include a bar and restaurant. Major credit cards accepted. Rua Vasco da Gama, Horta (phone: 92-23021). Moderate.

São Francisco – In the heart of town, this 32-room residential pension offers friendly service, quiet rooms, and something of the feel of a monastery. No restaurant. 13 Rua Conselheiro Medeiros, Horta (phone: 92-22957). Inexpensive.

EATING OUT: ***Fayal*** – This hotel dining room serves well-prepared dishes such as pork chops "American-style" (grilled) and scallops of beef in madeira wine. Open daily. Reservations unnecessary. Major credit cards accepted. Rua Consul Dabney, Horta (phone: 92-22181). Moderate.

Vista da Baia – American Mary Vargas moved to Faial years ago with her Faial-born husband, Frank. Now they run a restaurant that overlooks the bay at Varadouro, on the island's west coast. Barbecued chicken is the specialty of the house, but this is also a great place to drop by for a drink and some small talk. Closed Mondays. Reservations unnecessary. Major credit cards accepted. Estrada do Varadouro (phone: 92-95140). Moderate.

O Tripeiro – By reputation, the best restaurant on the island. A short walk past the harbor, the setting is simple, and the seafood and fish are fresh and delicious. Closed Mondays. Reservations unnecessary. Major credit cards accepted. 24 Av. Marginal, Horta (phone: 92-23295). Moderate to inexpensive.

Café Sport – The "in" place for the at-anchor yacht crowd, this is also known as "Peter's café," or simply "Pete's," and it's known in sailing circles far beyond the shores of the Azores. It also attracts its share of locals, which makes for an interesting, high-energy mix when the drinks are flowing, as they usually are after 5 PM. The menu of fish and meat dishes is okay, but the bar and the crowd (and the interesting scrimshaw museum upstairs) are the real attractions. Open daily. Reservations unnecessary. Visa accepted. 9 Rua Tenente Valadim, Horta (phone: 92-22327). Inexpensive.

FLORES

The remotest islands of the Azores are Flores and Corvo, and of these, Flores, about 150 miles from Faial, is the westernmost island in the archipelago and the westernmost point of Europe. The island (11 miles long and 9 miles wide) offers surprisingly diverse beauty within its modest boundaries: rugged terrain, dramatic shoreline cliffs, lovely crater lakes, waterfalls, and everywhere the abundance of wildflowers that eventually gave it its name. Some visitors consider São Miguel the most beautiful of the Azores, but Flores has equally enthusiastic advocates. After its discovery in 1452, early attempts to colonize the island by Flemish settlers were unsuccessful, so that actual settlement did not begin until 1528, when farmers and herdsmen from northern Portugal arrived. During the 16th and 17th centuries, English privateers encroached on the island's serene isolation by using its waters as a base to attack Spanish galleons returning with treasure from the New World. In 1862, the Confederate privateer *Alabama,* outfitted by the British, used it as a base to attack American ships. Today the island's small population (about 4,350), engaged in agriculture and fishing, lives as peaceably as ever, mainly in two towns: Santa Cruz das Flores, in the middle of the island's east coast, and the smaller Lajes das Flores, in its southwest corner.

GETTING AROUND: Airport – Until fairly recently, the only way to reach Flores was by boat, as the old airport did not accommodate commercial airliners. Now the only way to reach the island (except from Corvo) is by plane: *SATA* (phone in Santa Cruz: 92-52425) flies to the island's newly renovated airport. Infrequent service, however, combined with stormy weather during winter months, makes a quick visit risky. Although the island can easily be seen in a day, it's not unusual for visitors to be stranded for a week or longer.

Car Rental – Rental cars are available from *Rent-a-Car Vila Flores,* Travessa de São José, Santa Cruz (phone: 92-52190).

Taxi – Taxis provide car-and-driver service for sightseeing out of Santa Cruz.

SPECIAL PLACES: Santa Cruz das Flores – Churches from the 16th through the 19th centuries provide this charming village with architectural significance. Among them are the parish church, Nossa Senhora da Conceição, a 19th-century building with an imposing façade, and São Pedro, an 18th-century rebuilding of a 16th-century structure, notable for its carved and gilded high altar.

Enxaréus Grotto – Boats take visitors along the deeply indented, cliff-lined coast for a visit to this dramatic sea cave about 3 miles south of Santa Cruz.

Vale da Fajãzinha – On the western coast of Flores, this is a valley with lovely waterfalls cascading to the sea and lush vegetation to give it a feel of the tropics. It's reached by a winding road that makes its way down from the main road leading from Santa Cruz to Lajedo, a 10-mile (16-km) trip that takes about 45 minutes.

Lagoa Funda – The prettiest of the seven crater lakes on the island is surrounded by hydrangeas. It's about a half-hour drive inland from Santa Cruz.

CHECKING IN: *Toste* – A 10-room *pensão residencial,* basic but comfortable. Breakfast is served, but there's no restaurant. There is, however, a small supermarket nearby. Rua Senador André de Freitas, Santa Cruz (phone: 92-52119). Inexpensive.

Vila Flores – This 9-room *pensão* is clean and comfortable, with a homey atmosphere and a restaurant (see *Eating Out*). Rua Senador André de Freitas, Santa Cruz (phone: 92-52190). Inexpensive.

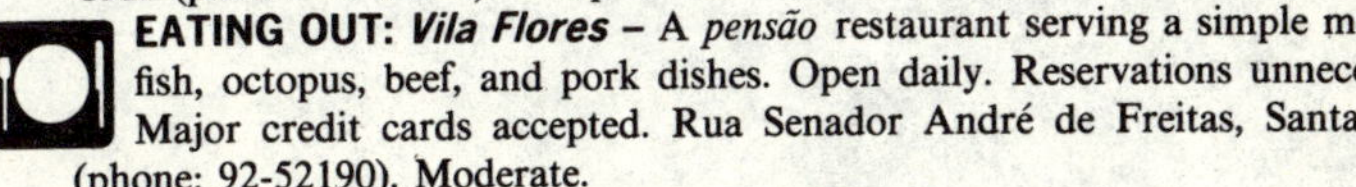

EATING OUT: *Vila Flores* – A *pensão* restaurant serving a simple menu of fish, octopus, beef, and pork dishes. Open daily. Reservations unnecessary. Major credit cards accepted. Rua Senador André de Freitas, Santa Cruz (phone: 92-52190). Moderate.

CORVO

The smallest of the Azores has a population to match its size: Only about 370 people call Corvo home. The island lies 15 miles northeast of Flores and was discovered the same year (1452), although it was settled later (1548). Its name dates back to days when both it and Flores were known jointly by one name, Ilha dos Corvos Marinhos, or "Island of the Sea Crows." Only about 4½ miles long and 3 miles wide, Corvo, like its sister islands, packs a great deal of natural beauty into a very small space. In the north is the Caldeirão, the extinct volcanic crater that formed the island, now carpeted in green and filled with two lovely lakes. From 2,200-foot-high Monte Grosso, atop the crater rim, the panoramic views are magnificent. In the south are the islanders' cultivated fields and pastures, and at the very southern tip, their only settlement, Vila Nova do Corvo, a typically picturesque town of red-roofed white houses laid out along narrow streets called *canadas.* The only way to reach Corvo is by boat from Santa Cruz das Flores. There are no rental cars, but a few taxis are available — and a taxi should be sufficient, since the island has a single road, about 5 miles long, linking the town in the south to Caldeirão in the north. There are no hotels or other hostelries. Camping out is one possibility; by asking around, you may find someone to put you up, pension-style. As for eating out, you're on your own.

Madeira

Lying nearly 400 miles off Morocco's Atlantic coast and nearly 600 miles southwest of the Portuguese mainland, Madeira rises from the sea in an angular assault of mountains, valleys, ravines, and cliffs, the result of millions of years of volcanic activity and erosion. On coastal lowlands and on steep hillsides, terraced fields and rustic homes replace the anarchy of once primeval forest with the geometry of human settlement. Only in a few places, where mountains and sea cliffs proved too vertical and too inaccessible for even the hardy Madeirans to colonize, can fragments of the dense forest that once dominated the island (Ilha da Madeira means "island of wood" in Portuguese) still be found, along with stark evidence of its volcanic past.

Madeira shares its oceanic isolation with a small fleet of neighboring islands that make up the Madeira archipelago. Porto Santo, 27 miles to the northeast across occasionally choppy seas, is comparatively low lying and the only other inhabited island in the group. It serves as a summer getaway for residents of the main island, thanks to sand dunes, beaches, and some of the islands' sunniest weather. To the southeast lie the rugged, unsettled Ilhas Desertas, often visible from Madeira in sharp-edged silhouette on the southeastern horizon. Still farther south, not far from Spain's Canary Islands, is a cluster of equally barren islets, the wild Selvagens.

Until 1964, when a jet airport finally was built on Madeira, visitors arrived aboard passenger ships that made Funchal, the only community on Madeira large enough to be called a city, a standard port of call on transatlantic and around-the-world cruises. Cruise ships still drop anchor at Funchal, which is built around a bay along the island's sheltered south coast, but it was the coming of the jets that opened Madeira to the European holidaymakers who have been arriving in increasing numbers ever since. With 100,000 people, more than a third of the island's population, and a year-round flow of visitors, Funchal is a bustling city that also serves as the capital of the archipelago, which is, in turn, an autonomous region of Portugal. Portuguese law applies, although the local legislature plays a significant role in administration, planning, and budgeting. As with most islands, where isolation establishes a reality that is somewhat different from life on the mainland, here, too, a well-defined individuality encourages consideration of full independence. It is a scenario, however, that practically no one takes very seriously.

For winter-weary Europeans, Madeira's climate is its primary attraction. Winter temperatures rarely dip below 50F, and average a comfortable 60F when most of Europe is 20 to 30 degrees colder. North Americans expecting a Portuguese version of the Caribbean, Mexico, or Hawaii, however, may find such temperate weather a surprise — and something of a disappointment. Summer temperatures are no more extreme, seldom topping the 70s. Indeed, springtime plots a 12-month course here, with one flower or another —

bougainvillea, hibiscus, begonias, birds of paradise, anthuriums, orchids, morning glories, hydrangeas — blooming and one fruit or another — mangos, papayas, figs, oranges, pears, avocados, guavas, passion fruit — ripening throughout the year. Few are indigenous; Madeira's subtropical climate and rich volcanic soil proved a hospitable habitat for plants brought by trading ships from all parts of the globe, tropical and temperate.

Because the island rises so precipitously from sea level to mountaintop, it has distinct zones of vegetation, and visitors can climb from sugarcane to pines and heather in the course of only a short drive. Madeira's steep rise from the sea is the cause of another peculiarity that may disappoint: its lack of sandy beaches. There are a few stretches of gravel or pebbles along the shoreline, and Porto Santo is well endowed with sand, but in the main, swimming on Madeira is confined to hotel pools or to small coves developed with cabaña facilities. Thus, for an American visitor, it is the charm of Funchal and the dramatic beauty of the landscape, not the lure of a tropical getaway, that makes a visit worthwhile.

Oblong in shape, roughly 35 miles from east to west and 13 miles from north to south, Madeira is traversed by well-maintained, well-marked roads. Panoramic vistas are a part of any drive, even within the confines of Funchal, where city streets climb 2,000 feet or more above sea level before surrendering to farmland, forest, and the jagged mountains seen from lookouts such as that atop 6,104-foot Pico Ruivo, the island's highest point. More than half of Madeira's inhabitants still live out in the countryside, particularly in the southern part of the island, where their terraced fields — called *poios* — create what seems a vast agricultural suburb extending nearly the full length of the south coast. Funchal itself retains the feel of a large village, with open markets, narrow streets, and a 17th-century scale, while actual small villages such as Ribeira Brava and Machico, west and northeast of Funchal respectively, and São Vicente, on the north coast, evoke the atmosphere and scale of traditional Madeira, with whitewashed, tile-roofed houses and the distinctive square bell towers of Madeiran churches dominating the skyline. Yet growth has been explosive for the past several decades, fueled by expanding tourism that has left casino gambling, high-rise resort hotels, and condominium apartments in its wake, and by agricultural exports and the money sent back to families by citizens living and working overseas.

Madeirans have been shipping out to parts unknown for several centuries, first drawn aboard as sailors and later enticed by opportunities offered in places as far afield as New England, Hawaii, South Africa, and Australia. Although legend credits the shipwrecked English adventurer Robert McKean (also spelled Machim) with the island's discovery in 1346, better-documented evidence reserves that honor for João Gonçalves Zarco, a Portuguese explorer who, with his fellow sailor Tristão Vaz Teixeira, first spotted the island of Porto Santo (in 1418) and then Madeira (in 1419), and claimed them on behalf of Prince Henry the Navigator, who had sponsored the expeditions.

Many other explorers followed, along with settlers, as Madeira became a popular port for ships heading off across the mysterious Atlantic during the age of exploration, and the first of a string of colonies that would make tiny Portugal a major world power by the mid-16th century. What had been a wilderness was soon home to tens of thousands of Portuguese drawn to this new mid-ocean frontier as sailors, fishermen, farmers, herdsmen, and tradesmen. They established ports, cleared most of the forest, and built the extensive network of irrigation ditches (called *levadas*) that still carry water from the cloud-banked interior and the rainy north coast to the drier south, where settlement was heaviest.

Although Spain controlled Madeira from 1580 to 1640 (when Spanish kings sat on the Portuguese throne), it was the British who ultimately provided a more lasting influence. Links to Britain were forged in 1662, when Catherine of Bragança married King Charles II of England and granted favored status to English settlers on Madeira. British traders strengthened those links, shipping large quantities of sugar, the crop that had brought the island its first taste of prosperity, and wine, which still contributes to Madeira's wealth. The British then took advantage of the commercial links when, in the guise of protector during the Napoleonic era, they sent troops to occupy the island, first in 1801, and then again from 1807 to 1814. Napoleon himself anchored off Funchal in 1815 — as a prisoner en route to exile on the isolated south Atlantic island of St. Helena. The British consul in Madeira, the only visitor allowed the emperor, presented Napoleon with a gift of madeira wine.

Sugarcane, imported from Sicily early in the 15th century, was Madeira's original cash crop. Today, bananas and grapes dominate, the former exported fresh, the other fermented to produce the distinctively rich-flavored wines that have a centuries-long reputation. The first vines, brought to Madeira from Crete during the 15th century, produced sweet wines of the *malvazia,* or, to the British, malmsey type. They were known early and well in England — a 15th-century Duke of Clarence, brother of King Edward IV, was rumored to have been drowned in a cask of madeira, and madeira wine is mentioned in Shakespeare's plays. English wine merchants soon set up shop on the island, and began to export wine to the mother country and the colonies so extensively that by the 18th and 19th centuries, the English, with the Americans, were Madeira's major customers.

George Washington, John Adams, and Thomas Jefferson were all enthusiasts, but the wine they drank was not like the earliest madeira. Over the years, it was discovered that fortifying the local wine with brandy not only increased its alcoholic content, but also made it less likely to spoil during long ocean voyages. Then it was noticed that the heat to which the wine was unavoidably subjected during long months at sea resulted in added body and shelf life. Eventually, the heating stage (called *estufagem*) was made a part of the basic fermentation process. Today, the results can be tasted when visiting the São Francisco Wine Lodge in Funchal, where the four classic types of madeira, named for the grape variety used to produce each — dry sercials, semidry verdelhos, semisweet boals, and sweet malmseys — are fermented and stored. Storage racks still hold bottles dating from the 1830s, their contents still drinkable, evidence that madeiras are among the longest lasting of all wines.

The British, again, are credited with creating a market for Madeiran embroidery and building a reputation for quality that continues to this day. In 1856, Elizabeth Phelps, daughter of a British wine merchant, set up a workroom on the island to turn out the embroideries that were so prized by the ladies of the Victorian era. The enthusiastic British response soon had thousands of Madeiran women embroidering for export. An estimated 70,000 still carry on the craft today, as the abundance of embroidered tablecloths, napkins, nightgowns, and other clothing in Funchal's well-stocked shops confirms.

And it was the British, late in the 19th century, who first made Madeira a favorite getaway for sun seekers. That was the era when the legendary *Reid's* hotel, built by a Scot, opened, bringing a touch of Victorian Britain to Funchal. Wealthy British, particularly those in search of a salubrious climate to nurse frail health, soon turned Madeira into something of a private country club, an outpost of the British Empire rather than of the Portuguese. Today, the hotel, which hosted Edward VII while he was Prince of Wales, Winston Churchill, and others, remains the quintessence of British gentility (and still serves afternoon tea), though dozens of other hotels and rental condominiums have opened their doors over the years to accommodate the sharp increase in visitors.

Luckily, the island seems to have absorbed the growth in the number of visitors while maintaining its authenticity. This is due largely to the fact that most Madeirans retain family ties to the land, still hand-tending the terraced fields that have been built and expanded over the centuries as the population has grown. Man and nature do mix surprisingly well on Madeira, as can be seen in precisely this green, terraced sea (a match in scale and beauty for the terraced farmlands of Bali and the Philippines, which are perhaps more familiar). It can also be seen in the seemingly random placement of what look like miniature houses, sprinkled over the dramatic, flowing landscape. The addition of other manmade details make each vista an image of harmonious juxtaposition. Some of the details are hard to bring into focus. Take Madeira's ample population of cows, for instance. A traveler could spend a week in the countryside without ever suspecting they were there, unless he or she happened to look into one of the thatch-roofed huts, called *palheiros,* that dot the hillsides. The terraced fields may provide enough fodder for the cows' feed, but they offer too little space for free grazing and too much risk that a stray might tumble off the edge.

Other images of this amply flowered island complete a picture of great serenity: the brilliant afternoon light on the boats and harbor at the fishing village of Câmara de Lobos; a misty afternoon in the forest near the highland village of Camacha; Funchal at dusk, with city lights serving as a glowing highlight against the sun's last traces. Madeira is a rare travel fantasy come true, and it lingers in the memory like the sweet aftertaste of a sip of madeira wine.

SOURCES AND RESOURCES

TOURIST INFORMATION: The Regional Tourist Office of Madeira has its headquarters (and a well-supplied street-level office) in the heart of town (18 Av. Arriaga, Funchal; phone: 91-25658); smaller branches on the island are in Machico (Edificio Paz; phone: 91-965712) and at the airport (phone: 91-522933).

Several informative tourist publications are available, including the *Madeira Tourist Guide, Madeira: Somewhere Special,* and *Madeira Tourist Information,* in addition to maps of Funchal and Madeira. Free visitor publications, including the *Madeira Island Bulletin,* a monthly tabloid, are also available at most hotels. *Madeira Holidays,* a magazine with text in English, French, German, and Portuguese, contains a useful "Information and Shopping Guide" and costs about $2. Note that Madeira Tourist Radio broadcasts in English between 5:45 and 6:30 PM daily except Saturdays (1485 on the AM dial).

Porto Santo's Tourism Office is in Vila Baleira, the island's main town (Av. Vieira de Castro; phone: 91-982361). Maps of the island and town are available; in addition, most guides to Madeira include a few pages about Porto Santo.

Local Coverage – The *Diário de Notícias,* Madeira's daily newspaper, provides a sense of local concerns, as well as information on special events.

TELEPHONE: The area code for all of Madeira (including the island of Porto Santo) is 91. If calling from mainland Portugal (or Porto Santo), dial 91 before the local number.

CLIMATE: A spring-like climate makes Madeira a year-round destination. Fahrenheit temperatures range from the 50s and 60s in winter (November through April) to the 60s and 70s in summer, with warm periods pushing up into the 80s. December through February are the coolest and rainiest months. July and August are the "season," drawing large crowds of vacationing Europeans.

GETTING THERE: *TAP Air Portugal* flies nonstop daily from Lisbon, and less frequently from Porto, the Azores (São Miguel and Terceira), Spain's Grand Canary, and several European capitals. Once a week, the *TAP* flight from Lisbon to Funchal continues to the island of Porto Santo, 20 minutes away. Porto Santo is also served by daily flights from Funchal aboard the smaller, non-jet planes of *Linhas Aéreas Regionais* (*LAR*), a domestic carrier whose flights can be booked through *TAP* offices. *TAP*'s main office is in Lisbon (3A Praça Marquês de Pombal; phone: 01-544080); they also have an office in Funchal (8-10 Av. das Comunidades Madeirenses; phone: 91-30151). While there is no scheduled boat service to Madeira, numerous cruise ships make calls at Funchal. Porto Santo can be reached by ferry from Funchal, but during the winter, when the seas around these islands are prone to be rough, boat service may be canceled.

SPECIAL EVENTS: Funchal is the prime focus of the special events calendar, setting things going with a magnificent fireworks display over the city on *New Year's Eve.* See the spectacle from land or head out to sea for a deck-top view. From mid-December through the beginning of January, most of the city center's trees and streets are lit up by thousands of colored lights. *Carnaval* arrives in February or early March and features several parades complete with extravagant floats, musicians, and dancers in costume. The *Festa da Flor* (Flower Festival), lasting 3 days in April, celebrates the island's botanic abundance with flower-decked floats and a parade of 2,000 children carrying blossoms pieced together as a floral Wall of Hope. The festivities have a heavy folk flavor, with plenty of Madeiran music, singing, and dancing. The grape harvest begins in late August, and late September sees the *Festa do Vinho* (Wine Festival), when local wine cellars are open, *fados* are sung, folk dances are performed, and traditional Madeiran foods are served. In late October, brass bands from villages all around the island hold forth in a good-natured competition — with a parade that is an important part of the revelry.

SPORTS AND FITNESS: Deep-Sea Fishing – Blue marlin, tuna, bonito, and barracuda can be caught in Madeiran waters, where world records have been set. The *Madeira Game Fishing Centre–Turipesca* offers charter services for up to four anglers. Prices, including crew, insurance, tackle, and bait, vary between $500 and $565 per charter, depending on the season. Inquire at the entrance to the town pier

(Marina) or call 91-31063 or 91-42468. In Machico, contact *Turipesca* at the *Dom Pedro Machico* hotel (phone: 91-962751). Big-game fishing excursions aboard the *Missil* are another possibility; capacity is four to five people, and the price is $120 per person for the day. Contact Captain Laquai (phone: 91-933414).

Golf – Madeira's new 18-hole golf course is in the village of Santo da Serra, near the airport, a 30-minute drive from Funchal. Designed by Robert Trent Jones, Sr., it offers spectacular views over Zarco's Bay. The clubhouse has a restaurant, a bar, a lounge, and a changing room; golf club rentals and caddies are available (phone: 91-552139). Scheduled to open sometime this year is Madeira's second golf course, *Palheiro Golf.* The par-71 layout, designed by British architect Cabell Robinson, is located next to the famous Quinta do Palheiro Ferreiro gardens, 5 miles (8 km) east of Funchal.

Hiking – The tourist office can supply information on a number of recommended trails, which range in difficulty from relatively flat walks following the course of the island's irrigation canals (*levadas*), suitable for almost anyone, to strenuous walks in the vicinity of Pico Ruivo, suitable only for very experienced walkers accustomed to heights. Note that it takes only about half an hour for total darkness to fall, so any walks should be timed accordingly. *Savoy Travel,* at the *Savoy* hotel in Funchal (phone: 91-31151), offers a half-day *levada* walking tour for those who prefer not to go alone.

Horseback Riding – The facilities of the *Associação Hípica da Madeira* are 5½ miles (9 km) from the center of Funchal at Quinta Vale Pires, accessible via Caminho dos Pretos. About 50 horses are here, as well as two open riding areas and a covered one. Horses can be rented for rides through the countryside at about $7 per hour, including insurance. Make reservations through the *Dorisol* (phone: 91-32658) or *Buganvilia* (phone: 91-31015) hotels.

Snorkeling and Scuba Diving – Equipment is available from *Manta Raener Madeira* (phone: 91-932410) at the Tourist Center Galomar in Caniço de Baixo, several miles east of Funchal; from the *Madeira Carlton* hotel (formerly the *Sheraton;* phone: 91-31031); and from *Madeira Dive* (phone: 91-22031, ext. 250), in the *Savoy* hotel.

Swimming – Except for a small one at the eastern tip of the island, sand beaches are lacking on Madeira, and since the coast is generally too rocky for easy ocean access, most swimming is done in hotel pools or in one of several rock-sheltered, manmade pools just to the west of Funchal. These offer cabañas, lounge chairs, food, and drink. The *Lido* (Rua do Gorgulho; phone: 91-762217), the *Clube Naval* (235 Estrada Monumental; phone: 91-22253), and the *Clube de Turismo* (179 Estrada Monumental; phone: 91-762559) attract a mix of Madeirans and visitors. Both guests and non-guests can rent cabañas at the *Savoy* hotel's swimming pools. The island of Porto Santo makes up for the lack of beaches on Madeira with its 4-mile-long strand.

Tennis – The best public facility is at the *Quinta Magnólia* (Rua do Dr. Pita; phone: 91-764013), where the courts have been placed in a garden setting swept by cool breezes. In addition, the *Madeira Palácio* (phone: 91-30001), *Reid's* (phone: 91-23001), the *Savoy* (phone: 91-22031), *Casino Park* (phone: 91-33111), and *Duas Torres* (phone: 91-30061) hotels all have tennis facilities, and most provide court time for non-guests. Few are equipped for night play.

Windsurfing – Lessons and equipment can be obtained in Funchal at the *Savoy* hotel (Av. do Infante; phone: 91-22031), and in Machico at the *Dom Pedro Machico* hotel (phone: 91-962751).

MADEIRA

Funchal, the island capital, is set on a bay on Madeira's south coast, and attracts by far the greatest number of visitors, although Machico, east of

the harbor, the towers of the Old City, and a heavily populated mountainside that ultimately surrenders to wilderness.

The Old City of Funchal is east of the hotel zone, stretching roughly between two forts, São Lourenço to the west and São Tiago to the east. Running along the waterfront between them is the Avenida do Mar, a seaside promenade intersected midway by the small town pier. Funchal's main thoroughfare, Avenida Arriaga, is behind Avenida do Mar and parallel to it, with a statue of the island's discoverer, João Gonçalves Zarco, at one end and the Sé, Funchal's 15th-century cathedral, at the other. This, the heart of the Old City and the first Portuguese cathedral to be built "overseas," combines elements of Manueline and baroque design. The structure is made of lava rock and stucco; its interior highlights include a wonderful ceiling of cedar inlaid with ivory, the 17th-century chancel woodwork, the beautiful Flemish paintings above the 16th-century altar, and the gilded wood of the Chapel of the Holy Sacrament.

The city's best shopping streets are near the cathedral, as are alfresco cafés at which to sip richly flavored Brazilian coffee and watch the passing scene. Before taking it easy, however, take a tour of the *São Francisco Wine Lodge* (28 Av. Arriaga; phone: 91-20121), run by the Madeira Wine Company, the largest exporter of madeira wines. After an informative film, the tour visits the lodge's wine cellars and aging rooms, where still-capped 19th-century vintages are to be found, and ends in the tasting room, where numerous brands are sold. The lodge is open weekdays from 10 AM to 1 PM and from 2:30 to 6 PM (Saturdays by appointment); tours (1 hour) take place at 10:30 AM and at 3:30 PM (bookings are necessary for groups, and there is a charge for the tour). On the same street is the *Museu Cristovão Colombo* (48 Av. Arriaga; phone: 91-36192), a museum and library with nearly 500 titles relating to Columbus and other rare pieces, including a great number of books on Madeira and a fine collection of old prints (open Mondays through Fridays from 10 AM to 1 PM and from 2 to 7 PM; admission charge).

Among several other museums of interest is the *Museu de Arte Sacra* (Museum of Sacred Art; 21 Rua do Bispo; phone: 91-28900), only about 10 minutes on foot from Avenida Arriaga. Housed in the former Episcopal Palace facing Funchal's mosaic-covered Praça do Município, it contains paintings from the 15th to the 18th centuries — Portuguese and Flemish painters are well represented — as well as gold and silver plate, ivory sculpture, and gilded wood ornamentation. Another 10 minutes away is another museum, set in the *Quinta das Cruzes* (1 Calçada do Pico; phone: 91-22382), a 15th-century country house built by the explorer Zarco, but now dedicated to the decorative arts. Portuguese furniture of the 16th century, Chinese porcelain, and French enamel are displayed in rooms that were once the villa's wine cellar; 1 flight up are French and English furniture and a collection of ivory carvings. The building is surrounded by a botanical garden of several acres of tropical and subtropical flowers. Both museums are open from 10 AM to 12:30 PM and from 2 to 6 PM; closed Mondays. Admission charge. Still another museum, near the *Quinta das Cruzes,* is the *Museu Frederico de Freitas* (Calçada de Santa Clara; phone: 91-20578), displaying art objects, furniture, and a unique collection of Madeiran watercolors in an 18th-century house (admission information is the same as for the two museums above, except that this one closes at 6:30 PM). The Convento de Santa Clara, founded by two of Zarco's granddaughters on the site of a church he had chosen as a burial place for his family, is on the same street. Now it's run as a kindergarten by nuns, but visitors are welcomed at the door to the right of the church, whose interior, beautifully covered in *azulejo* tiles, contains Zarco's Gothic tomb. Not far away is the *Museu Vicentes* (43 Rua da Carreira; phone: 91-25050), formerly a leading island photographic studio and now a repository of over 100,000 glass negatives constituting a history of the island and those who have visited it (open Mondays through Fridays from 2 to 6 PM; no admission charge).

Nothing typifies Funchal's authenticity better than the *Mercado dos Lavradores* (Workers' Market) at the eastern edge of the Old City. It's best in the morning: Arrive between 7 and 11 AM (closed Sundays) and see the market come alive with the animated dealings of farmers, fishermen, and price-conscious local shoppers. Flower vendors stationed at the door wear traditional Madeiran garb (cap, red vest, ruffled white blouse, and full skirt). The produce arrayed inside — everything from carrots, onions, chestnuts, and papayas to scabbard fish, tuna, swordfish, and eel — serves as an introduction to the fare available at local restaurants. Plan to spend an hour or two wandering about (and note that several blocks farther east is the Barreirinha district, a still-proletarian fishermen's quarter where upscale restaurants provide alfresco dining).

The Jardim Botânico, in the hills at Caminho do Meio, in the Bom Sucesso district (about 15 minutes by car from Avenida Arriaga), is another must-see, open from 8 AM to 6 PM; closed Sundays; admission charge. Just about every flower, plant, or tree that grows on Madeira is represented here, laid out on terraces surrounding an old country house. The noteworthy views of the city and harbor are an added attraction. Close by, and also well worth seeing, is the Jardim dos Louros, home to more than 500 tropical birds from around the world (open from 9 AM to 6 PM daily; admission charge). More of Madeira's floral abundance can be seen in the gardens of the Quinta do Palheiro Ferreiro, a private estate 5 miles (8 km) east of the center, open to the public from 9:30 AM to 12:30 PM weekdays (except public holidays); admission charge. Orchids in particular are at Quinta Boavista (27 Rua Albuquerque), 5 minutes from the center and open from 9 AM to 5:30 PM Mondays through Saturdays; no admission charge.

ELSEWHERE ON THE ISLAND

Monte – This hillside community, nestled amid towering trees and an abundance of flowers, is about 3 miles (5 km) and 1,800 feet above the Old City. Once popular as a country retreat, it is now more a suburb of Funchal, but its cool climate, luxuriant vegetation, and panoramic views still attract visitors. The Nossa Senhora do Monte church, built late in the 18th century, provides an unexpectedly sophisticated baroque façade preceded by a steep staircase. Inside, the silver tabernacle above the main altar houses a small statue of Our Lady of the Mount, found in the 15th century at the very spot in Terreiro da Luta where the Virgin Mary is said to have appeared to a young shepherdess. Since that time, Our Lady of the Mount has been Madeira's patron saint, and the church is the object of pilgrimage every *Assumption Day* (August 15), when some of the faithful climb the stairs on their knees. The church also contains the tomb of Charles I, the last of the Austro-Hungarian emperors, who died here in 1922. The famous toboggan ride (see *Getting Around*) begins near the steps of the church.

Câmara de Lobos – Drive 5½ miles (9 km) west of Funchal along Route 101, passing terraces dense with bananas, to reach this picturesque fishing village of whitewashed, red-tile-roofed houses built around a cliff-sheltered harbor and a rocky beach. Named for the seals once abundant in coastal waters, the village was a favorite of Winston Churchill, who often set up his easel here during visits to Madeira. A roadside viewpoint overlooks the harbor and its colorful array of fishing boats, with the dramatic sea cliff of Cabo Girão as a backdrop. Arrive by 8 AM and you're likely to see fishing boats being unloaded after a night at sea. By midday, the scene is more tranquil, as fishermen cluster amid their boats to play cards and women do their wash in the Ribeira do Vigario. The walk along the harbor breakwater provides additional panoramic views.

Cabo Girão – The 1,900-foot headland, the second-highest promontory on earth, lies 7 miles (11 km) west of Câmara de Lobos. Follow Route 101 as bananas give way to vines, then turn left onto the clearly marked road to the lookout at the summit. The view down the almost sheer drop to the pounding sea is magnificent; even here, several hundred feet below, small patches of terraced fields cling to the cliff edges wherever possible.

Serra de Agua – Continue west from Cabo Girão and turn inland at Ribeira Brava. About halfway between the island's north and south coasts is this rustic riverside village, which benefits from a wonderful setting of sharply eroded mountains rising precipitously from terraced hillsides that are often shrouded in mist and clouds. Bamboo and weeping willows line the river, adding a romantic touch to what is otherwise a workaday farm settlement. The road climbs from Serra de Agua to the 3,304-foot-high Encumeada Pass, where new panoramas take in the descent toward the north coast and São Vicente.

São Vicente – This small town on Madeira's north coast, about an hour's drive from Funchal, is set where a river of the same name meets the sea. The views as the road winds its way down from the mountains into town are particularly beautiful, although there is little to see in São Vicente itself, apart from a small cluster of shops. The town does, however, provide a midday stop for a number of motorcoach tours of the island, as well as for sightseers touring on their own. More views are in store as Route 101, which makes a complete circuit of the island, leads west of São Vicente, climbing to cliffside heights and offering sweeping views of Madeira's north coast. Because portions of the road are narrow and unpaved, careful attention to driving is necessary, as is an occasional bit of maneuvering when confronting oncoming traffic.

Porto Moniz – A sheltered anchorage formed by a narrow peninsula that points toward a picturesque islet, Ilhéu Mole, is the setting for this charming fishing village on the northwest coast of Madeira. A further attraction, besides the scenery, is the large natural ocean pool set amid lava rock that attracts swimmers during the summer months. (Winter weather and rough surf can make a swim uninviting and dangerous.) At Porto Moniz, the around-the-island road turns inland to wind its way south and eventually back east to Funchal.

Eira do Serrado – This 3,385-foot lookout point is about 8 miles (13 km) northwest of Funchal, reached by taking the Pico dos Barcelos road and driving approximately 20 minutes through countryside rife with eucalyptus trees and native forest. The lookout sits atop the sawtooth crater of one of Madeira's great formative volcanoes, and the view down into the crater encompasses, surprisingly, not only farmland, but also the whitewashed village of Curral das Freiras. The name of the village means "nuns' shelter," because it was to this spot that the sisters of Funchal's Convento de Santa Clara escaped in the 16th century, in retreat from French pirates who had attacked and pillaged the city. Eventually, the settlement became permanent, and only recently was its isolation infringed upon by more than a footpath. Now there is a road, but the trip from the lookout down to the village is worthwhile only if you've time to spare. At the lookout, vendors sell well-priced handicrafts, and a path leads to additional panoramas.

Pico do Arieiro – No place on Madeira reveals its volcanic nature better than its second-highest peak, 14 miles (22 km) north of Funchal — on a clear day, that is. Often, while the rest of the island is basking in sunlight, this 5,939-foot peak may well be covered in clouds, mist, and rain. When skies clear, the summit lookout reveals a landscape covered in volcanic debris and the eroded mountains that have been created in the millions of years since Madeira surfaced from the sea. Fortunately, the road goes right to the top of Pico do Arieiro, so no mountain climbing is necessary to see the view.

Pico Ruivo – At 6,104 feet, this is Madeira's highest peak, a prize to be gained only by those who make the effort; unlike Pico do Arieiro, no road leads to the top. There is a 4-mile (6-km) trail from Pico do Arieiro that takes about 3 hours of hiking and entails a few treacherous stretches without the benefit of safety rails. Otherwise, a trail from Parque das Queimadas (at the end of a 3-mile/5-km road from Santana, a village on the island's northeastern coast) leads to the heather-covered summit. From here, Madeira's tallest mountains rise all around, and long-distance views take in the valleys of the island's north coast, Ponta de São Lourenço at its easternmost tip, as well as

Santana and the village of São Jorge at its northeastern corner. The trip is worthwhile for those with the stamina and the time, and — provided arrangements have been made with the tourist office in Funchal beforehand — it's possible to spend the night in the rustic refuge — *casa de abrigo* — a few minutes' walk from the top.

Camacha – The quiet highland village is just 6 miles (10 km) northeast of Funchal, at an altitude of almost 2,300 feet. The surrounding groves of willows provide the material for making the wickerware that is the village specialty; the wicker shops are worth a visit even for those who don't intend to buy. Try to come to town on a Sunday, when it's buzzing with residents of the area gathered to socialize and promenade.

Machico – It was here, 16 miles (26 km) northeast of Funchal, that the Portuguese explorer João Gonçalves Zarco and his crew made their first landfall on Madeira, in 1419. Thus, the bay fronting the town is known as Zarco's Bay. According to legend, Machico was also the place where the Englishman Robert McKean (or Machim) was shipwrecked with his bride, Ana d'Arfet, in 1346. The young couple died, but the unlikely story has other survivors of the ship taking to sea in a raft and ending up in Morocco, after having been captured by Arab pirates. Eventually, word of Madeira's existence is supposed to have reached Portugal, resulting in the voyage of discovery led by Zarco, along with Tristão Vaz Teixeira, a fellow sailor, who became governor of this part of the island. Machico's parish church and the Capela São Roque both date from the 15th century. At the Capela dos Milagres (Chapel of Miracles), rebuilt in 1829 after having been destroyed by a flood in 1803, a framed cross is said to be the one originally left on the graves of the ill-fated McKean and his wife.

SHOPPING: Embroidery, wine, and wickerware are Madeira's most distinctive products, but a shopping spree on Madeira (and that, for the most part, means Funchal) can also turn up good prices on tooled leather, handmade shoes, and high-fashion European clothing. The best browsing is along Rua do Aljube and the cluster of streets bordered by Avenida Zarco, Rua 5 de Outubro, and Avenida do Mar. Shops are generally open Mondays through Fridays from 9 AM to 1 PM and again from 3 to 7 PM, Saturdays from 9 AM to 1 PM. The lunchtime closing is an eleventh commandment, so make shopping plans accordingly. Outside Funchal, shopping is likely to be limited to wicker, another island specialty. The village of Camacha, about 6 miles (10 km) from Funchal, is the center of this activity.

An Englishwoman established Madeiran embroidery during the Victorian era, and today thousands of Madeiran women embroider under contract to makers and retailers of table linen, children's wear, women's lingerie, and other fashions. Prices vary considerably, so shopping around is warranted, but since Madeirans know what the market will bear, don't expect fantastic bargains. Prices, in fact, can be surprisingly high, with a large, intricately embroidered Irish linen tablecloth (napkins included) topping $2,500. But there are lovely things for far less.

Artecouro Leather Shop – The leather is from mainland Portugal, but the bags and belts that are the shop's specialties are made on Madeira with great skill and style; there are also wallets, sandals, and children's boots. 15 Rua da Alfândega, Funchal (phone: 91-37256).

Bazar do Povo – This commercial center, housing several boutiques, restaurants, and a hairdresser, also comprises what appears to be a five-and-dime store from another era, which sells inexpensive odds and ends. 1 Rua do Bettencourt, Funchal (phone: 91-22055).

Camacha Wickerworks – Room after room of things made of wicker, from giraffes and other animals to furniture. Items too large to be carried can be shipped home. Largo da Achada, Camacha (phone: 91-922167). There is also a showroom and shop at the *Centro Comercial do Infante Shopping Center,* 75 Av. Arriaga, Funchal (phone: 91-34586).

Casa do Turista – A showcase for Portuguese crafts — crystal, porcelain, ceramics, wickerware, dolls, and more, including embroidery — displayed in an old mansion. 2 Rua Conselheiro José Silvestre Ribeiro, Funchal (phone: 91-24907).

Cloe Leather – Everything from shoes to bags to high-fashion accessories in calf, mustang, and more exotic skins. 13 Largo do Phelps, Funchal (phone: 91-27711).

Hélio – The source of well-priced Charles Jourdan shoes — the shop is Madeira's exclusive Jourdan agent. 65 Rua do Aljube, Funchal (phone: 91-23447).

H. Stern – Brazil's ubiquitous gemstone jeweler has shops in three Funchal hotels — the *Madeira Carlton,* formerly the *Sheraton* (Largo António Nobre; phone: 91-36605); the *Madeira Palácio* (Estrada Monumental; phone: 91-34352); and the *Casino Park* (Av. do Infante; phone: 91-25442).

Jabara – Madeiran embroidery; opened in 1908, the store is a downtown landmark. 59 Rua Dr. Fernão de Ornelas, Funchal (phone: 91-34318).

Lãs Voga – An old-fashioned, abundantly stocked yarn shop. 60 Rua Dr. Fernão de Ornelas, Funchal (phone: 91-38228).

Leacocks – Manufacturers and exporters of quality embroidery and tapestries. 13 Rua Major Reis Gomes, Funchal (phone: 91-22065 or 91-36613).

A Loja Nova – Sophisticated European women's wear. 45 Rua do Aljube, Funchal (phone: 91-20322).

Maria L. Kiekeben – Manufacturers of Gobelin-style tapestries and tapestry kits, petit point embroidery, needlepoint, and high quality handmade rugs, made to order. The factory is at 194 Rua da Carreira, Funchal (phone: 91-22073; fax: 91-31201); the retail shop, *Madeira Gobelins,* is at 2 Av. do Infante, Funchal (phone: 91-27857).

Nova Minerva – It bills itself as "creative shirtmakers," with a very nice collection of shirts for men. 31 Rua da Alfândega, Funchal (phone: 91-37627). The shop for women is at 40 Av. Arriaga, Funchal (phone: 91-28264).

Oliveiras – One of the widest selections of embroidery in town. The workroom on the floors above is one of a couple of dozen such factories in Funchal. Ask to visit, and see what it takes to create a finished tablecloth or negligee (and ask for the 25% factory discount). At two adjoining downtown locations: 22 Rua dos Murças, Funchal (phone: 91-29340) and 11 Rua da Alfândega, Funchal (phone: 91-20245).

Patrício E. Gouveia – An extensive stock, featuring every variety of embroidery. 34 Rua do Anadia, Funchal (phone: 91-20801).

São Francisco Wine Lodge – Run by the Madeira Wine Company — the place to go for seven of the better-known labels, including Leacocks, Blandys, and Cossart Gordon. 28 Av. Arriaga, Funchal (phone: 91-20121).

Teixeiras – Still more Madeiran embroidery. This is the place for something special; the prices are a bit higher, but the quality is a bit better, too. 13 Rua do Aljube, Funchal (phone: 91-36616).

NIGHTCLUBS AND NIGHTLIFE: *Fado* is popular here, as it is in Lisbon. If you like its soulful sound, head to *Bar Marcelino Pão e Vinho* (22A Travessa das Torres; phone: 91-34834). Also check with the major hotels — *Madeira Carlton, Savoy, Casino Park, Madeira Palácio, Reid's* — to see if *fado* or folk performances are scheduled. The *Savoy* hotel (Av. do Infante; phone: 91-22031) has a rooftop nightclub, *Galaxia,* with panoramic views and its own band (folk dancing on Tuesdays and Thursdays); *Safari* (5 Rua do Favila; phone: 91-20455) follows a disco beat, as does *Baccara* (phone: 91-31121), a new dance spot located in the casino (see below). The *Prince Albert* (86 Rua da Imperatriz Dona Amélia; phone: 91-31793), a pub with Victorian ambience, is quieter, allowing conversation. *Joe's Bar* (1 Beco Imperatriz Dona Amélia; phone: 91-29087) is intimate and charming, with nightly piano music and a lovely terrace. Salsa Latina (101 Rua da Imperatriz Dona Amélia; phone: 91-25182) has live (quiet) music and serves light meals; *Berilights* (23 Rua do Gorgulho; phone: 91-62535) is a bar and meeting place for young people.

The *Casino da Madeira,* adjoining the *Casino Park* hotel (Av. do Infante; phone:

91-33111), is open daily from 4 PM to 3 AM (jackets required after 8 PM). Slot machines, craps, blackjack, and American and French roulette are played in the three gaming rooms — an American Room, a European Room, and a private room (Salle Privée), reserved for the casino's best customers. There is a nominal entrance fee for the gaming rooms, and foreigners are expected to present a passport.

CHECKING IN: Although there are several small hotels in outlying towns such as Ribeira Brava, most visitors stay in either Funchal or Machico. Funchal offers elegant high-rise hotels clustered to the west of the port, a few condominiums, and a range of lovely small hotels and pensions on the narrow streets of the Old City. Machico is Madeira in a resort mode, with a number of large hotels. Also available — under Portugal's *Turismo de Habitação* network — are rooms in privately owned manor houses and stately homes (see *Accommodations,* GETTING READY TO GO). Expect to pay $150 or more a night for a double room at properties listed below as very expensive, $75 and up in a hotel listed as expensive, from $40 to $70 in a moderate one, and $35 or less in an inexpensive one. As on the mainland, breakfast is included; any establishment designated as "residential" does not have a restaurant and usually serves breakfast only. Hotels, large and small, are generally well maintained and well managed, catering primarily to visitors from Great Britain, Germany, France, and Scandinavia.

FUNCHAL

Casino Park – Part of the casino–conference center–hotel complex designed by Oscar Niemeyer, the architect of Brasília, this is ultramodern in style: simple yet elegant. The 400 rooms offer sweeping views of the sea and Funchal's harbor; facilities include a large pool with landscaped lounging areas, a children's pool, a health center, tennis courts, shops, and more than 1 dining room serving good food. Of the top hotels, this is also the closest to the center of town, a 10-minute walk away. Av. do Infante (phone: 91-33111; fax: 91-33153). Very expensive.

Madeira Carlton – Stylish decor, rooms with panoramic ocean views, 2 large swimming pools, tennis, a sauna, water sports, and a central location within walking distance of downtown (it's not much farther out than the *Casino Park*) describe this high-rise, which used to be the *Sheraton.* With 372 rooms, it's the island's largest hotel. Largo António Nobre (phone: 91-31031; fax: 91-27284). Very expensive.

Madeira Palácio – On the outskirts of town, on a hillside that affords beautiful views of the 2,000-foot sea cliffs at Cabo Girão. Friendly service by a well-informed staff is a major plus, as is the decor in the 260 rooms (comfortably contemporary). There's fine dining, and other facilities include tennis courts, water sports, and an oversize pool with Madeira's dramatic landscape as a backdrop. A free shuttle bus links the hotel to several downtown locations, a 10-minute drive. Estrada Monumental (phone: 91-30001; fax: 91-25408). Very expensive.

Reid's – The quintessential colonial hotel, an outpost of 19th-century propriety, where guests still linger in the lounge or parade through the lobby in tuxedoes and evening gowns. Built in 1891, the hotel has been beautifully maintained and, where necessary, modernized. It offers sweeping coastal views from many of its 152 rooms and 21 suites, 10 acres of florally landscaped grounds, 2 lovely heated oceanside swimming pools, water sports, tennis, some of Madeira's best dining options (see *Eating Out*), and a central location within walking distance of the Old City. The price for such pleasures is the highest on Madeira. 139 Estrada Monumental (phone: 91-23001; fax: 91-30499). Very expensive.

Savoy – Kitsch says it all for this 350-room oceanfront property, which is even older than *Reid's* and is its traditional rival. Actually, beyond the garish grandeur of the lobby, it tones down considerably. Poolside is the *Savoy* at its best, however — there are 2 large pools and plenty of space for lounging. Water sports, tennis, and miniature golf are available on the property. Av. do Infante (phone: 91-22031; fax: 91-23103). Very expensive.

Estalagem Quinta da Bela Vista – A participant in the government's *Turismo de Habitação* program, this beautiful old house is appointed with antique furniture and offers 36 rooms and 4 suites. There's an attractive garden and a good French restaurant on the premises, too. 4 Caminho Avista Navios (phone: 91-764144; fax: 91-765090). Expensive.

Estalagem Quinta Perestrelo – Another *Turismo de Habitação* property, this modern 28-room inn boasts a pleasant swimming pool and a central location, across from the *Quinta Magnólia* gardens (see *Eating Out*). 3 Rua do Dr. Pita (phone: 91-763720; fax: 91-763777). Expensive.

Quinta do Sol – Mid-size at 116 rooms, it offers friendly service in a park-like setting within walking distance of downtown Funchal. It's adjacent to the grounds of the *Quinta Magnólia* (see *Eating Out*), and benefits from easy access to the facilities there. 6 Rua do Dr. Pita (phone: 91-764151; fax: 91-766287). Expensive.

Eden Mar – A nice, recently built apartment-hotel set about 50 yards from the sea. It's located west of the center, in the heart of the tourist zone that surrounds the *Lido* swimming pool complex, and it has 37 studios and 68 junior suites with kitchenettes. 2 Rua do Gorgulho (phone: 91-62221; fax: 91-761966). Expensive to moderate.

Quinta da Penha de França – A large townhouse has been converted into an inn of 35 rooms, with lots of local character, a restaurant and snack bar, gardens, and a swimming pool. It's set in quiet surroundings, close to the *Casino Park* and the other leading hotels. 2 Rua da Penha de França (phone: 91-29080; fax: 91-29262). Expensive to moderate.

Windsor – A middle-of-the-road choice in more ways than one, since this is neither large nor small (67 rooms), quite nice, reasonably priced, and the only one of its category in the center of town; rooftop pool. 4C Rua das Hortas (phone: 91-33083; fax: 91-33080). Expensive to moderate.

Monte Carlo – It occupies the crest of a hillside in the Old City, so there are breathtaking views of ocean, mountains, and red tile roofs from the balconies, the dining room, poolside, and many of the 45 rooms — about 20 of which are in the main house, a rococo palace that is something of a landmark in its own right. A friendly atmosphere prevails; reserve in advance, especially during peak seasons. 10 Calçada da Saúde (phone: 91-26131; fax: 91-26134). Moderate.

Reno – An apartment-hotel overlooking the heart of the Old City, within a short walk of Funchal's shops. Studios and 1-bedroom units are available, all with kitchenettes. 15-25 Rua das Pretas (phone: 91-26125; fax: 91-26125). Moderate.

Santa Clara – A wrought-iron gate and a walkway lined with hibiscus lead to this 16-room *pensão residencial* (residential pension), only a block away from the *Quinta das Cruzes* museum and gardens. Inside, the house has a turn-of-the-century, Victorian feel, which means a bit stuffy, but by no means unfriendly. The view from the dining room, swimming pool, and rooftop solarium is particularly beautiful, embracing sea, city, and mountains. 16B Calçada do Pico (phone: 91-24194; fax: 91-21080). Inexpensive.

ELSEWHERE ON THE ISLAND

Atlantis – One of the island's top properties, this high-rise was originally built as a *Holiday Inn.* Set on Zarco's Bay, about 35 minutes from Funchal by taxi or bus, it has 312 rooms, all with balconies and sea views. Guests also appreciate the indoor and outdoor pools, rooftop grill, nightclub, gamerooms, cinema, tennis courts, and shops. Agua de Pena, Machico (phone: 91-962811; fax: 91-965859). Expensive.

Dom Pedro Machico – A self-contained resort overlooking Zarco's Bay. It has 218 rooms, a heated saltwater pool, a discotheque, tennis courts, and other amenities, including the necessary equipment for windsurfing and deep-sea fishing. Estrada São Roque, Machico (phone: 91-962751; fax: 91-966889). Expensive to moderate.

BravaMar – Those in the mood to stay in a smaller Madeiran town should try this 36-room hotel. The decor is simple, in fact a bit spartan, but there's privacy, a quiet setting, and plenty of exploring to do in the surrounding countryside. Rooms have ocean views and kitchenettes. Rua Gago Coutinho, Ribeira Brava (phone: 91-952220; fax: 91-953132). Moderate.

Estalagem do Mar – Right on the ocean, this rustic *Turismo de Habitação* inn offers guests an impressive view of the breathtaking cliffs and mountains on the island's north coast. There are 45 double guestrooms, plus a restaurant that serves local fare. About an hour from Funchal, in São Vicente (phone: 91-842615; fax: 91-842765). Moderate.

Pousada do Pico do Arieiro – A member of Portugal's *pousada* chain, it's set on top of the second-highest mountain on the island. Fireplaces and winter gardens contribute to the inn's atmosphere, and the 22 rooms have terraces from which to admire the superb view. Reserve through *Enasol,* 2 Rua da Sé, Funchal (phone: 91-24707); through the chain's US representative, *Marketing Ahead* (phone in the US: 212-686-9213); or directly through the inn. Pico do Arieiro (phone: 91-48188; fax: 91-48119). Moderate.

Pousada dos Vinháticos – This woodsy 12-room inn, opened in 1940 as the first *pousada* in all of Portugal, is on the mountain-rimmed road that leads to the scenic Encumeada Pass. It's a great place to stay for those who want to go hiking (there are numerous trails nearby), and then spend the night in magnificent mountain quiet. Reserve through *Enasol,* 2 Rua da Sé, Funchal (phone: 91-24707); through the chain's US representative, *Marketing Ahead* (phone in the US: 212-686-9213); or directly through the inn. Serra de Agua (phone: 91-952344; fax: 91-952540). Moderate.

EATING OUT: There are perfectly acceptable restaurants in all of the large hotels, clusters of restaurants taking advantage of the island's natural beauty spots, even fast-food restaurants; most of the better places are in Funchal, although there are eating places in many towns around the island. Note that Funchal Marina, to the west of the town quay, offers a string of moderate and inexpensive restaurants within a short distance of each other — the area is pleasant and frequented by people of all ages. Madeiran specialties include *sopa de tomate e cebola* (tomato and onion soup), *caldeirada* (fish soup), *bife de atum e milho frito* (grilled tuna steak with fried corn meal), *espada* (black scabbard fish) prepared a variety of ways, and *espetada* (skewered beef, fragrant with laurel and garlic, grilled over charcoal). Pastries may look better than they taste, but *bôlo de mel* (treacle cake) is an exception. Expect to pay $35 to $45 for a meal for two without drinks at restaurants listed below as expensive, from $20 to $30 in those listed as moderate, and under $15 in the inexpensive ones.

FUNCHAL

Arsenio's – A favorite with Madeirans and visitors. Fine food (local seafood and continental specialties) is complemented by *fado* singers and Brazilian rhythms. Open daily. Reservations necessary. Major credit cards accepted. 169 Rua de Santa Maria (phone: 91-24007). Expensive.

Caravela – Many Madeirans consider this Funchal's best. The menu is mainly continental, but includes local seafood and fish dishes as well. The setting combines casual, contemporary decor with views of the harbor. Open daily from noon to 10 PM. Reservations necessary. Major credit cards accepted. 15 Av. do Mar (phone: 91-46484). Expensive.

Casa dos Reis – For candlelit dinners in a mahogany- and brass-accented setting that still manages to be warm and friendly, this spot is only a short walk from the *Casino Park, Madeira Carlton,* and *Savoy* hotels. Fish, lamb, and specialties of the charcoal grill are the fare. Open for lunch and dinner daily. Reservations necessary. Major credit cards accepted. 101 Rua da Imperatriz Dona Amélia (phone: 91-25182). Expensive.

Casa Velha – A 19th-century Madeira residence redone as a restaurant with gently revolving ceiling fans, lace curtains, and blue tiles. Both local and international dishes are served. Open for lunch and dinner daily. Reservations necessary. Major credit cards accepted. By the west entrance of the *Casino Park* hotel. 69 Rua da Imperatriz Dona Amélia (phone: 91-25749). Expensive.

Don Filet – A Brazilian-style charcoal grill makes this place a favorite with locals, who also come for the Wednesday-night *fado* performances. The rest of the week, there's live music at the piano bar. For tourists, the restaurant provides a free shuttle van to and from nearby hotels. Reservations necessary on weekends. Major credit cards accepted. 7 Rua do Favila (phone: 91-764426). Expensive.

Les Faunes – Madeira at its most elegant. Customers pay for swank surroundings (several Picasso lithographs adorn the walls), quality service, delicious continental fare, and an oceanfront view. Open for dinner nightly, from 7:30 to 11:30 PM. Reservations necessary. Major credit cards accepted. *Reid's Hotel,* 139 Estrada Monumental (phone: 91-23001). Expensive.

Golfinho – The nautical decor matches the menu of this restaurant in the Old City: catch-of-the-day fish and seafood. Closed Sundays. Reservations necessary. Major credit cards accepted. 21 Largo do Corpo Santo (phone: 91-26774). Expensive.

Solar do F – Portuguese regional cooking is served in this bar/grill/restaurant, where there's also dining on a garden terrace. The surroundings are pleasant and secluded, only 250 yards from the *Madeira Carlton* hotel. Open for lunch and dinner daily. Reservations necessary. Major credit cards accepted. 19 Av. Luís de Camões (phone: 91-20212). Expensive.

Gavina's – Always crowded, lively, and enjoyable, this oceanfront eating place serves fish and seafood — shrimp, lobster, octopus, sea bass, *espada, sargo* (sea bream), *bodião* (parrot fish), *salmonete* (red mullet), and others are all on the menu. A free shuttle van picks up diners and then drops them off at Funchal's major hotels, just 5 to 10 minutes away. Open daily. Reservations necessary. American Express and Visa accepted. Rua do Gorgulho (phone: 91-62918). Expensive to moderate.

Jardin – One of several good restaurants in the Old City specializing in seafood and continental dishes. Dine alfresco or inside, amid Victorian decor. Open for lunch and dinner daily. Reservations advised. Major credit cards accepted. 60 Rua Campo Dom Carlos I (phone: 91-22864). Expensive to moderate.

Vagrant – Once a yacht owned by the *Beatles,* it's now a restaurant anchored on the east side of the town quay. A large selection — from seafood to sandwiches — is offered. Open daily. Reservations advised. Major credit cards accepted. Av. das Comunidades Madeirenses (phone: 91-23572). Expensive to moderate.

Vila Cliff – Specialties from mainland Portugal and Madeira served in an eatery overlooking the sea. Open daily for lunch, tea, and dinner. Reservations necessary. Major credit cards accepted. Estrada Monumental, next to the entrance to *Reid's* hotel (phone: 91-23015). Expensive to moderate.

O Celeiro – Madeiran cooking is served here, in the middle of town, just off the main street, and the atmosphere is pleasant. Open for lunch and dinner daily. Reservations advised. Major credit cards accepted. 22 Rua dos Aranhas (phone: 91-37322). Moderate.

Lido Mar – Within the *Lido* swimming pool complex west of town, this place offers fish and shellfish specialties and selected meat dishes. Open for lunch and dinner daily. Reservations advised. Major credit cards accepted. Rua do Gorgulho (phone: 91-762212, ext. 59). Moderate.

Portuguese Grill – Smart, quiet, and near the *Lido* pool complex west of town. Open for lunch and dinner daily. Reservations advised. Major credit cards accepted. 21 Caminho da Ajuda (phone: 91-30043). Moderate.

Quinta Magnólia – Don't let its status as a hotel-school restaurant serve as a deterrent. The food is some of the best in Madeira, the service (by a staff in training for coveted jobs in the food and beverage field throughout Portugal) is exceptional, and the setting, an elegant old mansion amid botanical gardens — the former *British Country Club* — is perfect. Since the restaurant serves lunch (a set menu, at 1 PM; bar opens at noon), not dinner, spend the morning at the estate's pool or tennis courts or simply walking the grounds, and make lunch the big meal of the day; reservations necessary. Otherwise, stop by for tea (at 4 PM); reservations unnecessary. Closed Sundays. No credit cards accepted. 10 Rua do Dr. Pita (phone: 91-64614 or 91-64013). Moderate.

São José – The menu features local specialties such as *galinha regional* (chicken in tomato sauce), as well as duck *à l'orange* and tournedos Orsini. The decor, with entry via a Moorish arch, is as eclectic as the menu. Good value for the money. Reservations unnecessary. Major credit cards accepted. 11 Largo do Corpo Santo (phone: 91-23214). Moderate.

O Almirante – A central location, a casual atmosphere, good food, and good prices are the lure. Fish and grilled meats are the specialties. Reservations advised. Major credit cards accepted. 1 Largo do Poço (phone: 91-24252). Moderate to inexpensive.

ELSEWHERE ON THE ISLAND

O Galo – A coastal restaurant facing the sea in a small village 7 miles (11 km) east of Funchal. The fish specialties make it worth the trip. Open for lunch and dinner; closed Mondays. Reservations advised. Major credit cards accepted. Caniço de Baixo (phone: 91-932220). Expensive to moderate.

Lagoa – Frequented by lots of locals, this seafood restaurant is near the *Madeira* golf course, half an hour by car from Funchal. Open for lunch and dinner daily. Reservations necessary. Major credit cards accepted. Santo da Serra (phone: 91-552118). Expensive to moderate.

Montanha – This place serves charcoal-grill specialties in a spectacular setting overlooking Funchal Bay, 10 minutes east of the city on the old airport road. Open daily. Reservations advised. Major credit cards accepted. 101 Estrada Regional, Neves (phone: 91-793500). Expensive to moderate.

Orca – Set in a picturesque village at the northwest corner of the island where there is bathing in rock pools by the sea, this spot serves Madeiran specialties, as well as international dishes. Open for lunch and dinner daily. Reservations advised. Major credit cards accepted. Porto Moniz (phone: 91-852359). Expensive to moderate.

A Rede – Fresh fish and other seafood, plus rice with lobster, crab, shrimp, limpets, clams, and octopus, are the draw; located on the coast 7 miles (11 km) east of Funchal. Open for lunch and dinner daily. Reservations necessary. Major credit cards accepted. Caniço de Baixo (phone: 91-933425). Expensive to moderate.

Roca Mar – Also on the east coast, this is a country restaurant facing the ocean and serving regional and international specialties. Open for lunch and dinner daily. Reservations advised. Major credit cards accepted. Caniço de Baixo (phone: 91-932999). Expensive to moderate.

Xadrez – Popular and packed with Madeirans, it's a 5-minute drive from the *Dom Pedro Machico* hotel. Open for lunch and dinner; closed Mondays. Reservations necessary. Major credit cards accepted. Caramachão Machico (phone: 91-965889). Expensive to moderate.

O Boieiro – A unique eatery, 15 minutes east of Funchal on the new road to the airport, it serves a good variety of dishes, brought to you in a bullock cart. Open daily from noon to midnight. Reservations advised. Major credit cards accepted. Caniço de Baixo (phone: 91-932123). Moderate.

Café Relógio – A great place to stop while touring the eastern part of the island. Those in the mood for a sandwich or a good cup of espresso can stay downstairs, where the scene is alive with local color on weekends. Upstairs, there's a restaurant serving regional specialties. Open daily. Reservations advised. Major credit cards accepted. Largo da Achada, Camacha (phone: 91-922114). Moderate.

O Facho – Regional cooking, with fish and seafood specialties, make this Machico's best. Open daily. Reservations advised. Visa, MasterCard, and Diners Club accepted. Machico (phone: 91-962786). Moderate.

Quebra-Mar – Set on a rocky shelf along the coastal road on Madeira's northern side, with panoramic views and exceptional seafood — fresh shrimp, lobster, squid, and octopus. A prime stop for cars and buses touring the island, it can become quite crowded despite seating for several hundred. Open daily. Reservations advised. Visa accepted. São Vicente (phone: 91-842338). Moderate.

A Seta – Head for the hillside village of Monte for a 7-course meal of regional specialties including *espada, espetada,* roast chicken, cod, and *bôlo do caco,* the delicious Madeiran country bread made with sweet potatoes. Dinner is followed by folk music and dancing that ends with audience participation. Open daily. Reservations advised. Major credit cards accepted. 80 Estrada do Livramento, Monte (phone: 91-47643). Moderate.

PORTO SANTO

In contrast to mountainous Madeira, which is 27 miles to the southwest, Porto Santo is a low island — its highest point, Pico do Facho, rises little more than 1,600 feet above sea level. Set in the lee of the clouds attracted to Madeira's higher peaks, it is also far drier and several degrees warmer, on average, than Madeira. The island's limited rainfall and chalky soil result in a further stark contrast: its sparse vegetation versus Madeira's green exuberance. Within the 16 square miles of Porto Santo, however, there is one feature of the landscape that Madeira cannot claim: A 4-mile-long sandy beach attracts not only visitors from abroad but also the Madeirans themselves.

Though it may lie low on the horizon, Porto Santo was the first island of the Madeira archipelago to be discovered. That was in 1418, when Zarco and Teixeira, sailing for Prince Henry the Navigator, found refuge here during a raging Atlantic storm. In honor of the sanctuary it provided, they named the island Porto Santo, or "Holy Port." Settlement began the following year, with farmers using windmills to draw water to irrigate sugarcane, grains, and grapes. Christopher Columbus, who married Isabel Moniz, the daughter of the island's governor, lived here for a brief time before heading off on the voyages that would make him famous.

Today, about 5,000 people call Porto Santo home; Vila Baleira, roughly in the middle of the south coast, is both the "capital" and the largest town. Most islanders continue to till the soil, harvesting tomatoes, watermelons, figs, grapes, and grain — the few windmills still to be found are a reminder of the difficulties of island agriculture. Other islanders set out to fish, although fewer than before seem willing to put in the time and effort needed to make fishing a career. Summer brings an influx of visitors, but not enough to crowd the beach. Off-season has its appeal, but with temperatures generally in the 60s, it's a bit chilly for swimming. Some visitors arrive on day trips from Madeira. Others, who appreciate Porto Santo's away-from-it-all pace and mood, stay a while.

GETTING AROUND: The island is small, only 7½ miles long and 4 miles wide, so getting around is easy. For those who prefer to leave the arrangements to others, full-day excursions from Madeira are offered by *AB Tours,* 177 Rua dos Ferreiros, Funchal (phone: 91-25134).

Airport – Flights arrive daily from Funchal and land at the Aeroporto de Porto Santo, 2 miles (3 km) from Vila Baleira; taxis are available.

Car Rental – In Vila Baleira, rental cars are available from *Atlantic Rent-a-Car* (Av. Vieira de Castro; phone: 91-982630; fax: 91-983434) and *Moínho Rent-a-Car* (Rua Dr. Estêvão Alencastre; phone: 91-982780; fax: 91-762125). If you're staying in Vila Baleira, however, a rental car is not really necessary, because taxis can be hired for sightseeing excursions.

Ferry – Ferries link Funchal and Vila Baleira; in winter, service is frequently canceled because of rough seas.

Taxi – There are taxi stands in the center of town (Largo do Pelourinho; phone: 91-982160; and on Rua Dr. Nuno Teixeira; phone: 91-982118). *AB-Tours* (7 Rua João Gonçalves Zarco; phone: 91-982175) and *Blandy Brothers* (Av. Dr. Manuel Pestana Junior; phone: 91-982114) both offer sightseeing tours of the island.

SPECIAL PLACES: Vila Baleira – Also called simply Porto Santo, the island's main town lies toward the center of the 4-mile-long beach. Besides the beach, several pensions, restaurants, facilities for changing money, and the local tourist office (on Av. Vieira de Castro; phone: 91-982361), its attractions include the small, white Piedade church and the adjacent town hall. Nearby, on Rua Cristovão Colombo, but not open to the public, is the house in which Columbus is said to have lived.

Portela – This lookout point, on a hillside north of Vila, offers an island-wide panorama.

Pico do Castelo – A road lined with cedar trees leads north from Vila almost to the top of this 1,445-foot peak, the island's second highest. The views include most of the island and Madeira's distant mountains.

Ponta da Calheta – The island's southwestern extremity; a lookout here takes in the desolate Baixo islet.

CHECKING IN: The choices are limited to two hotels and several pensions. Advance bookings are necessary in summer, although those who want to take a chance might be able to find an empty room without one. Prices are a bit lower than on the main island of Madeira. Expect to pay $65 or more for a double room in the expensive category, $35 to $60 for a moderate one, and $30 or less for an inexpensive one.

Porto Santo – This 2-story hotel, a bit over a mile (1.6 km) southwest of Vila Baleira, offers 100 rooms with private bath, a beachfront setting, a swimming pool, and a tennis court. Campo de Baixo (phone: 91-982381; fax: 91-982611). Expensive.

Palmeira – A 25-room *pensão* on Vila Baleira's beachfront avenue, it has a pleasant setting and a friendly staff. Av. Vieira de Castro (phone: 91-982112). Moderate.

Praia Dourada – Nicely maintained and well operated, it has 35 rooms, all with private bath. It's in Vila Baleira, a short walk from the beach. Rua Dr. Pedro Lomelino (phone: 91-982315; fax: 91-982437). Moderate.

Zarco – A small, homey *pensão residencial* of 22 rooms, within a short walk of the beach in Vila Baleira. Rua João Gonçalves Zarco (phone: 91-982273). Inexpensive.

EATING OUT: Fish and seafood predominate. Although many restaurants open only in summer, there are several to choose from throughout the year. Expect a meal for two without drinks to cost $10 to $20 in a moderate restaurant, under $10 in an inexpensive one.

Asia Mar – As its name suggests, this popular new eatery specializes in Chinese food; the Peking duck is highly recommended. Closed Tuesdays. Reservations necessary. No credit cards accepted. Off the main road near the beach, in Campo de Baixo (phone: 91-982468). Moderate.

Estrela de Calheta – Fish and seafood specialties are served in this restaurant by the beach, near the end of the road to Ponta da Calheta. Open daily. Reservations advised. No credit cards accepted. Calheta (phone: 91-822145). Moderate.

Teodorico – Traditional skewered and grilled beef — *espetada* — is the specialty. The restaurant is in the hills in scenic Serra de Fora, northeast of Vila. Open daily. Reservations advised. No credit cards accepted. Serra de Fora (phone: 91-982257). Moderate.

Baiana – A café–snack bar–restaurant in the center of Vila, it serves the catch of the day, plus regional dishes. The covered outdoor patio is a pleasant place to dine alfresco. No credit cards accepted. Rua Dr. Nuno Teixeira (phone: 91-982209). Moderate to inexpensive.

INDEX

Index

NOTES

NOTES

NOTES

NOTES